RESEARCH HANDBOOK ON EUROPEAN STATE AID LAW

D1744595

RESEARCH HANDBOOKS IN EUROPEAN LAW

This important series presents a comprehensive analysis of the latest thinking, research and practice across the field of European Law. Organised by theme, the series provides detailed coverage of major topics whilst also creating a focus on emerging areas deserving special attention. Each volume is edited by a leading expert and includes specially-commissioned chapters from distinguished academics as well as perspectives from practice, providing a rigorous and structured analysis of the area in question. With an international outlook, focus on current issues, and a substantive analysis of the law, these *Handbooks* are intended to contribute to current debate as well as providing authoritative and informative coverage.

Forming a definitive reference work, each *Handbook* will be essential reading for both scholars in European law as well as for practitioners and policymakers who wish to engage with the latest thinking and ongoing debates in the field.

Research Handbook on European State Aid Law

Edited by

Erika Szyszczak

University of Leicester, Littleton Chambers, Temple, UK

RESEARCH HANDBOOKS IN EUROPEAN LAW

Edward Elgar
Cheltenham, UK • Northampton, MA, USA

Published by
Edward Elgar Publishing Limited
The Lypiatts
15 Lansdown Road
Cheltenham
Glos GL50 2JA
UK

Edward Elgar Publishing, Inc.
William Pratt House
9 Dewey Court
Northampton
Massachusetts 01060
USA

A catalogue record for this book
is available from the British Library

Library of Congress Control Number: 2011925783

ISBN 978 1 84980 274 1 (cased)

Typeset by Servis Filmsetting Ltd, Stockport, Cheshire
Printed and bound by MPG Books Group, UK

Contents

Contributors

Christian Ahlborn is a lawyer in the Competition and Antitrust Department of Linklaters LLP, London.

Andreas Bartosch is partner of Kemmler Rapp Böhlke, Brussels.

Andrea Biondi, Kings College, London.

Alexander Birnstiel, Rechtsanwalt, Partner, Noerr LLP, Munich, Germany.

Michael Blauberger, TranState Research Centre, University of Bremen and Jean Monnet Fellow (2010–2011) at the Robert Schuman Centre for Advanced Studies, EUI Florence, Italy.

Lorenzo Coppi, Compass Lexicon and College of Europe, Bruges.

Maja-Alexandra Dittel, Marine Environment Division at the International Maritime Organization, London.

Michelle Everson, Faculty of Law, Birkbeck College, London.

Martin Farley, Associate, Hogan Lovells, Fellow of the Centre of European Law, Kings College, London.

Leigh Hancher, University of Tilburg, Of Counsel, Allen and Overy, Amsterdam.

Helge Heinrich, Rechtsanwalt, Senior Associate, Noerr LLP, Munich, Germany.

Herwig C.H. Hofmann, University of Luxembourg.

Klaus-Otto Junginger-Dittel, Deputy Head of the Regional Aid Unit, European Commission, Brussels.

James Kavanagh, Senior Consultant, Oxera, Oxford.

Markus Krajewski, University of Erlangen-Nuremburg, Germany.

Rike Krämer, TranState Research Centre, University of Bremen.

Thibaut Kleiner, Head of Unit, State Aid Case Support and Infringement Coordination, European Commission, Brussels.

Antigoni Lykotrafiti, Jean Monnet Post-doctoral Fellow, Robert Schuman Centre for Advanced Studies EUI, Florence.

Claire Micheau, European Commission.

Alessandro Morini, Assistant, University of Luxembourg.

Paolisa Nebbia, Italian Competition Authority, Rome.

Gunnar Niels, Director, Oxera, Oxford.

Daniel Piccinin is a lawyer at Brick Court Chambers.

Simon Pilsbury, Managing Consultant, Oxera, Oxford.

Francesco Salerno, Senior Attorney, Cleary Gottlieb, Brussels.

Michael Schütte, Rechtsanwalt / Avocat (Munich), Schuette Law SPRL, Brussels.

Erika Szyszczak, University of Leicester, Barrister, Littleton Chambers, London.

Preface

For many decades State aid law and policy were neglected aspects of the EU integration project. With the start of the new millennium and the ensuing dramatic enlargement of the EU, State aid law has become a central focus of attention. Along with procurement policy, State aid was seen as one of the remaining difficulties in creating an integrated single market. This invited greater attention from the Commission in formulating long-term policy alongside its day-to-day State aid enforcement role. At the same time, issues arising from State aid became increasingly contested by non-State parties, mainly competitors, in the national courts. This invited participation in the State aid discourse by a wider group of actors as well as confronting the Commission with the need to ensure the good administration of State aid notifications and complaints and a careful analysis of the effects of State aid.

Attempts to modernise State aid became central to the Lisbon process which started in 2000, whereby the aim was to encourage 'intelligent' State aid by reducing aid to specific sectors and by making better use of aid for horizontal projects which were central to EU integration concerns. In 2005 the Commission presented the ambitiously titled *State Aid Action Plan Less and Better Targeted State Aid: A Roadmap for State Aid Reform 2005–2009*. This policy framework has under-pinned the new approach to State aid policy in the EU in recent years and informs many of the chapters in this book.

At the same time, new and unforeseen issues confronted the EU. For example, the effects of liberalisation, the consequences of enlargement, the growth of regionalism, the need to tackle climate change with sustainable energy policies, and questions concerning the role of public services in liberalised and competitive markets arose as policy concerns. Moreover the economic and financial crisis at the end of the last decade propelled State aid to the centre stage of competition policy, thereby moving it from a concern solely for a discrete group of specialists and with the term 'State aid' thereby entering popular discourse and public debate. After 2007 State aid has become a central issue in the future of the whole EU integration process.

Thus, when asked to edit this book, I wanted to provide a modern snapshot of the way in which State aid has become a central aspect of EU integration and a major concern of national economic policy. Several excellent practitioner handbooks exist, providing detailed coverage of the soft and hard law, European Court and Commission Decisions. These texts have allowed scope for this research handbook to widen the discussion towards a critical and inter-disciplinary analysis of the way in which State aid law and policy has accommodated the new demands of integration and the role expected from regulation of State intervention in competitive markets.

My thanks to the contributors who have participated in this project, offering a range of perspectives on the breadth and complexity of the modern use of State aid in Europe.

Erika Szyszczak,
University of Leicester and Littleton Chambers, Temple, London.
January 2011

Abbreviations

AA	Association Agreements
AMS	Aggregate Measurement of Support
AoA	Agreement on Agriculture (WTO)
CJEU	Court of Justice of the European Union
DSB	Dispute Settlement Body
EA	Europe Agreements
EEA	European Economic Area
EU	European Union
EU ETS	European Union Emissions Trading System
GATT	General Agreement on Tariffs and Trade
GATS	General Agreement on Trade in Services
GBER	General Block Exemption Regulation
MEIP	Market Economy Investor Principle
NAFTA	North American Free Trade Agreement
NAP	National Allocation Plan
OCCP	Office of Competition and Consumer Protection
OPEC	Office for Protection of Economic Competition
PPAs	Power Purchase Agreements
PPP	Polluter Pays Principle
PSO	Public Service Obligation
RAG	Regional Aid Guidelines
RAGBER	Regional Aid Block Exemption
RTA	Regional Trade Agreement
R&R	Rescue and Restructuring
R&R aid	Rescue and Restructuring aid
R&D&I Guidelines	Research and Development and Innovation Guidelines
SAAP	State Aid Action Plan
SAMO	State Aid Monitoring Office (Hungary)
SANI	State Aid Notifications Interactive (System)
SCM	Subsidies and Countervailing Measures (WTO)
SGEI	Service of General Economic Interest
SGI	Service of General Interest
SSGI	Social Service of General Interest
SME	Small and Medium Enterprises

TFEU	Treaty on the Functioning of the European Union
USO	Universal Service Obligation
WTO	World Trade Organisation

Table of equivalences

NOTE ON CITATION

The European Courts are referred to as the General Court (ex-Court of
First Instance (CFI) and the CJEU (Court of Justice of the European

Union). In the text of this book the Treaty of Lisbon 2009 re-numbering of the Treaty Articles is used. To keep the text easy to read a Table of Equivalences is provided. Where appropriate, for example, in a quotation, the old numbering of the EEC and EC Treaties is retained.

Table of cases before the Court of Justice of the European Union (CJEU)

Table of cases before the General Court

1   Modernization of State aid policy
*Thibaut Kleiner**

I.   INTRODUCTION

When looking at the analysis of State aid policy development in the recent literature, one may be reminded of the Quarrel of the Ancients and the Moderns at the *Académie française* in the early 1690s. Whereas the Ancients considered that the classical Graeco-Roman culture had reached perfection, the Moderns considered that the writers of the time were able to innovate and to overcome antique authors. A somehow similar debate seems to have gained prominence in the field of State aid, with certain scholars, mostly economists, praising the introduction of a refined economic approach in State aid (Hancher 2006; Heidhues and Nitsche 2006; Röller and Stehmann 2006) as a way towards modernization, and others, essentially lawyers, criticising it as a threat to State aid discipline, and calling for going 'back to basics' (Buendia 2006; Buendia and Smulders 2008).

This chapter looks critically at the development and structuring of EU State aid policy over the last twenty years, with a particular focus on the State aid reform programme introduced by Commissioner Neelie Kroes through the *State Aid Action Plan* (SAAP).[1] First of all, the chapter presents an analytical framework to examine what can be defined as modernization, on the basis of three models of influence for State aid policy. The chapter then looks at the recent period of State aid reform to analyse to what extent it can be analysed as an attempt towards one type of modernization. Finally the chapter looks at the deliverables of the SAAP and the Commission's State aid policy in the financial crisis, to examine whether the objectives of State aid reform have achieved some results.

II.   MODERNIZATION IN CONTEXT: THREE MODELS OF INFLUENCE FOR STATE AID POLICY

When trying to describe the many changes that have affected State aid policy over the past twenty years, it may be useful to first present some conceptual framework for looking at it and to refer to some models or ideal-types to guide the analysis of it. Modernity refers to a stage of development following a traditional, pagan or medieval era and modernization is the process through which certain practices and issues become structured and rationalized (Weber 2003). Its use is widespread and has been instrumentalized to portray in a positive light the introduction of change. Modernization is therefore generally understood as an improvement of a given area of life. In the case of State aid, as Pesaresi and Van Hoof (2008) recall, the history of State aid looks like a ugly duck turning into a swan, as State aid has lagged behind other areas of competition policy in obtaining academic and professional recognition. Similarly, Lowe (2009) viewed modernization as a process incorporating not only legal instruments but also organizational dimensions and priority-setting. In order to be able to appreciate to what extent State aid reform corresponds to a modernization, it may be useful to refer to three models of influence for State aid law and policy.

II.i.   The Derogatory Model, where State Aid Policy is Attached to the Protection of the Single Market

As Buendia Sierra (2006) argues, State aid policy has many chromosomes of a single market policy. Conceptually, State aid in a common market can be very detrimental because it may cancel out the effect of removing trade barriers. Suppose the trade of textiles is subject to a 10% duty on imported goods. By creating a common market this duty is eliminated, thus reducing the price of importing goods by 10%. Suppose that at the same time, a State aid to national producers, corresponding to a subsidy of 10% of the selling price is introduced. The effect of the abolition of the tariff is completely cancelled out: imported goods are put at a disadvantage through the State aid that is equivalent to the abolished tariff. This is why a common market should in theory not allow for subsidies to national producers.

In the derogatory approach, State aid control is first and foremost associated with the preservation of the single market. Because State aid is by its very nature contrary to the single market, this perspective views the identification of State aid in the broadest possible context as the duty of the Commission, so that it can be properly controlled. Any measure that may be qualified as State aid must be pursued to the full, in order to make sure that the Commission can prohibit measures that may impede the single market.

The derogatory model leads to a vision of State aid as a legal process of formal typology, categorizing some State actions as aid and designating formal areas of derogation to the general prohibition of State aid.

According to Friederiszick et al. (2006) State aid legal procedures, due to the intrinsically political nature of State aid, would largely reflect the desire to limit political influence, rather than to focus on economic effectiveness. This is also the perspective put forward by Ehlermann (1995) then Director General of DG Competition, when he evaluates the success or failure of State aid control in relation to the shrinking in the political margins of Member States and the increasing of the overall responsibilities of DG IV. Accordingly, a strict legal tradition has developed in which State aid is deemed illegal, unless certain (largely form-based) criteria are met.

Modernization, in the perspective of the derogatory approach, corresponds to a situation where State aid law is properly enforced and expands in all possible areas of Member States' activities, so that any State intervention is subject to the scrutiny of the Commission, and can be controlled and possibly amended before it is authorized. This perspective, incidentally, has also an institutional angle, because modernization is more or less equivalent with the attainment of a stage where the Commission receives more power, to the detriment of Member States, and EU law is properly enforced. The dark age of the derogatory approach is by contrast a stage where Member States basically ignore EU law and their responsibilities in terms, for instance, of stand-still obligations and notification of any new aid. Modernization in this perspective corresponds to strong enforcement.

II.ii.   The Competition Model

The second model for describing State aid corresponds to the competition model, where State aid is essentially about preventing negative spill-overs from State aid on competition. The competition model to State aid focuses on the distortionary effects of State aid on markets and between firms and tries to provide some rationale for the compatibility of State aid. Whereas the derogatory model essentially conceives State aid a *per se* distortionary, the competitive model recognizes the possibility for *good* State aid too. Instead of using presumptions as regards the negative effects of State aid, it tries to demonstrate *in concreto* in which circumstances State aid is detrimental (Crocioni 2006).

The competition model is based on the perspective that the Treaty of Rome introduced the State aid provisions within the chapter on competition and builds a common corpus between State aid and the rest of competition policy (antitrust and merger control). Whereas the derogatory model sees State aid as belonging more to the single market body, and the prohibition of State aid as necessary for the preservation of the single market, the competition model sees State aid control as one way to promote the good functioning of markets, in particular by addressing market failures that prevent markets from delivering optimum outcomes.

The competition model also aims at making sure that State aid analysis properly reflects economic and business reality. It favours an effects-based approach to a more legal and formalistic application of EU rules. Importantly, this also opens the possibility to move away from a 'one size fits all' approach based on formal criteria, and towards a more systematic assessment of the positive and negative effects of the aid which is warranted to better distinguish 'good aid' from 'bad aid' (Friederiszick et al. 2006).

The competition model goes with the view that substantial analysis should direct the priorities of State aid and that it should be inscribed in methodologies and narratives. Nikolaides and Rusu (2010) consider that economics can offer methods to assess State aid, as well as plausible stories to justify decisions and normative guidance as to where society and consumers gain or lose out from different business practices, corporate strategies, and public policies. By looking at the positive and negative effects of State aid, it is possible to best evaluate whether they contribute to objectives of common interest (Kleiner and Alexis, 2005).

Finally, the competition model goes together with the idea that the Commission should not be doing everything, but only focus on meaningful distortions (Lowe, 2009). Contrary to the derogatory model, which is essentially trying to cover the full ground of State economic involvement, the competition model is more restrictive and considers that only where there are negative spill-overs on Member States should the Commission get involved in refraining national initiative (Crocioni, 2006).

II.iii.   The Political Integration Model

Finally, a third model is available to describe State aid modernization, and can be called the political integration model. In this model, State aid is first and foremost conceived as a means to controlling governments and coordinating their economic policies. It is viewed as a policy, rather than merely the application of law. In that perspective, the purpose of the policy is to foster deeper integration between national economies.

State aid belongs to policies that have been traditionally associated with the concept of 'negative integration' (Scharpf 1996). Negative integration is often seen as the establishment of the single market and competition policy. Lawton (1996) defines Europeanization as a transfer of sovereignty from the national to the European level. This corresponds to the controlling dimension of State aid. State aid control, negatively, has the property to also guide Member States in a given direction, corresponding to the permissible areas where Member States are not infringing State aid rules. Spector (2006) has explained that State aid control may be desirable because national public authorities may not be able to resist lobbying pressure, because of the wasteful effect of subsidy awards or because of negative externalities on neighbouring countries that cannot be internalized. Dewatripont and Seabright (2006) also argue that State aid control is useful to limit the risk that national politicians fund wasteful projects.

There is another side to State aid too, as a vector of positive integration. Börzel (1999) defines Europeanization as a process by which national policies become increasingly influenced by European policy-making, which corresponds to the coordination of national policies resulting from the Community State aid policy. Even though State aid does not eliminate the potential conflicts between national and European common interest and can only neutralize them, State aid rules can define the common European interest in a way that makes it possible to coordinate national actions (Le Berre 2009). Hix (1999) considers for instance that competition policy was enhanced in the wake of the Single European Act 1986 and did not lead to a race to the bottom, whereby Member States reduce the level of regulation under the pressure of, notably, businesses. Mörth (2003) shows the emergence of new rules of the game that can structure the policy processes at the European level and the domestic, using the example of defence equipment.

Under the political integration model, State aid is an instrument not only of negative integration, but also of positive integration by prescribing how Member States should design their economic policies and where they should target their spending. It contributes to economic integration and supports the perspective of a common economic government by coordinating Member States' actions. Modernization in that model corresponds to the progress towards positive integration.

III.   THE EARLY YEARS

In more than fifty years of State aid control, it is clear that this policy has experienced different fortunes and degrees of enforcement. As Mederer (2008) explained, the framework of State aid control has been established in a regular and constructive dialogue with Member States, with a high degree of continuity in its underlying principles associated with a deepening of the enforcement of the State aid discipline. However, until recently, most general courses on EU law would refer to it only in passing (Quigley 2003). The question may therefore be asked, why State aid did not attract greater attention earlier, by comparison to other areas of competition policy. This in turn leads to looking at the overall development of competition policy and the role of State aid in it. What comes out is the finding that State aid was exposed to a long period of ineffective enforcement by Member States in the 1970s and 1980s, and that it took repeated efforts by the Commission and some Court judgments favouring the institutional position of the Commission to allow a first modernization, at the end of the 1990s.

III.i.   The Expansion of State aid Control

The Spaak report, at the origins of the original EEC Treaty, gave State aid control some prominence in protecting competition and defending the Common Market. The first years of the Common Market correspond to a promising period for State aid control, with the perspective of expanding in a series of areas of State intervention. For instance, even in 1961, the then Court of Justice indicated that the notion of aid is wider than that of a subsidy (Grespan and Santamato 2008). It remains that from the late 1960s, the Commission was in a difficult position to establish a level-playing field and to contain Member States' attempts to outbid each other in some forms of subsidy wars (Mederer 2008). In fact, according to Cini (2000), it was only with the appointment of Peter Sutherland as Competition Commissioner in the late 1980s and Leon Brittan as his successor that the policy started to take shape. During the economic crisis of the 1970s and early 1980s, the Community seemed paralysed. It was unable to contain national protectionism motivated by domestic political pressure in a context of growing unemployment, leading to subsidy wars in particular in the field of textiles and steel.

According to Rawlinson (1993), the Commission was unable to resist political pressure before it developed some sets of rules to constrain the possibilities for them to grant aid. At the beginning of the 1980s, the Commission could only express frustration at the lack of discipline among Member States in terms of notification of aid before implementing it (Smith 1996). Transparency of State aid enforcement and decisions left much to be desired, as only negative decisions were published in the official journal. Strikingly enough, the Commission had to withdraw a proposed Regulation because Member States were likely to use this opportunity to limit its abilities (Sinnaeve and Slot 1999). The Commission as a result had to resort to soft law to regulate State aid by limiting its own power instead of using Council Regulations.

After a long period of ineffective enforcement of State aid control, sometimes qualified as 'dark age' (Pesaresi and Van Hoof 2008), the Commission finally succeeded in the 1980s and 1990s in adopting a series of important rules and Regulations. The approach followed was, however, quasi regulatory, despite the fact that it was about the Commission's self-limitation (Cini, 2000). It benefited from the combination of individual decisions by the Commission, and by overall policy initiatives, like the 1993 White Paper on growth, and of Court judgments (for example, *Philip Morris, Boussac*) to formalize statements and criteria. Whereas the Commission had failed to convince the Council in the 1970s to adopt an effective procedural Regulation, it was finally successful in having two Regulations adopted: one as regards procedures (Sinnaeve and Slot 1999) and the other concerning a Block Exemption Regulation, whose purpose was to define some State aid measures that governments could adopt without needing to notify them to the Commission. To a large extent, the strategy followed by the Commission in the 1990s established the path in the next years of State aid reform and modernization. In the mid-1990s, State aid control came to the fore through some landmark decisions (*Crédit Lyonnais, Air France, Volkswagen*), which demonstrated the ability of the Commission to impose some conditions on companies despite the political resistance of Member States (Ehlermann 1995; Smith 1998).

All these developments can be seen in parallel with an expansionary effect of the State aid doctrine allowed by the Courts and leading the Commission to very much enhance its competencies and jurisdiction. In fact, the history of State aid law is very much about the expansion of State aid control into many areas of national policies. The Commission's juris-diction increased over time according to the type of aid: direct subsidies, direct taxation, indirect taxation, other advantages. It also increased in terms of the scope of the measures: direct support to a single company, a sector, an activity, and their objectives: regional aid, restructuring aid, public service obligations. This was made possible notably because of a very wide interpretation by the Court of the notion of aid in terms of effects on competition and on trade (Grespan and Santamato 2008) and judgments enhancing the procedural powers of the Commission, in particular recovery of illegal aid.[2]

III.i.a.   The first modernization of state aid

Pullen et al. (2000) consider that a first modernization of State aid took place at the end of the 1990s resulting from a series of changes taking place at the time, in particular around the treatment of procedures and sectoral rules. For instance, the Commission attacked the unlimited guarantees benefiting German regional banks. It also applied strict rules to the pro-hibition of sectoral aids in the field of textiles, steel or shipbuilding. This was embedded in a series of rules, not only sectoral but also procedural.

Most notably were the procedural Regulation of 1999, establishing for the first time a comprehensive corpus of rules for Member States and the Commission to comply with, and the enabling Regulation of 1998 setting up the possibilities for block exemptions and *de minimis* aid.

Interestingly, State aid's development until 2000 appears as an institutional conquest where the Commission tries to increase the enforcement of the Treaty's provision. It best corresponds to the first model of modernization, whereby State aid expands through legal jurisdiction. Legal constraint and the obligation for Member States to obtain the Commission's agreement before implementing State measures correspond to a situation where the European influence shapes Member States' policies. This results in changes in the way State aid is designed and granted, or even in a prohibition of State intervention in some areas.

One may question whether this expansion of State aid was really foreseen by the founding fathers, or endorsed by Member States. For instance the qualification as economic activity of an increasing number of functions historically performed by the State exclusively, was questioned by Member States and they criticized the interpretation of the Commission concerning the effect on trade. By expanding State aid control, the combined action of the Commission and of the Court increasingly subjected any State intervention in the economy to a prohibition principle. This led to a very restrictive stance towards Member States' ability to act in the economy, with little consideration to the actual negative effects on other Member States.

The CJEU put some limitations on the expansion of State aid at the beginning of the 21st Century. Between 2000 and 2003, the Court used a series of judgments to redefine the notion of State aid and to reduce substantially the possible scope of the previously rapidly expanding regime of State aid law and to progressively consolidate the discipline (Braun and Kühling 2008). Judgments in *Preussen Elektra*, *Ferring* or *Altmark* spring to mind in that context. For further discussion see Chapter 13.

Around the same period, as the Courts were bringing a halt to the expansionary ambitions of the Commission, some economists were saying that State aid was in need of an economic framework, pointing to the remarkable lack of it in the Commission's practice (Besley and Seabright 1999). By comparison, the reform of antitrust and merger control at the end of the 1990s and beginning of the 2000s was very much about re-focusing the Commission's intervention and to embracing a more economics-based approach.

III.i.b.   The reform of antitrust and merger control

The modernization of State aid cannot be properly appreciated without looking at the changes affecting antitrust and merger control around the same period. The so-called modernization of antitrust and merger control has been analysed at length (Vives 2009). It corresponds in particular to the decentralizing of EU law to national competition authorities. It is also associated with the introduction of more economic and effects-based analysis of restrictions to competition. As Kleiner (2008) explained, the reforms of antitrust and merger control were a source of inspiration for the reform process conducted in the field of State aid.

What is interesting for State aid is that the modernization of antitrust pre-dates by a number of years similar development in its field. Already in the 1990s, when State aid was emerging from a difficult period in merely ensuring that Member States have a 'minimum of compliance with the Treaty rules, antitrust policy experienced its own transformation, which led to the adoption of the Modernization Regulation.

The reform of Article 101 TFEU by means of Regulation No 1/2003 initiated an exception system in Europe. The new regime changed the interpretation of the two elements (1) 'may affect trade between Member States' and (2) 'which have as their object or effect the prevention, restriction or distortion of competition' in Article 101 (1) TFEU as well. By applying the so-called 'more economics based approach', the economic assessment in Article 101 TFEU became much more detailed. Regulation No 1/2003 with the shift to the authorization system as well as the introduction of the more economics based approach changed the application of Article 101 TFEU (Hildebrand 2009).

The modernization of antitrust was therefore much about a dual change of paradigm: on the one hand a departure from a form-based approach of restrictions of competition towards a more effects-based approach (Roeller and Stehmann 2006) and on the other hand a decentralization of European law within a network of competition authorities. The White Paper on modernization[3] set out very clearly that the objectives of the changes were as much on substance as on the administration of the law. It recognized that it was essential to adapt the system to the economic and social changes which have occurred since 1962 so as to relieve companies of unnecessary bureaucracy, to allow the Commission to become more active in the pursuit of serious competition infringements and to increase enforcement of the competition rules by the national authorities and courts.

The modernization of merger control followed a similar path, in so far as both the jurisdiction of the Commission and the substantial analysis conducted in merger control were reformed, to improve the focus of the Commission's action, develop a more effects-based approach underpinned by economic analysis, and to provide greater guidance as to the Commission's assessment and procedures, so that the jurisdiction of the Commission and that of national competition authorities would be more harmonious (Vives 2009). The reform of antitrust and merger control therefore fit nicely with the competition model described above.

IV.   THE STATE AID ACTION PLAN: A PLATFORM FOR MODERNIZATION

The State Aid Action Plan (SAAP) was adopted by the Commission at the beginning of the mandate of the Competition Commissioner Neelie Kroes. It constituted an ambitious work program of revising basically all existing State aid rules over a five-year period. It also provided a conceptual framework for this reform programme, which it incidentally even categorized as modernization.[4] The SAAP is considered as a turning point in the development of State aid policy. It moved State aid closer to other areas of competition policy and introduced the conception of State aid as an instrument (and not an end in itself) to support wider policy objectives (Zemplinerova 2010; Kleiner 2008). What is interesting in SAAP is that it was both a conscious attempt at reform and a wish list, expressed as a consultation document, thus leaving open the level of ambition the Commission would ultimately opt for.

IV.i.   A Political Re-foundation

The origins and motivations of the SAAP have been described elsewhere (Kleiner 2008). It benefited from a unique configuration of opportunities: unfinished reforms from Commissioner Monti's tenure; a new Commission with a clear objective around growth, a series of Guidelines coming to an end, which opened the possibility for some institutional entrepreneurship on the part of the Commission (Blauberger 2009). What is striking about the SAAP is that it starts not with a work programme, but rather with a question: why does the EU need a State aid policy? The SAAP has at its origins a quest for meaning and purpose. As a consultation document, it tried to validate with Member States and stakeholders the direction to be given to this policy. In addition, the SAAP offered an overall strategy to respond to well identified challenges.

When presenting her reform programme, Commissioner Neelie Kroes insisted that the plan was motivated by procedural shortcomings and by generally a lack of clarity as to the conceptual framework and basic justifications underpinning State aid control:

I have identified a series of specific points on which the existing rules are less than satisfactory. The objectives of State aid discipline are neither well understood, nor well served by the current framework. State aid control has evolved over the years into an unnecessarily complicated set of rules, exemptions, and guidelines. It has had to intervene in rather insignificant cases, for example on individual swimming pools. The procedures have grown lengthy and cumbersome. And Commission approval of State aids is still too often seen as just one additional bureaucratic formality to be jumped at the end, once the decision to grant aid has already been taken.

The reform we are proposing will give State aid policy a clearer meaning and a clearer direction, so that European citizens can see that their concerns are being listened to, and are being addressed in an appropriate and unbureaucratic way by the European Union. (Kroes 2005)

Interestingly, the objectives pursued appear as a retrenchment rather than an expansion of the Commission's control. The message is no longer that Member States are ignoring the law. It is rather that the law, as developed by the Commission, is not understandable and its procedures are cumbersome. The objective is not to go against the granting of State aid, but rather to give a meaning and better administer a policy controlling it.

It is nevertheless important to recall the degree of ambition of the plan laid down by the Commission at this occasion, as a response to a series of policy, rather than legal, challenges identified in 2005: enlargement, the Commission's strategy for growth and jobs, excessive complexity and bureaucratic burden, the need for Member States to enforce the rules, transparency and advocacy. The response to these many challenges was to change more or less everything, but to do it in a consistent manner, on the basis of some guiding principles:

To face the new challenges requires a thorough modification of the existing State aid rules, as regards both substance and procedures. Any effective assessment of the allocation or distribution effects of State aid must take into account their actual contribution to commonly agreed, politically desirable objectives. The aim is to present a comprehensive and consistent reform package based on the following elements:

– less and better targeted State aid;
– a refined economic approach;
– more effective procedures, better enforcement, higher predictability and enhanced transparency;
– a shared responsibility between the Commission and Member States: the Commission cannot improve State aid rules and practice without the effective support of Member States and their full commitment to comply with their obligations to notify any envisaged aid and to enforce the rules properly (SAAP para. 18).

The SAAP aimed at providing a complete response to the modernization of State aid, not only at the level of substance but also at the level of procedures. To that extent, it aimed no less than offering a re-foundation to the compromise between the Commission and Member States as regards the purpose of this policy.

IV.ii.   Mainstreaming State Aid Policy by Making it a Tool for Competitiveness

The SAAP has as its subtitle 'less and better targeted aid', which is the objective repeatedly invoked in the Lisbon strategy for growth and jobs. This was a novel perspective to expressly relate State aid to other policies of the Commission, and to explain its purpose in relation to policy goals in the EU interest.

In addition to questioning the justifications and meaning of State aid policy, the SAAP went on with an overall strategy to address well-identified challenges. By presenting State aid as an instrument, the SAAP changed the perspective followed so far by the Commission. It promoted a new role for State aid, not as a legal control mechanism refraining Member States' from intervention in the economy, but rather as a policy supporting common goals of the Union.

Commissioner Neelie Kroes explained that competition policy, and in particular State aid, was not an end in itself but rather a means to an end (Kroes 2007). This perspective departs from the conception of competition as an independent agency, a model sometimes favoured for antitrust and merger control, to put it at the centre of the Commission, as one pillar of the EU economic policy-making. Similarly, Kleiner (2005) outlined how SAAP had devised a framework to contribute to the Lisbon Strategy for growth and jobs. The SAAP offered a framework to contribute to the Commission's overall objectives, by categorizing objectives of common interest either as efficiency or equity. It explains that efficiency objectives can be supported through State aid, when it targets market failures. State aid may also be needed when market forces produce undesirable results, for instance, social or regional inequality, to correct the action of well functioning markets, thereby fulfilling the equity objective of State aid.

Through this categorization, however, the SAAP introduced the view that Member States had to better justify the purpose of their intervening in the economy. Besides, by putting State aid policy somehow at the service of broader policy objectives of the Commission, it put it closer to the centre of gravity. As Herbert Ungerer, Deputy Director General in charge of State aid, explained: 'One may say that the State aid Action Plan integrated EU State aid control into mainstream EU.' (Ungerer 2008).

This mainstreaming can also be related to the political integration model. By favouring certain objectives and developing narratives in favour of 'less and better targeted aid', the SAAP promoted a common framework for Member States, in line with the Commission's overall economic governance. It therefore promoted coordination among them and positive integration.

IV.iii.   Refined Economic Analysis

The introduction of a refined economic analysis in State aid is the novelty of the SAAP that caught most attention among scholars and practitioners, and led to sometimes vivid debates. It is also probably the cornerstone of the reforms introduced, as it was the main instrument to design changes at the level of State aid rules and decision practice. The pros and cons of a refined economic analysis have been amply analysed (Buendia and Smulders 2008; Derenne and Merola 2007; Friedricszick et al. 2006; Hildebrand and Schweinsberh 2007) and we only need to remind ourselves of its main features.

The SAAP explains that the refined economic approach is a tool for the Commission to better design its rules and support a better targeting of State aid towards competitiveness, in particular by verifying that State aid is properly addressing market failures. A refined economic approach provides a common narrative to State aid policy and a consistent framework, which makes it possible to better define the positive and negative effects of State aid and to delineate good from bad aid (Lowe 2009; Roeller and Stehmann 2006).

Besides and importantly, the SAAP proposed to use a refined economic analysis to better identify where the Commission should focus its scrutiny.[5] This relates to the introduction of a General Block Exemption Regulation, to authorize an increased number of measures without the need for Member States to notify them, because the Commission would consider that distortions of competition are limited enough. Similarly, the SAAP announced an increase in the amount of the *de minimis* aid.

Finally, the SAAP presented the methodology that the Commission follows to examine the compatibility of a State aid, in a series of steps, which became known as the 'balancing test'. The balancing test looks at the positive and negative effects of aid and compares them to determine whether on balance the aid should be authorized. This opened up the possibility for the Commission to move towards an effects-based approach in State aid, and to therefore bring it closer to the type of analysis done in antitrust and merger control.

In short, the refined economic approach is probably the element in

SAAP that was most clearly expressed and that is closest to the competition model. It promoted a vision of modernization as convergence with antitrust and merger control, while also maintaining some originality for State aid (Kleiner 2008). This being said, the economic framework presented in SAAP, and in particular the request that Member States better define the motivation of their spending was attacked notably by Germany, as going beyond the control of competition externalities on other Member States (Blauberger 2009). This shows that the refined economic approach also borrowed from the derogatory model, since it expanded the scope of review for the Commission.

IV. iv.   Improving the Enforcement of State Aid: Recovery, Notification Obligation, Transparency

The aspect that attracted most of the positive comments in the consultation following the publication of the SAAP was not the introduction of a refined economic approach, but rather the willingness to improve State aid procedures and enforcement. The proposals made in the SAAP as regards procedures, despite being considered as vague (Derenne 2005) covered a large number of areas. In particular, it distinguished between two tracks. The first track, without resorting to a new Council procedural Regulation, would pursue improvements in terms of dialogue with Member States and efficiency of internal procedures. There, the focus was on partnership with Member States, along the political integration model rather than trying to impose EU law upon them, like the derogatory model. As Commissioner Neelie Kroes put it: 'The Commission cannot deliver effective State aid administration without a true partnership with dedicated and committed counterparts in the Member States.' (Kroes 2005b). This included the creation of a State Aid Network of national authorities.

In addition, SAAP called for a better enforcement of State aid law: 'The effectiveness and credibility of State aid control presupposes a proper enforcement of the Commission's decisions, especially as regards the recovery of illegal and incompatible State aid' (para. 53). Finally, the SAAP anticipated the possibility to introduce a new procedural Regulation, but did not provide a great deal of details about what could be introduced, only listing the objectives of such review: transparency, notification obligations, efficiency.

All these elements nicely fit with the derogatory model, of improving the enforcement of State aid and expanding its scope.

In conclusion, one can recognize in SAAP some links with the three models of State aid modernization. Admittedly, the influence of the competition model is strongest, around the introduction of the refined economic approach in particular. This corresponds to the trend experienced by antitrust and merger control earlier. But the derogatory model is not totally absent either from SAAP, in particular in reference to a stricter enforcement of EU law. What is striking is the attempt of the SAAP to transform State aid into an instrument of policy coordination, in line with the political integration model. This is probably a distinctive feature of State aid reform compared to antitrust and merger control.

V. MODERNIZATION OR NOT: STATE AID REFORM AND THE FINANCIAL CRISIS

Even though the SAAP had a strong programmatic character, it is also striking that it left many options open. First of all, it was presented as a consultation document with the view that effective changes would only be introduced at the level of individual soft law proposals (Buendia and Smulders 2008). Secondly, while offering an overall philosophy and listing proposals, the document was not extremely precise. To that extent, it is important to verify whether the SAAP delivered on its promises.

V.i. State Aid Action Plan: Delivered?

First of all, as regards the work programme in terms of adoption of new documents and Guidelines, it is fair to say that the SAAP has been delivered to a great extent. As Ungerer (2008) explained, the resulting revision of State aid rules has resulted in:

- The publication of the SGEI (Services of General Economic Interest) Exemption Decision and Framework of 2005 that clarified under which conditions public intervention in these areas falls under Article 106 (2) TFEU and not under Article 107 TFEU, and how the Commission will assess such measures (discussed in Chapter 13);
- The Risk Capital Guidelines, Export Credit Communication, the Regional Aid Guidelines and the Research and Development and Innovation Framework of 2006 (discussed in Chapter 10);
- The Environmental Guidelines (including Climate Change aid) and the reference rate Communication and Guarantee Notice of 2008 (discussed in Chapter 11);
- Broadcasting and Broadband Guidelines in 2009;
- The *de minimis* Regulation clarified that minor aid amounts (€200 000 over three years) would not be considered by the Commission as aid falling under Article 107 (1) TFEU.

And, as the major omnibus Regulation of the reform, the General Block Exemption of 2008 which put under a single umbrella all existing block exemptions and extended the concept of block exemption to a number of new areas (the General Block Exemption Regulation (GBER) as issued in August 2008 now covers 26 measures as compared to only 10 under the pre-existing block exemptions)

In addition, as regards procedures, the Commission adopted a package of procedural measures in 2008 (Simplification Package):

- A Notice on a simplified procedure aimed at a substantial rationalization of the process wherever we can undertake a standard
  assessment of measures notified to the Commission;
- A Best Practice Code for streamlining the procedures for the
  remaining more complex cases;
- The Notice on the enforcement of State aid rules by national courts
  which substantially clarifies rights of complainants before national
  courts.

Commissioner Kroes expressed satisfaction at the achievements of the State aid Action Plan, considering that virtually all State aid rules had been modernized. In fact, compared with the initial programme, very few gaps can be identified from the initial objectives. The Commission only refrained from publishing some Notices that mostly have to do with the notion of aid rather than with compatibility (fiscal aid, forms of aid, market economy investor principle), and from proposing a new Council procedural Regulation. Interestingly, State aid reform was successful in increasing the consistency of the compatibility reasoning across Guidelines. More explanation is provided in Guidelines about the motivations for certain measures, and they are justified on the basis of market failures or equity considerations. The balancing test was therefore positive in developing State aid as a discipline, and not merely a catalogue of rules not always easy to understand. These narratives, about why State aid may be acceptable, or not, were also instrumental during the financial crisis.

V.ii.   Less and Better Targeted Aid?

As regards the targeting of State aid, it is fair to say that before the financial crisis, some good progress could be identified as can be seen from the State aid scoreboard (2009). Looking at the trend from a long-term perspective, the overall level of State aid in the 1980s was in the region of 2% of GDP, fell to just below 1% in the 1990s and now stands at around 0.5%–0.6%. Total State aid (less railways) granted by the Member States in 2007 stood at €65 billion or 0.53% of EU Gross Domestic Product (GDP). Aid for industry and services amounted to €49 billion or 0.40% of GDP. In that context, one could say that the objective of the SAAP of 'less and better targeted aid' was at least well on track until the financial crisis.

V.iii.   Improved Architecture and Less Red Tape?

The Commission delivered also on the introduction of the refined economic approach in its new Guidelines. Whereas it increased the scope of block exemptions, it also introduced a detailed assessment for cases of higher aid amount, which are to be examined on the basis of an effects-based approach, the so-called 'balancing test'. This has been introduced in the Research and Development and Innovation, Risk Capital, Environmental Protection, Large Investment projects under Regional Aid, Employment, Training and Broadcasting. In addition, the DG Competition published a staff working paper on guiding principles for the analysis of compatibility, which has not however been endorsed yet by the Commission.

Some observers have considered that whereas this was positive at the level of Guidelines and in some cases, the Commission was not properly equipped because it lacked investigative powers to step up its ability to analyse markets (Morgan de Rivery et al. 2007). At the same time, the scrutiny of larger aid amounts seems to have increased. According to Kerber (2010), the current economic approach to EU State aid policy tends to be more a general control of the effectiveness of all subsidies in the Member States, which goes far beyond the initial intention of the EU competition rules of Article 107 to 109 TFEU that wanted to control subsidies in regard to their distorting effects on competition through spill-over effects between Member States.

Again, looking at the facts described in the State aid scoreboard, one has to notice that the Commission's strategy developed in the SAAP has started to deliver the expected results. In 2007, there were 777 cases notified by Member States. While the number of notifications is lower than the exceptionally high level in 2006 (922 notifications), it remains significantly above the level in 2004 and 2005. Moreover, the decrease is in line with the Commission's commitment to facilitate the granting of aid through block exemptions and focus its scrutiny on the most distortive types of aid. In 2007, Member States were able to introduce more than 1100 measures without prior notification to the Commission. This compares with 410 block exempted measures in 2006 (European Commission Scoreboard 2009).

The SAAP acknowledged the existence of shortcomings in the length and predictability of State aid procedures and called for actions to modernize them. According to the Scoreboard, the Commission has since made efforts to improve its internal practice and increase efficiency in the State aid field. It has recently started a dialogue with Member States on how to further improve the efficiency of State aid procedures and has adopted internal measures to reduce the time required to treat State aid notifications. Thanks to these measures, the average length of the preliminary examination procedure for a notified case fell by 1.4 months over the last five years. The average duration is now around 5 months. As to the proportion of cases closed within a certain period of time, the results show that 46% were closed within 4 months and 70% were closed within 6 months (European Commission Scoreboard 2008).

Some improvements were noticed along the competition model of modernization, even though these were more evolution than revolution. The Commission still has to deal with a large number of notifications; it still lacks investigative tools to look very precisely at the effects of State aid.

V.iv.   Stronger Enforcement?

It is difficult to assess whether the enforcement of the Commission became stricter or not after SAAP, in particular because it is not easy to find any appropriate measurement of it. In particular, if Member States better conform to State aid rules, this should lead to a lower number of negative decisions. In short, the better the enforcement, the lower the need to sanction Member States with negative Decisions. At the same time, the number of detailed investigations opened and the number of negative Decisions could be an indication of the degree of aggressiveness in the Commission's enforcement. With this caveat in mind, it is possible to extract some numbers from the Commission's case database.[6]

The table shows that, in proportion to the number of notifications received, the Barroso Commission overall opened fewer detailed investigations (9% against 12%) and took fewer negative decisions or withdrawal decisions (5% against 8%) than the Prodi Commission. The trend is even stronger for selected horizontal objectives, which may indicate learning by Member States.

As regards recovery of illegal aid, the Commission's track record shows some considerable progress in the aftermath of the SAAP. The purpose of recovery of unlawful and incompatible aid is to re-establish the situation that existed on the market prior to the granting of the aid. This is necessary to ensure that the level playing field in the internal market is maintained. In line with the SAAP, recent efforts have resulted in a marked improvement in the execution of recovery decisions, leading to an increase in the amount of incompatible aid recovered and a decrease in the backlog of

*Table 1.1   Comparison of decision types between the Prodi and Barroso
            Commissions*

	01/11/1999– 01/11/2004'	01/11/2004– 01/03/2010'	%	%	evolution
Number of notifications	2851	3106			9%
Number of opening decisions	352	286	12%	9%	−25%
Number of negative decisions and withdrawals	235	160	8%	5%	−38%
R&D	12	6	5%	2%	−66%
Number of notifications R&D	230	343			
Environmental protection	28	12	16%	4%	−74%
Number of notifications environmental protection	173	285			
Regional aid	60	32	20%	8%	−60%
Number of notifications regional aid	293	388			

Source: European Commission database, available at: <http://ec.europa.eu/competition/state_aid/register/>

pending cases. As a result, €7 billion or 92% of total illegal and incompatible aid had effectively been recovered by June 2008 (Scoreboard, 2009).

V.v.   Which Model Did Prevail?

The above analysis shows that the modernization of State aid following the SAAP was significant, but not as clear-cut in its direction as one may have expected from the intentions expressed in the SAAP. As anticipated from the analysis of the SAAP, it appears that State aid modernization was very much along the competition model path. This corresponds notably to a clearer test of compatibility (with the balancing test), introduced rather consistently in almost all State aid Guidelines, and providing narratives and justifications for State aid. This corresponds also to the new architecture of State aid with a greater focus on more distortive cases.

One also has to notice that this move was incomplete. First, the Commission's lack of investigative powers is limiting its ability to fully move to an effects-based assessment comparable to antitrust. It is also clear that State aid will always leave a greater degree of political appreciation (Friederisczik et al. 2006). Second, the number of notifications to the Commission is still arguably quite large, with notification thresholds in the GBER as low as 2 million (for training aid for instance) and a level for *de minimis* aid still fairly low (€200,000 over three years). These limitations and the remaining important part of formalistic criteria in State aid practice, and the arguably increased scrutiny of the justification of State aid and increased enforcement at the level of illegal aid show that the derogatory model is still very influential in the development of State aid. It seems however to have been stopped as regards the expansion of the notion of aid.[7]

As regards the political integration model, it is probably the most remarkable element in the SAAP and it got some following from Member States, even though the State aid scoreboard shows large discrepancies between them in the way they have implemented the common strategy (Scoreboard 2008). Blauberger (2009) thus considers that the Commission succeeded in creating positive integration from above and increasingly influences the objectives of national State aid policies.

V.vi.   Financial Crisis: Unexpected, but Benefiting from the Reform

An overview of the modernization of State aid policy would not however be complete without a look at the financial crisis and its handling by the Commission under the State aid rules. Admittedly, the financial crisis was not anticipated by the Commission. For that reason, the attempt to modernize State aid rules did not specifically focus on any crisis management. However, the Commission was confronted with an unprecedented challenge when governments were obliged to massively intervene to preserve the financial system in September 2008, following the bankruptcy of Lehman Brothers. The financial crisis prompted public intervention in the economy of a scale unheard of since World War II. This led to a level of State aid in the region of 2% again, like in the 1980s, according to the State aid scoreboard 2009. At the end of September 2008, the Commission was confronted with a call for some regulatory holidays from State aid rules. The worry was that it would not be possible for the Commission to cope with the amount of aid measures on the table and that applying State aid rules would hinder Member States in their salvation expedition.[8]

Instead of giving up its powers, the Commission rapidly set up a strategy to cope with the financial crisis. Since the beginning of the crisis, the

Commission's objectives in applying the competition rules have been two-fold. First, to support financial stability by giving, as quickly as possible, legal certainty to rescue measures taken by EU Member States. Second, to maintain a level playing field in Europe and ensure that national measures would not export problems to other Member States.

As speed was of the essence in order to prevent financial markets from collapsing, decisions on State measures in support of financial institutions were taken within days (Editorial Comment 2010). The Commission then issued a series of Guidelines to coordinate Member States' actions in the crisis and avoid them resorting to beggar-thy-neighbour policies (Brisse 2010). The same principles were applied to the crisis as those developed for the SAAP. It led to providing meaning and legitimacy to State aid in times where natural reflexes of Member States would be to protect their markets and therefore resort to subsidy wars to protect national employment. The risk of State aid policy being on holiday due to the crisis was avoided in particular because of the ability of the Commission to demonstrate that without the Commission, Member States would undermine their individual attempts to cope with solutions.

In that context, modernization of State aid can be identified by comparing the results obtained by the Commission in terms of coordinating Member States' actions with what happened in the crisis of the 1970s and 1980s. As Commissioner Kroes put it on 29 September 2009:

> Overall, this crisis has been handled well compared to the Great Depression and previous threats of protectionism. Indeed, the Commission has been quick and loud in resisting protectionism. And we have shown the value of competition policy in safeguarding the Single Market. But the speed and scale of the financial crisis also brought another trend into the limelight: the Commission's role as an enabler. Enforcement remains our core business, of course. But in the urgency and confusion after the Lehman Brothers collapse the Commission was able to work with the European Central Bank, national central banks and Member States – in new ways – to deliver the legal certainty needed for bail-outs and a measure of stability in the financial sector. (Kroes 2009a)

The protection of the single market as negative integration and the coordination efforts of the Commission as positive integration show that the Commission's role in the financial crisis was leaning towards the political integration model. Soltesz and von Köckritz (2010) also consider that the European Commission assumed as a result a powerful role turning into a supervisor of restructuring efforts of banks. In the end, Commissioner Neelie Kroes considered that:

> Overall, yes the system is working. We have juggled many balls during these last five years but we have delivered our promises. The long term trend in State aid

is better value for money for taxpayers; and our work has been a major factor in limiting the damage caused by the crisis. (Kroes 2009b)

In fact, even taking into account the very extreme measures taken in 2008 and 2009 to save the financial system and limit the effects of the economic crisis, Member States continued on the trend of more horizontal aid (European Commission Scoreboard 2010). It can therefore be expected that once the temporary crisis measures come to an end, Member States will continue on the long-term trend supported by the SAAP. It can also be hoped that the measures taken to support the financial system will not prove as costly as could be inferred from the nominal values of the support. In fact, State guarantees may have a limited impact on States' budgets if they are not called in, and they will bring some revenues to Member States in the meantime, thanks to the pricing conditions imposed by the Commission, and the State capital provided by governments should be repaid and provide some revenues too, rather than overall costs.

VI.   CONCLUSION

This chapter has analysed the modernization of State aid and found that a period of 'dark age' in the 1970s and 1980s had slowed down the development of State aid compared to antitrust and merger control towards a competition model. The SAAP in 2005 was very much about convergence with the rest of competition policy in that respect, but not only that. In fact, it also pursued the derogatory model of increased enforcement and control, and most remarkably promoted State aid as an instrument for coordinating Member States' economic policies. Increased legitimacy for State aid control was achieved on the back of agreed common objectives, which made it possible for the Commission to resist protectionist pressures when the economic crisis erupted. This shows that State aid modernization was influenced by three models but that the influence of the derogatory model was greatest in the 1990–2005 period, that the influence of the competition model was greatest with the launch of the SAAP and its refined economic approach, and that the political integration model was essential to preserve the Commission's standing all along, and in particular during the crisis.

To that extent, it appears that the modernization of State aid is essentially about promoting a professional space of technical expertise between Member States and the Commission, through the development of conceptual frameworks explaining how State aid can have negative effects on competition and how public spending can be beneficial. This requires however that the political integration model for State aid is sufficiently developed as otherwise Member States will only consider the Commission as an unnecessary bureaucratic hurdle in their attempt to maximize the welfare of their national citizens. This also requires a professional community of lawyers and economists to feed the process.

Contrary to what Buendia and Smulders (2008) seem to imply, the SAAP did not lead to a weakening of State aid discipline to the benefit of richer Member States. To the contrary, by equipping the policy with narratives and a strategy to cope with objectives outside the mere expansion of State aid law, the SAAP was a very useful preparation for the financial crisis. It helped resist calls for altogether eliminating State aid control as a bureaucratic obstacle, much in contrast to what happened 25 years before in another crisis situation. It also helped change the approach towards delivering decisions more efficiently.

In fact, it appears that the recent modernization of State aid resulted in a compromise situation. The Commission seems to have limited its ambition as regards the expansion of the notion of State aid. The Commission has followed the Court in accepting that some measures do not constitute State aid, notably as regards SGEI, measures not financed through State resources, *de minimis* aid, non-economic activities in the field of Research and Development and fiscal aid. But in exchange it has increased expectations as regards enforcement of State aid control: notification obligations, recovery of illegal aid, application of Commission's Guidelines for compatibility.

The Commission has also limited its scrutiny of State aid involving limited aid amount, through the introduction of the GBER. But in exchange, it requires more precise justification of State aid to make it compatible, and arguably a higher burden of proof for cases subject to detailed assessment, above a certain threshold.

Finally, the Commission did not succeed in eliminating differences between Member States nor to promote a network of State aid national authorities comparable to the antitrust European Competition Network. National preferences in terms of economic intervention have remained largely untouched and State aid does not appear to be a suitable instrument for harmonization between Member States. However, the Commission has succeeded in establishing common frameworks and in guiding Member States' actions towards more co-ordination.

The modernization of State aid in the last years should therefore ultimately be understood as a new compromise with Member States as regards the role and influence of the Commission. The acceptance of State aid control will continue to depend on the ability of the Commission to legitimize its action, by demonstrating its value-added in an increasingly complex and diverse Europe.

NOTES

* The views expressed in this chapter are the author's views only and not necessarily those of the European Commission.
1. State aid action plan – Less and better targeted State aid: a roadmap for State aid reform 2005–2009 (Consultation document) (SEC(2005) 795).
2. For example, Case 70/72 *Commission* v. *Germany* [1973] E.C.R. 813; Case 120/73, *Lorenz* [1973] E.C.R. 1471.
3. *White Paper on modernization of the rules implementing Articles 81 and 82 of the EC Treaty (formerly Articles 85 and 86 of the EC Treaty)*, O J 1999 C 132.
4. Part I of the SAAP is called 'A modernised State aid policy in the context of the Lisbon strategy for growth and jobs ' and part III talks about 'modernising State aid policy and practice'.
5. See SAAP, paras. 35–38.
6. <http://ec.europa.eu/competition/elojade/isef/index.cfm?clear=1&policy_area_id=3>.
7. The analysis of fiscal aid in particular experienced some tightening through judgments of the Court concerning regional selectivity, and some Commission Decisions concerning material selectivity embraced the same trend (cf. *Groepsrentebox; Spanish Goodwill*).
8. This rhetoric was witnessed in December 2008, when the Finance Minister of Sweden, Anders Borg, told the press it was time to call off the legions of State aid bureaucrats. See 'Brussels to be flexible on State aid', by Nikki Tait in Brussels and Scheherazade Dankeskhu and Ben Hall in Paris; *Financial Times*, 2 December 2008). Borg certainly did not realize that Roman legions numbered as many as 6,000 soldiers and DG Competition's State aid staff is a mere 300.

REFERENCES

Besley, Timothy and Paul Seabright (1999), 'The effects and policy implications of State aids to industry: an economic analysis', *Economic Policy*, **14:28**, 13–53.
Blauberger, Michael (2009), 'Of "Good" and "Bad" subsidies: European State aid control through soft and hard law', *West European Politics*, **32:4**, 719–737.
Börzel, Tanja A. (1999), 'Institutional adaptation to Europeanization in Germany and Spain', *Journal of Common Market Studies*, **37:4**, 573–596.
Braun, Jens-Daniel and Jürgen Kühling (2008), 'Article 87 EC and the Community Courts: from revolution to evolution', *Common Market Law Review* **45:2**, 465–498.
Brisse, Matthieu (2010), 'Le rôle juridique contrasté de l'Union européenne face à la crise: un tour d'horizon des mesures prises', *Revue du Marché commun et de l'Union européenne*, **534** (janvier), 20–25.
Buendía Sierra, Jose Luis (2006), 'Not like this: some sceptical remarks on the "refined economic approach" in State aid', *Proceedings of 4th EStAL Expert's Forum on New Developments in European State aid Law*, May 2006, Brussels.
Buendía Sierra, Jose Luis and Ben Smulders (2008), 'The limited role of the "Refined Economic Approach" in achieving the objectives of State aid control: time for some realism', in James Flett (ed), *EC State Aid Law: Liber Amicorum in Honour Francisco Santaolalla*, The Hague: Kluwer, Ch. 1
Cini, Michelle (2000), 'From soft law to hard law? Discretion and rule making in the State aid rule regime', *European University Working Papers*, RSC N° 2000/35, Badia Fiesolana: Italy.
Crocioni, Pietro (2006), 'Can State aid policy become more economic friendly?', *World Competition*, **29:1**, 89–108.
Derenne, Jacques (2005), 'State aid Action Plan, a practitioner's view', Presentation at the Global Competition Law Centre, 19 September 2005. Available at: <http://www.

coleurope.eu/content/gclc/documents/GCLC_lunch_talk_19_9_05%20-%20short%20vers ion.PPT>.

Derenne, Jaques and Massimo Merola (eds) (2007), 'Economic analysis of State aid rules – contributions and limits', Proceedings of the Third Annual Conference of the Global Competition Law Centre (GCLC), Brussels 21–22 September 2006, Berlin: Lexxion.

Dewatripont, Matthias and Paul Seabright (2006), 'Wasteful public spending and State aid control' *Journal of the European Economic Association*, **14:2/3, A**.

Editorial Comment (2010), 'From rescue to restructuring: the role of State aid control for the financial sector', *Common Market Law Review*, **47**, 313–318.

Ehlermann, C-D (1995), 'State aid control in the European Union: success or failure?', *Fordham International Law Journal*, **18**, 1212–1229. Also available at: <http://ec.europa.eu/competition/speeches/text/sp1995_001_en.html>.

European Commission (2003), *White Paper on modernization of the rules implementing Articles 81 and 82 (formerly Articles 85 and 86) of the EC Treaty*, available at: <http://europa.eu/legislation_summaries/other/l26059_en.htm>.

European Commission (2006), *Results of the Consultation on the State aid Action Plan* – 9 February 2006, Available at: <http://ec.europa.eu/competition/state_aid/reform/com-ments_saap/index.html>.

European Commission (2008), *State aid scoreboard Spring 2008 update*, COM (2008) 304, final, 21 May 2008, includes a special focus chapter on State aid for environmental protection.

European Commission (2009), *Report on Competition Policy 2009*. Luxembourg: OPOCE, available at: <http://ec.europa.eu/competition/publications/annual_report/2009/en.pdf>.

European Commission (2009), *State aid scoreboard Spring 2009 update*, COM (2009) 164, 8 April 2009, special edition on State aid interventions in the current financial and economic crisis.

European Commission (2010), *State Aid Scoreboard Autumn Update*, COM (2010) 701, includes an update on State aid in the context of the financial and economic crisis.

Friederiszick, Hans, W., Lars-Hendrik. Röller and Vincent Verouden (2006), 'European State aid control: an economic framework', in P. Buccirossi (ed), *Advances in the Economics of Competition Law*, Cambridge, MA: MIT Press.

Grespan, Davide and Sardro Santamato, (2008), 'Favouring certain undertakings or the production of certain goods: Advantage', in W. Mederer, N. Pesaresi and M. Van Hoof (eds), *EU Competition Law, State Aid*, Leuven: Claeys & Casteels, Ch. 4.

Hancher, Leigh (2005), 'Towards an economic analysis of State aids', *European State Aid Law Quarterly*, **3**, 425.

Heidhues, Paul and Rainer Nitsche (2006), 'Comments on State aid reform – some implica-tions of an effects-based approach', *European State Aid Law Quarterly*, **1**, 23–34.

Hildebrand, Doris (2009), 'The role of economic analysis in the EC competition rules', in Jacques Derennes and Massimo Merola (eds), *Economic Analysis of State aid Rules – Contributions and Limits*, Berlin: Lexxion.

Hildebrand, Doris and A. Schweinsberh (2007), 'Refined economic approach in European State aid control – will it gain momentum?', *World Competition*, **30:3**, 449–462.

Hix, Simon (1999), *The Political System of the European Union*, Basingstoke: Palgrave.

Kerber, Wolfgang (2010), 'EU State aid policy, economic approach, bailouts, and merger policy: two comments', in Basedow, Jürgen, and Wolfgang Wurmnest (eds), *Structure and Effects in European Competition Law*, The Hague: Kluwer Law International, available at SSRN: <http://ssrn.com/abstract=1547790>.

Kleiner, Thibaut (2005), 'Reforming state aid policy to best contribute to the Lisbon Strategy for growth and jobs', *European Competition Newsletter*, **2** (Summer), 29–35.

Kleiner, Thibaut and Alain Alexis (2005), 'Politique des aides d'Etat: une analyse économique plus fine au service de l'intérêt commun', *Concurrences*, N° 4-2005, **n°356**, 45–52.

Kleiner, Thibaut (2008), 'The State Aid Action Plan (SAAP)', in W. Mederer, N. Pesaresi and M. Van Hoof (eds), *EU Competition Law, State Aid*, Leuven: Claeys & Casteels, Ch. 3.

Kroes, Neelie (2005), 'Reforming Europe's State aid regime: An action plan for change', speech at Wilmer Cutler Pickering Hale and Dorr/ University of Leiden Joint conference on European State aid Reform Brussels, 14 June 2005, available at: <http://europa.eu/rapid/pressReleasesAction.do?reference=SPEECH/05/347&format=HTML&aged=0&language=EN&guiLanguage=en>.

Kroes, Neelie (2005), 'The State aid Action Plan – delivering less and better targeted aid' speech – UK Presidency Seminar on State Aid, London, 14 July 2005, available at: <http://europa.eu/rapid/pressReleasesAction.do?reference=SPEECH/05/440&format=HTML&aged=0&language=EN&guiLanguage=en>.

Kroes, Neelie (2007), 'La libre concurrence n'est pas une fin en soi', *Concurrences*, N3-2007, **n°13832**, 1–2.

Kroes, Neelie (2009a), 'Lessons learned from the economic crisis', address to Committee on Economic and Monetary Affairs Brussels European Parliament, 29 September 2009, available at: <http://europa.eu/rapid/pressReleasesAction.do?reference=SPEECH/09/420&format=HTML&aged=0&language=EN&guiLanguage=en>.

Kroes, Neelie (2009b), 'Better targeted aid is the name of the game', London, UK European State Aid Law Institute, 28 November 2009, available at: <http://europa.eu/rapid/pressReleasesAction.do?reference=SPEECH/09/560&format=HTML&aged=0&language=EN&guiLanguage=en>.

Lawton, Thomas (1996), 'Industrial policy partners: explaining the European level firm-Commission interplay for electronics', *Policy and Politics*, **24:4**, 425–436.

Le Berre, Christophe (2009), 'État de nécessité et droit du marché', *Jurisdoctoria*, **n°2**, 47–72.

Lowe, Philip (2009), 'The design of competition policy institutions for the twenty-first century: the experience of the European Commission and the Directorate-General for Competition', in Xavier Vives, (ed), *Competition Policy in the EU: Fifty Years on from the Treaty of Rome*, Oxford: Oxford University Press, 21–41

Mederer, Wolfgang (2008), 'Evolution of State aid control', in W. Mederer, N. Pesaresi and M. Van Hoof (eds), *EU Competition Law, State aid*, Leuven: Claeys & Casteels, Ch. 2.

Morgan de Rivery, Eric, Sabine Thibault-Liger and Jacques Derenne (2007), 'Procedure', in Massimo Merola and Jacques Derenne (eds), *Economic Analysis of State Aid Rules – Contributions and Limits*, Berlin: Lexxion.

Mörth, Ulrika (2003) 'Europeanization as interpretation, translation and editing of public policies', in Kevin Featherstone and Claudio M. Radaelli (eds), *The Politics of Europeanization*, Oxford: Oxford University Press.

Nicolaides, Phedon and Ioana Eleonora Rusu (2010), 'The "binary" nature of the economics of State aid', *Legal Issues of Economic Integration*, 37:1, 25–40.

Pesaresi, Nicola and Marc Van Hoof (2008), 'State aid control: an introduction', in W. Mederer, N. Pesaresi and M. Van Hoof (eds), *EU Competition Law, State aid*, Leuven: Claeys & Casteels, Ch. 1.

Pullen, Mike, Paulette Vander Schueren, James Bergeron (2000), 'European Law', *International Lawyer*, **34:3** (Fall), 907–962.

Quigley, Conor and Andrew Collins (2003), *EC State Aid Law and Policy*, Oxford: Hart Publishing.

Rawlinson, Frank (1993),'The role of Policy frameworks, Codes and Guidelines in the control of State aid', in Ian Harden (ed.), *State Aid: Community Law and Policy*, Cologne: Bundesanzeiger.

Röller, Lars-Hendrik, and Oliver Stehmann (2006), 'The Year 2005 at DG Competition: the trend towards a more effects based approach', *Review of Industrial Organization*, 29:4, 281–304.

Scharpf Fritz (1996), 'Negative and positive integration in the political economy of European welfare states', in G. Marks, F. Scharpf, P. Schmitter and W. Streeck (eds), *Governance in the European Union*, London: Sage, 15–39.

Sinnaeve, Adinda. and Piet J Slot, (1999), 'The new regulation on State aid procedures', *Common Market Law Review*, **36**, 1153–1194.

Soltesz, Ulrich and Christian von Köckritz (2010), 'From State aid control to the regulation of the European banking system – DG COMP and the restructuring of banks', *European Competition Journal*, **6:1**, (April), 285–307.

Smith, Mitchell (1996), 'Integration in small steps: the European Commission and Member State aid to industry', *West European Politics*, **19:3**, 563–582.

Smith, Mitchell (1998) 'Autonomy by the rules: The European Commission and the development of State aid policy', *Journal of Common Market Studies*, **36:1**, 55–78.

Spector, David (2006), 'The economic policy of State aids: The assessment criteria', *Concurrences*, **2**, 4.

Ungerer, Herbert (2008), 'After the State aid Action Plan: – the EU's new State aid framework', Brussels, EU State Aid Summit, available at: <http://ec.europa.eu/competition/speeches/text/sp2009_11_en.pdf>.

Vives, Xavier (2009), *Competition Policy in the EU: Fifty Years on from the Treaty of Rome*, Oxford: Oxford University Press, 21–41.

Weber, Max (2003), *The Protestant Ethic and the Spirit of Capitalism*, translated by Talcott Parsons, 1958, New York: Dover.

Zemplinerova, Alena (2010), 'The Community State aid Action Plan and the challenge of developing an optimal enforcement system, in Alastair Sutton and Ioannis Lianos et al., (eds), *The Reform of EC Competition Law*, International Competition Law Series Volume 41, The Hague: Kluwer Law International, 521–535.

2   State aid control from a political science perspective

Michael Blauberger

This chapter provides an overview of the political science literature on the development of European Union (EU) State aid control and on its impact at the domestic level. First, while Treaty provisions on State aid have remained largely unchanged since the original Treaties of Rome of 1957, it took several decades for the Commission to realise true enforcement powers. The Commission's incremental soft law approach, supportive Court of Justice of the European Union (CJEU) jurisprudence, as well as private complainants, are considered in the literature as major factors that helped to overcome initial Member State resistance to State aid control. Partly under-researched, however, are the internal dynamics of the Commission shaping its particular mix of competition, regional, industrial policies which underlie European State aid rules. Second, the effectiveness of EU State aid control in restricting and/or redirecting Member State subsidies is discussed controversially in the political science and political economy literature. Several authors argue that EU State aid control is not only constraining Member States' ability to distort competition in the internal market, but it increasingly influences the targets of national State aid policies. Some, however, partly dispute these trends or they propose alternative explanations that focus less on European influences.

I.   INTRODUCTION

European State aid rule- and decision-making has always been politically sensitive.[1] In contrast to antitrust or mergers, the Commission's practice in the field of State aid control primarily targets Member State policies, and only indirectly firms (Ehlermann 1995). Moreover, given their strong distributive element, State aid measures may attract considerable public attention at the national level. Well-known examples range from Alitalia and Alstom to the Gdansk shipyard or Opel. If individual State aid measures get politicised to such an extent, the label 'political' often becomes synonymous to 'illegal' and/or 'economically irrational' from an EU perspective. In order to assure the credibility of EU State aid control, therefore, the Commission needs to avoid political conflicts about individual decisions. For decades, the Commission has sought to commit itself to strict State aid control by developing an increasingly complex system of soft and hard rules which are at the core of this volume (Rawlinson 1993: 57). More recently, the strengthening of economic analysis in the handling of individual cases was partly justified as an additional means to minimise the potential for political interference:

> I see no tension between the legal and the economic approach. Our objective is always the same: take the right decision, as close as possible to reality, and with the best possible factual underpinning! (. . .). So when some Member States call for state aid rules which reflect the so-called external aspects of competitiveness, my response is again based on economics rather than on politics. (Kroes 2006)

Today, open political conflict about individual State aid decisions clearly is the exception rather than the rule; even during the recent financial and economic crisis, the Commission has managed to sustain a rule-based approach and to temporally limit the exceptions made (see Chapter 7). Nevertheless, EU State aid control remains inherently 'political' in at least two respects: first, competition policy in general, and State aid control in particular, are horizontal policies which touch upon a broad variety of goals other than competition, for example, innovation, environmental protection, regional development. Apart from refined economic analysis, balancing these different goals against each other and setting priorities necessarily involves some kind of political judgement in the design of State aid rules.[2] Second, the enforcement of EU State aid rules heavily depends on their general acceptance by, and the cooperation of, Member State governments. In order to progressively develop EU State aid control and given its limited own resources, the Commission needs to be sensitive to what is politically feasible at the level of Member States.

Thus, by studying State aid control we can learn a lot about the interaction between the European and domestic levels as well as the interrelation of different policies in the EU. For a long time most political scientists interested in European integration largely neglected this policy field. In 2005, a bibliometric survey on all articles on EU policies published in three major political science journals between 1994 and 2004 identified competition policy as one of the major under-researched policy areas. The author of the survey concluded:

> In my view, the fact that there are twice as many articles on the European employment strategy as an open method of coordination (OMC) as there are on state aid is problematic. I recognize the novelty of the OMC. It is intellectually stimulating and deserves our scrutiny, but, in my view, the life of the

average European is likely to be more profoundly affected by the EU control of state aid. (Franchino 2005: 246)

More recently, political science research on competition policy seems to catch up with other policy areas, both quantitatively and qualitatively. State aid control is among those subfields that account for an overall increase in political-scientific research on EU competition policy (Karagiannis 2009: 8).

This chapter provides an overview of the contributions of political scientists to the study of EU State aid control which centre around two broad sets of questions. Part II focuses on the historical development and the *integration* of State aid control at the European level: How did the Commission manage to turn its potential competences established by the Treaty into actual powers vis-à-vis Member State governments? How far has the Commission used the regulation of State aid control to develop its own model of 'good' State aid policy? Part III addresses the *domestic impact* of EU State aid control. How far do we observe the Europeanisation of national State aid policies, that is, do we detect changes of national State aid policies which are systematically linked to European influences? By which instruments, and through which mechanisms, does European State aid control affect Member State policies? Part IV concludes by identifying *desiderata* for further research.

II.   INTEGRATION OF EUROPEAN STATE AID CONTROL

Many processes at the European and Member State levels interact with each other and can hardly be understood in isolation (Méndez et al. 2006). Nevertheless, for analytical reasons most political scientists researching the EU distinguish between processes of integration, that is, the transfer of competences to or the acquisition of competences by, the European institutions, and processes of Europeanisation, that is, the domestic impact of European integration and Member State compliance with EU rules. The following two subsections discuss a first strand of literature which mainly analyses the integration of State aid control.

II.i.   From Potential to Actual Power

Generally, most political science scholars of European integration may be grouped into either the camp of inter-governmentalism or the camp of neo-functionalism. On the one hand, inter-governmentalists emphasise the sovereignty of Member State governments as masters of the Treaty and their ultimate authority to advance or to roll back integration (Moravcsik 1993). On the other hand, neo-functionalists or supra-nationalists point to the autonomous role of EU institutions such as the Commission and the European Courts in promoting legal integration (Burley and Mattli 1993). As regards European State aid control, the slow pace of integration until the late 1980s might be interpreted as a confirmation of inter-governmentalist arguments, because Member State governments heavily constrained the Commission's autonomy. It seems fair to argue, however, that State aid control has increasingly become a challenge for inter-governmentalist accounts today. As a consequence, most political-scientific studies of State aid control do not question anymore *whether*, but *how* and *under what conditions* the Commission managed to successively expand its supra-national autonomy in this policy field, partly against the resistance of Member State governments (Doleys 2009: 5).

To begin with, the Commission itself has to be understood as a *supra-national entrepreneur* which acts strategically in order to overcome Member State resistance and to turn potential powers granted by the Treaty into actual powers. Apart from individual Decisions, the Commission's main instruments to promote State aid control are Guidelines and Frameworks on compatible aid. This particular 'soft law approach' (Cini 2001) was developed out of necessity after the refusal of Member State governments to adopt Council legislation in 1966 and 1972 (Lavdas and Mendrinou 1999: 29f.). What first appeared to be a weakness developed into a particular strength of EU State aid control. While the Commission still has a strong interest in securing broad Member State approval for its rules through consultations and multilateral meetings, no Council vote or even domestic transposition are required as in the case of normal secondary law. As it was shown for the Guidelines on regional aid for the period from 2000 to 2006, the Commission may even introduce changes into its soft rules after the final multilateral meeting with Member State representatives was held (Méndez, Wishlade and Yuill 2006: 593). Moreover, despite significant controversies about their legal basis and character,[3] the Commission's soft rules have become *de facto* and even *de jure* binding upon Member States. In order to 'convince' individual Member States to accept new rules, the Commission repeatedly employs a strategy that was described elsewhere as 'divide and conquer' (Schmidt 2000: 46f.). If a broad majority of Member States accepts new or revised Guidelines, the Commission may threaten governments which refuse their approval to open formal investigations concerning all existing aid covered by the new rules.[4] The obligatory character of State aid soft law became particularly obvious during the accession preparations of the Central and Eastern

European countries. According to the third Copenhagen criterion, candidate countries had to comply with the *acquis communautaire* and in the field of State aid, the *acquis* was defined as broadly as possible, including not only legislation, but all sorts of Commission Communications as well as the jurisprudence of the European Courts.[5] Finally, the Commission enjoys broad discretion in setting the agenda by its timing of the revision of State aid Guidelines and Frameworks. Cini and McGowan (2009: 177–180) describe in detail how the Commission took the opportunities of the single market initiative in the late 1980s and of the Lisbon Agenda in 2005 to systematically revise its State aid Guidelines and Frameworks. Conversely, when the financial and economic crisis led to an enormous increase in rescue and restructuring measures, the Commission apparently feared a detrimental effect on ongoing consultations and postponed the revision of the Guidelines on rescue and restructuring aid until 2012.[6]

Undoubtedly, the Commission's best ally in promoting the integration of EU State aid control in cases of Member State resistance is the CJEU (Smith 1998: 66f.). First and foremost, the ECJ decisively supported the Commission in interpreting the State aid prohibition broadly and, thus, often helped to counter Member States' 'creative' efforts to circumvent EU State aid control. As a matter of fact, the CJEU does not always support the Commission (Lehmkuhl 2008: 144f.). For example, the judgment in *Preussen Elektra*[7] was perceived as a serious limitation for EU State aid control. Yet even Commission 'defeats' in individual cases may have an empowering effect in the long run. If the Commission applies State aid rules too softly in an individual case, other Member State governments or competitors of the beneficiary can dispute the Decision in court (Smith 1998: 66). As a result, already the threat of a negative court judgment empowers the Commission externally vis-à-vis Member States as well as internally (DG COMP or the Legal Service) to apply EU rules strictly. Moreover, the ECJ significantly helped to improve the Commission's access to information in State aid cases, for example, by confirming the Commission's competence to decide negatively on the basis of incomplete information provided by a Member State. Last but not least, the most powerful tool of EU State aid control, the Decision to order recovery of illegally granted aid, was invented by a Court ruling in 1973. Once again, the Commission was sensitive as regards the political feasibility of tighter State aid control and it did not make use of its new power before 1984 (Smith 1998: 65, 68).

Apart from the Commission itself and the CJEU, private complainants played a significant, but ambivalent, role in the integration of EU State aid control. On the one hand, private complaints are one of the Commission's major sources to detect non-notified State aid measures.

On the other hand, increasing third party involvement in State aid cases is one of the main reasons for the Commission's chronic excess of workload. Dissatisfied with the Commission's treatment of their complaints, private parties have repeatedly challenged State aid decisions before the CJEU or the General Court (Smith 2001: 228f.). Thus, private complaints may empower and constrain the Commission at the same time. The initiative of DG COMP to regulate the procedure of State aid control in the late 1990s was partly a response to the increasing workload caused by private party involvement (Smith 1998: 231). Similarly, the expansion of Block Exemption regulations in recent years was mainly justified by the Commission as a means to better focus its own regulatory capacities on the most critical cases. These aspects of State aid control are discussed in Chapters 15 to 17 in this volume.

II.ii.   From State Aid Control to State Aid Policy?

In principle, competences appear to be clearly allocated between the European and domestic levels in the field of State aid. While the Commission *controls* Member State aid in order to prevent distortions of competition, Member States keep the autonomy to design their own State aid *policies*, as long as these do not violate EU competition law. As becomes clear from the latter qualification, however, deciding about the compatibility of State aid necessarily involves considerations about policy aspects as well. Various contributions from political scientists, therefore, analyse how the Commission tries to incorporate policy goals other than competition into EU State aid rules or how State aid control may even become an instrument to promote other EU policies.

First of all, these studies unanimously warn against treating the Commission as a unitary actor and try to investigate the internal dynamics between different Directorates-General or even within DG COMP (From 2002). In one of the earliest contributions on the policy aspects of EU state aid control, Lavdas and Mendrinou (1995) traced the evolution of the Commission's approach towards aid for small and medium-sized enterprises (SME), showing how the former DG III (Internal Market and Industrial Affairs) and DG IV (Competition) sought to accommodate their differing policy objectives. As a result, the authors argued, the Commission became more and more permissive towards aid for SME while the overall control of national state aid was tightened (ibid: 190). A more recent example of tensions between industrial and competition policy objectives is the regulation of so-called 'innovation aid'. While this new category of compatible aid was partly regarded with scepticism within DG COMP and the Legal Service, for example, as to how to identify 'innovation', its introduction was actively promoted by DG Enterprise and Industry (Blauberger 2009b: 723). Another field which traditionally involves tensions between different DGs and policy objectives is regional policy which is discussed in Chapter 10 (Cini and McGowan 2009: 182f.). When the Commission presented its Regional Aid Guidelines in 1998, one commentator questioned whether this was still competition policy or 'cohesion policy by the back door':

> This presentation of the Guidelines is notable for a number of reasons. First, it makes no mention of the perceived need to control regional aid in the context of distortions of competition (. . .) Second, it is very much concerned with the *substance* of regional policy. (Wishlade 2003: 89, emphasis in the original text)

More generally, these various examples have been interpreted as evidence of an evolving European model of 'good' State aid policy (Blauberger 2009b). Although State aid policy is not harmonised at the EU level, the Commission has adopted the Council's plea for 'less and better targeted aid' as its own reform slogan. Most explicitly, the Commission's State Aid Action Plan (SAAP) of 2005 defined substantive 'key priorities' for well-targeted aid and called for 'a modernised state aid policy in the context of the Lisbon strategy for growth and jobs' (European Commission 2005). An overview of the modernisation policy is provided in Chapter 1 of this book.

The policy considerations of the Commission are also present in its 'balancing test' mentioned above. In line with the jurisprudence of the CJEU, the balancing test requires all national State aid measures to be justified with regard to some 'common interest' of the EU (European Commission 2005: 4). The implications of this approach as well as its limits have become most obvious during the reform of the Regional Aid Guidelines in the context of Eastern enlargement. According to the Commission's original proposal, State aid should have been restricted to the most underdeveloped regions from a European perspective (Wishlade 2008: 756–759). After strong opposition from some 'old' Member States, the Commission returned to a less radical approach which still allows regional aid for these countries' least developed regions. It can only be speculated, whether the Commission's initial proposal was deliberately radical in order to yield concessions by some Member States or whether the Commission was partly surprised by the force of their opposition (Wishlade 2008: 759). The second element of the Commission's balancing test, the so-called 'incentive effect' was partly perceived as an unwarranted interference into national State aid policy as well. In its comment on the SAAP, the German government opposed the Commission's proposal:

The Commission possesses the competence neither to allocate resources nor to harmonise legal and financial policies nor to evaluate the success of national state aid policies' (Bundesministerium der Finanzen 2005: 2).

Nevertheless, the incentive test has subsequently been systematically introduced into European state aid rules (Neven and Verouden 2008: 1.51).

To sum up, State aid control inherently touches upon the objectives of national State aid policy and the Commission has increasingly developed an own model of what it considers to be well-targeted aid. Our knowledge about how these policy objectives are defined internally by the Commission as well as in exchange with Member State governments remains rather anecdotal. Given the overall tightening of European State aid control, Member State governments, while formally continuing to insist on their authority to design national state aid policies, appear to progressively accept the Commission's influence on the substance of State aid policy. We now turn to the question of the actual EU influence on national State aid policies.

III.   EUROPEANISATION OF NATIONAL STATE AID POLICIES

The term 'Europeanisation' refers to the domestic impact of European integration. Do EU Member States really grant 'less and better targeted' aid? And if they do so: are these trends caused by EU influences? A second strand of political science research on EU State aid control tries to identify its domestic impact, analyses the ways by which the Commission influences the design of national State aid policies and discusses alternative explanations for the observable trends.

III.i.   Empirical Evidence and Competing Explanations

Studies on the domestic impact of EU State aid control either follow a quantitative approach, investigating the development of State aid levels and objectives, or they analyse more qualitatively individual cases and processes of national policy adjustments. As regards quantitative studies, various political-scientific authors base their analysis on data from the EU State aid Scoreboard and the Commission's register of State aid cases (Smith 1996; Zahariadis 1997; Wolf 2005; Aydin 2007; Zahariadis 2008; Blauberger 2009a). The Commission's Scoreboard provides the most complete and up-to-date dataset on State aid, compared, for example, to OECD data (Aydin 2007: 121), which may partly explain the proliferation of quantitative studies based on this source. These studies largely confirm the Commission's own observation of a downward trend in State aid expenditure during the 1990s and most of the 2000s as well as a redirection of State aid towards horizontal objectives in recent years (European Commission 2008).

Apart from the overall trends, however, quantitative studies differ insofar as they attribute changes in national State aid policies only partly to European influences. Most sceptical as regards EU impact, Zahariadis (2002: 296) deduces from his comparison of State aid expenditures in EU Member and non-Member countries in the early 1990s that increasing trade linkages rather than formal EU membership explain State aid discipline. Other accounts of State aid expenditure focus on socio-economic and party political factors such as high levels of unemployment (Blais 1986), leftist governments (Zahariadis 1997; Cao et al. 2007), or political pathologies such as weak governments and lack of transparency (Neven and Röller 2000). Yet, these accounts hardly explain the long-term trends observed within the EU. In contrast, more recent comparisons of EU Member and non-Member States unanimously find that EU State aid control makes a difference. Wolf (2005) compares systems of State aid control across different levels, global (WTO), regional (EU), and national (German federalism), and concludes that EU State aid control is by far the most effective system in ensuring compliance (ibid.: 91). Aydin (2007) analyses State aid expenditure across 16 OECD countries, including EU and EEA Member States, candidate countries, Turkey, and Japan. Without denying the persisting differences between EU Member States' industrial policies, she finds strong evidence for lower State aid levels due to EU State aid control (ibid.: 122–125). Finally, Blauberger (2009a) compares State aid policies in Central and Eastern European countries before and after EU accession. While candidate countries partly used their 'last-minute' chance between the conclusion of accession negotiations and enlargement to grant considerable amounts of State aid, they largely brought their policies in line with EU requirements afterwards (ibid: 1037).

Qualitative studies complement these accounts of broader trends by focusing on individual cases of successful or unsuccessful State aid control. Their picture of the domestic impact of European State aid control is more nuanced. For example, a case study on German public banks analyses how European State aid control provided an opportunity structure for private competitors to complain and to build an alliance with the Commission which finally helped to overcome governmental resistance (Grossman 2006). Although the issue of German public banks under EU State aid control may not be settled once and for all, the analysis shows the Commission's ability to enforce EU State aid rules even against strong institutional inertia if it builds strategic alliances and if it uses its windows of opportunity when governmental resistance vanishes (ibid: 341).

Other studies are more sceptical and point to institutional incompatibilities between the EU and domestic levels which may lead to sub-optimal outcomes for both sides. Despite initial agreement on the direction of restructuring Olympic Airways, the positions of the Greek government and the Commission diverged over time and both parties ended up in a legal conflict before the CJEU (Featherstone and Papadimitriou 2007; see Chapter 6 of this volume). The Commission won the case in the CJEU, but taking the long duration of the conflict into account and the legal uncertainty involved, this result was clearly inferior to a cooperative solution. According to Featherstone and Papadimitriou both conflict parties contributed to this outcome (ibid: 51): On the one hand, the Greek government suffered from its shorter time horizon and multiple veto players in domestic policy-making. On the other hand, the Commission proved partly unable to proactively assist the Greek government in finding a workable restructuring strategy and sent inconsistent signals, thus increasing legal uncertainty. In a similar vein, the dispute over State aid to Volkswagen in Saxony serves as an example for Thielemann (1999) to illustrate different institutional logics of German federalism and EU State aid control. Three institutional features, the author argues, explain the Commission's 'blindness' to the peculiarities of German federalism and caused an evitable conflict (ibid: 411f.): centralized decision-making of DG COMP versus traditionally joint decision-making involving federal and regional authorities in Germany, discretionary versus legalistic decision-making, as well as horizontal versus vertical policy co-ordination (that is, the interference of DG COMP in what is considered to be a question of regional policy autonomy in Germany).

While this critical analysis of tensions between German federalism and the Commission's practice dates back to 1999 and some of the institutional incompatibilities may have been alleviated since then, more recent qualitative studies address the special circumstances of EU State aid control in Central and Eastern Europe. One of the major topics of debate during accession negotiations was regional aid, mainly through tax exemptions in so-called 'special economic zones' (Atanasiu 2001; Bohle and Husz 2005). The Commission concluded several transitional agreements on special economic zones with Poland, Hungary and other new Member States. In the case of Hungary, Bohle and Husz (2005: 94f.) argue, the concessions made by the Commission were not so much due to insurmountable governmental resistance, as the tax exemptions granted put a serious strain on public budgets, but rather resulted from successful lobbying of multinational companies who are the main beneficiaries of this type of regional aid. In Poland, domestic party politics and unstable governments were the main reasons why the introduction of State aid legislation was repeatedly delayed and hardly accomplished by the date of accession (Gwiazda 2007). Given that accession countries had no choice but to comply with EU demands, however, party political factors played a decreasingly important role towards the end of accession negotiations and after accession, even the eurosceptic Kaczyński government could not fundamentally oppose EU State aid control anymore (ibid.: 124).

In sum, a broad variety of political-scientific studies show that national State aid policies are partly 'europeanised', that is that EU State aid control has an identifiable impact on the overall design of Member States' policies as well as on individual State aid measures. While aggregate trends, however, tell us little about the instruments and mechanisms of EU influence on the ground, individual case studies sometimes provide very specific explanations that may only be representative for some cases, for example, depending on the applicable rules or the Member States involved. The remaining part of this chapter, therefore, discusses recurrent patterns of Member State compliance with EU State aid rules.

III.ii.   Patterns of Compliance with EU State Aid Rules

There exists an increasingly differentiated political science literature on why States (do not) comply with EU legal obligations and by which instruments the Commission is most successful in 'guarding the Treaty', that is, in making Member States comply (Börzel 2003; for a broad overview, see Treib 2008). Compliance with EU State aid rules is a special case in at least two respects. First, before initiating infringement proceedings, the Commission already possesses the specific tool of recovery decisions.[8] Second, in contrast to harmonised EU policies, 'compliance' with EU State aid rules is not accomplished once and for all by the domestic transposition and implementation of European secondary law, but continuously and often passively through not granting distortive aid (Blauberger 2009a: 1033).

In the most comprehensive discussion of various compliance mechanisms in the field of State aid control, Wolf (2005: 92–113) finds hierarchical forms of enforcement, monitoring and sanctioning through the Commission, judicial dispute settlement by the CJEU, most important for ensuring compliance with EU State aid rules. By contrast, inclusion and participation of the affected parties or discursive processes of mutual learning are found to be less decisive. Undoubtedly, the single most powerful instrument of the Commission is a negative decision (including the order of recovery of unlawful aid) or even the threat thereof. While the relatively low number of negative decisions might be interpreted to indicate weak enforcement by the Commission, it was noted quite early that it should rather be read as a sign of Member States' anticipatory obedience (Smith 1996: 568). Unlike infringement proceedings, which often take very long before they become costly for non-compliant Member State governments, the Commission's threat to decide negatively or even the opening of formal investigations immediately impose costs on potential State aid beneficiaries through creating legal uncertainty, thus reducing the attractiveness of receiving State aid in the first place. Hence, given that firms know about this legal uncertainty and also about the risk of losing governmental support during lengthy procedures, EU State aid rules serve to 'channel State aid demand' (Blauberger 2009a: 1041f.). Eventually, in cases of sustained ignorance of EU obligations by Member State governments, the Commission can still largely count on the support of the CJEU for its negative decisions (cf. Featherstone and Papadimitriou 2007) and it has significantly intensified its efforts to close pending recovery cases in recent years.

Apart from the most critical State aid cases, however, in which formal investigations and the threat of negative decisions exert a deterrent effect, compliance with EU State aid rules is largely assured at the early stages of policy formulation, based on the comprehensive regulation of State aid procedures and substance (Wolf 2005: 99f.). As regards compatible aid, the Commission managed to gradually increase and shift the burden of proof towards Member State governments. While the Commission automatically assumes all State aid to potentially distort competition, Member State governments, in order to pass the balancing test and to make final approval likely, need to design and justify their State aid measures along the lines of the Commission's Guidelines and Frameworks. Besides, the more detailed the criteria set out by the Commission in guiding its assessment of compatible aid, the more these rules provided an opportunity structure for private parties to either demand forms of compatible aid or to complain about distortive aid (cf. Grossman 2006).

Finally, the assertion that the inclusion of affected parties and mutual learning are less decisive for compliance needs to be partly qualified. Wolf (2005: 111) does not principally deny the importance of these factors, but argues:

> As such, the years up until the 1980s can be seen as a time of common learning and the discursive development of European state aid control law (. . .) However (. . .) the ratio of landmark cases to simple rule application cases has decreased rapidly over the last ten years because of the now well-established system of state aid control in the EU.

Yet, two more recent developments point to an ongoing relevance of participatory and discursive elements in ensuring Member State compliance. Firstly, the Commission's extensive use of public consultations during the revision of Guidelines and Frameworks.[9] Secondly, the training of competition experts in EU candidate countries during the accession preparations. Before accession, candidate countries are required to establish national State aid monitoring authorities that are supposed to play the role of, and to entertain close contacts with, the Commission. These authorities serve to build State aid expertise at the domestic level and to train staff for the Commission services. Lastly, high-profile cases such as the restructuring of Olympic Airways (Featherstone and Papadimitriou 2007) may serve as reminders not to underestimate the importance of multilevel cooperation in avoiding legal conflicts in the vast majority of cases.

IV.   CONCLUSION

The main goal of this chapter was to show that EU State aid control poses many interesting questions for political scientists and to provide a brief overview of the answers given so far. While EU State aid control did not attract broad attention by political scientists until the late 1990s, the body of literature has grown considerably during the last decade. Yet, there is still plenty of room for further research.

State aid during the financial and economic crisis, Member State policies as well as their treatment by the Commission, will certainly become a major research topic (cf. Wilks 2009: 273).[10] How far, and by which, strategies will the Commission be able to temporarily limit the exceptions made during the crisis and to return to strict enforcement of EU State aid rules? What will be the mid- and long-term effects of the crisis on Member States' expenditure for State aid? Other research gaps were already identified in previous parts of this chapter: What determines the Commission's evolving mix of policy goals incorporated into EU State aid rules? How far do Member States' policies converge towards a common European model of modern State aid policy and what accounts for persisting differences between national approaches? Finally, one may at least speculate about some issues that could gain relevance in the future: What is the role of EU State aid control in an increasingly global economy, for example, will the EU be able to export its State aid rules beyond Europe (cf. Aydin 2009). Or, from a normative perspective: taking into account ongoing debates about the EU's 'democratic deficit' (Höpner and Schäfer 2010: 362f.), is an increasingly powerful and differentiated EU system of State aid control still sufficiently legitimated by its promise to provide overall efficiency gains?

NOTES

1. I thank Umut Aydin, Markus Krajewski and Rike U. Krämer for their helpful comments on draft versions of this chapter.
2. A major element of the refined economic approach in State aid control is the introduction of the so-called 'balancing test' which aims at assessing more systematically the potential positive and negative effects of proposed State aid measures. Yet, this test cannot be conducted without prior definition of some criteria and policy objectives which are regarded to be in the common interest. For more detail, see Neven and Verouden (2008: 1.17). For a study which addresses the methodological limits of evaluating the effectiveness of State aid measures, see Nitsche and Heidhues (2006: 65f.). See also Chapter 4 by Coppi in this volume.
3. See for example, the discussion of soft law in the regulation of SGEIs by Szyszczak in Chapter 13 of this volume.
4. See Cini (2001: 201f.) for a detailed study of the Commission's strategic behaviour vis-à-vis Germany and Spain when these two countries refused to accept a new framework on State aid to the motor vehicle industry in 1989. A more recent example is Germany's initial refusal to accept the revised Guidelines on regional aid which had been accepted by all other 24 EU Member States in 2006. The heading of the Commission's Press Release (IP/06/851) showed quite openly the punitive character of its response: 'State Aid: 24 Member States Accept New Regional Aid Guidelines (2007–2013); Commission Opens Formal Investigation *against* Germany' (emphasis added).
5. As a consequence, some candidate countries like Poland engaged in enormous legislative activity, trying to transpose large parts of EU State aid Guidelines and frameworks into domestic law (Gwiazda 2007).
6. See the Commission's Communication of 2 July 2009, O.J. 2009 C 156/3.
7. Case C-379/98, *Preussen Elektra* [2001] E.C.R. I-2099.
8. Accordingly, the most appropriate indicators for Member State non-compliance with EU State aid rules are the number and volume of pending recovery cases. Apart from the Commission's own analyses published in the EU State Aid Scoreboard and the Competition Policy Newsletter (cf. Marinas 2005), however, this data (which is only available from 2000 onwards) has hardly been recognised in the political science literature. Most authors rather focus on individual cases or they interpret overall State aid reductions and redirections towards horizontal aid as indirect signs of Member State compliance.
9. The website of DG COMP provides a comprehensive overview of ongoing and closed consultations: <http://ec.europa.eu/competition/consultations/closed.html>
10. See, for example, the workshop on 'The European Union and State Aid: the Present Crisis and Beyond' which was held at the Centre for Competition Policy, Norwich, and which brought together lawyers, economists and political scientists. Online: <http://www.uea.ac.uk/ccp/events/pastevents/2009stateaid> (Last checked: 22 December 2010).

REFERENCES

Atanasiu, Isabela (2001), 'State Aid in Central and Eastern Europe', *World Competition*, **24**, 257–283.

Aydin, Umut (2007), 'Promoting industries in the global economy: subsidies in OECD countries, 1989 to 1995', *Journal of European Public Policy*, **14**, 115–131.

Aydin, Umut (2009), *Promoting Competition: European Union and the Global Competition Order*, Paper presented at the EUSA Eleventh Biennial International Conference, Los Angeles (23–25 April 2009).

Blais, André (1986), 'The Political Economy of Public Subsidies', *Comparative Political Studies*, **19**, 201–216.

Blauberger, Michael (2009a), 'Compliance with rules of negative integration. European State aid control in the new Member States', *Journal of European Public Policy*, **16**, 1030–1046.

Blauberger, Michael (2009b), 'Of 'good' and 'bad' subsidies: European state aid control through soft and hard law', *West European Politics*, **32**, 719–737.

Bohle, Dorothee and Dóra Husz (2005), 'Whose Europe is it? Interest group action in accession negotiations: the cases of competition policy and labor migration', *Politique Européenne*, **6**, 85–112.

Börzel, Tanja A. (2003), 'Guarding the Treaty. The compliance strategies of the European Commission', in Tanja A. Börzel and Rachel A. Cichowski (eds), *The State of the European Union VI: Law, Politics, and Society*, Oxford/New York: Oxford University Press, 197–220.

Bundesministerium der Finanzen (2005), *Stellungnahme der Bundesregierung der Bundesrepublik Deutschland zum 'Aktionsplan staatliche Beihilfen'*, Berlin.

Burley, Anne-Marie and Walter Mattli (1993), 'Europe before the court: a political theory of legal integration', *International Organization*, **47**, 41–76.

Cao, Xun, Aseem Prakash and Michael D. Ward (2007), 'Protecting jobs in the age of globalization: examining the relative salience of social welfare and industrial subsidies in OECD countries', *International Studies Quarterly*, **51**, 301–327.

Cini, Michelle (2001), 'The soft law approach: commission rule-making in the EU's State aid regime', *Journal of European Public Policy*, **8**, 192–207.

Cini, Michelle and Lee McGowan (2009), *Competition Policy in the European Union*, Houndmills/New York: Palgrave Macmillan.

Doleys, Thomas (2009), *Fifty Years of Moulding Article 87: The European Commission and the Development of EU State Aid Law & Policy (1958–2008)*, Paper presented at the ESRC Workshop 'The European Union and State Aid: The Present Crisis and Beyond', (9–10 July 2009) Norwich.

Ehlermann, Claus Dieter (1995), *State Aid Control: Failure or Success?* Brussels: European Commission.

European Commission (2005), *State Aid Action Plan. Less and Better Targeted State Aid: A Roadmap for State Aid Reform 2005-2009*, Brussels.

European Commission (2008), *State Aid Scoreboard. Autumn 2008 Update*, Brussels.

Featherstone, Kevin and Dimitris Papadimitriou (2007), 'Manipulating rules, contesting solutions: Europeanization and the politics of restructuring Olympic Airways', *Government and Opposition*, **42**, 46–72.

Franchino, Fabio (2005), 'The study of EU public policy. Results of a survey', *European Union Politics*, **6**, 243–252.

From, Johan (2002), 'Decision-making in a complex environment: A sociological institutionalist analysis of competition policy decision-making in the European Commission', *Journal of European Public Policy*, **9**, 219–237.

Grossman, Emiliano (2006), 'Europeanization as an Interactive Process: German Public Banks Meet EU State Aid Policy', *Journal of Common Market Studies*, **44**, 325–348.

Gwiazda, Anna (2007), 'Europeanization of Polish competition policy', *European Integration*, **29**, 109–131.

Höpner, Martin and Armin Schäfer (2010), 'A new phase of European integration: organised capitalisms in post-ricardian Europe', *West European Politics*, **33**, 344–368.

Karagiannis, Yannis (2009), *Still in the Era of Area Studies? Political-Scientific Perspectives on European Competition Policy in the 2000s*, Barcelona: IBEI Working Paper 2009/24.

Kroes, Neelie (2006), *The Refined Economic Approach in State Aid Law: A Policy Perspective*, Presentation at the College of Europe Conference, (21 September 2006) Brussels.

Lavdas, Kostas A. and Maria M. Mendrinou (1995), 'Competition Policy and Institutional Politics in the European Community: State Aid Control and Small Business Promotion', *European Journal of Political Research*, **28**, 171–201.

Lavdas, Kostas A. and Maria M. Mendrinou (1999), *Politics, Subsidies, and Competition. The New Politics of State Intervention in the European Union*, Cheltenham: Edward Elgar.

Lehmkuhl, Dirk (2008), 'On government, governance, and judicial review: the case of European competition policy', *Journal of Public Policy*, **28**, 139–159.

Marinas, Nuria (2005), 'Enforcement of State Aid Recovery Decisions' *Competition Policy Newsletter*, **11**, 17–21.

Méndez, Carlos, Fiona Wishlade and Douglas Yuill (2006), 'Conditioning and fine-tuning europeanization: negotiating regional policy maps under the EU's competition and cohesion policies', *Journal of Common Market Studies*, **44**, 581–605.

Moravcsik, Andrew (1993), 'Preferences and power in the European Community: a liberal intergovernmentalist approach', *Journal of Common Market Studies*, **31**, 473–524.

Neven, Damien J.and Lars-Hendrik Röller (2000), 'The political economy of State aid: econometric evidence for the Member States', Damien J. Neven and Lars-Hendrik Röller (eds), *The Political Economy of Industrial Policy in Europe and the Member States*, Berlin: edition sigma, 25–37.

Neven, Damien J. and Vincent Verouden (2008), 'Towards a more refined economic approach in State aid control', in Wolfgang Mederer and Nicola Pesaresi and Marc van Hoof (eds), *EU Competition Law Volume IV: State Aid*, Leuven: Claeys & Casteels, Ch. 4.

Nitsche, Rainer and Paul Heidhues (2006), *Study on Methods to Analyse the Impact of State Aid on Competition*, European Economy, No. 244, Brussels: European Commission, Directorate General for Economic and Financial Affairs.

Rawlinson, Francis (1993), 'The role of policy frameworks, codes, and guidelines in the control of State aid', in Ian Harden (ed) *State Aid: Community Law and Policy*, Köln: Bundesanzeiger Verlagsgesellschaft, 52–60.

Schmidt, Susanne K. (2000), 'Only an agenda setter? The European Commission's power over the council of Ministers', *European Union Politics*, **1**, 37–61.

Smith, Mitchell P. (1996), 'Integration in small steps: the European Commission and Member-State aid to industry, *West European Politics*, **19**, 563–582.

Smith, Mitchell P. (1998), 'Autonomy by the rules: the European Commission and the development of State aid policy', *Journal of Common Market Studies*, **36**, 55–78.

Smith, Mitchell P. (2001), 'How adaptable is the European Commission? The case of State aid regulation', *Journal of Public Policy*, **21**, 219–238.

Thielemann, Eiko R. (1999), 'Institutional limits of a 'Europe with the regions': EC State-aid control meets German federalism', *Journal of European Public Policy*, **6**, 399–418.

Treib, Oliver, (2008), 'Implementing and complying with EU governance outputs', *Living Reviews in European Governance* 3, available at http://www.livingreviews.org/lreg-2006-1 [25.01.2007].

Wilks, Stephan (2009) 'The Impact of the Recession on Competition Policy: Amending the Economic Constitution?' International Journal of the Economics of Business **16**, 269–288.

Wishlade, Fiona (2003), *Regional State Aid and Competition Policy in the European Union*, The Hague, London, New York: Kluwer Law International.

Wishlade, Fiona (2008), 'Competition and cohesion – coherence or conflict? European Union regional State aid reform post-2006', *Regional Studies*, **42**, 753–765.

Wolf, Dieter (2005), 'State aid control at the national, European, and international level', in Michael Zürn and Christian Joerges (eds), *Law and Governance in Postnational Europe. Compliance beyond the Nation-State*, Cambridge: Cambridge University Press, 65–117.

Zahariadis, Nikolaos (1997), 'Why State subsidies? Evidence from the European Community countries, 1981–1986', *International Studies Quarterly*, **41**, 341–354.

Zahariadis, Nikolaos (2002), 'The political economy of State subsidies in Europe', *Policy Studies Journal*, **30**, 285–298.

Zahariadis, Nikolaos (2008), *State Subsidies in the Global Economy*, New York: Palgrave.

3 State aid in the accession States
Alexander Birnstiel and Helge Heinrich

I. INTRODUCTION

As the title of this chapter indicates, the chapter is intended to give an overview of State aid in the so called 'accession States'. The term 'accession States' refers to European States which either have already become EU Member States during one of the last EU enlargement rounds (the so called new Member States) or which have applied for EU membership and have been granted the status of a candidate State.

Accession States are obliged to incorporate the *acquis communautaire* into their legal system. This obligation applies also to State subsidies and the underlying State aid policy which must comply with the EU State aid framework from the accession date. It may not be expected that most of the measures involving State aid in accession countries can be aligned with the State aid *acquis* from day one. The accession of new Member States always involves the considerable risk that State aid incompatible with the State aid *acquis* significantly hampers competition in the common/internal market.

In order to avoid such a scenario, it is obvious that a system needs to be developed and applied which allows for a smooth transition from State subsidies in the pre-accession period to State aid compatible with the common/internal market in the post-accession period. This mechanism must entail a fair balancing of the legitimate interests of the EU with regard to safeguarding an undistorted competition in the common/internal market on the one side, and the candidate countries with regard to the time and efforts it may take to adopt and implement a State aid policy compatible with the State aid *acquis*, on the other side.

The experience of the last enlargements indicates that a system of phasing in EU State aid rules by implementing a pre-accession system of State aid control in the candidate countries will best serve the purpose of a smooth transition. This is not to deny the institutional and political challenges that are inherent to this approach. After accession, however, there is no room for a 'gradual phasing-out of old interventionist habits' by stipulating certain transitional periods any more (Stobiecka-Kuik and Bomhoff 2008: 1.503).

For this reason, it seems worth placing the emphasis in this chapter on the description and analysis of the pre-accession systems of national State aid control that were successfully implemented in the Central and Eastern European candidate States during the enlargement rounds in 2004 and 2007, respectively. In 2004, Cyprus, Malta, Hungary, Poland, the Slovak Republic, Latvia, Estonia, Lithuania, the Czech Republic and Slovenia joined the EU, and, only three years later, Romania and Bulgaria in 2007.

Our analysis focuses on the following aspects:

- a description of the history of the 2004 and 2007 enlargements providing the factual background for the introduction of pre-accession national systems of State aid control (Part II);
- a State-by-State review of transitional arrangements including a discussion of problematic areas of State aid in candidate States (Part III);
- an analysis of the concept of existing aid which is the legal rationale behind the introduction of pre-accession national systems of State aid control (part IV);
- a discussion of possible lessons for future enlargements (Part V), and;
- as the concluding part of this chapter, an overview of the situation in current candidate and possible candidate States (Part VI).

II.   A SHORT HISTORY OF THE 2004 AND 2007 ENLARGEMENT

II.i.   Overview of Procedural Steps for EU Membership

Article 49 TEU provides that: '*Any European State which respects the values referred to in Article 2 and is committed to promoting them may apply to become a member of the Union.*' Any membership application will be submitted to the Council. If the Council unanimously agrees on a negotiating mandate, accession negotiations may be formally opened with the candidate country. As the EU acts as an Intergovernmental Conference regarding accession negotiations, the Member States are the parties to the accession negotiations so that each EU decision must be taken unanimously. The Presidency of the EU presents the negotiating positions agreed by the Member States and chairs negotiating sessions at the level of ministers or their deputies.

The negotiations concentrate on the terms under which the candidate States will join the EU and, in particular, adopt and implement the *acquis*. This includes the stipulation of possible transitional arrangements to allow the candidate State a longer implementation period of certain parts of the *acquis*. Such transitional arrangements may only be exceptionally granted, they must be limited in scope and duration (Känkänen 2003: 26).

The *acquis* is split up into separate negotiation chapters one of which relates to competition policy. The Commission closely monitors the progress of each candidate State and publishes annual reports on the progress already achieved. Negotiations are not completed before all 31 chapters have been closed.

The results of the negotiations will be incorporated in the Accession Treaty and Act. On the side of the EU, the assent of the Parliament and the approval of the Council are required. After signature, Member States and candidate States have to ratify the Treaty and Act. Upon completion of these acts, the Treaty will become effective and the candidate State becomes a Member State on the agreed date.

II.ii.   Political and Economic Circumstances of the 2004 and 2007 Enlargement

Soon after the fall of the Berlin Wall, the European Community established diplomatic relations with the countries of Central and Eastern Europe. During this process in the 1990s, so called Europe Agreements (EA) were concluded with Bulgaria, the Czech Republic, Hungary, Estonia, Latvia, Lithuania, Poland, Romania, the Slovak Republic and Slovenia preparing the way in the EU for these countries.[1] The EAs covered political cooperation, favourable trade relations, economic activities and cultural cooperation. The Association Agreements (AA) with Cyprus (1972) and Malta (1970) had already been signed and covered similar fields (except political dialogue).

In June 1993, at its Summit in Copenhagen, the European Council declared that 'the associated countries of Central and Eastern Europe that so desire shall become members of the Union' and laid down the following criteria which a candidate country is generally required to fulfil before accession negotiations may be started:

- stable institutions guaranteeing democracy, the rule of law, human rights and respect for and protection of minorities (political criteria);
- a functioning market economy which is able to cope with the pressure of competition in the internal market (economic criteria);
- adoption and implementation of the entire body of EU law (the *acquis communautaire*); and
- the ability to assume the obligations of membership including adherence to the objectives of political, economic and monetary union.[2]

The Luxembourg Summit of December 1997 agreed to launch the enlargement process and to start negotiations with the Czech Republic, Estonia, Hungary, Poland, Slovenia and Cyprus on 31 March 1998. Two years later, at the Helsinki European Council on 12 December 1999, the Member States decided to launch accession negotiations also with the remaining candidate States: Bulgaria, Latvia, Lithuania, Malta, Romania and the Slovak Republic. With the exception of Bulgaria and Romania, the negotiations with ten of the twelve candidate States could be completed at the Copenhagen Summit of 2002.

It is expected that applicant countries accept the *acquis communautaire* on joining the EU. The competition *acquis* is based on Article 37 TFEU (State monopolies of a commercial character), Articles 101–105 TFEU (rules applicable to undertakings), the EC Merger Regulation 839/2004, Article 106 TFEU (public undertakings and undertakings with special or exclusive rights) and Articles 107–109 TFEU (rules applicable to State aid) and at the time of last enlargement rounds, also Articles 65 and 66 of the ECSC Treaty, which expired in 2002. Part of the State aid *acquis* is addressed under other chapters such as transport, agriculture and fisheries.

Unlike in other areas, the EU deemed mere commitments in the field of State aid insufficient and provided therefore a system of pre-accession conditionality on State aid. This system comprised three elements: (i) implementing the necessary national legal framework regarding State aid, (ii) providing an adequate administrative capacity for monitoring and controlling State aid on the national level and (iii) a credible enforcement record of the national State aid controlling authorities (Känkänen 2003: 24; Schütterle 2003: 29; van de Casteele 2005: 39).

As a first step, all EAs contained in their Articles 63, 64 or 65 a ban on State aid corresponding to Article 107 TFEU (Atanasiu 2001: 259; Schütterle 2002: 578; Cremona 2003). Accordingly, any State aid distorting or threatening to distort competition by favouring certain undertakings or the production of certain goods was considered incompatible with the proper functioning of the EA if the State aid were to affect trade between the EU and the candidate country. Moreover, the majority of the EA envisaged the adoption of State aid implementing rules. According to the implementing rules candidate countries would establish national authorities to control and monitor the granting of State aid in the respective candidate countries (Cremona 2003: 268–269).[3] As the candidate countries were free to decide on how to establish their national State aid control systems, some decided for independent central bodies, while other candidate countries assigned this task to special units of ministries, usually the finance ministry.

In Hungary, for instance, the State Aid Monitoring Office (SAMO) was established as part of the Ministry of Finance for supervising aid granted by the Hungarian authorities prior to the accession. Today, SAMO is the responsible national coordinating body for State aid issues (Hargita and Filep 2004: 586). In Slovenia, the Commission for State Aid Control was established as an internal unit originally of the Ministry of the Economy and later the Ministry of Finance. With the accession, this Commission was replaced by a special department at the Ministry of Finance, the State Aid Monitoring Sector. This authority fulfils monitoring tasks and provides administrative assistance to grantors of State aid (Jagodič-Lekočevič 2004: 375–377). In the Czech Republic, the Office for Protection of Economic Competition (OPEC) acted as an independent authority, monitoring and supervising body responsible for the compliance assessment with the State Aid Act prior to the accession (Bednar 2005: 265). In Poland, the president of the Office of Competition and Consumer Protection (OCCP) is responsible for notifying planned aid measures to the Commission. Until accession, the president of the OCCP was authorized to supervise and monitor State aid. (Paczkowska-Tomaszewska, Jaros and Winiarski 2006: 670).

For the first time in accession history, the EU introduced a system of double review of the compatibility of State aid granted prior to, and still applicable after, the accession. This review was conducted first by the national authority and then by the Commission (Kuik 2004: 367; Stobiecka-Kuik and Bomhoff 2008: 1.443).

The EAs became obsolete with the accession to the EU. From this time, the competence to declare State measures compatible with the substantive (national) rules on State aid shifted from the national authorities in the candidate countries to the Commission which has the exclusive jurisdiction for declaring State aid compatible with the common/internal market. Most new Member States decided to maintain the national State aid control system to preserve the expert knowledge and experience already gained in the pre-accession years (Jagodič-Lekočevič 2004: 376; Hargita and Filep 2004: 586; Kuik 2004: 365).

III. OVERVIEW OF TRANSITIONAL ARRANGEMENTS AND TYPICAL FORMS OF PROBLEMATIC STATE AID DURING THE 2004 AND 2007 ENLARGEMENT

III.i. Overview of Transitional Arrangements State-by-State

III.i.a. Bulgaria

The competition chapter was finally closed in December 2004. Bulgaria demanded no transitional arrangements.

III.i.b. Cyprus

The competition chapter was closed in December 2002. For incompatible fiscal aid, a phase-out was agreed by the end of 2005.

III.i.c. Czech Republic

The competition chapter was closed in December 2002. Transitional arrangements have been concluded with regard to the restructuring of the Czech steel industry, which had to be completed by 31 December 2006.

III.i.d. Estonia

The competition chapter was closed in December 2002 without transitional arrangements.

III.i.e. Hungary

The competition chapter was closed in December 2002. The following transitional arrangements have been agreed upon with Hungary during the accession negotiations:

– The phasing-out of incompatible fiscal aid for SMEs by the end of 2011.
– The conversion of incompatible fiscal aid for large undertakings into regional investment aid. The maximum aid ceiling was restricted to 75% of the eligible investment costs if the company started the investment under the scheme before 1 January 2000 and to 50% if the company started the investment after 1 January 2000. In the motor vehicle industry the maximum aid was further limited corresponding to 40% of the maximum aid ceiling (i.e. 30% if the regional aid ceiling for other types of investment was 75%).
– The phasing-out of incompatible fiscal aid for off-shore companies by the end of 2005.
– The phasing out of incompatible fiscal aid granted by local authorities by the end of 2007.

III.i. f. Latvia

The competition chapter was closed in December 2002 without transitional arrangements.

III.i.g. Lithuania

The competition chapter was closed in December 2002 without transitional arrangements.

III.i. h.   Malta

The competition chapter was closed in December 2002. The following transitional arrangements have been agreed upon with Malta during the accession negotiations:

– The phasing-out of incompatible fiscal aid for SMEs by the end of 2011.
– The conversion of incompatible fiscal aid for large companies into regional investment aid. The maximum aid ceiling was restricted to 75% of the eligible investment costs if the company started the investment under the scheme before 1 January 2000 and to 50% if the company started the investment after 1 January 2000.
– Restructuring aid for the shipbuilding sector during a restructuring period until the end of 2008.
– The phasing-out of operating aid under the Business Promotion Act by the end of 2008.

III.i. i. Poland

The competition chapter was closed in December 2002. The following transitional arrangements have been agreed upon with Poland during the accession negotiations:

– The phasing-out of incompatible fiscal aid for small enterprises by the end of 2011.
– The phasing-out of incompatible fiscal aid for medium-sized enterprises by the end of 2010.
– The conversion of incompatible fiscal aid for large undertakings into regional investment aid. The maximum aid ceiling was restricted to 75% of the eligible investment costs if the company started the investment under the scheme before 1 January 2000 and to 50% if the company started the investment after 1 January 2000. In the motor vehicle industry, the maximum aid was further limited corresponding to 40% of the maximum aid ceiling (i.e. 30% of the eligible investment costs if the regional aid ceiling for other types of investment was 75%).
– Regarding State aid for environmental protection, transitional arrangements have been accepted for standard-related investments for which a specific transitional period had been agreed upon in the Environment Chapter. The aid intensity was limited to the applicable regional aid ceiling with a 15% supplement for SMEs. For existing IPPC installations covered by a transitional period under the Environment Chapter, a 30% aid intensity was accepted until

the end of 2010, while for IPPC-related investment not covered by a transitional period under the Environment Chapter, the 30% aid intensity was only limited until 31 October 2007. For large combustion plants, an aid intensity of 50% was held acceptable for investments relating to a specific transitional period stipulated under the Environment Chapter

- The restructuring of the steel industry by the end of 2006.

III.i.j.   Romania

The competition chapter was closed in December 2004. The following transitional arrangements have been agreed with Romania during the accession negotiations:

- The phasing-out of incompatible fiscal aid by 31 December 2011 under the Law on Free Trade Areas for undertakings which signed commercial contracts before 1 July 2002. The State aid may be granted for regional investments. The maximum aid intensity is 50% of the net grant equivalent and 65% for SMEs provided that the total net aid intensity does not exceed 75%. In the motor vehicle sector, the total aid is limited to a maximum of 30% of the eligible investments costs.
- The phasing-out of incompatible fiscal aid by 31 December 2010 under the GEO on Deprived Areas for undertakings which were given the permanent investor certificate before 1 July 2003. The State aid may be granted for regional investments. The maximum aid intensity must not exceed 50% of the net grant equivalent and 65% for SMEs provided that the total net aid intensity does not exceed 75%. In the motor vehicle sector, the total aid is limited to a maximum of 30% of the eligible investment costs.

III.i.k.   Slovakia

The competition chapter was closed in December 2002. The following transitional arrangements have been agreed upon with Poland during the accession negotiations:

- The conversion of incompatible fiscal aid and into regional investment aid regarding, however, only one beneficiary in the motor vehicle manufacturing sector. The maximum aid intensity was limited to 30% of the eligible investment costs.
- The phasing-out of incompatible fiscal aid to one beneficiary in the steel sector when the aid reaches a pre-determined amount or by the end of 2009, at the latest. The aid objective was to facilitate

an ordered rationalization process leading to a reduction of excess staffing levels.

III.i.l.   Slovenia
The competition chapter was closed in December 2002 without transitional arrangements.

IiI.ii.   Typical Forms of Problematic State Aid

III.ii.a.   Fiscal measures
Given the budgetary constraints in most of the Central and Eastern European countries, indirect State aid, in particular fiscal measures such as tax holidays, tax waivers and tax deferrals were widely used measures of industrial policy (Atanasiu and Oprescu 2004: 69; Atanasiu 2005: 597). It was therefore not a real surprise that the Commission found a number of tax schemes during the negotiations which did not comply with the State aid *acquis*, as can also be seen from the State-by-State overview above. Usually it will be possible either to agree on a phasing-out of these measures after a transitional period of some years or to convert the measures into compatible horizontal aid with clearly defined objectives such as regional, environmental or training aid.

III.ii.b.   Environmental aid
Only Poland required a transitional period for certain State aid measures related to the implementation of environmental standards. This came as a surprise as it seemed unlikely that undertakings in other new Member States would be able to implement all environmental standards before accession (Stobiecka-Kuik and Bomhoff 2008: 1.477). Therefore, it may be expected that environmental aid will become an issue in future enlargements of the EU.

III.ii.c.   Aid for the steel sector
For some new Member States such as Poland or the Czech Republic the steel industry was an extremely important part of their economies (Lienemeyer 2005: 94). In the past, the mostly State-owned steel companies had been heavily supported by a wide range of State measures, including operating aid, to compensate for the problems of over-capacity.

As the steel sector was in economic difficulties during the 1990s, the Protocols of the EAs concluded with Bulgaria, the Czech Republic, Hungary, Poland, Romania, Slovakia and Slovenia provided detailed rules for the implementation of restructuring plans for steel companies (see, for example, Article 8 (4) of the Protocol 2 of the EA with Poland).

According to Protocol 2, the aid beneficiaries had to be viable at the end of the restructuring period, the amount of aid had to be limited to the absolutely necessary amount for restoring viability and the restructuring had to be linked to a capacity reduction (Lienemeyer 2005: 94).

The restructuring should have been finalized within five years from the signature of the EAs. Poland, Bulgaria, the Czech Republic and Romania did not complete the restructuring process before the envisaged deadline and requested therefore an extension of the five-year grace period following the entry into force of the respective EAs.

The rules for restructuring State aid to the steel sector have been incorporated in the Accession Acts of the Czech Republic (Protocol 2 to the 2003 Accession Act), Poland (Protocol 8 to the 2003 Accession Act), Slovakia (Annex XIV to 2003 Accession Act) and Romania (Annex VII to the 2005 Accession Act). This incorporation was necessary as restructuring aid to the steel sector has been prohibited since 2002. The respective Protocols are considered *lex specialis* to both the general rules on State aid and the regular transitional rules in the Accession Treaty (Lienemeyer 2005: 95). Therefore, steel restructuring aids were not subject to the existing aid mechanism in the Accession Treaty. As the Protocols explicitly allowed for the recovery of incompatible and steel restructuring aid, the Commission was entitled to order the recovery of incompatible aid even before accession for non Member States (Stobiecka-Kuik and Bomhoff 2008: 1.482).

In a number of cases relating to Polish and Czech steel companies the Commission opened a formal investigation procedure because Poland and the Czech Republic did not fully comply with the national restructuring plan[4] or wanted to modify the conditions of individual restructuring plans.[5]

III.iii.   Summary

As all Central and Eastern European countries which became new Member States had been State economies with highly subsidized industries before the fall of the Iron Curtain, it was only natural that both the treatment of existing State aid as well as the stipulation of certain transition periods for the application of Articles 107 and 108 TFEU were crucial issues for most of the countries. In the meantime, most of the transitional arrangements are no longer applicable as they have to be limited in scope and time. However, they are still of interest today as they show typical areas of problematic State aid which may provide useful guidance for further enlargements.

IV.   THE CONCEPT OF EXISTING STATE AID AND ITS APPLICATION TO ACCESSION STATES

The treatment of State aid granted prior to and still applicable after the accession, is one of the core questions to be dealt with in the Accession Treaty. The other central question relates to temporary exceptions from the full application of State aid rules after accession by the stipulation of transitional arrangements. This question has been discussed in the preceding part of this chapter.

It should be remembered that all new Member States of the 2004 and 2007 enlargements had already been closely linked to the EU through Europe Agreements (EA) or Association Agreements (AA) prior to the accession. This common feature is important because these agreements provided, inter alia, the framework for the establishment of national State aid control systems in these countries prior to the accession to the EU. The situation was different from an immediate Accession Act as the system of a pre-accession double review of national aid allowed for a further development of the existing-aid concept (Stobiecka-Kuik and Bomhoff 2008: 1422; Cremona: 2003: 265).

The enlargements in 2004 and 2007 were, from an economic and institutional point of view, also quite different from the preceding enlargement in 1995 when Finland, Austria and Sweden joined the EU. At the time of their accession, the economic situation of Finland, Austria and Sweden had already been very similar to that of existing Member States. Regarding State aid control, the three new Member States had been subject to the supranational EFTA Surveillance Authority control of State aids. Accordingly, only State aid which was granted in contravention of the EEA Agreement or which was not notified to the EFTA Surveillance Authority was not accepted as existing aid (Roebling 2003: 34; Stobiecka-Kuik and Bomhoff 2008: 1.443 and 1.452).

IV.I.   The Definition of Existing State Aid

Article 108 (1) TFEU provides for the basic rule that governs the treatment of existing State aid in Accession States:

> The Commission shall, in cooperation with Member States, keep under constant review all systems of aid existing in those States. It shall propose to the latter any appropriate measures required by the progressive development or by the functioning of the internal market.

Prior to the enlargement in 1995 and the adoption of the Procedural Regulation 659/1999[6] any aid which was granted before the accession to the EU was deemed to be 'historical aid'. Article 1 (b)(i) of the Procedural Regulation provides for the following definition of existing State aid which is relevant in the enlargement context:

> (. . .) All aid which existed prior to the entry into force of the Treaty in the respective Member States, that is to say aid schemes and individual aid which were put into effect before, and are still applicable after, the entry into force of the Treaty.

The Commission cannot declare existing aid incompatible and order the recovery of aid disbursed in the past under existing aid measures, which is mainly due to reasons of the protection of confidence (Roebling 2003: 33). Instead, the Commission is restricted to launching the appropriate measures procedure with the Member State's authorities. Under this procedure, the Commission may only suggest appropriate measures for the future amendment of State aid measures. Moreover, appropriate measures are only binding upon Member State approval. Without approval, the Commission must open a formal investigation procedure, which it may conclude by deciding that the future application of the aid will be incompatible without amendments. The procedure is laid down in Chapter 5 of the Procedural Regulation.

All State measures which are not qualified as existing aid according to the definition provided in the relevant Accession Act, have been considered as new aid within the meaning of Article 108 (1) TFEU. Accordingly, these measures have been subject to the notification and standstill obligation laid down in Article 108 (3) TFEU.

IV.i.a Development of the notion of existing State aid during the 1994 and 2004 enlargement

During the 1994 enlargement, when Austria, Finland and Sweden joined the EU, this general approach was somewhat refined. Before the accession, these countries had been already subject to the control and review of State aid by the EFTA Surveillance Authority. According to Article 172(5) of the 1994 Accession Act, State aid which was granted in contravention of the EEA Agreement in 1994 or which was not notified to the EFTA Surveillance Authority was not considered as existing State aid.

Chapter 3 of Annex IV to the 2003 Accession Act and Chapter 2 of Annex V to the 2005 Accession Act introduced the following – further elaborated – notion of existing aid within the meaning of Article 108 (1) TFEU and Article 1(b)(i) Procedural Regulation, respectively:

(a) Aid measures put into effect before 1st December 1994;
(b) Aid measures listed in the Appendix to the Annex of the Act;

(c) Aid measures which prior to the date of accession were assessed by the State aid monitoring authority of the new Member State and found to be compatible with the acquis, and to which the Commission did not raise an objection on the grounds of serious doubts as to the compatibility of the measure with the common market, pursuant to the procedure set out in paragraph 2.

Stobiecka-Kuik and Bomhoff note that the Commission has not identified many State aid measures in the new Member States which are covered by point c) above. Due to certain administrative hurdles, Member States did not make extensive use of the possibility to list State aid measures in the Appendix to the Annex of the Accession (see point b) above).

The interim measure (see point c) above) was based on point 2 of Chapter 3 of Annex IV to the 2003 Accession Act and point 2 of Chapter V of the 2005 Accession Act, respectively. It introduced a system of double review of the compatibility of State aid which can be described as follows. At first, the national State aid monitoring authority had to approve the measure. In a second step, the national authority submitted summary information on the measure to the Commission. If the Commission did not raise objections to the measure because it seriously doubted the compatibility with the common/internal market within three months, the measure was considered as existing aid. The second step involved a 'retroactive application' of EU State aid rules (Kuik 2004: 367). The Commission could also request additional information within the three-month period. If the serious doubts were not relieved, the Commission could take a Decision to initiate the formal investigation procedure, which would become effective only with the accession date (Roebling 2003: 36; Stobiecka-Kuik and Bomhoff 2008: 1.457). Under the interim mechanism, the new Member States (except Bulgaria and Romania) have notified 559 measures to the Commission (Kuik 2004: 366).

With regard to Romania, the 2005 Accession Act provided for a specific safeguard clause postponing the accession date by one year to January 2008 and also specific rules for the interim procedure as the Commission had noted a lack of a credible enforcement record in Romania's State aid control regime (Atanasiu and Oprescu 2004: 73; van de Casteele 2005: 40). This was the reason why the Commission was entitled to object to any aid measure granted between 1 September 2004 and the starting date of the interim mechanism (1 May 2006) by decid-ing to initiate a formal investigation procedure. As the time between the introduction of the interim procedure (1 May 2006) and the accession to the EU (1 January 2007) was rather short, the interim measure was only of limited use (van de Casteele 2005: 41; Stobiecka-Kuik and Bomhoff 2008: 1.458).

IV.i b   Aid put into effect prior to the accession

In order to apply the interim mechanism and to qualify a measure as existing aid, the measure had to be put into effect before accession. The Commission had the chance to review and to clarify the scope of this requirement in a number of Decisions.[7] According to the Commission, the decisive question is whether the whole measure is covered by a legally binding act of the respective Member State. If not, the interim mechanism was not applied and the Member State invited to re-notify the State aid according to the regular procedure laid down in Article 2 Procedural Regulation.

IV.i.c.   Aid still applicable after the accession

In order to apply the interim mechanism and to qualify a measure as existing aid, the measure had to be applicable after the accession. In their analysis of this requirement, Stobiecka-Kuik and Bomhoff note that the appropriate measures procedure of the Procedural Regulation was introduced only with regard to aid schemes so that it was rather an inappropriate means to avoid last-minute aid grants to individual beneficiaries (Stobiecka-Kuik and Bomhoff 2008: 1.467). For this reason, the 2003 and 2005 Accession Acts provided the following safeguard:

> All measures still applicable after the date of accession which constitute State aid and which do not fulfill the conditions set out above shall be considered as new aid upon accession for the purpose of the application of Art. 88(3) of the EC Treaty.

Accordingly, all aid measures granted prior to and still applicable after the accession without meeting all requirements of existing State aid within the meaning of the Accession Acts at the same time, were considered new State aids. This involved a particular risk for measures which had not been notified to the Commission under the interim mechanism if the Commission later found that these measures contained State aid applicable after the accession. If so, these measures were treated as new aid, as of the date of accession.[8]

Whether a State measure is applicable after the accession or not has to be decided in light of the legal and economic effects following from the measure for the State budget. Accordingly, aid schemes and individual aids which were not limited in time or which did not specify the final amount of the Member State's liability before accession, are considered applicable after the accession. If not, such measures are past aid which is beyond the scope of Commission review.[9]

The mainly budget-related interpretation of the interim mechanism provisions by the Commission was tested in a number of individual aid cases. For instance, certain formulae were deemed too imprecise for future calculations of State aid and therefore applicable after the accession, if the amount depended on the beneficiary's behaviour[10] or if the Member State had to bear most of the economic risks.[11]

IV.ii.   State aid in the transport and agricultural sector

For State aid in the transport and agricultural sector (except for fisheries), the notion of existing State aid has been subject to the further requirement that the Commission was informed within four months after the accession of State aid put into effect prior to and still applicable after the accession. This is usually referred to as the 'sunset clause'. Any State aid which is deemed incompatible with the State aid rules and is still applicable State after 1 May 2007 is considered new aid. Consequently, if the procedural requirements were met, all State aid measures put into effect prior to and still applicable after the accession, were considered existing aid for the first three years after accession. The sunset clause applied also to Bulgaria and Romania (Stobiecka-Kuik and Bomhoff 2008: 1.455).

V.   LESSONS TO BE LEARNED FROM THE 2004 AND 2007 ENLARGEMENTS FOR FUTURE ENLARGEMENTS?

Sometimes it is argued that the pre-accession preparation appears to be a win-win situation as it enables candidate countries to become accustomed to the EU State aid rules due to the phasing-in of competition rules, while the internal market is protected at the same time from delayed phasing-out of anti-competitive subsidizing practices by applicant countries (Stobiecka-Kuik and Bomhoff 2008: 1.441). Although pre-accession preparation may be described as a win-win situation in the end, it may nevertheless take a candidate country several years to comply with the EA requirement to adopt national State aid legislation due to domestic political resistance against the required changes in national State aid policy, and in particular against the introduction of an effective national State aid control system. For instance, only in 2000 did Poland manage to comply with the State aid requirements contained in the EA of 1991 (Pelka 2004). A significant factor was the opening of accession negotiations in 1998 (Gwiazda 2007: 116–120).

Domestic political opposition may also be the reason why in many candidate States appropriate enforcement activities were only started significantly more slowly than in the antitrust field (Känkänen 2003: 25).

Moreover, the case of Romania shows that a very strict approach at the early stages is required in order to avoid recourse to emergency measures only shortly before conclusion of the Accession Treaty (Stobiecka-Kuik and Bomhoff 2008: 1.445).

Independent from the political and administrative difficulties the introduction of a pre-accession State aid control system may face at the national level, such system allows for an early identification of problematic areas of State aid which is necessary to assess legitimate needs of candidate countries for transitional arrangements. In order to establish a credible enforcement record by the national State aid controlling authority, it seems preferable to entrust a truly independent authority with this task as such authority may be better suited than a ministerial unit to enforce national State aid rules in case of political resistance.

Once the accession to the EU transforms from merely a faraway political vision more and more into a realistic political option for the candidate State the introduction of pre-accession national State control systems is likely to become a success story as the pre-accession national State control is a perfect means for the candidate State to learn to play the game of EU State aid (Blauberger 2007: 4). This is demonstrated by an analysis of State aid amounts granted by the new EU-10 members, before and after, the accession. While the Commission found that the new EU-10 countries (1.42%) spent more than the EU-15 (0.42%) on State aid to undertakings as a percentage of their GDP[12] and aid amounts significantly peaked in the years immediately preceding the accession, the aid amounts were already falling to levels comparable to those of old Member States in the first years after the accession (Blauberger 2007: 8–10).[13] The expectation that without the carrot of accession conditionality new Member States would rather abstain from complying with EU State aid rules, has therefore not been fulfilled. Rather the opposite is true: new Member States have a considerable compliance record and brought their policies quickly in line with the requirements of EU State aid rules (Blauberger 2009: 1037).

For future enlargements, the experience gained with regard to typical areas of problematic indirect State aid for the EU may prove very helpful to appropriately address such measures and, in the best case, to diminish the need for transitional periods. The clarification and further development of the notions of aid put into effect before and still applicable after accession during a number of Commission Decisions will make the use of the interim mechanism for candidate States more predictable. Candidate States may also expect a less lenient review of national decisions by the Commission under the existing aid mechanism as the Commission will not be faced with such a heavy workload of national decisions compared to the last enlargement rounds with 10 (or rather 12) new Member States.

VI.   THE SITUATION IN THE CURRENT CANDIDATE AND POTENTIAL CANDIDATE STATES

At present, Turkey, Croatia, the Former Yugoslav Republic of Macedonia and Iceland have the status of candidate States. Albania, Bosnia and Herzegovina, Kosovo (under UN Security Council Resolution 1244), Montenegro and Serbia are considered potential candidate States. Except for Kosovo, the EU and its Member States have concluded Stabilization and Association Agreements (SAA) with Albania, Bosnia and Herzegovina, Montenegro and Serbia between 2006 and 2008.[14]

In light of the experience with the late adoption of implementing rulers (IR) in some cases the Commission insisted that the SAAs with Croatia, the Former Yugoslav Republic of Macedonia, Albania, Bosnia and Herzegovina, Montenegro and Serbia directly contained provisions corresponding to the IRs of previous EAs (Stobiecka-Kuik and Bomhoff 2008: 1.429). For instance, Article 71(3)(4) of the SAA with Albania provides:

> Albania shall establish an operationally independent authority which is entrusted with the powers necessary for the full application of paragraph 1(iii) within four years from the date of entry into force of this Agreement. This authority shall have, inter alia, the powers to authorize State aid schemes and individual aid grants in conformity with paragraph 2, as well as the powers to order the recovery of State aid that has been unlawfully granted.

Regarding Croatia, The Council adopted the new Accession Partnership on 12 February 2008.[15] According to this Partnership, Croatia is expected to carry out the following actions in the area of State aid: (i) adoption of a National Restructuring Programme for the steel sector that ensures the viability and respect for EU rules on State aids; (ii) adoption of individual restructuring plans for each of the shipyards in difficulties which have to be incorporated in a National Restructuring Programme (in line with EU rules on State aids), (iii) completion of the legislative alignment with EU State aid rules in the area of fiscal aid as well as alignment of all other remaining aid schemes identified in the State aid inventory as being incompatible with EU rules; (iv) adoption of the regional aid map. In its 2009 Progress Report, the Commission noted a reasonable level of alignment while stressing the need for sustained efforts to complete the restructuring of the shipyards.[16] On 30 June 2010, Croatia opened the last three policy-related negotiating chapters and provisionally closed two.

The Former Yugoslav Republic of Macedonia was granted candidate status on 16 December 2005.[17] According to the Accession Partnership adopted by Council Decision on 18 February 2008 the Former Yugoslav

Republic of Macedonia is expected to complete the following actions in the area of State aid: the establishment of effective ex-ante control of State aid.[18] In the 2009 Progress Report, the Commission noted that the number of ex-ante State aid decisions increased although some institutions, in particular those providing indirect aid, are still reluctant to send notifications to the Commission for Protection of Competition.[19] So far, no recommendation on the start of accession negotiations has been made by the Commission.

Iceland applied to join the EU on 16 July 2009 and on 17 June 2010, the European Council decided to open negotiations with Iceland.

Turkey has so far neither adopted State aid legislation nor established an operationally independent authority to monitor State aid. Some progress was made as regarding State aid to the steel industry when Turkey submitted a revised 'National Restructuring Plan' for the steel sector in June 2009.[20]

NOTES

1. The full text of the EA with the candidate countries can be found at <http://www.consilium.europa.eu/App/accords/Default.aspx?command=searchResult&lang=EN&id=297&doclang=EN&searchTitle=europe%20agreement&fromDate=01/01/0001&toDate=01/01/0001> (last accessed on 23 December 2010).
2. European Council in Copenhagen, 21–22 June 1993, Conclusions of the Presidency, DOC/93/3; for a discussion of these Copenhagen Criteria see Cremona 2005.
3. Decision No 3/2001 of the EU-Poland Association Council of 23 May 2001 adopting the implementing rules for the application of the provisions on State aid referred to in Article 63(1)(iii) and (2) pursuant to Article 63(3) of the Europe Agreement establishing an association between the European Communities and their Member States, of the one part, and the Republic of Poland, of the other part, and in Article 8(1)(iii) and (2) of Protocol 2 on European Coal and Steel Community (ECSC) products to that Agreement, O.J. 2001 L 215/39.
4. Commission Decision of 5 July 2005 in Case C-20/2004, Restructuring aid to steel producer Huta Czestochowa S.A., O.J. 2006 L 366/1.
5. Commission Decision of 13 September in Case N-350/2006, Change of restructuring plan of MSO, O.J. 2006 C 280/04.
6. O.J. 1999 L 83/1.
7. See, for example,. Commission Decision of 7 April 2006 in Case C-5/2005, Frucona, O.J. 2007 L 112/14.
8. Commission Decision of 4 June 2008 in Case C-41/05, O.J. 2009 L 225/53 (92).
9. Commission Decision of 28 January 2004 State aid CZ 14/2003–Czech Republic Česka spořitelna, a.s.
10. Commission Decision of 18 July 2007 in case C-27/04, Agrobanka, O.J. 2008 L 67/3.
11. Commission Decision of 25 September 2007 in Case C-43/2005, Polish stranded costs, O.J. 2009 L 83/1.
12. *State Aid Scoreboard, Autumn 2004 update*, COM(2004)750 final, p. 5.
13. *State Aid Scoreboard, Spring 2005 update*, COM(2005)147 final, p. 49.
14. The texts of the SAAs can be found at: <http://ec.europa.eu/enlargement/potential-candidates/index_en.htm> (last accessed 8 January 2011).

15.   2008/119/EC: Council Decision of 12 February 2008 on the principles, priorities and conditions contained in the Accession Partnership with Croatia and repealing Decision 2006/145/EC, O.J. 2008 L 42/51.
16.   Croatia 2009 Progress Report (Commission Staff Working Document), COM(2009) 533, 35.
17.   Decision 2006/57/EC, O.J. 22008 L 80/32.
18.   2008/212/EC: Council Decision of 18 February 2008 on the principles, priorities and conditions contained in the Accession Partnership with the Former Yugoslav Republic of Macedonia and repealing Decision 2006/57/EC, O.J. 22008 L 80/32.
19.   The Former Yugoslav Republic of Macedonia 2009 Progress Report (Commission Staff Working Document), COM(2009) 533, 38.
20.   Turkey 2009 Progress Report (Commission Staff Working Document), COM(2009) 533, 49.

REFERENCES

Atanasiu, I. (2001), 'State aid in Central and Eastern Europe', *World Competition*, **24**, 257–283.

Atanasiu, I. (2005), 'EC State aid policy with respect to soft budgetary constraints: tax and social security contribution payment arrears', *European State Aid Law Quarterly*, **4**, 597.

Atanasiu, I. and G. Oprescu (2004), 'State aid to the Romanian steel and coal sectors: issues related to accession', *Romanian Journal of European Affairs*, **4**, 59–80.

Bednár, J. (2005), 'The State aid control procedures in the Czech Republic', *European State Aid Law Quarterly*, **4**, 265–267.

Blauberger, M. (2007), 'European State aid control in the new Member States – The examples of Poland and the Czech Republic', available at <http://aei.pitt.edu/7704/?> (last accessed 27 December 2010).

Blauberger, M. (2009), 'Compliance with rules of negative integration: European State aid control in the new member States', *Journal of European Policy*, **16**, 1030–1046.

Cemnolonskis, S. (2005), 'The State Aid Control Procedure in Lithuania', *European State Aid Law Quarterly*, **4**, 269–273.

Cremona, M. (2003), 'State aid control: substance and procedure in the Europe agreements and the stabilisation and association agreements', *European Law Journal*, **9**, 265–287.

Cremona, M. (2005), 'EU enlargement: solidarity and conditionality', *European Law Review*, **30**, 3–22.

Gwiazda, A. (2007), 'Europeanization of Polish competition policy', *European Integration*, **29**, 109–131.

Hargita, E. and Z.R. Filep (2004), 'State aid control in Hungary', *European State Aid Law Quarterly*, **3**, 585–590.

Jagodič-Lekočevič, L. (2004), 'State aid control in Slovenia', *European State Aid Law Quarterly*, **3**, 375–379

Lagzdina, D. (2005), 'The State aid control procedure in Latvia', *European State Aid Law Quarterly*, **4**, 267–269.

Lienemeyer, M. (2005), 'State aid for restructuring the steel industry in the new Member States', *Competition Policy Newsletter*, **1**, 94–102.

Känkänen, J. (2003), 'Accession negotiations brought to successful conclusion', *Competition Policy Newsletter*, **1**, 24–28.

Kuik, K. (2004), 'State Aid and the 2004 accession – overview of recent developments', *European State Aid Law Quarterly*, **3**, 365–373.

Paczkowska-Tomaszewska, A., K. Jaros and K. Winiarski (2006), 'Monitoring State aid in Poland', *European State Aid Law Quarterly*, **5**, 669–682.

Pelka, P. (2004), 'State aid control in Poland', *European State Aid Law Quarterly*, **3**, 380–382.

Roebling, G, (2003), 'Existing aid and enlargement', *Competition Policy Newsletter*, **1**, 33–37.

Schütterle, P. (2002), 'State aid control – an accession criterion', *Common Market Law Review*, **39**, 577–590.

Schütterle, P. (2003), 'Enlargement: pre-accession State aid after accession', *European State Aid Law Quarterly*, **2**, 29–38.

Schütterle, P. (2004), 'Beihilfenkontrolle in den neuen Mitgliedstaaten', *EWS,* **11**, 485–489.

Smith, M. P. (1996), 'Integration in small steps: the European Commission and Member-State aid to industry', *West European Politics*, **19**, 563–582.

Smith, M. P. (1998), 'Autonomy by the rules: the European Commission and the development of State aid policy', *Journal of Common Market Studies*, **36**, 55–78.

Stobiecka-Kuik, A. and A. Bomhoff (2008), 'External aspects of State aid policy (Part 2 – accession)', in Wolfgang Mederer, Nicola Pesaresi and Marc van Hoof (eds), *EU Competition Law*, **IV**, Book One, Leuven, Belgium, Claeys & Casteels, 147–185.

van de Casteele, K. (2005), 'Next EU enlargement: Romania and State aid control', *Competition Policy Newsletter*, **1**, 39–42.

Vosu, A. (2004), 'State aid control in Estonia', *European State Aid Law Quarterly*, **3**, 382–384.

4 The role of economics in State aid analysis and the balancing test

Lorenzo Coppi

> Economics did not suddenly drop out of the sky in 2005 like the famous apple which hit Isaac Newton on the head. Like gravity, economics have always been there, playing a part in determining whether a measure constitutes state aid or not, and whether or not it should be allowed. But if truth be told, even if we knew economic analysis was useful, we did not always make systematic use of it. With the State Aid Action Plan, we therefore set out to refine our thinking, and to develop a single methodology to assess the effects of aid – the so-called 'balancing test'. Neelie Kroes 2007.

Article 107(1) TFEU states: 'Save as otherwise provided in the Treaties, any aid granted by a Member state or through state resources in any form whatsoever *which distorts or threatens to distort competition* by favouring certain undertakings or the production of certain goods shall, *in so far as it affects trade between Member States*, be incompatible with the internal market' (emphasis added). Articles 107(2) and 107(3) lay out several exceptions, that is, circumstances in which the aid may be considered compatible with the Treaty.

The concepts of *distortion of competition* and *effects on trade* in the general prohibition of State aid are eminently economic concepts, suggesting that an economic analysis should be required in order to determine whether aid would be in violation of Article 107(1) TFEU. Yet case law largely established the presumption that State aid would result in distortions of competition and effects on trade, leaving little room for economics in the determination of whether State aid would violate Art.107(1).

Because the exceptions in Article 107(2) and (3) TFEU are exhaustively spelt out, and the necessary compatibility analysis identified in a detailed manner in various European Commission Guidelines, economics also did not play a significant role in the assessment of the compatibility of the aid.

For this reason, State aid is the area of EU competition law in which economics has traditionally played the least significant role, being largely confined to the application of the Market Economy Investor Principle, which is used to identify whether the transfer of state resources constitutes aid.

In recent years, however, State aid has started to join other areas of competition law in the gradual move from a purely form-based approach towards an effects-based approach which emphasises the economic implications of State aid. The impetus for this change came from the Commission's 2005 State Aid Action Plan, which advanced a 'refined economic approach' and the adoption of an effects and efficiency-based approach.[1] This agenda, which has been publicly restated by the Commission in several occasions,[2] has been developed in several discussion papers and contributions by members of the Commission.[3] The results from the ensuing economic debate have been summarised and condensed on a new framework for economic analysis which is described in the 2009 *Common Principles* staff discussion paper: the so-called *balancing test*.[4]

While the new framework does not really advocate a more economic approach to Article 107(1) TFEU, and in particular to the requirement that distortions of competition and effects on trade be substantial, it does address the issue of State aid compatibility under Article 107(3) TFEU advancing a more economic approach to the analysis.

In particular, the new framework recommends a *balancing test* whereby State aid should be declared compatible whenever its benefits (in terms of economic efficiency or equity) outweigh the distortions of competition that the aid is likely to cause. This *balancing* framework, with its focus on economic efficiency, is firmly rooted in modern public economics and is thus sound from the perspective of the welfare analysis of neoclassical economics.

The refined economic approach to State aid is a welcome development, as it helps clarify the compatibility criteria ex Article 107(3), especially when the aid is *ad-hoc*, that is, not covered by any of the specific Guidelines: it is in the interest of good enforcement policy that the analysis be spelt out in detail. From a policy perspective, a more explicit and rigorous analytical framework provides the opportunity for reducing the level of political interference in State aid control and for furthering the role of economic and legal analysis.

However, the new economic framework has been criticised for its narrow focus on economic efficiency, which is seen by some as resulting in an unwarranted expansion of the negative prohibition of Article 107(1) TFEU. From an economics perspective, the balancing framework is indeed somewhat limited in scope. Conspicuously absent from the balancing framework are:

(i)   a number of common market failures or efficiency justifications for the state intervention in the economy;
(ii)   a rigorous analysis of how one should address equity and solidarity considerations, which are often a key driver of State aid; and
(iii) a discussion of the effects on the internal market and trade between Member States.

Moreover, the *Common Principles* paper in which the balancing framework is epitomised is understandably an exercise in economics *realpolitik*. In order to maintain consistency with the traditional (but rather economics-illiterate) State aid analysis, the *Common Principles* paper tends at times to bend at times the intellectual rigour of the economic framework. Hence, a total (or social) welfare standard is preferred to the consumer welfare standard guiding other competition law enforcement; market power, while a market failure, is not to be addressed by State aid; and any distortion of the competitive process is considered a negative to be outweighed, even when it might have positive efficiency outcomes (at least in a static sense). It is precisely in those parts of the *Common Principles* paper which echo the traditional approach to State aid analysis that the proposed economic framework becomes less convincing.

The effect of these omissions and bending of the economic reasoning may be one of reducing the possible justifications for State intervention in the economy and thus the type of aid that will be deemed compatible. Thus the developing economic framework may indeed be a tool in achieving less aid, as set out in the SAAP.

It is still too early to judge how soon the refined economic framework which is embedded in the balancing test will be applied widely to State aid cases. This *balancing* framework is strongly supported by the economists at the Commission (both within DG Comp and DG EcFin), as well as some Member States, and seems to have become the embodiment of post-SAAP State aid analysis. The framework has already started to permeate soft law, and in particular the Environmental, Research and Development and Innovation, Employment, Training and Risk Capital Guidelines. However, the need to maintain consistency with past decisions and case law means that the framework is at times stretched or ignored as in the case of the Commission's approach to Rescue & Restructuring aid, and even – in some cases – of the application of the 'economics-savvy' Environmental Guidelines.

Thus, economic analysis of State aid, although increasingly popular, is still at an early stage and it is still an open question as to whether it will provide a more rigorous analytical framework to State aid, or whether the political pragmatism which is the hallmark of State aid control will continue to trump the more analytical framework that is being advanced.

These themes are discussed in the rest of this chapter. Part I carries out a brief historical review of the emergence of economic analysis in State aid control; Part II outlines the refined economic framework for assessing the compatibility of State aid with EU law; Part III comments on the economic framework from the perspective of the economics literature; and Part IV concludes with commentary.

I   THE EMERGENCE OF ECONOMICS IN STATE AID ANALYSIS

Thirty years ago in the United States and up to fifteen years ago in the European Union, competition law consisted primarily of form-based, *per se* rules, bright line prohibitions, and specific exemptions. At that time economic analysis was not necessary to determine whether business practices violated competition law.

The success of the law and economics movement in the US first, and in Europe later,[5] has fostered a shift towards a case-by-case, effects-based, rule of reason approach to evaluating business practices. Under this modern effects-based approach, competition authorities and courts are frequently required to determine which business practices are anticompetitive and which are not on the basis of their economic effect on the market. One after another, all the areas of competition law have opened up to economic analysis.

State aid is one of the last areas to be affected by this trend towards effects-based analysis and economics.[6] The traditional role of economics in State aid proceedings was very limited: the only application of economic concepts was in the area of the Market Economy Investor Principle, the key test to identify whether a transfer of State resources should be considered State aid (see Chapters 5 and 6 for a detailed discussion of the application of this test).

Article 107(1) TFEU postulates that only aid which distorts competition and affects trade between Member States is incompatible with the internal market. Distortions of competition and effects on trade would appear to be areas in which economic analysis would be relevant. However, historically, the existence of such distortions has been largely presumed whenever aid was present, as case law established a very low threshold to find the existence of distortions of competition and effect on trade under Article 107(1) TFEU.[7] Accordingly, economic analysis has had a fairly limited role in this regard, even though recent case law may indicate that the aid's effects on trade may need to be analysed in more depth in the future.[8]

The compatibility analysis under Article 107(2) and 107(3) TFEU was also traditionally carried out without recourse to economics, because the steps of the analysis were identified in a detailed and rather formalistic manner in various Commission Guidelines. This meant that State aid was traditionally the area of EU competition law in which economics played the least significant role. However, in the last few years, economics has started playing an increasingly important role in State aid analysis.

I.i.   The State Aid Action Plan: the need for a More Refined Economic Approach

The impetus for a more significant role of economics in State aid analysis was given by the Commission's 2005 consultation document, State Aid Action Plan (SAAP).[9] The SAAP notes the political mandate for a significant review of State aid policy,[10] and anticipates the need for the modernisation of State aid control, on the basis of four main objectives: (1) less and better targeted State aid; (2) a refined economic approach; (3) more effective procedures and enforcement, greater predictability and transparency; and (4) sharing of responsibility between the Commission and the Member States. For further analysis see the discussion by Kleiner in Chapter 1.

The second objective (a refined economic approach) is considered an important tool to maximise the benefits of State aid, while minimising its negative effects on competition and the internal market.[11] In particular, the SAAP focuses on the concept of *market failure* and on its importance as the justification for public intervention.

There was a relatively broad consensus in the responses from Member States regarding the goal of 'less and better targeted aid'; on the role of economic analysis in delivering that role (in particular on the view that the focus on State aid should be on remedying market failures); and on the necessity to balance the positive and the negative effects of the aid.[12] However, several Member States also pointed out that the economic framework advanced in the SAAP was very generic and that more flesh was needed on those bones.

The flesh was added in successive Discussion Papers authored by the Commission's economists. Members of the Chief Economist Team published a Working Paper discussing the more refined approach to State aid and how that could result in 'less and better targeted aid'.[13] That paper in essence contained all the elements of the new economic framework, and in particular of the *balancing test* as a way to weigh the positive effects of the aid (that is, its contribution towards a goal of common interest) against its negative effects (that is, distortion of competition and trade).

This balancing test soon became the official Commission tool to deliver a refined economic approach on State aid, and was publicly endorsed by the then Commissioner Kroes.[14]

More importantly, the balancing test found its application in a number of 'soft-law' provisions introduced since 2005, such as: the R&D&I Guidelines;[15] the Guidelines for Aid to Small and Medium Enterprises;[16] the Environmental Guidelines;[17] the Training Aid Guidelines;[18] and the Guidelines for Aid to Disabled and Disadvantaged Workers.[19]

The position of the Commission and the application of the balancing test to State aid have been crystallised in the Commission's Staff Working Paper *Common principles for an economic assessment of the compatibility of state aid under Article 87.3 EC-Treaty* (*Common Principles* paper).

II. THE IMPLEMENTATION OF THE ECONOMIC APPROACH: THE BALANCING TEST

As discussed, the centrepiece of the refined economic approach in the State aid reform package is the so-called *balancing test*, which focuses on the conditions for compatibility with ex Article 107(3) TFEU.

The most complete discussion of the precise economic criteria and methodology used to implement the balancing test is in the *Common Principles* paper. The balancing test has three stages.

1. First, it considers whether the aid is aimed at a 'well-defined object of common interest', which 'can include both efficiency and equity objectives.'
2. Second, the balancing test considers whether the proposed aid is a 'well-designed instrument' with which to deliver the objective identified above.
3. Finally, the potential negative effects of the aid (that is, the 'distortive effects on competition and trade') need to be considered and weighed against the positive effects of achieving the objective of common interest.

These three steps are described in more detail below.

II.i. Step 1: a Well-defined Object of Common Interest

Economists agree that, in several circumstances, State aid may have a role in increasing economic welfare. There are two key ways in which State aid may increase welfare: by improving *efficiency* when the market fails to deliver an optimal economic outcome; and, depending on social and political preferences, by improving *equity*, when the market outcome is characterised by significant socio-economic inequality.[20] In non-technical terms, the first objective (efficiency) is commonly referred to as 'making the pie larger', while the second objective (equity) is commonly referred to as 'sharing the pie fairly'.

Efficiency can be improved by the correction of a *market failure*; that is, by action to tackle cases where the market alone fails to provide the optimal level of a good or service. The concept of market failure is linked to the first fundamental theorem of welfare economics. Loosely speaking, this theorem states that the market, left to its own devices, will achieve the most efficient economic outcome unless there are market failures, such as: externalities are present, markets are incomplete, consumers and producers do not all behave competitively, and/or no market equilibrium exists. In these circumstances a more efficient outcome can be achieved by removing the market failure, possibly through the use of State aid.

In a nutshell, the quantity produced and consumed of a particular good will be inefficiently low or high in the presence of market failures, and a removal of those market failures will bring about an expansion in economic activity (or a reduction in a negative element of economic activity), which can deliver an unequivocal improvement in welfare, often called a *Pareto improvement*, that is, a situation in which no economic actors will be worse off and at least some actors will be better off.[21]

The *Common Principles* paper notes three sources of market failures in particular: externalities, imperfect information, and coordination problems.

Economic theory shows that markets fail to deliver the efficient outcome in the presence of *externalities*. Externalities are aspects of transactions which affect economic agents other than those who take the investment, production, or consumption decision, and as such these wider 'external' effects to society at large will not in general be taken into consideration by a private investor when deciding how much to invest, produce or consume. This implies that the private investor, disregarding external effects on other actors, will generally invest, produce or consume too little or too much from a public interest perspective. Thus correction for externalities can offer an improvement in efficiency that increases overall social welfare, and thus can justify State aid.[22]

It is important to note that externalities result in market failures only if there are *incomplete markets*. An efficient economic outcome would be attained even in the presence of externalities, if everything could be traded that is valued by an actor in the economy and involves interaction with one or more other actors. For instance, if a factory pollutes a river, it may create a negative externality for other economic actors (for example, a fish farm operating on that river). In the absence of a market for 'polluting rights' (that is, when markets are incomplete), the factory will choose an inefficiently high level of pollution as it does not bear its full cost. This inability of the market to deliver the efficient outcome because of the combination of a negative externality with an incomplete market is a market failure.

Asymmetric or imperfect information can also be a source of under-provision of a certain good or service and thus require State intervention to be rectified. For instance, if a proportion of the goods available are known to be of low value, but these goods cannot be differentiated by buyers from goods of higher value, the price that buyers are willing to pay for the good will fall to the point that no seller in possession of a higher-value product will offer it for sale, and so the market for the good will shrink and may collapse. This is known as the 'lemons' problem, after Nobel laureate George Akerlof's seminal contribution.[23] In general, when there is incomplete information (for example, when a bank is unwilling to make a loan to a low-risk customer, because it cannot be sure from the available information that the customer is indeed low-risk), the market will not achieve an efficient outcome.

The market is also prevented from delivering the efficient outcome whenever *coordination failures* are present (that is, when economic agents fail to coordinate to achieve a mutually beneficial outcome). For instance, two products which are used together may each need to be widely available in order for them to be valuable to consumers. In this case, it might be the case that neither product is marketed because the producers of the different products cannot coordinate on releasing their respective products. This coordination failure prevents products for which a demand would exist from reaching the market.

Although the *Common Principles* paper gives it a less prominent role, the provision of *public goods* is another area in which market forces are unable to achieve an efficient outcome. Public goods are defined as goods which can be enjoyed without reducing the amount available to others (non-rivalry in consumption) and which cannot be provided selectively to only certain members of the public only (non-excludibility). Although pure public goods are relatively rare (for example, policing, free-to-air TV, a beautiful landscape, or clean air), various goods present characteristics of non-excludibility (for example, open water, fisheries, also called *common goods*). Because of the (economic) impossibility of excluding non-paying agents and thus to profit from their provision, the market will always tend to provide an inefficiently low quantity of public or common goods, and State intervention may help achieve a more efficient provision of those goods.

In addition to its efficiency rationale, State aid is often justified on the basis of equity considerations. The *equity* motive for State intervention concerns the redistribution of resources in order to reflect the preferences of society in terms of wealth distribution. Thus, provided that its positive effects are felt in less developed regions or by socially disadvantaged groups, aid can be justified on the basis of considerations about equity and social cohesion. The *Common Principles* paper states that equity considerations often provide the main rationale behind regional aid;

employment aid; rescue and restructuring aid; and certain types of aid for services of general economic interest. However, the discussion of equity issues in the *Common Principles* paper is relatively short and high level, reflecting the standard view among economists that equity considerations are the domain of politics and that economics has relatively little to say about equity.

In conclusion, the Commission recognises that State aid may be an appropriate tool when markets fail to deliver an efficient outcome because of market failures, or when Member States want to purse equity, redistribution, or social cohesion goals.

II.ii.   Step 2: is aid the appropriate instrument to deliver the objective?

Once the presence of a legitimate goal for the aid has been ascertained, the second step of the balancing test considers whether the proposed aid is a 'well-designed instrument' with which to deliver the identified objective of common interest. There are three issues to consider here: selectivity, incentive effect, and proportionality.

First of all, the analysis needs to consider whether the aid is an appropriate policy instrument, that is, whether a *selective instrument* has advantages over other types of policy interventions, such as regulation, direct provision of goods or services, or fiscal instruments.

Second, it should be considered whether there is an *incentive effect*, that is whether the aid is likely to bring about the desired change in the behaviour of the beneficiary (as opposed to result simply in a windfall for the beneficiary). The *Common Principles* paper goes into some detail on how the notifying Member State may be able to show that such positive incentive effect is likely to materialise.[24]

Third, the *Common Principles* paper highlights that the aid should be *proportionate* to the problem tackled, taking a fairly strict view of proportionality, that is, that 'aid is considered to be proportionate only if the same result could not be reached with less aid and less distortion.'[25] In other words, the notifying Member States will have to show that the proposed aid is the *minimum necessary* to obtain the change in the beneficiaries' incentives needed to deliver the objective of common interest.

II.iii.   Step 3: Do the Positive Effects of Delivering the Objectives Outweigh the Negative Effects of the Distortions of Competition and Effects on Trade?

The final stage of the balancing test involves the consideration of the potential negative effects of the aid, primarily the 'distortive effects on competition and trade': aid will be found compatible only if the negative effects of the aid are more than offset by its positive effects.

Even though State aid can be justified on the basis of efficiency or equity considerations, it may also result in distortions of competition, or of the 'level playing field' between firms: it may crystallise inefficient industry structures; it may crowd out private investment; it may reduce effective competition by increasing market power or by reducing the incentives to compete; it may distort production and location decisions across Member States; and it may foster overly risky or inefficient behaviour.

It is quite correct for the Commission to be concerned about potential market distortions caused by State and: indeed this is the key reason why, in economic terms, State aid can be problematic. These distortions of competition may result in various types of market inefficiencies. It is useful to distinguish between static inefficiencies (or allocative and productive inefficiencies, in which (subsidised inefficient undertakings may produce or sell more than inherently more efficient ones); and dynamic inefficiencies (where incentives to compete are reduced or overly risky behaviour is incentivised as a result of the moral hazard spurred by State aid).

The traditional distortion of competition considered in State aid analysis is the productive inefficiency arising from allowing inefficient players to survive and to maintain their market share. The *Common Principles* paper echoes the traditional distinction between selective versus horizontal aid, the former being considered more distortionary. Schemes open to all undertakings are by their nature considered significantly less distortionary than aid reserved to a sub-set of undertakings, which may then be unfairly advantaged in the market.

Yet, the *Common Principles* paper highlights that from an economics point of view, dynamic considerations are more important: aid may help perpetuate failed business models; it may reduce the incentive to compete; and may create moral hazard by encouraging excessive risk-taking. These effects are likely to be more serious and long-lasting than mere distortion of the 'level playing field'. In particular, moral hazard is a key concern. An implicit promise of future aid may affect firms' incentives, and may result in moral hazard, which arises when a firm or individual is protected from the 'downside' of its risks, fostering overly risky behaviour. Repeated State aid may create the expectation that certain undertakings are 'too big to fail' (or too politically important to fail), and thus perpetuate overly risky or inefficient business practices.

Finally, the *Common Principles* paper states that the balancing exercise requires evaluating the positive and the negative effects 'in qualitative terms as well as, where possible, in quantitative terms'. In order to come to a conclusion as to the overall merits of the aid, a *social welfare policy standard* is advanced, which is defined as follows:

> Social welfare takes into account not only the sum of consumers' and producers' surpluses, but also how welfare is distributed across countries and citizens. Social welfare thus integrates efficiency elements (i.e. by looking at how much wealth is created by affecting consumers' and/or producers' surpluses) as well as equity elements (i.e. by looking at how this wealth is divided between Member States and citizens). A social welfare standard takes into account all the effects that may be generated by the aid.

As discussed in Part III.iv. below, this choice of policy standard is very different from that advanced in all other areas of EU competition law (a consumer welfare standard).

III.   IS THE ECONOMIC FRAMEWORK OF THE BALANCING TEST FULLY FORMED?

The balancing test is an important development, as it advances a much needed analytical approach to the compatibility criteria under Article 107(3)(c) TFEU, which should result in better and more predictable enforcement. Moreover, the balancing test brings State aid in line with the other areas of competition law which have already moved (or are moving) in the direction of an effects-based analysis.

The framework of the balancing test is not fully formed, and it may be expected that over time more thought will have to be given to a few features of the test. First, most of the focus of the balancing test is on economic efficiency, and while this is consistent with the goal of the SAAP of 'less and better targeted aid' it is somewhat at odds with the traditional rationale for State aid and State aid control.

Second, even accepting efficiency as the guiding principle for State aid control, the balancing test summarised in the *Common Principles* paper is not entirely consistent in its treatment of different market failures.

Third, it is cumbersome to carry out step two of the balancing test as indicated in the *Common Principles* paper, unless the Commission can provide more guidance on how to identify clearly the counterfactual which should be used to benchmark the effects of the aid.

Fourth, if the balancing exercise is to be meaningful, the analysis of the distortion of competition and effect on trade needs to be carried out in a much more detailed manner than in the traditional analysis, where, consistent with case law, these effects are assumed to arise whenever selective aid is present.

These points are discussed in more detail in the next four subsections.

III.i.   The Elephant in the Room: State Aid Control as a Budget Discipline Device

A common justification for supra-national State aid control is the need to avoid a 'wasteful subsidy race'. After all, this is the rationale behind the WTO scrutiny of state subsidies. If a country subsidises national producers of goods for which there is international trade, similar subsidies may be granted 'in retaliation' by other countries, which in turn creates an escalation in the level of subsidies. Indeed, the main rationale for including State aid control as part of the Treaty of Rome 1957 was to avoid protection of national champions and subsidy races that would jeopardise the creation of the internal market.

Over time, however, the objective of State aid control seems to have moved away from trade considerations and towards concerns of budget discipline. At the same time, case law has limited the relevance of distortions of trade in the general prohibition of Article 107(1) TFEU. The result has been a rather significant de-emphasising of the prevention of wasteful subsidy races as the key objective of State aid control.

This shift in the rationale of State aid control has been highlighted also by the Commission in a Discussion Paper. State aid control has evolved through time to encompass different objectives, 'The initial motivation of State aid control [was] to avoid trade disputes between Member States and collectively wasteful subsidy competition.'[26] More recently:

> [r]educing the overall level of state aid is a long-standing EU policy objective which is incorporated, along with better targeted aids, in the Lisbon Agenda and later became a leitmotif of the State Aid Action Plan. Reducing the volume of state aid is not only a question of budget discipline (although no part of government expenditure should be exempt from discipline); it also reflects a widespread view that a significant proportion of state aid is inefficient and distortive. Hence, state aid control is seen as being concerned not only with minimising distortions of competition but also with limiting government failures.[27]

The *balancing test* crystallises this shift from trade control to budget control theorised in the SAAP by focusing on the efficiency analysis of State intervention while omitting a requirement that State aid should only be deemed incompatible if it negatively affects trade. In other words, consistent with case law, the balancing test may deem 'wasteful' aid incompatible even if it does not *substantially* affect trade.

This means that State aid control can no longer be considered Europe's internal WTO, but should rather be considered a sort of European

Member States' financial controller with special responsibility for subsidies. While this is consistent with current case law and the stated political objectives of the SAAP, several commentators have perceived this as a potential encroachment on Member States' fiscal and government spending policies.[28]

This potential encroachment on Member States' fiscal policies and government spending appears even more serious if one considers that:

- not all State aid results in subsidy races (for example, State aid to undertakings active in markets which are essentially national or regional would not substantially affect trade and thus would not initiate subsidy races); and
- not all subsidy races are wasteful (for example, sometimes a subsidy race may be a market-oriented mechanism which determines the most efficient location of a production facility).

The modern economic literature on international trade shows that 'wasteful subsidy races' are more likely to arise when: (i) product markets are not competitive; (ii) there is significant trade between Member States but fairly limited trade with countries outside in the EU; and (iii) beneficiaries' locations are fixed or their location decisions create limited positive spill-overs for the economy.[29]

Yet the balancing test does not take any of these factors into consideration and may thus consider as incompatible even aid which is very unlikely to result in wasteful subsidy races or in any effect on trade at all. However, even if State aid does not create effects on trade which are detrimental for the internal market, it is always possible that State aid is 'wasteful' in that it does not have a justification from the point of view of economic efficiency or equity and that it is only undertaken as the result of lobbying from organised special interest groups.

This possibility is the current focus of State aid control: limiting 'wasteful' government intervention in the economy. Judging from the Member States' responses to the SAAP, some Member States (for example, the UK, France, and Italy) seem to agree that that is the direction towards which State aid control should move. Others (for example, Germany) are less convinced that limiting 'wasteful' government intervention in the economy is a legitimate aim of State aid control[30].

Thus then the question arises of why do we need a super-national authority in order to limit wasteful government spending? Why do Member States accept the bestowing this of 'financial controller' role upon the Commission? Why cannot Member States curb wasteful spending which does not have clear effect on inter-Community trade?

The answer may be that it is difficult for Member States to commit not to offer aid to certain economic sectors or undertakings, as it is often politically very difficult to deny aid. Thus Member States might welcome the intervention of the Commission which 'ties their hands' and does not allow them to squander fiscal resources in doubtful State aid schemes.[31] This would explain why Member States accept the Commission's supervision on government spending which poses limited or no threat to the internal market.

In conclusion, the balancing test seems unnecessary and inadequate if the aim is to protect the internal market and to prevent State aid from provoking wasteful subsidy races; but it is an appropriate instrument if the aim is to promote budgetary discipline with regard to Member States' fiscal spending.

III.ii.   Certain Possible Objectives of Common Interest have not been Fully Addressed

In general, the refined economic approach embodied in the balancing test and its efficiency objectives are appropriate and coherent, if one agrees with the goal of curbing wasteful (or inefficient) government intervention in the economy.

However, the treatment of equity objectives is rather vague, and certain market failures have not been explicitly considered in the *Common Principles* paper. It is unclear from the Commission's policy statements and recent decisions whether such vagueness and omissions should be read as a limitation of the set of acceptable objectives of common interests.

The *Common Principles* paper establishes two main general objectives of common interest: efficiency and equity. While efficiency is a well-defined economics concept, there is no consensus in economics on how to define *equity* and on what level of equity is desirable. Economics does not have commonly accepted prescriptions on which level of redistribution is justified, or a consensus on how to quantify the effects of such redistribution. The traditional economics view – that increasing equity (for example, through redistribution) would negatively affect agents' incentives, economic activity and ultimately growth – has been challenged in the 1990s by a number of empirical contributions showing that growth rates appear to be higher in countries where income inequality is lower.[32]

Given the ambiguous normative prescriptions from economics, the preferred level of equity is an eminently political decision. Depending on the socio-political preferences of a Member State, many different policies and aids may be justified on the basis of equity considerations.

The *Common Principles* paper does not provide much guidance in this area; while it spells out a number of areas in which aid may be targeted to equity objectives, almost all of them are the subject of specific Guidelines, and thus not covered by the balancing test. This vagueness on the application of the balancing test to equity objectives is natural given the lack of consensus in the economics literature on the subject. However, it is unfortunate, given that most State aid has to do with equity objectives (for example, regional aid, employment aid, and rescue and restructuring aid) rather than efficiency ones. This limits the application of the economic framework to a relative small portion of State aid cases.

Also, the *Common Principles* paper discusses various types of factors leading to market failure, but does not mention others, such as *incomplete markets* (that is, the inability to trade a good, or to sign 'futures' contracts for a good), and *commitment problems* (that is the inability of market participants to commit to an 'optimal' conduct). It is unclear whether the Commission considers these possible sources of market failure as legitimate objectives of common interest.

However, the omission of *market power* from the list of market failures that may be remedied through State aid is intentional. Market power is a pervasive market failure: when markets are not competitive, the efficient outcome is not achieved, prices are higher and quantity produced and consumed lower than the level that efficiency would dictate. Thus, market power results in a *deadweight welfare loss,* meaning that total welfare could be improved if prices were reduced and quantity increased towards the levels of a perfectly competitive market. In theory, State aid which reduces market power (for example, entry-inducing aid, or marginal cost-reducing aid) would tend to reduce the inefficiency associated with market power, and thus should be considered as satisfying step one of the balancing test. Yet, footnote 22 of the *Common Principles* paper states:

> Another reason why the market may not lead to an efficient outcome is the existence of market power, for instance in a situation of a monopoly. However, in most markets where some players enjoy a certain degree of market power, and where markets may not be considered fully efficient, the Commission will normally not retain this as a sufficient justification for granting state aid, i.e. to smaller or maverick players.

No reason is given for this determination. In fact, there is little economic justification for considering only certain types of market failure as addressable by State aid. This discrepancy is almost certainly due to the fact that using State aid as a tool to reduce market power might justify the old-style dirigiste industrial policy which the SAAP, consistent with the prescription of the current economic paradigm, views as negative and is trying to reduce. However, not considering market power as a market failure potentially addressable by State aid complicates step three of the balancing test, as discussed above.

In summary, the vagueness in the application of the balancing test to equity objectives and the omission of market power from the list of addressable market failures means that the balancing test may not be immediately applicable to a significant number of common aid categories.

III. iii.   Does the Requirement that State Aid is a 'Well Defined Instrument' Complicate the Analysis Unnecessarily?

The second step of the balancing test requires ascertaining whether State aid is a 'well-defined' instrument to deliver the selected objectives of common interest.

The first question to answer, in order to determine if State aid is a 'well-defined' instrument, is whether State aid is an *appropriate* instrument to deliver the objective of common interest. The *Common Principles* paper is not very clear as to the counterfactual to use in order to measure the appropriateness of State aid. On the one hand, it correctly states that the counterfactual scenario against which the aid should be analysed is the situation where no aid is given.[33] On the other hand, the *Common Principles* paper also suggests that the Commission will compare the aptitude of the aid to deliver the objective against that of other non-aid policies (taxation, regulation, direct provision of goods and services), suggesting that in fact the counterfactual scenario is one where an alternative (non-aid) policy is implemented instead of the aid.[34]

It would be inappropriate to use this 'alternative policies' counterfactual to analyse State aid. Thus, State aid is almost always a 'second best' instrument when it comes to remedying market failures: externalities can be better internalised by assigning ownership rights and allowing trading; appropriate legislation can better overcome coordination failures and inability to commit; government-mandated disclosure is often the best remedy to asymmetric or imperfect information; and public goods should be directly provided by the State. There is almost always a better way (in theory, at least) to remedy market failures than the provision of State aid, so if an 'alternative policy' counterfactual scenario is used in order to determine the appropriateness of State aid, very little (if any) State aid would be considered to be compatible.

The second question to answer in order to determine whether aid is a well-designed instrument is whether the aid is likely to bring about a change in the beneficiary's *incentives*. This is a tricky area, as the requirement that the beneficiary changes its behaviour as the result of the aid is very often in tension with the requirement that aid does not create distortions of competition, as these are often also generated by a change in stakeholders' incentives, as discussed above.

Finally, the issue of whether aid is the most appropriate instrument or less distortionary instrument exists returns to the analysis when the *proportionality* principle is applied. As the proportionality principle requires that the amount of aid is the minimum necessary to deliver the stated objective, the application of this principle may imply that an instrument different from State should be preferred when available. For instance, a government could pursue a certain project as a pure public good provision (which does not include aid), or it may want to lower the cost for the taxpayer by means of, for example, a public-private partnership, which may include some State aid, yet may be significantly cheaper for the State. Should the State have to spend more in order to minimise the level of aid, just to satisfy the proportionality principle?

In summary, the requirement that the aid is a well-defined instrument as required by the second step of the balancing test may be overly strict, to the point that, if the analysis is carried out rigorously, no aid might be considered with certainty to be appropriate and proportionate, because in principle there will almost always be a better (that is, less distortive) manner in which to achieve the objective of common interest. Unless it is more precisely defined, the application of this leg of the test may therefore grant the Commission significant discretionary power in determining whether aid is a well-defined instrument.

III.iv.   To What Extent Does State Aid Really Distort Competition?

The third step of the balancing test has to do with distortions of competition. The analysis of distortions of competition has always been part of the assessment of State aid and therefore its inclusion in the balancing test is not surprising.

What is novel, is that in the *Common Principles* paper the discussion of the distortions of competition does not major on maintaining a 'level paying field' among undertakings, but rather on the potential negative effects in terms of *producers' incentives* that the aid may have. This absence of focus on the 'unfairness' of selective aid is atypical of State aid discourse, where considerations about 'fairness' have often been the main element of the analysis of the distortions of competition.[35] This new focus on incentives is consistent with the refined economic approach where aid is judged on the basis of efficiency considerations, rather than fairness.

The *Common Principles* paper states that effects on social welfare (as opposed to consumer welfare) should be considered.[36] This is surprising, as most competition policy statements from the Commission are concerned with consumer welfare,[37] and current and past Commission's economists have explicitly advocated the use of the consumer welfare in State aid (adjusted to consider the tax-related cost of the aid), consistent with the stated policy standard of other provisions of EU competition law.[38]

It is in fact unclear why State aid should be judged on the basis of the effect on a broader number of stakeholders than a merger or an Article 101 or Article 102 TFEU case. Why should company profit, which, as a matter of stated policy, is irrelevant to the Commission's assessment of the competitive effects of mergers and other business practices, be a relevant consideration for State aid?

The likely reason for including producers' welfare in the policy standard has to do with the traditional focus of State aid analysis on the competitive disadvantage faced by the competitors of the beneficiary. It can even be argued that the traditional policy standard was an 'effect on rivals' standard, whereby the aid was assessed on the basis of whether it distorted the 'level playing field'.[39] Because in the traditional analysis the distortion of competition has often been equate to the negative effect on competitors, a consumer welfare standard which, by definition, would exclude the welfare of those producers from the analysis would have been too significant a departure from traditional State aid control. [40]

It is important to note that, in any event, the policy standard advocated in the *Common Principles* paper is vague. The reference to a 'social welfare' standard different from a total welfare standard allows the weighing of the interests of different stakeholders differently. The reason for the vagueness in the policy standard may have to do with the fact that, from a static point of view and assuming the presence of some market power, the distortions of competition that State aid brings about are not necessarily harmful.[41]

For instance, assume that a Member State gives an automaker a production subsidy of €1,000 per car; what would be the effect on competition of this subsidy? The aid recipient would have a lower cost of production, which would allow it to increase its production. In the presence of market power, the increase in production of the aid recipient would not completely crowd out the production of competing automakers, which would reduce their sales somewhat but not as much as the increase in the sales of the aid recipient. The outcome would be an increase in the production of cars and thus lower prices: with a clear benefit for consumers. It can also be shown that under fairly general market conditions, the overall effect on producer surplus is positive (in that the aid recipient's increase in profit outweighs the loss in profit of its competitors), and that total welfare will improve, even when one deducts the cost of the aid for the taxpayers.[42]

In other words, the static effect of State aid in the presence of market power tends to be one of output expansion, which is typically consumer (and total) welfare enhancing. Thus both a consumer and a total welfare standard would tend to find that many types of aid would result in a 'positive distortion of competition', at least in a static setting (or, in the short run).[43] The need to avoid such 'positive distortion of competition' may be one of the reasons why the *Common Principles* paper adopts a vague 'social welfare' standard in which the interest of various stakeholders might be weighted differently.

More importantly, as noted by all the contributions to the economic debate on State aid after the SAAP,[44] it is essential that a distortions of competition analysis should focus on the aid's *dynamic* effects on incentives and market structure, as opposed to the standard static effects of distortion of the level playing field, which do not appear to be significantly or even unequivocally harmful.

When considering the aid's *dynamic* effects on incentives and market structure, it is important to consider that aid dampens competition incentives and results in moral hazard only if it is foreseen and expected by the undertakings. If the granting of State aid is uncertain or unpredictable, even the *dynamic* distortions of competition would be limited. So, even this type of *dynamic* distortions of competition cannot simply be assumed, as they may not arise.

In summary, as indicated in the *Common Principles* paper, the analysis of distortions of competition needs to abandon the traditional focus on preserving a level playing field for undertakings, and refocus on the dynamic effects on incentives to compete. Only in this manner can the balancing test focus on the harmful effects of aid on consumer welfare, consistent with all other areas of EU competition law, instead of having to adopt a vague and unjustified 'social welfare standard' to avoid having to consider the 'positive distortions of competition' that State aid often brings about in the presence of market power.

III.v.   Will the Balancing Test Really be Applied by the Commission?

The balancing test has been included in various policy statements from the Commission, beginning with the SAAP,[45] and in a number of Guidelines for specific aid categories (for example, R&D&I, Risk Capital, and Environmental Aid).

However, the *Common Principles* paper notes that even in these economics-savvy Guidelines the balancing test is reflected 'with adaptations in the light of the specific policy context', meaning that the economic framework is to be applied only when there is little or no existing case law, and thus no need to maintain consistency with past practice. For instance, the balancing test is referenced as a key principle in the introduction of the Environmental Aid Guidelines, yet its application is limited to ad hoc cases which require a detailed assessment (section 5 of the Guidelines), while the assessment of the dozen types of environmental aid commonly granted is carried out in a rather formalistic manner, without a single reference to market failures or to the balancing of positive and negative effects of the aid (see sections 3.1.1 to 3.1.12 of the Guidelines). The need to maintain consistency with previously approved schemes or types of aid trumps the application of the more sophisticated economic framework.

This is a general feature of the more sophisticated economics approach: it does not apply to aid which falls within the scope of existing Guidelines. This means that aid for those specific objectives, but which does not meet all the conditions in their respective guidelines, cannot be declared compatible, even if it passes the balancing test. From a policy standpoint, it is unclear why this should be the case: there is no reason why, just by the nature of its objective, certain categories of aid should not benefit from being analysed under the balancing test, instead using the test as an additional compatibility criterion also for aid which is covered by the specific guidelines (but does not meet all their conditions).

Another limitation in the application of the more sophisticated economic framework is the existence of categories of aid which would be difficult to justify on the basis of the balancing test. One such example is rescue and restructuring aid. Much of the rescue and restructuring (R&R) aid is granted in order to maintain inefficient undertakings which have failed the test of a normally functioning market. It is hard to see what market failure this type of aid would address. In fact, it is the very nature of well-functioning markets that they lead to the exit of inefficient firms; and preventing their exit, rather than remedying a market failure, precludes the market from operating efficiently. Equity considerations (rather than efficiency objectives) are often quoted as the rationale for R&R aid; and given the aforementioned vagueness of the economic approach to equity objectives, one may consider R&R aid to have a well-defined objective of common interest. Yet, if equity is the objective of R&R aid, it is unlikely that such aid would pass the second step of the balancing test, as there are many other instruments which can deliver social objectives in a more appropriate, proportional and incentive-compatible manner.

Thus, the rigorous application of the balancing test to R&R aid would result in only a fraction of the R&R aid currently approved under the R&R Guidelines being considered compatible. The Commission is in the process of reviewing the R&R guidelines and has launched a consultation process which may lead to a more sophisticated economic approach to R&R aid. However, if the aid provided to financial institutions during the financial crisis can be of any guidance,[46] the Commission may find it difficult to move from the traditional approach to R&R aid to a more refined economic approach that is consistent with the SAAP.[47]

In summary, the application of the more sophisticated economic framework and the balancing test is severely limited by the need to maintain consistency with past Commission practice as codified in the case law and in the various Guidelines. The main application of the balancing test in the near future will therefore be in ad hoc cases for which there are no guidelines or fitting precedents. Over time, however, the more sophisticated economic approach should permeate the Commission's analysis more widely and eventually it should find its way into case law and the Guidelines.

IV.   CONCLUSION

Until recently, economics did not play a significant role in the determination of whether aid violated Article 107(1) TFEU or could be compatible under Article 107(2) or 107(3) TFEU; the role of economics in State aid proceedings was limited to the application of the Market Economy Investor Principle in order to determine whether a transfer of State resources constituted aid. Thus, State aid is the area of EU competition law in which economics has traditionally played the least significant role.

Starting with the Commission's 2005 State Aid Action Plan, however, State aid has started to join other areas of competition law in their gradual move from a purely form-based approach towards a more effects-based approach which emphasises the economic implications of State aid. The new framework for economic analysis is based on a *balancing test* which weighs the positive economic effects of the aid against its negative effect in order to determine whether aid should be deemed compatible under Article 107(3) TFEU.

The refined economic approach to State aid is a welcome development, as it provides a more rigorous analytical framework to the compatibility analysis of Article 107(3) TFEU, and thus the opportunity for reducing the level of political interference in State aid control and furthering the role of economic and legal analysis. Consistent with the stated aim in the SAAP ('less and better targeted aid'), the balancing test advanced by the Commission applies the underlying economic framework in a way which tends to reduce the possible justifications for State intervention in the economy and thus the type of aid that will be deemed compatible.

The balancing test is an important development, as it advances a much needed analytical approach to the compatibility criteria under Article 107(3)(c). However, the framework of the balancing test is not fully formed, and it may be expected that over time more thought will have to be given to a few features of the test, such as: the overall objective of a modernised state aid control regime; whether market power should be treated as a 'cognizable' market failure; whether step two of the balancing test (the 'well-defined instrument' criterion) needs to be clarified; and the need for a more detailed analysis of distortions of competition and effects on trade.

To what extent and how rapidly the economic framework will be adopted in the Commission's practice is an open question. The need to maintain consistency with past practice, case law, and existing Guidelines means that the economic framework is at times stretched or ignored. Yet, the framework has already started to permeate soft law, and in particular the Environmental and R&D&I Guidelines. Although the Guidelines and frameworks for specific aid measures still apply, an increasing number of ad hoc cases will be analysed using this economic approach, which does not mean that the analysis needs to be more complex, just more economically sound.

NOTES

1. Consultation document, *State Aid Action Plan: Less and better targeted State aid: a roadmap for State aid reform* 2005–2009, COM (2005) 107 final.
2. See in particular Kroes 2006; Kroes 2007.
3. See, in particular, Buelens et al. 2007; Friederiszick and Röller 2008. Another early contribution to the debate was Heidhues and Nitsche 2006.
4. Staff discussion paper, *Common Principles for an Economic Assessment of the Compatibility of state Aid Under Article 87.3*, 15 May 2009 (*Common Principles* paper).
5. The law and economics movement started in the late 1970s in the US with the work of economists like Aaron Director, and legal scholars such as Frank Easterbrook, Richard Posner, and Robert Bork. In Europe, while already in the 1960s the CJEU required an analysis of agreements in their economic context (market effects), economics started gaining more traction in competition law only after the 1997 Notice on market definition.
6. In Europe, the process of more economically sound, effects-based application of competition law started with the market definition Notice (1997); then proceeded to Article 101 TFEU (the Guidelines on Vertical Restraints, 2000); then mergers (with the Guidelines on the assessment of horizontal mergers, 2004, and those on the assessment of non-horizontal mergers, 2008); and more recently started to make inroads into Article 102 TFEU (with the 2008 Guidance on its enforcement priorities in applying Article 102 TFEU).
7. See Case C-73/79, *Philip Morris Holland BV* v. *Commission* [1980] E.C.R. 2671–2688, determining that the selective nature of the aid should be regarded as affecting competition and trade; Case C-296/82, 318/82, *Leeuwarder Papierwarenfabriek BV v. Commission* [1985] E.C.R. 809, requiring that the Commission sets out its reasoning for why aid is likely to result in distortions of competition and trade; and Case T-55/99, *Confederación Española de Transporte de Mercancías (CETM)* v. *Commission* [2000] E.C.R. II-3207 in which the General Court indicated that, provided it explains its reasoning as to how the aid in question distorted competition and affected trade, the Commission is not required to carry out an economic analysis of the actual situation on the relevant market.

8. See Case T-34/02, *Le Levant v. Commission* [2002] E.C.R. II-2803 and Case C-494/06 P, *Commission v. Italian Republic and Wam Spa* [2009] E.C.R. I-3639, para 61, where the Court held that 'Contrary to the claim of the Commission in that respect, the mere fact that Wam took part in intra-Community trade by exporting an important part of its production within the EU cannot suffice, in the particular circumstances of the case recalled in paragraph 55 of this judgment, to demonstrate those effects [on trade].'
9. European Commission 2005.
10. The SAAP states: 'The European Council of March 2005 has called on 'Member States to continue working towards a reduction in the general level of state aid, while making allowance for any market failures. This movement must be accompanied by a redeployment of aid in favour of support for certain horizontal objectives such as research and innovation and the optimisation of human capital. The reform of regional aid should also foster a high level of investment and ensure a reduction in disparities in accordance with the Lisbon objectives.' However, commentators have raised doubts as to the actual strength of such political mandate, see, for example, Kaupa 2009.
11. As the SAAP states: 'Making more use of a refined economic approach is a means to ensure a proper and more transparent evaluation of the distortions to competition and trade associated with state aid measures. This approach can also help investigate the reasons why the market by itself does not deliver the desired objectives of common interest and in consequence evaluate the benefits of state aid measures in reaching these objectives.'
12. See the Member States' response to the consultation document and in particular those of the UK, France, and Italy For a more nuanced support to the SAAP, see Germany's response to the consultation document.
13. For a final version of their views, see Friederiszick et al. 2007. As indicated by the authors: 'European state aid control is currently at a turning point. The European Union and its member states increasingly recognize the need to rethink the balance between the various objectives of state intervention. Constraints on state budgets and concerns about the effectiveness of state aid have increased the political pressure towards a more economics, effect-based approach in state aid and state aid control. Both at national and European level, the political mandate is for "less and better targeted state aid". In this paper, we explore how an increased reliance on economic insights in state aid control can contribute towards the objective of enhancing the effectiveness of state aid control.'
14. See Kroes 2007 for then-Commissioner Kroes's public pronouncements on the balancing test. See also the commentary to the Commission Communication: *Criteria for the compatibility analysis of state aid to disadvantaged and disabled workers* in Memo/09/260, June 2009.
15. Community Framework for state aid for Research and Development and Innovation, O.J. 2006 C 323/1.
16. Community Guidelines on state aid to promote risk capital investments in small and medium-sized enterprises, O.J. 2006 C 194/2.
17. Community Guidelines on state aid for environmental protection, O.J. 2008 C 82/1.
18. Criteria for the compatibility analysis of training state aid cases subject to individual notification, O.J. 2009 C 188/1.
19. Criteria for the compatibility analysis of state aid to disadvantaged and disabled workers subject to individual notification, O.J. 2009 C/6.
20. See, for example, the discussion in two articles from European Commission's officials, referenced at fn 3.
21. A (Pareto) efficient outcome is one in which no agent can be made better off without making someone else worse off. For a definition of market failure, see Ledyard 2008.
22. A common example of a positive externality is investment in basic (non-patentable) R&D. Basic non-patentable technical progress benefits everybody but the inventor is unable to appropriate the return from these benefits, so the market will deliver too little basic (non-patentable) R&D from the point of view of society as a whole.

23. Akerlof 1970.
24. See *Common Principles* paper, paras 35, 36, and 38.
25. *Common Principles* paper, para. 39.
26. Buelens et al 2007, 5 and 6.
27. Ibid. p. 8.
28. See, for instance, Kaupa 2009 and Spector 2008.
29. See Krugman 1991a; Brander and Spencer 1985; Krugman 1991b, Besley and Seabright 1999.
30. In its response to the SAAP consultation document, Germany states that the SAAP reveals an 'instrumentalisation' of State aid control, particularly for fiscal policy purpose. While Germany agrees that State aid measures should be evaluated for effectiveness, it also points out that that is not the role of the Commission, but rather that of member states. Germany also considers that with the SAAP the Commission may be extending state aid control beyond what is defined by the Treaty.
31. There is an ample economics literature on the inability of politicians to commit to curb wasteful subsidisation. For a discussion of this political commitment problem and how State aid control may solve it, see Dewatripont and Seabright 2006. See also Monti 2008 and Spector 2008 for a discussion of State aid control as a solution to Member States, inability to commit not to grant wasteful subsidies.
32. One of the first and most influential contributions to the new literature emphasising the positive effects of 'equity' on growth is Alesina and Rodrick 1994. For a complete survey of the economic literature on the relationship between economic inequality and economic growth, see Aghion, Caroli and Garcia-Peñalosa 1999.
33. *Common Principles* paper, para. 17.
34. *Common Principles* paper, paras 30 and 31.
35. See, for instance, Kroes 2010, an article in the *Competition Policy Newsletter,* where a 'level playing field' is mentioned five times in four pages.
36. Note that the *Common Principles* paper draws a distinction between 'social welfare' and 'total welfare', the latter being the sum of producers' and consumers' welfare, while the former includes equity considerations, presumably by giving more weight to the welfare of certain stakeholders.
37. See, for instance, *Guidelines on the application of Article 81(3) of the Treaty*, O.J. 2004 C 101/97, para. 13; *Guidelines on the assessment of horizontal mergers under the Council Regulation on the control of concentrations between undertakings,* at paras 8 and 79.
38. See Friederiszick and Röller 2008.
39. See, for instance, Heidues and Nitsche 2006; Friederiszick and Röller 2008.
40. See, for instance, Heidues and Nitsche 2006, proposing a total welfare policy standard as a compromise between the consumer welfare standard used in other areas of EU competition law and the 'effects on rivals' standard typical of traditional State aid analysis.
41. See, for instance, Heidues and Nitsche 2006; Friederiszick and Röller 2008.
42. A situation in which this result may be reversed is if the overall economic cost of each €1 of aid is larger than €1, because of distortive elements of taxation or of costly administration of public finances and aid. See, Collie 2000.
43. This effect is due to the fact that in this case aid tends to remedy the market failure represented by market power. The basic economic framework in the Common Principles paper is therefore intellectually sound: by 'distorting competition' State aid remedies a market failure, that is, market power, or imperfect competition. Yet, the *Common Principles* paper explicitly states that market power is not market failure addressable by State aid. For a more general analysis highlighting the efficiency benefits of subsidies in the presence of market power, see Besley 1989.
44. See, for example, Heidhues and Nitsche 2006.
45. See para. 11 of the SAAP and the pronouncements of then-Commissioner Kroes 2007.
46. The case of aid given to banks during the 2008–9 global financial crisis under Article 107(3)(b) TFEU is different from standard R&R aid under Article 107(3)(c) TFEU, as

the financial crisis had many elements of systemic market failure. Aid given to remedy such a systemic market failure can often be deemed compatible under the balancing test. Unfortunately, the Commission approached the aid given to financial institutions during the 2008–9 global financial crisis by and large under the traditional framework of R&R aid, instead of taking the opportunity of applying the more sophisticated economic framework and the balancing test. For an application of the balancing test to that aid, and for a critique of the Commission's policy in that context, see Coppi and Haydock 2009.

47.   For some of the challenges involved in applying the more economic approach and the balancing test to R&R aid, see Coppi et al.

REFERENCES

Aghion, Philippe, Eve Caroli and Cecilia Garcia-Peñalosa (1999), 'Inequality and economic growth – the perspective of the new growth theories', *Journal of Economic Literature*, **37:4**, 1615–1660.

Akerlof, George A. (1970), 'The market for 'Lemons': quality uncertainty and the market mechanism', *Quarterly Journal of Economics*, **84:3**, 488–500.

Alesina, Alberto and Dani Rodrick (1994), 'Distributive politics and economic growth', *Quarterly Journal of Economics*, **109:2**, 465–90.

Besley, Timothy (1989), 'Commodity taxation and imperfect competition: A note on the effects of entry', *Journal of Public Economics*, **40:3**, 359–367.

Besley, Timothy and Paul Seabright (1999), 'The effects and policy implications of state aids to industry: an economic analysis,' *Economic Policy*, **14:28**, 13–53.

Brander, James A. and Barbara J. Spencer (1985), 'Export subsidies and international market share rivalry', *Journal of International Economics,* **18:1-2**, 83–100.

Buelens, Christian, Gaëlle Garnier, Matthew Johnson and Roderick Meiklejohn (2007), 'The economic analysis of state aid: Some open questions', *European Economy*, Brussels: Directorate-General for Economic and Financial Affairs, European Commission, Economic Papers, No. 286 (September).

Collie, D R. (2000), 'State Aid in the European Union: The Prohibition of Subsidies in an Integrated Market', *International Journal of Industrial Organisation*, **18**, 867–84.

Coppi, Lorenzo and Jenny Haydock (2009), 'The approach to state aid in the restructuring of the financial sector', *Competition Policy International*, (November).

Coppi, Lorenzo, Urs Haegler and Ingrid Liedrop (2011), *LECG Response to the commission Consultation Paper on the Review of Rescue and Restructuring Aid Guidelines*.

Dewatripont, Mathias and Paul Seabright (2006), "Wasteful" public spending and state aid Control', *Journal of the European Economic Association*, **4:2–3**, 513–22.

European Commission (2005), *State Aid Action Plan: Less and better targeted state aid: a roadmap for state aid reform 2005–2009*", COM (2005) 107 of 7 June 2005.

Friederiszick, Hans and Lars-Herdich Röller, (2008), 'European state aid control: an economic framework', in Paolo Buccirossi (ed), *Advances in the Economics of Competition Law*, Cambridge MA: MIT Press.

Heidhues, Paul and Rainer Nitsche (2006), 'Study on methods to analyse the impact of state aid on competition', *European Economy*, Brussels: Directorate-General for Economic and Financial Affairs, European Commission, Economic Papers, **No 244**, (February).

Kaupa, Clemens (2009), 'The more economic approach – a reform based on ideology?', *European State Aid Law Quarterly*, **3:4**, 311–322.

Kroes, Neelie (2006), 'The refined economic approach in state aid law: a policy perspective', GCLC/College of Europe Conference, 21 September 2006 Brussels.

Kroes, Neelie (2007), 'The Law and Economics of State aid control – a Commission Perspective' Speech to the Joint EStALI/ESMT Conference, 'The Law and Economics of European State Aid Control', 8 October 2001 Berlin, available at: <http://europa.eu/

rapid/pressReleasesAction.do?reference=SPEECH/07/601&format=HTML&aged=0&language=EN&guiLanguage=en>.

Kroes, Neelie (2010), 'Competition policy and the crisis – the Commission's approach to banking and beyond' *Competition Policy Newsletter*, **No.1**, 3-6.

Krugman, Paul (1991a), *Geography and Trade*, Cambridge MA: MIT Press.

Krugman, Paul, (1991b), '*The move toward free trade zones*', *Economic Review*, Federal Reserve Bank of Kansas City, (**Nov**), 5–25.

Ledyard, John O. (2008), 'Market failure', Durlauf, Steven N. and Lawrence E. Blume. (eds), in *The New Palgrave Dictionary of Economics*, 2nd edn, Basingstoke: Palgrave Macmillan.

Monti, Mario (2008) 'Quelques aspects politiques et pédagogiques du contrôle des aides', *Concurrences*, **No 3**.

Spector, David (2008) 'Le rôle de l'analyse économique dans la politique des aides d'etat', *Concurrences*, **No 3**.

5 The market economy investor: an economic role model for assessing State aid

James Kavanagh, Gunnar Niels and Simon Pilsbury*

I. RELEVANCE OF THE MARKET ECONOMY INVESTOR PRINCIPLE

Economic logic, and legal principles, dictate that State aid, as a 'transfer of State resources conferring a benefit or advantage', occurs only when the State acts on terms that would not be acceptable to a private business. If a public authority grants funding to a firm on terms which the same firm could have obtained by going to a bank, or capital markets, then there is no 'advantage' conferred by State intervention. This is irrespective of whether the recipient is a government-owned entity (for example, a State-owned seaport or airport) or a private firm. A prime question in State aid law is how to assess whether the terms of the State action are in fact compatible with those acceptable to a commercial investor. This is known as the market economy investor principle: MEIP.

The MEIP is an interpretation of Article 107(1) TFEU and, more specifically, of the first and second criteria proposed for determining whether government funding constitutes State aid. Any measure that satisfies the MEIP is not considered State aid. In this case, the other two criteria for State aid, selectivity, and (actual or potential) distortion of competition and intra-community trade, no longer need to be assessed.

The MEIP was set out in the 1998 *Van der Kooy* case:

> It is of the essence of a State aid that it is non-commercial in the sense that the State steps in where the market would not. The state may have its reasons for doing so but they are not commercial in the ordinary sense of the word. Thus the state may subscribe for shares in a company or lend money, but when it does so to an extent or on terms which would not be acceptable to the commercial investor, it is granting aid which falls within Article [107 TFEU] if the tests of that provision are satisfied.[1]

To an economist, there is at first sight something inherently paradoxical in the MEIP. Does not the mere fact that the State spends money imply that no private party would do so? Indeed, some of the most publicised State aid cases have involved government rescues of failing firms or banks, which almost by definition would not meet the MEIP. Yet there is more to it. Many State-owned entities engage in normal commercial activity, which is fully in line with the principle of 'no prejudice of the system of property ownership' established in Article 345 TFEU. In such a mixed economic landscape, it makes sense to ask the question whether a particular State action does indeed qualify as commercial action, or whether an element of aid is involved. This application to State-owned firms operating in a commercial environment is one of the more straightforward uses of the MEIP.

The MEIP has been applied to other, perhaps less straightforward, situations. Public authorities may sell land to private parties, and the question becomes whether the price obtained reflects normal market conditions.[2] States may make capital investments in companies, and the MEIP would ask if a private investor would have made the same investment under normal market conditions.[3] Similarly, States may act as lenders to private companies. There appears to be a subtle legal difference between the private investor test and the private creditor test,[4] but both would follow the basic MEIP logic.

This chapter sets out the basic economic principles behind the MEIP. It illustrates these principles with several examples, including the 2008 *Ryanair/Charleroi Airport* case involving airport charges to an airline, and the less straightforward 2010 *Landesbank Hessen Thüringen Girozentrale (Helaba)* case involving the transfer of an investment fund from the State to a bank.

II.   ECONOMIC PRINCIPLES UNDERLYING THE MEIP

In undertaking an MEIP analysis, it is necessary to:

- consider the expected profitability of the investment;
- ring-fence the commercial activities from the functions that would be performed by the State even if it were a private investor;
- conduct a forward-looking, incremental analysis;
- use the appropriate discount rate or market-based return to compare with the expected profitability;
- focus on the actual decision made, rather than the process of decision-making.

We now consider each of these points.

II.i.   Expected Profitability of the Investment

An appropriate application of the MEIP requires an assessment of the expected profitability of the State's action. In essence, this comes down to measuring the intervention's rate of return, using standard investment appraisal techniques, in particular the net present value and internal rate of return.[5] If this return exceeds the cost of capital (the return required by providers of capital to the activity) it can be deemed consistent with the MEIP. This appraisal process is also normally undertaken, whether explicitly or implicitly, by private sector firms when considering whether to make an investment. Again, well-established financial techniques can be used to estimate the cost of capital in these cases and these are discussed below.

II.ii.   Ring-fencing Commercial Activities from other Activities of the State

Many State-owned operations have both commercial aspects (which are, or could be, run for profit) and other social, public-policy aspects (which require subsidisation from the government). A seaport or airport owned by the local government undertakes commercial activities that private port operators would also undertake, for example, charging shippers for port and handling services, but may also perform public functions such as providing basic infrastructure and promoting local employment and business activity. This distinction is not always straightforward, as the operations may be set up under a complicated legal ownership or organisational structure that makes it difficult to identify exactly where the commercial operations end and the other social aspects come in. Yet, from an economic perspective, it is often feasible to ring-fence the commercial aspects of the operations, thus rendering them independent of the legal structure. Only the costs and benefits related to these commercial activities are relevant for the MEIP test.

II.iii.   A Forward Analysis

The MEIP assessment should be made on an *ex ante* basis, taking into account only the information that could reasonably have been foreseen at the time the state decided to make the investment. While inevitably somewhat artificial (one has to go back in time), conducting the analysis in this way can affect a State aid decision in either direction since investments which have turned out to be profitable may in fact have been reasonably expected to be unprofitable before they were made, or vice versa. Hence, *ex post* information should not be used directly for the MEIP test. This was recognised in the 2002 *Stardust* case, where the CJEU established that:

> In this case, it is undisputed between the parties that, in order to examine whether or not the State has adopted the conduct of a prudent investor operating in a market economy, it is necessary to place oneself in the context of the period during which the financial support measures were taken in order to assess the economic rationality of the State's conduct, and thus to refrain from any assessment based on a later situation.[6]

Examining the *ex post* performance of the investment or the performance of similar companies can still serve as a sense-check of the *ex ante* assumptions, particularly where there are no unexpected changes in circumstances.

Furthermore, the MEIP should be applied on an incremental basis, that is, it should consider only the costs and revenues associated with the project at hand. The logic of this is as follows. Assume that a State-owned enterprise is losing €0.4m per year before a deal is signed; after the deal is signed for a new project, the enterprise's losses are reduced to €0.2m per year in the short run, and profits are anticipated for the long run. Although an assessment of the profitability of the State-owned enterprise as a whole will show that it is still loss-making at the time the project commences, the project itself is profitable and would therefore be likely to be undertaken by a private investor.

II.iv.   Analysis of the Discount Rate Used

Another important factor in assessing the profitability of a government investment is the discount rate used. As the MEIP involves an assessment of whether a private investor would have undertaken the State's action, profits should be discounted using the same rate that a private investor would have used. This rate is different from, and normally higher than, the rate at which governments can borrow money. A rational private investor will invest only if it expects to earn at least the opportunity cost of capital, that is, the return the investor would expect to obtain in the capital markets from other investments of similar risk profiles. The standard measure of this is the weighted average cost of capital (WACC). This is the average of expected rates of return to debt and equity, weighted by the relative proportions of debt and equity in a firm's capital structure. If the State is an equity investor, the appropriate required rate of return is the cost of equity, rather than the WACC. Conversely, if the State provides loans, the appropriate rate of return is the cost of debt. This should be equivalent to the true market cost of debt, excluding any effect of a State guarantee (which would artificially lower the cost of debt).

II.v.   Focus on the Actual Decision Made

Finally, it is important to focus on the *actual decision* that is made by the State, rather than the *process* by which the decision is made. For example, if a State-owned firm did not have a detailed business plan setting out the expected profitability of the deal at the moment of 'investment', this cannot in itself be construed as evidence that the firm did not act as a private investor. After all, quite a few real-world business decisions by private firms are taken without an explicit business plan. In determining whether the MEIP test is passed, the critical consideration is whether the decision would have been taken by a private investor, not whether that decision was reached by exactly the same process as would have been adopted by a prudent private investor. On the other hand, having a robust business plan in place at the time of the deal would of course help in supporting the case that it is indeed a commercial deal. Public entities are therefore well-advised to have such plans in place.

III.   THE *LINDE* CASE: ILLUSTRATING SOME OF THE MEIP CRITERIA

In a 2002 judgment, the General Court applied the MEIP to annul a Commission Decision establishing that aid given to Linde AG (in the form of a grant) was incompatible with the internal market.[7] Based on the application of this principle, the Court found that the German State had acted in the same way a private investor would have acted under the same market conditions. This case illustrates how the MEIP should focus on incremental investment decisions, as explained above.

In 1996/97, the German State-owned privatisation agency (THA/BvS), which owned a carbon monoxide plant at the chemical site of Leuna, incurred substantial losses associated with a below-cost long-term supply contract to Union Chimique Belge (UCB). Aid in the form of a DM9m grant was provided to a new investor, Linde, for the construction of a new carbon monoxide plant. In return for the grant, Linde took over the THA/BvS supply obligation to UCB. The Commission originally found that the grant did not comply with the MEIP because it allowed Linde to obtain a new production facility without having to bear the full costs. The General Court held that the Commission should have examined whether the subsidy reflected the market price that would have been agreed between agents operating under the same market conditions. This required the Commission to determine the equivalent price of the carbon monoxide supply obligation and to compare this with the grant given by the German State to Linde. If a private investor would have paid the same amount, such a grant could not be deemed State aid.

In light of the General Court's comments, the Commission reviewed its previous decision and found that:

> In the course of fulfilling its loss-making carbon monoxide delivery obligation, Germany tried to minimise its financial burden by finding a more economical solution, while honouring its contractual commitment to UCB. The decision by the THA/BvS to choose Linde for that purpose was, in that specific situation, objectively the most economical solution for the State.[8]

Furthermore, the Commission established that the grant did not distort competition since there was no other firm in the EU that could have supplied the carbon monoxide to UCB. Hence, the Commission found that the government subsidies did not constitute state aid.

IV. THE *RYANAIR/CHARLEROI* CASE: A 'STRAIGHTFORWARD' MEIP APPLICATION

A Court judgment in which the MEIP was considered applicable in a straightforward way involved the deal between Brussels South Charleroi Airport (BSCA) and Ryanair.[9] This case is discussed to further illustrate the economic criteria underlying the MEIP.

The agreement at issue was signed in November 2001 by Ryanair, BSCA and the Walloon government (which owns the airport), and concerned Ryanair basing aircraft at BSCA. A base is where aircraft remain overnight; it is important for an airport to have aircraft based at its location because this facilitates early outgoing flights and late incoming flights, thereby maximising the amount of time the airport is used and the number of air traffic movements it will receive. Prior to this agreement, Ryanair had already operated flights to and from BSCA under an earlier (1997) agreement, using aircraft based at other European airports.

The precise terms of the 2001 deal were crucial to the Commission's consideration of whether it represented State aid to Ryanair. Among the key terms were the following.

- The landing charges payable by Ryanair were approximately 50% lower than the general charges for using the airport, which were previously fixed by the Walloon Region (via a decree of the Regional

Parliament). The basis of charging was also different for Ryanair. While the standard tariffs were set on the basis of the weight of the aircraft, Ryanair paid charges according to the number of embarking passengers.

– Payments were to be made to Ryanair by BSCA at the start of the contract. A maximum of just under €3m could be paid, most of which was on the basis of €160,000 for each new route opened from BSCA to another airport.

– Ryanair was to pay a discounted fee for ground handling of €1 per passenger (compared with a standard fee of around €10 per passenger).

– A promotional arrangement ('Promocy') was set up, whereby Ryanair and BSCA each contributed €4 per passenger to a fund for advertising and promotion of flights to and from BSCA.

– Ryanair was to base between two and four aircraft at BSCA, and operate at least three rotations per day with each aircraft, for a 15-year period.

At its core, the arrangement was discounting standard airport rates in return for long-term commitments to provide a minimum level of service at the airport.

A first issue regarding the MEIP that emerged during the Commission's investigation was whether it could be applied at all to the specific deal signed by Ryanair. This proceeds from the Commission's characterisation of the fees paid by Ryanair to use the airport as 'taxes' (given that they were set by decree of the Walloon Parliament) rather than charges (which could be set by the airport independently of political authorisation). The Commission stated in its Decision that:

> . . . the Walloon Region has placed itself in a situation of confusion of powers. Instead of acting within the framework of its public powers, it deviated from the rules that it laid down itself by making the agreement . . . with Ryanair. The 'commercial need' to attract Ryanair to Charleroi thus made it move outside the applicable framework in relation to fixing charges in Wallonia . . . The principle of private investor in a market economy cannot be used as a basis for justifying this confusion of powers or the advantages granted to Ryanair.[10]

Due to this alleged confusion of roles between BSCA and the Walloon Region, the Commission concluded that the MEIP approach was not applicable to the relationship between the two parties and Ryanair. The corollary of this is that any price lower than that set by Parliamentary Decree would have represented State aid to Ryanair. As noted above, the more obvious approach from an economic perspective when applying the MEIP would be to ring-fence the activities which are of a commercial nature, and split them from the regulatory and governmental activities.

Despite considering the MEIP to be not applicable in the case of Ryanair's contract with BSCA, the Commission analysed the expected contribution of the agreement to the airport. The basis for doing this was a business plan covering the period up to 2010, which had been created by the airport prior to the signing of the contract with Ryanair. Analysis of this plan, by all parties to the proceedings, formed a large part of the case before the Commission. The plan covered all of the activities of BSCA, rather than just the costs and revenues that are associated with the Ryanair agreement.

The Commission identified a number of shortcomings in this business plan.

–   **Creation of passengers from full-fare airlines**. Prior to signing the agreement with Ryanair, BSCA received a very small number of passengers from full-fare airlines (fewer than 20,000 in 2001), and an even smaller number from charter airlines (fewer than 10,000). The business plan projected that the number of passengers from full-fare scheduled airlines would increase significantly over the course of the agreement (to 150,000 in 2007, and to 300,000 in 2010). The Commission criticised the lack of a rationale behind these projections, and particularly the fact that other papers submitted by the airport had indicated that it could hope to obtain significant full-fare traffic only in the event of capacity constraints at Zaventem (the main airport serving Brussels).
–   **Treatment of passengers from other low-fare airlines**. The business plan also included a significant uplift in passengers from other low-fare airlines, with numbers reaching 450,000 per annum by 2010. At the same time, Ryanair's passenger numbers were expected to plateau at 700,000 per annum from 2003 to 2010. The Commission argued in its decision that both of these projections were likely to be inaccurate. It considered that the other low-fare passengers should be reassigned in the business plan as if they were Ryanair passengers. This had the effect of reducing the projected profitability of these customers, as the contribution of €4 per passenger to Promocy had originally applied only to Ryanair passengers.

The Commission removed all passengers of other low-fare airlines from the business plan on the basis of the minutes from a BSCA board meeting held at around the time that the Ryanair agreement was concluded, which stated that it would be 'illusory to hope that another airline would establish a base at Gosselies' (the location of BSCA). Even if this were the case, it does not preclude from the likelihood of other low-fare airlines deciding to use BSCA as a destination rather than as a base. Furthermore, the Commission did not take into account the fact that even if it were inconceivable that another airline would wish to set up at BSCA before Ryanair did so (explaining the statement in the board papers), that does not mean that it would still be inconceivable for another airline to wish to do so after Ryanair's commencement of operations. There are several economic reasons for this.

First, Ryanair's presence at the airport demonstrates that there is demand at the airport, and that it is possible to operate profitably from it. This has the impact of reducing the perceived risk for other airlines considering setting up from BSCA, meaning that they would require a lower rate of return.

A second, and possibly more important, feature is the presence of network externalities at airports. In the case of non-hub airports, these network externalities are primarily two-sided. Consumers will place a greater value on flying to airports which have good transport links to onward connections, and, to a lesser extent, shopping and refreshment amenities. However, both transport operators and retailers will set up at airports only where there is a certain minimum throughput of potential customers. Consequently, boosting passenger numbers should increase other facilities provided, which in turn will increase passenger willingness to fly to the airport. The impact of Ryanair starting operations at BSCA would be expected to boost transport links and other amenities, and this would increase the expected profits of other airlines setting up at the airport. Consequently, Ryanair setting up a base at BSCA could, and indeed did, increase the willingness of other airlines to fly from the airport.

Ex post evidence would also tend to support the proposition that signing the agreement with Ryanair would encourage other airlines to use the airport. In July 2004 Wizz Air set up at Charleroi; in 2008 it flew 270,155 passengers from the airport, a figure not dissimilar to the 300,000 other low-cost passengers expected in the BSCA business plan for that year.[11] Onair began flights in 2005 from BSCA to Pescara, while Jetairfly opened a one-aircraft base at the airport in 2008. Overall passenger numbers (2.96m in 2008) were in fact higher than projected in the original business plan (2.42m), despite there being no passengers from full-fare airlines. *Ex post* evidence is not strictly relevant for the MEIP, which is an *ex ante* assessment (that is, before the business decision is taken), but it can provide a useful sense-check of the assumptions originally made in the business plan.

Another aspect of the MEIP debate concerned the treatment of the costs of fire and maintenance services. The Commission analysed at some length the funding of these costs at the airport. From 1990 to 2001 they were met by the Walloon Region rather than the airport itself. At the time of signing the agreement with Ryanair, BSCA was in a 'legal vacuum' whereby the Region had not agreed to extend the agreement to cover fire and mainte-nance costs. The Commission considered that €1.6m of these costs were fixed, and so should not be considered when analysing the profitability of the agreement with Ryanair, but that further fire and maintenance costs of around €1.5m per annum were due to the contract with Ryanair and should accordingly be taken into account.

As a result of all these findings, the Commission's revised business plan sharply reduced the expected profitability of the agreement between Ryanair and BSCA. The expected profit of €108.6m over the period 2001–15 was subject to deductions of €141.3m as a result of the identified issues, the largest of which was a reduction of €78.4m arising from the removal of passengers from full-fare airlines. Overall, the Commission's expectation was that the agreement would be loss-making from the per-spective of BSCA, and that therefore the MEIP was not satisfied by the agreement.

Ryanair appealed the Commission's Decision to the General Court on a number of grounds, including the following.

- That the Commission had treated BSCA and the Walloon Region as separate entities, when for MEIP purposes they should be taken as one and the same economic agent, through the owner-ship of BSCA by the Walloon Region, and the close relationship between the airport and the Region. Ryanair characterised what the Commission saw as 'confusion' between airport and Region as them in fact being a single economic entity.
- That the Commission should have assessed the measures taken by the Walloon Region with reference to the MEIP. In particular, Ryanair criticised the assessment by the Commission that by setting airport charges, the Region was acting as a regulator rather than as an economic agent (in this case, the owner of the airport).
- That the Commission's approach amounted to discrimination between private and public airports, because private firms would have a freedom of pricing denied to publicly owned airports. In particular, Ryanair argued that, under the Commission's approach, if the Region set airport charges then this would be a regulatory act, whereas if the Region entrusted the setting of charges to its wholly owned subsidiary airport, this would be a commercial act. Ryanair argued that this distinction was artificial.

– That the Commission had not fulfilled its obligation to provide reasons for taking a decision.

All of these points were disputed by the Commission, which stated before the Court that:

– taking the Region and BSCA together would have no impact on the findings, since the agreement with Ryanair did not confer any advantage on the Region;
– the suggested application of the MEIP is incompatible with the Commission's guidelines on the application of State aid law to the aviation sector, according to which public investment in airport infrastructure constitutes a general measure of economic policy;
– the fixing of landing charges to obtain access to infrastructure falls within the exercise of public authority powers.

IV.i.   The Court's Findings

When considering whether the Region and BSCA should be treated as a single entity or as separate, the General Court determined that the Walloon Region and BSCA should have been regarded as one single entity for the purposes of application of the MEIP. The main reason given by the General Court was that, when applying the MEIP, commercial transactions must be considered as a whole in order to consider whether the Region and BSCA behaved in a commercial manner. The General Court also noted that the Commission did not provide sufficient evidence to rule out the prospect that, due to the financial ties between the Region and BSCA, the Region obtained financial benefits from entering into the agreement.

This ruling from the General Court would appear to be important in the context of any reconsideration of State aid by the Commission, as it goes to the heart of the approach adopted in the decision. In several instances (for example, the treatment of fire and maintenance costs, and regarding the capping of payments to an environment fund in the business plan) the Commission treated the two entities as separate. Consequently, a potential new decision, or similar decisions concerning other airports, would have to be adopted on a somewhat different basis to the original one.

The second core finding of the General Court was that the actions of the Walloon Region in fixing airport charges should be considered economic activities. It stated that:

> the fixing of the amount of landing charges and the accompanying indemnity is an activity directly connected with the management of airport infrastructure,

which is an economic activity . . . The airport charges fixed by the Walloon Region must be regarded as remuneration for the provision of services within Charleroi Airport, notwithstanding . . . that a clear and direct link between the level of charges and the service rendered to users is weak.[12]

This is an important point since it helps clarify the extent of what will be considered an economic activity; even when prices are being set directly by an element of the government, they can be considered part of an economic activity so long as there is a payment for services rendered.

Following from this, the General Court found that the argument that airport charges may not be set by the airport itself is not sufficient to exclude the application of the MEIP to the agreement between BSCA and Ryanair. It went on to comment that the MEIP should have been applied, since the scheme reducing charges could have been introduced by a private operator. The Court found that the refusal to apply the MEIP to the agreement between Ryanair and BSCA created an error in law.

The actual application of the MEIP to the agreement between Ryanair and BSCA was not considered in detail by the General Court. However, the judgment did note that it cannot be ruled out that the application of the MEIP to the single body made up of the Walloon Region and BSCA might have led to a conclusion that there had been no State aid. This statement seems well grounded given that such an approach would most likely require a quite different treatment of key parts of the airport's business plan.

As a consequence of these findings, the General Court annulled the Decision by the Commission.

V. THE *HELABA* CASE: A COMPLEX FINANCIAL TRANSACTION

In March 2010, the General Court upheld the Commission's finding that the German state (*Land*) of Hessen acted as a private investor in transferring the €1.264 billion Housing and Future Investment Fund to Landesbank Hessen-Thüringen Girozentrale (Helaba).[13] The fund was established in 1998 and comprised Hessen's claims from a portfolio of low-interest social housing loans made between 1948 and 1998.

The *Land* transferred the fund to Helaba in the form of a silent partnership in December 1998. The Federal Banking Supervisory Office (Bundesaufsichtsamt für Kreditwesen) the relevant German regulator, recognised the contribution as hybrid equity capital which qualified as core capital (a bank's core capital is the buffer that the bank is required to hold to protect depositors and other stakeholders from any decline in the value of the bank's assets).

Remuneration for the *Land's* contribution was set at 1.4% of the nominal value. Although Helaba received the full amount in December 1998, remuneration was payable only on smaller phased amounts in the first four years (€310m, €610m, €820m and €1.02 billion). The portion of the contribution above these phased amounts was not remunerated, reflecting the fact that Helaba did not need the capital for capital adequacy purposes but only to fund growth. In the contested decision, the Commission held that while a private investor might have accepted a phased approach, it would have demanded some form of remuneration on the full amount of the contribution, regardless of Helaba's needs. It therefore imposed a rate of remuneration of 0.3% on the share of the contribution above the annual tranches and ordered Hessen to recover past unpaid amounts. The Commission held that, subject to this change, the contribution did not create an advantage for Helaba.

The Bundesverband deutscher Banken (BdB) challenged the Commission's decision that no advantage was conferred on Helaba by the transfer, since it was BdB's position that the agreed remuneration was less than what would have been accepted by a private investor, and therefore that the capital contribution amounted to State aid. Some of BdB's specific points were as follows.

- The contribution had more in common with riskier share capital than silent partnerships; the Commission was wrong to benchmark the remuneration against rates used in silent partnerships rather than share capital.
- The Commission incorrectly calculated the remuneration which would apply, even if the contribution were more akin to a silent partnership than share capital.
- The Commission was incorrect to allow phased remuneration in the first four years, since the state of Hessen lost the use of the full amount upon transferring it to Helaba.

In considering the classification of the contribution, the Court noted that the classification itself is less relevant than the specific risks faced by the contribution. In assessing these risks, the Court examined the priority of claims in the event of insolvency; the likely profitability profile of the investment (ie, fixed versus variable compensation); the liquidity of the investment; and the size of the contribution relative to the total capital of Helaba. While the Court noted that the contribution did not correspond exactly to either share capital or a silent partnership, it concluded on each point that the Commission had not made a manifest error in benchmarking the rates paid for Hessen's contribution against other silent partnership transactions.

The large size of the contribution relative to the total capital of Helaba (40%) was also cited by BdB to argue that the Commission had incorrectly calculated the remuneration to be paid by Helaba. The Court accepted that the significance of the contribution does increase the risk faced by Hessen, but noted that Helaba did not need a contribution of this size. If such a large capital injection had been required, the Court considered that Helaba would have been able to raise the capital in the market, from a number of investors. In other words, it was not a benefit for Helaba:

> . . . while the size of the Land's proportion of the core capital of Helaba entailed an increase in risk for the Land, it is not clear that that amounted to an advantage for which Helaba should have paid a premium.[14]

In considering the phased remuneration, the Court noted again that Helaba did not need a capital contribution for regulatory capital adequacy purposes and that its growth needs required only around €150m in new capital per year. It therefore held that Helaba behaved reasonably in demanding a two-tier remuneration system and that an investor in the State's position, which did not want to divide its contribution, would not have been able to achieve full rates on the entire amount. Furthermore, the Court noted that BdB had not alleged that the contribution afforded any advantage to Helaba. In sum, this case illustrates how the MEIP can be applied to complex financial transactions as well as commercial activities by the State.

VI.   CONCLUSION

The MEIP is central to determining whether a measure confers a benefit or advantage on the recipient and therefore whether the measure may constitute State aid. As its use by both the Commission and the European Courts increases, economic and legal practitioners will gain increased clarity on how and when the MEIP can be applied.

The cases discussed in this chapter illustrate some of the range of circumstances in which the MEIP can be used. The *Ryanair* case shows that the General Court is endorsing the use of the MEIP for commercial activities carried out by the State, in this case airport services to airlines, despite the Commission's initial reluctance. The *Helaba* case shows that the MEIP can also be used to evaluate more complex financial transactions where the State is involved; it cannot be taken for granted that such transactions always reflect State aid. Similarly, other recent decisions demonstrate that the MEIP can also be applied to cases involving fiscal measures. In *Eléctricité de France v. Commission*, the General Court found that the exemption from a tax could be evaluated under the MEIP as a capital contribution from the French State in its capacity as owner of EDF.[15]

All these cases demonstrate the rapid evolution of the MEIP as an economic tool in State aid analysis.

NOTES

*   The views expressed are those of the authors alone.
1.   Cases 67, 68 and 70/85, *Van der Kooy v. Commission* [1988] E.C.R. 219.
2.   For example, Case T-274/01, *Valmont v. Commission* [2004] E.C.R. II-3145.
3.   For example, Case C-142/87, *Belgium v. Commission* [1990] E.C.R. I-959.
4.   Bacon 2009: para 2.34.
5.   For a detailed discussion of these techniques and how they are used in a competition law context, see Oxera 2003.
6.   Case C-482/99, *France v. Commission* [2002] E.C.R. I-4387.
7.   Case T-98/00, *Linde AG v. European Commission* [2002] E.C.R. II-3961.
8.   Commission Decision of 19 March 2003 on State aid granted by Germany to Linde AG (Saxony-Anhalt)) (2003/687/EC), O.J. [2003] L 250/24, para 38.
9.   Case T-196/04, *Ryanair v. European Commission* [2008] E.C.R. II-3643. Oxera advised Ryanair in these proceedings.
10. Ibid, para 153.
11. Source: <http://www.charleroi-airport.com/raccourcis/detail-de-la-nouvelle/index. html?tx_ttnews%5Bpointer%5D=10&tx_ttnews%5Btt_news%5D=194&tx_ttnews%5B backPid%5D=20&cHash=33cf7d5d35> *Ryanair v. European Commission*, (accessed 26 May 2010).
12. Supra n.9, paras 88–89.
13. Case T-163/05, *Bundesverband deutscher Banken v. Commission* judgment of 3 March 2010.
14. Ibid, para 232.
15. Case T-156/04, *EDF v. Commission* judgment of 15 December 2009; on appeal: Case C-124/10P, O.J. 2010 C 161/16. See Szyszczak (2011).

REFERENCES

Bacon, Kelyn (2009), *European Community Law of State Aid*, Oxford: Oxford University Press.
Oxera (2003), 'Assessing profitability in competition policy analysis', *OFT Economic Discussion Paper 6*.
Szyszczak, Erika (2011), 'The survival of the market economic investor principle in liberalised markets', *European State Aid Law*, **1**, 35.

6 The intersection between the market economy investor principle and the one time-last time principle in the context of airline restructuring operations
Antigoni Lykotrafiti

I. INTRODUCTION

The chapter examines the intersection between the market economy investor principle (MEIP) and the one time-last time principle in the context of airline restructuring operations. The MEIP is a filtering mechanism designed to distinguish between cases of aid and cases of normal commercial transactions. In that sense, it constitutes the first step in a State aid analysis, being concerned with whether Article 107(1) TFEU applies or not. The one time-last time principle is a means to achieve optimal allocation of resources and therefore applies in a second step, when a finding of aid has already been reached and a compatibility assessment is pending. Since the principles in question are conceptually distinct, their intersection could not be easily ascertained. The only point where they seem to intersect is at the very end of a negative MEIP analysis and the very beginning of a compatibility analysis, that is, when a finding of aid at the end of the MEIP analysis triggers the application of the one time-last time principle at the beginning of the compatibility analysis.

Nevertheless, the application of the principles in the context of airline restructuring cases reveals a constant intersection. This is so because the MEIP is re-applied during the second step of the analysis, following a finding of incompatibility by virtue of the one time-last time limitation. Whilst in principle such a finding should entail the end of the State aid analysis and the prohibition of new aid, in practice it inaugurates the beginning of a second MEIP analysis. This occurs through the imposition of conditions on the aid recipient, whose fulfilment excludes the aid character of the planned operation. Although the latter practice is not necessarily illegitimate, it may become so if the conditions imposed do not reflect the reality of the private sector, but are simply used as a pretext to justify State action that would not otherwise be justified.

Before drawing any conclusions as to why this constant intersection occurs and what are its consequences for the fairness, effectiveness and credibility of the EU State aid regime, it would be useful to trace the application of the principles in question in the context of four high-profile airline restructuring cases, spanning over two decades of air transport liberalization, those of *Sabena, Air France, Iberia* and *Alitalia*.

II.   CASE LAW ANALYSIS

II.i.   *Sabena*

Well before the adoption of the 1994 Aviation Guidelines[1] and while the European skies were in a process of gradual deregulation, the Belgian flag carrier Sabena found itself in a maelstrom of financial difficulties that brought it to the door of the Commission, asking for approval of a package of restructuring measures. Low labour productivity and high personnel costs had contributed significantly to the very poor debt-equity ratio and the multi-billion losses suffered by the airline and its subsidiaries. Recapitalization under these conditions was deemed necessary.

The Commission considered that, in view of the accumulated debts and the costs of the restructuring programme, no private investor would have been prepared to participate in the company's restructuring. The operation therefore qualified as State aid within the meaning of Article 107(1) TFEU.[2] Despite the sweeping character of the proposed plan, the Commission found the aid compatible with the common market, subject, however, to a set of conditions, set in reality by the Belgian government itself. Although the sectoral framework applicable, namely the 1984 Aviation Memorandum,[3] was not unequivocal as to the one-off character of restructuring operations, the Commission formulated the government's undertaking to abstain from 'granting any further aid or other new measures favouring directly or indirectly Sabena or lowering the commercial risks of its shareholders' into a formal condition.

In May 1995 Swissair acquired a 49.5% stake in Sabena.[4] In January 2001 it undertook to become the majority shareholder in the latter, raising its holding to 85% over time. Six months later, and in view of Sabena's extremely precarious financial situation, a new agreement was reached, whereby the Belgian government and Swissair, Sabena's main shareholders, undertook to inject new capital of €430 million into the airline. At the beginning of October 2001, Swissair filed for bankruptcy, failing to honour its commitments towards its partner. The final countdown to Sabena's collapse had therefore begun. On 5 October 2001 the Brussels commercial court granted Sabena temporary protection from its creditors for a period of one month. The reaction of the Belgian government was immediate. Swissair's final instalment payment would be made good with a bridging loan of €125 million from the government, whereas Sabena would have in the meanwhile to find a new partner, prepared to continue managing the company. The urgency of the situation, reflected also in the expeditious adoption of the Commission's Decision on 17 October 2001, (in a period of less than two weeks since Sabena's first filing for bankruptcy protection), led the Commission to authorize the bridging loan as rescue aid in the context of pre-bankruptcy proceedings.[5] The Commission stressed that the aim of the aid was to permit the assisted firm to survive for a short period during which it had to assess in detail the prospects for future viability of the economic activities under threat. In any event, and in line with the one time-last time principle applicable under the 1999 Rescue and Restructuring (R&R) Guidelines to restructuring operations, the Commission made clear that as Sabena had already received restructuring aid in 1991, its restructuring plan could by no means include State aid of any kind.

Although the aid authorized had been explicitly tied to Sabena and its viability, the latter never used the loan. Given that no investor could be found to take over the company, the Belgian government came up with a plan whereby Sabena's subsidiary, Delta Air Transport (DAT), would guarantee the continuation of some of Sabena's services after the latter filed for bankruptcy. The green light from the Commission came soon after Sabena's official bankruptcy filing on 7 November 2001. Despite the fact DAT did not need, and, therefore, had not applied for rescue aid, the Commission saw no reason why Belgium's €125 million bridging loan could not be used as rescue aid by DAT,[6] subject to the same conditions defined by the Commission in its Decision of 17 October 2001.

Whether the thin line that divides rescue from restructuring operations in operational terms has been drawn correctly in the case of Sabena, so that the loan granted may not be used for restructuring purposes, is doubtful. The fungibility of money makes a distinction between rescuing with public funds and subsequent restructuring with the beneficiary's own means difficult. Given that Sabena had benefited from restructuring aid in the past, the one time-last time principle could only have been respected if the total of the bridging loan had been exclusively used to enable the basic airline business to continue operating during the time it takes to draw up a restructuring plan. In a different case, that is, if the whole or part of the loan had been used for DAT's restructuring, the once-only principle would have been violated. Whether a company that, as the Commission itself pointed out,[7] would have 'without the loan, to declare itself bankrupt in the next few days' could be seriously considered as capable of being born again from its ashes without any further aid is doubtful, albeit, apparently, credible to the Commission.

Under the 1999 R&R Guidelines repeated restructuring packages are prohibited by virtue of the one time-last time principle. The combination of restructuring aid with further rescue aid could be authorized, yet only under exceptional circumstances, unforeseeable and external to the company.[8] The Commission defined (in its 2004 version of the R&R Guidelines) an 'unforeseeable circumstance' as 'one which could in no way be anticipated by the company's management when the restructuring plan was drawn up and which is not due to negligence or errors of the company's management or decisions of the group to which it belongs'.[9] A finding that in the *Sabena* case rescue aid was justified, despite prior restructuring aid, due to such kind of circumstances, would require the examination of the restructuring plan implemented in 1991. It does not appear that the Commission engaged in an analysis of Sabena's constantly deteriorating finances in the light of previous restructuring efforts. Similarly, no exceptional, unforeseeable and external circumstances have been invoked as a justificatory basis for the bridging loan. Instead, the aid was deemed justified on acute social grounds since DAT's bankruptcy would add to the social upheaval caused by Sabena's collapse, leading to the loss of several thousand direct additional jobs.[10]

II.ii.   Air France

The first capital injections to Air France in 1991 and 1992 were authorized by the Commission in the light of summary proceedings. No formal proceedings were initiated, the decisions adopted never saw the light of day and all that is publicly known about the operations which took place and the relevant Commission approach has been encapsulated in two epigrammatic Press Releases.[11]

In February 1991 France notified the Commission of its intention to inject FF2 billion into the capital of Air France. Faced with considerable financial difficulties, Air France launched a strategic plan providing for significant staff reductions during the period 1991–1993 and an initial recapitalization of the airline amounting to FF 5.8 billion, to be realized in three tranches. Despite Air France's bad financial ratios, the Commission cleared the measures as being in line with the MEIP, considering that the past achievements of the company, the prospect of a major expansion of the Community civil aviation market, the group's particular strengths and the undertakings made in the restructuring plan, justified the classification of the State investment as a normal market economy operation. In July 1992 the Commission authorized two successive capital injections of FF 1.25 and 2.59 billion into Air France by BNP (a State-controlled investor) and a consortium of 21 banks respectively, as normal financial transactions. The Commission appeared equally optimistic as to the growth prospects of the sector. The restructuring underway was considered satisfactory, notwithstanding the airline's low net results, whilst the commercial terms of the operations were deemed to be in line with market conditions.

Nevertheless, some two years later, in May 1994, the French government's plans to inject FF20 billion into Air France as part of its restructuring obliged the Commission to open the formal investigation procedure under Article 108(2) TFEU, expressing doubts as to the compatibility of the measures with the State aid *acquis*. The urgency of the situation and the political pressure exercised on the Commission are evident from the speedy adoption of its Decision in July 1994, that is, in a period of less than two months from the start of the contentious procedure. Contrary to the fears expressed by interested parties, the Commission took the view that 'a genuine restructuring of Air France will contribute to the development of the European air transport industry by improving its competitiveness in the aviation sector and is therefore in the common interest'.[12] The aid was thus declared compatible with the common market by virtue of Article 107(3)(c) TFEU, provided that certain conditions were met. On the same day as the Commission authorized the aid, a separate Air France Decision was adopted, concerning the subscription by CDC-Participations, a French State-owned financial institution, to bonds issued by Air France.[13] This time the conclusion was reached that in view of the airline's economic and financial situation at the time the transaction was made and the terms and conditions of the bonds, a rational private investor would not have injected the capital in question. The investment was therefore held to constitute operating aid, incompatible with the common market. A recovery order was accordingly issued.[14]

The action for annulment against the Commission's Decision authorizing the aid brought before the General Court by a number of European airlines[15] did not prevent the release of the second and third tranches of aid in 1995 and 1997.[16] Nor had four years later the annulment of the Decision for insufficient reasoning on two matters of law any impact on the aid package authorized. Since the Court had not specifically ordered recovery, the Commission came up with a new Decision in July 1998, aligning its reasoning to the Court's observations.[17]

The restructuring plan implemented was meant to prepare Air France for privatization, turning it into '*une veritable enterprise*'. In mid-1996, several months before the official completion of the restructuring programme, Air France posted its first full-year operating profit since 1989.

By 1999 Air France's results were positive enough to induce a first round of privatization. More than 24.4% of the airline's capital was floated on the market by the State and institutional shareholders, reducing the State's shareholding to 54.4%. The second act of privatization took place in 2004, when a merger, unprecedented for European aviation standards, between Air France and the Dutch airline KLM successfully materialized. Air France was *de facto* privatized, the State's shareholding in the new group being mechanically diluted as a result of the Public Exchange Offer.

Judging by the result, Air France went through a genuine restructuring process, which not only restored its profitability in a relatively short period of time, but, in addition, brought it to the top of Europe's airlines. *Air France* is a reverse story. While normally an airline facing difficulties irreversible by its own means would ask for the Commission's clearance of restructuring aid obtained by the government and, thereafter, given the one time-last time limitation, would attempt to justify further injections of capital by employment of the MEIP, in *Air France* exactly the opposite happened. The Commission cleared the 1991 and 1992 equity increases as normal financial transactions. In these early years of deregulation, the transparency requirement was 'satisfied' simply with the issue of two laconic press releases. The airline's competitors, although unhappy, did not react. Only when a massive bailout of FF 20 billion was involved did the State aid rules, as formulated up until that point, that is, before the entry into force of the 1994 Aviation Guidelines,[18] come into play. Unlike the majority of flag carriers, Air France did not have to negotiate additional packages of aid. Having escaped the application of the one time-last time rule thanks to the characterization of the 1991 and 1992 operations as normal market economy transactions, the French authorities managed to negotiate with the Commission an extremely generous package of aid under Article 107(3)(c) TFEU, which by itself was capable of dramatically increasing Air France's capital. The subsidies involved, combined with a very good restructuring programme, soon got the airline out of the red.

II.iii.   *Iberia*

Iberia appeared in the State aid picture in February 1992, when the Spanish government made known to the Commission its intention to increase the airline's capital by PTA 120 billion, as part of a strategic plan covering the period 1992–1996. The Commission's handling of the case competes in opacity with the procedure followed in the 1991 and 1992 *Air France* cases. The *Iberia* decision, adopted in July 1992,[19] was never published, the only source of information made available by the Commission being a brief press release.[20] Although the aid notified appeared to be operating aid, aimed at the modernization of the fleet, the Commission refrained from attempting any relevant classification, finding it compatible with the common market under Article 107(3)(c) TFEU, provided that certain conditions would be met. Considering Iberia's bad and steadily deteriorating economic and financial situation, the Commission authorized the aid, in view of the firm undertakings given by the Spanish authorities that, *inter alia*, the operation would be of a one-off character.

In December 1994, and therefore before the completion of the four-year restructuring programme, the Spanish authorities asked for the Commission's approval of a further capital injection, amounting to PTA 130 billion. The Commission expressed doubts with regard to the subsidy-free nature of the capital injection, as well as with regard to the existence of unforeseeable, exceptional and external-to-Iberia circumstances, which could deactivate the condition set out in its 1992 Decision that no new aid should be granted throughout the duration of the programme. Although the magnitude of the planned injection was considered excessive from a rational investor's perspective and the financial risks associated with the operation too high, the plan was finally cleared in January 1996 as a normal commercial operation.[21] The readiness of Spain to amend the restructuring plan according to the Commission's recommendations, in conjunction with the firm commitments undertaken, as well as the supreme objective of preparing the airline for its future partial privatization, led to the approval of the plan as in line with the MEIP.

The 1996 *Iberia* decision is a clear illustration of the interrelation between the two pivotal principles governing restructuring, namely the MEIP and the one time-last time principle. Although *Iberia* is overall, like *Air France*, a success story in that the company underwent a restructuring process that restored its profitability, the authorization of a second package of aid under the private investor test has been much contested as running counter to the one time-last time principle. Undoubtedly, a negative Commission Decision would have caused major socio-political turmoil, potentially tackled through illegal granting of the planned aid against Commission opposition. Compliance with a negative decision could have supposedly led to further exacerbation of the airline's bad finances and finally to its bankruptcy. Whether the principle of proportionality could be legitimately employed when the two-pole 'MEIP/one time-last time' comes into play is an issue that merits attention (see below).

II.i v.   *Alitalia*

Unlike many other flag carriers that had inaugurated restructuring operations in the early 1990s, Italy first knocked on the Commission's door in

July 1996, notifying a restructuring plan for ailing Alitalia. According to Italy, the capital injection planned, amounting to Lit 3000 billion, was part of the airline's privatization process and had to be cleared as consistent with the MEIP. Following three successive adjustments of the plan addressing the Commission's reservations, the latter approved (under Article 107(3)(c) TFEU) a massive aid package of Lit 2750 billion to be granted in three tranches, provided that a number of conditions would be met, including the one time-last time limitation.[22] Italy appealed the Decision to the General Court in November 1997, claiming, *inter alia,* that the Commission had misapplied the private investor principle and had erroneously estimated the internal rate of return, as well as the minimum annual rate of return required by a private investor. Pending the Court's judgment, the Commission issued a further Decision authorizing the payment of the second instalment of restructuring aid to Alitalia.[23]

The Court gave judgment in December 2000,[24] annulling the Commission Decision as vitiated by an error of reasoning and two manifest errors of assessment, all related to the plea in law of misapplication of the MEIP. The Commission subsequently adopted a new Decision, revising its faulty reasoning and correcting the manifest errors of assessment identified by the Court.[25] Although the annulment of the 1997 Decision eliminated the legal basis for the subsequent authorization of the second tranche of aid, the Commission considered it logical not to object to its payment.[26] Despite the eventual release of the aid, Alitalia brought an action for annulment in November 2001, yet without success.[27]

The third instalment of aid was approved in July 2002.[28] On the very same day, the Commission adopted a further Decision regarding the recapitalization of the airline. In April 2002 the Italian authorities had notified a recapitalization plan, designed to increase Alitalia's capital by €1432 million. Despite the limited private sector contribution and although the restructuring of the company had not yet been completed, the Commission did not hesitate to clear the transaction as in line with the MEIP. Clearly, a classification of the capital increase as aid would have entailed prohibition of the plan by virtue of the one time-last time principle. The only way the operation could be approved was by recourse to the MEIP.

The Commission's optimism as to the profitability prospects of the airline proved, nevertheless, unrealistic, as in June 2004 the Italian authorities communicated to the Commission their Decision to grant Alitalia rescue aid in the form of a bridging loan of €400 million. A month later, the aid was officially authorized as in line with the 1999 R&R Guidelines.[29] Apparently, any doubts the Commission might have entertained as to the compatibility of the aid evaporated into thin air in the face of Italy's undertaking that Alitalia's restructuring would not contain any further State aid and, moreover, the State's share in its capital would be less than half (49%) within no more than 12 months, that is, that no re-capitalization by the State following restructuring would take place. It is of no surprise that the restructuring plan notified in October 2004,[30] despite being highly controversial, was eventually approved under certain conditions, whose fulfilment would entail compliance with the private investor test.[31]

Alitalia's efforts to comply with the conditions posed were primarily targeted at the reduction of the government's stake in the airline from 62% to less than 50%. To this end, in November 2005 the company raised €1 billion in new capital, the government buying almost half the stock on offer. The result of the new shares issue was the reduction of the Italian State's ownership to below 50%. A year later, Italy announced its plans to sell half of its 49.9% controlling stake. Yet, despite initial optimism, all efforts to privatize the company proved fruitless. The uncertainty as to the future of the airline, as well as its illiquidity, obliged Italy to advance a €300 million emergency loan to keep it afloat. Although this time the Commission could not but declare the aid incompatible with the common market and order its recovery,[32] it cleared (in a further Decision adopted on the same day) the sale of Alitalia's assets in the context of the special administration procedure to which it was admitted, aimed at its winding-up, as free of aid, on condition it takes place on market terms.[33]

Both Decisions have been challenged by Ryanair before the General Court.[34] Clearly, the Court's judgment is not really necessary for the interaction between the principles under examination to be confirmed.

III. SYNTHESIS

III.i. Theoretical Legitimacy of the Principles

The legitimacy of the MEIP as an instrument of State aid analysis could not be easily contested. Although the MEIP is not a Treaty-made concept, but merely an expression of the Commission's wide discretion in the sphere of State aid, it draws its legitimacy from a combined reading of Article 107(1) TFEU and Article 345 TFEU, that is, from the prohibition of aid in conjunction with the principle of neutrality regarding the system of property ownership. The right of the Member States to run a mixed economy necessitates the development of a method of differentiation between State action that falls into the remit of Article 107(1) TFEU and State action that is in line with private sector practices. The MEIP constitutes the benchmark employed by the Commission to perform such a distinction.[35]

The immediate judicial endorsement of the principle, confirmed on several occasions, reinforces its legitimacy as a method of assessment.[36]

For the purposes of our analysis, it suffices to mention that the application of the MEIP in the context of airline restructuring operations has been delineated in the 1994 Aviation Guidelines. To determine whether aid is involved, the Commission evaluates in the first stage the circumstances of the financial transaction in the light of the MEIP. In case aid elements are detected, the measure is, in a second stage, examined in the light of the derogation of Article 107(3)(c) TFEU.[37] Thereafter, the Commission may impose certain conditions on the aid beneficiary in order for the restructuring exemption to be granted. These conditions shall be determined in the light of the requirement that the aid does not adversely affect trading conditions to an extent contrary to the common interest.[38]

Similarly, the one time-last time principle does not derive its legitimacy directly from the Treaty.[39] Article 107(1) TFEU neither explicitly establishes such a principle nor implicitly alludes to a prohibition against more than one application for aid. More importantly, the exemptions, either mandatory or discretionary, provided for in paragraphs two and three respectively of Article 107 TFEU, have not been subjected to any frequency limitation as to their application in a particular case. Especially as far as the restructuring exemption is concerned (Article 107(3)(c) TFEU), the only limitation posed by the Community legislator is that this type of aid 'does not adversely affect trading conditions to an extent contrary to the common interest'. However, this does not mean that the Commission is not entitled to operationalize Treaty provisions through the promulgation of the necessary legislation, subject always to the control of the European Courts.

The one time-last time principle in the air transport sector is rooted in the 1984 Aviation Memorandum. Although the latter was drafted well before the deregulation of the European skies, in an era when State aid control was literally non-existent, it provided that 'restructuring aids' should 'form part of a programme, to be approved by the Commission to restore the airline's health, so that it can, within a reasonably short period, be expected to operate viably without further aid'.[40] A decade later the Commission, in line with the *Comité des Sages* recommendation for a clear and genuine one time-last time condition,[41] abandoned, (at least theoretically) its practice of limiting the effect of the principle to the duration of the restructuring programme, stating in its 1994 Aviation Guidelines that 'the programme must be self-contained in the sense that no further aid will be necessary for the duration of the programme and that, given the objectives of the programme to return to profitability, no aid is envisaged or likely to be required in the future'.[42] Second applications for aid will therefore only be evaluated in cases of exceptional circumstances, unforeseeable and external to the company.[43]

The issue of whether the Commission is empowered to approve aid for the purposes of airline restructuring subject to conditions has been theoretically contested.[44] The same applies to the nature of some of the conditions actually imposed by the Commission and to their ability, real and quantifiable, to minimize distortions of competition without unduly restricting the beneficiary airline's business. Nevertheless, the European Courts have, justifiably in the author's view, considered that the power conferred on the Commission by Article 108(2) TFEU to ask for the alteration of aid granted by a Member State or through State resources, when such aid is not compatible with the common market, could only be exercised in a proper way if the Commission were in a position to indicate the changes needed to be made in order for the competitive balance to be redressed.[45]

The Court had a specific opportunity to examine the consistency of the Aviation Guidelines with the Treaty rules in the 1998 *VLM* case.[46] The Commission's broad discretion in applying Article 107(3)(c) TFEU to rely on the criteria considered to be most appropriate for the assessment of the aid has only been subjected by the Court to the limitation that those criteria are relevant, having regard to Article 3(1)(b) TFEU and Article 107 TFEU. Given that the Court has rejected the applicant's contention that the Aviation Guidelines depart from the Treaty rules, both the MEIP and the one time-last time principle in the context of restructuring operations undeniably constitute a legitimate expression of the Commission's power to control State subsidies.[47]

III.ii.   Practical Application of the Principles

Having accepted the theoretical legitimacy of the principles in question, the delicate issue of their 'practical legitimacy' may now be examined. The mere description of the selected airline restructuring cases shows a clear interaction between the two principles. The assessment of a case in the light of these principles appears straightforward: if a private investor in a comparable situation with the State would not make the same investment the State intends to make upon and under the same conditions, there is aid involved, which can only be approved under the State aid rules if no other aid has been granted in the past 10 years. Limited exceptions are allowed. Therefore, the intersection of the principles in question should normally happen only once, at the initial stage of the Commission's investigation. It goes without saying that a positive application of the MEIP, that is, a finding that there is no aid involved, precludes altogether the application of the one time-last time principle.

In the Commission's practice, however, these rules seem to intersect continuously, not only when, at the end of a negative MEIP analysis, the one time-last time principle comes into effect, but also thereafter, when the Commission imposes specific conditions on the beneficiary in order for the aid to be cleared. It appears that the obstacle of the once-only restriction is overcome through recourse to the MEIP, which is in turn deemed satisfied if certain conditions are met.

This sequence of actions, which arguably complicates the State aid analysis unjustifiably, resulting potentially in absurdities, might be politically correct from a national point of view, yet from a Community point of view is politically incorrect. The Court has endorsed the imposition of conditions as a means to render an otherwise incompatible aid into aid compatible with the common market. It has by no means blessed the private investor test as a means to purify an aid, transforming it into a normal commercial transaction. The issue whether the Commission is entitled to impose any conditions at all in normal investment cases has been discussed by Balfour (1996), who has argued that there is a very great difference between conditions which a market investor might require the target-company to adopt and those imposed in connection with funding which constitutes aid. The purpose and legal justification of conditions in the latter case is the reduction of adverse effects on competition, whereas in the former case it is to make the company a more viable investment prospect. Balfour focuses mainly on the inflexibility which may characterize the conditions imposed by the Commission, especially from a private investor's perspective, concluding that:

> . . .the determination whether an investment satisfies the market investor principle probably does effectively permit the imposition of certain conditions, to the extent they are commitments which a market investor would be likely to require, but not necessarily the type of conditions which may be imposed in aid cases.

The distinction drawn by Balfour is important. In imposing conditions on the beneficiary company and possibly on the Member State concerned, so that the MEIP is satisfied, the Commission substitutes for the real private investor not only at the initial stage, when a proposed investment is assessed, but also at later stages, when a decision to invest has been basically taken by the private investor, provided that the company concerned will commit itself to a specific course of action either immediately or at a later point in time. This substitution for the private investor, especially when it goes that far in scope and in time, is awkward. This is so not only because it appears to swing from objectivity to arbitrariness according to the political circumstances and to the high or low profile of the case at hand, but mainly because it trespasses on the one time-last time principle, depriving it of meaning.

It would not be exaggerating to claim that in the context of air transport the Commission applies the rules not only selectively, but also inconsistently. The elasticity of the theoretical instruments used, whether and to what extent they expand or contract, is a function of the political gravity of the State aid case at issue. The more politically charged a case is, the more likely that the MEIP will prevail over the one time-last time principle and subsequently that Commission-made conditions will prevail over the MEIP. Is this criticism justified in the light of the outcome of each single airline restructuring case handled so far, that is, of the fact that certain restructuring operations, as authorized, constituted the salvation of heavily indebted and operationally bankrupt airlines, which are now pioneering the consolidation of the European skies?

III.iii.   Is There Any Room for the Principle of Proportionality?

The *Air France* and *Iberia* cases have both raised criticism as to the soundness of the Commission's analysis and its adherence to the EU State aid regime. However, both airlines, each one in its own way, have managed to restructure, distancing themselves from the State purse. The issue which arises is whether the turnaround results achieved could be attributed also to the Commission's handling of the cases, in other words, whether the outcome of the restructuring efforts would have been different, had the Commission applied the State aid rules without entertaining any considerations related to the effectiveness and proportionality of its Decision. Could the principle of effectiveness (*effet utile*) be considered a determinant of the conditions crafted by the Commission? Could the same be said for the principle of proportionality?

Clearly, if a national airline were to exit the market due to bankruptcy, the social upheaval caused would be major. Employment considerations can therefore only constitute a constant concern for the Commission when dealing with struggling airlines. In view of this reality, it could be argued that a strict application of the one time-last time principle would be disproportionate, as fettering the chances of an airline to genuinely restructure and continue operating on a sound basis. The precedents of Air France and Iberia are in this respect illustrative of the great potential national airlines have to overcome crisis situations.

Arguably, the fairness of the law applicable each time and its ability to generate good results should never be neglected or underestimated. Equally, the law should not be applied mechanically, without any consideration for its appropriateness. Whether the fairness of a certain rule is also a function of its actual application is probably an issue to be determined in the light of the principle of legal certainty.

Indisputably the law, either soft or hard, has a certain authority *erga omnes*. Its content cannot be negotiated. If the circumstances of a specific case justify the application of a certain piece of legislation, then it must be applied. The enforcer of the law has no discretion as to whether this piece of legislation will be applied or not. In a different case, legal certainty would be undermined and public order seriously disturbed. What, at most, could be acknowledged is the existence of certain pre-defined circumstances, that is, the fulfilment of certain conditions, which justify a differentiation in treatment. The differentiation in treatment could even take the form of an exemption from the general rule.

Although it is true that the Commission enjoys a margin of discretion in approving aid under Article 107(3) TFEU, provided for by the Treaty itself, such discretion is not unlimited and can by no means be exercised arbitrarily. Whilst, for instance, the Commission has a broad discretion in deciding how the MEIP applies in a specific case, it enjoys a much more limited discretion in deciding whether the MEIP is applicable in a specific case or not and no discretion whatsoever in deciding how and whether the one time-last time principle applies. This is so because, while the application of the MEIP is linked to certain business judgments, made with the use of appropriate benchmarks, the application of the one time-last time principle is straightforward and not dependent upon any kind of 'judgments'.

The jurisprudence of the European Court with regard to the limits of the Commission's discretion is clear; the Commission's discretion stops where the Court's reviewing power begins. The Court has no authority to substitute for the Commission in the latter's purely economic assessments and the Commission has no authority to substitute for the Court in the latter's determination and interpretation of the rules of law applicable in each case. This means in practice that the proportionality and effectiveness of a certain legislative instrument is not an issue to be decided *ad hoc* by the Commission. The content of the law, even if it is of a soft nature, cannot be determined by reference to the circumstances of each individual case. If in a civil law system the law provides and in a common law system the judge decides, in a mixed system, like that of the EU, the judge interprets the law and in the absence thereof, it creates it. These are competences reserved for the judiciary.

Obviously in the sphere of State aid, where the Commission's legislative powers are broad, the latter enjoys considerable freedom in shaping the EU State aid regime. However, this does not mean that the Commission is not bound by the rules it promulgates. Quite the contrary, the rules are as binding upon the Commission as upon their addressees.[48] By no means is the Commission entitled to bend its own rules in order to make them fit the reality of each of the various cases under investigation. In applying the State aid rules the Commission ought to be fair, respecting always the principle of equal treatment and sound administration.

However, the Commission can only be fair if the rules are fair. Being fair when applying unfair rules leads to 'Solomon' solutions that hardly fit in the EU legal order. Would it be realistic, nevertheless, to contend that Commission-made principles, like the MEIP and the one time-last time principle, benefiting from decades of application and having survived several attacks before the European Courts, are untenable? Could the rationality and the utility value of these principles be easily contested?

The principles in question are as fair as statutory, meaning man-made, law can be. They do not necessarily reflect a supreme natural law beyond any criticism. They are simply part of a system designed to achieve certain goals.[49] Considering the man-made origin of the principles, their imperfect nature is something that has to be accepted as part of their identity. The system can only be imperfect as derived from the people and destined for the people. Taking a pragmatic approach means accepting *a priori* its limitations and working constantly on its improvement.

The MEIP and the one time-last time rule are neither disproportionate in their conception nor ineffective. They exist to make sure that competition is not distorted. Their *raison d'être* and their effectiveness could hardly be contested, but could easily be undermined if misapplied. The Commission is not entitled to invoke socio-political or other reasons to avoid a proper application of the rules. If an airline, despite having been given the chance to restructure its operations, refuses to learn to fly solo, then it should be left to exit the market. The benefits on employment of having healthy and competitive operators in the market are multiple and, in any event, much greater than those resulting from keeping dying airlines artificially alive. Job security, in contrast to the great insecurity employees of ailing national carriers are obliged to live with, is a qualitative element and a comparable advantage that has been absolutely overlooked by the Commission in all its analysis. The level of pay has only been examined in the context of salary freezes as part of restructuring measures. Promotion prospects and related work opportunities figure nowhere in the Commission's employment considerations. Strikes and other forms of industrial action, a practice that has become synonymous with national flag carriers, have been unilaterally associated with losses suffered by the airline, the effect on the employees' income having been disregarded.

The answer to the principle of proportionality and effectiveness dilemma is clearly a negative one: the assessment tools employed by the Commission and in particular the private investor test and the once-only principle are already proportionate and effective. The invention of proportionality and effectiveness gaps could only make them disproportional and ineffective. The happy outcome of the Air France and Iberia restructuring has also been a function of the magnitude of the public funds made available to the airlines; funds that a private airline in a comparable situation would have never been in a position to draw from the private capital markets. The Commission cannot apply double standards, treating national companies more favourably. As private airlines have to find their way out of crisis situations on their own, so should national airlines have to find other means than State aid to remain viable.

IV. CONCLUSION

It is clear that the creation of a thorough and coherent State aid regime from, all in all, three schematic Treaty provisions is an ambitious goal. The tools employed by the Commission to make the EU subsidies mechanism operational need, in order to be useful and efficient, to be compatible with the mechanism. Whether the MEIP and the one time-last time principle are genuinely compatible with the system or whether the Commission tries on an *ad hoc* basis to appropriately programme them so as to be operational has given rise to some dispute.

Both principles are expressions of the Commission's competence to shape the State aid regime appropriately. The MEIP constitutes a filtering device, which streamlines the procedure, relieving both the Member States and the Commission of the duty to notify and assess respectively measures which raise no State aid considerations. The one time-last time principle is an illustration of the exceptional character subsidies ought to have in the financial life of the EU and therefore of their great potential to distort competition. In that sense, the one time-last time principle functions as a lever of pressure towards both the Commission, which is obliged to make sure that the aid package approved on each occasion has been carefully designed to restore the company's profitability without resort to new aid, and towards the Member States, who are obliged to safeguard the socially and economically optimum character of the subsidies granted out of tax-payers' contributions. At a second level, the once-only principle operates as a safety net, filtering out cases of companies which have the potential to restructure and of companies which can only stay afloat, provided that they are governmentally boosted.

The legality of the principles in issue could not be easily questioned. Both have successfully passed all the controls to which they have been subjected by the European Courts. Their judicial endorsement, on many occasions and over a long period of time, has reinforced their position in the subsidies control system, rendering them an integral part of each restructuring aid analysis. The same could not, however, be said about their actual application by the Commission in the context of airline restructuring cases, that is, about their operationalization. The intersection between these two principles, although marginal by definition, has often been exploited so as to serve other than Community objectives.

The legitimacy of the Commission's choice to significantly contribute to the politicization of its relations with the Member States, rather than attempting with the aid of the system of rules in place to de-politicize as much as possible the necessary interaction with national governments, is contestable. Having regard to the fact that the Commission is bound by its own rules, as well as to the fact that the EU State aid regime could be characterized, at this stage of development, as a rules-based system rather than as a system encouraging improvization, institutionally, the Commission is provided with sufficient means to impose its policy.

The answer to the question why, thus far, compliance with the State aid rules has not materialized has, therefore, to be sought not in the inappropriateness of the subsidies control mechanism, but in the entrenched mentalities, which oppose its operation. Clandestine leakages of aid are unavoidable so long as national governments have not been convinced of the absurdity of wasting State resources for the sake of operationally and financially bankrupt national champions. The role, therefore, of the Commission is above all an educational one. In order for illegal subsidies to be definitely phased out, the Commission must convince each and every actor in financial life, from the random air traveller to the national governments, that the way to achieve efficiencies in air transport, translated into reliable, convenient and economical quality services, is through undistorted competition.

NOTES

1. Application of Articles 92 and 93 EC and Article 61 of the EEA agreement to State aids in the aviation sector, O.J. 1994 C 350/7.
2. Commission Decision of 24 July 1991 on aid to be granted by the Belgian Government in favour of the air carrier *Sabena*, O.J. 1991 L300/48.
3. Second Memorandum of the Commission Regarding the Civil Aviation Sector (1984), Doc. Com (84) 72 final.
4. Commission Decision of 19 July 1995 on a procedure relating to the application of Council Regulation (EEC) No 2407/92 (*Swissair/Sabena*), O.J. 1995 L 239/19.
5. Press Release IP/01/1432, 17 October 2001.
6. Press Release IP/01/1558, 9 November 2001.

7.   Ibid.
8.   Point 38(2) of Aviation Guidelines and point 48 of 1999 R&R Guidelines.
9.   Fn 25 of 2004 R&R Guidelines.
10.   Press Release IP/01/1558, 9 November 2001.
11.   IP/91/1024, 20 November 1991 and IP/92/587, 15 July 1992.
12.   Commission Decision of 27 July 1994 concerning the notified capital increase of *Air France* (94/653/EC), O.J. 1994 L 254/ 73.
13.   Commission Decision 94/662/EC, O.J. 1994 L 258/26.
14.   Air France unsuccessfully challenged subsequently the Decision before the General Court: Case T-358/94, [1996] E.C.R. II-2109.
15.   Joined Cases T-371/94 and T-394/94, [1998] E.C.R. II-2405.
16.   See Commission letters to the French authorities on 5 July 1995 (O.J. 1995 C 295/2); 31 July 1996 (O.J. 1996 C 374/9); 10 June 1997 (O.J. 1997 C 374/6).
17.   Commission Decision of 22 July 1998 concerning the notified capital increase of *Air France*, O.J. 1999 L 63/66.
18.   The French authorities notified the Commission of their intention to grant aid in March 1994; the Aviation Guidelines came into force a few months later, in December 1994.
19.   Commission Decision of 22 July 1992, N 294/92.
20.   Commission Press Release IP/92/606, 22 July 1992.
21.   Commission Decision of 31 January 1996 concerning the recapitalization of *Iberia*, O.J..1996 L 104/25.
22.   Commission Decision of 15 July 1997 concerning the recapitalization of *Alitalia*, O.J. 1997 L 322/44.
23.   Commission Communication concerning the second instalment of aid for the restruc-turing of *Alitalia* approved by the Commission on 15 July 1997, O.J. 1998 C 290/3.
24.   Case T-296/97, *Alitalia v. Commission* [2000] E.C.R. II-3871.
25.   Commission Decision of 18 July 2001 concerning the recapitalization of *Alitalia*, O.J. 2001 L 271/28.
26.   See recital 37 of the 2001 Decision.
27.   The Court delivered its judgment in July 2008, confirming the validity of the Commission's 2001 Decision: Case T-301/01, *Alitalia v. Commission* [2008] E.C.R. II-1753; Press Release No 48/08, 9 July 2008.
28.   Commission Press Release IP/02/885, 19 June 2002.
29.   Commission Press Release IP/04/965, 20 July 2004.
30.   Commission Press Release IP/05/57, 19 January 2005.
31.   Commission Press Release IP/05/678, 7 June 2005 and Commission Memorandum MEMO/05/194, 7 June 2005.
32.   Commission Press Release IP/08/1692, 12 November 2008 and Commission Decision of 12 November 2008, O.J. 2009 L 52/3.
33.   State Aid Case N-510/2008 (Sale of assets of Alitalia), C(2008) 6745 final.
34.   Action brought on 28 March 2009, Case T-123/09, *Ryanair v. Commission*, O.J. 2009 C 141/45.
35.   See 1984 'Commission Communication on Government Capital Injections: Application of arts 92 and 93 of the EEC Treaty to public authorities' holdings', *Bulletin*, EC 9-1984, point 3.2.
36.   Case 234/84, *Belgium v. Commission* [1986] E.C.R.I-2263. See confirmation in, for example, Case C-301/87, *France v. Commission* [1990] E.C.R. I-307, para. 39; Case C-305/89, *Italy v. Commission* [1991] E.C.R. I-1603, para. 19.
37.   See para. 25 of Aviation Guidelines.
38.   See para. 37 of Aviation Guidelines.
39.   In this respect see, Soames and Ryan 1995, 305–306.
40.   Memorandum, at IV. 9, point 18.a.
41.   'Expanding horizons: civil aviation in Europe, an action programme for the future', Report to the Commission by the *Comitè des Sages*, January 1994.
42.   See point 38(2).

43. It has been argued by Frühling 2002, that the Commission introduced the strict criterion of 'exceptional, unforeseeable and external to the company circumstances' based on an improper interpretation of the *Aluminia Comsal* judgment (Case C-261/89, *Italy v. Commission* [1991] E.C.R. I-4437). A more careful reading of the 1994 Aviation Guidelines reveals that the reference made to the *Aluminia Comsal* judgment (and specifically to grounds 20–21) concerns the Commission's obligation in evaluating a second application for aid, to take into account all relevant elements, including the fact that the company has already received State aid.
44. See Balfour 1995 and 1996.
45. See, for example, the Court's judgment in the Cases T-244/93 and T-486/93, *TWD Textilwerke Deggendorf GmbH v. Commission*, [1995] E.C.R. II-2265, where Article 88(2) EC was interpreted as necessarily implying that 'a Commission decision authorizing aid under [Article 108 (3) TFEU] may be made subject to conditions for ensuring that authorized aid does not alter trading conditions in a way contrary to the Common interest'.
46. Case T-214/95, *Het Vlaamse Gewest v. Commission* [1998] E.C.R.-II 717.
47. In this respect see the analysis of Frühling 2002:141–142.
48. See, for instance, Case C-351/98, *Spain v. Commission* [2002] E.C.R.I-8031, para. 53, where the Court stated that the Commission is 'bound by the guidelines and notices that it issues in the area of supervision of state aid where they do not depart from the rules in the Treaty and are accepted by the Member States'. See also Case C-382/99, *Netherlands v. Commission* [2002] E.C.R. I-5163, para. 24, where again the Court declared that in so far as the guidelines of the Commission do not contradict Treaty rules, the policy rules which they contain are to be followed by the Commission.
49. For instance, the Court has stated that 'the Aviation guidelines concern a defined sector and are based on the desire to follow a policy established by it': Case T-214/95, *Het Vlaamse Gewest v. Commission* [1998] E.C.R.II -717, para. 89.

REFERENCES

Balfour, John (1995), 'State aid to airlines – a question of law or politics', *Yearbook of European Law*, **15**, 157.
Balfour, John (1996), 'The EC Commission's policy on State aid for airline restructuring: is the bonfire alight?', *Air and Space Law*, **20:2**, 60–67.
Frühling, Pierre (2002), 'The dissuasive "one time, last time" principle applied to european airlines state aid control', *Air and Space Law*, **27:2**, 135.
Soames, T. and A. Ryan (1995), 'State aid and air transport', *European Competition Law Review*, **16:5**, 290–309.

7 The Great Recession and other mishaps: the Commission's policy of restructuring aid in a time of crisis

Christian Ahlborn and Daniel Piccinin[1]

I. STATE AID AND THE FINANCIAL CRISIS: INTRODUCTION AND OVERVIEW

On 15 September 2008 Lehman Brothers files for bankruptcy. The financial markets and the world economy stare into the abyss.

The next four weeks witness government intervention in the financial sector at a scale previously neither seen nor imagined: the US Government takes control of AIG after an injection of US $85 billion, the same day as Lehman files for bankruptcy; the following weekend, the US treasury secretary, Henry Paulson, finalises the details of his US $700 billion 'bad bank' plan which, after some back and forth, is adopted by Congress on 3 October.[2]

A similar picture emerges on the other side of the Atlantic (albeit with a short delay): on 28 September 2008, the UK Government nationalises Bradford and Bingley and Germany underwrites a $35 billion bail-out of Hypo Real Estate; two days later sees the rescue of Dexia by the governments of Belgium, Luxembourg and France and of Fortis by the governments of Belgium, Luxembourg and the Netherlands; Ireland extends its bank guarantees the same day.[3] On 8 October 2008 the UK unveils a rescue plan for £250 billion for the UK banks.[4]

The European Commission plays a limited role in these rescue measures. However, Ireland's extension of its bank guarantees to Irish banks, covering an estimated €400 billion of bank liabilities, raises concerns that State rescue measures may distort competition and put other Member States at a disadvantage. A political consensus emerges that State aid control has a role to play in monitoring and controlling State intervention, which ensures that the Commission has an important role to play in the process of saving the banking system and the global economy.[5] Thus, as a result of the financial crisis, the spotlight falls on a policy instrument which until then had been the ugly duckling of EU competition policy; a policy instrument which had not yet been fully modernised, which heavily relied on form-based analysis and which (almost inevitably, given its nature) involved a strong element of political horse trading.

This chapter analyses how State aid control has fared in the process. Part I is an overview and introduction. Part II describes the origin and key factors of the financial crisis, and provides an overview of its impact on the financial sector and the impact of the subsequent recession on the real economy. Part III sets out the analytical framework of State aid control for support to firms in difficulties (so-called rescue and restructuring aid) and provides a rationale for the form-based approach. Part IV describes and assesses the Commission's State aid policy in the banking sector during the financial crisis. The focus is in particular on 'compensatory measures' to address distortions of competition. Part V deals with the Commission's State aid policy during the same period in the real economy. Part VI concludes.

II.   FINANCIAL AND ECONOMIC CRISIS

II.i.   Origin and Overview of the Financial Crisis

While there is still some disagreement about the main causes of the financial crisis, the overall story of how the financial crisis unfolded has by now been well rehearsed.[6] The principal underlying cause for the crisis was the abundance of cheap money in certain developed countries (especially the US and UK but also in Ireland and Spain amongst others) made available by the unprecedented growth in current account surpluses in countries such as China, Japan and large oil exporters.[7] The abundance of cheap credit led to asset price booms in real estate in the large current account deficit economies.[8] Banks in current account surplus countries like Germany also became exposed to the asset price booms in the current account deficit economies through their participation in asset backed securities.[9]

In response to the rising sub-prime mortgage defaults in the US in 2006, the real estate bubble finally burst and the US, the UK and other current account deficit countries, like Spain, saw a rapid decline in property prices. However, as Krugman and Wells (2010: 7) pointed out, the burst real estate bubble is not in itself enough to explain the catastrophe for the economy:

> The stock crash of 2000–2002 was a $5 trillion hit to US household wealth. It created a lot of pain for people counting on capital gains for their retirement, but it didn't trigger any broader systemic crisis. The housing bust was an $8

trillion hit – not all much bigger than the stock crash, once one takes into account both inflation and economic growth in the interim.

Other factors were at work which turned a real estate slump into a global financial crisis. The large inflows of cheap money led to a shift in the banking sector's reliance on wholesale borrowing and securitisation and increasingly risky lending practices (for example, sub-prime mortgages).[10] The burst of the North Atlantic housing bubble raised concerns about the soundness of banks, as financial institutions had significant exposure to losses from mortgage defaults. Lack of transparency caused by the securitisation process made it difficult to identify where the risks lay. A chain reaction ensued in which confidence in banks' balance sheets collapsed, liquidity in wholesale funding markets dried up (creating funding crises for banks that had relied on these markets) and prices collapsed for a wide range of assets in current account deficit countries (causing solvency problems for banks, particularly those with heavy exposures to mortgage and commercial real estate markets in these economies).[11] The disappearance of wholesale funding and the damage to banks' balance sheets had a dramatic impact on the real economy: at the end of 2008 and the beginning of 2009, the world faced a credit crunch and borrowing costs for private borrowers soared (to the extent that credit was available at all). The world economy stood at the edge of a precipice.

II.ii.   The Impact on the Banking Sector

II.ii.a.   The effect of the crisis
The financial crisis has caused massive losses in the banking system. Estimates for write-offs from expected or actual defaults of debtors and market losses from devaluation of assets and claims is currently set at US $2.2 trillion with more than 75% already reported.[12] The massive losses fed the general suspicion that banks may not be able to survive and undermined confidence in the creditworthiness of market counterparties. As Sinn (2010) reported:

> 2008 will go down in history as a year of bank failures, since well over 100 banks disappeared worldwide that year through bankruptcy and acquisition or were nationalised at the last minute.[13]

Examples of bank failures (in the sense of banks needing to be nationalised or acquired by other banks) include Fannie Mae and Freddie Mac, Lehman Brothers, Merrill Lynch and AIG in the US, Northern Rock, HBOS, Royal Bank of Scotland and Bradford and Bingley in the UK, and Sachsen LB and Hypo Real Estate in Germany.[14]

II.ii.b.   State support measures

In response to the serious threat posed by the financial crisis to the banking sector across Europe, almost all Member States committed vast amounts of aid to rescue the banks. These aid measures took a number of forms, principally including:

1. credit guarantee schemes to address banks' funding problems arising from the liquidity crisis in wholesale funding markets;
2. recapitalisations to improve banks' capital positions in light of impairments that they had suffered or expected to suffer; and
3. impaired asset schemes to protect banks against future unexpected impairments on their troubled asset portfolios and restore confidence in the banks.

In the period from October 2008 to March 2010, 18 European Member State Governments granted a total of approximately €994 billion of credit guarantees and €241.6 billion of recapitalisations to banks[15] with €827 billion and €142 billion taken up for credit guarantees and recapitalisations respectively in 2009 alone.[16] Together, these have accounted for nearly 10% of EU GDP.[17]

II.iii.   Outlook

The measures deployed to date have in large part been successful in preventing the collapse of the European financial system, with markets having made significant progress towards normalisation in the past 24 months. Nevertheless, lending remains tight and threats from a number of sources, not least recent concerns over sovereign debt in Europe, suggest that markets will remain fragile for some time and that further measures may be required to ensure confidence in the system is maintained.[18]

II.iv.   Impact of the Financial Crisis on the Real Economy

II.iv.a.   The effect of the crisis

The disappearance of wholesale funding markets and the huge losses which forced banks to shrink their lending activities caused a massive credit crunch. The inability of the banks to continue to play their role as financial intermediaries has led to the most severe contraction of economic activities since the Great Depression in the 1930s. Industrial output declined at a rate of around 10% until March 2009[19] while the volume of world trade declined by 22%.[20] While all countries have been affected by the Great Recession, the impact has varied. The domestic product of the

US, where the crisis began, shrunk by 2.6% in 2009, while that of the EU fell by 4.2%. Export-dependent Germany was hit harder (4.7%) as was the UK (5.0%) which was strongly dependent on the financial sector.[21]

II.iv.b.   State support measures

State intervention in the real economy took a variety of different forms, including the EU Temporary Framework and certain sector specific measures, such as the car scrappage scheme, as well as *ad hoc* rescue and restructuring aid.[22]

The EU Temporary Framework   The Temporary Framework was adopted on 17 December 2008 as part of the European Economic Recovery Plan to help facilitate companies' access to finance in order to boost demand, save jobs and restore confidence in the short term while encouraging 'smart investment' to yield higher growth and sustainable prosperity in the long term. The Temporary Framework which was originally applicable from December 2008 to December 2010 permits aid of up to €500,000 for companies facing a sudden shortage or unavailability of credit as a result of the current financial crisis; the aid may take the form of subsidised loan guarantees for payment of reduced premiums to encourage access to finance; aid in the form of interest rate reductions; aid for the production of green products; and aid to promote risk capital. However, as the crunch continues to bite in some Member States and the market outlook still gloomy for some companies more than others, the Commission announced an extension of the Temporary Framework until 2011 after consultations with Member States.[23]

Since the adoption of the Temporary Framework, the amount of aid granted by Member States has been relatively limited (both in relation to the aid granted in the banking sector and the size of the credit crunch). The UK for example has so far granted around about 1% (that is, €100 million) while Italy has spent 8% of the funds approved under the Temporary Framework. Germany has, however, been a major spender using up 78% of the approved funds under this measure.[24]

Ad hoc aid under the Rescue and Restructuring Guidelines   The financial crisis does not appear to have had a significant impact on the amount of aid granted *ad hoc* in the real economy to firms in difficulty. The number of restructuring cases post crisis (measured from 1 October 2008 to 30 September 2010) was not noticeably different to the preceding two years (19 versus 23).

While the total amount of aid approved post crisis has increased relative to the 2006–2008 period (from £327 million to £844 million), this increase is entirely due to aid notified prior to the financial crisis. Indeed, only 2 cases out of the 19 post crisis cases make reference to the financial crisis.

II.iv.c.   Outlook

In the same way that countries have been affected differently by the financial crisis and the resulting recession, their exit trajectories are also different. Growth in the US still appears to be sluggish, with an estimated rate for 2010 of around 2.7%, which may trigger further monetary policy measures by the US Federal Reserve.[25] Other countries are experiencing greater growth, notably Germany which is seeing its fastest growth rate in a decade.[26] Whatever the economic development of the various EU countries, it is safe to say that given the low levels of State aid granted to firms in the real economy, State aid measures are unlikely to have had any impact on that development.

II.v.   Light at the End of the Tunnel?

After the massive slump in 2009, most countries are back on a path of positive (albeit modest) growth. The EU is forecast to grow by around 1% and the US in excess of 2%.[27] As a result of the Great Recession (which has led to a significant reduction of public income), support measures for financial institutions and more general Keynesian support measures, public finances have suffered greatly. In several of the peripheral EU countries, in particular in the so-called PIGS countries (Portugal, Ireland, Greece and Spain), both deficit and debt have reached critical levels.[28] Despite massive protection mechanisms by EU countries and the IMF, markets are still nervous about the fate of the PIGS countries and the prices for credit default swaps (*de facto* insurance against default) for Ireland and Greece are still at record levels.[29] At the time of writing, it is not yet clear whether the worst of the Great Recession is over, whether we are heading for a 'double-dip' or whether we are facing a 'lost decade'.

III.   STATE AID CONTROL FOR FIRMS IN DIFFICULTY

III.i.   State Aid Control: the Ugly Duckling of Competition Policy

III.i.a.   Status quo

Unlike other areas of competition policy which have moved towards an economics based analysis, State aid policy, and in particular State aid policy regarding firms in difficulties, has changed relatively little over the last decade. Thus it remains essentially form-based, with heavy reliance on presumptions, both as to the benefits of aid, and the distortions of competition that may arise.

In the absence of any genuine modernisation of State aid control, the Commission has instead sought to classify aid according to the different objectives pursued by the aid so as to achieve at least some measure of control over where and how aid is granted. Accordingly, a plethora of special rules have been developed for each of the various categories of 'horizontal' and 'sectoral' aid (for example, Research and Development Aid, Investment Aid, Regional Aid).

The Commission's rules for aid to firms in difficulties are set out in the Rescue and Restructuring Guidelines (R&R Guidelines).[30] Issued in 2004, these Guidelines were due to be updated in 2009, but when the Commission found its hands full dealing with the financial crisis it decided to defer the updating process until at least October 2012.

The R&R Guidelines are technically limited to aid that is justified under Article 107(3)(c) TFEU, that is, aid to facilitate the development of certain economic activities or of certain economic areas. However, during the financial crisis, aid to banks in difficulty was approved under Article 107 (3) (b) TFEU as aid to remedy a serious disturbance in the economy. The Commission accordingly took advantage of the different legal basis to produce four new bank-specific rescue and restructuring guidelines in the course of seven months.[31] As is explained in more detail below, these Guidelines drew heavily on the R&R Guidelines for inspiration.

III.i.b.   Modernisation attempts

In fairness to the Commission, the failure to modernise the control of aid to firms in difficulty has not been for want of trying. In 2005 Commissioner Kroes launched the State Aid Action Plan[32] to much fanfare, promising to modernise State aid control one set of Guidelines at a time, ushering in a brave new world of a 'more economic approach'. This modernisation process has been relatively successful in some areas: notably the R&D, Risk Capital and the Environmental Aid Guidelines, that now include a mixture of form-based screening rules that reflect effects-based thinking, together with a (relatively) detailed rule of reason analysis of both social benefits and distortions of competition for the more difficult cases.

The Commission's 'more economic approach' was explained in detail in a staff working paper *Common Principles for an Economic Assessment of the Compatibility of State Aid under Article 87(3)*, which was a valiant attempt to create a coherent intellectual framework for European State aid control.[33] The paper explains the process by which social benefits and competitive distortions can be measured and remedied with a view to allowing only targeted aid that is on balance socially desirable and in principle could be applied to a wide range of State aid policy areas. However, as the paper itself acknowledges, the modernisation process under the State Aid Action Plan is not yet complete, and the staff working paper's balancing approach has no application in any of the policy areas that have yet to be modernised.[34] Unfortunately, aid to firms in difficulty is one such policy area. Thus, whereas the 'more economic approach' could offer much in the way of improving the targeting of rescue and restructuring aid, at the time of writing, the Commission is yet to attempt the process of modernising the Guidelines.

III.ii.   Rescue and Restructuring Aid: the Analytical Framework

III.ii.a.   The building blocks

The R&R Guidelines allow the Commission to approve aid to 'firms in difficulties'.[35] Accordingly, the key definition in the Guidelines that acts as a gateway to the grant of aid is of the term 'firm in difficulties'. In order to limit the scope of the Guidelines and ensure that aid is only made available as a last resort, the definition of 'firm in difficulty' is (in theory) tightly drawn. Thus, according to the Guidelines, a firm is only in difficulties if, 'without outside intervention by the public authorities, [it] will almost certainly condemn it to going out of business in the short or medium term'.[36]

The second general limiting principle in the guidelines that acts as a strict bar against abuse is the 'one time, last time' principle, which is designed to prevent hopeless firms from being kept on life support by repeated requests for aid, each of which may seem innocuous in isolation, but taken together amount to a serious drain on taxpayer resources and distortion of competition. Thus, the Guidelines refer to an (almost) absolute bar on rescue and restructuring aid being made available to a firm more than once in ten years.[37]

If a firm meets these two conditions, in principle it qualifies for rescue aid to keep it afloat for six months while a restructuring plan is prepared, and potentially also for restructuring aid thereafter to return it to viability. Restructuring aid is only available if the restructuring plan meets the three conditions set out in the Guidelines:

1.   the plan must ensure the beneficiary's return to viability without ongoing reliance on aid;
2.   the beneficiary must make a sufficient contribution to the cost of restructuring from its own resources; and
3.   compensatory measures must be imposed to address any distortions of competition arising from the aid.

If all of these conditions are met, restructuring aid should in principle be made available.

III.ii.b.   The policy in practice

The Commission does not use a 'rule of reason' type balancing approach to restructuring aid cases, instead preferring to apply relatively strict form-based rules to the approval of aid. In the sub-sections below, these rules are evaluated by comparing the social benefits of restructuring aid with the distortions of competition that are likely to arise so as to conduct a balancing analysis of restructuring aid in general.

III.ii.c.   Social benefits of restructuring aid

Restructuring aid covered by the R&R Guidelines is generally considered to be amongst the least beneficial forms of State aid. The policy objectives that the Commission identifies in the R&R Guidelines as legitimate to justify restructuring aid are:[38]

1. social or regional policy considerations;
2. the need to take into account the beneficial role played by SMEs; or
3. the need to avoid the demise of firms that would lead to a monopoly or tight oligopoly situation.

The Commission considers that these policy objectives are unlikely to be significant enough to justify aid in many cases, which is why it says that 'the general principle of the prohibition of state aid as laid down in the Treaty should remain the rule and derogation from that rule should be limited'.[39] Examples of restructuring aid that have been approved, albeit subject to tight conditions, are aid to struggling firms in the airline[40] and automotive[41] sectors. However, in none of these cases has the Commission made any serious attempt to assess the nature and scope of any benefits which may flow from the State aid, relative to the counterfactual of a 'no aid scenario', nor whether the aid is suitable or likely to realise the alleged objectives. Linnemeyer and Soukup reach the same conclusions:

> Looking at past decisions illustrates that the Commission has not verified this submission by the Member States, but accept the argument that with the bankruptcy the ailing company and its jobs would simply disappear. Moreover it has neither verified whether the aid had a positive effect on the number of job positions in the EU as a whole.[42]

III.ii.d.   Competition distortions arising from restructuring aid

The Commission's approach to analysing distortions of competition in restructuring aid cases is at most cursory.[43] As the Commission notes in the R&R Guidelines, restructuring aid is generally highly distortive because it allows a firm that would in the ordinary course have exited the market to remain in the market.[44] As a result, the Commission generally simply assumes that restructuring aid will be highly distortive of competition in all cases. This is reflected in the fact that the R&R Guidelines do not provide for any analysis to be conducted as to the effects that restructuring aid may have on competition.

III.ii.e.   Balancing of benefits and harm: the Commission's remedy policy

The R&R Guidelines clearly stipulate that 'in order to ensure that the adverse effects on trading conditions are minimised as much as possible, so that the positive effects pursued outweigh the adverse ones, compensatory measures must be taken'[45] and these 'measures must be in proportion to the distortive effects'.[46]

The particular measures envisaged by the Guidelines are 'divestment of assets, reductions in capacity or market presence and reduction of entry barriers on the markets concerned'.[47] According to the Guidelines, remedies should be designed on a 'case-by-case basis' and should focus on 'the market(s) where the firm will have a significant market position after restructuring'.[48] It is clear from the Guidelines that the compensatory measures must be painful for the firm, with the closure of loss-making activities not qualifying as compensatory,[49] but the Guidelines also call for the Commission to 'take account of the market structure and the conditions of competition to ensure that any such measure does not lead to a deterioration in the structure of the market'.[50]

III.iii.   Economic Assessment of the Commission's R&R Policy

From an economic perspective, the Commission's largely form-based policy would be justified if the form-based rules and remedy design largely reflected a broad effects-based analysis of the general characteristics of aid to firms in difficulty, and if there were good reasons not to conduct a full rule of reason analysis. As explained below, there are good reasons not to conduct a full rule of reason analysis for aid to firms in difficulty, and an economic analysis of restructuring aid can identify a number of conditions affecting the benefits and costs of aid under which the Commission's form-based approach would be sensible.

III.iii.a.   Social benefits

From an economic perspective, providing aid to firms in difficulty is typically not socially desirable. Although providing aid to maintain or increase the number of competitors in the market would ordinarily be expected to increase competition and improve outcomes for consumers, in competitive markets the cost to taxpayers and to competitors (including through reducing per-firm output and scale economies) would generally be expected to outweigh the benefits to consumers.

Moreover, if there is overcapacity in the market, competition is likely to be intense already and the aid will not have much effect on the total quantity produced for consumers (and thus will have only a small positive effect for consumers). Thus, the net effect of the aid on social welfare will be even more likely to be negative than in other circumstances. If the firm's difficulties are the consequence of an inefficient cost structure, the aid may allow the inefficient firm to remain in the market at the expense of more efficient firms (either by causing the exit of more efficient firms or preventing their entry). Again, if this is the case, there may be little or no benefit to consumers in terms of increased output or lower prices, but rather only increased production costs being met by taxpayers.

That said, in some circumstances there may be strong social policy justifications that outweigh the usual economic considerations. In particular, if a firm in difficulty is a critical source of employment in a region and in the absence of aid the firm would collapse suddenly, with its assets leaving the market and its employees becoming unemployed, the social and economic consequences of that collapse may be worse than the cost to taxpayers and competitors of providing aid to restructure the firm. Clearly, whether restructuring aid brings any material social benefits will depend on the particular circumstances of the case and the economic and social context in which the aid is given.

III.iii.b.   Distortions of competition

Set against any social benefits of restructuring aid are the costs of that aid from distortions of competition that may arise. These may arise in the short term from creating or increasing market power or in the long term by distorting competitive incentives.

Increased market power of the beneficiary   Restructuring aid could harm competition by leading to an increase in the market power of the recipient. It could, for instance, be used to finance or add credibility to a predatory pricing strategy to drive out or weaken competitors, thus eventually leading to higher prices or less choice for consumers. In many cases, however, this is unlikely to be a significant issue as, even with the aid, the recipient is generally in no position to pursue a strategy of aggressive expansion.

In principle, this concern about (creation or) reinforcement of market power of the aid recipient (or indeed previous unsustainable business practices) is not dissimilar to those raised in the context of Article 102 TFEU or under merger control. Although the mechanism by which the reinforcement of market power is brought about is different (State intervention rather than unilateral behaviour or a change in market structure), the overall analysis should follow similar lines: a theory of harm accompanied by evidence to support the likely creation or reinforcement of market power. This would require a formal market definition exercise, together with a detailed assessment of the nature of competition in the markets in which the concerns arise, together with an analysis of how the aid could affect the ability and incentive of the recipient to take action (e.g. predatory pricing) to increase its market power. As with Article 102 TFEU and merger control, the analysis required would be very fact specific and critically dependent on the characteristics of the market.

Moral hazard State aid may also adversely affect firms' incentives over time. The most significant objection in this category is that granting aid gives rise to moral hazard. Moral hazard is a species of what economists refer to as asymmetric information, where one entity (the principal) does not know how another (the agent) will behave in the future, and the dealings between the two entities incentivises the agent to take action that will be to the detriment of the principal.[51] Moral hazard often arises in the insurance context, where, for instance, someone who has purchased house insurance would thereafter have a reduced incentive to take care to avoid future burglaries (for example, by investing in good locks or burglar alarms) and would therefore increase the likelihood of a claim on the insurance policy.

Restructuring aid may give rise to moral hazard because when firms (recipients and their competitors) observe aid being given they anticipate that the aid will also be available to them should the need arise at a later stage. If firms can engage in risky behaviour that has some prospect of success but that carries downside risks that outweigh the potential gains, aid may encourage firms to undertake these risky strategies because they retain the 'upside' but not the 'downside' of the behaviour.

Other distortions of incentives In addition to moral hazard, aid can also mute firms' investment incentives because they anticipate that irrespective of their success (for example, through innovation or cost reduction programmes) they will never be able to drive competitors out of the market or expand to the full extent warranted by their success because the State will intervene to support their less successful rivals. By reducing the rewards for success and decreasing the costs of failure, State aid thereby reduces firms' efforts to succeed.

III.iii.c.   Balancing the social benefits and the impact on competition

In light of the generally weak policy rationale for restructuring aid outlined above, the fact that the aid is unlikely to bring benefits to consumers that outweigh the cost to taxpayers and that it may cause significant distortions of competition, with the exception of cases involving systemically important banks, it seems reasonable to assume that without measures to make the aid more palatable, restructuring aid is likely to be socially undesirable.

At the same time, restructuring aid cases often lead to significant political lobbying from the Member State government granting the aid. The saga over the intended rescue of Opel, General Motors' European car division, is a good illustration of the political dimension of rescue and restructuring aid.[52] There is a risk that if the Commission were to be required to conduct a rule of reason analysis, it would be unable to resist attempts by governments to skew the outcome of this analysis. The Commission's form-based rules may therefore have significant benefits of protecting against this political interference. However, even where aid is socially undesirable, prohibition of the aid may sometimes be politically unachievable, so the best outcome that may be possible is sometimes for the form-based rules to give approval to such restructuring aid subject to severe remedies.

III.iv.   The Rationale for Remedies in Restructuring Aid Cases

To address the impact of these competitive distortions and improve the social welfare impact of restructuring aid, the Commission imposes a number of conditions on aid recipients where it approves restructuring aid. The Commission tends to impose structural remedies (that is, divestments and capacity reductions) and behavioural remedies (such as market share caps and prohibitions on the recipient offering market-beating prices) to address the impact of aid on competition. These remedies are required to go beyond those necessary to restore viability and are designed to inflict 'pain' on aid recipients to lessen moral hazard and the distortion of investment incentives as well as to limit the market presence of the recipient to reduce the likelihood and severity of distortions arising from the possibility that the aid enhances the recipient's market power. These remedies, especially behavioural remedies, are likely to make matters worse for competition *ex post* (that is, after the clearance of the aid) by limiting the aid recipient's ability to compete and thus softening its rivals' incentives to compete.[53] There is therefore a trade-off between competitive distortions that are limited by the remedies (for example, moral hazard) and competitive distortions that are caused by the remedies (for example, the aid recipient's limited ability to compete).

In markets with substantial overcapacity, limiting the ability of the aid recipient to compete would not be very harmful for consumers because there would likely be ample competition from the remaining firms in any event. Such remedies may still have the effect of 'punishing' the aid recipient, however, so where there is substantial overcapacity it is likely that the positive effects of remedies will outweigh the negative effects.

Similarly, in markets where there is substantial scope for risk-taking activity or where innovation or investment incentives are important, the Commission's remedies may also be beneficial in that the distortive effects that are addressed by the remedies may be particularly large.

Although the Commission suggests that remedies should also be larger in cases where the recipient has a larger market presence, this is not obvious from a social welfare perspective. On the one hand, it may be that distortions of competition are larger (although as explained above this need not be the case); on the other hand, the benefits of keeping the recipient in the market (both from lower prices for consumers and any other public interest benefits motivating the aid) could also be expected to increase with the size of the recipient. Measures that weaken the recipient or reduce its presence could thus reduce the benefits of the aid without reducing the costs for taxpayers. Unless the effect of the compensatory measures on competition is clear and significant it is therefore not clear that more severe measures are socially desirable for larger firms.

In summary, the conditions imposed by the Commission in restructuring aid cases to address distortions of competition present a trade-off between the competitive distortions prevented by them and those that are caused by them. However, in a range of cases it is likely that the measures are beneficial relative to the alternative of approving the aid unconditionally.

III.v.   Preliminary Conclusions on the Economic Assessment of the Commission's Approach to Article 107(3)(c) TFEU Restructuring Aid Cases

The approach taken by the Commission in restructuring aid cases is broadly consistent with an economics-based assessment provided (at least some of) the following underlying conditions hold:

- the social policy objectives of the aid are relatively weak;
- there is significant overcapacity in the market;
- the recipient could plausibly pursue predatory strategies;
- the recipient is an inefficient producer;
- the aid is given in circumstances that are likely to arise again unless firms take costly measures to avoid them.

Where these conditions are satisfied, State aid is likely to be harmful unless compensatory measures are imposed. Moreover, in these circumstances the remedies employed by the Commission are more likely to be net beneficial than in other circumstances. Accordingly, where these conditions are satisfied, the Commission's form-based approach to restructuring aid is economically justified, especially in light of the costs of a rule of reason approach in the context of the intense political lobbying that accompanies restructuring aid cases.

IV.   RESTRUCTURING AID CASES IN THE BANKING SECTOR DURING THE FINANCIAL CRISIS

IV.i.   The Six Phases of State Aid Control in the Banking Sector during the Financial Crisis

IV.i.a.   Overview

The Commission's approach to Member State demands for State aid approval during the financial crisis evolved significantly as the financial crisis unfolded. As has been well documented elsewhere, there have been a number of sharp changes in direction in Commission policy.[54] In summary, the Commission's State aid control in the banking sector during the financial crisis to date can be understood as consisting of the following phases:

(i)   the period prior to October 2008 when all cases were dealt with under Article 107(3)(c) TFEU and the R&R Guidelines;[55]

(ii)   the period from October 2008 to late February 2009 when the Commission applied Article 107(3)(b) TFEU to approve a large number of aid measures in an extraordinarily short amount of time and subject to what appeared to be quite lax conditions;

(iii)   the period from late February 2009 to July 2009 in which the Commission started to assess restructuring plans for a significant number of aid recipient banks applying requirements closely modelled on the R&R Guidelines under the guise of Article 107(3)(b) TFEU;

(iv)   the period from July 2009 to December 2009 in which the Commission started to apply its new Financial Crisis Restructuring Guidelines,[56] which, as explained below, increased the restructuring obligations on aid recipient banks with a focus on industrial policy considerations through divestment remedies;

(v)   the period from January 2010 in which the Commission has been focussing on Ireland which raises special considerations (for example, the fragility of Ireland itself, the high concentration in the banking industry itself and the fact that virtually all domestic players have received State aid); and

(vi) the transition from Article 107(3)(b) TFEU back to standard R&R state aid rules that Commissioner Almunia has announced will take place by the end of 2011.[57]

IV.i.b.   Phase I: Application of the Rescue and Restructuring Guidelines

In the early stages of the financial crisis, before the collapse of Lehman Brothers, there was (understandably given the limited number of banks experiencing serious difficulties at that stage and the fear of opening up the floodgates to aid for struggling banks) no perceptible change in the Commission's approach to aid to banks suffering from the credit crunch. In a string of cases, including Northern Rock,[58] Sachsen LB[59] and IKB,[60] the Commission rejected submissions that the aid was necessary to 'remedy a serious disturbance in the economy of a Member State' as required by Article 107(3)(b) TFEU. Instead, in each case the Commission considered that the banks' problems stemmed from idiosyncratic flaws in their business models.

In each case in this first phase, the Commission therefore applied the standard approach under the R&R Guidelines and Article 107(3)(c). In Northern Rock's case, the UK Government offered remedies including a reduction in its balance sheet by 50% through a drastic reduction in gross lending and actively encouraging mortgage customers to migrate to Northern Rock's competitors.[61] The Commission responded by expressing doubts as to whether the restructuring plans represented a sufficiently drastic reduction in Northern Rock's activities.[62]

Formal Phase II conditional approval decisions were made for aid to Sachsen LB and IKB in June[63] and October[64] 2008 respectively. Sachsen LB committed to divesting or closing businesses that accounted for 25% of profits in 2008[65] and IKB committed to reduce its balance sheet by 47% from pre-crisis levels.[66]

IV.i.c.   Phase II: from Article 107(3)(c) TFEU to Article 107(3)(b) TFEU

The second phase of the Commission's response to the crisis saw it publish two sets of Guidelines: the Banking Communication[67] and the Recapitalisation Guidelines.[68] These Guidelines provided the framework for the Commission to approve vast amounts of aid under Member State schemes before (in most cases) reaching any decisions on the difficult question of restructuring. On this issue the Guidelines drew a sharp distinction between banks that were 'fundamentally sound' but suffering from the liquidity effects of the (exogenous) financial crisis and those that had endogenous problems. The Banking Communication said that the former would require less restructuring than the latter,[69] and the Recapitalisation Guidelines said that 'fundamentally sound' banks could avoid restructuring altogether.[70] The effect of this was that banks generally took the aid without knowing whether they would require restructuring at all, or what principles the Commission would apply to assessing restructuring plans if they were required.

An exception to the Commission's 'clear first, ask questions later' approach during this phase was its clearance decision for restructuring aid to Fortis on 3 December 2008. Perhaps the best illustration of the Commission's laissez-faire approach during this period, this highly complex case involving tens of billions of Euros worth of aid, the sale of part of the bank to the Dutch State and 75% of the remaining bank to BNP Paribas, was decided in just over two months, without an in-depth investigation and with only minimal compensatory measures (given that the relevant markets were predominantly national, it is hard to see how the separation of the Belgian and Dutch operations of Fortis could have had any effect on competition).[71]

IV.i.d.　Phase III: The pendulum swings back

From late February 2009, two key developments brought about a further change in the Commission's approach, with a return towards the approach under the R&R Guidelines. First, a number of banks that had received aid through schemes or *ad hoc* measures approved in late 2008 were due to submit restructuring plans or reports setting out their viability in accordance with the approval decisions given in the second phase of the Commission's approach. Second, there was a growing sense in the Commission that financial markets were stabilising and that something had to be done about the vast amounts of State aid that had been granted.[72]

Arguably the first clear sign of the Commission's new approach was the third set of Guidelines, published on 25 February 2009, this time to cover schemes to address the problems of banks' impaired assets (the 'Impaired Assets Guidelines').[73] These Guidelines essentially abandoned the distinction between 'fundamentally sound' and unsound banks, and emphasised the need for deep restructuring in a wider range of cases. Importantly, although the Commission suggested that some banks would not need deep restructuring measures, it no longer provided a 'safe harbour' from compensatory measures for banks meeting the criteria in the Recapitalisation Guidelines.

The fact that the Commission was effectively returning to its traditional

R&R Guidelines in the third phase can be seen from the fact that the two final decisions made during the third phase (*Commerzbank* and *West LB*) both involved remedies of a similar order of magnitude and type as those imposed during the first phase of the Commission's approach to the financial crisis. Commerzbank was required to reduce its balance sheet by 45% and comply with behavioural restrictions, and WestLB was required to shrink its balance sheet by 50%.[74]

IV.i.e.   Phase IV: State aid control as industrial policy

On 22 July 2009, the Commission finalised its Financial Crisis Restructuring Guidelines. These Guidelines represented a further hardening of the Commission's position with respect to State aid bank restructuring. Instead of focussing on reducing the scale of the aid recipient bank's activities and protecting competitors as in the R&R Guidelines, the Commission proposed to use aid recipient banks' restructuring plans to increase competition in banking markets through compensatory measures, calling for divestments to be made in national markets with high barriers to entry 'to enable entry or expansion of competitors'.[75] In its application of the new Guidelines to each of LBG, ING, RBS and KBC, the Commission required the divestment of stand alone retail and commercial banking businesses in recipient banks' home markets to address concerns about high market shares (although the extent of these divestments varied between cases). This approach stands in sharp contrast to the Commission's approach in cases decided during Phase II such as *Fortis* and even represents a substantial shift from the hardened position of Phase III with cases such as *Commerzbank*. During the earlier phases the Commission had considered that it was unnecessary to take action to address high market shares. Thus, in *Fortis* the Commission said:[76]

> With regard to that undertaking, the Commission notes that the difficulties encountered by Fortis Bank are not the result of an expansion strategy or a predatory-pricing policy on the Belgian market. It is therefore not essential that, in addition to the aforementioned reduction in size following the sale of FBN, Fortis Bank also reduces its size on the Belgian market which is the largest market on which Fortis Bank will remain active.

Similarly, in *Commerzbank*, although the Commission insisted on the divestment of Eurohypo which had market shares in the region of 25% in real estate financing markets, this remedy did nothing to address the competitive impact of those market shares since Eurohypo is required to be divested as a whole and Commerzbank does not otherwise compete in those markets.

IV.i.f.   Ireland: a special case

The Commission is currently dealing with the crisis in the Irish financial sector which has been a particular source of concern across Europe.[77] The Irish retail banking sector is concentrated with two banks (Bank of Ireland and Allied Irish Bank) having a combined market share of 65%.[78] This is unlikely to change as the crisis has increased concentration in some banking areas with no likelihood of competition except in the case of a new entrant into the market. The Irish Government adopted various measures including the nationalisation of Anglo Irish Bank in January 2009 (it has stated that the failure of Anglo Irish Bank would bring down the whole country),[79] the recapitalisation of the three major Irish banks: Bank of Ireland, Allied Irish Bank and Anglo Irish Bank which was approved by the Commission in March, May and June 2009 respectively, and a massive impaired asset scheme involving the purchase of €80 billion of real estate loans from all of the major Irish financial institutions.[80]

The Commission's response to dealing with the Irish situation is a delicate topic due to the fact that almost every market player has been in receipt of aid, and the impairments and losses to Anglo Irish Bank's commercial loan book have continued to increase due to the poor quality of the book and the drop in prices in the commercial property market combined with the crisis in the financial markets. The Commission found that the recapitalisation was indispensable to remedy Anglo Irish Bank's financial difficulties and maintain confidence in the Irish financial markets.

In November 2010, Ireland was under immense pressure (to which it succumbed) to receive loans from the European Central Bank and the International Monetary Fund in order to save its banks and prevent a ripple effect of a failure on the other parts of the EU.[81] The Commission is yet to make a final decision on the restructuring plans submitted by Anglo Irish Bank, Allied Irish Bank EBS and INBS.[82]

IV.i.g.   Transition from Article 107(3)(b) back to Article 107(3)(c) TFEU

The Commission is planning to bring the crisis regime, that is, State aid under Article 107(3)(b) TFEU, to an end by the end of 2011 and to reintroduce 'standard' rescue and restructuring guidelines for the banking sector by that time subject to prevailing market conditions. The transition which is proposed to be a gradual process taking into account the recovery that is noticed in the financial sector (albeit fragile) and that which is forecasted is expected to usher in the phase where the Commission returns to square one and the strict application of State aid along the lines of standard competition rules.[83]

IV.ii.   Underlying Assumptions for Aid to the Banking Sector during the Financial Crisis

After an initial period in which the Commission attempted to take into account the special nature of the financial crisis, the Commission reverted to a policy which largely applies the principles of restructuring aid. Indeed, in its fourth phase the Commission enforced these principles *à la rigeur*.

This would be a defensible approach (in other words consistent with an economics-based assessment) if the explicit or implicit assumptions underlying the restructuring aid principles were satisfied in the context of the banking sector in the financial crisis. As we will show in this next section, however, this is not the case.

IV.ii.a.   Is the social policy objective of the aid relatively weak?

Governments around the world were willing to intervene to support their banking sectors because of two particular features of financial systems. First, because of the interconnectedness of financial institutions and the crucial role that confidence plays in maintaining financial stability, the banking sector always carries a substantial degree of systemic risk. Were one bank to fail, the effect on the loss of confidence in other banks could have severe implications for the financial system overall. The collapse of Lehman Brothers provided an impressive illustration of that risk. Second, a functioning banking system is crucial to the performance of the wider 'real' economy.[84] That the present financial crisis caused one of the most precipitous collapses in economic activity in 100 years (even with the massive government intervention to prevent this) illustrates the extent to which the economy relies on the financial system.[85]

Despite the devastating effect of the financial crisis on the world economy to date, there is general agreement that the various State aid measures have helped stabilise the banking system and economy.[86] In particular, it is clear that aid recipient banks' competitors have benefited from the aid to the recipients as calm has been restored to financial markets. The improvement in financial stability has also benefited a number of economies, with the EU-27 as a whole already returning to economic growth albeit with some individual Member States still struggling.[87]

Given that State aid to banks in the financial crisis is necessary to avoid the total collapse of the financial system and to reduce the likelihood of a prolonged and deep economic recession, it is clear that aid to banks in the financial crisis provides large enough social benefits to outweigh any competition distortions that may arise.

The assumption of a weak policy objective clearly does not hold for banks in the circumstances of the financial crisis.

IV.ii.b.   Is there significant over-capacity in the market?

As the term 'credit crunch' makes clear, financial institutions (and their customers) did not operate in a market of over-capacity during the financial crisis; indeed, lending remains constrained, even in economies that have returned to growth. The burst of the asset bubble and subsequent fire sales led to a massive destruction of banks' equity capital which in turn forces banks to scale down their lending activities to bring their balance sheet back in line with minimum equity requirements. In addition, the financial crisis destroyed much of the financial wholesale market.

The result has been a collapse of private sector credit growth and a significant financing gap, that is, an excess of acute financing needs of the sovereign and private non-financial sector over the limited credit capacity of the financial sector. According to IMF estimates that financing gap will be around 15% of nominal GDP in the UK and around 3% in the Eurozone in 2009 and 2010.[88] Therefore, not only does the assumption of over-capacity not hold, the banking industry during the financial crisis operates at the opposite end of the spectrum, namely significant under-capacity.

IV.ii.c.   Could the recipient plausibly pursue predatory strategies?

A number of factors suggest that aid beneficiaries will not be able to pursue plausibly predatory strategies against rivals which did not receive State aid. First and foremost, the 'credit crunch' in the industry will make such a strategy impossible. In addition, aid was often made available at such unattractive terms that beneficiary banks will operate at a competitive disadvantage to non-aided banks. For example, the Asset Protection Scheme in the UK which was available to all UK banks contained such onerous terms that only banks without alternatives (in this case RBS) joined the scheme.

IV.ii.d.   Is the recipient an 'inefficient producer'?

Many banks which pursued a reckless strategy (that is, were 'inefficient producers') needed to be bailed out by their governments. However not every bank which needed State support was necessarily reckless. The Commission recognised this point when it distinguished in its Banking Communication between aid to 'fundamentally sound' and unsound banks.

By way of illustration, as the Bank of England highlighted in October 2008, UK banks that suffered the most during the financial crisis were those that focussed their activities on UK mortgages (as opposed to global investment banking activities or lending in foreign markets) and who relied most heavily on wholesale funding.[89] Although it is true that a bank pursuing a reckless expansionist strategy would have rated highly on both of these criteria, the same is true for any banks entering and competing primarily in the UK mortgage market. In particular, the main reason why wholesale funding has proved to be so much riskier than retail funding in the present crisis is that the latter benefits from explicit and implicit state guarantees whereas the former does not (at least until Member States began offering credit guarantees – albeit only for a fee).

The net effect is that it is very difficult to identify banks that are 'fundamentally sound' and whose difficulties are all exogenous and those who were largely responsible for their own demise. The assumption that the beneficiary is an 'inefficient producer' therefore only holds in part.

IV.ii.e.   The aid is given in circumstances that are likely to arise again unless firms take costly measures to avoid them

The Commission has made clear that (consistent with the jurisprudence of the European Courts) Article 107(3)(b) TFEU only applies in the context of a severe financial crisis where aid is needed to 'remedy a serious disturbance in the economy of a Member State'.[90] Given that such crises are (mercifully) extremely rare (as illustrated by the fact that the EU State aid regime has never had to deal with such a crisis before), the impact of the expectation that in such circumstances banks would receive aid free of conditions is unlikely to have much impact on the profitability or otherwise of any given business strategy (that is, because the financial crisis is such a low probability event).

IV.ii.f.   Preliminary conclusions

The circumstances in which financial institutions found themselves during the financial crisis differ at least in two fundamental ways from the underlying implicit assumptions of an economics-based application of the R&R Guidelines. First, the systemic risks in the banking sector and its importance for the wider economy provide a compelling social policy objective for the granting of State aid (as the Commission acknowledges[91]). Secondly, rather than occurring in the context of a crowded market with over-capacity, the credit crunch has left the banking market with a severe under-capacity.[92] As is explained below, this fundamentally alters the assessment of the potential for distortions of competition to arise.

For these reasons, it cannot be presumed that the aid measures 'are likely to produce negative effects on the market and to jeopardise the objectives produced by the Community Competition rules', a presumption which, in other areas of EU competition policy, is used as a benchmark for the Commission to apply a formalistic object-based analysis.[93]

Consequently, restructuring aid under Article 107(3)(b) TFEU, contrary to restructuring aid under Article 107(3)(c) TFEU does not lend itself to the application of a mechanic, form-based approach. An effects-based analysis of the social welfare benefits and potential competition distortions of aid is needed to ensure that State aid control intervenes in the right circumstances.

IV.iii.   Effects-based Analysis

While an effects-based analysis was largely absent from the cases which the Commission decided in the first three phases of its State aid policy, the Financial Crisis Restructuring Guidelines suggested a noticeable shift in the Commission's approach.

First, the Commission, in paragraph 28 of the Financial Crisis Restructuring Guidelines, identified a number of different types of competition distortions, namely (i) direct distortions of competition, including the risk of reinforcement of market power; (ii) distorting the incentives of unaided competitors; (iii) moral hazard; and (iv) harm to the Single Market, all of which are dependent on the position of the beneficiary and the nature of the affected markets.

Furthermore, the Commission stated clearly that any remedy measures should be '*tailor-made* to address the distortions identified on the markets where the beneficiary bank operates' (emphasis added).[94] Tailor-made remedies are incompatible with a one-size fits all analysis.

IV.iii.a.   The counterfactual
The starting point for any effects-based analysis, both in terms of assessing the distortions of competition as well as the social benefits of aid, is the identification of the 'counterfactual'. The counterfactual is the scenario against which the State aid scenario has to be measured.[95] In Article 107(3) (c) TFEU restructuring aid cases, the 'counterfactual' would normally be the scenario where the Member State in question does not provide any aid and the potential beneficiary is forced to exit the market.

Applying the counterfactual to Article 107 (3)(b) TFEU cases is essential to analyse the social benefits of the aid, but since the 'exit' of the potential beneficiary would, at least with some probability, lead to a financial meltdown of the financial sector, the counterfactual provides very limited guidance beyond this. In particular, it does not provide a framework for the assessment of any distortion of competition.

One solution to this issue is to take the decision to grant the aid as given (since preventing the meltdown of the financial sector always outweighs any distortions of competition) and to use the counterfactual merely for the identification of the optimal remedy. One would contrast the base case (restructuring aid without compensatory measures) against a range of counterfactuals (restructuring aid subject to various compensatory measures). Contrasting the base case against the counterfactual would consist of a three-step analysis: in a first step, the competition distortions of the aid would be assessed, ignoring the benefits of the aid (in other words contrasting the exit of the potential beneficiary against the scenario where it remains in the market, without taking into account the negative impact that the exit of the beneficiary would have on financial stability). In a second step the extent to which distortions of competition would be reduced by the proposed compensatory measures would be assessed (contrasted against the 'no remedy' scenario). Finally in a third step, the reduction in distortions of competition would be balanced against any effect the remedy may have on the social benefits of the aid. The remedies that are ultimately imposed should be those that have the largest net positive effect on welfare (taking into account the reduction in competitive distortions and any reduction in social benefits caused by the remedies), assuming that any remedies with net positive effects can be found.

IV.iii.b.   Distortions of competition

The Financial Crisis Restructuring Guidelines identified the following types of distortion.

First, among the most important concerns raised by the Commission is the potential for moral hazard:

> the current scale of the public intervention necessary for financial stability and the possible limits to normal burden sharing are bound to create even greater moral hazard that needs to be properly corrected to prevent perverse incentives and excessively risky behaviour to reoccur in the future and to pave the way for a rapid return to normal market conditions without State support.[96]

Secondly, the Commission was concerned about aid sustaining market power, particularly where that market power may have been the result of excessive risk taking:

> state aid prolongs past distortions of competition created by excessive risk-taking and unsustainable business models by artificially supporting the market power of beneficiaries.[97]

Thirdly, concerns were also raised about aid causing harm to competitors more generally:

> banks across the Community have been hit by the crisis to a very varying degree and state aid to rescue and restructure distressed banks may harm the position of banks that have remained fundamentally sound, with possible negative effects for financial stability.[98]

Finally, the Financial Crisis Restructuring Guidelines also express the concern that:

> national interventions in the current economic crisis will, by their very nature, tend to promote focus on the national markets and hence seriously risk leading to retrenchment behind national borders and to a fragmentation of the single market and that state aid may 'harm the level-playing field in the single market'.[99]

We shall address each of these concerns in turn.

Moral hazard   Moral hazard has been cited consistently by the Commission as a concern in financial crisis cases throughout each of the phases of the development of its approach to State aid in the financial crisis.[100]

The Commission's concern is that if State aid were to be granted without accompanying compensatory measures, all banks (including current aid recipients and those banks that have not needed to rely on aid) would infer that they were effectively benefiting from a free insurance policy against financial crises. As a result, they would be more willing to engage in risky strategies that would make a future financial crisis more likely.

For State aid in financial crises to create moral hazard, it must (a) reduce the deterrent effect of the prospect of losses in the next financial crisis through (b) permanently altering banks' expectations of what Member States and the Commission will do in future.

First, it is unlikely that the State aid granted to banks will have had any significant impact on the deterrent effect of prospective losses in the next financial crisis. The impact of the financial crisis on all banks, especially those who have received aid, has been devastating. Shareholders, bondholders, management and employees alike have suffered greatly. For instance, the UK banking sector saw average shareholder losses of approximately 50% from November 2007 to May 2009, and the aid recipient banks have suffered even more (indeed, some, such as Northern Rock and Bradford and Bingley have been nationalised). It is difficult to see how, if losses of this scale are insufficient to deter banks from undertaking risky activities in the future, imposing compensatory measures could make any difference to banks' strategies. Indeed, the Commission has acknowledged this point to some extent. In the Fortis case it accepted that the aid could not give rise to much moral hazard for Fortis Holdings (as opposed to Fortis Bank) since Fortis Holdings had lost more than 90% of its market value since 2006 and yet the aid to Fortis Holdings was worth only 5% of its 2006 market value.[101]

Secondly, it is also doubtful whether the actions by Member States and the Commission should be a good guide to the availability and terms of aid in the future. Not only was there a wide range of approaches to aid taken across different Member States, there is also no reason to expect that a similar approach will be taken next time as the next financial crisis to qualify under Article 107(3)(b) TFEU will (with any luck) be a long time in the future, against a backdrop of a vastly different economic, financial and political landscape.

More generally, the Commission's thinking on moral hazard lacks a coherent theory of banks' attitudes to risks of extreme financial crisis. The Commission's claim that banks took excessive risks before the crisis sits uneasily with the claim that granting State aid gives rise to moral hazard that did not exist before. Excessive risk taking implies that banks were either myopic or already assumed that they would be bailed out. If banks were myopic in the past, it is not clear why in the future they will act with more foresight. If banks assumed they would be bailed out in the past, it is not clear what difference realising those expectations would make to their expectations in future.

Furthermore, any effort to address moral hazard by 'punishing' aid recipient banks is likely to be relatively ineffective unless the Commission has a method for distinguishing clearly between those banks whose activities contributed to the extent of losses suffered in the crisis (for example, through risky business strategies) and those who followed prudent strategies but were nevertheless severely affected by the crisis. Although there is likely to be some correlation between the extent of a bank's losses and the riskiness of the strategies it pursued, in practice this correlation is likely to be weak for reasons set out above.

Finally, if the Commission's concern is to ensure that banks do not repeat the mistakes that led to the present financial crisis, State aid control must be among the weakest of policy instruments for addressing that concern. In light of the efforts being made towards financial market regulatory reform at the national, EU and global level,[102] it is hard to believe that State aid control addressing moral hazard concerns could have any noticeable effect on the frequency or severity of financial crises in the future.

Risk of aid supporting beneficiaries' market power   As far as the risk that aid might support the beneficiary's market power is concerned, in principle an Article 102 TFEU-type analysis could be applied to State aid cases. However, there is an additional complication in the financial crisis State aid cases due to the issue of the counterfactual: assessing the effect of the aid on competition involves a comparison of the level of competition with the bank receiving aid against a scenario in which the bank exits the market. Even ignoring the effects of this exit on financial stability (as one must if one is to be able to identify competition distortions at all), it is by no means obvious that the market would be more competitive without the aid recipient than with it.

This additional effect makes the analysis of market power concerns in financial crisis restructuring aid cases significantly more complex than the issues raised in merger control, Article 101 or 102 TFEU cases.

Harm to competitors   In principle, aid could harm competitors in two ways. It could harm them directly through 'crowding out' their activities or it could harm their incentives to compete because of the expectation that State aid will be available again in the future.

As mentioned earlier, predation strategies or crowding out effects are unlikely to arise in the banking sector during (and indeed post-) financial crisis. First, the 'credit crunch', that is, the inability of the banking sector to provide sufficient capital to the 'real economy' prevents crowding out or predation. In addition, aid has often been made available at highly unattractive terms and conditions (for those who can choose) and as a result, beneficiary banks may not operate at a cost advantage.

The concern over the effect of aid on the incentives of other banks to compete raises some of the same issues as the moral hazard concerns discussed above, namely that since firms' expectations of the future profitability of any given strategy are only affected in relation to profits earned in the event of a financial crisis that is extremely unlikely to occur with any frequency, the effect of aid under Article 107(3)(b) TFEU on dynamic competition should be extremely limited.

Effect on the Single Market   The Single Market concern has two key elements: that Member States will encourage aid recipient banks to favour the home Member State markets when devising their restructuring plans and that the advantages conferred by the grant of State aid may distort competition in markets that are wider-than-national.

The first issue is indeed a potential concern, although obviously it can only affect those aid recipient banks that have significant international operations. It is best addressed by close supervision by the Commission of the preparation of restructuring plans to ensure that there is no undue discrimination against activities in other Member States in the restructuring measures.

The second issue is less likely to be of concern since there are few banking markets with wider than national geographic boundaries that have any significant competition problems (that is, international markets such as those for large corporate banking or investment banking are generally fragmented and highly competitive). There may be some residual concerns about State aid distorting the flow of funds from international capital markets towards aid recipient banks, but this should be capable of being mitigated by ensuring that aid is limited to the minimum necessary (i.e. it should not be necessary to make aid recipient banks more sound than those that have not received State aid).

IV.iii.c.   Preliminary conclusion

The analysis above illustrates the complexity of the assessment of the competitive effects of State aid in the financial crisis. Fortunately, however, the most important issue, whether the grant of aid is socially desirable, is straightforward to answer: aid to banks in the financial crisis is unambiguously beneficial even without any compensatory measures. The aid may in some circumstances also give rise to distortions of competition, but it is by no means clear that these will arise in all cases and the analysis required to identify and quantify them is extremely complex and goes far beyond the analysis that is usually conducted in State aid cases. That said, the Commission has acknowledged in the Financial Crisis Restructuring Guidelines that it is necessary to analyse competition in detail in these cases, so it may be that the decisional practice of the Commission will evolve to take account of the issues discussed above.

IV.iv.   Assessment of State Aid policy

IV.iv.a.   Prohibitions and approvals

So far, the Commission has approved financial crisis aid to banks in all cases except one. The only exception was the credit guarantee given by Portugal to Banco Privado Portugues (BPP) in 2008, which was initially approved on a rescue basis but ultimately prohibited (with an order for recovery) in July 2010 because the guarantee fee was too low and because Portugal never submitted a restructuring plan for the bank at all.[103] BPP's banking licence was revoked and a liquidation process was put in place in April 2010, with the result that Portugal was required to pay the full loan amount under the guarantee, so it is perhaps unsurprising that a reasonable restructuring plan could not be prepared in the circumstances. The recovery order appears to be almost without consequence, however, given that its only effect appears to be that Portugal lists itself as an unsecured creditor of the (insolvent) bank for the difference between the guarantee fee charged and the price that the bank should have paid.

It is also striking how few banks have been closed during the financial crisis. Moreover, where closure has occurred it appears to have been largely the decision of the Member State concerned (see *Liquidation of Fionia Bank by Denmark*[104]) rather than at the request of the Commission.

This is not surprising, however, given the overwhelming case in favour of support of the banks and the banking sector.

Where aid has been approved, however, except for cases in which only limited amounts of aid were granted or in which the recipient banks themselves were very small, approval has almost always been subject to significant compensatory measures. The compensatory measures and other conditions which have been imposed have varied significantly over time (as Commission policy has adapted over time), however, and contrary to the Commission's claims to consistency between cases that were dealt with at the same time,[105] it is difficult to construct a coherent explanation of the Commission's decisional practice in the crisis even on that limited basis.

IV.iv.b.   Choice of remedies

The Commission has imposed a number of different types of compensatory measures as a *quid pro quo* for approving State aid to banks in the financial crisis. It has required banks to reduce the size of their balance sheets, or to commit to behavioural constraints (such as prohibitions on price leadership or limitations on balance sheet growth or on the amount of net lending) so as to reduce their market presence. It has also required banks to commit to divesting non-core (but profitable) assets and businesses.[106] More recently it has also required the divestment of core assets and businesses (or parts thereof) with a view to reducing market shares or fostering new entry.

Balance sheet reductions and behavioural constraints   Balance sheet reductions have been the remedy most consistently imposed through the phases of the Commission's approach to the financial crisis described in IV.i above. IKB, for example, committed to a 47% reduction in its balance sheet from pre-crisis levels in one of the last cases to be decided under Article 107(3)(c) in 2008. More recently and under Article 107(3)(b), Commerzbank and West LB committed to 45% and 50% balance sheet reductions respectively.

Behavioural restrictions have also been a consistent feature of the Commission's policy. In December 2008 at the height of the Commission's liberal second phase, the Commission prohibited Fortis from offering the most attractive prices in certain markets for which it has high market shares. Similar restrictions were imposed on Commerzbank during the third phase, albeit in markets for which Commerzbank had much lower market shares.

These remedies aimed at reducing the presence of aid recipient banks can cause a number of significant problems in the context of the financial crisis. First, behavioural constraints have the immediate effect of restricting static competition among banks in the market. Although the same is true when similar remedies are imposed in Article 107(3)(c) cases, in the context of a financial crisis the effect is potentially much more serious because there could be a number of aid recipients in the same market.

Moreover, as discussed above, given that the banking system is presently suffering from a severe shortage of lending capacity, remedies designed to limit banks' ability to lend (either directly or through limiting their access to deposits) could potentially have very serious adverse impacts on consumers and the wider economy. Output is already limited; to restrict it further artificially and to increase prices further would only make matters worse.

The Commission appeared to have recognised the issues associated with behavioural constraints (if not balance sheet reductions) in July 2009, however, as paragraph 44 of the Financial Crisis Restructuring Guidelines notes the potential for behavioural remedies to limit competition and says that where this is a significant issue alternative remedies should be found. However, in light of the Commission's decision to impose what the Commission described as 'the most far reaching' price leadership ban on ING in November 2009,[107] it is not clear what the Commission's current policy on this key issue is.

In any event, it is also not entirely obvious what competition distortions market presence remedies of either kind are designed to address. Clearly, concerns about 'predation' of competitors cannot be relevant given banks' lack of willingness to lend. Moreover, as described above, moral hazard is likely to be at most a second-order issue, if it can be identified at all.

Divestment of non-core assets   The divestment obligations imposed by the Commission up to and including what we describe as the third phase of the Commission's approach to the crisis focussed on non-core divestments. For instance, Sachsen LB was required to divest or close its Dublin-based structured finance business, while Commerzbank was required to divest a range of European private banking and wealth management businesses in addition to its divestment of Eurohypo – Commerzbank's real estate and public finance business.[108]

Remedies of this kind tend to have no direct effect on competition. This is especially so for remedies that involve the division of a bank along national borders (where markets are national) such as the split of Fortis's Dutch operations from its operations in Belgium and Luxembourg, or for the sale of a bank in its entirety (as Germany has committed to do with West LB).

At best it could be argued that the divestment of non-core assets represents an 'own contribution' from the recipient bank, which limits the amount of necessary aid and hence indirectly contributes to a reduction of distortion of competition. However, there is no evidence that divestment obligations have actually reduced the amount of aid. Moreover, given the Commission's approach of negotiating divestment obligations (up to six months) after the aid has been granted,[109] unless the Commission requires retrospective changes to the terms of the aid received, it is hard to imagine how these obligations could reduce the amount of aid to the bank.[110] If anything, in cases where the Member State has provided aid in the form of capital injections, divestment obligations that represent an 'own contribution' could increase the net burden on the State by decreasing the value of the State's shares in the bank.

While imposing obligations to divest non-core assets is unlikely to have any noticeable impact on distortions of competition, these obligations have drawn stinging criticism from officials and regulators in the financial sector. President Weber of the Bundesbank engaged in a public dispute with the Commission through the *Financial Times*,[111] claiming that the Commission's insistence on banks divesting foreign assets and withdrawing to their home markets would have the effect of undermining the Single Market.

The Commission's Financial Crisis Restructuring Guidelines reflect this criticism noting that restructuring measures may threaten the Single Market and that the Commission 'will view positively measures that contribute to national markets remaining open and contestable'.[112] This change in policy does also appear to have been reflected in practice, with the Commission increasingly requiring divestments in home markets along with those in other Member States.

Divestment of core assets   As described above, the key change in the Commission's approach in the fourth phase has been its calls for divestments of core businesses or parts thereof to increase competition in banking markets. Indeed, the Financial Crisis Restructuring Guidelines indicate that measures should seek to foster new entry in markets featuring high barriers to entry, 'including on the domestic retail market of the aid beneficiary'.[113]

At first glance this could be an attractive remedy from a competition perspective. Although as discussed above there may not be any serious distortions of competition for the remedy to address, unlike other remedies it would at least have the benefit of increasing competition (which could eventually lead to an increase in lending to the economy).

On closer inspection, however, these remedies are potentially quite dangerous. Since they are being applied to a number of banks across Europe simultaneously, the effect is that a significant number of banking businesses will be sold in 'fire sales' at approximately the same time. Uncertainty as to how and at what prices these sales could be achieved may threaten the stability of the fragile financial system today, especially given that the Commission has tightened its approach to divestment periods, requiring divestments within four years for each of ING, KBC, RBS and LBG when Commerzbank was given five and a half years to divest Eurohypo.

These remedies would also be value destructive in many cases as they often require assets to be carved out of existing businesses, with associated dis-synergies. Moreover, the long divestment periods are likely also to cause serious damage to the divestment businesses. This is why in merger control cases the Commission generally allows only six months for divestments to be made. This timescale would be impossible in the present climate for financial stability reasons (as the Financial Crisis Restructuring Guidelines acknowledge), but if a business were earmarked now for divestment in up to four years time, it is not clear that even the appointment of a powerful monitoring trustee could prevent the loss of morale, staff and customers as a result of the uncertainty over the future.

There is also a real danger that the new entry could have unintended consequences for competitors who have not received aid. First, it is clear that the new entrant would reduce the profitability of all firms in the market through increased competition. There is no rationale for harming banks that do not require aid. More significantly, however, there is a serious risk that the new entrant would – once the credit crunch has abated – crowd out and cause the exit of existing smaller financial institutions that have not received aid. For example, even in relatively concentrated markets like the UK there are a number of small building societies and banks that have so far managed to weather the crisis, but may be seriously affected by additional competition from a new entrant. Even if there are barriers to entry and expansion that protect the profitability of larger incumbents, it is not necessarily the case that the smaller players earn above normal profits.

IV.iv.c.   Preliminary conclusions

The Commission's State aid policy towards banks in the financial crisis avoided making the two most critical mistakes that could have been made: attempting to delay or block the approval of emergency rescue and restructuring measures or abandoning State aid control altogether and risking a potential subsidy race between Member States.

However, the Commission's performance in overseeing banks' restructuring plan design processes once the dust began to settle in 2009 strongly reflected the Commission's underdeveloped intellectual framework in the rescue and restructuring aid context. Thus, even in the post-Financial

Crisis Restructuring Guidelines phases, its assessment of competitive distortions has been cursory at best, its remedies could not conceivably have
been 'tailor made' to address such distortions as may have arisen, and
indeed many of the remedies may have caused significantly more harm
than good.

V. RESTRUCTURING AID CASES IN THE REAL ECONOMY DURING THE FINANCIAL CRISIS

V.i.   The Absence of the Financial Crisis in State Aid Control in the Real Economy during the Financial Crisis

The previous section described the massive State intervention in the
banking sector during the financial crisis (amounting to around 10% of
EU GDP)[114] and the resulting State aid investigations and approvals.
The focus on financial institutions (both in terms of aid and the control
of aid) is not surprising given the origin of the crisis, the fragility of the
banking sector and its importance as a financial intermediary for the real
economy.

What is surprising, by contrast, is the absence of any increase in *ad hoc*
restructuring cases in the real economy as a result of the financial crisis.
Twenty-three restructuring cases during the two years prior to October
2008 compared with 19 restructuring cases for the same period post
October 2008. Of the 19 cases decided after October 2008, the large majority concern aid granted prior to October 2008 and only two cases make a
specific reference to the financial crisis.[115]

This picture somewhat understates the role of State aid (and State aid
control) in the real economy as it does not take account of aid granted
under the Temporary Framework[116] (which permits aid granted to firms
up to a level of €500,000) as well as certain industry-specific support, such
as the car-scrappage scheme introduced in various Member States.[117]

Nevertheless, the reason why the financial crisis (and the subsequent
Great Recession) has not triggered a greater number of big restructuring
aid cases in the real economy remains a valid question. One reason may
simply be timing: the average duration of restructuring cases in the real
economy has been circa 21 months[118] and more cases may yet work their
way through the system. In addition, State support measures during the
crisis may have been less targeted at individual firms but rather been of a
more general nature, and hence have fallen outside the ambit of State aid
control. Finally, there may have been limited political support for firm-
specific bail-outs in the wake of a global crisis.

Whatever the explanation, even a small number of restructuring aid cases in the real economy triggered by the financial crisis and subsequent recession justifies questioning whether the current framework is appropriate in the circumstances.

V.ii. Underlying Assumptions for Aid to the Industrial Sector during the Financial Crisis

V.ii.a. Is the social policy objective weak?

The R&R Guidelines emphasise that only certain policy considerations will justify the approval of rescue and restructuring aid. The Guidelines list in particular (i) social and regional policy considerations; (ii) the beneficial role played by other SMEs; and (iii) exceptionally, the protection of a competitive market structure.

The restructuring cases over the last four years are almost exclusively based on these three justifications.[119] Well over 75% of restructuring aid (in terms of number of cases) was justified by 'social and regional policy' objectives and the majority of firms were based in assisted areas. Aid to SMEs was quoted as the second most frequent aid objective, in around a third of all cases.[120] Reference to the preservation of a competitive market structure is made in only two restructuring aid cases over the last four years and only as a secondary objective.[121]

Where restructuring aid is justified on the basis of social and regional policy objectives, the Commission's evaluation of benefits is in most cases limited to the confirmation that the beneficiary is located in a region which is eligible for aid under Article 107(3)(a) TFEU. In a small number of cases, the Commission makes reference to a more specific benefit, for example, that the demise of the beneficiary 'would have serious consequences' in terms of employment for the economy.[122]

The assessment of restructuring aid for the benefit of SMEs receives the same broad-brush treatment. Even in restructuring aid cases which are justified on the basis 'of the desirability of maintaining a competitive market structure',[123] which are limited to exceptional circumstances and where antitrust has developed an appropriate analytical framework, the Commission's assessment is cursory and tends to be limited to a few structural observations.

The Commission's approach has two important implications: first, cases with potentially strong policy objectives (that is, those where aid is likely to lead to significant benefits) are inevitably treated in the same way as those with weak objectives (and indeed those which are likely to lead to harm). Secondly, it is not possible to verify whether the assumption that restructuring aid cases have weak policy objectives generally holds true.

V.ii.b.   Is there significant over-capacity in the market?

In the large majority of restructuring aid cases (that is, in more than two-thirds of all cases), over-capacity does not appear to feature in the markets under consideration: in only around 10% of all restructuring aid cases over the last four years does over-capacity feature as a relevant issue in the Commission's considerations.[124] This may be the result of the stringent approach of the R&R Guidelines, which state that 'it would not be justified to keep a firm artificially alive in a sector with long-term structural cover-capacity'[125] and in such cases 'the reduction in the company's capacity or market presence may have to be as high as 100%'.[126] Member States may be deterred from granting (or at least deterred from notifying) aid to firms in sectors with structural over-capacity. At times, the Commission may also be reluctant to reach a finding of structural over-capacity where it is otherwise minded to approve the aid.[127]

What is surprising, however, is that even in cases where over-capacity appears to be a feature (for example, affecting a market generally associated with long-term structural over-capacity or raised as an issue by a third party), the Commission has frequently not expressly considered over-capacity as a factor in its assessment.[128] Overall, the assumption of significant over-capacity does not hold.

V.ii.c.   Could the recipient plausibly pursue predatory strategies?

For a predatory story to be plausible, a beneficiary (following the receipt of the state aid) must have significant market power. In the cases under consideration, the Commission generally does not provide a rigorous assessment of the relevant product and geographical markets in which the beneficiaries operate. At times, the Commission even leaves the market definition open where the alternative markets result in vastly different market shares for the beneficiaries. For example, in the case of Huta Cynku Miasteczko Slaskie, the beneficiary's market share at EU level was 3% while at national level it was 57%.[129] For these reasons, the Commission's analysis must be treated with caution.

Nevertheless, the following broad picture emerges from the restructuring cases over the last four years: in almost half of all cases,[130] the market position of the beneficiary was *de minimis* ('insufficient market position' or market share of less than 5%). At the other end of the spectrum, there are a relatively small number of cases (less than 20% of all cases over the last four years) where beneficiaries have market shares in excess of 25% and the possibility of a plausible predatory strategy cannot be excluded purely on the basis of market structure. These cases included in particular the airline and shipyard cases.[131] The assumption may hold in small numbers of cases but does not seem to be valid as a general proposition.

V.ii.d.   Is the recipient an inefficient producer?

In the vast majority of cases, internal problems (ranging from a lack of cost accounting to poor quality and production management) have been the only or key contributing factor for the difficulty in which a beneficiary finds itself. The assumption that the recipient is an inefficient producer therefore seems generally to be correct.

V.ii.e.   Is the aid given in circumstances that are likely to arise again unless firms take costly measures to avoid them?

Contrary to aid given to 'remedy a serious disturbance in the economy', restructuring aid under Article 107(3)(c) TFEU is frequently given in circumstances that are likely to arise again unless firms take costly measures to avoid them.

V.ii.f.   Preliminary conclusions

A closer review of the restructuring aid cases over the last four years raises significant doubts as to whether the underlying assumptions (which ensure that the form-based rules of the R&R Guidelines are consistent with an economic analysis) are correct even outside of the financial sector.

The majority of cases do not involve over-capacity (and in an even greater majority over-capacity is not a relevant consideration). Furthermore, most beneficiaries lack significant market power. These facts have important implications both for the assessment of competition distortion as well as the choice of remedies. This suggests that the current rather mechanical 'one size fits all' approach is not optimal and that a more tailored approach is required.

V.iii.   Effects-based Analysis

A more tailored approach requires (at least in part) an effects-based analysis and the building blocks are similar to those set out in the previous section. This said, an analysis of restructuring aid in the real economy tends to be simpler than in the financial sector as fewer interdependencies have to be taken into account.

The Commission paper on the *Common Principles for an Economic Assessment of the Compatibility of State Aid*[132] provides a general framework for such an effects-based analysis, including the assessment of social benefits, the assessment of competitive harm and the balancing of benefits and harm.[133]

V.iii.a.   The counterfactual

The greater simplicity in the analysis can be seen, for example, in the identification of the counterfactual. Contrary to aid in the financial sector, intended to remedy a serious disturbance in the economy where there is no workable direct counterfactual, the counterfactual for restructuring aid against which to determine both social benefits and distortions of competition is (at least in principle) more straightforward, because the failure of the beneficiary would not normally cause large scale market disruption in the same way as the failure of a bank would. However, as Oxera's study of the counterfactual in restructuring aid cases shows, it is not necessarily the case that the counterfactual will be a world where the beneficiary (to be) has failed and exited the market(s).[134]

In fact, Oxera found that 77% of firms that experience 'difficulties' but do not receive aid manage to remain active in the market three years later, albeit potentially under different ownership.[135] Accordingly, as Oxera argue, if a meaningful analysis of either the social benefits or the competitive effects of restructuring aid is to be conducted, it is important to give serious consideration to what would have become of the beneficiary in the absence of the aid.

V.iii.b. The social benefits

The *Common Principles* paper set out a general framework for analysing the social benefits of State aid that can be applied in a range of contexts, including (in principle) restructuring aid. The framework consists of two questions:

(i)   is the aid measure aimed at a well-defined objective of common interest?
(ii)   is the aid well designed to deliver the objective of common interest?

These questions are now addressed in turn.

(i) Is the aid measure aimed at a well-defined objective of common interest?

As noted above, the R&R Guidelines indicate the following social policy objectives for allowing aid for firms in difficulty:

(i)   social and regional policy considerations;
(ii)   the beneficial role played by other SMEs; and
(iii)   exceptionally, the protection of a competitive market structure.

Although in principle these may be reasonable objectives of common interest, they are not very well defined and may not arise in any given case. Importantly, identifying the objective of the aid involves more than just identifying something that the Member State would like to support (for example, jobs in the region, SMEs, or more competition). It requires the identification of a market failure or fairness objective, that is, an explanation as to why, without State aid, the market will fail to deliver the Member State's objective. That involves an assessment of how the Member State's objective would fare in the counterfactual.

According to Oxera, at least to the extent that the Member State's objective is to protect jobs and output in the beneficiary's region or industry, it is far from clear that there is always or even usually a serious problem that needs to be solved. Thus, as noted above, 77% of firms in distress are still present on the market three years later. Moreover, employment and revenues for the firm on average only fall by 30% and 20% respectively over that three-year period.[136] Moreover, although Oxera found 'mildly negative' spill-overs from redundancies at the distressed firm to job losses elsewhere in the region and industry, it found no evidence of spill-overs from reduced output at the distressed firm to reduced output elsewhere.[137]

Oxera's conclusions do not imply that aid to firms in difficulty is not aimed at appropriate social policy objectives, but they do suggest that a rigorous counterfactual analysis is necessary to ensure that State aid is only given where there is a genuine market failure to be addressed.

*(ii) Is the aid well designed to deliver the objective of common interest, i.e.
       does the proposed aid address the market failure or other objectives?*

The second question is subdivided into three different tests:

First: is the aid an appropriate policy instrument to address the policy objective concerned?

In the rescue and restructuring context, this issue largely turns on an assessment of the viability of the beneficiary's restructuring plan. Assuming that without the aid the firm would have failed and adverse social policy outcomes would have followed (which is the subject of the first question), the main question is whether the aid is capable of avoiding that outcome.

Second: is there an incentive effect, that is, does the aid change the behaviour of the aid recipient?

Given that the behaviour change that rescue and restructuring aid is primarily aimed at is avoiding the failure of the firm, this second aspect to the question again largely focusses on the viability of the beneficiary's restructuring plan. To the extent that the Member State has more specific policy objectives, such as local employment, the extent to which the aid is targeted at that specific objective is also relevant. For example, it is not inconceivable that aid could help restore a beneficiary's viability without maintaining local employment if the aid was used to restructure away from the region.

Third: is the aid measure proportionate to the problem tackled, that is, could the same change in behaviour not be obtained with less (or less distortive) aid?

The final aspect of the second question corresponds to the requirement that aid be limited to the minimum necessary and be structured so as to avoid adverse consequences for competition. In the rescue and restructuring aid context this primarily involves consideration of whether the restructuring could equally have been achieved with less aid and more of the beneficiary's own resources.

Harm to competition   The Commission's mantra that rescue and restructuring aid distorts competition 'by preventing the recipient from being forced out of the market and thus hindering the development of competing firms'[138] is of course a truism in so far as the competitive outcome would have been different in the absence of the aid.

This view seems to confuse, however, harm to competitors (which undeniably exists) with harm to the competitive process and harm to consumer welfare (which may or may not be an issue).

Contrary to the Commission's analysis in restructuring cases, the Commission's *Common Principles* provide a coherent starting point for the assessment of harm or distortions to competition[139] which consider similar issues to the ones the Commission considered in the banking sector during the financial crisis in particular moral hazard (impact on long-term incentives of the beneficiary), harm to competitors (crowding out, impact on long-term incentives to rivals of the beneficiary) and effect on the single market.

Moral hazard   For State aid to create moral hazard, (as discussed above) it must reduce the deterrent effect of prospective losses in the case of financial difficulties. In this crisis the decision makers (that is, managers and shareholders) for aided banks suffered devastating losses even where the banks did receive aid (which made moral hazard less of a concern in those circumstances). The same argument cannot be made in more general cases, however, where aid may indeed significantly reduce the deterrent effects of possible losses.

For State aid to create moral hazard, the approach taken by the Member States and the Commission in a particular case must also make a permanent difference to firms' expectations of what will happen next time. This raises a number of interesting points in the context of restructuring aid in the real economy.

First, as concerns the aid recipient itself, although in principle moral hazard could be expected to be a significant problem in light of the likelihood that the firm will find itself in difficulties again in the future, this problem is adequately addressed by the 'one time, last time' principle.

Second, across the EU, the Commission assesses around 10 cases of *ad hoc* restructuring aid per year. This contrasts with an average of around 145,000 insolvencies in the EU for the same period.[140] In other words, for around 14,500 insolvencies, one firm gets life support through restructuring aid. This suggests that, at least at this very high level, *ad hoc* restructuring aid is unlikely to have a material impact on expectations in the markets.

But the distortion of restructuring aid is neither uniform nor random across the economy and hence the potential for moral hazard can be significantly higher in particular instances. A number of particular instances spring to mind:

> *State-owned firms*: almost half of the beneficiaries in the 42 cases during the review period where either State-owned or had the State as a significant shareholder. Moral hazard should therefore be a more serious concern for State-owned (or partly State-owned) companies.
>
> *Sector-specific intervention*: a number of sectors received more than their 'fair share' of State aid. Of the 42 cases, this is in particular airlines (Austrian Airlines, Alitalia and Cyprus Airways) and ship building (with Stoczni Gdansk, Szczecin shipyard, Stocni Gdynia, Hellenic shipyard and Constructions Mecaniques de Normandie).

More generally it can be argued that moral hazard is more likely to be an issue with large firms where the ratio of aided firms to failing firms is higher than with smaller firms.

Supporting market power   By contrast to banking cases during the financial crisis where the credit crunch has left consumers with an undersupply of lending, and the loss of the aid recipient from the market would cause a significant reduction in competition, the situation in standard restructuring aid cases where there is either excess capacity or inefficiency on the part of the aid recipient is such that in principle an Article 102 TFEU-type analysis could be applied by analogy.

Harm to competitors   Short-term harm to competitors (crowding out) is a more serious issue in restructuring cases in the real economy, particularly in markets with significant over-capacity. Long-term harm to competitors through the effect of aid on the incentives of rivals to the beneficiary raises the same issue as moral hazard.

Effect on the Single Market   The Single Market issues with restructuring cases in the real economy are potentially more significant and difficult to resolve than the banking sector. Unlike financial markets, which insofar as competition issues are likely to arise are likely to be national in scope, many real economy markets are much wider. In those cases, restructuring aid may distort the location of economic activity within the EU.

The issue is made more complex by the fact that in the real economy context, the very objective of the aid is often a distortion of the Single Market, that is, the Member State granting the aid is seeking to support an industry within its State or a particular region.

V.iv.   Assessment of Competition Policy

V.iv.a.   Prohibitions and approvals
During the four years from 9 October 2006 until 30 September 2010, the Commission investigated 42 restructuring aid cases. Nineteen of these cases[141] fell into the 'post-Crisis' period (the two years after the bankruptcy of Lehman), 23 cases[142] fell into the 'pre-Crisis' period (the two years prior to Lehman's bankruptcy). The Commission prohibited nine of the 42 cases, concluded in six cases that the State measure did not amount to State aid and approved the aid in the remaining 27 cases (in seven cases without compensatory measures).

V.iv.b.   Prohibition cases
The Commission prohibited a total of nine cases during the four-year period, five during the post-Crisis period, and four in the pre-Crisis period.

Each of the prohibitions concerned a fundamental breach of the R&R Guidelines: in two cases the beneficiary was not viable, in one case the beneficiary had breached the one time, last time principle, in four cases no restructuring plan or no compensatory measures were submitted and two cases concerned misuse of aid under a specific derogation.

V.iv.c.   Choice of the remedies
The R&R Guidelines have a strong focus on remedies which reduce the beneficiary's presence in the market and this theme is reiterated in many of the R&R aid Decisions. The following statement from the *Vanyera 3* case is repeated in numerous other Decisions:

Table 7.1　Prohibitions and approvals of restructuring aid

Number of cases	Post-Crisis		Pre-Crisis	
	No. of cases	Amount of aid (in millions)	No. of cases	Amount of aid (in millions)
No aid	2	40.2 million	4	239.0 million
Prohibited	5	1,696.0 million	4	332.9 million
Approved with compensatory measures	9	843.6 million	11	327.5 million
Approved without compensatory measures	3	8.6 million	4	15.5 million
Total	**19**	**2,588.5 million**	**23**	**914.8 million**

> The aid shall not unduly distort competition. This usually means a limitation of the presence which the [beneficiary] enjoys on its markets at the end of the restructuring period. The compulsory limitation or reduction of the company's presence on the market represents a compensatory factor in favour of its competitors.[143]

The R&R Guidelines specifically mention 'divestment of assets, reduction in capacity or market presence and reduction of entry barriers'.[144]

The choice of the Commission remedies reflects this stated position. Over the last four years, the Commission imposed compensatory measures in 21 cases, many of which involved multiple compensatory measures. By far the most frequent compensatory measure imposed by the Commission is the reduction of capacity or a cap on production; this was imposed in 17 of the 21 cases. Divestment of non-core businesses or transfer of assets has been the second most popular remedy.

Before assessing the compensatory measures imposed in the various restructuring aid cases, a word of caution is required: many of the compensatory measures offered by the beneficiary will have been influenced by their business plans. While the disposal of a loss-making business can generally not serve as a compensatory measure (on the basis that the recipient would have had to sell the business to return to viability), the mere fact that a business is profit making does not lead to the conclusion that the aid recipient was planning to keep the business.

V.iv.d.　Production caps, capacity reductions and behavioural constraints

Compensatory measures involving capacity reductions were applied indiscriminately across cases of very different circumstances. In the seven cases post-Crisis, where the Commission forced the beneficiary to reduce or limit output, two cases concerned markets with over-capacity, in two cases over-capacity was not raised as an issue and three cases concerned markets with growing demand. The position is similar during the pre-Crisis period: capacity reductions and production caps were imposed in markets with over-capacity (for example, Daewoo FSO), without apparent over-capacity (for example, Bäcker Legat) and with growing demand (for example, Construction Mecanique de Normandie). The only case (other than SMEs) pre-Crisis where *no* output constraint was imposed on the beneficiary actually concerned a market *with* over-capacity.[145] The Decisions do not disclose in all cases the magnitude of the output constraint imposed on the beneficiaries. To the extent that such data is available, there is no clear correlation between the magnitude of constraint (in percentage terms) and other factors which one would expect to be relevant, such as over-capacity and market shares.

V.iv.e.   Divestment of non-core assets

The transfer of assets is the second most popular compensatory measure. As discussed in the previous section, it is a remedy in search of a competition concern; in other words, it is not clear what type of concern the transfer of assets is supposed to address: it generally does not weaken a beneficiary's market position but tends to transfer a market position to a third party. To the extent that the sale of the assets does not take place at a loss, there is also no impact on moral hazard.

Overall it is not entirely clear in what circumstances the Commission regards this type of compensatory measure as appropriate; furthermore, as with remedies imposing output constraints, there is no obvious correlation between the magnitude of the remedy and any facts which affect the size of competition distortion.

V.iv.f.   Divestment of core assets

The divestment of core assets (such that it leads to a reduction of market shares by the aid recipients rather than to a complete exit from the market) has not yet been imposed by the Commission in any real economy cases in the context of Article 107(3)(b) TFEU.

V.v.   Preliminary Conclusions

The Commission will only impose a prohibition in a restructuring aid case if one of the core principles of restructuring aid control is breached, for example, lack of viability or the one time last time principle. This makes the choice of remedy the key policy decision.

The following aspects of the Commission's choice of remedy are striking. Firstly, compensatory measures which constrain the beneficiary's output are clearly the default remedy in restructuring aid cases. Secondly, the choice of remedy does not seem to be affected by the specific circumstances of a case; nor does the magnitude of the remedy seem to be correlated with factors which are likely to affect the extent of competition distortions. Thirdly, in a number of cases the Commission does not seem to have established (or at least not disclosed in the decision) the key factors which are critical to understanding the impact of a remedy on social welfare.

VI.   CONCLUSION

State aid control was a key policy instrument during the financial crisis. The Commission has played an important role in this by testing the viability of beneficiary banks and by ensuring that there are no 'zombie banks' which are artificially kept alive by Member State governments.

The Commission's assessment of harm to competition and its policy of imposing 'compensatory measures' on aid recipients to address such harm has been less beneficial. Not only were there serious flaws in the Commission's analytical framework, but the remedies imposed were at best ineffectual (as, for example, in the case of divestment of non-core business) and at worst positively harmful (as was the case with balance sheet reductions and constraints on pricing).

In our view, the origin of these problems stem from the fact that the Commission, after a period of grappling with the peculiarities of the banking sector during the financial crisis, returned to the default position of its general rescue and restructuring aid policy which is geared towards reducing the market presence of the beneficiary through capacity reductions and divestments. While such a policy may be appropriate in the limited circumstances of markets with over-capacity it was entirely unsuited to the 'credit crunch' and made a bad economic situation worse.

However, even in rescue and restructuring cases in the real economy, a policy which aims to reduce capacity, production and/or presence of the beneficiary independently of market circumstances, such as the level of capacity available in the market, does not lead to the right policy outcomes.

The Commission is planning to review its rules on rescue and restructuring aid both for the banking sector (where Guidelines are planned for November 2011) and for the real economy (where the Commission aims for revised Rescue and Restructuring Aid Guidelines in the course of 2012). This is a golden opportunity to overhaul the system.

The starting point should be the classification of the objective of restructuring aid control: is it, as the present system suggests, the protection of competitors (even where such protection comes at a price for customers or the economy overall) or is it the protection of competition? The two may coincide but this is by no means always the case.

Assuming that the aim is ultimately the protection of competition, a coherent analytical framework for harm to competition needs to be developed. The Commission's *Common Principles*[146] provide an excellent basis. In every individual case, it is necessary (as in other areas of competition policy) to identify specific competition concerns and to support the story of harm with facts. And last, but by no means least, the remedies imposed by the Commission need to be designed to address the harm to competition identified. Moral hazard will require different remedies from those required to address the competition concern of crowding out equally (or more) efficient competitors.

NOTES

1.   We are very grateful to Oyebola Ajayi, Per-Axel Frielingsdorf and Elizabeth Hookham for their research assistance and help with this chapter. The views and any errors in this chapter are, however, our own.
2.   Raum, Tom, 'Bush signs $700 billion bail out bill', Associated Press, 3 October 2008.
3.   IMF, *Global Financial Stability Report*, October 2008, p. 8.
4.   HM Treasury, Financial Support to the Banking Industry, 8 October 2008, available at: <http://webarchive.nationalarchives.gov.uk/20100407010852/http://www.hm-treasury.gov.uk/press_100_08.htm> (last accessed 28 December 2010).
5.   See ECOFIN's call for the enforcement of State aid rules at p. 7 of its Press Release 13784/08 (Presse 279) on 7 October 2008, available at:
     <http://www.consilium.europa.eu/uedocs/cms_data/docs/pressdata/en/ecofin/103250.pdf> (last accessed 28 December 2010).
6.   See *'The Turner Review: A regulatory response to the global banking crisis'* March 2009 for a particularly thorough account; Ben S Bernanke: *The Causes of the Recent Financial and Economic Crisis, Statement before the Financial Crisis Inquiry Commission*, 2 September, 2010; Paul Krugman and Robin Wells: The Slump goes on: Why? *NY Review of Books*, 30 September 2010, available at <http://www.nybooks.com/articles/archives/2010/sep/30/slump-goes-why/> (last accessed 28 December 2010).
7.   *The Turner Review*, op. cit, pp. 12–13. Davies 2010.
8.   Ibid, 7.
9.   See, by way of illustration paras 5–6 of Commission Decision of 11 March 2008 in case C 10/2008 to approve restructuring aid to IKB.
10.   Bank of England, *Financial Stability Report*, October 2008, Issue 24, 7–8.
11.   Ibid, 10–13.
12.   IMF, *Global Financial Stability Report*, October 2010, 13.
13.   Sinn 2010: 47.
14.   Bank of England, *Financial Stability Report*, June 2009, Annex – Timeline of crisis events.
15.   See *Report from the Commission: State aid Scoreboard – Report on recent developments*

on crisis aid to the financial sector – Spring 2010 update, available at: <http://eur-lex.europa.eu/LexUriServ/LexUriServ.do?uri=CELEX:52010DC0255:EN:NOT http://europa.eu/rapid/pressReleasesAction.do?reference=MEMO/10/284&format=HTML&aged=0&language=EN&guiLanguage=en. http://www.ipex.eu/ipex/webdav/site/myjahiasite/groups/CentralSupport/public/2010/COM_2010_0255/COM_COM(2010)0255(COR1)_EN.pdf> (last accessed 28 December 2010).

16. At the time of writing, the exact information on the take up rate for 2010 was not available. See *Report from the Commission: State aid Scoreboard – Report on recent developments on crisis aid to the financial sector – Autumn 2010 update*, pp. 47–55 particularly footnote 118. Available at: <http://ec.europa.eu/competition/state_aid/studies_reports/2010_autumn_en.pdf> and its annex at: <http://ec.europa.eu/competition/state_aid/studies_reports/annex_2010_autumn_en.pdf> (last accessed 28 October 2010).

17. Ibid. The total amount of financial crisis banking State aid approved by the Commission between October 2008 and March 2010 accounted for approximately 33% of EU GDP, although the approved measures have not been fully implemented.

18. Bank of England, *Financial Stability Report*, June 2010, Issue No. 27, Overview.

19. *Global Economic Prospects 2010*: World Bank, 21 January 2010, 2.

20. Ibid, 36.

21. Eurostat: *Growth rate of GDP volume – percentage change on previous year* available at: <http://epp.eurostat.ec.europa.eu/tgm/table.do?tab=table&init=1&plugin=1&language=en&pcode=tsieb020> (last accessed 28 December 2010).

22. Commission Staff Working Document, *Facts and figures on State aid in the Member States, Autumn 2010 update*, ch. 3, 55–59, available at: <http://ec.europa.eu/competition/state_aid/studies_reports/annex_2010_autumn_en.pdf> (last accessed 28 December 2010).

23. Communication of the Commission – *Temporary Union framework for State aid measures to support access to finance in the current financial and economic crisis*, available at: <http://ec.europa.eu/competition/state_aid/legislation/temporary_framework_en.pdf>; see also, SPEECH/10/711 – *State aid: Commission prolongs crisis framework with stricter conditions – trend towards less and better targeted aid continues despite crisis-related spike*, available at: <http://europa.eu/rapid/pressReleasesAction.do?reference=SPEECH/10/711&format=HTML&aged=0&language=EN&guiLanguage=en> (last accessed 28 December 2010).

24. Ibid, 4–5.

25. See note 22 above.

26. Ibid.

27. Ibid.

28. See Eurostat News Release N° 170/2010available at: <http://epp.eurostat.ec.europa.eu/cache/ITY_PUBLIC/2-15112010-AP/EN/2-15112010-AP-EN.PDF> (last accessed 28 December 2010).

29. Abigail Moses, Ireland, 'Greece Debt Woes Reverse Sovereign Default Swaps Rally', Bloomberg, 29 October 2010.

30. *Community Guidelines on State Aid for Rescue and Restructuring Firms in Difficulty*, O.J. 2004 C 244/02.

31. *The application of State aid rules to measures taken in relation to financial institutions in the context of the current global financial crisis*, O.J. 2008 C 270/08; *Recapitalisation of financial institutions in the current financial crisis: limitation of the aid to the minimum necessary and safeguards against undue distortions of competition*, O.J. 2009 C10/02, *The treatment of impaired assets in the community banking sector*, O.J. 2009 C72/01; *The return to viability and the assessment of restructuring measures in the financial sector in the current crisis under the State aid rules* O.J. 2009 C 195/09.

32. *State Aid Action Plan – Less and better targeted state aid: a roadmap for state aid reform 2005 – 2009*, 7 June 2005, available at: <http://eur-lex.europa.eu/LexUriServ/

LexUriServ.do?uri=COM:2005:0107:FIN:EN:PDF> (last accessed 28 December 2010).

33.   Available at: <http://ec.europa.eu/competition/state_aid/reform/economic_assessment_en.pdf> (last accessed 28 December 2010).
34.   Ibid, para. 7.
35.   R&R Guidelines, para. 1.
36.   Ibid, para. 9.
37.   Ibid, para. 73.
38.   Ibid, para. 8.
39.   Ibid, para. 4.
40.   *Cyprus Airways C-10/2006*.
41.   89/58/EEC *Commission Decision of 13 July 1988 concerning aid provided by the United Kingdom Government to the Rover Group, an undertaking producing motor vehicles.*
42.   Lienemeyer and Soukup 2008.
43.   In this respect the Commission's approach is consistent with its approach to the assessment of distortions of competition in State aid cases in general, where the CJEU in Case 730/79, *Philip Morris* [1980] E.C.R. 2671 has endorsed the presumption that conferring a selective advantage on an undertaking will distort competition and in most cases has not required the Commission to conduct a formal analysis or a quantification of distortions of competition.
44.   R&R Guidelines, para. 4.
45.   R&R Guidelines, para. 38.
46.   R&R Guidelines, para. 39.
47.   Ibid.
48.   R&R Guidelines, para. 40.
49.   Ibid.
50.   R&R Guidelines, para 39.
51.   Eatwell, Murray and Newman 1987: 549.
52.   See 'State aid to Opel cannot be linked to German jobs, EU says', published at *EarthTimes*:   <http://www.earthtimes.org/articles/show/283561,state-aid-to-opel-cannot-be-linked-to-german-jobs.html>; European Commission statement of 11 September 2009 at <http://europa.eu/rapid/pressReleasesAction.do?reference=MEMO/09/389&format=HTML&aged=0&language=EN&guiLanguage=en>; and Tony Barber: 'BusinessEurope slams German Opel rescue', *Financial Times*, 17 September 2009 at <http://www.ft.com/cms/s/0/457a3d80-a363-11de-a435-00144feabdc0.html> (all last accessed 28 December 2010).
53.   Although divestments may not necessarily have this effect, they can give rise to dissynergies or distort competition in other ways (for example, giving rise to excessive entry). Moreover, to the extent that the divestment is at fair value it is not clear how it addresses moral hazard and to the extent that it is not an arbitrary advantage is being conferred on the purchaser.
54.   See Werner and Maier 2009, for an account of the evolution of the Commission's policy up to March 2009.
55.   *Community Guidelines on State aid for rescuing and restructuring firms in difficulty*, O.J. 2004 C 244/2 (Rescue and Restructuring Guidelines). See Nicolaides and Kekelekis 2005 for a review of the principles of the Rescue and Restructuring Guidelines.
56.   *Communication from the Commission – The return to viability and the assessment of restructuring measures*, O.J. 2009 C 195/9.
57.   See n 24 above. See also, Speech/10/703 – Joaquín Almunia Vice President of the European Commission responsible for Competition Policy, *Competition Policy: State of Play and Priorities European Parliament*, ECON Committee Brussels, 30 November 2010, available at: <http://europa.eu/rapid/pressReleasesAction.do?reference=SPEECH/10/703&type=HTML>.

58. Commission Decision of 2 April 2008 in Case C-14/2008 to open an in-depth investigation.
59. Commission Decision of 4 June 2008 in Case C-9/2008 to approve the aid to Sachsen LB subject to conditions.
60. Commission Decision of 21 October 2008 in Case C-10/2008 to approve the aid to IKB subject to conditions.
61. Commission Decision of 2 April 2008 in Case C-14/2008, para. 48.
62. Commission Decision of 2 April 2008 in Case C-14/2008, para. 126.
63. Commission Decision of 4 June 2008 in Case C-9/2008 in relation to Sachsen LB.
64. Commission Decision of 10 October 2008 in Case C-10/2008 in relation to IKB (in German).
65. Commission Decision of 4 June 2008 in Case C-9/2008 in relation to Sachsen LB, section 7.2.2.4.
66. Commission Decision of 10 October 2008 in Case C-10/2008 in relation to IKB (in German), section 2.7.
67. *Communication from the Commission – The application of State aid rules to measures taken in relation to financial institutions in the context of the current global financial crisis*, O.J. 2008 C 270/8.
68. *Communication from the Commission – The recapitalisation of financial institutions in the current financial crisis: limitation of aid to the minimum necessary and safeguards against undue distortions of competition*, O.J.2009 C 10/2.
69. *Banking Communication*, para. 14.
70. Recapitalisation Guidelines, paras 40–42.
71. Commission Decision of 3 December 2008 in Case NN-42/2008.
72. Speech/09/63 of Neelie Kroes, European Commissioner for Competition Policy, 'The road to recovery', Paris, 17 February 2009.
73. *Communication from the Commission on the treatment of impaired assets in the community banking sector*, O.J. 2009 C 72/01 (Impaired Assets Guidelines).
74. Case N-244/2009 in respect of Commerzbank and Case C-43/2008 in respect of WestLB.
75. Financial Crisis Restructuring Guidelines, para. 32.
76. Commission Decision of 3 December 2008 in Case NN-42/2008, para. 94.
77. Irish crisis shakes Europe, *The Wall Street Journal*, 1 October 2010, available at <http://www.efinancialnews.com/story/2010-10-01/ireland-crisis-shakes-europe> (last accessed 28 December 2010).
78. As of 2003 – OECD Policy Roundtables, Competition, Concentration and Stability in the Banking Sector 2010.
79. Brian Lenihan's (Ireland Finance Minister) interview with the *Financial Times*, 29 September 2010.
80. State aid N725/2009 – Ireland, Establishment of a National Asset Management Agency (NAMA): Asset relief scheme for banks in Ireland.
81. Fergal O'Brien and Simone Meier, 'Ireland Receives EU/IMF Bailout to Bolster Banks', Bloomberg (29 November 2010), available at: <http://www.bloomberg.com/news/2010-11-28/ireland-receives-eu-imf-bailout-to-bolster-banks-table-.html> (last accessed 28 December 2010).
82. Statement by Competition Commissioner Almunia on Irish banks, MEMO/10/465, 30 September 2010, available at: <http://europa.eu/rapid/pressReleasesAction.do?reference=MEMO/10/465&format=HTML&aged=0&language=EN&guiLanguage=en> (last accessed 28 December 2010).
83. See *Report from the Commission: State aid Scoreboard – Report on recent developments on crisis aid to the financial sector – Autumn 2010 update.*
84. See statements of the UK government in the 2009 Budget report, ch. 3, available at: <http://www.hm-treasury.gov.uk/d/Budget2009/bud09_chapter3_222.pdf>. See also 'US government rescues insurer AIG', BBC News 17 September 2008, available at: <http://news.bbc.co.uk/1/hi/business/7620127.stm>, and Press Release from the US

Department of the Treasury of 2 March 2009 at: <http://www.treasury.gov/press/releases/tg44.htm> (all last accessed 28 December 2010).

85. See Eichengreen, B. and K.H. O'Rourke. 'A Tale of Two Depressions' for a comparison of the current recession with the Great Depression. Advisor Perspectives, Inc., 2009, available at: <http://www.advisorperspectives.com/newsletters09/pdfs/A_Tale_of_Two_Depressions.pdf> (last accessed 28 December 2010).

86. See Commissioner Kroes' statements in 'State aid: Commission adopts guidance on bank recapitalisation in current financial crisis to boost credit flows to real economy', European Commission Press Release available at: <http://europa.eu/rapid/press-ReleasesAction.do?reference=IP/08/1901&guiLanguage=de> (last accessed 28 December 2010).

87. See Eurostat News Release No 148/2010, available at: <http://epp.eurostat.ec.europa.eu/cache/ITY_PUBLIC/2-06102010-AP/EN/2-06102010-AP-EN.PDF> (last accessed 28 December 2010).

88. IMF, *Global Financial Stability Report* , October 2009, 34.

89. Bank of England, *Financial Stability Report*, October 2008, Issue 24, Chart 4.9.

90. *Banking Communication*, para. 7.

91. See for instance *Banking Communication*, para. 4.

92. Banks' lending capacity has been substantially reduced and the UK Government adopted a series of measures to promote lending to businesses. See HM Treasury's statement to the House of Commons on Bank Lending of 19 January 2009 at: <http://www.hm-treasury.gov.uk/statement_chx_190109.htm> (last accessed 28 December 2010).

93. Para. 21 of the Guidelines on the Application of Article [101(3)TFEU] of the Treaty, O.J. 2004 C 101/08.

94. Financial Crisis Restructuring Guidelines, para. 30.

95. See Rainer Nitsche and Paul Heidhues: 'Study on methods to analyse the impact of State Aid on competition', Economic Papers, Commission, February 2006, sections 1.6.4, 3.7.4 and 4.6 available at: <http://ec.europa.eu/economy_finance/publications/publication804_en.pdf>. In July 2008 the Commission tendered a contract for a 'Study on counterfactual scenarios to restructuring state aid: observed developments when no aid is granted to firms in difficulty'. This contract was awarded to Oxera in December 2008. The Report was entitled *Should aid be granted to firms in difficulty? A study on counterfactual scenarios to restructuring state aid*, February 2010, available at: <http://www.oxera.com/main.aspx?id=8790> (all last accessed 28 December 2010).

96. Financial Crisis Restructuring Guidelines, para. 29.

97. Ibid, para. 28.

98. Ibid, para. 29.

99. Ibid, para. 29

100. See, for example, *Sachsen LB* (Case C-9/2008) para. 126 and *Fortis* (Case N-255/09) para. 104.

101. Commission Decision of 12 May 2009 in Case N-255/09, para. 104.

102. In July 2009 the UK government published a Paper on reforming financial markets available at: <http://www.hm-treasury.gov.uk/reforming_financial_markets.htm>. At the EU level there have also been initiatives to reform the European financial sector as can be seen in the Commission's Communication for the Spring European Council of March 2009 available at: <http://ec.europa.eu/commission_barroso/president/pdf/press_20090304_en.pdf>; see also Nikki Tait, 'EU taskforce proposes tougher regulation', *Financial Times*, 25-February 2009, available at: <http://www.ft.com/cms/s/0/346c05c8-031d-11de-b405-000077b07658.html>. In June 2009 the US Department for Treasury also published a White Paper on regulatory reform available at: <http://www.whitehouse.gov/the_press_office/President-Obama-to-Announce-Comprehensive-Plan-for-Regulatory-Reform/> (all last accessed 28 December 2010).

103. IP/10/972: *Commission orders recovery of illegal state aid from Banco Privado Português.*
104. Liquidation of Fionia Bank by Denmark, Case N-560/2009 – Aid for the liquidation of Fionia Bank.
105. *Financial Crisis Restructuring Guidelines*, para. 38.
106. For example Sachsen LB was required to divest or close its Dublin-based structured finance business and Commerzbank was required to divest a range of European private banking and wealth management businesses.
107. Commission Press Release, *State aid: Commission decisions on KBC, ING and Lloyds – frequently asked questions*, 18 November 2009.
108. The extent to which Eurohypo was a 'core' business is debatable, but it can certainly be distinguished from the core divestments that are designed to increase competition. Eurohypo conducted the entirety of Commerzbank's activities in its areas, so it is to be divested with its market share and competitive position intact.
109. This has been the case for example in Commerzbank, Hypo Real Estate and WestLB, where the actual negotiation of divestment obligations took place when the restructuring plan was notified to the Commission (six months after the rescue aid had been approved by the Commission and granted by the relevant Member States).
110. The Commission did, for instance, require ING to pay more for its State aid as part of its restructuring plan.
111. Interview with Axel Weber, *Financial Times*, 21 April 2009. See also Commissioner Kroes' response, '*European Commission responds to Axel Weber*', *Financial Times*, 22 April 2009.
112. *Financial Crisis Restructuring Guidelines*, para. 33.
113. *Financial Crisis Restructuring Guidelines*, para. 35.
114. See Report from the Commission: *State aid Scoreboard – Report on recent developments on crisis aid to the financial sector – Spring 2010 update* (see n 15 above).
115. See section II.iv.d. above.
116. At time of writing, the current consolidated version was available at <http://ec.europa.eu/competition/state_aid/legislation/temporary_framework_en.pdf>.
117. See n 21 above.
118. Average duration of review of all cases both pre- and post-Crisis, with the shortest duration being 1 month 10 days and the longest being 8 years and 7 months).
119. Except in N420/2008, *Restructuring of London & Continetal Railways (LCR)* (13 May 2009) where future competition and need to separate operations were the justifications given by the beneficiary.
120. The sum of all aid objectives exceed 100% as cases are at times based on more than one type of justification.
121. See para 65 of Commission Decision of 13 May 2009 in Case C20/2007 – *Pickman S.A. – La Cartuja de Sevilla* and para 35 of Commission decision of 30 January 2008 in Case N323/2007 – *Vanyera3*.
122. See para 17 of Commission Decision of 15 December 2009 in Case N488/2009 – POLFA and para 15 of Commission Decision of 27 January 2010 in Case N672/2008 – *Kalofolias*.
123. R&R Guidelines, para. 8.
124. Austrian Airlines, Hellenic Shipyard, Ottana Energia (rejected), Bison-Bial, Daewoo FSO.
125. R&R Guidelines, para 8.
126. R&R Guidelines, para 42.
127. In the Ottana Energia case, the Commission took the view that it 'could not uphold its observation of the opening decision that there was overcapacity in the Sardinian energy market. Although such overcapacity de facto exists, it is there only for the purpose of keeping always a certain reserve for supplying the island.' C 11/2007, para 56.
128. See Decisions C6/2009, *Restructuring of Austrian Airlines AG* (28 August 2009);

C18/2005, *Restructuring aid to Stoczni Gdansk* (22 July 2009); C26/2008, *Loan to Alitalia* (12 November 2008); C19/2005, *Restructuring aid for Szczecin shipyard* (6 November 2008); C17/2005, *Restructuring aid for Stoczni Gdynia* (6 November 2008); C14/2007, *Restructuring aid to NGP* (16 July 2008); C16/2004, *Hellenic Shipyards* (2 July 2008); N92/2008, C11/2007, *Restructuring aid to Ottana Energia* (2 July 2008); C51/2006, *Misuse of aid by Arcelor Huta Warszawa* (11 December 2007); C6/2007, C23/2006, *Technologie Buczek Group* (23 October 2007); C32/2006, N289/2007, *Restructuring aid to Fiem* (25 September 2007); C54/2006, *Restructuring aid for Bison-Bial* (12 September 2007); C 10/2006, *Cyprus Airways Public Ltd-Restructuring Plan* (7 March 2007); C3/2005, *Restructuring aid to DAEWOO – FSO* (20 December 2006).

129. Although the Commission found that there was no aid given to the beneficiary after a formal investigation procedure.
130. In 45% of all cases.
131. *Stoczni Gdansk* C-18/2005, para. 189, *Austrian Airlines* C-6/2009 para. 326; *Cyprus Airways* C-10/2006 para. 29.
132. Above n 30.
133. Ibid, para. 9.
134. Oxera, *Should Aid be Granted to Firms in Difficulty? A Study on Counterfactuals Scenarios to Restructuring State Aid*, February 2010.
135. Ibid, section 8.2.3.
136. Ibid, section 8.2.4.
137. Ibid, section 8.2.5.
138. See for example *FagorBrandt*, C-44/2007, para.76.
139. *Common Principles* paper, above n 30, 16.
140. *Insolvencies in Europe, 2009–2010*, A Survey by the Creditreform Economic Research Unit.
141. See Decisions: C-40/2008, *Restructuring aid to PZL Hydral* (4 August 2010); C38/2007, *Alleged aid to Arbel Fauvet Rail SA* (23 June 2010); N488/2009, '*Restructuring aid to POLFA* (4 March 2010); N672/2008, *Restructuring aid to Kalofolias* (27 January 2010); N604/2009, *Modification of previously approved restructuring aid to Fiem* (15 December 2009); C6/2009, *Restructuring of Austrian Airlines AG* (28 August 2009); C18/2005, *Restructuring aid to Stoczni Gdansk* (22 July 2009); C10/2005, *Restructuring aid to COMBUS A/S* (13 July 2009); N420/2008, *Restructuring of London & Continetal Railways (LCR)* (13 May 2009); C20/2007, *Pickman S.A. - La Cartuja de Sevilla* (13 May 2009); C43/2007, *Change of restructuring plan of Huta Stalowa Wola* (10 March 2009); C47/2008, *Restructuring aid to Przędzalnia Zawiercie* (03 March 2009); N212/2008, *Restructuring aid for PKS Wadowice S.A.* (28 January 2009); C52/2006, *Restructuring aid for Odlewni Zeliwa Srem* (10 December 2008); C26/2008, *Loan to Alitalia* (12 November 2008); C19/2005, *Restructuring aid for Szczecin shipyard* (06 November 2008); C17/2005, *Restructuring aid for Stoczni Gdynia* (06 November 2008); C44/2007, *Restructuring aid to FagorBrandt* (21 October 2008); N458/2008, *Restructuring aid to Götzke Natursteinwerk* (20 October 2008).
142. See Decisions: C14/2007, *Restructuring aid to NGP* (16 July 2008); C16/2004, *Hellenic Shipyards* (2 July 2008); N92/2008, *Restructuring aid to 'Der Bäcker Legat'* (2 July 2008); C11/2007, *Restructuring aid to Ottana Energia* (2 July 2008); C13/2007, *Restructuring aid to New Interline* (16 April 2008); N506/2007, *Restructuring of Hartwig Warszawa* (2 April 2008); N 472/2007, *Restructuring aid to Compel Rail* (2 April 2008); N323/2007, *Restructuring aid to Vanyera3* (30 January 2008); C51/2006, *Misuse of aid by Arcelor Huta Warszawa* (11 December 2007); C6/2007, *Restructuring aid for Techmatrans* (28 November 2007); C23/2006, *Technologie Buczek Group* (23 October 2007); C32/2006, *Restructuring aid to Huta Cynku Miasteczko Slaskie* (25 September 2007); N289/2007, *Restructuring aid to Fiem* (25 September 2007); C54/2006, *Restructuring aid for Bison-Bial* (12 September 2007); N561/2006, *Restructuration aid for Constructions Mécaniques de Normandie (CMN)*

(10 July 2007); C19/2006, *Restructuring aid for Javor Pivka* (10 July 2007); C20/2006, *Restructuring aid for Novoles Straza* (10 July 2007); C46/2005, *Mesures de sauvetage en faveur de 'Inter Ferry Boats' (IFB)* (24 July 2007); C32/2005, *Restructuration aid for Ernault* (4 April 2007); C 10/2006, *Cyprus Airways Public Ltd- Restructuring Plan* (07 March 2007); C3/2005, *Restructuring aid to DAEWOO – FSO* (20 December 2006); C42/2005, *Restructuring aid to KONAS – Slovakia* (26 September 2006); C49/2005, *Restructuring aid for Chemobudowa Krakow* (26 September 2006).
143.   Para. 28.
144.   Para. 39 of the R&R Guidelines.
145.   Commission Decision of 12 September 2007, C54/2006, *Restructuring aid for Bison-Bial.*
146.   *Common Principles* Paper, above n 30.

REFERENCES

Davies, Howard (2010), *The Financial Crisis: Who is to Blame?,* United Kingdom: Polity.

Eatwell, John, Murray Milgate and Peter Newman (1987), *The New Palgrave: A Dictionary of Economics, Volume 3*, London and New York: Macmillan and Stockton.

Krugman, Paul and Robin Wells (2010), 'The slump goes on: why?', *NY Review of Books*, 30 September 2010, available at: <http://www.nybodes.com/articles/archives/2010/sep/30/slump-goes.why/>.

Lienemeyer, Max and Karl Soukup (2008), 'The Rescue and Restructuring Guidelines – State aid to companies in difficulties', in *EU Competition Law, Volume IV State Aid Book Two*, Leuven: Claeys & Casteels, ch. 7, 1069–1121.

Nicolaides, Phedon and Mihalis Kekelekis (2005), 'When do Firms in Trouble Escape from State Aid Rules? Part II', *European State Aid Law*, **1**, 17–25.

Sinn, Hans-Werner (2010), *Casino Capitalism: How the Financial Crisis Came About and What Needs to be Done Now*, Oxford: Oxford University Press.

Werner, Philip and Martina Maier (2009), 'Procedure in crisis? Overview and assessment of the Commission's State aid procedure during the current crisis', *European State Aid Law*, **2**, 177–186.

8   The concept of selectivity?
Andreas Bartosch

Like a human being the concept of selectivity has two legs. One is its geographical dimension, the other its material one. Whilst the former has been clarified to a large extent by the EU Courts in the more recent past, the latter still remains a highly controversial subject as is evidenced by the numerous publications that have been dedicated to it.[1]

One of the conditions of the prohibition on the granting of State aid laid down in Article 107 TFEU is 'the favouring of certain undertakings or the production of certain goods' which is commonly referred to as the notion of selectivity. This concept of selectivity consists of two components, the first component being a *geographical* one, meaning in essence that a measure is selective if undertakings in a specific part of the entire territory of a Member State are treated differently, that is, more favourably than in the rest of this territory, and, the second component, a *material* one looking at all other forms of unequal treatment of undertakings by the intervention of a Member State.

This chapter covers both notions of selectivity, but places greater emphasis on the much more controversial concept of material selectivity. As will be explored in some detail on the basis of the pertinent jurisprudence of the EU Courts, I assert that the same rules apply when it comes to selectivity, whether material or geographical, inside and outside the area of fiscal measures.

I.   GEOGRAPHICAL SELECTIVITY

The notion of territorial or geographic selectivity has been largely resolved by recent jurisprudence.[2] Whether or not a given measure is geographically selective or not, depends first of all on the following:

- *First*, if the central government of a given Member State is competent to adopt a given measure and then decides to apply this measure only in a given geographical area that forms not the entirety, but only a part of its territory, this measure is per se geographically selective.
- *Second*, if the competence for the adoption of a given measure lies with a public body below the level of the central government, for

example, a regional or a local authority, the fact that one such body creates a measure more favourable than another one does not render this measure geographically selective. In this scenario it is not possible to identify any 'normal' measure on the central government level that the measure under (State aid) review would deviate from.

–   *Third*, if on the one side there is such a 'normal' measure on the central government level, but on the other side the central State has granted a certain degree of autonomous competencies to a specific region that then makes use of this autonomy, the measure under review will escape the verdict of geographical selectivity only if the competence of the autonomous body qualifies to be institutionally, procedurally and financially autonomous.[3]

Despite the Commission's attempt to argue in favour of a fourth criterion in the third of the aforementioned three scenarios, that is, that the autonomous body must play a fundamental role in the definition of the political and economic environment,[4] both EU Courts have unanimously rejected this proposition Moreover, the Courts stated that whenever the three forms of autonomy were present, the autonomous body automatically played a fundamental role in this region's political and economic environment.[5]

When it comes to the interpretation of the aforementioned three facets of autonomy the EU Courts have clarified as follows:

–   *First*, for the presence of institutional autonomy it suffices that the institutions of the region enjoy a particular political and administrative status without there being any requirement as to the latter's degree.[6]

–   *Second*, as for procedural autonomy the CJEU merely requires that the central government must not have the possibility to influence the content of the autonomous powers. The mere existence of a consultation mechanism that was regarded to exclude this criterion by the Advocate General in the *Azores* case[7] is no obstacle as long as the central government is not able to impose a certain measure in case the consultation process does not result in an agreement.[8] The General Court showed an even higher degree of liberalism in holding that it suffices that the central government never intervened in the exercise of the autonomous powers in practice whilst it held it to be immaterial if such a competence existed in a legal sense.[9]

–   *Third*, the financial autonomy is not jeopardized by the mere existence of a financial transfer or solidarity system by which the central government offsets losses of the autonomous region. Such a system, that was regarded against the existence of this third requirement in the *Azores* ruling, does not render the measure under review to be geographically selective. Moreover, the CJEU requires the existence of a causal link or relationship between the advantages granted and the compensatory transfers by the central administration.[10]

II.   MATERIAL SELECTIVITY

Contrary to the clarity achieved when it comes to the notion of geographical selectivity, the concept of material selectivity is still far from there. The concept of material selectivity has developed into the decisive tool by which the Commission and ultimately the European Courts determine the freedom (still) enjoyed by Member States to pursue their different policies (for example, environmental, social, economic) outside the ambit of the prohibition laid down by Article 107(1) TFEU and therefore outside any obligation to notify the Commission of a given measure.

Subsequent to two rulings by the General Court by which a more limited interpretation seemed to develop,[11] the CJEU has in the meantime overturned one of them by adopting a much more conservative approach.[12] The latter has also received some attention by academic writers.[13]

In general terms I hold, as briefly mentioned in the beginning of this contribution, that the rules pertaining to material selectivity are not at all limited to the field in which they have been discussed most frequently, that is, in the area of fiscal measures. The notion of material selectivity has a by far greater and more general role to play than only in the limited field of taxation where it is mostly discussed and debated. Without giving any particular justification or reason for this, the jurisprudence of the EU Courts has conducted the very same assessment as developed in relation to fiscal measures in a number of other areas. It has been applied to a reduction of licence fees granted by the State.[14] In the Dutch *NOx* case (which bears a particular importance with regard to this chapter) an emission trading system by which certain large undertakings were granted the right to trade emission certificates was assessed in this way.[15] In two different Spanish cases it was applied to cheap loans to facilitate the acquisition of commercially used vehicles and thereby the renovation of the fleets of such vehicles in the interest of road safety and ecology.[16] This shows that the specific assessment of material selectivity as it has conceived for the purposes of evaluating fiscal measures has spread to a number of other areas. It is submitted that the analysis as to material selectivity does not differ depending on whether a scheme of fiscal advantages or any scheme outside this (limited) area is under State aid review.[17]

II.i.   The Jurisprudence of the EU Courts

Before entering into a (first) analysis of how the jurisprudence has so far interpreted the concept of material selectivity, it seems appropriate to have a look at the way the Courts have conducted their assessment. The test regularly commences by step 1, intended to find out whether a given measure or scheme is prima facie selective, that is, whether it provides for an unequal treatment of at least two groups of undertakings that prima facie should be treated equally. If such can be ascertained, the analysis proceeds to step 2 by which the Courts ask whether such prima facie selectivity could still be justified by the nature or general scheme of the system the measure/scheme under (State aid) review belongs to.[18] However, at times the analysis does not strictly follow this pattern as some judgments tend to merge these steps.[19]

When looking at the jurisprudence of the EU Courts, one cannot fail to see that the notion of material selectivity is, from the perspective of the Member States, a worryingly broad one.[20] Only a very limited range of national measures are then capable of avoiding the verdict of falling under the State aid ban of the Treaty. First of all, there are all the measures that indiscriminately apply to all undertakings operating in a given Member State.[21] In a somewhat exceptional case the Commission has accepted once that a measure where the identity of its beneficiaries is not yet clear at the moment of its adoption may also escape the classification of being (materially) selective.[22] Otherwise, it has been held to be entirely immaterial that the beneficiaries are selected according to predetermined objective criteria, that the budget allocated to the measure under (State aid) review has been fixed or that an indefinite number of undertakings may qualify as beneficiaries.[23] Likewise the fact that the measure covers a whole sector of the economy[24] or even several[25] is not apt to put it outside this broad concept, either. The same applies if it is (only) certain objective criteria that predetermine the economic sectors that may benefit from a given measure.[26] Even if all economic sectors are covered, the differentiation between undertakings with, and without, export activities has been held to be sufficient to justify the finding of a (potential) selectivity.[27] The same applies if the Member State authority exercises any form of discretion in the selection of the beneficiaries or the extent to which they may benefit from a given scheme.[28]

The correctness of such a broad approach has been questioned in Opinions of different Advocates General and by a number of legal writers. Advocate General Jacobs remarked that the establishment of a general rule that aid in favour of the national production is per se not capable of constituting a general measure risked the dividing line between illicit State aid and general economic policy of a Member State becoming blurred.[29] Likewise, Advocate General Geelhoed expressed his concerns that an overly extensive concept of what is a (materially) selective (tax) measure could effectively deprive Member States of making use of competences that the Treaty had assigned to them.[30] Throughout the years academic writers have expressed similar thoughts, for example by deliberating whether the selectivity criterion could be used to introduce some 'rule of reason' test[31] into State aid law; whether an effects-based approach (relating to the mere effects of a measure under State aid review) would be the correct approach when looking at selectivity;[32] or, whether it would be best to distinguish between objectives of general policy/general interest which were to be permissible and other specific objectives that were not.[33]

The aforementioned represents only a very sketchy image of the notion of material selectivity. A closer look at the jurisprudence of the European Courts reveals however that this broadness reflected by so many judgments does not take into account the considerable degree of freedom that Member States (still) enjoy on its very basis.

II.i.a.   The objectives-oriented approach of *Adria-Wien*

In its landmark judgment in *Adria-Wien Pipeline*[34] the CJEU had to rule on whether the Austrian *Energieabgabenvergütungsgesetz*, a law granting a rebate on energy taxes to undertakings that were primarily active in the manufacturing of goods rather than in the provision of services, amounted to a selective advantage. In a first step the Court had regarded it to be material to enquire whether:

> . . .under a particular statutory regime, a State measure is such as to favour certain undertakings or the production of certain goods within the meaning of Article 92(1) of the Treaty (Article 107(1) TFEU) in comparison with other undertakings which are in a legal and factual situation which is comparable in the light of the objective pursued by the measure in question.[35]

For the first time in the jurisprudence of the EU Courts, the *objective* pursued by a Member State was regarded to be decisive for the determination of whether a State measure could be regarded to be prima facie selective. Following this initial statement the Court immediately continued by asking the further question whether the advantage conferred by the measure, 'is justified by the nature or general scheme of the measure *of* which it is part'.[36] In its further analysis the Court then remarked that neither could there be found a general principle in the statutory regime under review that undertakings primarily active in the manufacturing sector should benefit in a particular way nor that such undertakings were more energy-intensive than those active in the provision of services, nor that the environmental objectives underlying the measure under review justified any sort of differentiated treatment of these two groups of undertakings.[37]

The ruling in *Adria-Wien* seems to somewhat merge the two steps traditionally taken when assessing whether a measure under State aid review is to be classified as materially selective. Several judgments of the EU Courts[38] and the Commission Notice on the application of the State aid rules to measures relating to direct business taxation[39] regularly perform the above-mentioned two-step test asking, firstly, whether one group of undertakings is in receipt of an advantage denied to another group and secondly whether such differentiation is justified by the nature or general scheme of the measure of which it forms part. In *Adria-Wien* it has been clearly stated that the statutory Austrian regime was regarded to be selective, first, because the two groups of undertakings, that is, the ones primarily active in the manufacturing sector and the ones active in providing services, were seen to be in a comparable legal and factual situation with regard to the objectives pursued by the regime under review and, second, because these objectives provided no justification whatsoever to treat them any differently. However, the Court of Justice clearly accepted the primordial role to be played by the objectives defined by the Member State itself when devising a regime that differentiated between two (or more) different groups of undertakings. Whether this is done within step one, or step two, or even in both steps, is immaterial to the outcome of the exercise. What matters is that in *Adria–Wien* the Court was willing to accept a clearly objectives-based approach in the area of material selectivity.

II.i.b. The rulings of the General Court in *British Aggregates* and *Dutch NOx*

The acknowledgment of objectives pursued by a Member State in the assessment of whether a given regime may grant selective advantages to one or more groups of undertakings in relation to one or more others has been fully endorsed by the General Court in two subsequent rulings, one of which has since been set aside by the Court and with the other still under an appeal lodged by the Commission.

Interestingly, one of these judgments stems from the area of fiscal measures whereas the other concerns a completely different subject matter. Furthermore, the factual scenarios underlying these two rulings differ insofar as the first one is based on the complaint of a competitor, namely a competitors´ association that attacked the Commission´s finding of non-selectivity and the second one on the Member State´s viewpoint that a measure notified by it did not amount to an illegal State aid as it did not confer any selective advantage whereas the Commission adopted a (mere) compatibility decision. This further distinction should also be carefully kept in mind for purposes of the subsequent assessment of both rulings.

In *British Aggregates* the United Kingdom had imposed a levy on so-called 'virgin aggregates' extracted from nature, the so-called aggregates levy (AGL), whereas recycled aggregates were exempted from this. In this the Member State pursued the intention to encourage the use of recycled aggregates, whereas the need for the extraction of virgin aggregates from nature was meant to be reduced. The plaintiff, the British Aggregates Association, challenged the Commission's Decision holding that the scheme introducing the levy did not amount to an illegal State aid as it lacked the requirement of material selectivity.[40] The General Court upheld the Commission's assessment reasoning as follows: given the absence of any sort of harmonization as to environmental policies and referring to Article 11 TFEU calling for the requirements of the protection of the environment to be taken into account when interpreting the different provisions of the Treaty the Member States were deemed to be:

> . . . free, in balancing the various interests involved, to set their priorities as regards the protection of the environment and, as a result, to decide which goods or services they are to decide to subject to an environmental levy.[41]

The Court continued:

> .. the mere fact that an environmental levy constitutes a specific measure, that extends to certain designated goods or services, and cannot be seen as an overall system of taxation which applies to all similar activities that have a comparable effect on the environment, does not mean that similar activities, which are not subject to the levy, benefit from a selective advantage.[42]

Furthermore, the Court distinguished the factual scenario underlying this case from the one in *Adria-Wien* stating that in the latter case the CJEU had to consider not the material scope of an environmental levy as in the case at hand, but moreover the partial exemption from the payment of such a levy that had been granted to a certain group of undertakings.[43] Most strikingly perhaps the judges were willing to accept the power of the Member States to set their priorities in the economic, fiscal and environmental fields, 'even if based on the desire to maintain the international competitiveness of certain sectors', as was the declared aim of the levy imposed on 'virgin aggregates'.[44] As it is apparent from the brief summary of this ruling the judges granted a maximum of freedom to the Member States to pursue the different goals of their various national policies and did not establish any boundaries to such freedom, even allowing the express desire to enhance the competitiveness of certain economic sectors.

The further judgment of the General Court, concerning a system of emission trading notified by the Dutch government, is likewise remarkable as it not only provides a further example of the considerable leeway that this Court has been willing to grant to Member States in advancing their different policies (at least in the environmental field), but also pertains not to a fiscal advantage, but moreover to a quasi-direct grant.[45] Under the notified scheme certain large industrial facilities amounting to an approximate number of 250 were granted the right to freely trade emission certificates on the market. Hence, it was possible for any such large undertaking to observe the maximum thresholds for its NOx emissions either by way of modernizing its facilities or by acquiring the emission certificates from another undertaking or by a combination of these two methods. The tradability of these certificates granted to these large undertakings by the scheme under review for free in lieu of being sold or auctioned was classified as an advantage granted through State resources as the State chose to forgo revenues it would have had if it had opted for one of these other two possibilities.[46]

The General Court, in expressly relying on the *Adria-Wien* ruling, then identified the notified scheme as the 'measure in question' in relation to which it would have to assess whether the group of undertakings benefitting from the advantage (arising from the free tradability of the certificates), that is, the approximately 250 large facilities, and others not benefitting were in 'a comparable factual and legal situation'. This was answered in the negative as the measure was limited to those large undertakings which, in case they exceeded a maximum level of emissions set under the national legislation, were liable to pay fines whereas this did not apply to all other undertakings being smaller. Hence the scheme was not regarded to be prima facie selective. In the alternative, the General Court stated that, in case this argument of the lack of prima facie selectivity were not to be accepted, the differentiation would anyhow be justified by the ecological considerations which formed the nature and general scheme of the system under review.[47]

II.i.c.   The appeal ruling in *British Aggregates*

Both rulings of the General Court have been appealed, with one appeal decided and the other pending.[48] In the first appeal, decided on 22 December 2008, the CJEU fully endorsed the criticisms voiced in the Opinion of Advocate General Mengozzi delivered on 17 July 2008.[49] Both the Advocate General and the Court held that pursuant to a consistent jurisprudence of the CJEU the objective pursued by a measure under review was not capable of excluding the existence of an aid under Article 107(1) TFEU, but that this prohibition did not distinguish measures according to their causes or objectives, but merely defined them in relation to their effects.[50] On this premise the Court of Justice rejected outright the objectives-based approach followed by the General Court. Finally it saw its assessment confirmed insofar as the General Court had held that:

> potential inconsistencies in the definition of the scope of the AGL in relation to the environmental objectives pursued may be justified, even if they are based on objectives unrelated to environmental protection, such as the desire to maintain the international competitiveness of certain sectors.[51]

II.ii.   The Analysis of this Line of Jurisprudence

At a first glance there seems to be an irreconcilable tension between the older ruling in *Adria-Wien* that in principle accepts an objectives-based solution so as to exclude material selectivity and the blunt effects-based approach presented by the CJEU in *British Aggregates*. Therefore it is first to be ascertained whether *Adria-Wien* can still be regarded as 'good law' or whether it has effectively been overruled by the judgment of 22 December 2008. First, it is remarkable that this later judgment still expressly quotes *Adria-Wien*, but not in relation to the first step of the analysis, the prima facie existence of material selectivity, but only with regard to the second, that is, the justification by the nature and general scheme of the system of which it forms part.[52]

This would in principle allow for assuming the ongoing relevance of the 2001 ruling as it is impossible to reject the existence of an objectives-based approach and at the same time accept the relevance of such objectives when turning to the justification test. This might again not be the final answer as paragraph 54 of the *Adria-Wien* ruling (as referred to by the Court in its judgment of 22 December 2008) only concerns the (alternative) argument put forward that the objective to preserve the competitiveness of the Austrian manufacturing sector would not be capable of providing a justification for the prima facie selective differentiation between this and the services sector. In this the facts in *Adria-Wien* and in *British Aggregates* are identical insofar as both schemes under review, that is, the Austrian *Energieabgabenvergütungsgesetz* and the AGL had the express intention to improve the competitiveness of a specific sector of the (national) economy. This was (rightly) rejected by the CJEU in *Adria-Wien* and, in my view, surprisingly accepted by the General Court in *British Aggregates*. The express quotation of the older ruling may therefore not have any significance as to the (still) open question of whether it can still be relied on. It may therefore be more elucidating to have a closer look at those judgments which in *British Aggregates* the CJEU quoted in support of its effects-based approach. First, the Court quotes paragraph 79 of its ruling in *Kimberley Clark*[53] where the standard phrase can be found that Article 107 (1) TFEU does not distinguish between the causes and aims of a measure, but defines them in relation to their effects. However, the same paragraph likewise states that, if objectively justified by entrepreneurial reasons, the fact alone that a measure under review likewise pursues a political goal does not cast on it the verdict of falling under the State aid ban of the Treaty. Hence, quite to the contrary, an analysis of this first quotation moreover seems to support the finding that the fact that a scheme serves to implement a certain policy of the Member State does not automatically render it materially selective.

Second, in *France v. Commission*,[54] likewise quoted by the CJEU in *British Aggregates*, the Court had merely stated that the fact alone that the scheme under review in that case, (the *Fonds national de l'emploi*) pursued a goal of social policy could not automatically put it outside the ambit of the ban on State aid.[55] This statement is in no way incompatible with the principal acceptance of objectives pursued by a Member State to be taken into account when assessing whether a given scheme is materially selective. In *Adria-Wien* the Court expressed its willingness to accept the ecological goals of the *Energieabgabenvergütungsgesetz*, but then had to conclude that the differentiation between the manufacturing and the services sectors did not constitute a logical implementation of this goal. Moreover, it stated that another objective of this measure had been the improvement of the competitiveness of the Austrian manufacturing industry, the latter not qualifying as a permissible objective so as to exclude the existence of (material) selectivity. In *Kimberly Clark* the Court did not let the fact that the French FNE pursued goals of social policy suffice so as to immediately classify it to be materially selective. It merely regarded this not to be sufficient to rule out such a finding from the outset. The verdict of selectivity was moreover based, and fully consistent with, a constant line of jurisprudence initiated by this very judgment[56] on the presence of a discretion enjoyed by the FNE in determining the amount of its financial contributions.[57]

Thirdly, the famous *Maribel* ruling likewise quoted by the CJEU[58] in its judgment of 22 December 2008 contains exactly the same reasoning as that in *Kimberley Clark*. In that case it had not been the pursuit of social policy goals per se that automatically rendered the Belgian scheme by which social security contributions had been reduced to promote the creation of jobs to be materially selective, but moreover the exclusion of certain economic sectors from its ambit in contradiction to this very (social) aim.[59] In other words, it was not the fact that a given scheme had pursued certain goals which had been harmful, but moreover that the implementation of the scheme did not adequately reflect these goals.

Fourthly, in *Spain v. Commission*[60] likewise quoted in *British Aggregates*[61] one can only find the very general statement that State measures are not automatically exempt from the application of the ban on State aid because of their social character.[62] However true this is, it has no specific relevance to the notion of material selectivity as discussed herein. Solely the ruling in *Spain v. Commission*[63] is somewhat more ambiguous when it comes to the issue that forms the subject matter of my analysis. Here, a scheme was to be assessed which granted certain advantages both to individuals and to undertakings qualifying as SMEs in order to provide an incentive for them to renew their commercial vehicle fleets. On the one hand the Court expressly quotes the relevant paragraph 41 of the *Adria-Wien* ruling stressing the relevant 'statutory regime' and the 'objective pursued by the measure in question'.[64] Furthermore it states that Spain has not produced 'any evidence of any system of charges in the general interest'.[65] On the other hand, besides the general hint to the effects-based approach the CJEU likewise expressly states that, even if the Member State had been successful in providing evidence of such objectives, these would be, 'however legitimate', ineffective with regard to the assessment of a national measure under Article 107(1) TFEU.[66] Whereas the prima facie selectivity of the Spanish scheme is (correctly) answered in the positive on the basis of its differentiation between individuals and SMEs benefitting from it and large undertakings excluded from it, the Court nevertheless uses a very strong wording suggesting that it regards the pursuit of national policies to be immaterial when it comes to the assessment of whether a given measure is materially selective or not. Still, *Adria-Wien* is, somewhat contradictorily, expressly quoted in support of this premise. Moreover, the differentiation between these two groups did not seem to be justified in the light of the goals advocated by the Spanish government, i.e. the protection of the environment and the safety of road traffic as it did not become clear why these mandated the exclusion of large undertakings from benefitting from the scheme.

However unsatisfactory the outcome of this analysis may be, the overwhelming majority of statements made by the Court of Justice support the finding that, even after 22 December 2008, the *Adria-Wien* ruling can still be relied on when it comes to the assessment of a State measure under the heading of material selectivity.

III. OWN ASSESSMENT

III.i. The Distinction Between Permissible and Impermissible Objectives

Given the inconsistencies of the jurisprudence on the notion of material selectivity it is of foremost importance to find a concept that strikes the right balance between the protection of competition as mandated by Article 107(1) TFEU and a (sensible) degree of freedom enjoyed by the Member States to pursue different political goals without having to notify each and every measure pursuant to Article 108(3) TFEU. Material selectivity has therefore become the very battleground on which Member States are fighting for their freedom to pursue different policies of various kinds with immunity from the scrutiny exercised by the State aid watchdog.

Whereas in my view, as analysed in detail before, an objectives-oriented approach as introduced by *Adria-Wien* is (still) acceptable, it however becomes clear that State aid control would be deprived of all its meaning if Member States were permitted to use all sorts of political objectives that they may reasonably or unreasonably come up with in order to argue that a measure fails to qualify as materially selective.[67] Conversely, as it was most aptly expressed by the former Advocate General Geelhoed in his Opinion in the *GIL Insurance* case,[68] an overly extensive concept of selectivity will serve to deprive the Member States of competencies they enjoy pursuant to the Treaty provisions. In other words, if any sort of objective defined by a Member State justified a second guess to be exercised by the Commission in the framework of its compatibility assessment, such would paralyse Member States' legislative and administrative activities almost completely as one cannot possibly think of any measure adopted either in the fiscal area or otherwise that is not based on one kind of political objective or another, may this be economic, social, ecological.

It is submitted that in striking the right balance by differentiating between permissible or 'good' and impermissible or 'bad' objectives meaning that the former can be pursued by way of a measure granting advantages whereas the latter must not.

In this, ecological objectives seem to be prima facie 'good' ones. *Adria-Wien* has demonstrated that State aid law is in essence willing to accommodate a much broader concept of Member States' freedom when it comes to the assessment of whether a given measure is selective or not. The ecological concerns underlying the Austrian *Energieabgabenvergütungsgesetz* serve as a classic example. It may be inferred that other political motives, based on considerations of a social, cultural or educative kind may be just as good. Conversely, the jurisprudence has identified a number of objectives that would have to be qualified as 'bad' ones, meaning that if a Member State's measure pursued them, it would not be acceptable to define it as falling outside the concept of material selectivity. Such objectives are in particular economic ones, such as the tackling of unemployment in a particular region or the enhancement of the latter's attractiveness for (foreign) investors.[69]

For the same reason the Commission has regarded a number of national tax measures that were intended to attract multinational groups of under-takings to the territory of the Member State to be materially selective.[70] In *Adria-Wien* the Court had regarded it as a further argument underscoring its verdict that the provisions of the statutory measure under review con-stituted a materially selective aid, that the statement of reasons which had led to the bill for the Austrian *Energieabgabenvergütungsgesetz* had clearly stated that its intention was to enhance the competitiveness of the national manufacturing sector in relation to those of other Member States.[71]

The ruling of the General Court in *British Aggregates* was the very first that deviated from this clear line of jurisprudence as it evolved in the aftermath of *Adria-Wien* by holding that, even if the differentiation was spurred by the Member State's desire to enhance the competitiveness of a given sector, this could not give rise to any verdict of selectivity.[72] It was to be expected that the Court of Justice would correct this apparent devia-tion from its former jurisprudence[73] as such would have indeed opened the floodgates for Member States, inventiveness to argue the non-selectivity of measures even if they had clear-cut goals of distorting the competitive environment in favour of certain (domestic) industries or specific under-takings. This means that all considerations of improving the competitive-ness of certain undertakings, industries, sectors or regions are from the very outset impermissible and consequently give rise to selectivity. The same applies, as it has already been clarified by the judgment in *Adria-Wien* if these goals are not the principal ones pursued by a given scheme or measure, but moreover merely ancillary to the main goals which may be of a different, permissible nature.

III.ii. The Relevance of Mere Effects

The aforementioned suggestion does not solve the crucial issue raised by the appeal ruling in *British Aggregates* of whether (material) selectivity can possibly still be identified on the basis of mere effects of a State measure, whether direct or indirect, on competition. Following this an indissolu-ble tension seems to exist between the (still permissible) objectives-based approach in *Adria-Wien* and the mere effects based approach of the CJEU ruling in *British Aggregates*. If mere effects-on competition were to suffice, then one would have to seriously doubt whether there could still be any State measure conferring economic advantages (direct or indirect) that could escape State aid control. Even those schemes that apply to all undertakings active in a given Member State (and thereby falling outside the ambit of the notion of material selectivity) would then be caught as it is evident that they would improve the competitiveness of all sectors in a given Member State in relation to those in the other Member States.

This would run counter to another principle of State aid law that selective advantages may never arise by way of a comparison of diverging factual and legal circumstances as they exist in the individual Member States.[74] Even outside this extreme scenario every measure conferring advantages on undertakings will in one way or the other improve their competitive position, even if this is completely unintended by the scheme or other measure under review. A tax scheme that for example provides incentives for the renovation of old buildings (for reasons of planning considerations) will render their owners more competitive in the rental market. Likewise, a measure that provides tax advantages to the buyers of environmentally friendly cars will improve the competitive standing of those manufacturers that are the first movers in the related environmental technologies; moreover, it will grant a competitive edge to the developers and producers of such technology.

IV. CONCLUSION

This chapter on the concept of selectivity provides a concise, but thorough overview of the state of the EU Courts' jurisprudence and the Commission practice on the two limbs of the selectivity criteria. When it comes to *geographical selectivity*, a high degree of legal certainly in combination with a more liberal approach on autonomous regions and their competences is working very much to the delight of Member States. The same cannot be said in the area of *material selectivity*. Here, the jurisprudence of the EU Courts is highly casuistic, at times conflicting and in essence apparently advocating a wide concept of material selectivity. This appears to require the Member States to notify all, and every measure, that may grant economic advantages pursuant to Article 108(3) TFEU in order to abide by the State aid discipline of the EU. Foremost, but by no means exclusively, tax measures will in almost all cases involve such advantages. If all of these were to be notified, the Commission could eventually become the super board of control of national fiscal policies and end up being bestowed with the competence to revisit the pursuit of any sort of Member State policies, however unrelated these were to the competition concerns that the State aid rules are meant to address. In order to strike the right balance between an effective competition policy and enforcement on the one side and a proper respect for Member States´ sovereign right to conduct different policies that are untouched by harmonization measures on EU level, I suggest differentiating between permissible or 'good' objectives that Member States may pursue without having to justify them in terms of State aid control and impermissible or 'bad' objectives that render a given measure materially selective. For sure, despite the apparent attraction this approach has one should not underestimate the practical difficulties it may entail. Not every measure is based on clear-cut 'good' or 'bad' objectives. Many may feature a mixture of both. In many cases it may be uncertain which objective is the *main* objective and which one is a side or subsidiary objective. More seriously, the borderline between objectives and effects may be effectively blurred. Not all legislative acts may be so transparent as the *Energieabgabenvergütungsgesetz* in *Adria-Wien*. As in life generally, the fear that a task might be difficult to perform should not stop us from taking it on. Difficulties may indeed be lying in its path and not all of them might be resolved to the perfectionist's standards. But this is still much better than depriving Member States of their freedom to pursue independent policies without the undue interference of EU State aid control.

NOTES

1. See, inter alia: López 2010; Bartosch 2010; Honoré 2009; Cruz Vilaça 2009; Rossi-Maccanico 2009; Bousin and Piernas 2008.
2. See Case C-88/03, *Portugal v. Commission (Azores)* [2006] E.C.R. I-7115; Joined Cases C-428 to 434/06, *UGT Rioja et al.* [2008] E.C.R. [6747]. More recently, Case T-75/03, *Banco Comercial dos Acores v. Commission* [2009] E.C.R. 143.
3. Case C-88/03, *Portugal v. Commission (Azores)* [2006] E.C.R. I-7115, paras. 64 *et seq.*
4. This requirement had indeed been mentioned in the 2006 *Azores* ruling, ibid, para. 66.
5. Joined Cases C-428 to 434/06, *UGT Rioja et al.*, supra n. 2, paras. 53 *et seq.*; Cases T-211/04 and T-215/04, *Gibraltar v. Commission*, n.y.r., paras. 87–88.
6. Joined Cases C-428 to 434/06, *UGT Rioja et al.*, supra n. 2, paras. 77 *et seq.*
7. See the Opinion of Advocate General Geelhoed in Case C-88/03, *Portugal v. Commission (Azores)* [2006] E.C.R. I-7115, at para. 69.
8. Joined Cases C-428 to 434/06, *UGT Rioja et al.*, supra n. 2, paras. 96 *et seq.*
9. Cases T-211/04 and T-215/04, *Gibraltar v.* Commission, n.y.r., paras. 95–97.
10. Joined Cases C-428 to 434/06, *UGT Rioja et al.*, supra n. 2, paras. 135 *et seq.*
11. Case T-210/02, *British Aggregates v. Commission* [2006] E.C.R. II-2789 and Case T-233/04, *Netherlands v. Commission* [2008] E.C.R. II–591.
12. Case C-487/06 P, *British Aggregates v. Commission* [2008] E.C.R. 10505.
13. See da Cruz Vilaça 2009; Honoré 2009. Cf. in more general terms: Bartosch 2009, paras. 85 and 107.
14. Case T-475/04, *Bouygues v. Commission* [2007] E.C.R. II-2097, para. 106; confirmed by Case C-431/07 P [2009] E.C.R. 2665.
15. N 327/2008 and N238/2008.
16. Case T-55/99, *CETM* [2000] E.C.R. II-3207; Case C-501/00, *Spain v. Commission* [2004] E.C.R. I-6717.
17. Cf. Bartosch 2010.
18. Cf. the three-step approach also advocated in the more recent ruling in Joined Cases T-211/04 and T-215/04, *Gibraltar* [2008] E.C.R. II-3745. [On appeal: Case C-106-107/09P].
19. See the analysis provided by Honoré 2009: 530–31.
20. As to this criticism see also, most recently, López 2010: 807 *et seq.*
21. Case C-43/99, *Adria-Wien Pipeline* [2001] E.C.R. I-8365, para. 35; Case C-156/98, *Germany v. Commission* [2000] E.C.R. I-6857, para. 22.

22. N-674/01 – *Italy* – measures for the regularization of underground activities; compare however C 66/2002 – *United Kingdom* – *Gibraltar Government Corporation Tax Reform* where the small number of beneficiaries, that is, work-intensive undertakings, led the Commission to assume the selective character of the measure under review although it was in no way clear how these could be identified in an ex ante assessment.
23. Case T-55/99, *CETM* [2000] E.C.R. II-3207, para. 40.
24. Case C-75/97, *Belgium v. Commission (Maribel)* [1999] E.C.R. I-3671, para. 33; Case C-148/04, *Unicredito* [2005] E.C.R. I-11137, para. 45.
25. Case C-172/03, *Wolfgang Heiser v. Finanzamt Innsbruck* [2005] E.C.R. I-162, paras. 42–43.
26. Case 173/73, *Italy v. Commission* [1974] E.C.R. 709, para. 15; Case T-55/99, *CETM* [2000] E.C.R. II-3207, para. 40.
27. Case C-501/00, *Spain v. Commission* [2004] E.C.R. I-6717, para. 120.
28. Case C-241/94, *France v. Commission (Kimberley Clark)* [1996] E.C.R. I-4551, para. 24.
29. Opinion of 7 May 1996 in Case C-41/94, *France v. Commission* [1996] E.C.R. I-4551, para. 30.
30. Advocate General Geelhoed, Opinion of 18 September 2003 in Case C-308/01, *GIL Insurance* [2004] E.C.R. I-4777, para. 76.
31. Hancher 2003: 366–368.
32. Honoré 2009: 534 *et seq.*
33. Kurcz and Vallindas 2008: 177 *et seq.*
34. Case C-143/99, *Adria-Wien Pipeline* [2001] E.C.R. I-6857.
35. Ibid, para. 41.
36. Ibid, para. 42.
37. Ibid, paras. 48-52.
38. Case C-75/97, *Belgium v. Commission (Maribel)* [1999] E.C.R. I-3671, paras. 23 *et seq.* and paras. 32 *et seq.* Joined Cases T-227 to 229/01, T-265-266/01 and T-270/01, *Territorio Histórico de Álava et al.*, n.y.r.
39. O.J. 1998 C 384/3.
40. Commission, 24 April 2002, N 863/01.
41. Case T-210/02, *British Aggregates v. Commission* [2006] E.C.R. II-2789, para. 115.
42. Ibid.
43. Ibid, paras 120–121.
44. Ibid, para. 128.
45. Case T-233/04, *Netherlands v. Commission* [2008] E.C.R. II-591.
46. Ibid, paras. 63–78.
47. Ibid, paras. 86–99.
48. Case C-487/06 P, *British Aggregates v. Commission* [2008] E.C.R. I-10505; Case C–279/08 P, *Commission v. Netherlands* O.J. 2008 L 223/30.
49. Ibid.
50. See Opinion of 17 July 2008, para. 96 and judgment of 22 December 2008, para. 83.
51. Ibid, para. 88.
52. Ibid, para. 88.
53. Case C-56/93, *Belgium v. Commission* [1996] E.C.R. I-723.
54. Case C-241/94, *France v. Commission* [1996] E.C.R. I-4551.
55. Ibid, para. 21.
56. See Commission Notice on the Application of the State aid rules to Measures Relating to Direct Business Taxation, O.J. 1998, C 384/3, paras. 21–22; cf. Joined Cases T-127-129/99 and T-48/99, *Territorio histórico de Álava et al.* [2002] E.C.R. II-1275, para. 154.
57. Case C-241/94, *France v. Commission (Kimberly Clark)* [1996] E.C.R. I-4551, para. 23.
58. Case C–5/97, *Belgium v. Commission* [1999] E.C.R. I-3671, para. 22.
59. Ibid, paras. 29–31.
60. Case C-342/96, [1999] E.C.R. I-2459.
61. Case C-487/06 P, *British Aggregates v. Commission* [2008] ECR I-10505.
62. Case C-342/96, *Spain v. Commission* [1999] E.C.R. I-2459, para. 23.

63. Case C-409/00 *Spain v. Commission* [2003] E.C.R. I-1487.
64. Ibid, para. 47.
65. Ibid, para. 53.
66. Ibid, para. 54.
67. See also Kurcz and Vallindas 2008: 173.
68. Opinion of Advocate General Geelhoed in Case C–308/01, *GIL Insurance* [2004] E.C.R. I-4777, para. 76.
69. Joined Cases T-127/99-T-129/99 and T-148/99, *Daewoo Electronics Manufacturing España* [2002] E.C.R. II-1275, para. 167; Joined Cases T-346/99–348/99, *Territorio histórico dé Alava et al. v. Commission* [2002] E.C.R. II-4259, para. 63; Case T-445/05, *Assoziazione italiana del rispramio gestito et. al. v. Commission* [2009] E.C.R. II-289, para. 139; Case T-424/05, *Italy v. Commission* [2009] E.C.R. 23, para. 139.
70. See the detailed account presented by Rossi-Maccanico 2007.
71. Ibid, para. 54.
72. Case T-210/02, *British Aggregates v. Commission* [2006] E.C.R. II-2789, para. 128.
73. Case C-487/06 P, [2008] E.C.R. I-10505, para. 88.
74. Case T-308/00, *Salzgitter v. Commission,* [2004] E.C.R. II-1933, para. 81; cf. the Opinion of Advocate General Maduro of 12 January 2006 in Case C-237/04, *Enirisorse v. Sotacarbo* [2006] E.C.R. I-2843, paras. 43 *et seq.*

REFERENCES

Bartosch, A. (2009), *EU – Beihilfenrecht*, Munich. C.H. Beck.
Bartosch, A. (2010), 'Is there a need for a rule of reason in European State aid law? Or how to arrive at a coherent concept of material selectivity?', *Common Market Law Review*, **47:3**, 729–752.
Bousin, J. and J. Piernas (2008), 'Developments in the Notion of Selectivity', *European State Aid Law*, **7:4**, 634–653
Da Cruz Vilaça, J-L. (2009), 'Material and geographic selectivity in State aid – recent developments', *European State Aid Law,* **8:4**, 443–451.
Hancher, L (2003), 'Towards a new definition of a State aid under European Law: Is there a new concept of State aid emerging?', *European State Aid Law*, **2: 3**, 365–373.
Honoré, M. (2009), 'Selectivity and taxation – reflections in the light of Case C-487/06 P, British Aggregates Association', *European State Aid Law,* **8:4**, 527–537.
Kurcz, B.and Vallindas, D. (2008), 'Can general measures be . . .selective? Some thoughts on the interpretation of a State aid definition', **45**, *Common Market Law Review*, 159–182.
López, H. (2010), 'General thought on selectivity and consequences of a broad concept of State aid in tax matters', *European State Aid Law*, **9:4**, 807–819.
Rossi-Maccanico, P. (2007), 'Commentary of State aid review of multinational tax systems', *European State Aid Law*, **6:2**, 25–42.
Rossi-Maccanico, P. (2009), 'Community review of direct business tax measures: selectivity, discrimination and restrictions', *European State Aid Law*, **8:4**, 489–506.

9   State aid and taxation in EU law
Claire Micheau

I.   INTRODUCTION

The application of State aid law to taxation is a decisive regulatory instrument which can have a significant effect on the internal market. Given the critical importance of taxation systems in national economies, tax measures are a significant tool for Member States to introduce market distortions in order to strengthen some sectors or activities and thereby to support economic, political, strategic or social policies.

Empirical surveys show the importance of State aid in tax matters. It involves considerable amounts of money for the economic stakeholders involved. According to the Commission Scoreboard, tax exemptions accounted for 42% of the share of aid instruments in total aid for industry and services in the Member States in 2008. Consequently, State aids awarded through tax exemption represented the second most important conferral of aid instruments.[1] This amounted to around €19.8 billion.[2] Moreover, the comparison between the periods 2003–2005 and 2006–2008 shows that Member States increasingly introduced State aids in the form of tax exemptions while on average the use of grants remained stable.[3]

The adaptation of the rules governing State aid to direct taxation raises intricate issues, and is at the crossroads of different legal areas (those of tax law, competition law and EU law). It also involves sensitive questions subject to economic concerns. Above all, it deals with taxation which is a sovereign area of Member States. Therefore, applying State aid law to tax measures remains a subtle process where the right balance between political, economic and legal considerations should be found.

In the light of these foregoing considerations, this chapter seeks to provide an overview of the application of State aid law to tax measures. Issues in this regard remain complex and leave room for debate. The topical aspect of State aid law has given rise to an abundant literature.[4] After describing in broad outline the historical background of State aid law in tax matters over the last decades, the chapter will focus on the *substantive* legal framework of tax State aid law. To this end, it will address the definition of tax State aid. Special attention will be given to the decisive criterion of tax selectivity. The chapter will then address issues regarding the *enforcement* framework of tax State aid with regard to tax recovery.

II.   HISTORICAL BACKGROUND

Article 107 TFEU introduces the principle of prohibition of State aids: any aid which can distort competition by favouring certain undertakings or the production of certain goods is prohibited if trade between Member States is affected. This prohibition applies to any type of aid, regardless of its form. It follows that *tax* measures also fall within the scope of Article 107 TFEU. Moreover, although direct taxation is a sovereign competence of each Member State, the CJEU has consistently held that the Member States should exercise that competence consistently with EU law.[5]

In the light of these considerations, the CJEU has applied the rules governing State aids to tax matters since its early case law. The first case which involved tax State aid was referred to the Court in 1961 under the European Coal and Steel Community Treaty.[6] Regarding the application of the EEC Treaty provisions to tax State aids, the founding case was in 1974. In this *Italian textile* case,[7] the CJEU found that a reduction in social security contribution in favour of the textile sector was a State aid. Another noteworthy case, the *Banco Exterior de España* case[8] a ruling some twenty years after the *Italian textile* case, is also considered as a landmark case by the legal literature because it reviews the position adopted and developed by the CJEU in this regard.[9]

Nonetheless, despite the steady application by the CJEU of State aid rules to taxation, the Commission did not take the same approach. For decades, it tended to set aside tax measures from State aid review. The major reason for this reluctance lies in the peculiarity of tax matters. Direct taxation remains a sovereign area of Member States. As such, the Commission preferred not to systemically challenge national tax regimes, which might be inconsistent with Article 107 TFEU. But the situation evolved in the nineties. In order to contribute to the completion of the internal market, Commissioner Mario Monti introduced a new impulse by proposing a global tax strategy in March 1996 (Monti Memorandum).[10] It is against this background that the concept of *harmful tax competition* gained importance.[11]

The ECOFIN Council established a High Level Group which was in charge of addressing harmful tax competition. A second Monti Memorandum was issued in October 1996.[12] On this basis, the Commission published a Communication in 1997 dealing with the notion of harmful tax competition and its limits.[13] The Commission's efforts culminated with the adoption of its proposals by the ECOFIN Council on 1 December 1997. The Council adopted a 'Package to tackle harmful tax competition' which included a Code of Conduct.[14] This Code, which was a non-binding legal instrument, determined a number of criteria for tax measures, which could be considered effectively harmful to competition. On this basis, a Group of Code of Conduct (Primarolo Group, by reference to the group's chairman) identified 66 national tax measures which were regarded as potentially harmful within the meaning of the Code of Conduct.[15] In addition, in December 1998,[16] the Commission issued a Notice on the application of State aid rules to measures relating to direct business taxation in order to clarify the current state of law, to improve transparency and to ensure equality of treatment among the Member States. The Member States sought to roll back existing tax regimes which could challenge State aid discipline and to refrain from enacting new ones. In parallel, the Commission initiated procedures against several national tax schemes. In February 2004[17] the Commission, which had built up a certain body of experience in this regard, released an Implementation Report to provide further clarification on its practice.

To summarize, therefore, the application of State aid rules to taxation is both recent and topical. It is only within the context of harmful tax competition over the last decade that the Commission has systematically applied Article 107 TFEU to national tax regimes on the basis of the 1997 Code of Conduct. In the last ten years, the Commission has developed rules and taken new approaches. At the same time, one has to keep in mind that over a period of 50 years the CJEU had already introduced a legal framework for tax State aid. It is in light of this jurisprudential framework that the Commission has developed its stance. But a number of legal issues are debatable and some gaps remain. On this basis, the chapter will now address some issues regarding the substantive and enforcement frameworks of the law governing tax State aid.

III.   CRITERIA FOR TAX STATE AID

The notion of State aid is governed by substantive criteria which are laid down in the Treaty. The case law and the Commission's practice have applied these criteria to tax measures. By doing so, they have sought to *adapt* these criteria to the peculiarities of direct taxation. This section aims at stressing the main issues that EU practice has to deal with.

III.i.   Criterion of 'State-originated Resources'

According to Article 107 TFEU, a State aid should be granted 'by a Member State' or 'through State resources'. Despite the wording of Article 107 TFEU, the CJEU does not make a clear distinction between aids granted by a Member State or through its resources.[18] Rather, it interprets Article 107 TFEU in such a way that the aid should be *directly* or *indirectly* granted through State resources.[19] In tax matters, this means that the tax aid can be *directly* granted by the State, including not only central governments and national tax authorities but also infra-State entities which enjoy tax powers. In addition, aids can also be *indirectly* granted by State resources, that is, through funds under State control or through public funds performed by non-State bodies.[20]

The criterion of 'State-originated resources' raises interesting issues in tax matters. Firstly, the link between State-origin and advantage can be problematic. For instance, in *Germany* v. *Commission*[21] the German government introduced a tax measure whereby persons and entities established in Germany could set off certain gains arising from a hidden reserve against the cost of purchasing shares in capital companies having their central administration in the new *Länder* or in Berlin. Of particular concern was the fact that revenues saved by individuals were not systematically reinvested into the new companies. Rather, it depended on the individual to make this reinvestment. The CJEU found that there was an advantage *indirectly* granted to companies in the new *Länder* and in Berlin which consisted in enabling investors to take up holdings under advantageous tax conditions. Although investors remained independent in taking their decisions, there was a link between the criteria of 'State origin' and 'advantage' since 'the alteration of the market conditions which gives rise to the advantage is the consequence of the public authorities' loss of tax revenue'.[22] It follows that a tax measure which encouraged individuals or entities to invest in favour of certain undertakings satisfies the criterion of the origin of the advantage because the Member State had renounced tax revenue that it would have normally levied.

In addition, the issue of the transfer of State resources is questionable. It can be debatable whether or not a tax State aid should involve a charge on the public account. In tax matters, this issue is relevant in situations in which a new tax regime changes the legal situation of the undertaking concerned. For instance in *Sloman Neptun*,[23] a German measure enabled certain shipping undertakings flying the German flag to impose conditions and rates of pay less favourable than those applicable to German sailors on seafarers who were nationals of third countries. Although this deregulation of labour law led to a reduction of social security contributions and income tax, the CJEU found that the criterion of State resource was not established because the State was not involved in the relationship between the contributors of the aid (the seafarers who were nationals of third countries) and the recipients (the German ship-owners). This stance was confirmed in the *Preussen Elektra* case,[24] which considered that a new provision, imposing a transfer of funds between private undertakings in the electricity market, and indirectly involving a loss of tax revenue, was not a State aid if there was no direct or indirect transfer of State resource.

Another aspect related to tax aids is the potential positive effect on the public budget. From a Member State's perspective, a tax State aid consists in granting a tax break to certain undertakings. For the Member State, this involves a loss of tax revenue in its public account. However, the tax measure can also have the indirect consequence of attracting investments which have an overall positive effect on the public budget. Consequently, the measure does not result in a loss of revenue, but on the contrary in an increase of investment revenue which would not have been realised otherwise. The question arises then as to whether the measure constitutes a tax aid granted through public resources. However, although there is some force in this debate, the Commission's practice[25] and CJEU case law[26] have consistently refused to consider the indirect positive effects of a tax scheme on the Member State's budget. Only the tax revenue which would have been realized in the absence of the measure should be taken into account regardless of the potential economic effects of the measure.

In sum, it follows from the foregoing that the relevant element to assess the criterion of 'State-originated resources' is the charge on the public account. A State aid should necessarily involve a cost for the Member States' budget.[27] In tax matters, this involves in general a loss of tax revenue. On this basis, it is then irrelevant whether or not the measure is *directly* granted by the State or *indirectly* granted through State resources. In the same line of reasoning, it is unimportant whether the measure confers an advantage to the *direct* or *indirect* beneficiaries of the aids.

III.ii. Criterion of Tax Advantage

The second criterion for State aid is the 'advantage' conferred by the measure. In tax matters, some interesting questions arise from this criterion. An advantage is in general conferred where Member States provide for financial support to certain undertakings. In tax matters, Member States do not give incentives through direct payments, guarantees or benefits in kind. Rather, they introduce advantageous tax schemes which favour certain undertakings.[28] In that respect, one has to keep in mind that the notion of 'tax' is broadly interpreted, including for instance capital duties, social security contributions or royalties.

The notion of tax advantage can be complex in practice because it involves a very large number of possible tax measures. EU State aid law applies to any type of measure, regardless of its form. Hence, all types of tax scheme can be reviewed in the light of Article 107 TFEU. But there is no possible classification of all tax measures which can be termed

State aids given the diversity of national tax schemes and the absence of common tax standards among the Member States. It follows that an abundant range of measures can come within State aid law, such as tax credits, accelerated depreciation, reduced tax rates, advantageous transfer pricing rules or rescheduling of tax debt. Moreover, tax measures can apply at the different stages of the revenue-raising process (determination of tax base, assessment of tax liability and enforcement of tax claim).[29] Therefore, a tax advantage can take a wide-reaching range of forms which can be complex or technical. This requires a case-by-case analysis that can be subtle and intricate.

Given the multitude of forms of tax aids, EU law has taken the following approach: 'the measure must confer on recipients an advantage which relieves them of charges that are normally borne from their budget'.[30] To this end, one should distinguish between the general tax system and the preferential tax measure which affects positively the recipient's tax liability. As the Court put it, 'in order to identify what constitutes an advantage (. . .), it is imperative to determine the reference point in the scheme in question against which that advantage is to be compared'.[31] Therefore, the general tax system should first be determined. On this basis, a comparison should be made between the tax treatment provided by the measure and the tax treatment under the general tax system. But this approach can be subtle in practice because it involves determining a tax reference benchmark. This can raise intricate and challenging problems. The issue of the reference benchmark will be analysed further with regard to the selectivity criterion. Nonetheless, at this point of the analysis, one can already object that there is a problem of distinction between advantage and selectivity. The assessment of these two criteria is based on the same approach which consists in establishing a departure from the general tax system. The ultimate objective is to assess whether there is *a selective advantage*. These two criteria are however dissimilar. They have different objectives and rationales. But the similarity of their reviews and their interconnection can raise some difficulties in practice.

In view of the above, the question arises as to whether a derogatory tax scheme which *increases* the tax burden of certain undertakings can also be regarded as a State aid. This is the case in a situation where a tax is applied to certain undertakings while other undertakings are not subject to this tax. Instead of 'tax incentive', the question deals with 'tax disincentive'. The advantage would consist in the fact that competitors of the exempted undertakings are subject to the tax. Although in principle a 'disincentive' does not constitute a State aid,[32] the question involves however an analysis of the 'disincentive' with regard to the general tax system.

In summary, tax advantage generally takes the form of a *negative* aid, meaning that the State does not transfer a direct subsidy, but it rather allows for a tax break. Consequently, the main issue of assessing the tax advantage lies in the difficulty of determining which tax burden the Member State would normally have levied. This issue is closely related to the problem of the measure's selectivity which will now be examined in greater depth.

III.iii.   Criterion of Tax Selectivity

Selectivity is a decisive criterion in tax aid review. According to Article 107 TFEU, selectivity deals with the question as to whether a tax measure 'favours certain undertakings or the production of certain goods' over others. As a preliminary comment, it is worth noting that EU law does not limit its scrutiny to the direct recipients of the aids (for example, under-takings which benefit from tax breaks), but it also analyses other *indirect* beneficiaries of tax aids. For instance, tax allowances granted for private savings in a fund, which provided loans to certain undertakings under preferential rates, can be regarded as selective.[33] Likewise, tax-free bonuses conferred on coal mine workers can be selective to the benefit of coal mining undertakings in comparison with undertakings in other sectors.[34] For the analysis of tax selectivity, one has therefore to keep in mind that selectivity is assessed with regard to direct and indirect beneficiaries. That being said, the issue of tax selectivity commands attention. It will be addressed from two angles: that of material selectivity and geographic selectivity.

III.iii.a.   Material selectivity
Material selectivity is at the centre of State aid law in tax matters.[35] It covers measures which are restricted to one or more sectors of activity, types of undertaking or productions of goods. The decisive question is as to whether the tax measure is an exception to the general tax. A measure can be *de jure* selective, meaning that it applies *explicitly* to certain under-takings. More problematic are measures which are *de facto* selective. These concern measures which apply in principle to all undertakings, but which in practice are available only to a restricted number of undertak-ings. For instance, one can imagine a measure which provides a reduction of social contribution charges for female employees in order to support female work. This measure applies in principle to all undertakings. However, undertakings which employ a higher percentage of employees (for example, undertakings in the textile sector) could effectively benefit more from this measure than undertakings which have an equal or higher number of male employees (for example, undertakings in the road haulage

sector).[36] The *SEAS* case illustrates this issue. The Danish electricity company SEAS had suffered loss on various activities and intended to focus as for the future on electricity production and supply. But SEAS was not allowed to offset its deficit against electricity prices (which constituted its sole source of benefit). Against this backdrop, the Danish government introduced a tax regime which allowed electricity companies to incorporate their deficit into electricity prices. Although this tax measure was in principle available to all electricity companies in Denmark, the Commission found that the measure was designed in such a way that only SEAS could benefit from it in practice.[37]

In tax matters, the issue of *de facto* selectivity is of great importance because tax regimes are generally introduced by way of pieces of legislation or regulations which are framed in general terms. It is therefore necessary to go beyond the wording of the tax provisions and to carry out a case-by-case analysis. For instance, in the *Groepsrentebox* case,[38] the Netherlands had introduced an advantageous intra-group loan scheme. Although this regime seemed available to all companies, it was questionable whether it was not *de facto* selective because group companies benefited from it in comparison with stand-alone companies.[39]

The major issue regarding tax selectivity lies in the distinction between general and selective tax measures.[40] A measure is selective because it derogates from the general tax system. However, the dividing line between the selectivity and generality of the tax measure can be blurred. For instance, since vehicles using diesel are more fuel-efficient and produce less greenhouse gas, let us suppose that a Member State plans to support diesel vehicle manufacturers which are more environmentally friendly than gas vehicle manufacturers. To this end, the Member State introduces an advantageous tax regime which applies only to diesel vehicle manufacturers. The question would then arise as to whether this tax regime would be selective within the meaning of State aid law. One can question whether the tax regime constitutes an exception to the normal application of the tax regime since the car manufacturing market is equally divided between diesel and gas vehicle manufacturers. In this situation, where is the general tax system? Can one consider that the tax treatment of diesel vehicle manufacturers constitutes a derogation although it applies to a large part of the market of vehicle manufacturers? Moreover, it is uncertain that the reference system would be limited to the vehicle manufacturing market. In that instance, how could one determine the reference framework? Should it be the general system of corporate taxation?

This question is all the more complex with regard to the current CJEU's position. It seems that the dividing line between the general system and the selective measure cannot be found in the delimitation between majority of taxpayers and minority of recipients. In that respect, Advocate General Fennelly expressly refuted such a demarcation.[41] Furthermore, it is common ground that the number of recipients involved is not relevant when assessing the selectivity of a tax measure: a measure can cover an indefinite number of beneficiaries.[42] Moreover, the CJEU endorses the view that a measure can be termed selective although it applies to a very large number of undertakings or productions of goods in various sectors.[43] In the light of these considerations, it appears complex to identify the deviation from the general tax norm. It is therefore interesting to analyse the approach adopted by the EU case law to handle this decisive problem.

IV.   TEST OF TAX SELECTIVITY: A THREE-STAGE EXAMINATION

In order to assess the selectivity of a tax measure, CJEU case law and the practice of the Commission have introduced a so-called 'derogation test' based on three main steps. The underlying idea is to define the tax derogation from a reference benchmark. To this end, in the founding *Italian textile* case (1974) the CJEU held that a measure is selective where it was 'intended partially to exempt those undertakings from the financial charges arising from the normal application of the general system of compulsory contributions imposed by law'.[44] The CJEU has then used different terminologies: the measure should 'place certain undertakings in a more favourable situation than others';[45] the measure is liable 'to place the undertakings to which it applies in a more favourable situation than others, inasmuch as it allows them to continue trading in circumstances in which that would not be allowed if the usual insolvency rules were applied, since those rules are decisive when it comes to protecting creditors' interests';[46] the measure grants 'advantages accruing exclusively to certain undertakings or certain sectors';[47] the measure favours certain undertakings 'in comparison with other undertakings which are in a legal and factual situation that is comparable in the light of the objective pursued by the measure in question';[48] 'within the context of a particular legal system, that measure constitutes an advantage for certain undertakings in comparison with others which are in a comparable legal and factual situation';[49] the measure gives rise to an 'advantage for certain undertakings as compared with others which, within the legal framework in which that body exercises its competences, are in a comparable legal and factual situation'.[50]

In that respect, it is interesting to note that the Commission has also used different terminologies: the measure should constitute 'a departure from the generally accepted or benchmark tax structure, which produces a favourable tax treatment of particular types of activities or groups of tax-payers';[51] a measure should be 'an exception to the application of the tax system';[52] the measure should apply to companies which are 'in a legal and factual situation comparable to that of [other] companies'.[53]

In short, two main expressions emerge from these different terminologies. On the one hand, the measure is regarded as selective where it constitutes a deviation from the general tax system. On the other hand, the measure is analysed on the basis of a comparison between the tax treatment under the tax measure and the tax treatment under the general system. The intellectual process is not the same depending on the terminology used. One requires determining first the general tax system and then to examine the derogation from this system. The second involves identifying legal and factual situations to compare the two different tax treatments in the light of the objective pursued by the measure in question. However, the CJEU and the Commission do not seem to apply different tests. Rather, they apply the same test which is described in different manners. This test consists in analysing a derogation from the standard application of the tax measure. For this purpose, it is suggested to compare the tax treatment under the derogatory measure with the tax treatment under the general tax system. If a difference of treatment is established, then the tax measure can be regarded as a derogation from the general tax system.[54]

Moreover, at this stage of the analysis, it is worth noting that *the margin of discretion* conferred to national authorities for granting the aid is a decisive element. Discretional practice gives rise to a presumption of selectivity. Of particular concern is the opacity of the decision and the room for manoeuvre conferred to the national authorities.[55] The presumption based on discretionary practices is of great importance for cases dealing with ruling methods, transactions[56] or amnesty practices.[57] For example, the CJEU took the view that a joint financing by a Member State through a public fund, which had discretion to adjust its financial assistance, should be regarded as a selective measure.[58]

In addition, the selectivity of the measure can be *justified on the basis of the nature or general scheme of the system.* Interestingly, this justification was introduced by the CJEU in 1974 in the landmark *Italian Textile* case as an *obiter dictum.*[59] After this case, the CJEU did not mention any justification until the nineties. The notion was then developed and recognized as a valid element by the Commission Notice[60] and Court's case law.[61] Justification by the general tax system is significant because it allows for considering the logic and internal consistency of the tax regime in order to assess the selective nature of the measure. In some textbook cases, justification by the logic of the general tax system does not raise major difficulties. For example, non-profit-making undertakings such as associations or foundations are not taxed because no profit is made. Therefore, it is justified by the nature of the tax system that national tax systems have established derogatory rules for non-profit-making undertakings (in comparison with profit-making undertakings).

One has to keep in mind that the justification by the logic of the general tax system is a derogatory rule of the Treaty and, as such, it is narrowly interpreted. The CJEU accepts only a limited number of justifications, including the principle of tax neutrality,[62] the need to tackle tax avoidance,[63] the need to take into account specific accounting requirements,[64] the need to consider the peculiar nature of a sector or activity,[65] or the redistributive purpose of the tax.[66] Apart from these, EU law refutes other justifications which are put forward by the Member States. For instance, the justification based on the need to make undertakings more competitive has systematically been rejected.[67]

The introduction of the justification by the nature or general scheme of the tax system can be criticized on the basis that it may go beyond the meaning of the TFEU. The TFEU already provides some exemptions (Article 107(2) and (3)) which do not take into consideration the internal logic of a tax regime. But the justification by the system also allows a tax measure to fall outside the scope of State aid law although it is mentioned in the Treaty. In response to this remark, one can object that the nature or general scheme of the tax system is used to justify the *selectivity* of the measure (but not the measure as a State aid). In addition, scholars have pointed out the risk that Member States would interpret the justification broadly so that they would circumvent their obligation of notification.[68] One should however point out that the strict interpretation given to this justification as well as the developed position under EU law gives rise to a narrow margin of action for the Member States.

To summarize, therefore, the EU has developed a selectivity test based on the following three stages:[69]

(i)   determination of a tax system of reference;
(ii) identification of a derogation from the tax system of reference;
(iii) possible justification of the measure by the nature or general scheme of the tax system.

In practice, the application of this test leaves room for debate. The major issue lies in the choice of the reference framework. If a very large tax reference framework is determined (for instance, the general system of business taxation), any differential treatment from this tax system may be termed State aid. On the contrary, if a limited reference tax system is chosen (such as SME taxation, taxation of collective investments or taxation of dividends), the measure would be assessed against this sub-system of reference. But there is a risk that any tax measure would be regarded as non-selective if the subsystem of reference is limited to the extent needed. To illustrate this issue, let us suppose that a Member State has introduced a tax scheme where interests received from companies located abroad are taxed at a reduced tax rate while interest received from national companies are taxed at the general corporate tax rate. The objective is to attract foreign investment. This tax scheme introduces a difference of treatment between companies receiving foreign interests and companies receiving national interests. If the reference framework is the general corporate tax system, the measure is selective. However, if the reference framework is limited to income arising from abroad, then the measure is not selective.

In view of the above, EU practice tends to opt for a large reference framework which could be regarded as too extensive. For instance, in the *Adria-Wien Pipeline*[70] case discussed in Chapter 8 by Bartosch, the CJEU took the view that a tax measure which applied to undertakings which carried on activities in the production of goods was selective because it did not also apply to undertakings supplying services. The analysis assessed the tax measure against a very broad benchmark since it drew a comparison between primary, secondary and tertiary sectors. However, one could object that this application of the selectivity test is not satisfactory because the undertakings did not carry on economic activities in the same sectors. Undertakings producing goods and undertakings supplying services were *a priori* not in comparable legal and factual market situations. The position adopted by the CJEU can bring about debatable outcomes. To counterbalance the extensive application of the selectivity test, some alternative approaches have been proposed by legal scholars.[71]

V.   GEOGRAPHIC SELECTIVITY

In addition to material selectivity, the application of State aid law to tax measures raises complex issues with regard to geographic selectivity. Geographic selectivity, which constitutes a relevant aspect in tax aid review, can be defined as the selectivity of tax measures which are regional or local in scope. In tax matters, the issue is of great importance for measures which have been granted by infra-State authorities enjoying regulatory powers over their tax systems. It deals with Member States' devolutions of tax powers and constitutional systems.

At this point of the analysis, it is important to distinguish *symmetrical* from *asymmetrical* devolution of tax powers. *Asymmetrical* devolution of powers is characterized by tax autonomy conferred on only a limited number of infra-State entities. By contrast, there is *symmetrical* devolution of powers where all regions or local authorities enjoy equal tax powers. In the case of symmetrical devolution of powers, the situation is straightforward. There is no tax reference benchmark since all entities are equally entitled to set up their own tax provisions. Therefore, a tax measure cannot be found geographically selective. Consequently, although a tax measure can be more favourable to undertakings established in certain tax regions in comparison with undertakings established in other regions, the measure falls outside the scope of State aid law if there is a genuine symmetrical devolution of tax powers.[72]

In contrast, the assessment of geographic selectivity in the case of *asymmetrical* devolution of powers is far from being clear-cut. Until recently, EU law took the view that the tax reference framework was the tax system which applied in the entire territory of the Member State. Subsequently, a tax measure granted by a region which favoured undertakings established in this region in comparison with undertakings established in the rest of the Member State was selective within the meaning of Article 107 TFEU.[73]

In the decisive *Azores* case,[74] the CJEU adopted another approach by introducing an *autonomy test*. At issue was a tax regime introduced by the Azores Region which provided a reduction of the rate of income and corporation tax in favour of undertakings established in the Azores Region. These operating aids introduced a favourable tax treatment to the detriment of undertakings located in the rest of the Portuguese territory. The CJEU endorsed the view that the reference framework for assessing the selectivity of the measure could be limited to the geographical area where the regional or local authority 'occupies *a fundamental role in the definition of the political and economic environment* in which the undertakings present on the territory within its competence operate'.[75] In the light of this consideration, the CJEU introduced a three-stage examination to determine the tax autonomy of the regional or local authority involved: (i) the measure should be adopted by a regional or local authority which has, from a constitutional point of view, a political and administrative status separate from that of the central government; (ii) the measure should be adopted without the central government having the possibility to interfere in its substance; (iii) financial repercussions of a reduction of the national tax rate for undertakings established in the infra-State entity should not be compensated by incentives conferred by other regions or central government.[76] This test was therefore based on three main criteria:

institutional, procedural and economic autonomy. Interestingly, in the *Azores* case, the CJEU found that the economic autonomy of the Azores Region was not established. On this basis, the tax system was qualified as State aid.

The CJEU shed light on the autonomy test in the *UGT-Rioja* case.[77] It took the view that it is for the national court to determine the tax autonomy of the infra-State entity.[78] Regarding the criterion of procedural autonomy, the CJEU stated that some national procedures (for example, conciliation procedure to avoid legislative conflicts) can be accepted as long as the national government does not intervene directly in the process of adopting the tax measure. Furthermore, the criterion of economic and financial autonomy involves no financial transfers from the national government of other regions to the region at issue having the effect of compensating the cost of the tax measure.

The jurisprudential line introduced in the *Azores* case is open to criticism.[79] First, the CJEU focuses on three precise criteria to assess the tax autonomy of the region. But what matters in tax matters is the autonomy enjoyed by the region to confer the tax regardless of other economic or political considerations. Therefore, the CJEU's test reflects a formal approach which does not necessarily represent the general position and the tax autonomy of the region within the constitutional system of the Member State.

Furthermore, one could argue that the *Azores* test could encourage regions to gain more tax autonomy in order to confer tax advantages in favour of undertakings located within their territory. Nonetheless, given the narrow interpretation given to the three criteria, only few regions are concerned.[80] The *Azores* test is far from becoming a new Pandora's Box.

More generally, one can object that the *Azores* test may constitute an intrusion into the Member States' constitutional systems. EU law should respect the internal structures of the Member State without any interference.[81] It is the Member States' prerogative to establish tax decentralization under their respective rules and principles regardless of any intervention at the European level. Tax decentralization can take a wide-reaching range of forms which do not necessarily comply with the *Azores* test. In light of this consideration, the *Azores* test appears as a debatable review of the tax constitutional organization of the Member States.

Although there is some force in the above-mentioned criticism, one should above all welcome the CJEU's openness to the recognition of tax regional autonomy. Although the test needs to be developed and subject to a more flexible interpretation, it remains above all a decisive step towards the adaptation of State aid law to tax measures.

VI. AFFECTING COMPETITION AND TRADE

According to Article 107 TFEU, the aid should distort competition and affect trade between Member States. These two conditions are usually examined together because they are regarded as inextricably linked.[82] Regarding these conditions, the mere fact that the measure strengthens the position of the companies in comparison with other companies is sufficient to establish on effect trade.[83] Hence, 'it is clear from the Court's case law that the requirement of an effect on trade between Member States is easily satisfied'.[84] In tax matters, this criterion does not raise particular issues. Its application to tax measures is in line with the position adopted by the Commission and the CJEU.[85]

The criterion of effect on competition and trade is not subject to an actual analysis. As the Court put it, 'although the Commission is required, in the reasons for its decision, to refer at least to the circumstances in which aid has been granted where those circumstances show that the aid is such as to affect trade between Member States, it is not required to demonstrate the actual effect of aid already granted'.[86] In this regard, some scholars have suggested carrying out a real analysis of the criterion. Establishing the 'actual effect' of the tax aids could counterbalance the extensive application of the selectivity criterion. Such an analysis would be based on a more economic approach in order to identify the real effect of the aids on competition and trade.[87]

In summary, the criteria for State aids applied to tax measures show some interesting features which can raise complex issues. But the review of tax State aid should however not be confined to the analysis of the *substantive* criteria. The *enforcement* rules on State aids can also be problematic with regard to tax measures and merit closer examination.

VII. TAX RECOVERY

Under EU law, State aids which are in breach of Article 107 TFEU should be fully recovered. Although the Treaty remains silent in this regard,[88] the CJEU introduced this principle in 1973.[89] Regulation 659/1999 on State aid established this principle as a general obligation for the Commission.[90] The principle of full recovery seeks to re-establish the *status quo ante* in order to remedy the distortion of competition caused by the effects of the illegal aid. The reintroduction of the previously existing situation also involves the payment of interest for the corresponding time period.[91]

In tax matters, aid recovery can raise interesting issues. A tax aid should be fully recovered on the basis of the general tax system. To this end, the Notice suggests drawing a comparison between the tax actually paid and the tax that should have been paid under the reference framework.[92] The recipient should refund the difference between these two tax treatments (including the interest). Interestingly, the CJEU takes the view that the Commission is not in charge of determining the exact amount of tax aid which should be recovered. The Commission should only provide relevant indications.[93] Rather, the Member States, which have direct access to information regarding the tax treatments of the undertakings involved, should establish the exact amount of tax aid.[94]

In addition, consideration should be given to the impact of the tax system in determining the amount recovered. Recipients of the aid should only refund the net amount of the aid. This rule was introduced in the *Siemens* case concerning a scheme of operating aids introduced by the Belgian government. The Court took the view that national authorities can deduct certain sums for the calculation of aid recovery in accordance with their tax system.[95] On this basis, the question arises as to how national authorities should reconstitute the previous tax situations of the undertakings concerned. Of particular concern was the possibility of taking into account *possible* economic operations which could have taken place. In this regard, the CJEU held that it was not consistent 'to determine the amounts to be repaid in the light of various operations which could have been implemented by the undertakings if they had not opted for the type of operation which was coupled with the aid'.[96] It follows that national authorities can calculate the amount of tax recovery only on the basis of the most advantageous tax treatment which could have been applied without imagining past hypothetical events. But one can object that this stance can be challenging in practice. In certain cases, it can be difficult to reconstruct past events without inventing economic operations which could have been carried out.

Further consideration should be given to the recovery of a tax forming a part of the aid. Since its early case law, the CJEU considered that the method for financing the aid should also be considered.[97] In the noteworthy *Van Calster* case,[98] the CJEU took the view that a tax which has been exclusively introduced to finance an aid should also be qualified as an aid. Hence, the tax should also have been notified: 'where an aid measure of which the method of financing is an integral part has been implemented in breach of the obligation to notify, national courts must in principle order reimbursement of charges or contributions levied specifically for the purpose of financing that aid'.[99]

It is further noteworthy that the tax, in order to be part of the aid, must be 'hypothecated' to the aid, meaning that the benefit arising from the tax should systematically be allocated to finance the aid.[100] Only if there is such an automatic link between the aid and the tax, then the tax, as a method of financing the aid, should also be notified[101] and national courts must in principle order reimbursement of the tax.[102]

In the light of the foregoing considerations, the question arises as to whether taxpayers subject to a tax forming a part of the aid can either refuse to pay the tax or claim for the reimbursement of the tax (if they have already paid it). Taxpayers could argue that they are subject to a tax which is part of an illegal aid deemed to be recovered. In addition, the aid could also consist in a tax exemption. In this case, taxpayers could allege the tax is an integral part of the aid because the aid consists in the exemption from that tax. In a constant line of jurisprudence, the Court affirms that taxpayers subject to a mandatory tax cannot rely on the argument that there is a breach of Article 107 TFEU to avoid payment of the tax or seek restitution.[103]

But the situation differs where there are only a limited group of competing operators involved. The CJEU has shed light on this issue in two relevant rulings. The landmark *Ferring* case[104] dealt with only two competing operators in the medicine distribution channels in France: the wholesale distributors on the one hand and the pharmaceutical laboratories, which sold directly to pharmacies, on the other hand. Since only one group of operators (the wholesale distributors) was liable to certain impositions regarding public service obligations, the French government levied on the other group of operators (the pharmaceutical laboratories) a tax in favour of the wholesale distributors in order to counterbalance the situation. Against this background, the question arises as to whether the tax at issue was a State aid. The CJEU found that the tax was contrary to Article 107 TFEU 'only to the extent that the advantage in not being assessed to the tax on direct sales of medicines exceeds the additional costs that they bear in discharging the public service obligations imposed on them by national law'.[105] The CJEU took a further step in the well-known *Laboratoires Boiron* case.[106] In this case involving similar facts to those of the *Ferring* case, the CJEU ruled that the taxpayers could *claim reimbursement* from the relevant authorities. But this reimbursement could take place only to the extent of the overcompensation of the wholesale distributors.

This position is in line with the CJEU's jurisprudence regarding a tax forming an integral part of the aid. Accordingly, such a tax should also be termed aid. Therefore, it is consistent to allow the reimbursement of the tax in certain cases. This can, however, be subtle in practice. First, taxpayers claiming reimbursement can encounter practical difficulties in calculating the exact amount of aid granted to the recipients, bearing in mind that this aid corresponds to an overcompensation of public service obligations. Moreover, the CJEU's position applies only in a specific situation characterized by a limited and identifiable number of competitors in a given market. However, one asks whether the number of groups of competitors should necessarily be identifiable or limited. If so, the dividing line between the *Van Caslter* and *Laboratoire Boiron* cases may begin to blur. Therefore, special attention should be paid to the coming cases in this regard.

VIII.   CONCLUSION

This chapter sought to address a number of relevant issues related to the application of State aid law to tax measures. Although the CJEU has dealt with tax aids since its early case law, it is only in the nineties as part of an overall review of harmful tax competition that the Commission has systemically examined national tax regimes in the light of State aid law. To this end, it has taken relevant approaches and adopted pertinent interpretations. It has shed light on the criteria of State-originated resources, tax advantage and tax selectivity. In the same line, it has clarified aspects of tax recovery.

But despite the development of EU law with regard to tax aids, some gaps remain and some interpretations are debatable. Of particular concern is the selectivity criterion whose material and geographic tests may bring about debatable outcomes and introduce a certain degree of legal uncertainty. The subtle position adopted with regard to recovery of a tax forming a part of the aid could be open to criticism.

A debate has been launched in order to address these relevant issues. Within the framework of the 2005–2009 State Aid Action Plan, the Commission has explored interesting options. It considered revisiting the 1998 Notice on the application of the State aid rules to measures relating to direct business taxation published in 1998.[107] Special attention should be given to indirect tax measures which have been disregarded until now. Very interesting questions dealing with VAT measures or excise duties remain unanswered. Although it is important to clarify some rules, little progress has been made so far. It seems, therefore, that the decisive legal developments will arise from EU practice and case law. In the coming years, EU law will have to strike a balance between the strict application of State aid law and the need to introduce flexibility with regard to taxation.

ACKNOWLEDGEMENTS

Any opinions expressed by the author are personal and do not reflect the views of any institution or organisation. The chapter was written when the author was at the Law Faculty of the University of Luxembourg and before she joined the European Commission. The author is deeply grateful to J. Azizi (judge at the General Court) and Herung Hofmann (Professor at the University of Luxembourg) for their support and helpful comments.

NOTES

1. Commission Staff Working Document, *Facts and Figures on State Aid in the EU Member States*, SEC (2009) 1683, 7 December 2009, 33.
2. This data is based on the Commission Scoreboard which calculates total State aid up to around €47.2 billion (excluding crisis measures), ibid, 10.
3. Ibid, 35.
4. See in particular on this general topic Schön 1999, Schön 2006, Quigley 2009: 65–100; Quigley 2004, Kube 2001, Luja 2003, M.-A. Mamut 2008, P. Rossi-Maccanico 2009a, Triantafyllou 2008, Kube 2005, Sutter 2005, Jaeger 2006.
5. Case C-279/93, *Schumacker* [1995] E.C.R. I-225, para. 21; Case C-80/94, *G. H. E. J. Wielockx* v. *Inspecteur der Directe Belastingen* [1995] E.C.R.I-2493, para. 16; Case C-311/97, *Royal Bank of Scotland plc* v. *Elliniko Dimosio* [1999] E.C.R. I-2651, para. 19; Case C-251/98, *C. Baars* [2000] E.C.R. I-2787, para. 17; Joined Cases C-397/98 and C-410/98, *Metallgesellschaft Ltd and Others* [2001] E.C.R. I-1727, para. 37; Case C-443/06, *Erika Waltraud Ilse Hollmann v. Fazenda Pública* [2007] E.C.R. I-8491, para. 33.
6. Case 30/59, *De Gezamenlijke Steenkolenmijnen in Limburg v. High Authority of the European Coal and Steel Community* [1961] E.C.R. 50.
7. Case 173/73, *Italian Republic v. Commission of the European Communities* [1974] E.C.R. 709.
8. Case C-387/92, *Banco de Crédito Industrial SA, now Banco Exterior de España SA v. Ayuntamiento de Valencia* [1994] E.C.R. I-877.
9. O'Brien 2005.
10. Commission of the European Communities, *Taxation in the European Union*, Discussion Paper for the Informal Meeting of ECOFIN Ministers, SEC (96) 487 Final, Brussels, 20 March 1996.
11. Harmful tax competition can be defined as the excessive lowering of domestic tax burden by the Member States in order to provide an attractive tax system. For a thorough analysis of the notion of harmful tax competition within a EU context, see Pinto 2003; Carlos dos Santos 2009. Furthermore, it is notable that the debate on harmful tax competition has been launched in parallel in the OECD, see OECD, *Harmful Tax Competition – An Emerging Global Issue*, Report approved on 9 April 1998.
12. Commission of the European Communities, *Taxation in the European Union: Report on the Development of Tax Systems*, COM (96) 546 final, Brussels, 22 October 1996, 1–13.
13. Commission Communication, *Towards Tax Co-ordination in the European Union – A Package to Tackle Harmful Tax Competition*, COM (97) 495 final, Brussels, 1 November 1997.
14. Council, Conclusions of the ECOFIN Council Meeting, on 1 December 1997 Concerning Taxation policy, O.J. 1998 C2.

15. Report of the Code of Conduct Group (Business Taxation) to ECOFIN Council on 29 November 1999, Brussels, SN 4901/99 (Primarolo Report).
16. Commission Notice on the Application of the State Aid Rules to Measures relating to Direct Business Taxation, O.J. 1998 C 384/3 (Commission Notice).
17. Report on the Implementation of the Commission Notice on the Application of the State Aid Rules to Measures relating to Direct Business Taxation, C(2004)434 (Implementation Report) Brussels, 9 February 2004.
18. Joined Cases C-72/91 and C-73/91, *Firma Sloman Neptun Schiffahrts AG v. Seebetriebsrat Bodo Ziesemer der Sloman Neptun Schiffahrts AG* [1993] E.C.R. I-887, para. 19.
19. Case 82/77, *Ministère public du Kingdom of the Netherlands v. Jacobus Philippus van Tiggele* [1978] E.C.R. 25, para. 25.
20. See for instance: Case 173/73, *Italian Republic v. Commission of the European Communities* [1974] E.C.R. 709, para. 35.
21. Case C-156/98, Federal Republic of Germany v. Commission of the European Communities [2000] E.C.R. I-6857.
22. Ibid, para. 27.
23. Cases C-72/91 and C-73/91, *Firma Sloman Neptun Schiffahrts AG v. Seebetriebsrat Bodo Ziesemer der Sloman* [1993] E.C.R. I-887.
24. Case C-379/98, *PreussenElektra AG and Schleswag AG* [2001] E.C.R. I-2099.
25. Implementation Report, paras 19 and 20. See for instance Commission Decision of 17 February 2003 on the aid scheme implemented by Belgium for coordination centres established in Belgium, 2003/755/EC, O.J. 2003 L 282; Commission Decision of 17 February 2003 on the State aid implemented by the Netherlands for international financing activities, 2003/515/EC, O.J. 2003 L 180, para. 84; Commission Decision of 30 March 2004 on the aid scheme implemented by the United Kingdom in favour of Gibraltar Qualifying Companies, 2005/77/EC, O.J. 2005 L 29/24, 24-38, paras 58–59.
26. Joined Cases C-182/03 and C-217/03, Kingdom of Belgium v. Commission of the European Communities and Forum 187 ASBL v. Commission of the European Communities [2003] E.C.R. I-6887, paras 127–129; Joined Cases T-92/00 and T-103/00, Territorio Histórico de Álava – Diputación Foral de Álava, Ramondín SA, Ramondín Cápsulas SA v. Commission of the European Communities [2002] E.C.R. II-1385, paras 61 and 62.
27. Interestingly, certain other systems of law have adopted a different approach. For instance WTO law of subsidies does not consider that a 'cost of government' is relevant for the determination of a financial contribution by the government; see WTO Panel Report, Canada – Measures Affecting the Export of Civilian Aircraft, WT/DS70/R, circulated 14 April 1999, paras 9.111–9.120, confirmed by WTO Appellate Body Report, Canada – Measures Affecting the Export of Civilian Aircraft, WT/DS70/AB/R, circulated 2 August 1999, paras 149–161.
28. In this regard, the CJEU held expressly that aids are 'not only positive benefits, such as subsidies themselves, but also interventions which, in various forms, mitigate the charges which are normally included in the budget of an undertaking and which, without, therefore, being subsidies in the budget of an undertaking and which, without, therefore, being subsidies in the strict meaning of the word, are similar in character and have the same effect', in Case 30/59, *De Gezamenlijke Steenkolenmijnen in Limburg v. High Authority of the European Coal and Steel Community* [1961] E.C.R. 48.
29. Point 9 of Commission Notice.
30. Ibid.
31. Case T-308/00, Salzgitter AG v. Commission of the European Communities [2004] E.C.R. II-1933, para. 81.
32. In this sense, see Schön 2006: 252–253.
33. Case 102/87, French Republic v. Commission of the European Communities [1988] E.C.R. 4067, para. 5.

34. Case 30/59, *De Gezamenlijke Steenkolenmijnen in Limburg v. High Authority of the European Coal and Steel Community* [1961] E.C.R. 1. For other examples, see Case C-172/03, *Wolfgang Heiser v. Finanzamt Innsbruck* [2005] E.C.R. I-1627, para. 47; Case C-382/99, *Kingdom of the Netherlands v. Commission of the European Communities* [2002] E.C.R. I-5163, paras 55–67; Case C-156/98, *Federal Republic of Germany v. Commission of the European Communities* [2000] E.C.R. I-6857, paras 22–23; Case T-34/02, *Le Levant v. Commission of the European Communities* [2006] E.C.R. II-267, paras 118–120; Case T-445/05, *Associazione italiana del risparmio gestito and others v. Commission of the European Communities* [2009] E.C.R. II-289, paras 126–165.

35. For further development on this topic, see Da Cruz Vilaça 2009, Rossi-Maccanico 2009b, Rossi-Maccanico 2009c, Rossi-Maccanico 2007, Luja 2010, Luja 2009, Nicolaides 2007, Aldestam 2005, Kurcz and Vallindas 2008, Bousin and Piernas 2008, Van de Casteele and Hocine 2008, Micheau 2008, Waelbroeck 2005, Carlos dos Santos 2009.

36. See for instance Case 203/82, *Commission of the European Communities v. Italian Republic* [1983] E.C.R. 2525.

37. Commission Report, *XXIVth Report on Competition Policy*, 1994, 347 and Annex II, 513–514. For another example, see Commission Decision of 12 May 2004, Reduction of a VAT debt owed by Umicore SA, C 76/2003, O.J. 2004 C 223/2, para. 51.

38. Commission Decision of 8 July 2009 on the *Groepsrentebox* scheme which the Netherlands is planning to implement, N 465/2006, O.J. 2009 L 288/26.

39. At issue was also the question as to whether the tax regime was more advantageous for international groups than national groups since international groups could likely deduct more than 5% of the taxation of interests in other Member States. The Commission finally endorsed the view that the tax regime did not involve any legal and economic obstacles and was therefore open to all undertakings, since it is easy to create a group in the Netherlands (Commission Decision of 8 July 2009 on the *Groepsrentebox* scheme which the Netherlands is planning to implement, N 465/2006, O.J. 2009 L/288 para. 127. For an analysis of the *de jure/de facto* selectivity of intra-group taxation schemes, see Luja 2009.

40. Regarding the distinction between selective measures and general measures, see Wishlade 1997, Bacon 1997, Kurcz and Vallindas 2008.

41. 'The application of the aid rules under the EC Treaty does not necessarily turn on the question whether the specifically favoured economic actors are in a minority relative to those subjected to the "normal" or general regime', Opinion of A.G. Fennelly, 21 September 2000, in Case C-390/98, *H.J. Banks & Company Limited v. The Coal Authority and the Secretary of State for Trade and Industry*, para. 19. Applied to the extreme, this position could however involve that a general tax system which applies only to a limited number of companies could be the reference framework while the derogatory tax measure would be available to the major part of companies. See also Opinion of A. G. Tizzano, Case C-53/00, *Ferring SA v. ACOSS*, para. 39.

42. It only shows that the measure is not an individual aid; Case T-55/99, *Confederación Española de Transporte de Mercancías (CETM) v. Commission of the European Communities* [2000] E.C.R. II-3207, para. 40.

43. Case C-75/97, *Kingdom of Belgium v. Commission of the European Communities* [1999] E.C.R. I-3671, para. 32.

44. Case 173/73, *Italian Republic v. Commission of the European Communities* [1974] E.C.R. 709, para. 33.

45. Case C-241/94, French Republic *v.* Commission of the European Communities [1996] E.C.R. I-4551, para. 24.

46. Case C-200/97, Ecotrade Srl *v.* Altiforni e Ferriere di Servola SpA (AFS) [1998] E.C.R. I-7907, para. 41.

47. C-75/97, Kingdom of Belgium v Commission of the European Communities [1999] E.C.R. I-5331, para. 26.

48. Case C-143/99, *Adria-Wien Pipeline and Wietersdorfer & Peggauer* [2001] E.C.R. I-8365, para. 41. See also Case C-88/03, *Portuguese Republic v. Commission of the European Communities* [2006] E.C.R. I-7115, para. 54; Case C-308/01, *GIL Insurance Ltd and others* [2004] E.C.R. I-4777, para. 68; Case C-172/03, *Wolfgang Heiser v. Finanzamt Innsbruck* [2005] E.C.R. I-1627, para. 40.
49. Case C-487/06 P, *British Aggregates Association v. Commission of the European Communities* [2008] E.C.R. I-10505, para. 82.
50. Case C-169/08, *Presidente del Consiglio dei Ministri v. Regione Sardegna* [2009] E.C.R. I-10821, para. 61.
51. Annex I, para. 10.5 of the *Third Survey on State Aids in the European Community in the Manufacturing and Certain Other Sectors, Communication from Sir Leon Brittan to the Commission*, SEC (92) 1384 final, July 1992.
52. Point 16 of Commission Notice.
53. Commission Decision of 8 July 2009 on the *Groepsrentebox* scheme which the Netherlands is planning to implement, N 465/2006, O.J. L 288, para. 103.
54. It is interesting to note that the Commission considers that tax measures of a purely technical nature, or measures pursuing economic policy objectives related to specific sectors, fall outside the scope of Article 107 TFEU if they apply without distinction to all undertakings of productions of goods (point 13 of Commission Notice).
55. Point 22 of Commission Notice.
56. See for example Commission Decision of 12 May 2004, Reduction of a VAT debt owed by Umicore SA, C 76/2003, O.J. 2004 C 280, para. 55.
57. See for instance Commission Decision of 12 May 2004, Reduction of a VAT debt owed by Umicore SA (formerly Union Minière SA), O.J. 2004 C/10.
58. Case C-241/94, *French Republic v. Commission of the European Communities* [1996] E.C.R. I-4551, paras 22-24.
59. Case 173/73, *Italian Republic v. Commission of the European Communities* [1974] E.C.R. 709, para. 33.
60. Points 23 *et seq.* of Commission Notice.
61. See for instance Case T-211/05, *Italian Republic v. Commission of the European Communities* [2009] E.C.R. II-2777, para. 117; Case C-487/06 P, British Aggregates Association *v.* Commission of the European Communities [2008] E.C.R. I-10505, para. 76; Case C-148/04, Unicredito Italiano SpA *v.* Agenzia delle Entrate, Ufficio Genova [2005] E.C.R. I-11137, para. 51; Case C-75/97, Kingdom of Belgium *v.* Commission of the European Communities [1999] E.C.R. I-3671, para. 33.
62. Commission Decision of 5 June 2002 on State aid granted by Italy in the form of tax exemptions and subsidised loans to public utilities with a majority public capital holding, 2003/193/EC, O.J. L 77.
63. Case C-308/01, *Gil Insurance Ltd and others* [2004] E.C.R. I-4777.
64. Point 27 of Commission Notice.
65. Commission Decision of 11 December 2001 on the tax measures for banks and banking foundations implemented by Italy, 2002/581/EC, O.J.L 18, para. 32; Joined Cases T-92/00 and T-103/00, *Territorio Histórico de Álava – Diputación Foral de Álava, Ramondín SA, Ramondín Cápsulas SA v. Commission of the European Communities* [2002] E.C.R. para. 60; Joined Cases T-127/99, T-129/99 and T-148/99, *Territorio Histórico de Álava (Diputación Foral de Álava and Others) v. Commission of the European Communities* [2002] E.C.R. II-1275, para. 164.
66. Point 24 of Commission Notice.
67. See, for instance, Commission Decision of 17 February 2003 on the State aid implemented by the Netherlands for international financing activities, 2003/515/EC, O.J. 2003 L 180.
68. Wouters and Van Hees (2002).
69. In that respect, see Cases T-211/04 and T-215/04, *Government of Gibraltar*, [2008] E.C.R. II-3745.

70. Case C-143/99, *Adria-Wien Pipeline and Wietersdorfer & Peggauer* [2001] E.C.R. I-8365.
71. For a review of some approaches proposed by the legal literature, see Micheau (2010). For a critical analysis, see chapter 8 by Bartosch in this volume and Bartosch 2010.
72. See, for instance, Commission Decision of 7 December 2005 on IRAP deductions-Law n° 80/2005, art. 11-ter, N 198 / 2005, O.J. 2006 C/42.
73. Point 17 of Commission Notice. See, for instance, Commission Decision of 11 December 2002 on the part of the scheme adapting the national tax system to the specific characteristics of the Autonomous Region of the Azores which concerns reductions in the rates of income and corporation tax, 2003/442/EC, O.J. 2003 L 150/52; Commission Decision of 11 July 2001 on the State aid scheme applied by Spain to certain newly established firms in Navarre (Spain), 2002/893/EC, O.J. 2002 L 314/17. See also, for examples of case law: Joined Cases T-127/99, T-129/99 and T-148/99, *Territorio Histórico de Álava – Diputación Foral de Álava, Comunidad Autónoma del Pais Vasco, Gasteizko Industria Lurra, SA, Daewoo Electronics Manufacturing España, SA v. Commission of the European Communities* [2002] E.C.R. II-1275; Joined Cases C-183/02 P and C-187/02 P, *Daewoo Electronics Manufacturing España SA (Demesa), Territorio Histórico de Álava – Diputación Foral de Álava*, [2004] E.C.R. I-10609.
74. Case C-88/03, *Portuguese Republic v. Commission of the European Communities* [2006] E.C.R. I-7115.
75. Ibid, para. 66 (emphasis added by the author).
76. Ibid, para. 67.
77. Joined Cases C-428/06 to C-434/06, *Unión General de Trabajadores de La Rioja (UGT-Rioja)* [2008] E.C.R. I-6747.
78. One can object that it gives rise to an excessively broad margin of discretion for national jurisdictions. This can challenge the principles of equality and legal security, see Da Cruz Vilaça 2009.
79. For a critical review of geographic tax selectivity under EU law, see Rydelski 2006, Lindsay-Poulsen 2008, Kurcz 2007, Da Cruz Vilaça 2009, Bousin and Piernas 2008, Moreno Gonzalez 2007, Arhold 2006, Jaeger 2007.
80. See for instance, Cases T-211/04 and T-215/04, *Government of Gibraltar v. Commission of the European Communities* [2008] E.C.R. II-3745.
81. Article 4(2) TEU.
82. Joined Cases T-298/97, T-312/97, T-313/97, T-315/97, T-600/97 to 607/97, T-1/98, T-3/98 to T-6/98 and T-23/98, *Alzetta Mauro and others v. Commission of the European Communities* [2000] E.C.R. II-2319, para. 81; Case T-288/97, *Regione Friuli Venezia Giulia v. Commission of the European Communities* [1999] E.C.R. II-1871, para. 41.
83. Case 730/79, *Philip Morris Holland BV v. Commission of the European Communities* [1980] E.C.R . 2671, para. 11.
84. Opinion of A.G. Jacobs, 23 March 1994 in Joined Cases C-278/92, C-279/92 and C-280/92, *Kingdom of Spain v. Commission of the European Communities*, para. 33.
85. Point 11 of Commission Notice.
86. Case T-445/05, *Associazione italiana del risparmio gestito and others v. Commission of the European Communities* [2009] E.C.R.II-289, para. 10. See also Case T-424/05, *Italian Republic Commission of the European Communities* [2009] E.C.R. II-23, para. 153.
87. See for instance, Garcia and Neven 2005, Fingleton, Ruane and Ryan 1999, Da Cruz Vilaça 2009, Heidhues and Nitsche, 2006, Garcia and Neven 2005.
88. Article 108(3) TFEU only restrains Member States from enacting measures before the Commission adopts a final Decision.
89. . Case 70/72, *Commission of the European Communities v. Federal Republic of Germany* [1973] E.C.R. 813, para. 13.
90. Council Regulation No 659/1999 of 22 March 1999 laying down detailed rules for the

application of Article 93 (now Article 108 TFEU) of the EC Treaty, O.J. 1999 L 83/1, para. 14.

91. The interest rate is fixed by the Commission Regulation (EC) No 1935/2006 of 20 December 2006 amending Regulation (EC) No 794/2004 implementing Council Regulation (EC) No 659/1999 laying down detailed rules for the application of Article 93 of the EC Treaty, O.J. 2006 L 407.

92. Point 35 of Commission Notice.

93. See for instance Case 102/87, *French Republic v. Commission of the European Communities* [1988] E.C.R. 4067, para. 33.

94. See for example Case C-480/98, *Kingdom of Spain v. Commission of the European Communities*, [2000] E.C.R. I-8717, para. 26; Case C-382/99, *Kingdom of the Netherlands v. Commission of the European Communities* [2002] E.C.R. I-5163, para. 91; Case T-354/99, *Kuwait Petroleum (Nederland) BV v. Kingdom of the Netherlands* [2006] E.C.R.II-1475, para. 67.

95. Case T-459/93, *Siemens SA v. Commission of the European Communities* [1995] E.C.R. II-1675, paras. 83–84. This stance has been confirmed in Case T-67/94, *Ladbroke Racing Ltd v. Commission of the European Communities* [1998] E.C.R. II-1, para. 188. See also Notice from the Commission, *Towards an effective implementation of Commission decisions ordering Member States to recover unlawful and incompatible State aid*, O.J. 2007 C 272, para. 50.

96. Case C-148/04, *Unicredito Italiano SpA v. Agenzia delle Entrate, Ufficio Genova 1* [2005] E.C.R. I-11137, para. 114.

97. 'In its appraisal, the Commission must therefore take into account all those factors which directly or indirectly characterize the measure in question, that is, not only aid, properly so-called, for selected national activities, but also the direct aid which may be constituted both the method of financing and by the close connection which makes the amount of aid dependent upon the revenue from the charge': Case 47/69, *Government of the French Republic v. Commission of the European Communities* [1970] E.C.R. 487, para. 17.

98. Joined Cases C-261/01 and C-262/01, *Eugene Van Calster* [2003] E.C.R. I-12249.

99. Ibid, para. 54.

100. Joined Cases C-128/03 and C-129/03, *EM SpA, AEM Torino SpA v. Autorità per l'energia elettrica e per il gas and Others* [2005] E.C.R. I-2861, para. 46; Joined Cases C-393/04 and C-41/05, *Air Liquide Industries Belgium SA v. Ville de Seraing and Province de Liège* [2006] E.C.R. I-5293, para. 46; Joined Cases C-266/04 to C-270/04, C-276/04 and C-321/04 to C-325/04, *Distribution Casino France SAS* [2005] E.C.R. I-9481, para. 40; Case C-175/02, *F.J. Pape v. Minister van Landbouw, Natuurbeheer en Visserij* [2005] E.C.R. I-127, para 15.

101. Joined Cases C-261/01 and C-262/01, *Eugene Van Calster* [2003] E.C.R. I-12249, para. 51.

102. Joined Cases C-261/01 and C-262/01, *Eugene Van Calster* [2003] E.C.R. I-12249, para. 54; Joined Cases C-192/95 to C-218/95, *Société Comateb and others* [1997] E.C.R. I-165, para. 20; C-174/02, *Streekgewest Westelijk Noord-Brabant v. Staatssecretaris van Financiën* [2005] E.C.R. I-85, para. 16.

103. Case C-390/98, *Banks* [2001] E.C.R. I-6117, para. 80; Joined Cases C-266/04 to C-270/04, C-276/04 and C-321/04 to C-325/04, *Distribution Casino France SAS* [2005] E.C.R. I-9481, para. 42; ECJ, Joined Cases C-393/04 and C-41/05, *Air Liquide Industries Belgium SA v. Ville de Seraing and Province de Liège* [2006] E.C.R. I-5293, para. 43.

104. Case C-53/00, *Ferring SA and ACOSS* [2001] E.C.R. I-9067.

105. Ibid, para. 29.

106. Case C-526/04, *Laboratoires Boiron SA* [2006] E.C.R. I-7529.

107. Commission State aid action plan – Less and better targeted state aid: a roadmap for state aid reform 2005-2009 (Consultation document), COM/2005/0107 final, para. 64.

REFERENCES

Aldestam, M. (2005), *EC State aid rules applied to taxes – An analysis of the selectivity criterion*, Doctoral Thesis, Uppsala: Iustus Förlag.

Arhold, C. (2006), 'Steuerhoheit auf regionaler oder lokaler Ebene und der europäische Beihilfenbegriff – wie weit reicht das Konzept von der regionalen Selektivität', *Europäische Zeitschrift für Wirtschaftsrecht*, 717–721.

Bacon, K. (1997), 'State aids and general measures', *Yearbook of European Law*, **17:1**, 269–321.

Bartosch, A. (2010), 'Is there a need for a rule of reason in European State aid law? Or how to arrive at a coherent concept of material selectivity?', *Common Market Law Review*, **47**, 729–752.

Bousin, J and J. Piernas (2008), 'Developments in the notion of selectivity', *European State Aid Law Quarterly*, **4**, 634–653.

Carlos dos Santos, A. (2009), *L'Union européenne et la régulation de la concurrence fiscale*, Brussels: Bruylant.

Da Cruz Vilaça, J-L. (2009), 'Material and regional selectivity in State aids – Recent developments', *European State Aid Law Quarterly,* **4**, 443–451.

Fingleton, J., F. Ruane, and V. Ryan (1999), 'Market Definition and State Aid Control', *European Economy Report and Studies*, **3**, 65–88.

Garcia, J-A and D. Neven (2005), 'State aid and distortion of competition – A benchmark model', *HEI Working Paper*, **6**, 1–31.

Heidhues, P and R. Nitsche (2006),'Comments on State aid reform: some implications of an effects-based approach', *European State Aid Law Quarterly*, **1**, 23–34.

Jaeger, J. (2006), *Beihilfen durch Steuern und parafiskalische Abgaben*, Dissertation Universität Salzburg.

Jaeger, T. (2007), 'Ende der ,Organisationsblindheit' der Gemeinschaft im Beihilferecht: keine automatische Selektivität regionaler Steuermaßnahmen', *Recht der internationalen Wirtschaft*, 120–125.

Kube, H (2001), 'National tax law and the translational control of State aids', *EUI Working Paper*, Law, 9.

Kube, H. (2005), 'Nationales Steuerrecht und europäisches Beihilfenrecht', in U. Becker and W. Schön (eds), *Steuer- und Sozialstaat im europäischen Systemwettbewerb*, 99–117.

Kurcz, B. (2007), 'How selective is selectivity? A few thoughts on regional selectivity', *Cambridge Law Journal*, **66:2**, 313–324.

Kurcz, B. and D. Vallindas (2008), 'Can general measures be. . ..selective? Some thoughts on the interpretation of a State aid definition', *Common Market Law Review*, **45:1**, 2008, 159–182.

Lindsay-Poulsen, W. (2008), 'Regional autonomy, geographic selectivity and fiscal aid: between "the rock" and a hard place', *European Competition Law Review*, **29:1**, 43–49.

Luja, R. (2003), *Assessment and Recovery of Tax Incentives in the EC and the WTO: A View on State Aids, Trade Subsidies and Direct Taxation*, Antwerp: Intersentia.

Luja, R. (2009), 'Group taxation, sectoral tax benefits and de facto selectivity in State aid review', *European State Aid Law Quarterly*, **4**, 473-487.

Luja, R. (2010), 'Revisiting the balance between aid, selectivity and selective aid in respect of taxes and special levies', *European State Aid Law Quarterly*, **1**, 161–168.

Mamut, M-A. (2008), 'The State aid provisions of the EC Treaty in tax matters', in M. Lang, P., Pistone, J. Schuch, C. Staringer (eds.), *Introduction to European Tax Law: Direct Taxation*, London: Spiramus, 65–94.

Micheau, C. (2008), 'Tax selectivity in State aid review: a debatable case practice', *EC Tax Review*, **17**, 276–284.

Micheau, C. (2010), 'Tax selectivity – critical review and alternative approaches', in *Conflict of Norms in International Tax Law series*, IBDF.

Moreno Gonzalez, S. (2007), 'Regional fiscal autonomy from a State aid perspective: The ECJ's Judgment in Portugal v. Commission', *European Taxation*, 328–338.

Nicolaides, P. (2007), 'Developments in fiscal aids: new interpretations and new problems with the concept of selectivity', *European State Aid Law Quarterly*, **1**, 43–49.

O'Brien, M. (2005), 'Company Taxation, State aid and fundamental freedoms: is the next step enhanced cooperation?', *European Law Review*, **30:2**, 219.

Pinto, C. (2003), *Tax Competition and EU Law*, The Hague: Kluwer Law International.

Quigley, C. (2004), 'Taxation and State aid', in A. Biondi, P. Eeckhout and J. Flynn (eds.), *The Law of State Aid in the European Union*, Oxford: Oxford University Press.

Quigley, C. (2009), *European State Aid Law*, Oxford: Hart Publishing.

Rossi-Maccanico, P. (2007), 'The specificity criterion in fiscal aid review: proposals for state aid control of direct business tax measures', *EC Tax Review*, **16:2**, 90–103.

Rossi-Maccanico, P. (2009a), 'European Commission competence in reviewing direct business tax measures', *EC Tax Review*, **5**, 221–235.

Rossi-Maccanico, P. (2009b), 'Community review of direct business tax measures: selectivity, discrimination and restrictions', *European State Aid Law Quarterly*, **4**, 489–506.

Rossi-Maccanico, P. (2009c), 'The notion of indirect selectivity in fiscal aids: a reasoned review of the Community practice', *European State Aid Law Quarterly*, **2**, 161–176.

Ruane, F. and V. Ryan (1999), 'Market definition and State aid control', *European Economy Report and Studies*, **3**, 65–88.

Rydelski, M. (2006), 'Geographically limited national tax rate variations and State aid', *European Law Reporter*, **10**, 402–407.

Schön, W. (1999), 'Taxation and State aid law in the European Union', *Common Market Law Review*, **36:5**, 911–936.

Schön, W. (2006), 'State aid in the area of taxation', in L. Hancher, T. Ottervanger and P.J. Slot (eds), *EC State Aids*, London: Sweet & Maxwell.

Sutter, F.P. (2005), *Das EG-Beihilfenverbot und sein Durchführungsverbot in Steuersachen*, Linde.

Triantafyllou, D. (2008), 'La fiscalité façonnée par la discipline des aides d'Etat', in *Liber Amicum Francisco Santaolalla Gadea, EC State Aid Law – Le droit des aides d'Etat dans la CE*, The Hague: Wolters Kluwer, 409–424.

Van de Casteele, K. and M. Hocine (2008),' "Favouring certain undertakings or the production of certain goods": Selectivity', in *EU Competition Law, State aids, Volume IV*, Leuven: Claeys & Casteels, 247–271.

Waelbroeck, D. (2005), 'La condition de "sélectivité" de la mesure', in M. Dony and C. Smits, *Aides d'Etat*, Université de Bruxelles, 79–95.

Wishlade, F. (1997), 'When are tax advantages State aids and when are they general measures', Regional and Industrial Research Paper, Glasgow: European Policies Research Centre, 20.

Wouters, J. and B. Van Hees (2002), 'Les règles communautaires en matière d'aides d'Etat et la fiscalité directe: quelques observations critiques', Institut de droit international K.U. Leuven, Working Paper, 18.

10 Regional State aid

*Maja-Alexandra Dittel and Klaus-Otto Junginger-Dittel**

I. INTRODUCTION

This chapter first outlines the general architecture of State aid rules in the area of regional aid. Subsequently, it analyses the objectives and types of regional aid, explains the rules for establishing regional aid maps and regional aid ceilings, presents the compatibility criteria that apply to the different types of regional aid, and addresses the specific rules for the assessment of large investment projects. In its final section, it gives an outlook on the future of regional aid rules.

The key regional aid rules are laid down in the 2006 Regional Aid Guidelines 2007–2013 (RAG)[1] and are taken over by the 2006 Commission Regional Aid Block Exemption Regulation[2] (RAG BER), which was superseded by the 2008 General Block Exemption Regulation[3] (GBER). This chapter normally refers to the RAG. The corresponding rules in the RAG BER and the GBER are given in footnotes.

II. THE ARCHITECTURE OF STATE AID RULES IN THE AREA OF REGIONAL AID

Unlike most other types of State aid, such as aid for small and medium sized enterprises (SMEs), research, development and innovation (RD&I), and environmental aid, regional State aid is directly referred to in the Lisbon Treaty (TFEU). The initial Treaty of Rome 1957 allowed, declaring as compatible with the common market:

> (a) aid to promote the economic development of areas where the standard of living is abnormally low or where there is serious underemployment,[4] . . .
> (c) aid to facilitate the development of certain economic activities or of certain economic areas, where such aid does not adversely affect trading conditions to an extent contrary to the common interest;[5]

These Treaty provisions remained largely unchanged, one exception being that the Lisbon Treaty 2009 brings all outermost areas (listed in Article

349 TFEU), independently of their socio-economic situation, under the scope of subsection (a):

> (a) aid to promote the economic development of areas where the standard of living is abnormally low or where there is serious underemployment, and of the regions referred to in Article 349, in view of their structural, economic and social situation.

Article 92(2)(c) EEC also affected regional State aid control since it declared compatible all aid compensating for the economic effects of the division of Germany. This Article became the main legal basis for aid in the former West-German 'Zonenrandgebiet' and in West-Berlin. Today, Article 92(2)(c) EEC is primarily of historical interest.[6]

Regional aid became one of the first fields in which the Commission exerted State aid control, by adopting, until the mid nineties, a multitude of separate rules.[7] These rules were codified only in 1998 by the Regional Aid Guidelines 1998 (RAG 1998),[8] as part of a first comprehensive reform of State aid rules. This first reform included in particular the adoption of the Council 1998 Procedural Regulation,[9] the Council 1998 Enabling Regulation,[10] and the replacement (in principle) of several sector specific texts on regional aid to so called sensitive sectors (for example, cars,[11] synthetic fibres[12]), by a Multisectoral Framework[13] containing rules applicable to regional investment aid to large investment projects in all sectors.

The present State aid architecture in the field of regional aid relies basically on the innovations introduced in 1998, in particular

- on the principle to define simultaneously, for all Member States, regional aid maps, which must be drawn up within the limits of an EU wide population coverage ceiling for assisted areas and allocated national quotas, and which remain applicable for the duration of a Structural Funds Programming Period (RAG 1998),
- the possibility to exempt some types of aid, including regional aid,[14] under certain conditions from the notification obligation laid down in Article 108(3) TFEU[15,16];
- the obligation to notify individually regional aid for large investment projects, as introduced by the Multisectoral Framework 1998 (and maintained in the Multisectoral Framework 2002).

Today, the 2006 Regional Aid Guidelines for 2007–13 (RAG), the 2006 Appropriate Measures on Regional Aid, the 2006 Regional Block Exemption Regulation (RAG BER), and the 2008 General Block Exemption Regulation play a fundamental role in regional State aid.

The RAG provide an interpretation of Articles 107(3)(a) and (c) TFEU. They contain mapping rules and criteria that allow the creation, for all Member States, of lists of regions that are eligible for regional aid pursuant to Articles 107(3)(a) and (c) TFEU for the 2007–2013 period. Member States must notify national regional aid maps that were drawn up in line with the above criteria. The RAG define compatibility criteria the Commission will apply when assessing aid schemes and *ad hoc* aid Member States might wish to put into place during the validity of the regional aid maps in the eligible regions.

In order to ensure that all regional aid schemes which are in place during the 2007–13 period respect the compatibly criteria laid down in the RAG, the Commission proposed, pursuant to Article 108(1) TFEU to limit the application in time of all existing regional aid schemes to aid to be granted before 2007.[17] The proposal was accepted by all Member States and thus became binding under Article 19 of the Procedural Regulation. Consequently, all regional aid measures (to be) granted after 2007 had, in principle, to be newly notified pursuant to Article 108(3) TFEU. Paragraph 3 of the RAG BER[18] of 24 October 2006 exempted all transparent non sector specific investment aid schemes and supplementary[19] *ad hoc* aid that met the compatibility criteria of the RAG from that notification obligation, provided an individual notification threshold for large investment projects defined under Article 7(e) was not exceeded. As a consequence, only intransparent or sector specific[20] investment aid schemes, operating aid, regional aid to newly created enterprises, *ad hoc* aid, and individually notifiable cases of application of block exempted aid schemes had to be notified.

Transparent aid is defined by Article 2(1)(i) of the RAG BER as aid where it is possible to calculate precisely the gross grant equivalent as a percentage of eligible expenditure ex ante without need to undertake a risk assessment. Article 2(2) of the RAG BER identifies as intransparent aid schemes in particular schemes which use State guarantees and public loans which are not backed by normal security and involve abnormal risks. However, such guarantee and loan schemes can be made transparent if, before the implementation of the scheme, the methodology to calculate the aid intensity of the State guarantee has been accepted following notification. Several Member States, including Austria, France, Germany, and Hungary, used this possibility and put guarantee schemes based on approved methodologies into effect on the basis of the RAG BER.

The RAG BER was replaced in 2008 by the GBER which integrated the provisions of the RAG BER. New elements are that under its Article 14 aid schemes for newly created enterprises can now also be block exempted, and that following the entry into force of the 2008 Reference Rate Communication[21] which provides differentiated risk margins depending on the rating of the beneficiary and the level of collateralisation of the loan, all public senior loan measures can be block exempted;[22] the adoption of the 2008 Guarantee Communication[23] which provides safe harbour fees for SMEs provides for block exempted guarantee schemes for SMEs even in absence of an approved methodology to calculate the aid intensity.[24] Aid schemes that were block exempted under the RAG BER continue to be block exempted pursuant to Article 9(2) of the RAG BER until the date of expiry of the approved regional aid maps.

The compatibility criteria for the assessment of the regional aid to large investment projects were complemented in 2009 by the adoption of the Communication on the in-depth assessment of regional aid to large investment projects.[25]

III.   OBJECTIVES AND TYPES OF NATIONAL REGIONAL AID

Paragraph 2 of the RAG clarifies that 'national regional aid promotes the economic, social and territorial cohesion of Member States and the European Union as a whole' by 'addressing the shortcomings of disadvantaged regions'.

According to paragraph 3 of the RAG, national regional aid is designed to assist the development of the most disadvantaged regions by supporting investment and job creation; its purpose is to promote 'the expansion and diversification of the economic activities of enterprises located in the less-favoured regions, in particular by encouraging firms to set up new establishments there'.

Paragraph 6 recognises that in certain cases 'the structural handicaps of a region may be so severe that regional investment aid, (. . .) may not be sufficient to trigger a process of regional development,' and thus needs to be supplemented by regional operating aid.

Paragraph 7 admits that the formation of new enterprises is hampered by barriers which are particularly acute in disadvantaged regions, and which require a specific instrument to encourage small business start-ups there.

As a result, the RAG distinguish between three types of regional aid:

- initial investment aid,
- operating aid, and
- aid for newly created small enterprises.

Whereas the first two categories were already used by the Regional Aid Guidelines 2000–2006 (and before), the last category was newly introduced.[26]

III.i. Aid for Initial Investment

Paragraph 34 of the RAG[27] defines initial investment as an investment in material and immaterial assets relating to:

- the setting up of a new establishment,
- the extension of an existing establishment,
- diversification of the output of an establishment into new, additional products, and
- a fundamental change in the overall production process of an existing establishment.

Paragraph 35 adds a further category: the acquisition of assets directly linked to an establishment, provided the establishment has closed, or would have closed had it not been taken over by a new investor. The new investor has to be independent from the earlier owners.

The notion of establishment is not explicitly defined by the RAG but understood as a production site belonging to an enterprise, and distinct from the legal entity of an enterprise.[28]

Neither replacement investment,[29] nor the sole acquisition of the shares of the legal entity do qualify as 'initial investment'.[30]

In many situations, investment projects include elements of extension, modernisation, and diversification.[31]

III.ii. Operating Aid

Paragraph 76 of the RAG defines operating aid as regional aid aimed at reducing a firm's current expenses. The reference to regional aid refers to the objective of the aid, namely to contribute to the economic development of a region. Operating aid which is granted in assisted areas for other purposes, for example, in the context of an operation to rescue or restructure a firm in difficulty,[32] does not fall under the notion of regional operating aid.

Paragraph 81 defines a specific sub-category of regional operating aid, namely aid intended to partly offset additional transport costs that may arise related to economic activities in outermost areas and low population density areas.

III.iii.   Aid for Newly Created Small Enterprises

Paragraph 84 of the RAG[33] clarifies that aid for newly created small enterprises constitutes aid granted in addition to regional investment aid to provide incentives for the support of business start-ups and the early stage development of small enterprises. Small enterprises are defined within the meaning of Article 2 of the Annex I to Commission Regulation (EC) No 364 or any successor regulation. The business start-up and early stage development is supposed to cover a period of up to five years, as from the date of creation of the enterprise.

IV.   RULES ON THE IDENTIFICATION OF REGIONS ELIGIBLE FOR REGIONAL AID AND FOR THE DEFINITION OF REGIONAL AID MAPS

Paragraph 5 of the RAG emphasises that ' regional aid can only play an effective role if it is used sparingly and proportionately and is concentrated on the most disadvantaged regions of the European Union'. It notes that greater distortions of competition can be accepted in regions eligible under Article 107(3)(a) TFEU than in those under Article 107(3)(c) TFEU. The principles of concentration and proportionality (regarding aid intensity ceilings for investment aid) are implemented by concise mapping rules laid down mainly in sections 3 and 4.1.2. of the RAG.

IV.i.   Overall Population Coverage

Following the accession of ten new Member States in 2004, more than 50% of the EU 25 population lived in recognised assisted areas by the end of 2006. To restore the principle of 'concentration', paragraph 13 of the RAG limits the overall population coverage (population living in areas eligible for regional aid pursuant to Articles 107(3)(a) and (c) TFEU) in principle to 42% of the EU 25 population[34] for the period 2007-13. However, to ensure a minimum of continuity of support measures, a 'safety net' is introduced by paragraph 14 to ensure that no Member State loses more than 50% of the coverage of its population covered during the period 2000–2006. The safety net increases the eligible population to 43.1% of the EU 25 population, or, following the accession of Bulgaria and Romania, to 46.6% of the EU 27 population.[35]

IV.ii.   Regions Eligible for Regional Aid Pursuant to Article 107(3)(a)

Section 3.2 of the RAG defines eligible regions as all regions at NUTS II level[36] with a per capita gross domestic product in purchasing power standards of less than 75% of the EU 25 average. Paragraph 17 of the RAG grants this status to all outermost regions covered by Article 299(2) EC (now Article 349 TFEU), independent of the level of their per capita GDP.[37]

Section 3.3. creates a temporary Article 107(3)(a) TFEU status until 31 December 2010 for the so called 'statistical effect 2-regions'. These are regions at NUTS II level with a per capita GDP between 75% of the EU 25 average, and 75% of the EU -15 average, that is, regions which would be eligible for a-status if the 2004 enlargement by ten Member States had not reduced the EU per capita GDP average. The individual statistical effect regions will benefit from regional aid pursuant to Article 107(3)(c) TFEU from 2011–2013 unless a review of their socio-economic situation, to have been carried out by the Commission in 2010, confirms on the basis of the most recent statistical data that their per capita GDP fell below 75% of the EU 25 average.

Annex V to the RAG identifies all regions at NUTS II level of the EU 25 which qualify for regional aid pursuant to Article 107(3)(a) TFEU, including the statistical effect regions. Bulgaria and Romania are eligible for Article 107(3)(a) TFEU in their entirety.

IV.iii.   Regions Eligible for Regional Aid Pursuant to Article 107(3)(c) TFEU

Regions under Article 107(3)(c) TFEU do not have to fulfil specific requirements regarding per capita GDP. To become eligible under Article 107(3)(c) TFEU, a region has to be proposed by a Member State within its population coverage, and to fall into one of the categories identified by paragraphs 30, 31, and 95 of the RAG. Accordingly, they have to qualify as one of the following:

- Economic development region (former a-region which does not qualify as statistical effect region).
- Low population density area (population density below 12.5 inhabitants per km² at level NUT III, or below 8 inhabitants at level NUTS II; some flexibility is allowed).
- Contiguous zones with a population exceeding 100 000, or islands and other regions categorised by similar geographic isolation, or entire NUTS III regions, situated in a NUTS II or NUTS III region,

or constituting a NUTS III region, with either a per capita GDP below the EU 25 average, or an unemployment rate exceeding 115% of the national average.

- Islands and other regions categorised by similar geographic isolation, with less than 5000 inhabitants.
- (part of a) NUTS III region adjacent (land border, or sea border of less than 30 km) to a region eligible under Article 107(3)(a) TFEU, or a State which is not a Member State of the EEA or EFTA.
- Areas with a minimum population of 50 000 which are undergoing major structural change, or are in serious relative decline.
- Areas with a minimum population of 20 000 characterised by very localised regional disparities (so called paragraph 31 regions).
- Regions which were eligible under Article 87(3)(c) EC in 2000-2006, and which benefit from transitional arrangements for 2007–2008 under paragraph 95.

IV.iv. National Population Coverage

According to section 3.4.1 of the RAG, the population coverage of a Member State for the full period 2007–13 results from the population living in its areas recognised as eligible for regional aid under Article 107(3)(a) TFEU, including the statistical effect regions, and its quota in the EU 25 population coverage eligible for Article 107(3)(c)TFEU. The EU 25 population coverage eligible for Article 107(3)(c) TFEU is derived as residual, by subtracting from the overall EU 25 population coverage the population of the areas recognised as eligible for regional aid under Article 107(3)(a) TFEU, including the statistical effect regions. The EU-25 population coverage eligible for Article 107(3)(c) TFEU is allocated to the various Member States by a two-step approach: in a first step, individual Member States receive the population of their regions qualifying as economic development and low population density regions. The remainder of the EU 25 Article 107(3)(c) TFEU coverage is distributed, in a second step, by applying a distribution key to Member States. The distribution key takes account of variations in GDP per capita and unemployment between the regions, both in a national and a Community context. Details of the underlying methodology that was already applied for 2000–2006, are laid down in Annex IV to the RAG.

IV.v. Proportionality

The principle that regional aid should be proportional to the regional handicaps is ensured through differentiated aid intensity ceilings for investment aid, the restriction of access to regional operating aid to regions eligible under Article 107(3)(a) TFEU and low population density areas, and a modulation in the aid amounts and aid intensity ceilings available for aid to newly created enterprises. The regional aid maps that are the result of the precise 'mapping rules' laid down in the RAG include only information on aid intensity ceilings for investment aid.

IV.v.a.   Aid intensity ceilings for investment aid

Maximum aid intensity ceilings for investment aid are defined mainly in section 4.1.2 of the RAG. Aid intensity is the discounted value of aid payments divided by the discounted value of eligible expenditure incurred.[38] Contrary to the RAG 2000–2006 which defined aid intensity ceilings for investment aid in net grant equivalents (after deducting taxes payable on aid), the aid ceilings under the RAG are defined in gross grant equivalents.

IV.v.b.   Standard aid intensity ceilings

The standard regional aid ceilings that apply to large undertakings are the following:[39]

- areas eligible for Article 107(3)(a) TFEU with per capita GDP below 45% of the EU 25 average: 50%
- areas eligible for Article 107(3)(a) TFEU with per capita GDP below 60% of the EU 25 average: 40%
- areas eligible for Article 107(3)(a) TFEU with per capita GDP below 75% of the EU 25 average: 30%
- statistical effect regions during 2007–2010: 30%
- statistical effect regions eligible for Article 107(3)(a) TFEU after 2010 with per capita GDP below 75% of the EU 25 average: 30%
- statistical effect regions areas eligible for Article 107(3)(c) TFEU after 2010 with per capita GDP above the EU 25 average: 20%
- areas eligible for Article 107(3)(c) TFEU with per capita GDP above the EU 25 average and an unemployment rate below the EU 25 average: 10%
- areas eligible for Article 107(3)(c) TFEU for 2007–2008 under paragraph 95: 10%
- areas eligible for Article 107(3)(c) TFEU as low population density areas: 15%
- areas eligible for Article 107(3)(c) TFEU adjacent to a-areas, or bordering States which are not Member States of the EEA or EFTA: 15%. For areas adjacent to areas eligible under Article 107(3)(a) TFEU the aid intensity may exceed 15%, if the increased intensity is

needed to ensure that the differential between the two regions does not exceed 20%
- areas eligible for Article 107(3)(c) TFEU under paragraph 31 'very localised regional disparity' zones: 0%
- all other areas eligible for Article 107(3)(c)TFEU: 15%.

In addition, transitional arrangements apply under paragraphs 92 and 93 of the RAG to NUTS II regions which were eligible for regional aid under (then) Article 87(3)(a) in 2000–2006, where the difference between the applicable aid intensity ceilings 2000–2006 and 2007–2013 exceeds 15%. In these situations, a reduction of at least 10% (net to gross) compared to the 2000–2006 ceiling applies for 2007–2010, and the definite ceiling applies as from 2011.

Outside assisted areas, investment aid to large undertakings is prohibited.

IV.v.c.   Increased aid intensity ceilings for SMEs
The aid intensity ceilings set out above may be increased, in line with paragraph 49 of the RAG, by SME-bonuses, for:

- small enterprises by 20%
- medium-sized enterprises by 10%.

In areas eligible under paragraph 31 of the RAG, small enterprises may receive up to 30%, medium-sized enterprises up to 20%, provided the eligible expenditure of the investment does not exceed €25 million.

The increased aid ceilings for SMEs are not applicable for large investment projects, with eligible expenditure exceeding €50 million, nor for investments in the transport sector.

Outside assisted areas, SMEs may benefit from investment aid in accordance with Article 15 of the GBER.

IV.v.d.   Adjusted aid intensity ceilings for large investment projects
For large investment projects with eligible expenditure exceeding €50 million, adjusted aid intensity ceilings apply pursuant to paragraph 67 of the RAG following a scaling down mechanism:

- for the first €50 million, the standard regional aid ceiling applies,
- for the next €50 million, half the standard regional aid ceiling applies,
- for eligible expenditure exceeding €100 million, 34% of the standard regional aid ceiling applies.

The underlying rationale is that large projects are less affected by regional handicaps than smaller projects, whilst aid to large projects is likely to have a stronger impact on trade and competition.[40]

iv.vi. Regional Aid Maps

The mapping rules described so far explain the criteria and limits Member States have to observe when notifying regional aid maps, and which the Commission considers in its compatibility assessment. Paragraph 96 of the RAG 2007–13 defines as the regional aid map of a Member State the regions eligible for regional aid pursuant to Article 87(3)(a) and Article 87(3)(c) EC, and the regional ceilings on the intensity for initial investment aid.

The Commission approved regional aid maps following their notification pursuant to Article 108(3) TFEU in 2006 and 2007, for the period 2007–2013. These maps are published in the *Official Journal*, and are considered to constitute an integral part of the RAG.

The regional aid maps were defined, in order to ensure continuity, for the programming period 2007–13. Paragraph 104 of the RAG offers Member States the possibility to carry out a mid-term review of their maps in 2010 and to notify amended regional aid maps before April 2010. Three Member States (France, Ireland, Italy) used this option.

V. COMPATIBILITY CRITERIA FOR REGIONAL AID

V.i. Compatibility Criteria for Investment Aid[41]

To be in conformity with the compatibility criteria under the RAG, the regional investment aid has to respect a series of requirements. First, the aid has to address an initial investment project, as defined above: the Commission assumes that the initial investment requirement ensures that the investment leads to the creation of a new or reinforced economic activity that creates new jobs and revenues. Second, the aid has to be in conformity with the regional aid map: to meet this requirement, the investment project must be carried out in an assisted area, identified in the applicable regional aid map, and the aid has to be granted within the period of validity of this regional aid map. Where the granting of the aid requires *ex ante* Commission approval following an Article 108(3) TFEU notification, the aid has to be notified during the period of validity of the map. In addition, the total public support for the project has to respect the regional aid ceiling, again defined by the regional aid map, that applies at the point in time when the aid is granted.[42] Under the rules on cumulation of aid laid down in section 4.4 of the RAG,[43] the notion of total public support is broadly defined. To be included under this notion, it is irrelevant:

- in which form the aid is granted,
- whether it comes from local, regional, national or Community sources,
- whether it is granted from one or several regional investment aid schemes or via *ad hoc* aid (individual aid not covered by an existing aid scheme),
- or whether some of the support qualifies as *de minimis* aid in the meaning of the applicable *de minimis* Regulation.[44]

Third, the aid has to be calculated with respect to eligible expenditure as prescribed by the RAG. Recognised eligible expenditure is defined either in reference to material and immaterial investment costs resulting from the initial investment project, or with regards to estimated wage costs for jobs directly created by the investment project.[45] In accordance with paragraph 51 of the RAG, the cost of preparatory studies and consultancy costs linked to an investment are also eligible, with a maximum aid intensity of 50% of the costs incurred. Eligible material investment costs consist of costs for assets relating to land, buildings, and plant/machinery.[46] Only investment costs related to new material assets are admitted, except where the initial investment is carried out by a SME, or refers to the takeover of the assets of an establishment which is closed, or will be closed in the absence of its takeover by a new, independent investor.[47] In the case of takeovers, the transaction has to take place under market conditions, and the acquisition of assets to which aid had already been granted at an earlier stage, is not eligible.[48]

Costs related to the acquisition of plant/machinery under lease are eligible only if the lease takes the form of financial leasing and contains an obligation to buy the leased asset at the end of the leasing contract. For costs related to the acquisition of land and buildings under lease to be eligible, the contract has to cover a period of at least five years after completion of the investment (three years for SMEs).[49]

Eligible immaterial investment costs consist of costs entailed by the transfer of technology through the acquisition of patent rights, licences, know-how or unpatented technical knowledge. For large undertakings, immaterial investment costs are eligible only up to 50% of the total eligible investment expenditure for the project.[50] Under the provisions of paragraph 56 of the RAG, it must be ensured that the intangible assets remain in the assisted area, and that the aid does not benefit other areas: to that end, eligible assets must be used exclusively in the establishment receiving the aid, amortisable, purchased from third parties under market conditions, and included in the assets of the firm and remain in the establishment for at least five years after completion of the investment (three years for SMEs).

Section 4.2.2 of the RAG stipulates that where the investment aid is calculated with regards to the eligible wage costs arising from job creation as a result of an initial investment project, the eligible costs are the wage costs of persons hired, calculated over a period of two years. Wage costs include the total amount payable by the firm, comprising the gross wage, before tax, and the compulsory social security contributions. Only the net job increase by the investment is taken into account, with net job increase being defined as the number of employees directly employed in a particular establishment after completion of the investment, compared with the average over the previous 12 months.

Where the aid calculated on the basis of material and immaterial investment expenditure is combined with aid calculated on the basis of wage costs, the eligible expenditure of the project is limited to the higher of the two possible definitions of eligible expenditure.[51]

Fourth, the formal incentive effect rules laid down in paragraph 38 of the RAG have to be respected;[52] these rules do not apply to aid granted under existing tax aid schemes where a tax exemption or reduction is granted automatically with respect to identified eligible expenditure without any discretion on the part of the authorities, but only to discretionary aid, whether it is granted on the basis of a scheme, or as *ad hoc* aid. They stipulate that projects are only eligible if two conditions are fulfilled: first, the aid beneficiary applied for aid before the start of works, that is, the start of the construction work or the first firm commitment to order equipment. The acquisition of land, or prefeasibility studies, is not taken into account to define the 'start of works'. Second, the authorities in charge of the scheme confirmed in writing before the start of the works that subject to detailed verification the project in principle meets the eligibility criteria for the scheme. In case of *ad hoc* aid, this confirmation is replaced by the requirement to send a letter of intent to award aid before the start of works.

Fifth, the rules on the minimum own contribution by the beneficiary laid down in paragraph 39 of the RAG have to be respected: these rules apply only where the aid is calculated on the basis of investment costs; they require that the aid beneficiary provides a financial contribution of at least 25% from its own resources, or external financing, in a form which is free of any public support, including support granted under the applicable *de minimis* rule. These rules are considered necessary to ensure that a minimum risk resulting from the implementation of the investment project remains with the beneficiary, so as to ensure that the investment project is as such viable and sound.

Sixth, in order to ensure that the aid has a real and sustained effect on regional development, the provisions on the maintenance of the investment and of the posts created by it, laid down in paragraph 40 of the RAG, have to be fulfilled: to that end, the aid must be made conditional on the maintenance of the investment project in the assisted region for a minimum period of five years after completion of the investment. In addition, where the aid is calculated with regard to wage costs for jobs directly created by the project, the posts have to be filled within three years after completion of the works, and have to be maintained for a minimum period of five years. Where the project is carried out by a SME, the maintenance periods for the investment and the created posts are reduced to three years.

Seventh, where the investment project concerns a large investment project with eligible expenditure exceeding €50 million, specific rules for regional aid to large investment projects have to be respected which are explained below.

V.ii. Compatibility Criteria for Operating Aid

The compatibility criteria for regional operating aid are laid down in section 5 of the RAG which emphasises that access to regional operating aid is normally prohibited, and can be granted only exceptionally if certain conditions are met:

First, the operating aid has to support an economic activity which takes place in a region which is eligible for operating aid. Such regions are regions eligible under Article 107(3)(a) TFEU, including the outermost areas, the least populated regions (8 inhabitants per km^2), and low population density areas. In addition, operating aid can be granted transitionally, to phase out operating aid schemes which existed in areas that lost their eligibility under Article 107(3)(a) TFEU.

Second, the operating aid has to fulfil a well defined purpose: in regions eligible under Article 107(3)(a) TFEU the aid has to be justified in terms of its contribution to regional development and its nature. It must be targeted at well defined shortcomings of the region with the aim to overcome delays and bottlenecks in regional development. In outermost regions the aid may in particular serve to offset the additional costs of economic activities, resulting from the specific constraints of remoteness, insularity, small size, difficult topology and climate, and dependence on a few products that hamper their economic development. In the least populated regions, the aid may serve to prevent or reduce the continuing depopulation of these regions. In the outermost areas and the low population density areas, aid may also be granted to partly offset additional transport costs.

Third, the level of the aid has to be proportional to the importance of the shortcomings it seeks to alleviate: the RAG do not normally define further the notion of proportionality for operating aid, but leave the proportionality issue to be assessed on the basis of the merits of the individual case.[53]

Fourth, the availability of operating aid to support certain economic activities has in principle to be limited in time. This limitation does not apply where the operating aid becomes necessary due to a permanent shortcoming, for example, where it serves to offset the additional costs of an economic activity in an outermost area, is intended to prevent or reduce the depopulation of the least populated areas, or is intended partly to offset the additional transport costs affecting outermost and low population density regions.

Fifth, operating aid has to be digressively reduced, except in situations where it addresses permanent, in particular geographic, shortcomings.

Sixth, operating aid, except where it is granted under general schemes to offset additional transport or employment costs, must not be granted to financial services and intra-group activities[54] since aid for these activities is unlikely to promote regional development, but likely to lead to major distortions of competition.

Seventh, regional operating aid to promote exports is excluded.

Eighth, regional operating aid should in principle be calculated with respect to a pre-defined set of eligible expenditures or costs, for example, cost of replacement investments, transport costs, labour costs, and be limited to a certain proportion of these costs.

Ninth, the specific provisions on the offsetting of additional transport costs laid down in paragraph 81 of the RAG on operating aid must be respected:

- The aid has to be limited to additional transport costs of goods produced in the eligible regions and which occurred within the national borders. The costs of transporting primary commodities, raw materials, or intermediate products from the place of their production to the place of final processing in the outermost region may be included. No aid must be granted for the transport of products which depend for the production on the availability of natural resources, and which cannot be produced elsewhere for that reason (e.g. products of the extractive industries); in addition, the transport aid must not be allowed to become export aid.

- The aid amount necessary to offset the additional transport costs has to be based on the most economical form of transport and the shortest route; in addition, the aid must be objectively quantifiable in advance, on the basis of an aid-per-passenger or aid per t/km basis.

V.iii.   Compatibility Criteria for Aid to Newly Created Enterprises

Aid for this new type of regional aid has to respect the compatibility criteria laid down in section 6 of the RAG.[55]

First, the aid has to be limited to the eligible beneficiaries, that is, small enterprises in their start-up and development phase within a period of five years following their creation.

Second, as regional investment aid, aid to newly created enterprises has to be in conformity with the regional aid map: to meet this requirement, the business creation and development has to be carried out in an assisted area, identified in the applicable regional aid map, and the aid has to be granted within the period of validity of this regional aid map.

Third, certain rules on the modulation in the aid amounts and aid intensity ceilings available for aid to newly created enterprises have to be respected:

> Paragraph 88 of the RAG establishes aid intensity ceilings for aid to newly created enterprises: these ceilings are defined with regard to the relevant eligible expenditure, and amount:

- in areas eligible under Article 107(3)(a) TFEU, to 35% in the first three years, and 25% in the subsequent two years.
- in areas eligible under Article 107(3)(c) TFEU, to 25% in the first three years, and 15% in the subsequent two years.

> These ceilings are increased by 5%:

- in areas eligible under Article 107(3)(a) TFEU with a GDP per capita below 60%
- in low population density areas with less than 12.5 inhabitants per km^2
- in small islands and other communities suffering from similar isolation, with less than 5000 inhabitants.

Paragraph 86 limits the total amount of aid for newly created enterprises over the eligible five year period to:

– €2 million in areas eligible under Article 107(3)(a) TFEU
– €1 million in areas eligible under Article 107(3)(c) TFEU.

Paragraph 90 stipulates that the above ceilings and maximum aid amounts are respected, taking into account all forms of public support, including support under the *de minimis* rules.

Fourth, the aid for newly created enterprises has to be granted with regard to certain eligible expenses, defined in paragraph 87 of the RAG. These expenses consist of the legal, advisory, consultancy and administrative costs directly related to the creation of the enterprise, and certain running costs which are incurred within the five-year period of eligibility. These running costs include interests on external finance, or a dividend on own capital employed, fees for renting production facilities and equipment, energy, water heating, taxes (except VAT and direct business profit/ income taxes) and administrative charges. Depreciation, fees for leasing production facilities and equipment, and wage costs, including compulsory social charges may be included as eligible expenses provided the underlying investments or job creation and recruitment measures have not benefitted from other aid.

VI. SPECIFIC RULES APPLICABLE TO REGIONAL AID TO LARGE INVESTMENT PROJECTS[56]

VI.i. Definition of Large Investment Project

Section 4.3 of the RAG lays down specific rules applicable to large investment projects. Large investment projects are defined in this context as investment projects with eligible expenditure exceeding €50 million, calculated at prices and exchange rates applicable on the date the aid is granted or notified.[57] The eligible expenditure to be taken into account are the eligible immaterial and material investment costs, unless the wage cost based eligible expenditure, as defined above, is higher. The RAG specify that in addition, the 'single investment project' rule applies, according to which all initial investment projects which consist of fixed assets combined in an economically indivisible way, and which are undertaken by one or more companies in a period of three years are considered to be one single investment project. To verify whether several projects are economically indivisible, account is taken of their technical, functional and strategic links and their immediate geographic proximity.[58]

VI.ii.   Increased Transparency Requirements for Large Investment Projects

Paragraph 64 of the RAG[59] stipulates that Member States have to inform[60] the Commission of the granting of aid to regional investment projects that was not individually notifiable within 20 days of the granting of the aid. The Commission verifies that the aid was granted in line with the provisions of the applied aid scheme and publishes the information on its website.[61]

VI.iii.   Individual Notification Requirement

According to paragraph 68 of the RAG,[62] regional investment aid exceeding a certain threshold has to be notified individually, even if it is granted on the basis of an aid scheme. This threshold depends on the standard regional aid ceiling applicable to large undertakings in the region where the investment is to be carried out, and amounts to 75% of the aid amount an investment with eligible expenditure of €100 million could receive if the standard regional aid ceiling was applicable to the whole amount of €100 million. The regional aid maps foresee already adjusted aid intensities (scaling down) for eligible expenditure exceeding €50 million, and the applicable threshold for individual notification corresponds to the maximum aid amount an investment project with eligible expenditure could receive if the adjusted aid intensity ceiling was fully applied.

VI.iv.   Compatibility Criteria for Regional Aid to Large Investment Projects

Individually notified regional aid to large investment projects has to respect all standard compatibility criteria for investment aid. It should be noted in this context that the regional aid maps foresee adjusted regional aid ceilings for large investment projects, as described above.

Where the notified aid amount exceeds the individual notification threshold mentioned above, the aid can only be approved within the preliminary investigation phase, if the aid project meets two tests defined in paragraph 68 of the RAG 2007–2013, namely:

- the 'market share' test (or paragraph 68(a)-test),
- and the 'capacity increase in an underperforming market' test (or paragraph 68(b)-test).

Under the 'market share' test, the Commission tries to address situations where a significant market position of the aid beneficiary that could be used for anti-competitive behaviour, could be reinforced by the aid. Under the test, the market share of the aid beneficiary must not exceed 25% of the relevant market which is addressed by the investment project. To carry out this test, it is first necessary to identify the *product (directly) concerned* by the investment. Normally, this product is the product covered by the investment project, and where the project concerns several products, all products involved. The product concerned may also include products which could, without major additional investment and cost, be produced in the aided production facility. Where the production concerns an intermediate product of which a substantive part is used by the aid beneficiary in captive production, the downstream (final) product may also be a product concerned.

In a second step, the relevant *product market* has to be identified: the relevant product market includes the product concerned and its substitutes, both from the demand and production side. Substitutes from the demand side are products which are considered, taking into account relative prices, by the consumers (or users of intermediate goods) to be able to replace the product concerned in its intended use, whereas substitutes from the production site are products which the producer could manufacture instead of the product concerned through flexibility of the production installations.

In a third step, the relevant *geographic market* for the product or products concerned has to be established. The formulation in paragraph 70 of the RAG 2007–2013 seems to suggest that the relevant geographic market should normally be defined at EEA level, but offers some flexibility where another generally accepted market segmentation for which statistical data are readily available seems more relevant. De facto, the Commission assesses markets for the market share test on the basis of the most relevant data and market segmentation, taking into account factors such as trade flows, exports intended by the aid beneficiary, relevant transport costs, and other barriers of trade that might segment markets for the definition of the relevant geographic market.

The 'market share' test is met if the market share of the beneficiary does not exceed 25% on any of the markets that are considered.

Under the 'capacity increase in an underperforming market' test, the Commission tries to address problems that might arise if a major aided investment project addresses a market characterised by overcapacities, since in this situation the risk exists that competitors will be crowded out. The test is carried out in two parts:

- in the first part of the test, the Commission establishes whether the investment project increases the production capacity by more than 5% of the market. The market is measured using apparent consumption data. Apparent consumption is defined for this purpose as production minus exports plus imports of the product concerned. This test is carried out at the level of the EEA, even if the geographic market concerned is defined at a different level.

– In the second part of the test, the Commission tries to establish whether the market concerned is growing slower than the GDP of the EEA. To that end, the average annual growth rate of the market over the last five years is compared to the corresponding growth rate of the EEA. Again the market is measured in terms of apparent consumption at EEA level. The test is normally carried out in volume terms (annual growth in units compared to real GDP growth), and where available, in value terms (annual growth in value terms, compared to the growth of the EEA nominal GDP). The value terms test is of particular importance in situations that are characterised by growing volumes and sinking prices, where an analysis which is solely based on volume terms could hide situations of overcapacities.

The 'capacity increase in an underperforming market' test is not met if both the capacity increase exceeds 5% of the market, and the markets grows slower than the EEA GDP.

The Commission can approve a regional aid to a large investment project on the basis of the preliminary investigation only if all standard compatibility criteria of the RAG 2007–2013 are respected, and both the 'market share' and 'capacity increase in an underperforming market' tests raise no problems. Where an aid project does not meet the standard compatibility criteria applicable to regional investment aid, where the Commission is unable to establish without doubt that the tests under paragraph 68 are met, or where these tests are clearly not met, the Commission has to open the formal investigation pursuant to Article 108(2) TFEU. Where the Commission is unable to confirm in the formal investigation that the tests under paragraph 68 are met, it has to carry out an in-depth assessment of the compatibility of the aid.

In the in-depth assessment of the compatibility of regional aid to large investment projects, the Commission carries out a 'detailed verification that the aid is necessary to provide an incentive effect for the investment and that the benefits of the notified aid measure outweigh the resulting distortion of competition'.[63] Details of the way the Commission intends to carry out this in-depth assessment are laid down in a Commission communication concerning the criteria for an in-depth assessment of regional aid to large investment projects which was published in September 2009[64] (IDAC). So far, such an in-depth assessment was carried out in only one case, concerning regional aid to Dell in Poland.[65] The application of the IDAC and the interpretation of its provisions certainly needs some further testing; in two other cases[66] where the Commission opened the formal investigation in late 2009, the Commission may be able to gain further experience in carrying out such in-depth assessments.

The key element and point of departure for the in-depth assessment is the verification of the incentive effect. In this incentive effect test,[67] the Commission determines whether the aid actually contributes to changing the behaviour of the beneficiary and is decisive for the location of the project in the assisted area: an incentive effect can be proven in two scenarios:

– In the first scenario, the aid gives an incentive to adopt a positive investment decision in favour of the beneficiary region in a situation where in the absence of the aid the project would not be profitable for the beneficiary at any location;
– In the second scenario, the aid gives an incentive to locate the investment in the beneficiary region rather than elsewhere since it compensates for the region's net handicaps and costs.

Where no incentive effect can be proven, the aid is considered incompatible.

In a second step, the Commission verifies whether the amount of the aid is proportional. This proportionality test[68] implies that:

– under scenario 1, the aid is in line with the normal rate of return on investment applied by the company in other investment projects, with the cost of capital of the company as a whole, or with returns commonly observed in the sector concerned;
– under scenario 2, the aid does not exceed the difference between the net costs for the beneficiary company to invest in the interested region and the (lower) net costs to invest in an alternative location, and thus compensates for the lower profitability of the project in the assisted region.

The standard situation seems to be the situation under scenario 2. The probability that a firm invests into a non viable project only because of the availability of aid seems rather remote. It is also rather difficult to imagine that a State could grant aid from scarce public resources to support an economic activity which might not be sustainable.

Under scenario 2, by definition, the counterfactual analysis[69] suggests that the investment would take place at any event. If the aid is proportional, any possible distortions of competition that might result from high market shares or an increase in capacity in an underperforming market would happen to the same extent without the aid. The aid does not increase the distortion of competition, but contributes (as has also to be proved under the in-depth assessment[70]) to the achievement of a regional development objective. It can therefore normally[71] be approved unless it has a negative effect on cohesion within the EU. Such an anti-cohesion effect would exist if the investment project would have located in the absence of any aid in a region which is poorer, or has the same level of handicaps, as the target region. If the aid would prevent an unaided investment in a region with the same, or a higher regional aid ceiling, the outcome of the overall balancing test which is carried out within the in-depth assessment would therefore be negative.

In the unlikely case of a scenario 1 project, the in-depth assessment will have to take account of a series of further negative effects of the aid which cannot all be presented here.[72] The overall balancing of positive and negative factors is likely to lead to a negative result in particular where the aided (*per se* non viable) investment adds capacity to a market in absolute decline, and thus contributes to the crowding out of more efficient firms.[73]

VII. OUTLOOK

VII.i.   The Interaction of Regional Aid with Measures under the Temporary Framework

In December 2008 the Commission adopted the Temporary Framework Communication.[74] The Communication defines the criteria the Commission will apply to declare certain aid measures compatible to remedy a serious disturbance in the economy of a Member State, a derogation provided for in Article 107(3)(b) TFEU. This is discussed further in Chapter 7.

Key measures under the Temporary Framework are:

- limited amounts of compatible aid (up to €500,000 per beneficiary for inter alia the financing of investments and the covering of operating costs, including replacement investments);
- subsidised loans and interest rate subsidies, equally available, inter alia, to finance investment projects and to cover operating costs, including replacement investments;
- subsidised guarantees to cover loans for financing initial and replacement investments, as well as working capital loans.

Such measures, which are subject to notification, can and have been approved during the period of validity of the Temporary Framework, and within time limits defined in the Framework, for the whole territory of a Member State. Since the Temporary Framework makes available investment aid to large firms outside assisted areas which is normally prohibited there, and allows for operating aid outside regions eligible for regional aid pursuant to Article 107(3)(a) TFEU, it leads temporarily to a reduction of the level of preferential treatment created by the RAG.

VII.ii.   The Review of the Regional Aid Rules for the Period after 2013

The present Regional Aid Guidelines, Block Exemption Regulations, regional aid maps and schemes all expire at the end of 2013. A new Structural Funds programming period starts on 1 January 2014.

Work on the review of the Regional Aid Guidelines and the linked block exemption provisions started in 2010. At this stage, it is difficult to predict whether, and in which areas, this review will lead to dramatic changes compared to the present rules.

The discussion will certainly focus on a series of cornerstones for regional aid control, in particular:

- the overall population coverage, the criteria for the definition of areas eligible for regional aid under Article 107(3)(a) TFEU, and the method for the distribution of areas eligible for regional aid pursuant to Article 107(3)(c) TFEU between Member States;
- detailed rules for the delimitation of areas eligible under Article 107(3)(c) TFEU;
- the general level of regional aid ceilings, and the modulation of the ceilings between different types of regions;
- national regional aid as an element contributing to the relocation of activities within the EU, and the role of regional aid in a more and more globalised economy in the light of the Europe 2020 objectives;
- the full integration of the 'enhanced economic approach' into regional aid rules, in particular regarding the rules on 'incentive effect', 'necessity of aid', and 'proportionality of aid', and the treatment of aid for sectors facing structural difficulties and concerning markets in decline.

The discussion will also include a substantial review of the rules applicable to the assessment of aid to large investment projects, and may possibly lead to the integration of the criteria for in-depth assessment laid down in the IDAC into the future Guidelines.

NOTES

*   The author is an official of the European Commission. The views expressed are purely those of the author and may not in any circumstances be regarded as stating an official position of the European Commission.
1.   *Guidelines on National Regional Aid For 2007–2013*, O.J. 2006 C 54/13.
2.   Commission Regulation (EC) No 1628/2006 of 24 October 2006 on the application of Articles 87 and 88 of the Treaty to national regional investment aid, O.J. 2006 L302/29.
3.   Commission Regulation (EC) No 800/2008 of 6 August 2008 declaring certain categories of aid compatible with the common market in application of Articles 87 and 88 of the Treaty, O.J. 2008 L 214/3.
4.   Article 92(3)(a) EEC , now Article 107(3)(a) TFEU.
5.   Article 92(3)(c) EEC, now Article 107(3)(c) TFEU.
6.   The TFEU reads: '(c) aid granted to the economy of certain areas of the Federal Republic of Germany affected by the division of Germany, in so far as such aid is required in order to compensate for the economic disadvantages caused by that division. Five years after the entry into force of the Treaty of Lisbon, the Council, acting on a proposal from the Commission, may adopt a decision repealing this point.'
7.   For an overview on the evolution of regional State aid control, see Olofsson 2005. Key texts adopted were the Council Resolution of 20 October 1971, O.J. 1971 C 111/ 1, the 1979 *Commission Communication to the Member States on Coordinating Principles,* O.J. 1979 C 31/9, and the 1988 *Commission Communication to the Member States on the method for the application of Article 92(3)(a) and (c) to national regional aid,* O.J. 1988 C 312/ 2
8.   Guidelines on National Regional Aid, O.J. 1998 C 74/9.
9.   Council Regulation No 659/1999 of 22 March 1999 laying down detailed rules for the application of Article 93 (now Article 88) of the EC Treaty, O.J. 1999 L 83/1.
10.   Council Regulation (EC) No 994/98 of 7 May 1998 on the application of Articles 92 and 93 (now 107 and 108 TFEU) of the Treaty establishing the European Community to certain categories of horizontal State aid, O.J. 1998 L 142/1.
11.   Community framework on State aid to the motor vehicle industry, O.J. 1997 C 279/1.
12.   Code on aid to the synthetic fibres industry, O.J. 1996 C 94/11.
13.   1998 Multisectoral framework on regional aid for large investment projects, O.J. 1998 C 107/7, replaced by Multisectoral framework on regional aid for large investment projects, O.J. 2002 C 70/8, and amended by *Commission communication on the modification of the Multisectoral Framework on regional aid for large investment projects* (2002) with regard to the establishment of a list of sectors facing structural problems and on a proposal of appropriate measures pursuant to Article 88 paragraph 1 of the EC Treaty, concerning the motor vehicle sector and the synthetic fibres sector (O.J. 2003 C 263/3); for an analysis of the Multisectoral Framework 2002 see Cavallo and Junginger-Dittel, 2004.
14.   Article 1 b of the Council Enabling Regulation allows the Commission to adopt exemption regulations for, and to declare as compatible 'aid that complies with the map approved by the Commission for each Member State for the grant of regional aid'.
15.   The exemption possibility was introduced by the 1998 Enabling Regulation.
16.   This possibility was applied in 2001 for regional investment aid in the 2001 Commission SME exemption Regulation (Commission Regulation No 70/2001 of 12 January 2001 on the application of Articles 87 and 88 of the EC Treaty to State aid to small and medium-sized enterprises, O.J. 2001 L 10/ 33) ; its recital 2 explicitly refers to regional aid.
17.   See RAG, para.107.
18.   It should be noted that the sectoral scope of application of the RAG and the RAG BER differ slightly. Pursuant to section 2 of the RAG, the RAG apply to aid in every sector of the economy apart from the fisheries sector and the coal industry, and the production

of agricultural products listed in Annex 1 of the EC Treaty, with the exception of the processing and marketing of such products. In the latter sector, and in several others (transport, shipbuilding) special rules apply. Aid to the steel and synthetic fibres sectors is prohibited. Article 1(2) of the RAG BER excludes also the shipbuilding, coal and synthetic fibres sectors. The same scope of application applies for the GBER.

Regional aid to firms in difficulties within the meaning of the Community Guidelines on state aid for rescuing and restructuring firms in difficulty (RRG), O.J. 2004 C 244/2 is equally prohibited by the RAG, unless it is granted in accordance with the provisions of the RRG.

19. See Article 3(3) RAG BER which allows exemption of *ad hoc* aid from the notification requirement if it forms part of an aid package that is predominantly based on block exempted aid schemes.
20. See RAG BER, para. 7(b).
21. *Communication from the Commission on the revision of the method for setting the reference and discount rates*, O.J. 2008 C 14/6.
22. See Article 5(1)(b) GBER.
23. *Commission Notice on the application of Articles 87 and 88 of the EC Treaty to state aid in the form of guarantees*, O.J. 2008 C 155/10.
24. See GBER, Article 5(1) 9 (c) (iv).
25. *Communication from the Commission concerning the criteria for the in-depth assessment of regional aid to large investment projects*, O.J. 2009 C 223/3.
26. Aid schemes for newly created small enterprises were approved by the Commission for example for France (N38/07), Luxembourg (N 142/08), and Malta (N 622/07). These aid schemes are now block exempted under the GBER.
27. See also Article 2 (1) 9(c) RAG BER and Article 12(1) GBER.
28. In the context of a single investment project an establishment may also be operated by several enterprises.
29. In practice, it is sometimes difficult to define the limits between a fundamental modernisation, and replacement investment, since most replacement of equipment involves assets which allow a higher production efficiency, or need less energy, raw materials, etc. In these situations, an assessment on the individual merits of the case becomes necessary.
30. See RAG, fn 36 and 37.
31. See for example N 635/2008 – Italy: LIP Fiat Sicily.
32. In the meaning of the *Community Guidelines on State Aid for rescuing and restructuring firms in difficulty*, O.J. 2004 C 244/2.
33. See also Article 14 GBER.
34. Bulgaria and Romania were not yet members of the EU when the RAG 2007–13 where adopted.
35. Para. 95 of the RAG established an additional, transitional safety net which applied until the end of 2008. Under these transitional phasing out arrangements, an additional coverage was given to ensure that up to 66% of the population of regions that benefitted from regional aid pursuant to (then) Article 87(3)(c) EC in 2000–2006 could be assisted during a two-year transition period.
36. The NUTS system was developed for statistical purposes. A NUTS I region includes normally several NUTS II regions, a NUTS II region several NUTS III regions. Details are laid down in Regulation (EC) No 1059 of 26 May 2003 on the establishment of a common classification of territorial units for statistics, O.J. 2003 L 154; NUTS II regions have a minimum population of 800 000 inhabitants, and a maximum population of three million.
37. The Lisbon Treaty 2009 introduces their a-status explicitly, see Article 107(3)(a) TFEU.
38. See also Articles 2(1)(h) RAG BER and 2(5) GBER.
39. Specific aid intensities apply for investments in the processing and marketing of agricultural products: see specific references in individual regional aid maps and Article 4(10) RAG BER and Article 13(9) GBER.
40. See Multisectoral Framework 2002, section 2.

41. See Articles 4 RAG BER and 12–13 GBER.
42. Where the individual aid has to be notified, the regional aid ceiling that applies at the point in time when the aid is notified, has to be respected.
43. See also Articles 6 RAG BER and 7 GBER.
44. At present, the relevant *de minimis* Regulation is Commission Regulation No 1998/2006 of 15 December 2006 on the application of Articles 87 and 88 of the Treaty to *de minimis* aid, O.J. 2006 L 379/5.
45. See RAG, para.36, and Articles 2(1)(e) (f), (k)–(m) RAG BER and 2(10)–(11) and (13)–(15) GBER.
46. See RAG, para. 50.
47. See RAG, para.54.
48. See RAG, para.54.
49. See RAG, para.53.
50. See RAG, para. 55.
51. See RAG, para. 72, and fn 67.
52. See also Article 5 RAG BER; it should be noted that Article 8 GBER contains somewhat different provisions; in fact, the 'confirmation of eligibility in principle' before 'start of works' is completely abandoned for SMEs, and replaced for large undertakings by a provision which stipulates that the Member State, before granting the aid, verifies that documentation prepared by the beneficiary establishes 'that the project would not have been carried out as such in the assisted region concerned in the absence of the aid' (Article 8(3)(e) GBER).
53. Such an assessment was, for example, carried out for a series of German guarantee schemes for working capital loans; see for example N 439/2007 – Germany: Federal guarantee scheme
54. As defined by Section J (codes 65, 66, and 67) and Section K (code 74) of the NACE code
55. See also Article 14 GBER.
56. For a more detailed analysis see Dittel and Junginger Dittel 2006.
57. See also Articles 2(1)(g) RAG BER and 2(12) GBER (which limits the definition to capital costs).
58. In many notified cases the Commission had to establish whether the project for which aid was notified, did not constitute a single investment project with an earlier also aided investment project. In several cases the Commission opened the formal investigation to clarify the issue, for example, in the Sovello case (C 21/2008 – Germany)) which was still decided under the slightly different rules of the Multisectoral Framework, and in the Deutsche Solar case (C 34/2008).
59. See also Articles 8(1) RAG BER and 9(4) GBER.
60. Standard summary information form.
61. About 60–100 summary information sheets are submitted to the Commission under this transparency mechanism per year. For a more detailed analysis, see de Vreese 2007.
62. See also Articles 7(e) RAG BER and 6(2) GBER.
63. RAG, para 4.1.2.
64. *Communication from the Commission concerning the criteria for the in-depth assessment of regional aid to large investment projects*, O.J. 2009 C 223/3.
65. C46/2009 – Poland: Dell.
66. C 34/2009 – Portugal: Petrogal, and C 46/2009 – Hungary: Audi Hungary.
67. IDAC, section 2.3.
68. IDAC, section 2.4.
69. IDAC, para. 40.
70. Para.14 of the IDAC contains a series of elements that might allow proof of the positive effects of the aid.
71. Para. 54 of the IDAC stipulates that substantial job losses – in a relocation situation – in existing locations within the EU have to be taken into account in the balancing exercise.

72. See IDAC, section 3.
73. See IDAC, para. 47.
74. *Communication from the Commission – Temporary framework for State aid measures to support access to finance in the current financial and economic crisis* – adopted on 17 December 2008, O.J. 2009 C 16/1.

REFERENCES

Cavallo, Silvia and Klaus-Otto Junginger-Dittel (2004), 'The Multisectoral Framework 2002: new rules on regional aid to large investment projects', *Competition Policy Newsletter*, **No. 1**, 78.

de Vreese, Leen (2007), 'Transparency system for large regional investment projects', *Competition Policy Newsletter*, **3.**

Dittel, Maja-Alexandra and Klaus-Otto Junginger-Dittel (2006), 'The Multisectoral Framework 2002 and its successor rules under the Regional Aid Guidelines 2007-2013: Regional investment aid to (very) large investment projects', in Leigh Hancher, Tom Ottervanger, and Piet Jan Slot (eds), *EC State Aids* (3rd edn), London: Thomson/Sweet and Maxwell, ch. 14, 344.

Olofsson, P. (2005), 'L'évolution de la politique des aides à finalité régionale 1956–2004', *Competition Policy Newsletter*, **No. 3**, 17.

11 State aid in the energy sector
Leigh Hancher and Francesco Salerno

I. INTRODUCTION

The European Union rules on State aid are of considerable importance to the energy sector given the traditionally high level of involvement of governments in energy production and supply. The opening up of the energy market in 2007 by means of EU legislation has been accompanied by vigorous enforcement of the competition rules as well as the State aid rules. Indeed, the Commission's Energy Sector Inquiry of 2007 announced that it would apply Articles 107 and 108 TFEU more rigorously in the energy sector, especially to preferential tariffs and to long term contracts.[1]

More importantly, State aid is an important instrument for stimulating environmental protection and climate change, which appears to enjoy centre stage amongst the different facets of energy policy in the EU, as highlighted also in the Lisbon Treaty 2009. As is well known, energy policy in the EU rests on three pillars, that is, internal market, climate change and security of supply.[2] While the Lisbon Treaty 2009 has introduced a new chapter on energy, thus providing a legal basis for energy policy, it has at the same time made clear that security of supply rests in the hands of the Member States.[3] With respect to the two other pillars, the Commission's success in mustering support for a common EU policy has certainly been greater in the climate change area compared to the internal market. The recent calls by the Commission on 20 Member States to *implement and apply Single Market rules without delay* bear eloquent testimony to that effect.[4] This should be contrasted with the ambitious targets for CO2 emission reduction and the promotion of renewable energy now enshrined in EU legislation.

For this reason, this chapter will focus on State aid for environmental protection, as this area is at the intersection between the State aid policy and the energy policy of the Union. In addition, aid earmarked for environmental protection represented around 12.7 billion euros by the end of 2008, which is approximately 24% of total horizontal aid (that is, the second largest type of aid after regional aid).[5]

Environmental aid has been the preferred course of action by some Scandinavian countries, the Netherlands, Germany, and the United Kingdom, whereas in other southern European countries the use of this tool is less prominent in relation to total aid for horizontal objectives. As explained below the rules on environmental aid have become highly complex. At the same time, and despite their complexity, it would appear that they have provided the Commission with a sound basis to declare most national aid to be compatible with the Union's environmental goals.

This chapter will first examine some of the controversies in applying the State aid rules to the energy sector. The second part of the chapter will go on to examine how the legal uncertainties which have surrounded the application of the State aid rules to the energy sector are becoming even more complex in the context of State support for climate change and the transition to a low carbon economy.

II. THE CONCEPT OF AID

II.i. Introduction

In principle, in order for a measure to fall within the scope of Article 107(1) TFEU, the measure in question must confer a benefit or advantage and all of the following conditions must be met:

(i)   the aid has been granted or imposed by a public authority;
(ii)   the measure results in a transfer of resources from the State or the State receiving less resources;
(iii)   the aid distorts competition by favouring certain undertakings or the production of certain goods; and
(iv)   the products or services in question are traded within the EU.

Before turning to the various aspects of the definition, a preliminary clarification is in order on the concept of 'beneficiary', that is, the recipient of aid. First of all, it is well settled in the case-law that recipients of aid are those who actually benefit from it.[6] In this context, it is worth pointing out that, in the identification of a beneficiary, the Commission has a wide discretion in determining whether companies forming part of a group must be regarded as an economic unit or as legally and financially independent for the purposes of applying the State aid rules.[7]

Second, it is equally well settled that Article 107 TFEU prohibits aid granted by a State or through State resources in any form whatsoever, without drawing a distinction as to whether the aid-related advantages are granted directly or indirectly.[8] The only proviso is that there must be a causal link between the aid granted through State resources and the benefit.[9]

Finally, in order to be caught by the application of the State aid rules, a beneficiary must be an 'undertaking'. This term is usually defined broadly, covering any entity engaged in an economic activity.[10]

II. ii.   The Concept of Advantage

The core of the concept of State aid is that it confers an economic advantage on the (potential) recipient, that is, an advantage that the recipient would not enjoy under normal market conditions. Combined with the Courts' insistence that the form of the measure is irrelevant and that it is the effect of the measure that is of key importance, this means that a wide variety of State action can potentially fall within the scope of the Treaty State aid regime, provided of course that the cumulative criteria as set out above are met. The two examples below are illustrative of the Commission's approach to this issue in the energy sector.

II.ii.a.   The concept of advantage in the Hungarian and Polish power purchase Agreements

In the Hungarian and Polish Decisions on long term power purchase agreements (PPAs),[11] in order to determine whether these contracts provided an economic advantage to power generators, the Commission had to assess whether, via the PPAs, generators obtain economic advantages that they would not obtain from the market. PPAs could provide eligible generators with an advantage if the parties to these agreements are placed in a better economic position than other companies. Even though the details of individual PPAs may vary, in the Commission's view, all PPAs were structured around a core, invariable principle: the mandatory purchase of most (sometimes all) of the electricity generated by the companies concerned, at a price reviewed periodically in accordance with the principle that the total costs (fixed and variable) of generating electricity, plus a profit margin, are passed on to the consumer.[12]

This meant that the commercial risk associated with operating the power plants was borne by the buyer of the electricity, that is, PSE in Poland and MVM in Hungary. This included the risk associated with fluctuations in electricity generation costs and, in particular, fuel costs, the risk associated with fluctuations in end-user electricity prices, and the risk associated with fluctuation in end-user electricity demand. These are the typical risks that any power generator without a PPA would bear itself.

In the Commission's view, the PPAs transferred more risks to the State-owned buyers than standard commercial practices (as applicable as of May 2004) and prevented both MVM and PSE from diversifying their portfolios and furthermore forced both companies to purchase more than they would need in the future.

On the basis of its assessment of the Hungarian PPAs, compared with 'standard practices' elsewhere in Europe, the Commission concluded that:

> . . . the main terms and conditions of the purchase obligation enshrined in the PPAs, i.e. the capacity reservations and minimum guaranteed off-take by MVM under such conditions as to ensure the return on investment of the power plants by shielding them from the commercial risks of the operation of their plant, constitute State aid within the meaning of Article 87(1) of the EC Treaty. This State aid is achieved by the combination of the capacity reservations, the minimum guaranteed off-take, the pricing mechanism based on a capacity fee and an energy fee meant to cover fixed, variable and capital costs, over a long duration beyond normal commercial practice (at para. 340).

II.ii.b.   Recent tariff cases

In the 2007 Energy Sector Inquiry, the Commission also took issue with regulated supply tariffs because 'such supply tariffs have adverse effects for competition and thus for consumers in the longer run', mentioning that it had received a complaint concerning Spanish tariffs and that it was investigating whether 'any violations of State aid or antitrust rules have taken place'.[13] In January 2007 the Commission started a State aid investigation on the Spanish regulated tariffs,[14] and in June of the same year it also started a State aid investigation on regulated supply tariffs in France.[15] While these investigations are still pending, in 2009 the Commission adopted a final Decision on another State aid case relating to tariffs for certain energy-intensive users in Italy (the *Alcoa* case).[16]

The conditions under which Alcoa purchased electricity had first been assessed by the Commission in 1996.[17] At that time, the Commission examined the electricity tariff, which ENEL charged the plants in question. The Commission took the view the tariffs did not constitute State aid because ENEL was behaving like an operator acting under normal market conditions. This decision was in line with earlier case-law and decision practice on electricity tariffs.[18] In the 1996 Alcoa Decision, the Commission was satisfied that this requirement was met because the tariff covered the marginal cost and at least a proportion of the fixed costs of the supplier, in circumstances where there was overcapacity and Alcoa was amongst the largest consumers.

Nevertheless the Commission now took issue with a change in the mechanism of the tariff. This is because the measure no longer consisted in ENEL applying a tariff for the supply to Alcoa, which was equivalent to a market price, but in the grant of a reimbursement by a public fund, financed through State resources (in order to offset the difference between the price paid to the supplier and the tariff approved by the Commission in 1996). Contrary to its 1996 Alcoa Decision and the 2000 EDF Decision, in the 2009 Alcoa Decision the Commission was no longer concerned about the level of the tariff. According to the Commission, the mere existence of a component designed to mitigate the price paid by the consumer was in and of itself conferring an advantage on the latter, regardless of (i) the price actually charged by the supplier; and/or (ii) the level of support provided by the State. In other words, the Commission seemed minded to regard as a measure of aid any State intervention, which might diminish electricity costs.

II.iii.   The market economy investor test and the EDF ruling

As is discussed in more detail in the chapters by Coppi, Kavanagh *et al.* and Lykotrafiti the Courts draw a distinction between State participation through acts of public prerogative and intervention through other means in their national economy. If a State intervenes as a market investor then this will not confer an advantage on the target company (MEIP principle). Several recent cases have thrown some light on how the Courts will deal with measures which take the form of fiscal measures but which nevertheless can be deemed, for various reasons to have the same effect as the intervention of a normal private investor. In *EDF v. Commission* the Court was requested to examine the legality of a Commission Decision condemning various fiscal measures adopted in the context of the restructuring of EDF in order to remedy the company's under-capitalisation in relation to its transmission network.[19]

The French government had, *inter alia*, waived payment of certain taxes due by EDF following a revision of its accounting system as part of its 'contrat d'entreprise' with the French State for the period 1997–2000, and in preparation for the liberalisation of the electricity market as required by EC Directive 96/92.[20] The Commission had considered certain of these measures to constitute aid and had opened a formal investigation under Article 108(2) TFEU.[21]

In December 2003 the Commission adopted a final Decision in which it held that the non-payment of company tax by EDF amounted to aid and directed the French State to recover some 14 billion FFr from EDF. The French authorities claimed that these various measures did not amount to aid but should have been seen as a normal investment. The Commission rejected this argument on the grounds that the MEIP principle did not apply in the context of the operation of the exercise of State prerogative powers, including fiscal powers. A State could not combine both roles or functions.

EDF appealed this Decision to the General Court. That Court upheld EDF's plea in this respect. It recognised that the established jurisprudence indeed drew a distinction between the State's obligations as owner and its obligations in regard to the exercise of its public powers. However, the Court also held that it was necessary to look not only at the *form* of the measure in question, but also its *effect*. In this case, the French State was the sole shareholder and was entitled as such to select the most effective means to restructure EDF's financing, including measures relating to the exercise of its fiscal powers. The Court therefore annulled the Commission's decision in this respect.

II.iv.   The MEIP and 'aid' through public undertakings

The MEIP also applies to investments made by public undertakings in so far as the resources in question of these entities can be deemed to be State resources and the measure can be attributed to the State, as discussed above. Two cases are illustrative of this approach.

II.iv.a.   The 2000 EDF Decision
In the 2000 EDF Decision, concerning the legality of rebates made by EDF to firms in the paper industry, the Commission considered that EDF had acted in accordance with the MEIP. EDF had granted certain advances to paper mills for the purpose of installing electrical infrared paper drying equipment. These advances corresponded to a reduction in the price for electricity normally consumed by the dryer for the duration of the six year supply contract.

The investigation concerned rebates granted between 1990–1996, that is, before the adoption of the first Directive on the internal electricity market, at a time when EDF disposed of overcapacity in nuclear energy. In a situation of overcapacity and in the absence of competition, the Commission considered that a private operator would rather sell an additional unit of electricity without covering the total cost for that unit rather than not sell it all. Hence EDF's behaviour was justified on commercial grounds, and the rebates did not constitute State aid. It is of interest to note that the Commission emphasised that the Decision should be seen in the context of the prevailing circumstances on the French market in the past, and should not be seen as preventing the Commission from examining the creation of the said overcapacity and its implications in the context of the ongoing liberalisation of the electricity market.[22] As mentioned above, a similar approach was also taken in the 1996 Alcoa Decision.

II.iv.b.   The 2004 British Energy Decision
In its Decision to open a formal procedure against the UK in connection with the aid package to British Energy (BE), the Commission initially

formed the view that BNFL, a publicly owned company, was not operating as a private investor in agreeing to re-negotiate a number of nuclear fuel supply contracts with British Energy, but that BNFL's agreement to conclude more favourable contracts was to be imputed to the State. Furthermore, BNFL as BE's largest creditor had agreed more favourable standstill conditions than those agreed with private creditors.[23]

In the Decision of 22 September 2004, the Commission established that BNFL acted in conformity with market creditor principle and that BNFL acted independently of the UK government. Thus the measures were not imputable to the State.[24]

II.v. State Resources

If the measure in question constitutes an economic or financial advantage for the recipient, it must then be ascertained whether or not that benefit is financed by or through State resources.

In the *PreusssenElektra* case,[25] the Court held that compensation provided to a regional supply undertaking participating in a so-called feed-in scheme did not involve any direct or indirect transfer of State resources to undertakings and therefore did not constitute State aid. The measures in question concerned a State-imposed minimum price which consumers had to bear and a quota system, which impacted on all electricity distribution companies. No transfer of State resources as such was involved. Thus, provided they respect the conditions set out in the *PreussenElektra* judgment, feed-in tariffs to support renewable energy sources fall outside the State aid rules. The Court did not take up the Commission's suggestion that a concept of a 'measure having equivalent effect' to a State aid measure should be embraced so as to prevent Member States from adopting minimum price regulations and quotas which essentially have the same protective effect as a State aid. Nevertheless the scope for Member States to avoid the reach of State aid control is relatively restricted, as subsequent case law has confirmed.

For instance, in *GEMO*,[26] a case decided shortly after *PreussenElektra*, the Court ruled that a measure requiring private undertakings to collect and dispose of animal waste and carcasses amounted to a State aid in favour of the beneficiaries of that disposal service (farmers and slaughterhouses). In this case the measure was financed by a tax incentive, which was in turn financed by a levy on supermarkets, hence the financial resources at the disposal of public undertakings as well as private undertakings controlled by the State could be subject to the Treaty discipline on State aid.

Moreover if the State intervenes in collecting and distributing any additional charge levied on consumers with a view to promoting renewable energy or for compensating past 'stranded investments' then irrespective of whether they originate from energy consumers, these funds are considered to be under the control of the State and therefore State aid. This has been confirmed by the Courts in the recent *Essent* and *Iride* cases.[27]

If there is no intervention by the State and the resources mobilised to purchase minimum quantities of renewable energy are both private and public, then there is no aid involved. A useful illustration is the Commission Decision on an obligation to promote PV panels entrusted to Flemish local grid operators, these being public and privately owned companies.[28]

Nevertheless the question of whether or not State resources are involved remains contentious and problematic as illustrated by the feed-in tariff Decisions in Austria. In 2006, the Commission required the Austrian authorities to notify a feed-in tariff implemented by the Austrian Green Electricity Act in order to support electricity production from renewable sources. Under the Austrian scheme, the shortfall between the fixed feed-in tariff at which an 'eco-balance group' purchased green electricity generated, and the fixed transfer price at which Austrian electricity traders were subsequently obliged by law to purchase that electricity, was compensated through the use of a levy or special tax imposed on the consumption of electricity by final consumers.[29]

In 2008, the Austrian authorities notified an amendment to the scheme, insofar as they intended to raise the level of the tariffs for renewable energy sources.[30] Similarly, in 2009 the Commission adopted a positive decision concerning feed-in tariffs in Luxembourg, which the Commission found a measure of aid because it involved a levy to compensate the shortfall between the price paid and the remuneration for the electricity at market prices.[31]

II.vi.   Imputability to the State

In *France v. Commission (Stardust Marine)* the Court provided a further clarification on the interpretation of Article 107 TFEU concerning the involvement of State resources as a constituent element of an aid measure. It held that even though resources which may eventually be at the disposal of the State may be deemed to be 'State resources' , it is also necessary to show that the actual deployment of those resources for the benefit of a particular undertaking can be attributed to some form of government decision. Merely 'organic' forms of public control over such resources are not in themselves sufficient.[32]

In the *Olympic Airways* case the Court made clear in its ruling on non-payment by Olympic of airport charges to Athens Airport, operated as a private undertaking, that the Commission must state clear reasons as to why it considers a measure to be imputable to the State.[33]

The implications for the energy sector of the 'Stardust' ruling are nonetheless of some importance given that several Member States still own or control parts of their countries' energy enterprises. Should a government (whether national or local) seek to exert control or influence over, for example, the tariffs charged to certain groups of users or to ensure that capacity in pipelines, electricity networks, storage facilities or interconnectors is reserved to particular undertakings, or for the dispatch of renewable forms of energy, State aid issues may well arise. The case of the French regulated tariff, mentioned above, provides a good illustration, as the Commission, following the *Stardust Marine* jurisprudence, imputed to the State a tariff adopted by EDF.[34]

II.vii.   Selectivity

As discussed in more detail in Chapter 8, general measures which can benefit the entire economy, such as a lowering of tax rates or interest rates do not create a selective benefit. The Courts have generally found the 'selectivity criteria' to be easily met. Hence in *Adria-Wien Pipeline*[35] the Court held that an Austrian tax measure awarding a rebate on energy taxes charged on supply of natural gas and electricity to undertakings active (i) in the manufacture of goods (ii) in so far as energy taxes exceeded 0.35% of the production value was in fact a selective measure.

Similar considerations on the need to distinguish between the object of the measure (relevant for the compatibility assessment) and its effects (relevant for the qualification of the measure as aid) underpinned the decision by the CJEU to set aside a judgment by the General Court. In *British Aggregates*, the General Court had accepted that the Commission was right in holding that the pursuance of environmental protection rendered a dedicated levy non-selective.[36] However, the CJEU found a fault in this reasoning, by re-stating that, 'Article 87(1) EC does not distinguish between the causes or the objectives of State aid, but defines them in relation to their effects', thus annulling the judgment.[37]

It may be also noted that the TFEU does not deal with the issue of whether a specific tax system imposing a surcharge tax on a certain economic sector constitutes a selective advantage in favour of those undertakings that are excluded from tax. In accordance with Articles 4(c) and 67(3) of the now-expired ECSC Treaty special charges on steel and coal producers were prohibited. Although there is little case-law on this issue, the Commission has dealt with the matter in the area of energy taxes, where it recognises that specific or special charges are solely concerned with a Member State's discretion in forming its tax system and do not constitute aid within the meaning of Article 107 TFEU.[38]

Moreover, at paragraph 13 of its *Notice on aid through direct taxation* the Commission observes that Member States maintain their power to spread their tax burden as they see fit across the different factors of production.[39] Nevertheless, in *AEM SpA*,[40] an increase in taxation for certain types of electricity was deemed to constitute aid for all other energy producers. The Court considered the aid measure justified by advantages arising from the liberalisation of the energy market.

II. viii.   Tradable Certificates and Permits

The Commission has usually considered tradable permits in the energy sector (notably emission permits) as falling under the State aid rules.[41] In the Dutch tradable Nox credits scheme, the Commission similarly held that credits corresponded to the absolute emission standard imposed by the State but were provided free of charge, so State revenues were foregone. The Commission considered the scheme was selective as it benefited a selected group of large industrial undertakings. On appeal, however, the General Court quashed the Commission Decision because of the measure's lack of selectivity.[42] In particular, the Court found that the criterion for application of the measure in question was an objective one, without any geographic or sectoral connotation. Moreover, since the measure in question was aimed at the undertakings which are the biggest polluters, that objective criterion was furthermore in conformity with the goal of the measure, that is the protection of the environment, and with the internal logic of the system.[43]

II.ix.   Effect on Trade

Given the structure of Articles 107 and 108 TFEU, and the system of prior notification of all planned State aid, it is not incumbent on the Commission to establish that the measure in question can appreciably effect competition or inter-State trade. It is sufficient that the Commission can establish a link between the measure in question and the likely or potential effect on competition and trade. However, as a general rule, the Commission must at least provide reasons as to why it assumes there is a foreseeable prospect for the measure to affect trade.[44]

III. COMPATIBILITY

Although an aid measure may be characterised as State aid within the meaning of Article 107(1) TFEU, this does not mean that it is prohibited: Article 107(1) TFEU is a conditional prohibition in the sense that a State aid measure may nevertheless be deemed to be compatible with Article 107(2) or 107(3) TFEU. This next section will examine the application of these exemptions to the energy sector. It will also include a short discussion the potential application of Article 106(2) TFEU to financial support measures for services of general economic interest in the energy sector.

III.i. The Automatic Exceptions: Article 107(2) TFEU

With regard to the exceptions listed in Article 107(2) TFEU it is well established that the Commission has no discretion in their application. Its primary task is to ensure that the conditions for exemption are met.

Article 107(2)(a) TFEU provides that aid having a social character and granted to individual consumers is compatible with the common market provided that the aid in question is granted without discrimination with regard to the origin of the products or service concerned. It must be ascertained whether consumers benefit from the aid in question irrespective of the economic operator supplying the product or service capable of fulfilling the social objective relied on by the Member State concerned.

If, for example, a social form of aid was provided to consumers to instal smart meters in their homes allowing them to switch easily between energy suppliers but the aid in question would only be disbursed if the consumers either purchased meters from locally based companies or had such meters installed by a local company, then Article 107(2)(a) TFEU could not apply.[45]

III.ii. The Discretionary Exceptions: Article 107(3) TFEU

In order to assist Member States and potential aid recipients the Commission has published numerous Guidelines and Notices on the conditions under which certain types of aid may be considered compatible with Article 107(1) TFEU. These various Guidelines and Notices are considered to be binding on the Commission and on the Member States if the latter have agreed to their contents.[46]

Between 2006–7 a large number of the existing Guidelines, including the Environmental Aid Guidelines, discussed in detail below, came up for renewal and reassessment. This reassessment was carried out in accordance with the objectives of the State Aid Action Plan (SAAP). It should be stressed that aid falling within the scope of a particular set of Guidelines must still be notified for eventual clearance, albeit that if the notified measure or scheme fulfils the criteria set out in the Guidelines, this should allow the Commission to reach a positive Decision on the notified measure or scheme at the end of its preliminary investigation.

The absence of a relevant set of Guidelines does not of course mean that the aid in question is likely to be declared compatible. If no Guidelines are applicable, the Commission must deal with the State measure on a case-by-case basis. Similarly, if a case cannot be disposed of under the relevant Guidelines, the Commission is still bound to examine the possible application of Article 107(3)(c) TFEU.

It should be noted that, in response to a steady flow of national measures intended to rescue and restructure both financial institutions and to provide support to firms in the 'real economy', the Commission adopted a Temporary Community Framework to support access to finance for the period December 2008 to 31 December 2010.[47]

The Temporary Framework places importance on the production of more environmentally friendly products, for which access to finance may become difficult.[48] The Environmental Aid Guidelines already provide considerable scope for declaring 'green subsidies' to be compatible with the EU State aid regime. Therefore, the focus on the environmental measures is relatively limited in the Temporary Framework to rules on interest-rate reduction.[49] It is important to stress that the Temporary Framework allows aid to be granted under more flexible conditions, but nevertheless the national aid schemes in question must be notified to the Commission in advance for approval.

III.iii.   State Aid and Compensation for Public Service Obligations

Article 106(2) TFEU may be relevant in examining whether a particular measure of financial support in the energy sector confers an advantage and thus aid at all within the meaning of Article 107(1) TFEU. In accordance with the judgment *Altmark*, in July 2003,[50] if the four cumulative criteria set out in that judgment are met, the measure is not aid, and need not therefore be notified.[51] If, any one of the *Altmark* criteria is not met, the measure will be deemed to be a State aid measure and must be notified to the Commission.

In the recent Decisions of 2008 and 2009 concerning the Polish and Hungarian long-term power purchasing agreements (PPAs), the generators who were parties to the respective PPAs argued that these contracts conferred SGEIs upon them and that therefore the PPAs fell outside the scope of Article 107(1) TFEU. The Commission rejected these arguments.[52] Although it acknowledged that Member States have a wide margin of discretion to define the scope of SGEIs the existence of this wide margin of discretion does not mean that just *any* State intervention with a policy motivation can be characterised as an SGEI.[53]

The interested parties also invoked environmental protection as one of the SGEIs to be implemented by the PPAs. The Commission considered that the requirement to fulfil environmental standards does not exhibit any special characteristics as compared with the constraints imposed on all companies active in an industrial sector.

Albeit that environmental protection is quoted as one of the possible areas for public service obligations in Article 3 of Directive 96/92/EC,[54] and subsequently in Directive 2003/54/EC,[55] these obligations must exhibit special characteristics as compared with the normal business environment of companies in the sector.

The interested parties also invoked security of supply as one of the SGEIs that the PPAs can fulfil. But the Commission countered that, as a preliminary matter, security of supply could only be an SGEI, provided that the generators concerned comply with sector specific regulation and use indigenous primary energy fuel sources, and that the total volume of energy does not exceed in any calendar year 15% of the total primary energy necessary to produce the electricity consumed in the Member State concerned.[56]

In view of the above, the Commission concluded that the Treaty provisions on SGEIs do not apply to PPAs.[57] The parties also argued that Article 106(2) TFEU would apply to the PPAs even if they did not fulfil the criteria of the *Altmark* judgment. The Commission took the view that Article 106(2) TFEU can apply only to companies which have been entrusted with providing genuine SGEIs, which was not the case. Finally, compensation for providing the SGEI must be proportionate to the costs incurred; so that it must be possible to carry out an assessment of the scope of the SGEIs in order to calculate the associated costs, a condition that again was not fulfilled.[58]

III.iv.   The General Block Exemption and the Environmental Aid Guidelines

Overall, State aid policy is to be seen as a complementary tool to provide incentives to firms to address the problems identified, in the absence of an available solution by the market. In this way, State aid policy is complementary to regulation, taxation or other forms of market-based instruments like the Emission Trading System. The 2008 Environmental Aid Guidelines (2008 Guidelines), replacing their predecessor text, published in 2001 (2001 Guidelines) are intended to incorporate the priorities of the European climate and energy package, adopted in 2007.[59] If one takes, for example, the recently adopted Renewable Energy Directive, the Environmental Aid Guidelines foresee that State aid is possible to compensate for the additional cost of the undertakings, either in the form of investments or operating aid.

The 2008 Environmental Guidelines must be read together with the General Block Exemption Regulation (GBER).[60] In combination, the two pieces of legislation are intended to eliminate the obligation on Member States to notify certain aid measures that do not meet minimum notification thresholds, thereby reducing the administrative burden resulting from the large number of minor aid amounts notified to the Commission.

The two texts are therefore designed to afford the Commission greater opportunity for a detailed examination of large amounts of State aid, which have a correspondingly greater potential to distort competition. In particular, the 2008 Guidelines set out a 'detailed assessment' for such large amounts of aid. Within these lower and upper amounts of aid, a 'standard assessment' is employed to determine the compatibility of State aid for environmental protection with the terms of the Treaty, while the 2008 Guidelines also set out specific rules for assessing aid in the form of tax exemptions or reductions.[61]

III.iv.a.   The GBER

The GBER consolidates a number of different Block Exemptions that had previously provided a patchwork exemption from the State aid rules for certain categories of horizontal aid. It exempts certain categories of aid for environmental protection from the notification obligation mandated by Article 108(3) TFEU.[62] The exempted measures may be implemented without the need to obtain prior authorisation from the Commission.

Whereas, the 2008 Guidelines cover both various forms of investment and operating aid, and tax exemptions/reductions, the GBER concerns only investment aid and fiscal exemptions/reductions. Moreover, the assessment of eligible costs under the GBER is less detailed than the assessment under the 2008 Guidelines, and the aid intensities envisaged by the GBER are less than those provided for in the 2008 Guidelines.

III.iv.b.   The 2008 Guidelines

There are seven principles underlying the entire design of the 2008 Guidelines:

(a)   the polluter-pays principle;
(b)   the fact that the aid should be designed in a way to incentivise change in the behaviour of the companies concerned;

(c)   the aid must be proportionate;
(d)   the concept of eligible costs;
(e)   the provision for detailed assessments;
(f)   the distinction between investment aid and operating aid; and finally
(g)   the permissive approach to larger aid intensities for SMEs.

The Commission's assessment varies according to the different types of measures but also in terms of the size of the project. The Commission has now examined a certain number of schemes implemented by Member States but there are also situations where it has been required to look in more detail into individual measures.

a.   'Polluter-pays' principle   The key tenet of the Guidelines is the polluter pays principle (PPP), according to which a polluter should pay all the costs of its pollution, including the indirect costs borne by society.[63]

The PPP provides a benchmark for the Commission against which to determine whether a measure constitutes State aid within the meaning of Article 107(1) TFEU since a measure will constitute State aid where it relieves an undertaking's liability under the PPP to bear the costs of their pollution. Second, the Commission uses the PPP '*in a prescriptive way as a policy criterion*', relying on the PPP as the reason why the costs of environmental protection should ultimately be borne by the polluters themselves, rather than by the States.[64]

The Commission considers the PPP to be of cardinal importance: the use of State aid to correct negative externalities is, by contrast, only a 'second best option'. Two factors limit, in practice, the feasibility of a pure application of the PPP. First, it is technically difficult to calculate the exact cost of pollution, and therefore how much the 'polluter' should pay. Second, since full adoption of the PPP might raise polluters' costs so quickly as to cause market shocks, a more incremental implementation of the PPP is necessary.[65]

b.   Incentive effect and necessity of aid   Of major importance is the principle that any environmental protection aid granted must create an incentive for undertakings to adapt their behaviour towards more environmentally friendly measures, so as to raise overall levels of environmental protection across the Union. Accordingly, the Commission excludes the authorisation of aid in all cases in which the project in question has already started prior to the application for aid by the beneficiary to the national authorities.[66]

The burden of proving the incentive effect of the aid rests on the applicant,[67] who must provide evidence that in the counterfactual, in which the undertaking did not receive the aid subject to examination, it would not have adopted the more environmentally friendly alternative solution in respect of which the aid is proposed.[68]

c. Proportionality of aid The third general principle and the corollary of the incentive effect, is the proportionality principle, according to which aid is only proportional where the same result could not be achieved with less aid.[69]

Accordingly, the amount of aid granted to the undertaking must be limited to the minimum required for the undertaking to realise the environmental protection measures in question. In cases where it is impossible to calculate the amount of aid on the basis of the extra cost, the 2008 Guidelines provide that proportionality must be ensured through conditions and criteria for granting the exemptions and reductions, which ensure that the beneficiary does not receive excessive advantages, and that the selectivity of the measure is limited to the strict minimum.

This is the case, for example, with respect to aid in the form of environmental tax exemptions or reductions, and aid in the form of tradable permit schemes.[70] The Commission relaxes the proportionality principle with respect to SMEs, on whom, proportionally; the burden of environmentally friendly reforms may fall more heavily.[71]

d. The concept of eligible costs The 2008 Guidelines express the authorised aid intensity, i.e., the authorised gross amount of aid that an undertaking may receive, as a percentage of the undertaking's 'eligible costs'. The calculation of eligible costs involves,[72] first, establishing the cost of an investment by reference to the counterfactual (the 2008 Guidelines refer to both 'counterfactuals' and 'reference investments' but both are means of achieving the same goal, that is, identifying a benchmark against which an undertaking's costs and efficiency can be assessed.

The second stage in the calculation of eligible costs involves the deduction of operating benefits and the addition of operating costs. Operating benefits are advantages accruing to an undertaking from the realisation of a particular investment or implementation of particular operations, such as cost savings or ancillary production volumes or efficiencies.[73] Operating costs comprise, for example, additional production costs that flow from the extra investment for environmental protection.[74]

e. Detailed assessment The 2001 Guidelines contained an obligation to notify individual investment aids where such aids exceeded certain defined threshold amounts, the rationale being that such large volume aids inherently carry a greater risk of market distortion. The 2008 Guidelines retain

Table 11.1   Aids subject to a detailed assessment of their compatibility
with Article 107(3)(c) TFEU

Category of aid authorised under the 2008 Guidelines	Threshold for detailed assessment
All investment aid	Aid amount exceeds 7.5 million euros for one undertaking
Operating aid for energy saving	Aid amount exceeds 5 million euros per undertaking for five years
Operating aid for the production of renewable electricity and/or combined production of renewable heat	Beneficiary is a renewable electricity installation in a site where the resulting renewable electricity generation capacity exceeds 125 MW. Beneficiary is a new plant and receives operating aid on the basis of a calculation of the external costs avoided
Operating aid for the production of biofuel	Aid is granted to a biofuel production installation at a site where the resulting production exceeds 150,000 tonnes per year.
Operating aid for cogeneration	Aid is granted to a cogeneration installation with the resulting cogeneration electricity capacity exceeding 200 MW. Aid for the production of heat from cogeneration will be assessed in the context of notification based on electricity capacity.

the detailed assessment for certain types of aid, setting thresholds that relate either to the amount of aid granted or the size of the beneficiary installation.[75]

Whereas the detailed assessment provided for in the 2001 Guidelines utilised the same criteria as the 'standard' assessment, the 2008 Guidelines set out detailed criteria for the economic assessment of individual cases.[76] These criteria include:

The incentive effect. As part of this assessment, the Commission will:

(i)   verify whether the State aid is targeted at the market failure identified;

(ii)   assess, by reference, for example, to Member State impact assessments, whether State aid is an appropriate instrument for granting support to the undertaking concerned, as compared with other less distortive instruments, in particular given that the State aid may conflict with the overarching 'polluter pays' principle;

(iii) consider, *inter alia*, evidence of the counterfactual (that is, the conduct that the undertaking would have adopted absent the aid);

(iv) assess whether the aid granted is necessary to realise the envisaged benefit, limited to the minimum required to realise such benefits, and granted pursuant to a non-discriminatory, transparent and open selection process that does not unnecessarily exclude companies offering competing projects.

Analysis of competitive distortions resulting from the aid measure. The Commission, having identified the positive effects of the grant of aid, will balance these positive effects against any resulting distortions in trade. The Commission will therefore examine the benefits that may be realised by undertakings receiving State aid in order to adopt more environmentally practices, including:

(i) The extent to which the investment may result in a reduction in production costs, brand labelling or image benefits, or the realisation of a first mover advantage through the production of newer or higher quality products.[77]

(ii) Whether such a first mover advantage may reduce the incentives of other undertakings to innovate, thereby crowding out investment in that technology in other Member States.[78]

(iii) The Commission is also sensitive to the risk that State aid for environmental measures may be used as a means of keeping afloat less efficient undertakings. In order to determine whether this is the case, the Commission will examine the productivity and financial health of the beneficiaries, and the ability of other undertakings in the sector to reach comparable levels of environmental protection without aid.[79]

(iv) Using concepts borrowed from the enforcement of Articles 101 and 102 TFEU and in merger analysis (e.g., countervailing buyer power, leverage into and foreclosure of new, ancillary markets) the Commission will analyse whether the environmental protection given to the beneficiary may be used to strengthen or maintain a position of market power on the relevant market.

(v) Finally, the Commission will consider the effect on trade, specifically, whether the grant of aid risks shifting profits to a different Member State by encouraging companies to relocate to the Member State granting aid.

f.   Distinction between investment and operating aid   The 2008 Guidelines distinguish between investment aid and operating aid.

Investment aid. Investment aid is aid intended to make investment in environmentally friendly production process and technologies more economically attractive by compensating in part the additional costs associated with the investment in the more environmentally friendly measures.

An example of investment aid for an environmentally friendly measure might be the grant of aid to a non-combustion installation that generates reduced levels of nitrogen oxide emissions and particulate matters, which cause increased ground-level ozone (i.e., smog) and acid rain.[80]

The 2008 Guidelines provide for investment aid intensity of between 50% and 70% of the additional cost attributable to the use of the environmentally friendly process, depending on the size of the beneficiary undertaking.[81]

Operating aid. As compared with investment aid, operating aid is intended to facilitate improved access to the market for production processes that are beneficial to the environment but which are more costly for the undertaking than processes and techniques that generate higher levels of pollution. Operating aid therefore covers the difference (that is, the shortfall) between the production costs of the more environmentally friendly techniques, and the market price of the energy produced using such techniques.

An example of operating aid for an environmentally friendly measure might be the grant of aid in the form of an excise duty reduction for biofuels. Such aid lowers the cost of bringing the biofuel to market, and thereby reduces the difference between the cost of producing the biofuel and its value.[82]

The Commission adopts a more benign approach towards investment aid. With respect to a number of potentially environmentally beneficial measures, the Commission authorises investment aid (up to certain defined levels) but does not permit operating aid at all.[83]

Operating aid alleviates an undertaking from the burden of certain costs that it would otherwise have to pay for its current activities, but without any guarantee, as a result of sunk costs and infrastructure investment, that the change in the undertaking's behaviour will outlive the grant of financial support in the form of State aid.[84]

g.   Larger aid intensity for SMEs   Under the 2008 Guidelines, SMEs systematically qualify for a greater intensity of State aid than larger undertakings,[85] and the intensity of this aid has also been raised across the board for undertakings of all sizes.[86]

The more permissive aid intensities for SMEs are applied across the range of State aid measures envisaged in the 2008 Guidelines, with the exception of aid for the remediation of contaminated sites, aid involved in tradable permit schemes, and aid in the form of reductions of or exemptions from environmental taxes, for which an SME may be eligible, but in respect of which no preferential treatment is applicable.

h.   Individual aid measures covered by the 2008 Guidelines   The 2008 Guidelines include a number of environmental protection aid measures that were previously covered by the 2001 Guidelines:

- Aid for undertakings which go beyond Community standards or which increase the level of environmental protection in the absence of Community standards
- Aid for energy saving
- Aid for renewable energy sources
- Aid for cogeneration
- Aid for the remediation of contaminated sites
- Aid for the relocation of undertakings

The 2008 Guidelines provide for the compatibility with the Treaty of the following additional measures:

- Aid for the acquisition of new transport vehicles which go beyond Community standards, or which increase the level of environmental protection in the absence of Community standards
- Aid for early adaptation to future Community standards
- Aid for environmental studies
- Aid for energy-efficient district heating
- Aid for waste management
- Aid involved in tradable permit schemes

II.iv.c.   Selected discussion of measures previously covered
In what follows below, we provide a discussion of certain measures covered by the Guidelines, selected either because of their interaction with EU legislation or because of the interrelations with the concept of aid.[87]

a.   Investment and operating aid for the promotion of energy from renewable energy sources.   Under the Renewable Energy Directive, Member States are bound by certain targets in terms of the share of generation from renewable energy sources. Measures to stimulate initiatives to achieve such targets which fulfil the definition of State aid, are subject to the 2008 Guidelines.

In particular, aid granted for the investment in and/or operations of the promotion of energy from renewable energy sources may be justified where it meets the criteria set out in the 2008 Guidelines, and where there are no mandatory Community standards governing the share of energy that an individual undertaking must generate from renewable energy sources.

The 2008 Guidelines define renewable energy sources as wind, solar, geothermal, wave, tidal, hydropower installations, biomass,[88] landfill gas, sewage treatment plant gas, and biogases.[89] Detailed provisions govern the eligible portion of investment costs that may be met by the State. The costs eligible for aid are calculated net of operating benefits and costs related to the extra investment for renewable sources of energy that arise during the first five years of the life of the investment.

The 2008 Guidelines provide that the calculation of operating benefits and costs will be made according to the 2008 Guidelines principles for identifying the part of the investment directly related to environmental protection.[90] The authorised volume of aid varies in accordance with the size of the undertaking recovering the aid. Tender process conducted as the basis of clear, transparent and non-discriminatory criteria can be used to authorise aid of up to 100% of the eligible investment cost.[91]

The 2008 Guidelines explain that operating aid may be authorised where it covers the difference between the costs of producing energy using renewable energy sources and the market price of the form of energy concerned.[92] There are three different options for a Member State wishing to grant operating aid for renewable energy sources to undertakings:

(i)   To grant operating aid to the undertaking to compensate for the difference between the cost of producing energy from renewable energy sources and the market price at which the energy produced can be sold.

(ii)   To organise green certificates or tender schemes.

(iii) To offer financial support to undertakings involved in the production of energy from renewable sources to compensate the higher costs of production, that is, either grant the aid on a decreasing basis over five-years (support should not exceed 100% of the extra production costs in the first year, decreasing in a linear fashion to zero by the end of the fifth year), or to grant aid that does not decrease over time but does not exceed 50% of the extra production costs over the five-year period.[93]

While all of the options discussed above can be seen as a response by Member States to EU legislation, the Commission will nonetheless require notification under the State aid rules before their implementation, and carry out a review of their compatibility there to. Interestingly, in the Accompanying Document to the Proposal for the New Renewable Energy Directive,[94] the Commission listed a number of State aid Decisions concerning national support for electricity from renewable sources.

b. Aid involved in tradable permit schemes. The 2008 Guidelines also provide for the granting of aid to introduce market-based instruments targeting environmental objectives to offset negative externalities, specifically through the grant of aid to undertakings participating in tradable permit schemes.

Emissions trading schemes involve a central authority setting a limit or cap on the overall levels of pollution that may be generated. A scheme in theory achieves a compromise between the need to limit the overall level of externalities (in the form of emissions pollution), the imperative of creating an incentive for undertakings to reduce their polluting emissions, and the pragmatism of recognising that undertakings that are less able to reduce their emissions (for example, because they are engaged in an inherently high polluting activity) are deserving of some degree of flexibility and differential treatment.

The 2008 Guidelines are intended to interact with, and will be subject to amendment to ensure their consistency with, the Commission's flagship EU Emissions Trading System (EU ETS).[95] Under the EU ETS, Member States draw up a National Allocation Plan setting out the total quantity of allowances within a given trading period that a Member State will allocate to domestic energy producers, and how those credits will be allocated. The scheme is currently in its second trading period, which began on 1 January 2008 and runs for five years until the end of 2012.

The Commission has set an ambitious emissions reduction target for the second period, capping national emissions from EU ETS sectors at approximately 6.5% below 2005 levels, in an attempt to meet the EU's commitments (and those of Member States) under the Kyoto Protocol.[96]

In accordance with the case law, the 2008 Guidelines require that, in order to produce an overall positive effect on the level of environmental protection in the Community, the number of permits involved in tradable permit schemes should be inferior to the global amount of permits granted by the Member State, thereby forcing a polluting undertaking to either buy supplementary allowances or reduce its pollution levels. The 2008 Guidelines also require that a trading scheme's objectives go beyond those of the mandatory Community standards applicable to the undertakings concerned, and that allowances be allocated to undertakings in a fair and transparent manner.[97]

The NAP methodology should not favour certain undertakings or sectors unless such preference follows from the environmental logic of the scheme or is necessary to ensure consistency with other environmental policies. By the Commission's own admission, the EU ETS has not been wholly successful to date in this regard.[98] Member States, with the autonomy to draw up national emissions allocation plans, have had an incentive to grant their own industry more favourable treatment than that enjoyed by (competing) undertakings in other EU Member States. Arguably, this lack of uniformity in the EU ETS runs contrary to the principle of non-discrimination in the 2008 Guidelines.[99] A further three conditions are imposed on the grant of aid through a tradable permit scheme:

1.   Beneficiaries of aid will be chosen according to objective and transparent criteria, and the aid will be granted in a non-discriminatory manner for all competitors in the same factual situation and market/sector.
2.   Full auctioning must lead to a substantial increase in production costs for each sector or category of individual beneficiaries, and this increase may not be passed on to customers without leading to substantial reductions in sales.
3.   It must be impossible for individual undertakins in the sector to reduce emission levels in order to be able to support the price of the certificates. The benchmark for the irreducible consumption level is the emission level derived from best performing technique in the EEA, and any undertaking reaching that best performance technique, is permitted to benefit from an allowance only up to the level of the increase in production cost resulting from the tradable permit scheme that results from use of the best performance technique, less any production costs that might be passed on to consumers.

While allocations are State-specific, geographic 'markets' may comprise more than one Member State, and as a result under the present system of national allocation plans, a new entrant in one Member State may receive allowances on more favourable terms than a rival in another Member State. Nevertheless, the NAP system has been abolished for the trading period starting in 2013 (ending in 2020).

As of 2013, emission permits will be allocated by means of an auction process, with the total volume of emissions credits available throughout the Common Market capped centrally by the Commission. However, the Commission plans to amend its Environmental Aid Guidelines in order to accommodate the continuation of free emission allowances to the power sectors of new Member States (notably those which rely on coal as a primary fuel) and certain industries which are at risk of 'carbon leakage'.

In updating the rules, the Commission may also try and make it clearer when and how such aid could be compatible with State aid rules to make it easier for Member States to design compatible support schemes.

C. Categories of measures that may be found to be compatible with Article 107(3) TFEU, aid in the form of tax reductions or exemptions Environmental taxes are imposed upon activities that have an unequivocally negative impact on the environment. Such 'eco-taxes' are a 'stick', creating incentives for undertakings to adopt more environmentally friendly business activities by financially penalising the undertakings' failure to adopt pro-environment methods. As noted by commentators, while eco-taxes are common, the considerable variation between the number, variety and intensity of such taxes between EEA States means that there is considerable scope for this tax treatment to distort conditions across the common market. National 'eco-taxes' usually meet the selectivity criterion.[100]

Eco-taxation schemes can contribute to the promotion of environmental protection and recognise the resulting risk of a temporary loss of international competitiveness for firms in Member States that have introduced such taxes as long as there is no harmonisation of eco-taxation at European level. The 2008 Guidelines eliminate the distinction drawn in the 2001 Guidelines between full tax exemptions and partial tax exemptions. Under the 2008 Guidelines, where the reduction/exemption relates to a harmonised environmental tax,[101] the exemption is authorised for a period of ten years on the condition that the beneficiary pays at least the Community minimum tax level set by the applicable Directive. As for reductions/exemptions relating to non-harmonized taxes, these are authorised for a period of ten years provided the specified conditions are met.

A second difference is that the distinction between existing and new taxes no longer features in the 2008 Guidelines. In the past, the Commission had taken the position that exemptions from pre-existing taxes could not be permitted, since they could not have an incentive effect and therefore would not decrease overall environmental pollution levels. However, the differential treatment of existing and new taxes proved too blunt to be of practical utility.[102]

Third, the 2008 Guidelines provide for the assessment of the necessity and proportionality of exemptions and reductions from non-harmonised taxes that fall below the Community minimum.[103] In this connection, the 2008 Guidelines introduce a new element to the proportionality test, according to which undertakings (primarily those in energy intensive industries with levels of energy consumption that are difficult to reduce)

adopting the best performing technique may benefit, at most, from a proportionate reduction in their tax bill that corresponds to the increase in
production cost resulting from being subject to the tax, less any increase in
costs that the undertaking is able to pass on to consumers.

IV.   CONCLUSION

The case law reviewed in the section on the concept of aid demonstrates
that the State aid rules have a potentially far-reaching impact on the
energy sector and that a large variety of State measures can fall within the
definition of a State aid and must therefore be notified to the Commission
for clearance. Nevertheless, if it is possible to argue that the measure does
not confer an advantage, for example, because it can be justified under the
market investor test, or even if an advantage is conferred, that advantage
is not selective or it is not financed by State resources, then Article 107(1)
TFEU cannot apply.

It is not always easy to establish whether the market investor test or
the selectivity tests are met. The case-law on State resources illustrates
that few measures may indeed escape this particular element of the test,
however. Given this legal uncertainty, many governments choose to
notify a measure for reasons of legal certainty only, claiming that it is
not a State aid within the meaning of Article 107(1) TFEU. That strategy
may produce mixed results as the Dutch NOx saga case illustrates. This
measure was notified for reasons of legal certainly only, in 2002, but the
Commission took a different view and held that the measure was compatible aid. The General Court quashed the Commission's Decision and the
Commission has in turn appealed that judgment to the CJEU.

As the *CELF* line of cases (discussed in Chapter 17 of this volume) has
underlined,[104] this makes it difficult to know when a national measure can
be legally implemented or not. A negative Decision from the Commission
implies that the national measure should not be implemented. If that
Decision is quashed by the General Court however, then the Decision is
void and the 'standstill' obligation presumably no longer applies. If the
General Court's ruling is in turn quashed on appeal, then the 'standstill'
obligation is re-instated. This is not without financial consequences for the
recipients of the aid in question.

This situation is lamentable given the acknowledged need to tackle
climate change both rapidly and effectively. Notification is therefore
always the safer option. At the same time the Commission cannot
process large numbers of cases and has now tried to streamline its own
administrative procedures and ensure that it can prioritise complex cases.

The Commission's 2008 Guidelines on Environmental Aid offer a good example of this approach. Indeed, thanks to the Guidelines, the application of the exemption provisions as set out in Article 107(3) TFEU has become clearer and more predictable.

The EU's commitment to a 'carbon-free' economy will require an even higher effort from the Commission to clarify the application the State aid rules to the energy sector, given that the latter will be one of the main protagonists in the efforts needed to achieve the EU's ambitious environmental targets. Thus, further updates will be needed to clarify the State aid aspect inherent in dealing with the heightened challenged of maintaining competitiveness and respecting the environment.

NOTES

1. DG Competition Report on Energy Sector Inquiry, 10 January 2007, available at <http://ec.europa.eu/competition/sectors/energy/inquiry/index.html>. (last accessed 31 December 2010).
2. See Szyszczak 2009.
3. See Article 194(2) TFEU: *Such measures shall not affect a Member State's right to determine the conditions for exploiting its energy resources, its choice between different energy sources and the general structure of its energy supply, without prejudice to Article 192(2)(c).*
4. See Press Release of 24 June 2010, available at: <http://europa.eu/rapid/pressReleasesAction.do?reference=IP/10/836&format=HTML&aged=0&language=EN&guiLanguage=en> (last accessed 31 December 2010).
5. A large part of this amount of aid is made up of tax revenues foregone following reductions of or exemptions from environmental taxes, as opposed to direct grants, and can therefore not be used as an exact proxy measure of the environmental benefit brought by the tax.
6. See, for example, Case C-303/88, *Italy v. Commission* [1993] E.C.R. I-2098, para. 57.
7. See Case T-394/94, *British Airways v. Commission* [1998] E.C.R. II-2405, para. 314. Case T-234/95, *DSG v. Commission* [2000] E.C.R. II-2603, para. 124; and Case T-303/05, *AceaElectrabel v. Commission* [2009] E.C.R. I-13 [confirmed on appeal: Case C-480/09P, Judgment of 16 December 2010].
8. See recently Case T-445/05, *Associazione italiana del risparmio gestito and Fineco Asset Management v. Commission* [2009] E.C.R. I-289, para. 127.
9. See Case C-382/9, *Netherlands v. Commission* [2002] E.C.R. I-5163 and the Advocate General's Opinion in that case, especially para. 130. See also Case C-156/98, *Germany v. Commission* [2000] E.C.R. I- 6857.
10. See, for example, Case C-41/90, *Höfner and Elser* [1991] E.C.R. I-1979, para. 21.
11. See Commission Decision of 4 June 2008 in Case C 41/05 on State aid awarded by Hungary through power purchase agreements, O.J. 2009 L 225/53 and Commission Decision of 25 September 2007 on State aid awarded by Poland as part of power purchase agreements and the State aid which Poland is planning to award concerning compensation for the voluntary termination of power purchase agreements, O.J. 2009 L 83/1.
12. The Polish electricity regulator, URE, indirectly retained the right to check whether the costs charged to PSE are justified and reasonable, but the Commission held that

in practice URE used this power only to check that the costs were actually linked to electricity generation.

13. See Sector Inquiry, paras. 610–612.
14. See Case C3-2007, O.J. 2007 C-43/9.
15. See Case C17-2007, O.J. 2007 C-164/9. In 2009, the Commission took note of a change in the original measure under investigation and adopted a Decision extending the scope of the investigation (see O.J. 2009 C-96/18).
16. See Case C-36b/2006. O.J. 2010 L227/62. See also Case T-332/06, *Alcoa Trasformazioni v. Commission* [2009] E.C.R. 29, a judgment issued on the Commission Decision to start the investigation. [on appeal: Case C-194/09P].
17. O.J. 1996 C 288/4.
18. See Case 67/85, *Van der Kooy v. Commission* [1988] E.C.R. 219 and Commission Decision of 11 April 2000 on the measure implemented by EDF for certain firms in the paper industry (O.J. 2001 L 95/18) (2000 EDF Decision).
19. Case T-156/04, [2009] E.C.R. II-4503 [on appeal C-124/10]. See Szyszczak (2011).
20. O.J. 1997 L 27/20.
21. O.J. 2002 C 280/8.
22. IP/00/370, 11 April 2000.
23. O.J. 2003 C 180/5 at pt. 119 *et seq.*
24. Case C (2004) 3474, O.J. 2004 L 142/26.
25. Case C-379/98, *PresussenElektra AG v. Schleswag AG* [2001] E.C.R. I-2099.
26. Case C-126/01, *Ministère de l'Économie, des Finances et de l'Industrie v. GEMO SA* [2003] E.C.R. I-13769.
27. Case C-206/06, *Essent Netwerk Noord BV and others* [2008] E.C.R. I-5497 and Case T-25/07 *Iride SpA and Iride Energia SpA v Commission* [2009] E.C.R. II-245.
28. Case N-254/06C (2006) 4956.
29. See Commission Decision of 4 July 2006 in Case NN 162/A/2003 and N 317/A/2006 Austria – Support of electricity production from renewable sources under the Austrian Green Electricity Act (feed-in tariffs), O.J. 2006 C 221/8.
30. See Commission Decision of 10 June 2008 in Case N 47/2008 Austria – Modification of feed-in tariffs for electricity from renewable sources, O.J. 2008 C-253/3.
31. See Commission Decision of 28 January 2009 in Case C-43/2002 (ex NN 75/2001) Luxembourg-concernant l'aide sous la forme de la création d'un fonds de compensation dans le cadre de l'organisation du marché de l'électricité mise à exécution par le Luxembourg, O.J. 2009 C-255/15.
32. Case C-482/99, *French Republic v. Commission* [2002] E.C.R. I-4397, para. 52.
33. Case T-68/03, *Olympiaki Aeroporia v. Commission* [2007] E.C.R. II-2911.
34. Where special derogations or exemptions arise from EU measures, for example, taxation measures, then the exemption is not attributable to a Member State, but to the Union institution and Article 107(1) TFEU does not apply. See Case T-351/02, *Deutsche Bahn AG v. Commission* [2006] E.C.R. II-1047.
35. Case C-143/99, [1999] E.C.R. I-8365.
36. Case T-210/02, *British Aggregates Association v. Commission* [2006] E.C.R. II-2789.
37. Case C-487/06 P, *British Aggregates Association v. Commission* [2008] E.C.R. I-10505.
38. Commission Decision of 24 April 2002 on State Aid N 863–UK, Aggregates Levy, O.J. 2002 C-133/12, upheld in Case T-210/02, *British Aggregates*, ibid. See also the Opinion of the Advocate General Geelhoed of 18 September 2003 in Case C-308/01, *Gil Insurance* [2004] E.C.R. I-4777.
39. Commission Notice on the application of the State aid rules to measures relating to direct business taxation in O.J. 1998 C 384/3.
40. [2005] E.C.R. I-2861.
41. Decision of 28 November 2001, and see also N653/99 – Denmark, CO 2 quotas and N123/2000, UK Climate Change Levy.
42. Case T-233/04, *Netherlands v. Commission* [2008] E.C.R. II-591.

43. Ibid., para 84–100.
44. See Case T-156/04, *Électricité de France (EDF) v. Commission* [2009] E.C.R. I-4503 [on appeal: case C-124/10]. See also Case T-303/05, *ACEAElectrabel v. Commission* [2009] E.C.R. II-137 where the Court held that an aid measure to support the construction of a district heating network in the Rome area can affect trade given that aid to the recipient will strengthen its position vis-à-vis other energy suppliers. [On appeal: Case C-480/09P].
45. See in particular, Case T-116/01 and T-118/01, *P&O Ferries (Vizcaya) v. Commission* [2003] E.C.R. II-2957, para. 63.
46. Article 107(3)(e) TFEU provides for such categories of aid as may be specified by Decision of the Council acting by a qualified majority on a proposal from the Commission. Council Regulation 1407/2002 on State aid to the coal industry after expiry of the ECSC Treaty is based on this provision, in O.J. 2002 L 205/1.
47. O.J. 2009 C 16/1.
48. It is to be noted that this measure addresses the possibility to subsidise products, rather than production processes or technologies.
49. See Temporary Framework, para. 4.5 'Aid for the production of green products'. Measures of this kind that have received Commission approval include a UK scheme providing interest rate subsidies for businesses investing in the production of cars that meet high environmental standards (see IP/09/333), and a similar scheme launched by Spain (see IP/09/499).
50. Case C-280/00, *Altmark* [2003] E.C.R. I-7747. See the discussion in Chapter 13.
51. See Commission Decision of 16 December 2006 in Case N-475/2003 Ireland – Public Service Obligation in respect of new electricity generation capacity for security of supply, O.J. 2004 C 34/8.
52. Commission Decision of 4 June 2008 in Case C 41/05 on State aid awarded by Hungary through Power Purchase Agreements, op cit., para. 254 *et seq.*
53. Case C-179/90, *Merci convenzionali porto di Genova SpA v. Siderurgica Gabrielli SpA* [1991] E.C.R. I-5889, para. 27.
54. O.J. 1997 L 27/20.
55. O.J. 2003 L 176/37.
56. See Article 15(4) of Directive 2009/72/EC of the European Parliament and of the Council of 13 July 2009 concerning common rules for the internal market in electricity. See also Commission Decision of 25 July 2001 in Case N-34/99, O.J. 2002 C 5/2; Commission Decision of 25 July 2001 in Case NN-49/99, O.J. C 268/7; Commission Decision of 30 October 2001 in Case N 6/A/2001, O.J. C 77/26; Commission Decision of 2 February 2005 in Case C 7/2005 in O.J. 2007 L 219/9.
57. Commission Decision of 4 June 2008 in Case C-41/05 on State aid awarded by Hungary through Power Purchase Agreements, op. cit., paras. 255–276.
58. Commission Decision of 4 June, 2008 in Case C-41/05 on State aid awarded by Hungary through Power Purchase Agreements, op. cit., paras. 268–270.
59. Community Guidelines on State Aid for Environmental Protection, O.J. C 82/1.
60. Commission Regulation (EC) No 800/2008 of 6 August 2008 declaring certain categories of Aid Compatible with the Common Market in application of Article 87 and 88 of the Treaty. O.J. 2008 L 214/3.
61. See N. Imbert, 'Les aides d'Etat au coeur des défis nouveaux en matière d'environnement et d'énergie', Speech, Les mardis du droit européen de la concurrence, 8 December 2009, Brussels.
62. The conditions for exemption are set out in Articles 17–25 GBER.
63. 2008 Guidelines, para. 24.
64. Opinion of Advocate General Jacobs of 30 April 2002 in Case C-126/01, *Ministre de l'Économie, des Finances et de l'Industrie v. GEMO SA* [2003] E.C.R. I-14243, paras. 68–70.
65. 2008 Guidelines, paras. 24(a) and 24(b).

66. Ibid., para. 143.
67. Ibid., paras 144–145.
68. Ibid., para. 146.
69. Ibid., para. 30.
70. Ibid., para. 33.
71. Ibid., para. 34.
72. The calculation methodology for eligible costs under the Block Exemption is a simplified version of the calculation used under the 2008 Guidelines. See Recital 49 of the General Block Exemption.
73. 2008 Guidelines, para. 70(20).
74. Ibid., para. 70(21).
75. The 2008 Guidelines also provide for the detailed scrutiny of measures that are subject to a duty to notify aid individually under the Block Exemption Regulation.
76. See 2008 Guidelines, paras. 165–188.
77. Ibid., para. 177.
78. Ibid., para. 179.
79. Ibid., para. 180.
80. Commission Decision of 10 July 2008 in Case N 265/2008 Czech Republic – Investment aid scheme for the reduction of NOx emissions and particulate matters from non-combustion installations, O.J. 2008 C 250/4.
81. N. Imbert, 'Les aides d'Etat au coeur des défis nouveaux en matière d'environnement et d'énergie', Speech, Les mardis du droit européen de la concurrence, 8 December 2009, Brussels.
82. Commission Decision of 20 August 2008 in Case N 63-2008 Italy – Excise duty reduction for biofuels O.J. 2008 323/4. See also, Commission Decision of 21 December 2007 in Case N-478/2007 Netherlands – Stimulating renewable energy, modification of the MEP, O.J. 2008 C 39/3.
83. This is the case, for example, for aid for undertakings, which go beyond EU standards or which increase the level of environmental protection in the absence of EU standards, aid for energy-efficient district heating, and aid for waste management.
84. See also, Soltész and Schatz 2009:158.
85. The 2008 Guidelines provide that SMEs are defined by reference to EC Regulation 70/2001 on the application of Articles 87 and 88 of the EC Treaty to State aid to small and medium-sized enterprises, O.J. 2001 L 10/33 (as amended), itself referring to the definition used in Commission Recommendation 2003/361/EC concerning the definition of micro, small and medium-sized enterprises, O.J. 2003 L 124/136. See the 2008 Guidelines, para. 70 (16). Under the terms of the GBER, references to EC Regulation 70/2001 are to be construed as referring to the GBER. The definitions used are, in any event the same. A small enterprise is defined as an enterprise, which employs fewer than 50 persons and whose annual turnover and/or annual balance sheet total, does not exceed 10 million euros. A medium sized enterprise is an enterprise, which employs fewer than 250 persons, and whose annual turnover does not exceed 50 million euros or whose annual balance-sheet total does not exceed 43 million euros. There is no distinction under the GBER or 2008 Guidelines for micro enterprises.
86. In addition, the possibility for aid to be granted up to an intensity of 100% where such grant follows a competitive tender process has been introduced. See, for example, Chérot, Derenne and Giolito 2008:137.
87. For a fuller discussion, see Allibert and Jones 2008.
88. The 2008 Guidelines note with respect to biomass that only aid for investment in or the operation of aid for the production of sustainable biofuels will be authorised under the provisions of the 2008 Guidelines relating to the promotion of energy from renewable energy sources.
89. 2008 Guidelines, para. 70. The Commission's list of renewable energy sources is exhaustive, perhaps a regrettable absence of flexibility, given the fast rate of technological development in the renewables sector. See, 'Response of the Dutch

authorities to the 2nd consultation document of the European Commission relating to: Community Guidelines on State Aid for environmental protection', 3.

90. Ibid., paras 81–83, See above, for a detailed discussion of how the eligible costs are calculated. During the consultation period, the concern was expressed that the requirement for eligible investments costs to be calculated net of any operating benefits and costs related to the extra investment for renewable sources of energy and arising during the first five years of the life of the investment was too demanding, and might deter investments by companies expecting to make returns on their investment within two to three years following the investment (See Comments of Business Europe, 'Community guidelines for State aid for environmental protection – preliminary draft 3', 5 November 2007.

91. 2008 Guidelines, para. 104.

92. Ibid., para. 107.

93. Ibid., paras. 100–111.

94. SEC(2008) 57.

95. 2008 Guidelines, para. 55. The 2008 Guidelines were adopted before the revised EU ETS was finalised. The 2008 Guidelines therefore provide for their own revision once a new Directive on the EU CO2 emissions trading system is introduced, to ensure compatibility with the trading system. Reports indicated that the necessary amendments would be implemented before the end of 2010. See P. Koh, 'EC to amend environmental guidelines by year-end', Mlex, 5 March 2010. It is more likely that new rules will be adopted by the end of 2011.

96. The Commission has also reviewed certain national schemes operating outside the EU ETS. See Commission Decision of 20 July 2005 in Case NN 12/2004 United Kingdom – Horticulture – Climate change level, O.J. C 262, 21 October 2005, p. 9; Commission Decision of 16 March 2005 in Case C-35/2003 (ex N-90/2002) Italy-Lazio-Reduction of greenhouse gas emissions, O.J. L 244, 7 September 2006, p. 8; Commission Decision of 23 November 2005 in Case-C 44/2004 (ex N 402/2004) Slovenia – Modification of Case SI 1/03 (The reduction of burdening of the environment of emissions with carbon dioxide), O.J. 2006 L 268, 19.

97. 2008 Guidelines, para. 140.

98. See, for example, <http://europa.eu/rapid/pressReleasesAction.do?reference=MEMO/08/35&format=HTML&aged=0&language=EN&guiLanguage=en#fnB1> (last accessed 31 December 2010).

99. 2008 Guidelines, para. 140(d). See 2008 Guidelines, para. 141.

100. Case C-143/99, *Adria-Wien Pipeline* [2001] E.C.R. I-836.

101. The only EU-wide harmonised tax is that provided for by the 'Energy Tax Directive', which sets minimum taxation rates for motor fuel, motor fuel for industrial or commercial use, heating fuel and electricity (Council Directive 2003/96/EC restructuring the Community framework for the taxation of energy products and electricity). As shown by Case 41/2006 Denmark – Modification of the CO^2 tax for quota-regulated fuel consumption in the industry, an exemption or reduction that complies with the requirements of Council Directive 2003/96/EC is not necessarily a State aid compatible with the common market.

102. See Kutenicova and Seinen (2008): paras 4.505–4.507. In 2002, the Commission approved adjustments made to the exemptions provided for in the German eco-tax despite the fact that the tax pre-dated the issuing of the 2008 Guidelines (Commission Decision of 13 February 2002 in Case N-449/2001, Germany – Ecological tax reform after 31 March 2002, O.J. 2002 C 137/24, 8 June 2002, p. 24; Commission Decision of 30 March 2004 in Case NN 61/2003, Germany – Ecotax from 1 January 2003 – Spitzenausgleich, O.J. 2005 C 133/2, p. 2; Commission Decision in Case N-775/2006, Germany – Tax reductions for manufacturing, agriculture and forestry and tax cap (Spitzenausgleich) for energy intensive users, O.J. 2007 C 152/1. However, the German eco-tax case involved the legislative amendment of the terms of an existing tax. An incentive effect could therefore still be found, since the Member State was

reforming the tax law in order to create an incentive for undertaking to work towards the new provisions. As such, despite the 2008 Guidelines removing the distinction between new and old taxes, it remains uncertain whether a pure pre-existing tax, without a legislative reform that adjusts the terms of that pre-existing tax and can therefore be interpreted as creating an incentive effect, would be authorised by the Commission even under the 2008 Guidelines. However, in theory, tax exemptions and reductions will fall within the scope of examination of the 2008 Guidelines irrespective of whether the tax for which the exemption is created was introduced prior to or before the introduction of the 2001 Guidelines.
103. Where the beneficiary pays at least the minimum level of tax required under Community law, no notification is required.
104. Case C-199/06, *CELF v. SIDE* [2008] E.C.R. 1-460.

REFERENCES

Allibert, B. and C. Jones (2008), 'Energy (including nuclear and coal)', in *EU Competition Law Vol IV State Aid*, Leuven: Claeys & Castells, ch. 4.
Chérot, J-Y., J. Derenne, and C. Giolito (2008), 'La Commission europeéenne adopte un nouvel encadrement des aides d'Etat en faveur de l'environnement pour les années 2008–2014', *Concurrences: Aides d'Etat, Chroniques*, **2**, 137–150.
Kutenicova, E. and A.T. Seinen (2008), 'Environmental Aid', in *EU Energy Law* Leuven: Claeys & Castells, ch. 3.
Soltész, Ulrich and Felix Schatz (2009), 'State aid for environmental protection: the Commission's new Guidelines and the new General Block Exemption', *Journal for European Environmental & Planning Law*, **6:2**, 141–170.
Szyszczak, E. (2009) 'Lisbon – Kyoto – Moscow: Joining the Dots?', *Fordham Environmental Law Review*, **19**, 287.
Szyszczak, E. (2011), 'The survival of the market economic investor principle in liberalised markets', *European State Aid Law Quarterly*, **1**, 35.

12 The relationship between State aid and the single market

*Andrea Biondi and Martin Farley**

I. INTRODUCTION

Since the adoption of the Treaty of Rome in 1957 the creation of the European single market has been fundamental to the European integration process. One of the principal methods by which the rules of the single market have sought to achieve European-wide integration has been through the imposition of limits on national economic policies so as to ensure the free-flow of trade. Central to this aim is the prohibition on Member States from seeking to influence or affect inter-State trade. This prohibition is embodied within the free movement provisions, which outlaw regulatory measures that create an obstacle to the free movement of goods, capital, workers, or services.

In addition to the protection of these 'four freedoms', the Treaty of Rome, and now the Treaty on the Functioning of the European Union (TFEU), also included provisions prohibiting the introduction of discriminatory tax measures by Member States that could have an effect on inter-State trade, as well as rules governing the creation of State monopolies. Each set of these provisions, however, is a specific embodiment of a more fundamental, underlying principle: Member States must not favour certain (usually national) undertakings to the disadvantage of undertakings from other Member States. It is this basic premise that forms the basis on which the realisation of the single market is built, and a principle that is expressly embodied in Articles 107 and 108 TFEU, which govern the granting of financial aid by Member States to private undertakings.

The question, therefore, is: if the provisions relating to the four freedoms, taxation etc. constitute a specific application of the principle that Member States must not favour certain undertakings over others, how do each of these provisions relate to the express manifestation of that principle as it appears in the rules on State aid. As the case law of the CJEU has repeatedly reaffirmed, although, constitutionally, the provisions on State aid and free movement should be considered as separate and distinct bodies of rules, these provisions have a common objective: to facilitate free trade between Member States under the normal conditions of competition.[2] As such, understanding the relationship between the rules on State aid and the four freedoms is key to developing a truly single market throughout the EU. This is true not only from a substantive point of view, and the need to ensure that the different provisions of the Treaty are applied in conformity with one another, but also from a jurisdictional point of view in respect of who may rely on which provisions and before which court. For example, with the exception of the last part of Article 108(3) TFEU, which contains a standstill provision addressed to the Member States and can be directly challenged by individuals, the rules on State aid are not directly effective.[3] This can raise jurisdictional questions in situations where all or part of the aid in question also infringes free movement provisions[4] or the specific provisions contained in Article 110 TFEU relating to Member States' internal tax regimes,[5] all provisions which are directly effective.

In addressing the relationship between the Treaty provisions on State aid and other Treaty provisions regulating the single market, this chapter will first examine the CJEU case law on the underlying, constitutional principles that govern the relationship between the State aid rules and the provisions on free movement, before focusing on the application of those principles in the following areas: (a) State aid and the four freedoms; (b) State aid and State monopolies and (c) the rules on internal taxation and parafiscal charges.

II.   STATE AID AND FREE MOVEMENT: GENERAL PRINCIPLES

When examining the relationship between the free movement provisions and the rules governing State aid two principal questions come to the fore. The first is whether the two sets of provisions should be considered as being mutually exclusive, despite the fact that they both work to achieve the same aims; and the second is whether the same wide definition applied by the CJEU to the test of 'restriction on trade' as it appears in the free movement provisions also applies to the 'effect on trade' test within the meaning of Article 107 TFEU.

The leading authority in this area continues to be the *Iannelli v. Meroni* judgment, which has constituted good law since it was handed down in 1977.[6] The case addressed the question whether a national court could, when asked to rule on a question of State aid, take into account a possible violation of Article 34 TFEU on the free movement of goods as well as a violation of Article 107 TFEU. In its ruling, the CJEU first dealt with the question of whether 'obstacles to trade' covered by other provisions of the Treaty could be applied in the context of Article 34 TFEU. The CJEU began its reasoning by acknowledging that a State aid regime is likely to have at least an indirect effect on trade. The CJEU went on to consider, however, that, as a general principle it was not possible to take the 'obstacles to trade' test as it applied in one section of the Treaty and apply it to a different section. Instead, the particular purpose of the Treaty provision in question needed to be taken into account, as did the provision's position in the general context of the aims of the Treaty and the scope of its application.

In seeking to analyse the purpose and context of the State aid regime in *Iannelli v. Meroni* the CJEU focused on the fact that Article 107 TFEU is not mandatory in nature. In doing so, the CJEU highlighted the fact that although Article 107(1) TFEU sets out a general prohibition on the granting of State aid, Articles 107(2) and (3) TFEU list a series of exceptions to the general prohibition and confer a wide discretion on the Commission to accept that a State aid system merits derogation from the general prohibition. In addition, the Commission enjoys full responsibility for carrying out an analysis of whether a national measure is contrary to the single market. By comparison, the CJEU considered that the purpose and context of the free movement provisions was mandatory, explicit and unconditional in nature and could be invoked directly before national courts. The CJEU concluded, therefore, that:

> the effect of an interpretation of Article 30 of the Treaty [now Article 34 TFEU] which is so wide as to treat an aid as such within the meaning of Article 92 of the Treaty [now Article 107 TFEU] as being similar to a quantitative restriction referred to in Article 30 would be to alter the scope of Articles 92 and 93 of the Treaty [now Articles 107 and 108 TFEU] and to interfere with the system adopted in the Treaty for the division of powers by means of the procedure for keeping aids under constant review as described in Article 93.[7]

The distinction between State aid and free movement provisions, therefore, is 'constitutional' rather than functional, and is based on the allocation of competence as set out in the Treaty.[8] The Commission has sole discretion to evaluate the compatibility of a State aid measure with the single market, whereas, individuals, and, given the direct effectiveness of the provisions, national courts, may challenge national measures as being contrary to the free movement provisions. It is impossible, therefore, to use the State aid measures and free movement interchangeably.

The CJEU reasoning is based on the assumption that both sets of rules are pursuing an identical aim: that of ensuring the free movement of goods, services, workers and capital under normal conditions of competition.[9] The prohibition contained in the free movement provisions against any possible obstacle to the free flow of goods and the prohibition contained in Article 107(1) TFEU on aid that affects trade, therefore, have the same legal consequence: the national measure in question is incompatible with EU law.[10] Only by keeping this functional identity in mind, can one fully understand the approach taken in respect of the mutual exclusivity of the two sets of provisions.

As is well known, contrary to the Opinion of Advocate General Warner, in *Iannelli v. Meroni* the CJEU, held that:

> Those aspects of aid which contravene specific provisions of the Treaty other than Articles 92 [now Article 107 TFEU] and 93 [now Article 108 TFEU] may be so indissolubly linked to the object of the aid that it is impossible to evaluate them separately so that their effect on the compatibility or incompatibility of the aid viewed as a whole must therefore of necessity be determined in the light of the procedure prescribed in Article 93. Nevertheless the position is different if it is possible when a system of aid is being analysed to separate those conditions or factors which, even though they form part of this system, may be regarded as not being necessary for the attainment of its object or for its proper functioning.[11]

The CJEU concluded that where it was possible to separate out the conditions that are not necessary for the attainment of the objects of the aid measure, the national court should be allowed to determine whether these separate factors constituted possible violations of the free movement provisions. Where this was not the case, however, then the measure, in its entirety, falls within the ambit of the State aid rules, and the jurisdiction of the Commission.

This so-called 'severability' test has been severely criticised for lacking clarity and for its difficult application.[12] When looked at in the above context, the test is clearly aimed at ensuring the effective application of EU law and at the dismantling of possible national barriers. In the vast majority of cases, where the issue of the relationship between State aid and free movement has been raised, the CJEU invariably managed to spell out how a particular contested measure could be severed from a general State aid regime, and thus be made subject to scrutiny under the free movement provisions.

The *Buy Irish* judgment is a good example of how the CJEU manages to sever measures from the State aid regime.[13] The case concerned an advertising campaign financed by the Irish Government, and was aimed at promoting sales of Irish products. Advocate General Capotorti, in a very strong Opinion, argued that such a campaign should not have been considered as a measure having equivalent effect, as the contested measures were 'in their nature not barriers or obstacles to trade established by the public authorities but rather of public aid whereby it sought to give domestic producers a competitive advantage over foreign producers'.[14]

The CJEU held instead that the mere fact that the campaign itself was directly financed by State resources did not mean that it could escape the prohibition laid down in Article 34 TFEU. Behind the ECJ's very curt response to Advocate General Capotorti's Opinion lies the assumption that State aid and free movement provisions serve the same purpose. The Court identified the substitution of domestic products for imported products on the Irish market as the Irish Government's true intention – an intention that was both anti-competitive and liable to hinder trade and, therefore, chose to assess the measure under the free movement provisions rather than the State aid rules.

The CJEU adopted the same approach in its ruling in *Commission v. France*, which concerned a tax advantage that was granted to newspaper publishers on the condition that the newspapers were printed in France. The CJEU stated once again that 'the provisions relating to the free movement of goods, the repeal of discriminatory tax provisions and aid have a common objective, namely to ensure the free movement of goods under normal conditions of competition'.[15] Thus, the mere fact that a national measure could be defined as an aid did not prevent the CJEU from deciding the case on the basis of the prohibition on obstacles to trade under the free movement provisions. The effect on market access, therefore, undoubtedly plays a role in the assessment of State aid.

Even in more recent cases the CJEU seems to apply the two sets of provisions somehow contemporaneously. In the *Presidenza del Consiglio dei Ministri v. Regione Sardegna*, the CJEU was asked to rule on a regional tax that was imposed on stopovers flights. The tax only applied, however, to undertakings that had their tax domicile outside of that region.[16] The CJEU considered the measure both as a violation of the free movement of services and as an aid, and focussed its reasoning on the differential treatment between flights operated by persons having their tax domicile within the region and those established in other Member States. Such differential treatment created an advantage that could be classified as both an obstacle to free movement and as a State aid.

In conclusion, it could be argued that the test adopted by the CJEU does not really focus on the possible severability of the State aid/free movement aspects of the measure, but rather on ensuring the effective application of EU law to national measures constituting an obstacle to trade. It should also be stressed that most of the cases where the Court found in favour of a possible application of the free movement provisions concerned non-notified aids. In those circumstances the only possibility for national courts (and thus for individuals) to review a system of aid arises under Article 107 TFEU, on the basis that the Member State failed to wait for Commission approval before implementing the aid.[17]

The willingness of the CJEU to apply the free movement provisions in the first instance, rather than the State aid rules is not, however, merely based on the desire to grant direct recourse to individuals, but can also be justified on the constitutional hierarchy of the Treaty. The CJEU summed up the effect of this hierarchy in its ruling in *Commission v. Italy (Sovrapprezzo)*.[18] In this case, the Court developed the idea that 'the general plan' of the Treaty requires that the application of State aid rules must never produce a result which is contrary to the Treaty rules governing free movement. The Court's approach was aimed at accommodating the fact that, unlike the free movement provision, the State aid rules are neither situation nor sector specific and can, therefore, be applied in circumstances not otherwise covered by the free movement provisions. Applying this hierarchical distinction in the *Sovrapprezzo* case, the CJEU held that although the procedure in Articles 107 and 108 TFEU left a wide discretion to the Commission as to whether an aid could be considered as compatible with the single market, the exercise of that discretion must not produce a result that would be contrary to any other specific provisions of the Treaty.[19]

III. STATE AID AND THE FOUR FREEDOMS

By its very nature, State aid necessarily involves some form of discrimination. This is apparent from the wording of Article 107(1) TFEU, which provides that in order for a measure to be classified as State aid, it must distort competition by 'favouring certain undertakings or the production of certain goods'. In many cases, the purpose of favouring one undertaking over another will be to promote a national champion or to provide an advantage to undertakings based in the Member State in question. While such measures run contrary to the principle of non-discrimination on the grounds of nationality, as set out in Article 18 TFEU, this, in itself, is insufficient to declare a measure as incompatible with the single market, where the other conditions set out in Article 107(1) TFEU have not been satisfied.[20]

In order to reject a selective measure, which would not otherwise constitute State aid as contrary to the internal market the national measure has to be examined against provisions such as Article 34 TFEU on the free movement of goods, Article 45 TFEU on the free movement of workers, Article 49 TFEU on the freedom of establishment, or Article 56 TFEU on the free movement of services, each of which constitutes a specific application, in the context of the internal market, of the general prohibition on discrimination on grounds of nationality in Article 18 TFEU.[21]

For instance, in *FEDICINE v. Spain*[22] a complaint was brought before the CJEU in respect of Spanish legislation that entitled film distributors to a licence to dub films from third countries. Such a licence would only be granted, however, if the distributors agreed to distribute Spanish films as well. It was argued before the Court that such a measure induced distributors to favour the distribution of Spanish films to the detriment of films from other countries. Although the Court held that this measure constituted an infringement of the prohibition of restrictions on the freedom to provide services and was contrary to Article 56 TFEU, it rejected the argument that the measure also fell within the scope of Article 107(1) TFEU. The Court based this decision on the ground that there was no transfer of State resources and no financial favouring of certain undertakings, therefore key elements of the test under Article 107(1) TFEU were missing.

In the *UTECA* case, which raised similar issues to those in *FEDICINE v. Spain*, the CJEU was asked to rule on a Spanish law that required television operators to earmark 5% of their operating revenue for the funding of European cinematographic films and films made for television, and to spend 60% of that funding for the production of films of which the original language was one of the official languages of Spain (not only Spanish, but also catalán, gallego, euskera).[23] The Court found that the legislation in question did breach the free movement principles, but was justified by the cultural aim of promoting Spanish multilingualism. The CJEU agreed, however, to at least consider a possible violation of State aid provisions. On this point the CJEU ruled that the measure did not constitute an advantage granted either directly or indirectly by the State or through State resources as the burden was not shouldered by the State but by television operators. As such, the measure was not contrary to the State aid rules.

Even in cases where State resources have been involved where there is a clear infringement of the freedom to provide services the attraction of the free movement principles has proved to be too difficult to resist, not only for the CJEU, but also for the Commission. One such example involved an order by the Commission addressed to the German Government requiring it to repeal a memorandum obliging certain civil servants to fly exclusively with Lufthansa or, failing that, with foreign companies that were associated with the German national airline.[24] While the Commission acknowledged that the memorandum in question constituted a State measure in favour of a public undertaking, and was clearly in breach of Article 107(1) TFEU, following the CJEU preference, when faced with a choice to rely on free market provisions rather than State aid provisions, the Commission based its decision on Article

56 TFEU on the freedom to provide services rather than on the State aid rules.

Free movement of establishment and capital also become relevant in the context of State aid control, particularly with reference to direct taxation mesures. In this area questions of competence are very prominent, because the regulation of national tax regimes falls within the competence of Member States and not the EU. It is up to Member States, and not the Commission, therefore, to devise the system of taxation best suited to the national economy.[25] Member States' competence to devise and regulate their own internal tax regimes is limited, however, to the extent that such regimes must not conflict with the provisions of the Treaty. For example, while a national tax regime can confer an advantage on certain undertakings over others, provided that such differentiations are non-discriminatory and justified by the nature of the tax system, the regime will still be contrary to the Treaty where such differences are based on the grounds of nationality or residency.

The CJEU has thus repeatedly held that granting tax benefits only to residents of a Member State or taxing non-residents at a higher rate of tax may constitute indirect discrimination by reason of nationality.[26] As such, the Commission will not approve aid that is granted through tax exemptions if the benefit of those taxes is restricted on the grounds of nationality.[27] In judgments such as *Marks & Spencer*[28] and *Cadbury Schweppes*,[29] the Court also went as far as considering measures permitting the transfer of losses from a subsidiary to its parent company, on condition that the former was either resident in the UK or economically active there, as a violation of freedom of establishment rules. The primary effect of this case law is of course to remove the possible discriminatory effects of different taxation levels between Member States. Nonetheless it – albeit indirectly – restricts a Member State's choice when developing an internal selective tax regime, as the European Courts will always assess whether such a measure constitutes an obstacle to trade. Such an effect is clear for instance in the *Italian banking foundation* judgment, which dealt with a tax reduction for banking foundations in Italy. In this case, the CJEU had no hesitation in holding that such a measure constituted State aid and further specified that the advantage, in terms of competitiveness, that was created by the tax reduction for operators established in Italy made it even more difficult for operators in other Member States to penetrate the Italian market. Despite the Member States' wide powers in tax matters they must still 'endeavour to ensure that the choices made in tax matters take due account of the consequences which may flow therefore for the proper functioning of the internal market'.[30]

IV.   STATE AID AND MONOPOLIES

State aid law also has a role to play in relation to State-run monopolies. State-run monopolies are prevalent in the transport and utilities sectors, and often have the common theme that, due to the need to service an entire community and the high sunk costs involved in entering the market, it is more profitable for a single entity to provide a service throughout the entire region than it would be for multiple competitors to fight over the provision of services. One such example is national postal systems, which require the creation of an entire collection and distribution network in order to provide an effective service. While competition may exist in certain areas of the postal service – such as special or guaranteed delivery – normal postal services are best carried out by a single operator. If the Member State in question helps finance such services then questions arise, not only as to whether this constitutes illegal State aid, but whether the specific Treaty provisions on State monopolies are infringed as well.

State monopolies are principally regulated by Articles 37 and 106(2) TFEU. Article 37 TFEU deals with State monopolies that have a commercial character and prohibits any discrimination between nationals of Member States regarding the conditions under which goods are procured and marketed.[31] In respect of the relationship between Article 37 TFEU and the provisions on State aid, in the case of *Hansen v. Hauptzollamt Flensberg*, which concerned a German monopoly in spirits,[32] the CJEU was called upon to address the constitutional relationship between these two sets of rules. In addressing the State aid element of the case, CJEU held that:

> State measures, inherent in the exercise by a State monopoly of a commercial character of its exclusive right must, even where they are linked to the grant of an aid to producers subject to the monopoly, be considered in the light of the requirements of Article [37 TFEU].

In the constitutional hierarchy of the Treaty the CJEU considered that the State aid provisions were subject to, and must be applied in light of, the prohibition in Article 37 TFEU. In this way, Article 37 TFEU needs to be complied with when assessing the compatibility of aid measures in the context of State monopolies having a commercial character. As such, and as was seen in the context of the four freedoms the Commission cannot grant clearance to a proposed State aid measure, if such measure infringes the prohibition set out in Article 37 TFEU.

The Treaty also regulates the application of the State aid rules to undertakings falling within the scope of Article 106(2) TFEU, by establishing a constitutional hierarchy similar to the one that exists between the State aid rules and the four freedoms. Article 106(2) TFEU regulates undertakings that are entrusted with the operation of a service of general economic interest or have the character of a revenue-producing monopoly. In contrast to situations covered by Article 37 TFEU, Article 106(2) TFEU applies when the State has outsourced the provision of, for example, a utility to a third-party, private sector undertaking, and granted the undertaking a monopoly over the provision of such service so that it can properly fulfil the tasks that it was entrusted with. Given the high demands, and the need to provide universal services – even where it may not be profitable to do so – Member States often need to entice private-sector entities to undertake the required services by offering fiscal or competitive advantages. It is at this point that the State aid rules and Article 106(2) TFEU begin to inter-relate.

An example of the inter-play between Articles 106(2) and 107 TFEU arose in the case of *Banco Exterior de España*.[33] The case concerned a Spanish measure exempting public credit institutions from taxation. In its ruling, the CJEU held that the power of the Commission under Article 107 TFEU to keep aid under constant review and supervision also covers State aid granted to the undertakings referred to in Article 106(2) TFEU. As such, the distinction made in Article 108 TFEU between existing and new aid also applies to aid granted to undertakings covered by Article 106(2) TFEU. In the context of the tax relief granted in *Banco Exterior de España*, this constituted existing aid, and, as such, the CJEU was not required to consider whether the aid was capable of falling outside the scope of the prohibition in Article 107 TFEU by virtue of Article 106(2) TFEU.

Following the ruling in *Banco Exterior de España*, the Commission considered that the procedure under Article 106 TFEU prevails over that in Article 108(3) TFEU but that a Member State may not invoke Article 106(2) TFEU to evade the notification requirements in Article 108(3) TFEU.[34] This approach was subsequently confirmed in *France v. Commission (CELF)*,[35] where the CJEU held that not only the obligation to notify State aid but also the suspension obligation under Article 108(3) TFEU applied to aids falling within the scope of Article 106(2) TFEU. Furthermore, while the mere fact that an aid measure satisfies the conditions of Article 106(2) TFEU will not necessarily mean that the aid in question is compatible with the single market, the Commission has discretion to use its powers to approve the aid under Article 108 TFEU where it is of the opinion that such approval is appropriate.[36] This is consistent with the Commission's standard approach in other areas of first considering the measure in the context of other specific single market provisions before turning to assess the aid on the basis of Articles 107 and 108 TFEU.

V. STATE AID, TAXATION AND PARAFISCAL CHARGES

It is important to remember that the rules governing the single market extend beyond the four freedoms and have an equally important role to play. One such area, and one that keeps creating specific problems for the European judiciary, especially with regard to its relationship with the State aid rules is the rules of indirect taxation. In addition to the general principle of non-discrimination on the grounds of nationality set out in Article 18 TFEU, Article 110 TFEU sets out specific provisions in respect of internal taxation, which prohibit Member States from imposing internal taxation of a discriminatory nature. The aim of such a provision – as the Court repeatedly held – is that of ensuring free movement of goods between the Member States in normal conditions of competition through the elimination of all forms of protection which may result from the application of internal taxation that discriminates against products from other Member States and the complete neutrality of internal taxation as regards competition between domestic products and imported products[37] As such, if a tax measure involves discriminatory taxation Article 110 TFEU will prohibit the tax measure even though the taxation in question may form part of an aid within the meaning of Article 107 TFEU. Conversely, however, the mere fact that the financing of an aid scheme does not infringe Article 110 TFEU does not necessarily mean that the scheme will be compatible with the requirements set out in Articles 107 and 108 TFEU.[38] In order for a tax measure, which constitutes aid, to be valid the Commission must, therefore, be satisfied that the measure in question, firstly, does not infringe Article 110 TFEU, and secondly, satisfies all of the relevant conditions set out in Articles 107 and 108 TFEU.

The same obligations also apply to national courts. For example, the *Nygård* judgment[39] concerned a levy imposed by Denmark on the production of live pigs for export. The national court had no doubts about the compatibility of such a measure with the free movement of goods. It was unsure, however, whether the authorisation granted by the Commission under Article 107(3) TFEU to the Danish scheme of production levies, could preclude it from setting aside a levy used to finance the authorised aid. On a preliminary reference the CJEU held that although only the Commission is competent to decide whether an aid scheme is compatible with the internal market, it also recognised that national courts have a responsibility to check whether any other directly effective provisions might have been violated, especially 'with a view to remedying, if necessary, infringements of Community law which have not been confirmed in the procedure provided for under Article 88 of the Treaty'.[40]

Perhaps one of the most challenging forms of aid related tax measures that the Commission and the European Courts have had to face, however, concerns parafiscal charges. Parafiscal charges are charges dedicated to a particular purpose,[41] and are often levied on a particular industrial sector so as to finance activities benefiting the sector as a whole. The funds generated by parafiscal charges are often used to finance promotional and marketing activities[42] or collective research.[43] In many cases the beneficiaries of parafiscal charges are institutions that do not carry on economic activities, and which do not, therefore, constitute undertakings for the purposes of the Treaty provisions. In such cases Article 107 TFEU will not apply and questions of State aid will not arise.[44]

Where the beneficiaries of funds levied by parafiscal charges are undertakings, however, two issues may arise in the context of the State aid rules: first, whether the funds constitute aid; and second, if the funds do constitute aid, can the charges be challenged under Articles 107 and 108 TFEU. In respect of the first question, the CJEU held in *Compagnie Commerciale de l'Ouest*, that the application of funds financed by parafiscal charges do constitute State aid for the purposes of Article 107 TFEU where the effect of the allocation of such funds is to favour certain undertakings over others, and that such aid measures had to be considered pursuant to the procedure laid down in Article 108(2) TFEU, subject to the jurisdiction of the national court where there is a breach of Article 108(3) TFEU.[45]

The second question, whether parafiscal charges could be challenged under Articles 107 or 108 TFEU, is more difficult to answer. Article 107 TFEU does not, on its face, prohibit the imposition of a tax or charge, even where the funds of such a charge are used to finance State aid. In its ruling in *France v. Commission*,[46] the CJEU acknowledged that a close relationship exists between an aid and a charge that finances that aid. The CJEU emphasised that in order to apply Article 107(1) TFEU it is necessary to consider all of the legal and factual circumstances surrounding the aid, including whether there is an imbalance between the charges imposed and the benefits derived from the aid. As such, the aid cannot be considered separately from the way in which it is financed. Finding a connection between the aid measure and the method of financing still stops considerably short, however, of allowing applicants to challenge parafiscal charges that fall within the ambit of a Member State's internal tax regime.

The CJEU sought to clarify the position of parafiscal charges in its rulings in the *Van Calster*[47] and *Streekgewest*[48] cases. The *Van Calster* case concerned a reference for a preliminary ruling in proceedings brought by Van Calster and Cleeren for reimbursement of a parafiscal charge that had been levied by the public authorities on trade in cattle. The funds levied from the charges were used to fund measures to combat animal disease and improve animal health and hygiene. Neither party disputed the fact that the use of the funds constituted State aid. Such aid had, however, been approved by the Commission. The question was whether the retroactive imposition of parafiscal charges under the scheme was prohibited under Articles 107 and 108 TFEU. The CJEU began its ruling by reiterating its position in *France v. Commission*, and concluded that the State aid rules do not cover the method of financing an aid where that method 'forms an integral part of the measure' in the sense that the charges are designed 'specifically and exclusively' to finance the aid.[49] Where the aid measure and the method of financing are so closely linked, the notification of the aid under Article 108(3) TFEU must also cover the method of financing, so that the Commission may consider the measure on the basis of all the facts.[50] The CJEU went on to conclude that if a charge, which is integral to an aid measure, is implemented in breach of the obligation to notify, the national courts must order reimbursement.[51] Therefore, parafiscal charges will only fall within the scope of the State aid rules where such charges are 'integral' to the aid in question. In such a case the Member State must notify both the aid and the charge to the Commission for its approval. Failure to notify the charges will entitle applicants who have paid the charge to seek reimbursement before their national courts.

The CJEU subsequently had the opportunity to develop the concept of a charge being 'integral' to the aid measure in its ruling in the *Streekgewest* case. As was the case in *Van Calster*, the applicant sought the reimbursement of a charge, this time in relation to a Dutch waste levy. In its ruling, CJEU considered that:

> Taxes do not fall within the scope of the provisions of the Treaty concerning State aid unless they constitute the method of financing an aid measure, so that they form an integral part of that measure.
>
> For a tax, or part of a tax, to be regarded as forming an integral part of an aid measure, it must be hypothecated to the aid measure under the relevant national rules, in the sense that the revenue from the tax is necessarily allocated for the financing of the aid. In the event of such hypothecation, the revenue from the tax has a direct impact on the amount of the aid and, consequently, on the assessment of the compatibility of the aid with the common market. . .The Court thus held that, where there is such a link between the aid measure and its financing, the notification of the aid provided for in Article 93(3) of the Treaty [now Article 108(3) TFEU] must also cover the method of financing, so that the Commission may consider it on the basis of all the facts. If this requirement is not satisfied, it is possible that the Commission may declare that an aid measure is compatible when, if the Commission had been aware of its method of financing, it could not have been so declared.[52]

The test for determining whether a parafiscal charge can be challenged under the State aid rules, therefore, turns, in the first instance, on whether the charge forms an integral part of the aid, to the extent that the proceeds of the charge are specifically allocated for the purposes of financing the aid. The lack of such hypothecation will mean that undertakings will not be able to challenge the parafiscal charges on the basis of Articles 107 and 108 TFEU. Following the CJEU ruling in *Van Calster* even where the charge is integral to the aid measure, an applicant may only seek reimbursement of the charge to the extent that the charge was not included in the Member State's notification to the Commission prior to implementing the aid measure.

While the CJEU case law in this area means that where a charge is not integral to the financing of an aid measure disadvantaged undertakings will not have recourse to a remedy under the State aid rules, such a result is necessary in light of Member States' competence to regulate their own internal tax regimes. As was stated above, Article 107 TFEU does not prohibit the imposition of charges or taxes. While such a prohibition may appear conspicuous by its absence, this position is, by necessity, correct if the CJEU is to ensure that Member States remain competent for their own internal tax regimes and that the Commission con only intervene where it can be clearly demonstrated that a tax regime is contrary to a specific Treaty provision. It is this balance that the CJEU has sought to strike with the principle of hypothecation.

VI.   CONCLUSIONS

The above discussion illustrates that, despite the best efforts of the CJEU to clarify the situation, the exact contours of the relationship between the State aid rules and the Treaty provisions governing the single market remain elusive. The development of tests such as severability and references to the constitutional hierarchy of norms within the Treaty go some way towards explaining the inter-play between the two sets of rules, but, in reality, the fact that the provisions inherently serve the same purpose – the furtherance of the internal market – means that is its almost impossible to delineate their application completely.

The guiding principle, as always, in respect of EU law, is that the Treaty principles should be interpreted and applied in a way that gives effect to their aims. The advantage in this case is that both sets of rules have the same aim. When faced with a situation where it is unclear, therefore, whether the State aid rules, or the Treaty provisions specifically designed to regulate the single market are more appropriate, approach the issues from both sides and leave it to the courts to decide which approach it prefers.

NOTES

* The views expressed in this article are solely those of the authors and may not under any circumstances be regarded as stating the position of any organisation with which the authors are associated.

1. See Case 17/84, *Commission v. Ireland* [1985] E.C.R. 2375; Case 103/84, *Commission v. Italy* [1986] E. C.R. 1759; Cases C-78/90 to C-83/90, *Compagnie Commerciale de l'Ouest* [1992] E.C.R. I-1847; Case C-21/88, *Du Pont de Nemours Italiana* [1990] E.C.R. 889.
2. Case 120/73, *Lorenz v. Germany* [1973] E.C.R. 1471.
3. Case 74/76, *Iannelli & Volpi v Meroni* [1977] E.C.R. 557.
4. Case 28/67, *Molkerei-Zentrale Westfalen v. Hauptzollamt Paderborn* [1964] E.C.R. 143.
5. *Iannelli & Volpi v Meroni*, supra n. 3, para. 10.
6. *ibid.*, para. 12.
7. See further, Biondi and Eeckhout 2003.
8. See Case 17/81, *Pabst & Richarz* [1982] E.C.R. 1331; Case 17/84, *Commission v. Ireland* [1985] E.C.R. 2375. 2375; Case 103/84, *Commission v. Italy* [1986] ECR 1759; Cases C-78/90 to C-83/90, *Compagnie Commerciale de l'Ouest* [1992] E.C.R. I-1847; Case C-17/91, *Lornoy* [1992] E.C.R. I-6523; Cases C-113/00 and C-114/00, *Spain v. Commission* [2002] E.C.R. I-7601.
9. Case C-21/88, *Du Pont de Nemours Italiana* [1990] E.C.R. I-889.
10. *Iannelli & Volpi* v *Meroni*, supra n. 3, para. 14.
11. Dashwood 1977.
12. Case 249/81, *Commission v. Ireland* [1982] E.C.R. 4005.
13. *ibid.* para. 4031.
14. Case 18/84, *Commission v. France* [1985] E.C.R. 1339.
15. Case C-169/08, *Presidenza del Consiglio v. Regione Sardegna* [2009] E.C.R. 16908.
16. *Lorenz,* supra n. 2.
17. Case 73/79, *Commission v. Italy* 1980] E.C.R. 1533. See also Cases 142 and 143/80, *Amministrazione delle Finanze dello Stato v. Essevi and Salengo* [1981] E.C.R. 1413 and Case 71/81, *Pabst & Richarz v. Hauptzollamt Oldenburg* [1982] E.C.R. 1331.
18. See also Case C-113/00, *Spain v. Commission* [2002] E.C.R. I-7601; Case C-114/00, *Spain v. Commission* [2002] E.C.R. I-7657. See in general Giolito 2008.
19. Case T-158/99, *Thermenhotel Stoiser v. Commission* [2004] E.C.R. II-1.
20. Case 36/74, *Walrave and Koch v. Association Union Cycliste Internationale,* [1974] E.C.R. 1405; Case 13/76, *Donà v. Mantero* [1976] E.C.R. 1333 and Case C-10/90, *Masgio Bundesknappschaft* [1991] E.C.R. I-1119.
21. Case C-17/92, *FEDICINE v. Spain* [1993] E.C.R. I-2239.
22. Case C-222/07, *UTECA* [2009] E.C.R. I-1407.
23. *Twentieth Report on Competition Policy* (1990), para. 357.
24. Joined Cases T-211/04 and 215/04, *Gibraltar a.o. v Commission a.o.* [2008] E.C.R. II-3745.
25. Case C-175/88, *Biehl v. Administration des contributions du Grand-duché de Luxembourg* [1990] E.C.R. 1779.
26. For example, see Case C-156/98, *Germany v. Commission* [2000] E.C.R. I-6857, para. 85, where the CJEU approved the Commission's refusal to authorise a scheme of aid whereby tax relief was granted for the reinvestment of profits in companies established in West Berlin or the former East Germany.
27. Case C–446/03, *Marks & Spencer plc v. David Halsey* [2005] E.C.R. I-10837.
28. Case C-196/04, *Cadbury Schweppes plc and Cadbury Schweppes Overseas Ltd v. Commissioners of Inland Revenue* [2006] E.C.R. I-7995. See further de Cecco 2007.
29. Case C-222/04, *Cassa di Risparmio di Firenze* [2006] E.C.R. I-289.
30. See Buendia Sierra 1999.
31. Case 91/78, *Hansen v Hauptzollamt Flensberg* [1979] E.C.R. 935.
32. Case C-387/92, *Banco Exterior de España* [1994] E.C.R. I-877.
33. *Twenty-fourth Report on Competition Policy* (1994), para. 492.

34. Case C-332/98, *France v. Commission (CELF)*, [2000] ECR I-4833. See also, Cases C-261 and 262/01, *Belgium v Van Calster* [2003] E.C.R. I-12249.
35. Case C-280/00, *Altmark Trans and Regierungspräsidium Magdeburg* [2003] E.C.R. I-7747
36. See, *inter alia*, C-213/96, *Outokumpu Oy* [1998] E.C.R. I-1777; Case C-383/01, *De Danske Bilimportører* [2003] E.C.R. I-6065.
37. Roth and Rose 2010:1611.
38. Case C-234/99, *Niels Nygård* v, *Svineafgiftsfonden* [2002] E.C.R. I-3657.
39. *ibid.* para 60.
40. See AG Stix-Hackl's Opinion in Joined Cases C-34-38/01, *Enirisorse v. Ministero delle Finanze* [2003] E.C.R. I-14243, para. 167.
41. Case 78/76, *Steinike und Weinlig v. Germany* [1977] E.C.R. 595.
42. Case 47/69, *France v. Commission* [1970] E.C.R. 487.
43. Joined Cases C-266/04 to C-270/04, C-276/04 and C-321/04 to C-325/04, *Distribution Casino France and Others* [2005] E.C.R. I-9481.
44. *Compagnie Commerciale de l'Ouest and Others*, supra n. 9. See also Case C-206/06, *Essent Netwerk Noord and Others* [2008] E.C.R. I-5497.
45. *France v. Commission*, supra n. 42, paras 7–8.
46. Joined Cases C-261-262/01, *Belgium v. Van Calster and Cleeren* [2003] E.C.R. I-12249.
47. Case C-174/02, *Streekgewest* [2005] E.C.R. I-85.
48. *Van Calster*, supra n. 46, paras 44–49.
49. *ibid.*,paras 50–51.
50. *ibid.*, paras 52–54.
51. C-174/02, *Streekgewest*, [2005] E.C.R. 1-85, paras 24–26.

REFERENCES

Biondi, A. and P. Eeckhout (2003), 'State aids and barriers to trade', in A. Biondi, Eeckhout P. and J. Flynn (eds), *The Law of EC State Aids*, Oxford: OUP, 103.
Buendia Sierra, J. (1999), *Exclusive Rights and State Monopolies under EC law*, Oxford: OUP.
Dashwood, A (1977), 'Preliminary Rulings on the EEC state aid provisions' *European Law Review*, **2**, 367.
de Cecco, F. (2007), 'The many meaning of "competition" in EC state aid law', *Cambridge Yearbook of European Law*, **9**, 130.
Giolito, C. (2008), 'La Procedure de contrôle des aides d'état peut-elle être ultilisée pour contrôler la bonne application d'autres dispositions de droit communautaire?' in J. Flett (ed), *Achieving the Objectives of State Aid Control: Time for Some Realism in EC State Aid Law: Liber Amicorum Francisco Santaolalla*, The Hague: Kluwer, 145.
Roth, P. and V. Rose, (2010), *Bellamy & Child: European Community Law of Competition*, 6th edn Oxford: OUP.

13 *Altmark* assessed
Erika Szyszczak

> Since the nineties, the place of public services within the single market has been a persistent irritant in the European public debate.[1]

This chapter explores the *Altmark* ruling in the context of modernising public services.[2] Thouvenin (2009) places the *Altmark* ruling of 24 July 2003 as one of the few cornerstones which constitute the main foundations of EU law, placing *Altmark* alongside the landmark rulings of *Van Gend en Loos,*[3] *Costa* v. *ENEL,*[4] *Simmenthal,*[5] *AETR*[6] and *Rutili.*[7] Viewing the ruling in this light allows an interrogation of the role of State aid law and policy, moving beyond an analysis of how the European Courts and the Commission have moderated the balance between protecting fundamental ideological principles of the Member States in providing public services against the countervailing tendencies of competition, free movement and liberalisation, by asking *how Altmark* has contributed to the modernisation of the functioning of public services.

I. *ALTMARK* IN CONTEXT

Public services have occupied an awkward role in the integration process. Bauby (2011) notes that, with the exception of what is now Article 93 TFEU (in the Chapter on Transport), the original EEC Treaty declined to acknowledge the role of public services in the European integration project. Instead the Treaty re-invented the concept of public services as 'services of general economic interest', as a *derogation* from the fundamental economic policy provisions of the EEC in what is now Article 106(2) TFEU.[8] An uneasy relationship developed between the Member States and the EU institutions, each straining to take competence over the role of public services in EU markets. Articles 37 and 106(1) TFEU provide a legal basis to challenge the distortive role of State monopolies in the free trade and competition[9] aspirations of EU integration, but from the 1990s a new phase of litigation emerged where the *funding* of public services became the focus of challenge as markets were opened up to competition.

The liberalisation programme which swept across Europe created new concepts of universal service obligations regulated by national and

EU law and the focus of attention turned away from challenges to State monopolies under Article 106(1) TFEU to negotiation of the content and extent of the reserved sectors and universal service obligations, especially in the networked industries.[10] Article 106(2) TFEU did not become wholly redundant as the emphasis of Article 106(2) TFEU shifted to scrutiny of the role of State aid to fund public services.[11] Difficulties emerged as a State aid approach looked to the distortive effects of a subsidy where a specific undertaking obtains an advantage from the funding ostensibly granted for the provision of a public service. The Commission was not consistent in its handling of such subsidies and the European Courts joined the Commission in oscillating between taking a 'State aid' approach and a 'compensation' approach in scrutinising the compatibility of public services and EU law.[12]

In the 'State aid' approach public subsidies are seen as State aids, unless they fall within one of the exemptions set out in Articles 107(2) and (3) TFEU, secondary legislation and soft law communications. In contrast a 'compensation' approach sees the 'subsidy' as covering the extra costs of providing a public service.[13]

The Commission and the General Court preferred to see the payment for public services as a State aid issue but the State aid rules contained few escape clauses to capture the range and level of State funding for public services.

In contrast Article 106(2) TFEU contained a 'Community' concept of 'services of general economic interest' and is seen as an exception, a justification, derogation, escape clause or a switch rule (Baquero Cruz 2002) to the free market and competition rules of the EU.[14]

A compromise resulted in the European Courts and the Commission allowing the Member States to control the definition of a SGEI by only allowing for review in cases of manifest error. The framework of review, and by implication, Europeanisation, of SGEIs, was extended by the European Courts developing concepts of 'economic' and 'non-economic' activity to capture the wider range of public services being delivered in competitive markets. This was complemented by the Commission using soft law communications to create a policy framework in the absence of consensus from the Member States (and the EU institutions) for binding EU regulation.[15]

Thus, State aid policy became a central tool for the assessment of *how* public services are to be provided in the EU but with a limited capacity to accommodate public services, especially where the activity was of a social nature. This harsh approach was eventually mitigated by the CJEU in *Altmark*. Public service compensation (PSC) is *not* a State aid if four conditions/criteria are met:

1) the recipient undertaking has clearly defined public service obligations (PSO) to perform;
2) the parameters on which public service compensation (PSC) is calculated are established in advance in a transparent and objective manner;
3) the compensation does not exceed the cost of performing the obligations, taking into account relevant receipts and a reasonable profit; and
4) the recipient undertaking was chosen to perform the SGEI in a public procurement procedure allowing performance of the services at the lowest cost or, if not, the level of compensation needed is based upon the costs of a typical, well-run undertaking with adequate funding.

The first two criteria were seen in the European Courts' case law. In relation to the fourth criterion the Commission had been pushing for the greater use of procurement and had already used the ideas in the *Communication from the Commission on the application of State aid rules to public service broadcasting*.[16]

The approach of *Altmark*, set in the context of public services delivered in a commercial environment, became the benchmark for addressing the funding requirements of *all* SGEIs in the EU where sector-specific rules are absent. However, in areas where *social* public services are provided, and hence greater political sensitivity is required, the *Altmark* framework required adaptation.

II.   THE REACTION TO *ALTMARK*

Overnight the *Altmark* ruling questioned the funding, and thereby the operation of, SGEIs across the EU, opening them to potential litigation. Although the Court had endorsed the Commission's approach to the funding of SGEIs it had also opened the door for the Member States to self-assess their own funding operations and avoid scrutiny by the Commission of the proportionality of their measures.

II.i.   The European Courts

In the cases which reached the European Courts there is an uneven application of the criteria. The criteria were not discussed in the ruling in *GEMO*,[17] with the Court focusing upon the definition of whether the measure was a State aid. A supermarket brought a challenge against a subsidy system which provided farmers and slaughterhouses with the free collection and disposal of animal carcasses and slaughterhouse waste and was designed to ensure that the waste found unfit for human and animal consumption was disposed of without risk to public health. The Court found that:

> In the present case, the fact that, in France, the costs of carcass disposal are borne neither by farmers nor by slaughterhouses necessarily has a positive impact on meat prices, thus making that product more competitive on the markets of the Member States where such costs are normally paid out of the budgets of competing traders.
>
> Against that background, it is clear that a measure of this sort constitutes an advantage for French exports and affects intra-Community trade.[18]

The Court declined to follow the Opinion of Advocate General Jacobs (delivered on 30 April 2002) who had conducted an in-depth analysis of the classification of how services of general economic interest can be funded under EU law.

In contrast, in *Enirisorse*, a user of a port challenged the system whereby a public body active in providing port services received a significant proportion of compulsory port taxes.[19] Enirisorse did not use the port services but loaded and unloaded goods itself. The Italian government argued that trade between the Member States was not affected by the scheme. Issues of Article 106 TFEU and SGEIs were not raised. The Court refers to, and applies, the first two *Altmark* criteria. Firstly, finding from its previous case law that the operation of a commercial port does not automatically constitute a public service obligation and in this case there was no evidence that public service duties had been entrusted to the port operator and that in any event an entrustment must be clearly defined. Secondly, in looking to see if the parameters on the basis of which the compensation is calculated had been established in advance in an objective and transparent manner the Italian government had argued that the allocation of a major part of the port charges to the operator, together with the rates charged, was essential in order to maintain those rates at a level which the traders could bear and for the port to continue to operate.

The Court did not find this sufficient evidence. The content of the public service was not clear (for example, whether it concerned only loading and unloading in the ports in question, or whether services such as docking safety are also covered) there was no clear indication of the cost of those services or of the assessment of the compensation. The amount of payment varied with the level of activity in the port. Thus the Court found that a State aid was present. In relation to the port charges these were found to constitute internal taxation within the meaning of Article 110 TFEU where they did not fall within the ambit of Articles 30 and 34 TFEU. In the absence of any unequal treatment discriminating against goods from other Member States, the Court held that a measure by virtue of which a Member State provides for the collection of such charges and the allocation of a significant proportion of the charges to a public undertaking, when the sum corresponds to a service actually provided by that undertaking, does not infringe Article 110 TFEU.

The General Court applied the *Altmark* criteria in *Danske Busvognmænd*,[20] rejecting the Commission's position that the *Altmark* criteria were fulfilled. In the ruling in *Traghetti* the CJEU found that none of the *Altmark* criteria were fulfilled where payments were made on account without establishing prior and stringent criteria for a public service obligation.[21]

The *Altmark* criteria were followed closely in *Servizi Ausilliari*.[22] The Court found an Italian measure by which a Member State provides for the payment of compensation from State funds to certain undertakings responsible for helping taxpayers in connection with the completion of tax declarations and filing them with the tax authorities was a State aid where the level of the compensation exceeded what is necessary to cover all, or part, of the costs incurred in the discharge of public service obligations, taking into account the relevant receipts and a reasonable profit for discharging those obligations. The compensation was not determined on the basis of an analysis of the costs which would be incurred by a typical undertaking, well run and adequately provided with the means required to be able to meet the necessary public service requirements.

The *BUPA* case is discussed below.[23] Here the *Altmark* criteria were adapted to the specific facts (and sector) in conjunction with an application of Article 106(2) TFEU. The ruling of the General Court was not taken on appeal to the CJEU and thus leaves open the question of *where* the case sits within the framework of funding for SGEIs with a special social dimension.

II.ii. The Commission

The Commission's response to the *Altmark* ruling was pragmatic. Firstly, it seized back the scrutiny of potential State aid by encouraging notification of proposed funding for SGEIs for analysis against the *Altmark* criteria and continuing to offer the opportunity of using Article 106(2) TFEU (and the principle of proportionality) to review funding for SGEIs enabling a balance between competing public service (social) interests against economic (competition) interests.

Secondly, the Commission refocused its soft law communications towards State aid issues and created a new package of measures to accommodate the *Altmark* ruling. It adopted a Framework[24] and a Decision[25] and a revision of the Transparency Directive,[26] along with two soft law communications of *Frequently Asked Questions*.[27] This is often referred to as the 'Monti-Kroes package'. The legal basis of the Framework and the Decision is not transparent. Both appear to operate as Block Exemptions to the State aid rules but do not use Article 109 TFEU as the legal base .

Under the Commission Decision public service compensation that amounts to State aid is permitted (that is, it falls within Article 106(2) TFEU and does not need to be notified to the Commission) if:

1. it is less than 30 million euros per annum paid to undertakings with an annual turnover of less than 100 million euros, or is paid to hospitals or social housing undertakings or certain small air or maritime undertakings, airports and ports carrying out a SGEI;
2. there is an official act (for example, a statutory rule) specifying the undertaking's precise public service obligation, the parameters for calculating, controlling and reviewing the public service compensation and the arrangements for avoiding over-compensation;
3. the amount of public service compensation does not exceed the costs involved in performing the PSO, taking into account relevant receipts and a reasonable profit; the compensation is only used for the SGEI concerned.

These conditions reinforce the transparency and efficiency objectives for public service obligations inherent within *Altmark* but carve out some exemptions for 'social' public services as well as introducing (in contradiction to the CJEU ruling in *Altmark*[28]) a *de minimis* rule.

In the Framework, public service compensation which does not satisfy the *Altmark* criteria or the Decision must be notified to the Commission as a State aid in the usual way. The Framework addresses when Article 106(2) TFEU will apply. The Framework is identical to the Decision, except for the fact that where State aid falls within the Decision it does not have to be notified to the Commission, thus the Commission is obviously concerned with larger amounts of State aid and wants the opportunity to scrutinise it, and may impose conditions on the grant of the aid.

Where the public service compensation does not fall under the conditions of *Altmark*, the Decision or the Framework the State aid rules may still apply, including the application of Article 106(2) TFEU.

The Commission also stated its intention to adopt a 'more economic approach' to the application of the State aid rules in its State Aid Action Plan. In the assessment of SGEIs Point (i) states:

> compensations granted should make the performing of public service missions feasible without leading to overcompensation and undue distortions of competition .[29]

III. A CLOSER LOOK AT THE COMMISSION AND EUROPEAN COURTS' PRACTICE

The creation of a clearer set of criteria against which public services could be scrutinised has given the Commission greater confidence to investigate how a public service has been defined. As Hancher and Larouche (2011) point out the evolution of public services at the national level may result in a 'pot pourri' of historical entrustments without clearly defined regulation, and often without market testing. For example in *Irish Buses* the Commission expressed doubts as to whether a 'Memoranda' of understanding could be classified as a public contract for the purposes of the *Altmark* criteria.[30] This can be contrasted with the *BUPA*[31] ruling where the General Court found that a SGEI can be conferred by general and regulatory measures and may also consist in an obligation imposed on a large number of, or indeed on all, the operators active on the same market. In the *Cumbria Broadband* Decision the Commission found that a negotiated procurement procedure would not satisfy the *Altmark* criteria but was willing to exempt the subsidy using Article 107(3) TFEU.[32]

In other cases we see the Member State engaging with a detailed explanation of how new forms of multi-media can have a regional and social benefit as a public service. For example in *Pyrenenees Atlantique* the broadband network was found to contribute to regional development as well as containing a high educational content by providing free access to all schools, and access to e-health and e-government for the local population.[33] Here all four *Altmark* criteria were met. The wide discretion of Member States to finance public service broadcasting is seen in the judgment of *TV2/Danmark*.[34] The General Court endorsed the Member States' broad powers to define public service broadcasting, referring to the Amsterdam Protocol on public broadcasting,[35] a Resolution of the Council[36] and relevant case law. The Court rejected the argument of commercial broadcasters that the definition of services of general economic interest must be dependent on a comparative analysis of programming. The Court has also held that the provision of compensation does not preclude commercial activities.[37]

In relation to the second criterion, which addresses the parameters of compensation, the Member States have been obliged to give greater transparency as to *how* public services are funded. The *exact* amount of compensation does not need to be pre-determined but now the Member States must be able to show that there is a *method* by which compensation is determined. For example, compensation for public bus services in the Czech Republic was established on the price of a journey per kilometre, based upon statistical data to ensure that the price was established on the basis of the costs of a typical undertaking, but not necessarily an efficient undertaking.[38] In contrast, the modification of the parameters for the compensation for a public service in the maritime transport sector (ferry routes between Sicily and smaller islands) *after* the conclusion of the contract did not satisfy the *Altmark* criteria.[39]

The third and fourth criteria have proved to be the most contentious in the post-*Altmark* era. The third criterion addresses over-compensation of public services and is closely linked to the aim of improving efficiency and competitiveness of public services. There must be an appropriate accounting system.[40]

In *F-Broadband* the criterion was fulfilled by way of a claw-back clause where the profits exceeded a certain amount.[41] But in *Danish Bus Services* where compensation was calculated on the basis of the reduction of the price, and not on the basis of cost, the Commission was not satisfied that such a methodology would eliminate over-compensation.[42] Where there is compensation of fixed sums for passengers with a clause to avoid over-compensation and deduct excessive profit from the following year's compensation, the Commission has found this approach to satisfy the *Altmark* criterion.[43]

Where an unclear, or incorrect, definition of an SGEI is made it is difficult to distinguish between SGEI costs and normal business operations; it becomes impossible to define the parameters for compensation and in particular chart over-compensation.[44] In *Enirisorse*, for example, the levying of a charge at Italian ports using two thirds of the proceeds to compensate port operators did not satisfy the *Altmark* criteria because the definition of the public service task was too broad, it was not clear what it comprised, there was no identification of the possible extra costs incurred in providing a PSO and no system for providing for avoiding or mitigating over-compensation.[45]

In a Decision in the partially liberalised postal sector the Commission found Deutsche Poste had received illegal State aid because part of the public service compensation for the postal services' public service obligation was used to cross-subsidise pricing below the cost of parcel delivery in the part of the business not subject to the public service obligation.[46] The Commission argued that it held the discretion to choose the method for determining if there was over-compensation. The General Court (confirmed by the CJEU) annulled the Commission Decision, holding that the Commission does not have the discretion to choose the method of calculation of costs but it must be able to show whether the total amount of transfers exceeds the total amount of additional costs from the SGEI (in this case cost of SGEI was 20,426 million euro). This suggests that the State needs to show a sophisticated accounting system that can allocate costs and revenue, allocate fixed costs and prevent cross-subsidies to prevent over-compensation and to determine a reasonable profit. Such a system involves, by necessity, appropriate administrative procedures.

To achieve transparency and to allow the State aid rules to function there must be account separation. In *Antrop* Carris provided public transport services in Lisbon and received compensation.[47] It also competed with other undertakings on other routes and the Court found that aid was not compatible with the State aid rules because Carris did not have separate accounts for the services subject to the public service obligation and non-public service obligation services. The Transparency Directive[48] was amended in 2006 to show the separation requirement between SGEI activities and non-SGEI activities.[49]

In preventing over-compensation the Commission has held in *Aid to TV2* that where compensation is granted in advance or through an automatic levy there must be a procedure for eliminating over-compensation at the end of the accounting year. Excess compensation may be transferred to the next accounting year and deducted from compensation that year and reserves may be built up but they have to be regularised at fixed times to eliminate over-compensation.[50]

The fourth criterion introduces the use of procurement procedures as a means of avoiding the application of State aid rules. Schemes which have involved procurement have been praised as offering the best quality for the lowest cost.[51] The Commission has engaged with an analysis of the quality of the methodology used in the procurement procedure, especially in relation to avoiding over-compensation:

> The Commission has to verify whether the characteristics of the procurement procedure at stake are such as to actually allow for the selection of the supplier capable of providing those services at the least cost to the community. This is a material analysis which is different and goes beyond the mere respect of the applicable public procurement rules.[52]

Finding a benchmark for the comparison of the costs involved in subsidising a public service is a difficult task. For example, where there are few operators in a market which has historically been closed to competition it may be difficult to find an appropriate benchmark comparator undertaking. The concept of a benchmark comparator is not clear because the fourth criterion refers to both a 'typical' and 'well-run' undertaking. These are not necessarily the same. The first category suggests an 'industry-average' whereas the second category is pointing to a 'well-run' undertaking, suggesting efficiency. In *Postbus* the Commission finds that achieving the costs of a 'well-run' undertaking is the not the same as achieving the costs of a 'well-run' undertaking in a market where, historically, only a few tenders for bus services in the Austrian Tyrol had been granted.[53]

Other examples include *Poste Italiane*,[54] where the remuneration for distribution of postal savings books was lower than remuneration obtained on the market. In Slovenia a programme for the recovery of stranded costs was notified to the Commission. The scheme was introduced in 2001 in order to support the generation of electricity from renewable sources and combined heat and power generation in Slovenia and to secure a reliable supply of energy from indigenous sources. The authorities did not produce an analysis of costs of a typical undertaking but were able to show that the proposed solution was least costly and there was no evidence that the undertaking was not run efficiently.[55]

In *Postbus* the Commission accepted the method to ensure that there was no over-compensation, by the use of three different ways of comparing the price asked by the undertaking with the averages found in the (bus) sector concerned.[56] To calculate the remuneration, the contract distinguished between *Beistellleistungen* and *Bestandsleistungen*. The contract defined *Beistellleistungen* as the core provision of bus transport services for which fixed compensation was paid and 204 807 km of travel were accounted for by the *Beistellleistungen*. On the question of the benchmark of comparing the costs in an average undertaking or the costs in a well-managed undertaking the Commission found that the costs of the public service matched those of an average undertaking in the sector. On the question of whether the costs in *Postbus* also corresponded to the costs in a well-managed undertaking the issue was more difficult because the bus transport sector, had been dominated by monopolies and contracts had been awarded without tenders for a long time. Thus an undertaking operating in such a market is not necessarily a well-managed undertaking. The Austrian authorities had not explained how these parameters represent the average in a well-managed undertaking. By way of example, the Commission considered that Austria could have taken as a basis the average costs in undertakings which have won a significant number of tenders in the sector in the last few years. The Commission also noted that there was a difference of 0.80 euro per km between the price for the *Bestellleistungen* and the price for the *Bestandsleistungen*. This implied that *Postbus* had a certain margin for improving its efficiency as regards the *Bestellleistungen*. Thus the fourth criterion of *Altmark* was not met.

Inefficiency was found in Spain where a scheme for financing of workforce reduction in the public service broadcaster RTVE was found to be incompatible with the *Altmark* criterion because the Commission concluded that an efficient undertaking would not have built up such a superfluous and excessive workforce and would not have needed compensation for reducing the workforce.[57] However Article 106(2) TFEU was satisfied because the compensation was proportionate to the costs incurred in the workforce reduction plan and would reduce public service costs and the overall use of State resources. All the costs created by the SGEI are covered in the determination of the compensation, but the costs do not have to be those of an efficient operator.[58]

The fourth criterion may be an impossible, or hypothetical, exercise to undertake, where the service being provided is complex and there are different quality standards between public and commercial service standards. The fourth criterion is rendered even more hypothetical because of the lack of guidance on the cost standard to be deployed, leaving the Commission with a wide discretion and the General Court reluctant to intervene where complex assessments are involved. Where the market is liberalised there may be a range of competitors from different geographical locations where there are advantages in, for example, production costs, transport costs, employment and social standards, taxation or industrial organisation. Liberalisation has created hybrid markets with some sectors using partial liberalisation techniques, leaving incumbents with an unusual role.[59]

IV.   *ALTMARK*-COMPATIBLE CASES

Very rarely has the Commission found that all four of the *Altmark* criteria were satisfied.[60] Examples of successful cases reveal the necessity of tight criteria to be used in the funding arrangements for a public service. In *Public Bus Transport Services in Wittenberg* (*Student Bus Service*)[61] there was an open competition to supply bus services for students and the compensation was based upon cost calculations from previous (stable) numbers of students. A quality service was demanded with a list of specific schools, the number of routes (and alternative routes) involved, specific timetables with the number of bus stops required (and waiting times), inter-connection with other transport systems and a choice of ticketing. The aid could be allocated as a lump sum per student but not for non-student passengers.

The four *Altmark* criteria were met in the *Slovenian Energy Tariffs* case.[62] Firstly, because the Commission accepted that security of supply is a well-defined SGEI, secondly, the parameters of compensation were objective and transparent because the aid was in the form of a fixed purchase price; thirdly there was no over-compensation because the purchase price covered only the cost of electricity production with no profit. The fourth criterion was not met through a public procurement procedure but the Commission found that there was no evidence that the plant was not run efficiently.

In *Poste Italiane*, the Commission found that there was a proper public service definition and assignment of the provision of the public service obligation, in this case the provision of postal savings books.[63] The parameters of the compensation had been established in agreement with the Poste Italiane and the Treasury, there was no over-compensation. The Commission found the Poste Italiane to be a well-run undertaking because remuneration was comparable to the market rate for distribution of similar products.

Another example is seen in *Pyrenees Atlantique* where a general access to the broadband infrastructure for all of the population was recognised as a SGEI.[64] The parameters of the subsidy were pre-defined in a concession contract and there was no risk of over-compensation because the calculation of the subsidy was based upon specific data provided by the public authority with a claw-back clause if profits exceeded a certain amount. The procedure for awarding the provision of the SGEI was based upon a thorough and detailed analysis of the project requirements and tenders from potential candidates with the criteria of award based upon the most efficient candidate.

V.   *ALTMARK*: A RESIDUAL APPROACH?

The criteria from *Altmark*, the Commission's State aid practice and the Monti-Kroes 2005/2007 package of measures creating the core of EU regulation for residual public services not covered by EU liberalisation regulation created a complex and fragmented policy approach to a fundamental issue in European integration.

Additional to the fragmentation of the treatment of SGEIs under the State aid rules is the complexity created by the new constitutional commitments towards public services as a result of the Treaty of Lisbon 2009. Article 16 EC marked a turning point in the recognition of public services as a shared value of the Member States and the EU and as a positive signifier shifting the role of public services in the EU away from a derogation to a positive obligation in the EU integration project.[65] The Treaty of Amsterdam 1997 ushered in a new role for SGEIs but the Commission has been slow to develop this role, largely because discussion of the role of SGEIs has continued to be placed in the rules of competition where the dominant discourse is upon exceptions, derogations, justifications or the carving out of safe harbours for special relaxation of the competition rules.

Article 16 EC is re-numbered as Article 14 TFEU and now creates a legal base for legislative measures.[66] Moreover, Protocol 26 to the TEU and TFEU is of special significance since Article 1 of this Protocol provides recognition of the special role of SGEIs in Europe drawing attention to a high level of quality, safety and affordability, equal treatment and the promotion of universal access and of user rights in the provision of SGEIs:

> The shared values of the Union in respect of services of general economic interest within the meaning of Article 14 of the Treaty on the Functioning of the European Union include in particular:
>
> – the essential role and the wide discretion of national, regional and local authorities in providing, commissioning and organising services of general economic interest as closely as possible to the needs of the users;
> – the diversity between various services of general economic interest and the differences in the needs and preferences of users that may result from different geographical, social or cultural situations;
> – a high level of quality, safety and affordability, equal treatment and the promotion of universal access and of user rights.

These are principles and values drawn from the qualitative criteria used in defining universal services obligations in the liberalisation legislation of the EU. By doing this the Treaty of Lisbon 2009 recognises the growing importance of universal service obligations as the basis for a modern and Europeanised approach to delivering quality services to consumers at affordable prices.[67]

Article 2 of the Protocol protects non-economic services of general economic interest from the reach of Union law:

> The provisions of the Treaties do not affect in any way the competence of member States to provide, commission and organise non-economic services of general interest.

Thus, for the first time, the EU Treaties recognise non-economic (sometimes referred to as 'social') services of general interest.

These commitments provide the potential framework for shifting the focus of attention onto the values inherent in the integration process and qualitative criteria for the provision of public services in the post-Lisbon era. On the one hand these commitments draw firmer bright lines between the Member States' competence to regulate non-economic services and place the regulation of economic services within the domain of EU law while recognising that they have role to play in enhancing the social dimension of European integration which can complement the role assumed by the nation-State.

On the other hand the Treaty of Lisbon 2009 also re-instates the ideological formal lines between State ownership of these services and EU competence, a line which is not so easy to sustain in the modern world of liberalisation and privatisation of State services. The Commission needs to harness the development of a SGEI policy as a social dimension to EU integration rather than continuing to see SGEIs as the irritant of the integration process. The Protocol could be used as to assess the role and delivery of SGEIs providing a wider set of benchmarks than the single issue of funding arrangements which can only indirectly assess the quality of SGEIs through an efficiency benchmark. In contrast the Protocol has a new set of qualitative benchmarks which are modern in their approach, drawn from ideas found in the criteria set in the liberalisation processes for USO: pluralism, quality, safety, affordability and equal access. Additionally the Charter of Fundamental Rights of the European Union contains a clause on access to SGEIs[68] along with other provisions which address public services (vocational training health care, consumer protection, environmental protection), as well a horizontal principles found in the Chapter III rights to equality.

The continued reliance upon Article 106(2) TFEU provides a transitional approach: to balance Member State and public interest objectives against the market-oriented EU norms. It is an approach which is particularly useful for the modernisation of State aid where there is partial liberalisation, or regulated markets in hybrid (competitive and reserved sector) markets with an aspiration towards market-based systems. The recognition that public services can be delivered and protected in competitive markets is a transformation of the competence divide between Member State autonomy and the imperatives of market integration.

Two case studies, social housing and health care, will reveal the struggle to find a normative basis in current EU policy for the application of the State aid rules to sensitive social activities of the Member States. But first an examination of the special case of public service broadcasting (PSB) is made as a study of how the Commission is able to retain control over sensitive SGEIs.

VI.   PUBLIC SERVICE BROADCASTING: A SPECIAL CASE?

Many of the Commission Decisions involve public service broadcasting where the proportionality principle of Article 106(2) TFEU is to the fore in the reasoning because of the sensitive nature of public broadcasting and the special status accorded to it in EU law and by the Commission, as is explained by the General Court:[69]

> Although the public service of broadcasting is considered to be an SGEI and not a service of general non-economic interest, it must none the less be pointed

out that that classification as an SGEI is explained more by the de facto impact of public service broadcasting on the otherwise competitive and commercial broadcasting sector, than by an alleged commercial dimension to broadcasting. As is clear from the Amsterdam Protocol, public service broadcasting 'is directly related to the democratic, social and cultural needs of each society'. To the same effect, the Resolution of the Council and of the Member States of 25 January 1999 concerning broadcasting states that that public service, 'in view of its cultural, social and democratic functions which it discharges for the common good, has a vital significance for ensuring democracy, pluralism, social cohesion, cultural and linguistic diversity, [and] must be able to continue to provide a wide range of programming . . . [for] society as a whole' (recital B and point 7 of the resolution).

That specific status for public service broadcasting is, moreover, the basis for the freedom accorded by the Amsterdam Protocol to Member States in the award of broadcasting SGEIs. It explains and justifies the fact that a Member State cannot be required to have recourse to competitive tendering for the award of such an SGEI, at least where it decides to ensure that public service itself through a public company, as in this case.[70]

The special status of PSB is such that the General Court suggests that PSB is 'almost a non-economic activity'.[71]

In *BBC Digital Curriculum*[72] (the first Decision after *Altmark)* the Commission was prepared to examine the issue of funding under Article 106(2) TFEU where there was no evidence of how costs could be compared to a typical undertaking and no procurement exercise had been carried out. The sensitive nature of public broadcasting[73] has allowed a sector-specific approach to emerge where the *Altmark* ruling receives marginal attention.[74] In other cases the Commission is willing to adapt the *Altmark* criteria. For example, in *BBC Digital Curriculum*,[75] the Commission found that the fourth *Altmark* criterion had not been met but when applying Article 106(2) TFEU found that where public service broadcasting was concerned it was possible for an undertaking to receive State aid which exceeded the costs of an ideal, efficient undertaking without there being over-compensation to invoke the State aid rules.

The wide discretion of Member States to finance services of general economic interests in the PSB is seen also in the judgment of *TV2/Danmark*.[76] In rejecting the argument of commercial broadcasters that the definition of SGEI must be dependent on a comparative analysis of programming, the General Court endorsed the Member States' broad powers to define public service broadcasting, referring to the Amsterdam Protocol on public broadcasting,[77] the Resolution of the Council[78] and relevant case law.

More recently public service broadcasting has come under pressure from the creation of new multi-media platforms, forcing the Commission to review its *Communication* in 2009.[79] Point 5 of the new Communication states:

> . . . technological changes have fundamentally altered the broadcasting and audiovisual markets. There has been a multiplication of distribution platforms and technologies, such as digital television, IPTV, mobile TV and video on demand. This has led to an increase in competition with new players, such as network operators and Internet companies, entering the market. Technological developments have also allowed the emergence of new media services such as online information services and non-linear or on-demand services. The provision of audiovisual services is converging, with consumers being increasingly able to obtain multiple services on a single platform or device or to obtain any given service on multiple platforms or devices. The increasing variety of options for consumers to access media content has led to the multiplication of audiovisual services offered and the fragmentation of audiences. New technologies have enabled improved consumer participation. The traditional passive consumption model has been gradually turning into active participation and control over content by consumers. In order to keep up with the new challenges, both public and private broadcasters have been diversifying their activities, moving to new distribution platforms and expanding the range of their services. Most recently, this diversification of the publicly funded activities of public service broadcasters (such as online content, special interest channels) prompted a number of complaints by other market players also including publishers.

Thus the Commission acknowledges that PSB may reflect the changes through development and diversification of new digital technologies and audiovisual services on all distribution platforms. The Commission acknowledges the moves towards pay services for broadcasting media are inevitable by including advertising, as well as payment for specific services, and pay service charges related to the payment of network distribution fees or copyright fees as falling within the PSB remit.[80] A caveat is entered into in Point 83. The Commission states that remuneration is one of the aspects to be taken into account when deciding if activities fall within the PSB remit since payment for services may affect the universality and overall design of the service on offer and its impact on the market. Grespan (2010: 85) argues that the concepts drawn from USO obligations on 'affordable price' would be one method whereby PSB could offer differentiated and premium services within the PSB remit.

The new *Communication* of 2009 reinforces the European Courts' jurisprudence in limiting the Commission's powers to review a PSB remit except in cases of manifest error:

> It is not for the Commission to decide which programmes are to be provided and financed as a service of general economic interest, nor to question the nature or quality of a certain product.[81]

The Commission gives guidance on what would constitute a manifest error, extending the list of examples from the 2001 *Communication*: activities which would not meet the Amsterdam Protocol's criteria of 'the democratic, social and cultural needs of each society', interpreted as advertising, e-commerce, teleshopping, the use of premium rate numbers in prize games, sponsoring or merchandising.

Reflecting the *Altmark* ruling and the 2005 Framework, Point 51 of the new *Communication* states that the entrustment of the PSB must specify the precise nature of the PSO and the conditions for providing the compensation for the PSB along with methods for avoiding and clawing back over-compensation. The Member States must provide for a regular and effective control by an independent body of the use of public funding to prevent over-compensation and cross-subsidisation and to scrutinise the level and use of public service reserves. Grespan (2010) points out that this new requirement is in response to the General Court annulment of the Commission Decision in *SIC* where the Court found that the Commission did not have sufficient reliable information to test the allegation of over-compensation.[82]

VII.   THE REGULATION OF SOCIAL MARKETS

The example of public service broadcasting has shown that the Commission is willing to carve out special rules from the State aid rules in sensitive sectors. The biggest challenge for the EU will be whether the post-*Altmark* policy-approach can be adapted to tackle the emergent problems as social markets are increasingly turned over to market-based principles. On the one hand, the EU recognises that there are certain areas of social activity where EU competence to legislate is limited. On the other hand, the Treaty of Lisbon 2009 breaks down the rigidity of 'social v. economic' competence lines by encouraging a greater role for social activities in European integration. The European Social Model emerging from the Treaty of Lisbon 2009 acknowledges the wide political differences on the future direction of European integration by combining a mix of competition, free market and solidarity based principles. Article 3 TFEU refers to the concept of a 'social market economy', and the Union is to address the sustainable development of Europe based upon balanced economic growth and price stability, a highly competitive social market economy aiming at full employment and social progress and a high level of protection and improvement of the quality of the environment. This consolidates and constitutionalises the attempts by the Court, and the political institutions, to obtain a better balance between the 'economic' and the 'social' dimension of European integration.

The EU approach to accommodate social activities with economic activities has been to carve out safe havens from the full impact of EU law.

Examples are seen in the exceptions found in the Services Directive[83] and the 2005 Framework and Decision 'Monti-Kroes package'. Also, within the procurement rules, social procurement activities are given a special status.[84] Where special rules do not apply for social markets in the absence of EU-level hard law, the disadvantage of the current *Altmark*-Article 106 TFEU approach is that each case continues upon a case-by-case approach with the Commission encouraging notification and scrutiny of the proposed subsidies. This is important in ensuring that there is transparency in tendering and financing processes but can result in an *ad hoc* approach, based upon the specifics of each case. The process creates dependency on the Commission, restoring the centrality of Commission's role in regulating State aid in the internal market. Two more case studies reveal the difficulties of accommodating SGEIs and social services of general interest (SSGI) into the fragmented and complex EU framework.

VII.i.   Social Housing

Subsidies for social housing are used for different policy reasons and this has created litigation in the United Kingdom, Ireland and the Netherlands (and, under the EEA Agreement for Iceland and Norway). Social housing was identified as an area exempted from the State aid rules in the Commission Decision of 2005.[85] This was an exemption, irrespective of the amount of compensation provided. The reasons for exempting social housing in this way are set out in Recital 16 of the 2005/842/EC Commission Decision:

> undertakings in charge of social housing providing housing for disadvantaged citizens or socially less advantaged groups, which due to solvability constraints are unable to obtain housing at market conditions. . .

A clear definition of social housing is not found in the Commission Decision, leaving the definition to the Member States' entrustment of a SGEI:

> Public service compensation granted to . . . social housing undertakings carrying out activities qualified as services of general economic interest by the Member State concerned.

The definition of social housing has proved to be narrow in two rulings under the EEA (which is substantively and procedurally the same as EU State aid law). The first decision concerns the Norwegian Husbanken, a scheme of housing loans established after World War II.[86] The original aim of the scheme was to facilitate universal access to housing with an emphasis upon disadvantaged groups. Over time new aspirations for the scheme emerged in promoting environmentally friendly, universally designed housing and promoting residential areas. Under the scheme loans were open to applicants on a non-means tested basis but with conditions attached to the nature of the housing. For example there should be a minimum floor space, and minimum quality standards to be met. The loan could exceed 80% of the building costs. The loans were set at the cost of State borrowing plus 0.5% which was lower than the normal private loan market rate. The Husbanken was not a normal banking operation and operated only in the housing loan market. The scheme was approved by the European Surveillance Authority as a SGEI derogation under Article 59(2) EEA citing the objective of providing affordable housing and satisfying territorial cohesion objectives. But the EFTA Court held that:

> These questions call for complex analyses and assessments which the Court cannot carry out but which must be done by the EFTA Surveillance Authority. Article 59(2) EEA calls for an application of a proportionality test to assess whether the required balance has been struck between the common interests of the Contracting Parties to the EEA Agreement and the legitimate interests of Norway. The common interests require extensive freedom in the field of services whereas the interests of Norway could be said to be that the Government and Parliament must be permitted to regulate Norwegian housing policy according to the political goals set. In other words, the EFTA Surveillance Authority must strike a balance between the right of Norway to invoke the exemption and the interest of the Contracting Parties in avoiding distortions of competition. For these reasons, the Court concludes that the EFTA Surveillance Authority, by not carrying out the tests described, wrongly interpreted and applied Article 59(2) EEA. Accordingly, the Decision under scrutiny must be annulled. (para. 70).

Iceland operated a social housing scheme where housing loans were granted. The aim of the scheme was to provide universal, non-means-tested, affordable housing in the interests of territorial cohesion. Lending could only be given to a maximum of two houses per applicant. Up to 90% of the purchase price was available and at a rate equivalent to the State funding plus 0.35%. The European Surveillance Authority classified the scheme as a SGEI but the EFTA Court annulled the ESA decision because there were no limits as to the size or value of the housing covered by the favourable loans.[87]

In 2005, the Commission had expressed doubts about the social housing system in the Netherlands after complaints from Dutch house-building companies that, with the help of State aid, social housing corporations were steadily expanding their commercial activities instead of using State funding to provide social housing. The State support for social housing corporations mainly takes the form of loan guarantees and grants. The

CJEU declined the opportunity to examine the Dutch social housing scheme in the light of Article 106(2) TFEU in *Sint Servatius*, analysing the scheme only in the context of the free movement of capital.[88] Not surprisingly the Court found that a prior authorisation scheme for cross-border investment projects constituted a restriction on the free movement of capital but it could be justified by an overriding reason of general interest (the rule of reason). Thus the Court missed the opportunity to examine whether Article 106(2) TFEU could be applied and the latitude of discretion left to a Member State in determining the scale of a SGEI in such a sector.[89]

On 15 December 2009, the European Commission endorsed commitments made by the Dutch authorities to bring the social housing system into line with EU State aid rules as a SGEI.[90] State funding is not to be used for commercial activities and is allocated in a transparent manner based on objective criteria. The Commission approved new State aid of 750 million euros for social housing projects in declining urban areas over a ten-year period. The State support for social housing corporations mainly takes the form of loan guarantees and grants. Following the Commission's investigation, the Dutch authorities have undertaken to change the social housing system to make it more transparent and focus on a clearly defined target group of socially less advantaged persons. Commercial activities, by contrast, can no longer benefit from aid. On commercial housing markets, social housing corporations will have to compete on the same conditions as other operators. In the interest of a social mix and social cohesion, 90% of the dwellings in each housing corporation will be rented to a pre-defined target group of socially less advantaged persons. The remaining 10% may be allocated to other groups, but on the basis of objective criteria with an element of social prioritisation. The Commission concluded that social mix and social cohesion are valid public policy objectives, for which State aid may be justified.

VII.ii.   Health Care

Health care is second case study where the EU law struggles to place the increasingly liberalised and commercial activities of a social activity, located firmly within Member State legislative competence in Article 168 TFEU, within an economic regulatory framework of competition law and free movement law.[91] The Framework exempts from the State aid rules subsidies paid to hospitals without a cap on the amount of the subsidy. This safe harbour for hospitals allows subsidies without an enquiry as to whether the behaviour of hospitals may create distortive effects within a Member State, for example, where subsidised hospitals compete with non-subsidised hospitals and other health care providers and distortions may occur across borders as health care increasingly becomes a cross-border and global service. In case law the CJEU has held that the Spanish health care authorities could be shielded from the competition rules by linking the economic purchasing activities to the social, non-market objectives the goods were used for.[92] In other cases the Court has used the notion of a non-undertaking or non-economic activity[93] or the use of Article 106(2) TFEU to protect health care related activity from the full thrust of the market rules.[94] Concerns are raised where there is a lack of transparency in the funding of health care increasing the risk of cross-subsidisation and over-compensation and complaints from Ireland,[95] Germany,[96] Belgium[97] and France[98] have been made to the Commission.

Three instances of Commission Decisions reveal the inconsistency in the approach towards State aid and health care. In Ireland a risk equalisation scheme between private providers of supplementary health care insurance was assessed against the criteria for a State aid under Article 107(1) TFEU. The health care insurance was fully-funded from private insurance premiums. The issue at stake was whether the risk equalisation scheme was a form of State aid. The Commission used the compensation approach seeing the State aid as a payment for a PSO. The requirements of necessity and proportionality were met. The Irish scheme contained incentives towards efficiency because the compensation was calculated on the market average and new entrants were encouraged by a waiver from contributing to the scheme for the first three years on entry. The Commission also acknowledged that Article 106(2) TFEU would be satisfied even if a State aid was found.[99]

The Netherlands also introduced a risk equalisation scheme for health insurance. Private insurers would cover the entire population of the Netherlands and former public insurers and cooperative insurers were allowed to retain their financial reserves when privatised.[100] The Netherlands' scheme was funded by providing health insurers with 50% of their funds from a public fund financed by income related social insurance contributions. The scheme demanded publicly defined minimum benefits, public supervision, universal coverage, open enrolment and community rating. The risk equalisation scheme compensated for the open enrolment requirement at 50% of the expected costs on an *ex post* basis. The strong aspect of the scheme was that it was seen '. . . as a system of double solidarity: among the insured population and between persons with various income levels (progressive financing).' (Sauter and van de Gronden 2010: 24). The Commission decided that this kind of scheme did not restrict competition, but indeed, promoted competition. However the Commission found that there was State aid present because the fourth *Altmark* criterion was not satisfied. This was because all insurers received compensation and thus there were no incentives for efficiency. The reserves retained by the former public and cooperative institutions were also partly classified as a State aid. The risk equalisation scheme was found to be a SGEI that was necessary to maintain stability in the health care market and provide universal access to affordable health care. Even though the compensation was *ex post* it was limited to the necessary minimum of compensation and thus the proportionality test was met. The scheme could be shielded from the full force of the competition rules on State aid through Article 106(2) TFEU. The retention of reserves by the former public and cooperative institutions was dealt with under Article 107(3) TFEU as an aid for the development of certain kinds of economic activity, here the liberalisation of health insurance markets.

In the *Brussels Hospitals* case compensation was made under a statute to cover the costs necessarily incurred as a public service obligation for intramural hospital care in the IRIS-Z region of Brussels.[101] The hospitals' duties were governed by a board consisting of representatives from the social services of the local authorities and these boards imposed universal service obligations to treat all patients irrespective of their social or health situation. To compensate for this public/universal service obligation the hospitals received extra funding above the funding which was paid to other hospitals in the private sector in Belgium. Normally there were very long delays in the payment of the public service compensation and therefore the Brussels IRIS-Z municipality paid the compensation as a temporary advance. The Commission found that the conditions for a State aid were met and that the fourth *Altmark* criterion was not satisfied. In applying Article 106(2) TFEU, the Commission was satisfied that the proportionality of the measures was appropriate.

The Commission's Decision of 2003 in the Irish health care scheme was challenged. In *BUPA*[102] the General Court gave notice that the *Altmark* criteria were not set in stone and that, without expressly alluding to the point, there was an element of flexibility and non-applicability in the criteria where social markets for health care were concerned. In Ireland the financing scheme for health care provided for *ex post* compensation of costs incurred by insurance companies in risk equalisation scheme (RES). The Irish private insurance system operated concurrently with a tax based system. Around 50% of the Irish population had taken out private insurance with one of the three private insurers operating on the Irish market. The risk equalisation scheme aimed to ensure that certain public interest objectives were met where private operators competed with a State health care scheme: open enrolment (anyone under the age of 65 should be accepted), lifetime cover, community rating (that is, no premium differentiation) and minimum benefits policy. The risk equalisation scheme (RES):

> . . .is essentially a mechanism which provides for payment of a charge to the Health Insurance Authority (HIA) by Private Medical Insurance (PMI) insurers, whose risk profile is healthier than the average market risk profile, and for a corresponding payment by the HIA to PMI insurers whose risk profile is less healthy than the average market risk profile. Those payments are made through a fund specially established for that purpose and administered by the HIA. (para. 27)

Determination of RES payments was linked to the differential between the risk profiles of the PMI insurers, taking into account a number of risk factors: the age and sex of the persons covered and, if appropriate, a weighting known as the 'health status weight', based on hospital bed utilisation. The costs PMI insurers incur may differ considerably and there was a cost differential, determined on the basis of the comparison between the actual costs (on the basis of the insurer's real risk profile) and the hypothetical costs (on the basis of the insurer's average market risk profile). This was the basis for calculating the equalisation payments, made after the costs had been incurred. This approach is criticised for not creating incentives to contract and purchase care in a more efficient way and compared with the Dutch scheme, which is mainly based on an *ex ante* scheme when risks are known in advance before actual costs incurred (Sauter: 2009). In contrast in the Netherlands the health care system is based completely on compulsory private insurance encompassing income solidarity and affordability of health care for everyone. In Ireland the private insurance system operated alongside the tax-financed health care system.[103]

In *BUPA* an SGEI is derived from the context of the activity. In *BUPA* the General Court develops the Commission's practice of giving further refinement to an EU definition of a SGEI, moving beyond the 2005 package of measures. In *BUPA* a definition of 'universal service' is set out where there is no obligation to cover an entire population and there can be limitations on the users and the territory covered. What is essential is the compulsory nature of the obligation (the obligation to deal on consistent conditions and the inability to reject the contracting party). Furthermore from *BUPA* it would seem that a universal service provision does not necessarily have to be affordable and the SGEI does not have to be free or non-profit-making.

In the Netherlands' health care scheme there was open enrolment, a community rating, minimum benefits were offered and regulatory supervision. However, the Commission came to the conclusion that the State aid provisions were applicable. The Dutch health insurance companies were 'undertakings' using a risk equalisation scheme, managed by a State body and which provided for the compensation of the differences in risks health insurance companies incur. The Commission used a flexible approach, accepting that health insurers can be undertakings entrusted with SGEI without being explicitly charged with such a mission by a legislative act or a public concession.

In *Brussels Hospitals* the regional and local authorities set the requirements for the SGEI which included a duty to serve all patients in all circumstances, to have available multi-site intra-mural care in addition to the general USO imposed on all hospitals.[104] The entrustment of the SGEI and the compensation for the public service had been determined by a law of 1987 and this set clear and transparent parameters on which the compensation was calculated.

In applying the *Altmark* conditions in *BUPA* to assess whether the RES scheme constituted State aid the General Court gives the Member State a wide margin of discretion. In relation to the first condition, the General Court concluded that, irrespective of the optional, complementary and 'luxury' nature of the PMI services, the PMI obligations aimed to ensure a certain level of PMI services to all persons living in Ireland, at an affordable price and on similar quality conditions. The Commission was correct in finding these obligations to satisfy a SGEI. The General Court referred to *minimum* criteria that must be taken into account:

> In that regard, the Court notes at the outset that even though the Member State has a wide discretion when determining what it regards as an SGEI, that does not mean that it is not required, when it relies on the existence of and the need to protect an SGEI mission, to ensure that that mission satisfies certain minimum criteria common to every SGEI mission within the meaning of the EC Treaty, as explained in the case-law, and to demonstrate that those criteria are indeed satisfied in the particular case. These are, notably, the presence of an act of the public authority entrusting the operators in question with an SGEI mission and the universal and compulsory nature of that mission. (para. 172.)

In finding the second *Altmark* condition satisfied, the General Court held that it is established case law that:

> . . . the Member State has a wide discretion not only when defining an SGEI mission but also when determining the compensation for the costs, which calls for an assessment of complex economic facts [. . .]. It is precisely because the determination of the compensation is subject to only restricted control by the Community institutions, moreover, that the second *Altmark* condition requires that those institutions must be in a position to verify the existence of objective and transparent parameters, which must be defined in such a way as to preclude any abusive recourse to the concept of an SGEI on the part of the Member State. (para. 214.)

Applying the third condition, the Court states that its review of the proportionality of the RES scheme is necessarily limited and only amounts to a *marginal review* of the Commission Decision:

> Given the discretion enjoyed by a Member State in defining an SGEI mission and the conditions of its implementation, including the assessment of the additional costs incurred in discharging the mission, which depends on complex economic facts, the scope of the control which the Commission is entitled to exercise in that regard is limited to one of manifest error. (para. 220).

Echoing the *Chronopost* litigation,[105] the General Court states that the RES cannot fulfil the third condition of *Altmark*, as the RES is not intended to compensate for an identified cost occasioned by the supply of the service in question.

In relation to the fourth condition, the Court held that:

> . . .accordingly, the Commission was entitled in this case to consider that in the context of the analysis of the existence of State aid within the meaning of Article 87(1) EC, there was no need to draw a comparison between the potential recipients of the RES payments and an efficient operator. (para. 248).

The reason is that the RES does not intend to offset the costs which might result from inefficiencies on part of the insurers.

In *BUPA* the Commission found the four *Altmark* conditions were fulfilled, even the fourth condition because all insurers, irrespective of how efficient they were, receive compensation. The General Court failed to address, or provide guidance on, how *ex post* compensation can be reconciled with competition law principles given that *ex ante* compensation is seen as more effective in providing incentives for efficiency. Similarly, when applying Article 106(2) TFEU the Commission found that the risk equalisation scheme was necessary to address the danger of risk selection by health insurers and to ensure the stability of the health insurance system. Although not articulated as clearly as in public service broadcasting policy, the Commission and the General Court appear to have carved out a special approach to the application of the State aid rules where health care is provided, but using different policy approaches.

VII.iii.   A Soft Law Approach to SSGIs

The increasing litigation and legal uncertainty over the application of the Treaty rules to SSGIs[106] led the Commission to issue a new Communication, *Services of general interest, including social services of general interest: a new European commitment*, complemented by two 'working documents': *FAQs concerning the application of public procurement rules to services of general interest'* and FAQs *on the application of Article 86(2) to State aid in the form of public aid compensation.*[107] From 2008 the Commission has published a biennial report on SSGIs as a staff working document. These developments contribute to a Europeanisation of SSGIs, with horizontal policies drawn up within the Commission through the Directorate on Competition and Employment, Social Affairs and Equal Opportunities.

VIII.   THE LEGACY OF *ALTMARK*

The ruling in *Altmark* can be placed within an historical context of removing the qualitative conditions for the provision of residual public services away from the competence of the Member States and modernising the conceptual framework within which public services are funded. Hancher and Larouche (2011) see this as a significant shift from the formalist paradigm inherent within Article 106(2) TFEU towards, what they describe as 'a more integrative paradigm', which can accommodate the funding of public services without a harsh and formal rule/exception relationship.

Altmark is of significant importance in the implicit recognition that State monopolies are no longer privileged undertakings operating in a *sui generis* 'market'. Public services can be (and often are) economic activities that are delivered in competitive markets and the EU competition rules can be used to foster competition, efficiency and consumer satisfaction. It is prescriptive approach in guiding the Member States towards the *ex ante* regulation of public services, rather than the old model of abolition or adaptation of existing State monopolies when measured against EU law in litigation. Thus *Altmark* sits between the regulatory approach of the EU in creating universal service obligations and the State aid rules which favour efficiency and transparency in competitive markets.

The difficulty for the EU is the management of the reform of SGEIs. The EU has limited specific legislative competence to regulate SGEIs, with legal bases found only in Articles 14 TFEU and Article 106(3) TFEU. But the competence creep of the free movement of services in particular has gradually embraced a number of services previously seen as social or non-economic public services which are now provided on an economic footing as Member States liberalise markets and attempt to reduce budget deficits. The cases which are brought to the CJEU challenge the operation and existence of national public services and often result in the re-organisation of such services and even de-regulation. Part of the problem is the reliance on the use of the State aid rules which are prohibitive in nature without a wider social basis for the evaluation of the compatibility of national SGEIs with EU integration principles. Thus the potential to balance social interests against competition interests when SGEIs are used is not fully articulated unless resort is made to Article 106(2) TFEU. On the other hand, there is greater potential to address the *qualitative* nature of SGEIs through the liberalisation processes, especially in the criteria for the creation of universal service obligations and this is recognised implicitly in the Protocol of the Treaty of Lisbon 2009. Until recently little litigation has emerged at the EU level on the scope of universal service obligations in the liberalisation legislation.

IX. FUTURE DIRECTIONS

The post-*Altmark* era may be regarded as a transitional and experimental period where the Member States and the EU (particularly through Commission practice) have brokered a new relationship towards the regulation of public services using the State aid rules. However, there are still many elements of uncertainty in both Commission practice and Court jurisprudence. There is both a Member State and EU benefit in the fluidity of application of the legal rules. Where there is no sector-specific legislation there is greater flexibility to negotiate the evolution and recalibration of the provision of public services. The Commission is taking stock of this new relationship through a stakeholder consultation, eliciting feedback on three broad issues related to stakeholders' interests:

1. from public bodies: is the package sufficiently user-friendly and does it allow provision of SGEI to citizens?
2. from SGEI users: does the package allow for provision of good-quality and cost-effective services?
3. from providers: does the package ensure a level playing field with competitors without creating unnecessary obstacles?

The Member States were asked to report on the implementation of the Monti-Kroes package during 2009.[108] This element of review reveals the weaknesses of self-reporting. Many reports are not very detailed, and Member States must be reluctant to open up their internal organisation of SGEIs to too much scrutiny. Some States express concerns over issues of legal certainty connected to the *Altmark* rulng and Monti-Kroes package, especially around the notions of economic activity, effect on trade, the relationship between State aid/public procurement and how to control of over-compensation. The lack of legal certainty raises concerns within the Member States and the Commission as to whether rules are always applied correctly. Many Member States would like to see the *de minimis* threshold raised and the creation of more safe harbours, especially for SSGIs.

The consultation was short: it started on 10 June 2010 and closed on 10 September 2010. Yet the consultation received a number of contributions, the most emanating from France, Germany, Italy and Belgium.[109] The Commission intends to produce a comprehensive report on the application of the Kroes-Monti package in early 2011 based upon the Member State responses and the consultation exercise. Only if deemed appropriate, a new legislative proposal may follow, coordinated with other initiatives, for example, a quality framework, the use of the new Article 14 TFEU legal base, the reform of the public procurement rules and the follow-up to the 2010 Monti Report.

X.   CONCLUSION

The *Altmark* ruling has attracted much critical attention. However, arguing its place as a cornerstone in the history of European integration may be precipitous. As this discussion shows, the significance of *Altmark* lies in the Commission's response to the ruling, allowing for the modernisation of public services and debate on *how* public services should function in the EU.

NOTES

1.   Mario Monti, *A New Strategy for the Single Market. At the Service of Europe's Economy and Society. Report to the President of the European Commission Jose Manuel Barroso*, 9 May 2010, 73. Referred to as the 'Monti Report' in this chapter.
2.   Case C-280/00, *Altmark Trans GmbH, Regierungspräsidium Magdeburg v. Nahverkehrsgesellschaft Altmark GmbH, third party: Oberbundesanwalt beim Bundesverwaltungsgericht* [2003] E.C.R. I-7747.
3.   Case 26/62, *Van Gend en Loos* [1963] E.C.R. 3 (direct effect).
4.   Case 6/64, *Costa* v. *ENEL* [1964] E.C.R. 1194 (supremacy).
5.   Case 106/77, *Simmenthal* [1978] E.C.R. 629 (supremacy).
6.   Case 22/70, *AETR* [1971] E.C.R. 263 (external competence).
7.   Case 36/75, *Rutili* [1975] E.C.R. 1219 (public order and free movement).
8.   Bauby 2011.
9.   Cf. Bekkedal 2011.
10.   See Szyszczak and Davies 2011.
11.   Szyszczak 2007.
12.   The Commission was asked to clarify the law on SGEIs following the European Nice Council 2000. See *Report to the Laeken European Council: Services of General Interest* COM (2001) 598 final followed by a *Non-paper on services of general economic interest and state aid*, 12 November 2002.
13.   Szyszczak 2002.
14.   The availability of Article 106(2) TFEU as a derogation or justification from the free movement rules is contentious, see: Bekkedal 2011. See the strict interpretation

of when Article 106(2) TFEU can apply in relation to a free movement of capital/ golden shares infringement: Case C-543/08, *Commission v. Portugal* judgment of 11 November 2010.

15. *Green Paper on Services of General Interest*, COM(2003) 270 final (21 May 2003); *White Paper on Services of General Interest*, COM(2004) 374 final (12 May 2004).
16. O.J. 2001 C 320/5.
17. Case C-126/01, [2003] E.C.R. 13769.
18. Paras 42 and 43.
19. Joined Cases C-34/01 et al., [2003] E.C.R. 14243.
20. Case T-157/01, *Danske Busvognmænd v. Commission* [2004] E.C.R. I-917.
21. Case C-140/09, *Fallimento Traghetti del Mediterraneo SpA v. Presidenza del Consiglio dei Ministri* judgment of 10 June 2010, n.y.r.
22. Case C-451/03, *Servizi Ausiliari Dottori Commercialisti Srl v. Giuseppe Calafiori* [2006] E.C.R. I-2941.
23. Case T-289/03, *BUPA* v. *Commission* [2008] E.C.R. 81.
24. Community Framework for state aid in the form of public service compensation, O.J. 2005 C 297/4.
25. Commission Decision of 28 November 2005 on the application of Article 86(2) of the EC Treaty to State aid in the form of public service compensation granted to certain undertakings entrusted with the operation of services of general economic interest, Document number C(2005) 2673, O.J L 2005 L312/ 67.
26. Commission Directive 2006/111/EC of 16 November 2006 transparency of financial relations between Member States and public undertakings as well as on financial transparency within certain undertakings (codified version) O.J. 2006 L 318/17.
27. Commission Staff Working Document, *Frequently asked questions in relation with Commission Decision of 28 November 2005 on the application of Article 86(2) of the EC Treaty to State aid in the form of public service compensation granted to certain undertakings entrusted with the operation of services of general economic interest, and of the Community Framework for State aid in the form of public service compensation. Accompanying document to the Communication on 'Services of general interest, including social services of general interest: a new European commitment'* COM(2007) 725 final, SEC(2007) 1514, SEC(2007) 1515.
28. Case C-280/00 *Altmark Trans* [2003] E.C.R. I-7747, para. 81. See also Case C-34/01 to C-38/01 *Enirisorse* [2003] E.C.R. 14243, para. 28: 'It must be recalled that there is no threshold or percentage below which it may be considered that trade between Member States is not affected. The relatively small amount of aid or the relatively small size of the undertaking which receives it does not as such exclude the possibility that trade between Member States might be affected. . ..'.
29. COM(2005) 107 final, 10.
30. C-31/2007 (ex NN 17/07), O.J. 2007 C 217.
31. Case T-289/03, *BUPA* v. *Commission* [2008] E.C.R. 81.
32. Cumbria Broadband Project Access, N282/2003, C(2003) 4480fin, available at: <http://ec.europa.eu/eu_law/state_aids/comp-2003/n282-03.pdf> (last accessed 3 January 2010).
33. Case N-381/2004.
34. Joined Cases T-309/04, T-317/04, T-329/04 and T-336/04, *TV2 Danmark* [2008] E.C.R. II-2935.
35. Available at: <http://eur-lex.europa.eu/en/treaties/dat/11997D/htm/11997D. html#0109010012> (last accessed 3 January 2011).
36. O.J. 1999 C 30/1.
37. T-442/03, *SIC* v. *Commission* [2008] E.C.R. II-1161 and T-309/04 *et al., TV2 v. Commission* [2008] E.C.R. II-2935.
38. Public service compensation for Southern Moravia Bus Companies (CAS Services, Czech Republic, C-3/2008 ex NN. 102/2005, O.J. 2008 C 48/19.

39.   Aide au transport maritime-Società Ustica Lines e Società N.G.I. N265/2006, O.J. 2007 C 196/3.
40.   T-156/04, *EDF v. Commission* [2009] E.C.R. II-4503. [on appeal Case C-124/10P].
41.   Haut débit en Pyrénées-Atlantiques – France, N 381 / 2004. See also Commission, *Community Guidelines for the application of State aid rules in relation to rapid deployment of broadband networks*, O.J. 2009 C 235/7.
42.   Compensation to long-distance bus operators for discounts given to certain types of passengers using long-distance bus services, N 332/2008, O.J. 2009 C 46.
43.   N 604/05, N 207/09 and N 206/09.
44.   Electricity in Poland, Decision 2009/287, O.J. 2009 L 83/1.
45.   Above n. 19.
46.   Commission Decision of of 19 June 2002 on measures implemented by the Federal Republic of Germany for Deutsche Post AG, O.J. 2002 L 247/27.
47.   C-504/07, *Associação Nacional de Transportadores Rodoviários de Pesados de Passageiros (Antrop) and Others v. Conselho de Ministros, Companhia Carris de Ferro de Lisboa SA (Carris) and Sociedade de Transportes Colectivos do Porto SA (STCP)* [2009] E.C.R. I-3867.
48.   Commission Directive 80/723/EEC, O.J. L 195/35 (as last amended by Directive 2005/81/EC, O.J. L 312/47).
49.   Commission Directive 2006/111/EC of 16 November 2006 on the transparency of financial relations between Member States and public undertakings as well as on financial transparency within certain undertakings, O.J. 2006 L 318/17.
50.   Commission Decision on aid to TV2, Denmark C2/2003), O.J. L 85/2006.
51.   N 46/2007, *Welsh Public Sector Network Scheme*; UK, O.J. C 207/157; N 604/05, N 207/09 and N 206/09, *D Bus Services.*
52.   Public Service Obligation in respect of new electricity, Ireland, N 475/2003 generation capacity, available at: <http://ec.europa.eu/eu_law/state_aids/comp-2003/n475-03.pdf> (last accessed 3 January 2010).
53.   Commission Decision of 26 November 2008 on State aid granted by Austria to the company *Postbus* in the *Lienz* district C 16/07 (ex NN 55/06), O.J. 2009 C 306/26.
54.   Commission Decision C(2006) 5478 final of 22 November 2006, C 49/06 (ex NN 65/06) Italy, Poste Italiane, Postal Savings, O.J 2007 C 31/11.
55.   Commission Decision of 24 April 2007 on the State aid scheme implemented by Slovenia in the framework of its legislation on qualified energy producers – Case No C 7/2005 , O.J. 2007 C-219/9.
56.   C 16/07 (ex NN55/06) O. J. 2007 L 306/26.
57.   Financing of workforce reduction measures for RTVE, NN 8/2007, O.J. 2007 C 109.
58.   Financing of workforce reduction measures of RTVE., Spain, Case NN 8/2007, RTVE, available at: <http://ec.europa.eu/competition/state_aid/register/ii/doc/NN-8-2007-WLWL-07.03.2007.pdf> (last accessed 3 January 2011).
59.   See for example, the acceptance of the sharing of fixed costs according to volume of services in Case C-341/06 P, *Chronopost* [2008] E.C.R.I-4777.
60.   See Case T-266/02, *Deutsche Post AG* v. *Commission* [2008] E.C.R. II-1233, para. 74: 'It follows that, where State resources were granted as compensation for additional costs associated with the provision of a service of general economic interest under the conditions set out in paragraphs 72 and 73 above, the Commission, if it is not to render Article 86(2) EC entirely ineffective, cannot classify as State aid all or part of the public resources granted, as long as the total amount of those resources remains below the additional costs generated by carrying out the public service mission (see, to that effect, *FFSA and Others v. Commission*, paragraph 55 above, paragraph 188).'
61.   O.J. 2006 C 49.
62.   C 7/2005, O.J. 2007 C L 219.
63.   C 49/06, O.J. 2009 C 189.
64.   Haut débit en Pyrénées-Atlantiques, N 381/2004, O.J. 2005 C 162.
65.   Ross 2000.

66. Article 14 TFEU states: Without prejudice to Article 4 of the Treaty on European Union or to Articles 93, 106 and 107 of this Treaty, and given the place occupied by services of general economic interest in the shared values of the Union as well as their role in promoting social and territorial cohesion, the Union and the Member States, each within their respective powers and within the scope of application of the Treaties, shall take care that such services operate on the basis of principles and conditions, particularly economic and financial conditions, which enable them to fulfil their missions. The European Parliament and the Council, acting by means of regulations in accordance with the ordinary legislative procedure, shall establish these principles and set these conditions without prejudice to the competence of Member States, in compliance with the Treaties, to provide, to commission and to fund such services.

67. See, for example, Case C-265/08, *Federutility*, judgment of 20 April 2010, n.y.r. where the Court held that a Member State may determine the price level for the supply of natural gas by the definition of 'reference prices' where the policy pursues a general economic interest consisting in maintaining the price of the supply of natural gas to final consumers at a reasonable level having regard to the reconciliation which Member States must make, taking account of the situation in the natural gas sector, between the objective of liberalisation and that of the necessary protection of final consumers pursued by the gas liberalisation Directive 2003/55 provided the measure is in the general economic interest, limited in time, is clearly defined, transparent, non discriminatory and verifiable, and guarantees equal access for EU gas companies to consumers.

68. Article 36 reads: The Union recognises and respects access to services of general economic interest as provided for in national laws and practices, in accordance with the Treaty establishing the European Community, in order to promote the social and territorial cohesion of the Union.

69. COM(2000) 580 final, 53; Point 6 2001 Communication.

70. Case T-442/03, *SIC* [2008] E.C.R. II-1161 paras 153–154. See also: COM(2000) 580 final, 53; *Communication from the Commission on the application of State aid rules to public service broadcasting*, O.J. 2001 C 320/5, Point 6.

71. Grespan 2010.

72. Case N-37/03-BBC Digital Curriculum O.J. 2003 C 271/47.

73. Set out in Case T-442/03, *SIC* [2008] E.C.R. II-1161, para. 153.

74. The Commission Communication on State Aid 2001 set out criteria for funding of public service broadcasting which are the precursor to the criteria used in the *Altmark* ruling: there must be a clear definition of the SGEI remit; the activities of PSB are expressly conferred; there must be a transparent separation of PSB and commercial activities; the funding should be proportionate but allow a reasonable profit (*Communication from the Commission on the application of State aid rules to public service broadcasting*, O.J. 2001 C 320/5).

75. BBC Digital Curriculum, UK, Case N-37/03, BBC, O.J. 2003 271/47.

76. Joined Cases T-309/04, T-317/04, T-329/04 and T-336/04, *TV2 Danmark* [2008] E.C.R. II-2935.

77. Available at: <http://eur-lex.europa.eu/en/treaties/dat/11997D/htm/11997D.html#0109010012> (last accessed 3 January 2011).

78. O.J. 1999 C 30/1.

79. *Commission Communication on the State aid rules to public service broadcasting*, O.J. 2009 C 185/1.

80. Point 83. Cf. Commission Decision of 24 April 2007 Case E3/2005 Financing of public service broadcasters in Germany para. 239, O.J. 2007 C 185/1; Commission Decision 27 February 2008 Case E4/2005 State financing of RTE and Teilifís na Gaelige (TG4) para. 137, O.J. 2008 C 121/5.

81. Ibid. Point 48.

82. See Commission Decision of 20.4/2005 E 10/2005 France – Licence fee payments to France 2 and France 3, O.J. 2005 L C240/20.

83. Directive 2006/123/EC, O.J. 2006 L 376/36.
84. See Case C-160/08, *Commission* v. *Germany*, 29 April 2010, n.y.r.
85. Commission Decision of 28 November 2005 on the application of Article 86(2) of the EC Treaty to State aid in the form of public service compensation granted to certain undertakings entrusted with the operation of services of general economic interest, Document number C(2005) 2673, O.J L 2005 L 312/ 67.
86. Case E-4/97, *Norwegian Bankers' Association* v *EFTA Surveillance Authority*, EFTA Court Ruling of 3 March 1999, E4/97. Available at: <http://www.eftacourt.int/images/uploads/E-4-97_Judgment.pdf> (last accessed 3 January 2011).
87. EFTA Court ruling of 7 April 2006, Case E-9/04.
88. Case C-567/07, [2009] E.C.R. 9021.
89. See van de Gronden 2011b.
90. Existing law and financing methods for Dutch Housing Corporations, The Netherlands, E 2/2005, O.J. 2010 C 250. The Commission is currently investigating the Bavarian *Einheimischenmodell* of selling land at a lower price than the market price to local residents depending upon how long they have lived in the area and other (social) factors such as the number of children, the family income or the number of family members in need of care. The Commission finds this discriminatory and contrary to the free movement and non-discrimination rules of the TFEU.
91. See van de Gronden *et al.* 2011a.
92. Case C-205/03P, *FENIN v. Commission* [2006] E.C.R. I-6295, para 37.
93. Case C-264/01 *et al.*, *AOK Bundesverband* [2004] E.C.R. 2493. Cf. Case C-300/07, *Oymanns/AOK Rheinland* judgment of 11 June 2009, n.y.r. Here the CJEU held that statutory health insurance funds are public contracting authorities for the purposes of procurement law and therefore their service agreements are subject to public procurement law. See also Case C-160/08, *Commission v. Germany* judgment of 29 April 2010.
94. See for example, Case C-475/99, *Glockner* [2001] E.C.R. I-8089.
95. Decision of the Commission of 13 May 2003 with regard to State aid N46/2003 – Ireland – risk equalisation, O.J. 1999 L 83/1.
96. See Koenig and Paul 2010.
97. Case T-137/10, *Coordination bruxelloise d'Instituions sociales et de santé (CBI) v. European Commission*, pending.
98. Case T-397/03, removed from the Register 18 November 2005.
99. Decision of the Commission of 13 May 2003 with regard to State aid N46/2003 – Ireland – risk equalisation, O.J. 1999 L 83/1.
100. Decision of the Commission of 3 May 2005 with regard to state aid N 541/2004 and N542/2004 – The Netherlands – risk equalisation system and retention of reserves, O.J. 2005 C 108.
101. Commission Decision C(2009) 8120 final COR; on appeal: Case T-137/10 *Coordination bruxelloise d'Institutions sociales et de santé (CBI) v. Commission*, pending.
102. Case T-289/03, *BUPA v. Commission* [2008] E.C.R. 81.
103. See Sauter 2009.
104. Supra n. 101.
105. Case C-341/06 P, *Chronopost* [2008] E.C.R.I- 4777.
106. The term SSGI has appeared in Commission communications. It does not have a legal definition in the Treaties. In the 2007 Communication, *Services of general interest, including social services of general interest: a new European Commitment, accompanying the Communication, A Single market for the 21st century Europe*, COM(2007) 724 final, the Commission differentiates between health services and other SSGIs which can comprise statutory and complementary social security schemes covering major risks (health, ageing, occupational accidents, unemployment, retirement, disability) and other essential services provided directly to persons that play a preventative and social cohesion role of customised assistance to facilitate social inclusion and safeguard fundamental rights. A more recent definition of

'What is a SSGI?' can be found in Belgian Presidency, 3rd Forum on Social Services of General Interest, General Background Note, 26 of 27 October 2010: '. . . activities supplied by public authorities or entrusted by them to private entities, to which missions of general interest are entrusted for the purpose of social protection, social and territorial cohesion, national solidarity and implementation of fundamental rights.' Available at: <http://www.socialsecurity.fgov.be/eu/docs/agenda/26-27_10_10_gbp_ssig_en.pdf (last accessed 3 January 2011).
107. Communication, *Services of general interest, including social services of general interest: a new European Commitment, accompanying the Communication, A Single market for the 21st century Europe*, COM(2007) 724 final.
108. <http://ec.europa.eu/competition/consultations/2010_sgei/reports.html>.
109. Ninety six contributions were received with thirty five from SGEI providers, twenty eight from public bodies, twenty eight from other interest groups and organisations and five from private parties and academia. The Commission announced the reforms in the Communication from the Commission to the European Parliament, the Council, the European Economic and Social Committee and the Committee of the Regions, *Reform of the EU State Aid Rules on Services of General Economic Interest* COM (2011) 146 final.

REFERENCES

Baquero Cruz, J. (2002), *Between Competition and Free Movement*, Oxford: Hart Publishing.
Bauby, P. (2011) 'From Rome to Lisbon: SGEIs in primary law' in E., Szyszczak, J. Davies, M. Andenas and T. Bekkedal (eds), *Developments in Services of General Interest*, The Hague: TMC Asser Press.
Bekkedal, T. (2011), 'Article 106 TFEU is dead – long live Article 106 TFEU!', in E. Szyszczak, J. Davies, M. Andenaes and T. Bekkedal (eds), *Developments in Services of General Interest*, The Hague: TMC Asser Press.
Grespan, D. (2010), 'A busy year for State aid control in the field of public service broadcasting', *European State Aid Law Quarterly*, **1**, 79–98.
Hancher, L. and P. Larouche (2011), 'The coming of age of EU Regulation of network industries and services of general economic interest', in P. Craig and G. De Búrca, *The Evolution of EU Law*, Oxford: OUP.
Koenig, C. and J. Paul, (2010), 'State aid screening of hospital funding exemplified by the German case', *European State Aid Law Quarterly*, **4**, 755.
Ross, M. (2000), 'Article 16 E.C. and services of general interest: from derogation to obligation?', *European Law Review*, **25**, 22.
Sauter, W. (2009), 'Annotation: Case T-289/03, *British United Provident Association Ltd (BUPA), BUPA Insurance Ltd, BUPA Ireland Ltd v. Commission of the European Communities*, Judgment of the Court of First Instance of 12 February 2008 nyr', *Common Market Law Review*, **46.1**, 269–286.
Sauter, W. and J. van de Gronden (2010), ' Taking the temperature: A survey of the EU law on competition and state aid in the healthcare sector', TILEC Discussion Paper No. 2010/038, available at: <http://papers.ssrn.com/sol3/papers.cfm?abstract_id=1702832> (last accessed 8 January 2011).
Szyszczak, E. (2002), 'Financing services of general economic interest', *Modern Law Review*, **65**, 229–241.
Szyszczak, E. (2007), *The Regulation of the State in Competitive Markets in the European Union*, Oxford: Hart Publishing.
Szyszczak, E. and J. Davies, (2011), 'Universal service obligations: fulfilling new generations of services of general economic interest', in E. Szyszczak, J. Davies, M. Andenas and T. Bekkedal (eds), *Developments in Services of General Interest*, The Hague: TMC Asser Press.

Szyszczak, E., J. Davies, M. Andenas and T. Bekkedal (eds), *Developments in Services of General Interest*, The Hague: TMC Asser Press.
Thouvenin, J-M. (2009), 'The *Altmark* case and its consequences', in M. Krajewski, et al. (eds), *The Changing Legal Framework for Services of General Interest in Europe*, The Hague: TMC Asser Press.
van de Gronden, J. *et al.* (eds), (2011a), *Health Care and EU Law,* The Hague: TMC Asser Press.
van de Gronden, J. (2011b), 'Social services of general interest and EU law', in E. Szyszczak, *et al.* (eds), *Developments in Services of General Interest*, The Hague: TMC Asser Press.

14 European economic rights and national State aids policy in conflict: the problem of the democratic securing of welfare
Michelle Everson

I. THE MISMATCH BETWEEN SUPRANATIONAL ECONOMIC POLICIES AND NATIONAL WELFARE

The co-ordination of economic and welfare (or social policies) within the EU is well documented. Clearly, the problem largely remains one of the level at which each set of policies is pursued, and the subsequent difficulties of national/supranational policy co-ordination: even post conclusion of the Treaty of Lisbon 2009, the EU's social competence remains very weak when compared with its economic role; Member States continue to bear the primary responsibility for the formulation and management of socially-redistributive mechanisms. Alternatively, where Member States remain jealous of their interventionist competence, and the EU is still denied meaningful fiscal powers in order to enable its own form of social intervention, conflict cannot but arise – for a highly topical example – between the fiscal probity demanded by the 'Growth and Stability Pact' at supranational level and the socially-corrective interventionist demands (home State welfare and host State support for the movement of labour) arising out of such fiscal commitments at national level.

So far, so conventional: and yet, such an obvious lack of political, social and economic co-ordination is merely the tip of an iceberg of a continuing chasm between the deep *structural/constitutional* commitments of the Member States to redistributive economic policies and a body of EU law that is deeply anchored within the efficiency paradigms of economic rationality and, more particularly, in the assumption of *separate* pursuit of identifiable socially-redistributive goals within a distinct social budget. In stark contrast to the apparent political consensus since the 1980s that an efficient economic policy can and should be pursued in isolation from social goals – which are accordingly apportioned to the social budget – our national constitutions often stubbornly retain their post-war commitments to structural corporatism, to a comprehensive politically interventionist economic competence.

At one level, such residual national structural constitutional corporatism proves highly disruptive within EU law as application of the EU legal economic competence to national provisions can give rise to wholly unexpected conflict with the complex constitutional provisions of the Member States. As this brief entry demonstrates, the case of *Rüffert*, decided by the CJEU in 2009,[1] might have been thought by the European Justices to have been a mere matter of the adjustment of the public procurement policies of German *Länder* to the Article 56 TFEU commitment of the Treaty to freedom of services. However, having considered the matter outside the provisions of EU State aid law, the CJEU was nonetheless to find itself in potential conflict with the powerful German Constitutional Court (*Bundesverfassungsgericht*), and more particularly that Court's earlier treatment of the same material within a national constitutional State aids framework which privileges a politically interventionist discretion above economically rationalising arguments.

At yet another level, however, residual structural corporatism also poses a heightened challenge to EU law. Certainly, from the point of view of the CJEU, it is surely tempting to view such national constitutional peculiarities as the swansong of the post-war constitutional settlement, and to happily set them aside in line with the motto 'the structural flesh may be weak, but the political will (for economic rationality) is strong'. Nonetheless, when set in the parallel context of the *Bundesverfassungsgericht*'s judgment on the compatibility of the Lisbon Treaty with the German Constitution (*BundesverfG*, 2BVE 2/08), it becomes readily apparent that what might be dismissed as outdated national corporatism is also an expression of intricate legal and constitutional considerations on the *democratic* legitimacy of the conduct of economic and social policy.

II   RÜFFERT VERSUS THE CASE OF THE '*VERGABEGESETZ*'

The case of *Rüffert* is surprising for a variety of reasons, and not least for the fact that, in a case concerning public procurement within the German state of Lower Saxony, the CJEU made no reference to Directive 93/37/EC as since amended by Directive 2004/18/EC.[2] The striking nature of the Court's failure to consider EU public procurement provisions was, however, easily matched by the depth of its disagreement with its own Advocate General. Confronted with a Lower Saxony law (*Landesvergabegesetz*) requiring all public procurement contracts within the state to be concluded in conformity with local collective bargaining agreements on wage rates, which were argued to be 'disproportionately' more favourable to home than host state workers since they exceeded the minimum established by the federal German bargaining agreement (*TV Mindestlohn*), Advocate General Bot chose to reject the challenge made to the law by Mr Rüffert, who was acting as an agent for 'imported' non-German workers. The *Landesvergabegesetz* could not be considered to negate the potential wage rate advantages of host workers since, firstly – or so the Advocate General opined – Article 7 of the Rome Convention 1980 in any case subjected host workers to the '*loi de police*' of the host country, including *all* collective bargaining agreements. Equally, Article 23 of Directive 93/37/EC[3] stated that public procurement contracts should be in conformity with 'the working conditions in force in the place of employment' and thus likewise required host workers to abide by local bargaining agreements. Thirdly, however, Advocate General Bot rejected Rüffert's reliance on the Posted Workers Directive (97/71/EC)[4] giving effect to the free movement of services (for contracted workers) and, more particularly, Article 3(1) of that Directive, stating that contracted workers should be subject to 'universally applicable' working conditions in the host State, and thus *only* to the 'universal' minimum wage. Instead, since the subsequent Article 3(7) stated that Article 3(1) 'shall not prevent application of terms and conditions . . . more favourable to workers', Article 151 TFEU, might finally be called into play to give precedence to Article 3(7) above 3(1), since Directive 97/71/EC was surely also designed to improve the living standards of workers in line with the EU's normative Treaty commitment to this effect.

The CJEU nonetheless demurred. Ignoring all references to the Rome Convention, Directive 93/37/EC, and Article 56 TFEU, the Justices curtly concentrated their efforts on securing the economic efficiency securing potential of the freedom to provide services (Article 56 TFEU). The economically allocative efficiency (justice) of wage rate competition surely prevailed in the Court's mind above the goal of raising living standards when it chose to follow its own decisions in *Viking* and *Laval*.[5] In line with *Viking*, then, a national provision would not be allowed to deprive the freedom of services of its core purpose of allowing appropriate competition between national workforces. By the same token, however, *Laval*'s injunction that Article 3(7) of the Posted Workers Directive should not be read so as to demand that host service providers are required to observe provisions in excess of universal provisions (as laid down in Article 3(1) (c)), determined that the *Landesvergabegesetz* was to be considered disproportionate – an undue restriction on contracted host workers who would be required only to observe the terms of the federal *TV Mindestlohn*.

This treatment of German state-level public procurement with reference to the freedom to provide services rather than public procurement provisions of EU law, becomes even more striking, however, to the degree that it thus represents an example of 'diagonal' conflict between supranational and national competences, an instance of spill-over from supranational jurisprudence on freedom of services into national jurisprudence on State aids. The specific material treated within the case of *Rüffert* was one that had already created a large degree of controversy within the Federal Republic. Above all, potential mismatches between collective bargaining policy at federal and at State level had determined that the issue of the *Vergabegesetzen* of the *Länder* (state procurement policies) would demand a mediating judgment on the part of the *Bundesverfassungsgericht*. However, within a wholly German context, the clash between the competences of state and federation within public procurement was to be treated within the realm of national State aids law, with radically different results from those arrived at by the CJEU.

Called upon to judge the constitutionality of Berlin's *Vergabegesetz* – in substance and form identical to that of Lower Saxony's – the *Bundesverfassungsgericht* chose to adopt a seemingly wholly formalistic legal approach and to approve the provision, which was a explicit measure of State aid designed to ensure local employment, on the basis of paragraph 97(4) Gesetz gegen Wettbewerbsbeschrar unger (GWB) (competition law) providing that 'extensive conditions may only be imposed upon contractors where this is provided for by federal or state law'. Equally, however, the imposition of local collective bargaining agreements upon public contractors was neither considered to be a breach of freedom of association under the constitution (9(3)Grundgesetz (GG)), nor was it deemed a breach of the freedom to exercise a profession (12(1)GG). Instead, the legislative mandate was given precedence above fundamental rights. Competition law provided for the state level regulation of public procurement. Accordingly, state level public procurement law might demand that contractors observe local collective bargaining agreements.[6]

III   THE SOCIAL CONSTITUTION AND THE DISEMBEDDED EUROPEAN MARKET

An immediate response to the diagonal conflict and spill-over between supranational rights of free movement and national State aid law might, as noted, be a legal shrugging of the shoulders; an assertion that German State aids law can and should be made compatible with EU free movement jurisprudence, and especially so, in view of prevailing political commitments to government by means of economic rationality. Nonetheless, this all too ready acceptance of the economically-rationalising legitimacy of

European law and its mission to overturn residual national corporatism may yet be premature. Joerges and Rodl (2009) have tellingly pinpointed the core *lacuna* of the European project:

> The problem of the welfare state is the practical-political *bête-noire* of the European project. What is left to us when we postulate that the ability to create an economic and social order is a constitutive pre-condition for democratic legitimacy, but simultaneously recognise that the EU harmonisation of the economic and labour constitutions of the Member States is impossible, so that Europe must reckon with lasting socio-economic divergence between its constituent Member States?

The vital point here is the relationship between the 'ordering' – that is the constitutional ordering – of economic and social policy, as well as democratic legitimacy, or due political process. All, in this analysis, are intimately linked with one another, such that the European project, if it continues – through diagonal, as well as direct, conflict – fatally to undermine the links between the economic and the social, the political and the constitutional, will founder in its own democratic deficit.

To German constitutionalists the problem is all too apparent. Granted, the post war political championing by the famous finance minister, Walter Erhardt, of 'ordo-liberal' thought – the Hayekian notion that the economy can be structured and protected (from the State and private individuals) by primary legal provisions (the Economic Constitution) – may give the impression that the Republic is distinguished by its dedication to creation of an autonomous economy; a dedication famously reflected within its constitutional commitment price stability. Nonetheless, the early proponents of ordo-liberalism in German (Walter Eucken) were similarly clear that social and economic orders were linked orders within the political constitution, such that economic autonomy, efficiency and rationality were subject always to the imperative of constitutional commitment to the *Sozialstaat* and the principle of democratic determination.[7] It was only later, in the wake of ever more powerful processes of European integration that purist ordo-liberal theorists, such as Hans Peter Ipsen and Ernst-Joachim Mestmäcker began to postulate the potential inherent to a European economic community founded in functional economic purpose and competition between constitutional orders.[8] But even these theorists began to baulk in the face of a Delors programme and the drive for the integration of a single market, which, by virtue of negative judicial integration and diagonal conflicts of spill-over – clearly reproduced in the case of *Rüffert* – was to find its counterpart in the 'disembedding' of national economies from their social-political constitutional frameworks and the establishment of the 'mastery of markets over the state'.[9]

IV   RESIDUAL CONSTITUTIONAL CORPORATISM RE-ASSESSED: LEGAL CAUTION AND POLITICAL DISCRETION

Seen in this light then, the CJEU's strange refusal to approach the case of *Rüffert* within the EU's own State aids regime and its creation of diagonal conflict between EU and German law may, nevertheless, seem to be less a matter of necessary constitutional adjustment of conflicting economic orders to reflect an assumed post-corporatist political consensus, and more a matter of importune judicial intervention. Certainly, the primary justification for the Court's final decision may carry with it a hint of an attempt to establish individual justice, as the Court asks why more advantageous local bargaining agreements should be applied only in the public sector:

> The case-file submitted to the Court contains no evidence to support the conclusion that the protection resulting from such a rate of pay – which, moreover, as the national court also notes, exceeds the minimum rate of pay applicable pursuant to the AEntG – is necessary for a construction worker only when he is employed in the context of a public works contract but not when he is employed in the context of a private contract (paragraph 40).

However, at the same time, such an *evidential* demand for *economic proof* just as surely reveals an anti-democratic tendency within the Court, a total commitment to an economic theory of efficiency and a judicial monomania that is strangely reminiscent of the infamous early 20th century arrogance of the US Supreme Court:

> This case is decided upon an economic theory which a large part of the country does not entertain. If it were a question whether I agreed with that theory, I should desire to study it further and long before making up my mind. But I do not conceive that to be my duty, because I strongly believe that my agreement or disagreement has nothing to do with the right of a majority to embody their opinions in law.[10]

Justice Holmes thus gently reminds the US Constitutional Court that it is not the province of the jurist, and more particularly, the constitutional jurist, to adopt the mantel of the political economist; a mantel to which the jurist is singularly ill-suited. Instead, the primary function of the constitutional jurist is one of the upholding of the democratic process. And it is here, in a final closer analysis, that the judgment of the *Bundesverfassungsgericht* on the issue of the *Berliner Vergabegesetz*, cannot simply be dismissed as an outdated judicial commitment to residual national economic corporatism.

Instead, the German Justices remain true to the antecedents of ordo-liberal theory, establishing a direct connection between economic and social ordering within the German Constitution. Peering beyond economic theory to identify the purpose of state demands that local collective bargaining agreements be respected by contracting parties within public procurement, the Court admits of the constitutional status – under the *Sozialstaatsprinzip* – of efforts to combat unemployment (1 BvL 4/00, paragraph 88). Equally, and perhaps more importantly, however, the *Constitutional* Court strictly delimits its own functions and competences. Within a national constitution of intertwined social, political and economic orders, it is not for the Court to decide upon the appropriate means to achieve a given economic or social aim. Instead, 'proportionality' must be a procedural rather than substantive mechanism of constitutional review, whereby the legislator need only demonstrate that her proposed means of achieving a goal, has a possibility of achieving that goal and might accordingly deploy her political *discretion* to bring her own economic, employment, social and political experience and aspirations to bear, in order to ensure 'the common good' (1 BvL 4/00, paragraph 92).

V. THE CONSTITUTIONAL-POLITICAL LIMITS TO ECONOMICALLY-EFFICIENT EUROPEAN INTEGRATION

Rüffert and the case of the *Berliner Vergabegesetz*, the clash of national with European State aid policy – or the assertion of European economic rights above national State aid law – thus teach us a series of vital lessons. Firstly, we might not assume that corporatism – the use of economic policy to pursue political/social goals – is dead within Europe. Instead, the potential for corporatist economic management is structurally assured by national constitutional law. Far more importantly, however, judicial support for apparently corporatist regulation at national level should likewise not simply be assumed to represent outmoded legal adherence to economic concepts that have now seen their day. Instead, such support is, far more, a feature of the integrated nature of the post-war national constitution, of the linking of political, social and economic orders within the national constitutional settlement in order to ensure continuing political ownership of the common good. Set in the context of the *Bundesverfassungsgericht*'s judgment on the compatibility of the Lisbon Treaty 2009 with the German Constitution, this accordingly determines that there are also clear political-economic limits to the process of

European integration. Where national constitutions maintain a commitment to welfare or the social state (2 BVE 2/08, paragraph 257) and where the constitutional order similarly recognises the political discretion of the national legislator to secure social welfare, then a EU, which continues to lack a social competence (2 BVE 2/08, paragraph 258), must take care to avoid any form of conflict with the democratically-legitimated economic/social orders of the Member States:

> A structural democratic deficit that would be unacceptable pursuant to Article 23 in conjunction with Article 79.3 of the Basic Law would exist if the extent of competences, the political freedom of action and the degree of independent formation of opinion on the part of the institutions of the Union reached a level corresponding to the federal level in a federal state, i.e. a level analogous to that of a state, because for instance the legislative competences, which are essential for democratic self-determination, were exercised mainly on the level of the Union. If an imbalance between character and the extent of the sovereign powers exercised and the degree of democratic legitimisation arises in the course of the development of the European integration, it is for the Federal Republic of Germany due to its responsibility for integration, to work towards a change, and if the worst comes to the worst, even to refuse to further participate in the European Union (2 BVE 2/08, paragraph 264).

Educing from one of the most powerful of constitutional courts within the EU, the threat of discontinued participation within the European integration project is one that should not be taken lightly. Accordingly, a final lesson might be drawn from *Rüffert* and the case of the *Berliner Vergabegesetz*, one that is specifically tailored for the CJEU. The enduring mystery of *Rüffert* must surely be one of the question of why the Court ignored the injunctions of its own Advocate General and chose to treat the material, not within the regime of EU State aid law but rather within the ambit of the freedom to provide services. To this exact degree then, the Court can and must be criticised: where a politically-legitimated regime for the regulation of national public procurement policies exists at European level, the legitimacy of assertion of economic rights above this regime must just as surely be questioned. The CJEU need not have created a diagonal conflict between EU economic rights and national State aid law, need not have bitten so deeply into the German constitutional order and need not have further disembedded the European market. Seen in this light, the time has now surely come to review and delimit the reach of the *Laval* and *Viking* jurisprudence of the CJEU, at least as regards its application to the area of State aid policy.

NOTES

1. Case 346/06, [2009] E.C.R. 1989.
2. O.J. 2004 L 134.
3. O.J. 1993 L199/54.
4. O.J. 1997 L 347/42.
5. Case C-438/05, *International Transport Workers' Federation, Finnish Seamen's Union* v. *Viking Line ABP, OÜ Viking Line Eesti* [2007] E.C.R. I-10779; Case C-341/05), *Laval un Partneri Ltd* v. *Svenska Byggnadsarbetareförbundet, Svenska Byggnadsarbetareförbundet, avd. 1, Svenska Elektrikerförbundet* [2007] E.C.R. I-11767.
6. *BundesVerfG*, 1 BvL 4/00, 11 July 2006.
7. See, for details of the tradition, Wegmann 2002.
8. Most famously, Ipsen 1972.
9. Mestmäcker taking extreme exception to the incursion of EU economic law into areas of national social policy, see, for example his interview, 'Dem EuGH fehlt Legitimation für Beschränkung direkter Steuern' (*Betriebs-Berater*, BB 43.2008, 20 October 2008, 16). In a similar vein, see Majone 2005. The reference to the disembedding of markets draws on the apocalyptic analysis provided by Polanyi 1944. The reference to the mastery of markets over the state is to Foucault 2008.
10. Mr Justice Holmes, dissenting, *Lochner v. New York* 198 U.S. 45, 25 S.Ct. 539.

REFERENCES

Foucault, Michel (2008), *Birth of Biopolitics: Lectures at the College de France, 1978-79*, London: Palgrave MacMillan.
Ipsen, H. P. (1972), *Europarecht,* Tübingen: Mohr-Siebeck.
Joerges, C. and F. Rödl, (2009), 'Informal politics, formalised law and the "social deficit" of european integration: Reflections after the judgments of the ECJ in Viking and Laval', *European Law Journal*, **15:1**, 1–19.
Majone, G. (2005), *Dilemmas of European Integration: the Ambiguities and Pitfalls of Integration by Stealth*, Oxford: Oxford University Press.
Polanyi, Karl (1944), *The Great Transformation,* (2001 edn) New York: Beacon Press.
Wegmann, M. (2002), Früher Neoliberalismus und europäische Integration: Interdependenz der nationalen, supranationalen und internationalen Ordnung von Wirtschaft und Gesellschaft (1932-1965), Baden-Baden: Nomos.

15 Procedural aspects of EU State aid law and practice
Michael Schütte

I. INTRODUCTION

According to Article 108 TFEU, any State aid measure must be notified beforehand to the European Commission, giving it the possibility to assess the measure under EU State aid rules. Member States are under an obligation *not* to implement the aid measure before the Commission has taken its position and either declared the measure compatible with the internal market under Article 107 TFEU, has not raised any objections or considers that the measure does not constitute aid.

These basic rules, as simple as they may sound in principle, provide many pitfalls in practice. One of the main difficulties stems from the fact that Article 108 TFEU – and the Procedural Regulation that has been adopted to make the process more transparent and predictable[1] – only apply to measures that constitute a State aid within the meaning of Article 107(1) TFEU. If a measure is not a State aid, then no notification to the European Commission is necessary, and the Member State is free to implement the measure without waiting for any reaction from the Commission.

A measure that does constitute a State aid, and that has been implemented without prior notification to the European Commission, is considered an *unlawful aid*, even if it may be declared compatible with the internal market under Article 107 TFEU. The distinction between unlawful or illegal aid – aid that has not been duly notified – and incompatible aid – aid that is not compatible with the internal market under Article 107(2) TFEU or cannot be declared compatible with the internal market under Article 107(3) TFEU is an important one, and the two terms should not be confused.

The fact that a measure is considered an unlawful aid has two basic consequences: first, and at the very minimum, the beneficiary of the aid will have to pay interest on the benefit obtained, from the granting until the aid is declared compatible,[2] and second, a competitor has the right to ask national Courts to take action against the granting of such unlawful aid, possibly forcing the recovery of the aid.[3] Article 108(3) TFEU is a provision that has direct effect, and on which third parties can rely directly before national courts.[4]

The Commission, by contrast, has to assess the compatibility of any aid measure – unlawful aid[5] or notified aid – with the internal market[6] and will only order the recovery of the aid if the aid is considered incompatible with the internal market under Article 107 TFEU, save in truly exceptional circumstances that may justify the immediate recovery of the aid during the period of assessment by the Commission.

In practice, the granting of unlawful aid is most often not the consequence of a deliberate act of a Member State to grant an unlawful and incompatible aid measure, but the consequence of a misjudgment of the classification of a measure as a State aid. For instance, a Member State may consider that a measure complies with the market economy investor principle, and thus does not constitute aid. If it does, and the assessment of the Member State is correct, then there is indeed no aid and no need to notify the measure to the Commission. Article 108 TFEU would not apply, and the measure would not be considered an illegal aid. If, by contrast, the Commission considers that the measure does not fully meet the market economy investor principle, it would consider the measure to constitute a State aid – and, since it has not been notified, it would be an unlawful aid that was granted in breach of Article 108(3) (3rd sentence) TFEU. The same situation may arise if the interpretation of an approved aid scheme differs between a Member State and the Commission: the Member State may consider the granting of an aid under that approved scheme meeting all the conditions, whereas the Commission may consider that one of the conditions of the scheme is not fully met. If that was the case, then the granting of the aid would indeed not fall under the approved scheme, but constitute a 'new' aid rather than an 'existing' aid under an approved scheme, and it would be an unlawful aid because it had not been notified.[7] Obviously, it is not up to the Commission to decide whether a measure constitutes a State aid – the provision of Article 107(1) TFEU contains legal terms that are subject to full review by the European Courts.[8] In practice, however, the position of the Commission is of paramount importance: its Decisions are considered binding and valid unless (and until) they are lifted by a judgment from the European Courts.

The procedural rules to be applied under Article 108 TFEU have been set out in more detail in Council Regulation No 659/1999 laying down detailed rules for the application of Article 93 of the EC Treaty [now Article 108 TFEU][9] (Procedural Regulation). This has been complemented by Commission Regulation (EC) No 794/2004[10] (Implementing Regulation). The Implementing Regulation has been amended several times, modifying the notification forms and detailed rules on how to notify aid measures.[11]

By contrast to other competition procedures, where the parties concerned are directly involved and have procedural rights on their own, the

State aid procedure is a procedure between the Member States and the European Commission. Third parties, such as the beneficiary or a competitor, do not have a real role to play[12] other than being an 'informant'.[13] In practice, well-advised beneficiaries and competitors will cooperate with the Member States so as to provide all necessary information and guide the notification process with the Commission. Their direct participation in the procedure is, technically speaking, limited to submitting written observations in the course of the formal procedure under Article 108(2) TFEU. The institutions, let alone the Member States, have yet to take steps to increase the participation of the parties directly concerned by State aid measures, which has been demanded repeatedly.[14]

II.   PROCEDURE FOR NOTIFIED AID

Article 108 TFEU requires Member States to notify the introduction of a new aid or the modification of an existing aid. In both cases, the State aid is considered 'new aid', as is clear from Article 2 of the Procedural Regulation. This means that any such aid must not be implemented or granted before the Commission has approved it.

II.i.   Definition of New Aid and Existing Aid

Article 1 Procedural Regulation contains the relevant definitions of 'aid', 'existing aid' and 'new aid'. 'New aid' is defined as any aid that is not 'existing aid', but includes any existing aid that is being modified. Thus, it is important to check whether an aid is considered as an 'existing aid' under Article 1 Procedural Regulation. Apart from aid that Member States had introduced prior to acceding to the Treaty,[15] the most relevant category of existing aid relates to aid measures approved by the Commission.

This applies, in particular, to aid schemes: any individual aid granted under an approved aid scheme is considered an 'existing aid' under Article 1(b)(ii) of the Procedural Regulation. Cases of aid deemed approved because the Commission has failed to take a decision within the deadlines according to Article 4 (6) of the Procedural Regulation – and which are thus 'existing aid' – are rather rare, if they exist at all; the same is true for aid that has been granted more than ten years prior to the Commission investigating it (Article 15 of the Procedural Regulation).

Finally, Article 1(b)(v) of the Procedural Regulation provides that any measure that had formerly not been considered as an aid, but is now considered a State aid due to the development of Community law, constitutes 'existing aid'. This applied, for instance, to the Belgian co-ordination centres: a co-ordination centre in Belgium of a group of companies (most often European Headquarters, or centres where the treasury of the group was managed) were getting favourable tax treatment under Belgian law. The Commission had originally considered this scheme not to constitute an aid. As EU State aid law developed, this seemed no longer appropriate, and the Commission insisted that the benefits be abolished.[16] Similarly, the Commission for a long time had considered airports not to be economic operators, but to be providers of infrastructure that would not be considered an 'undertaking' under Article 107 TFEU. The judgment of the General Court in *Aéroports de Paris* marked an important change: since then, airport operators are considered as economic operators,[17] and thus undertakings under Article 107 TFEU, and consequently, State measures to support them may constitute State aid.

The most important consequence of the classification of an aid as 'existing aid' is that the recovery of existing aid from the beneficiary is excluded. The Commission can re-assess the measure, and if it considers that the measure must be modified or abolished to be in line with current EU law, it can ultimately force the Member State to comply, under Article 108 TFEU. Consequently, an existing aid may have to be abolished, but only *ex nunc*. The Commission cannot order the recovery of an existing aid, even if it is, or has become, incompatible with the internal market. Thus, the classification as existing aid provides significant procedural protection to the beneficiary.

II.ii.   The Notification Process

The notification by the Member State follows the detailed procedure of the implementing Regulation, Regulation 794/04.[18] Special forms have been developed to facilitate the notification of different types of aid. In view of the increasing number of aid measures that have to be notified, and which are most often approved, the notifications have to be filed electronically with the Commission by means of the so-called State Aid Notification Interactive System (SANI system). Member States complete the notification online on the SANI forms and upload supporting documentation, and their Permanent Representative authenticates the submission of the final notification to the Commission.

Once the notification is complete and the SANI notification has been authenticated, the Commission assesses the compatibility of the aid with the internal market. This can be done in an informal procedure, if the Commission raises no objections or considers the aid to be compatible with the internal market. Should the Commission have doubts as to the compatibility of the aid, it must open the formal procedure under Article 108(2) TFEU.

II.ii.a.   Informal procedure

According to Article 4(5) of the Procedural Regulation, the Commission has two months for its initial assessment in the informal procedure. The two-month period begins with the submission of complete information by the Member State. In principle, the deadline is compulsory; if the Commission fails to take a position within that time period, the aid is deemed to be existing aid under Article 15 of the Procedural Regulation. What sounds like a hard deadline is, in fact, not a hard deadline at all. In almost all cases, the Commission has additional questions and needs additional information to take a position on the compatibility of the measure. Each request for new information (submitted in accordance with Article 5 of the Procedural Regulation) extends the deadline by another two months, counting from the date of the response by the Member State (Article 4 (5)(2nd sentence) of the Procedural Regulation). Consequently, in most cases, the actual time period for the compatibility assessment by the Commission is significantly longer than the two months foreseen by the Regulation. Furthermore, if a Member State fails to reply to a request for information despite a reminder from the Commission, the Commission may consider the notification withdrawn, Article 5(3) of the Procedural Regulation. This would be exceptional; in practice, the Member State and the Commission would normally agree on extensions of the deadlines.

The informal procedure normally ends with one of three possible Decisions:

a. either the Commission considers that the measure does not constitute aid (Article 4(2)); or
b. it considers the measure to be compatible with the internal market (Article 4(3)); without formally declaring the measure to be compatible, the Commission often merely states that it 'raises no objection' against the measure; or
c. it has (serious) doubts as to the compatibility of the aid with the internal market, and decides to open the formal procedure under Article 108(2) TFEU.

In practice, however, the Decision that a measure does not constitute aid is often avoided. The Commission does not particularly like to take this kind of Decision, since its assessment is subject to full legal review by the European Courts: whether or not a measure is an aid is a question of law. It is not subject to a Decision by the Commission, nor does the Commission have a large margin of discretion in this respect.[19] Thus, in practice, unless there are particular interests of the beneficiary involved who needs a 'no aid' Decision for reasons of legal certainty, Member

States may be encouraged to withdraw the notification since the measure constitutes no aid, thus relieving the Commission from having to take a 'no aid' Decision. In this type of situation, the withdrawal of the notification terminates the procedure.[20]

The informal procedure between the Commission and the Member State is not transparent, and potential beneficiaries have little or no possibility to discover what the exact contents of the notification are. In fact, a Member State may provide explanations to the Commission, or may even give one-sided commitments to the Commission as to the way in which the notified aid measure – for instance, an aid scheme that would apply to a multitude of beneficiaries – will be applied in practice. These explanations and commitments are considered by the Commission to be part of the notification, and if the aid measure is declared compatible with the internal market, they form part of that Decision. In other words, any deviation from such explanations and commitments by an authority of a Member State will deprive the aid measure of the 'existing aid' status and expose the beneficiary to recovery. The views of third parties, such as the beneficiary or a competitor, do not have to be taken into account by the Commission in this phase of the procedure.[21]

It should be noted that in the informal procedure, the Commission cannot technically impose conditions or obligations on the Member State – it assesses the notification by the Member State as it has been submitted. If the Commission is dissatisfied with the notification and considers that the measure is not compatible with the internal market without a certain condition or obligation imposed on the company or some clarification or commitment from the Member State, this would mean that the Commission has 'doubts' as to the compatibility, and thus must open the formal procedure. In practice, however, such doubts are discussed between the Commission and the Member State, and the Member State is, of course, free to offer one-sided commitments, which the Commission can then accept, as a precondition to its decision to consider the measure compatible with the internal market. Consequently, the one-sided commitments given by a Member State in the course of an informal procedure (which are *de facto* agreed with the Commission) have the same binding character as any obligation or condition imposed on a measure as part of the approval Decision in a formal procedure.

Where the Commission declares an aid measure to be compatible with the internal market, it will publish the decision on its website, and a short summary will be published in the *Official Journal*. It is currently under dispute whether the fact that the Commission declared a measure compatible with the internal market, and that its Decision is published in the *Official Journal* and accessible on the website is capable of providing legal certainty, or even creating legitimate expectations, to the benefit of beneficiaries. According to a judgment of the General Court (that is currently under appeal[22]) a beneficiary who benefited from an aid scheme in the form of a law which had been approved by the Commission, cannot rely on either the principle of legal certainty or legitimate expectations if the actual application of the law according to its wording violated an explanation given by the Member State to the Commission in the course of the notification process.[23] If the judgment were upheld by the European Court, beneficiaries will have to check all correspondence and exchange of information between a Member State and the Commission during the notification process to be certain that the granting of the aid is indeed covered by the Commission Decision approving the aid scheme.[24]

II.ii.b.   Simplified procedure
Given the fact that the vast majority of State aid cases that are notified to the Commission are considered compatible with the internal market and are often simple and straight forward, the Commission has introduced a 'simplified procedure'[25] which Member States can use for cases which are fully in line with the communications and frameworks of the Commission, and can thus easily be declared compatible with the internal market. The simplified procedure can be used for three categories of aid:

(i)   aid measures falling under the standard assessment under existing guidelines and frameworks;
(ii)   aid measures corresponding to well-established Commission decision-making practice; and
(iii) prolongation and extensions of existing schemes.

The simplified procedure can only be applied to notified aid. Sensitive sectors, such as agriculture, fisheries, textiles are not eligible for the application of the simplified procedure. In order to further facilitate the procedure, in particular on simple cases, the Commission has published a 'Best Practices' Code for State aid procedure.[26] Respecting the Best Practices should facilitate a smooth running of the procedure, and arriving at a positive decision swiftly.

II.ii.c.   Duration of the informal procedure
Article 108 TFEU is tacit as to the details and the duration of the procedure before the Commission. The CJEU ruled, however, that there must be clear limits to the duration of the procedure, and it decided that, if the Commission had not taken a position within two months of the notification, the Member State was free to implement the measure,

but had to inform the Commission thereof.[27] The two month deadline has been taken up by the Procedural Regulation.[28] It has, however, been watered down significantly by the fact that the deadline only commences once the Commission considers the notification 'complete'. As long as the Commission requests additional explanations, the two-month deadline starts over again with each new request. Consequently, this mechanism is sometimes used by the Commission merely to gain time; if it repeats a request for information on which a Member State has previously responded, however, the deadline is no longer extended.[29] The Member State can then implement the measure, but must inform the Commission, which can only stop the implementation by opening the formal procedure.

In practice, the informal procedure for notified State aid takes significantly longer than the two months that the European Court of Justice had in mind. Since the internal decision-making process within the Commission can easily take six weeks, from the time the case team has reached a clear position on the case, even rather simple cases are bound to take four months or more; six months is a more realistic estimation in most cases. Much depends, of course, on how the notification process is prepared. Pre-notification meetings in which the planned measures are discussed are a great help to accelerate the notification process.[30] Of course, the actual deadlines only begin once the notification has been formally submitted.

It should be noted that the two-month deadline applicable to the informal procedure only applies in case of notified aid measures. Any aid that is unlawful because it has been implemented without prior notification will initially be investigated in an informal procedure as well, but the Commission is not bound by the deadlines applicable to notified aid.

II.iii.   Formal Procedure

II.iii.a.   When to open a formal procedure
In cases where the Commission has (serious) doubts as to the compatibility of the aid, it shall open the formal investigation procedure, Article 108(2) TFEU and Article 4(5) of the Procedural Regulation. The Commission must open the procedure where doubts remain as to the compatibility of the aid, following the initial assessment in the informal procedure. It cannot deny the opening of the formal procedure on the basis of administrative convenience or other reasons.[31] It does not have a margin of discretion whether or not it opens the formal procedure, if it faces serious difficulties.[32] With regard to the assessment of the difficulties, the Commission can, however, attempt to solve them in a dialogue with

the Member State during the informal procedure. If and when doubts remain, the formal procedure must be opened.[33]

The Commission publishes its Decision to open the formal procedure in the *Official Journal.* That Decision should contain a description of the basic facts and the reasons for which the Commission has doubts as to the compatibility.[34]

The opening of the formal procedure is a challengeable act to the extent that it affects the legal position of the applicant. A procedure affecting a new aid will affect the position of the Member State, since Article 108(3) (3rd sentence) TFEU does not allow the Member State to grant the aid until the Commission has completed its assessment. Consequently, the application for annulment by a Member State is admissible.[35] By contrast, with regard to a beneficiary or other third party, the Decision to open the formal procedure normally constitutes only an interim step in the administrative procedure and does not affect its legal position, unless it relates to a measure that had not been considered a State aid by the Member State concerned, was in the course of implementation and was then classified by the Commission as 'new aid'.[36]

The opening of the formal procedure allows for limited participation of third parties, who can submit their comments within one month from the publication of the opening decision in the *Official Journal.* Third parties, which include the beneficiary, its competitors and any other party that considers itself affected by the Decision, do not become active participants in the procedure, however. Their procedural position, according to the European Courts, is that of an 'informant'.[37] They can provide factual elements, evidence as well as arguments. In cases concerning regional aid, for instance, the positive effects of the aid on the development of the region may well be demonstrated by local authorities, universities, whereas competitors will emphasise the distorting effects of the aid on competition and provide information on how the market should be defined.

As a consequence of the limitations of the procedural rights, the beneficiary and other third parties are bound to respect the deadlines to submit their written comments. Any facts or arguments submitted at a later point in time may be ignored by the Commission, unless they have been submitted by the Member State itself. The position of the Member State is a strong one: it controls the procedure, since it has filed (and can withdraw) the notification, and it can provide arguments and facts until the Commission has reached its conclusion on the notification.

II.iii.b.   Conclusion of the formal procedure

To conclude the formal procedure, the Commission takes one of the following Decisions:

(i) A Decision that the measure does not constitute aid, Article 7(2) of the Procedural Regulation;

(ii) A positive Decision, declaring that the measure is compatible with the internal market under Article 107(2) TFEU or is declared compatible with the internal market under Article 107(3) TFEU.

(iii) A negative Decision, declaring the measure incompatible with the internal market under Article 107 TFEU. Negative Decisions are normally combined with an order for recovery of the non-compatible aid, provided that the aid was granted unlawfully, that is, without prior notification.[38]

The positive Decision concluding a formal procedure may be subject to conditions or obligations, restricting the scope of the positive Decision and imposing certain duties on the Member State and the undertaking concerned. For instance, in restructuring cases, the Commission will always impose the obligation to carry out the restructuring plan in full, perform certain investments, cut capacity, respect capacity and/or production limitations, and report regularly on the progress of the restructuring process. Not respecting these conditions and obligations will affect the positive decision:[39] the State aid will be considered to not have been approved, or the aid misused,[40] leading to a recovery of any aid granted.[41] In practice, the Commission may adapt the positive Decision, provided that the deviations from the conditions and obligations are formally notified to it and can be justified by the Member State and do not run counter to the common interest.

II.ii.c. Duration of the formal procedure

According to Article 7(6) of the Procedural Regulation, the Commission shall conclude the formal procedure within 18 months from the opening Decision. This deadline is not a binding deadline, and is often exceeded. In practice, many formal procedures take significantly longer than the 18-month period foreseen in the Procedural Regulation. The reasons for this are manifold. Often, the beneficiary and the Member State will need a significant amount of time to provide the data and evidence supporting their position that the aid measure is compatible with the internal market. Rebutting arguments and alleviating the doubts of the Commission may require extensive economic analysis, the preparation – and the assessment – of which takes time. Since it is in the interest of the beneficiary to obtain the aid or have it approved ('better late than never'), this may involve getting experts (for example, economists) on board who then analyse the underlying data, trade flows. The doubts that the Commission raises can rarely be alleviated in a very short period of time. Concluding a formal procedure within a period of four months can be considered as 'record speed' and an exception,[42] which requires full cooperation from all side and the political will of the Commission and the Member State to arrive at a decision rapidly.

II.iv.   Procedure for Non-notified Aid

Under Article 108 TFEU, Member States shall notify any aid measure to the Commission, prior to implementing it. Article 108(3) TFEU specifically prohibits the granting of any State aid before the Commission has been in a position to assess its compatibility with the internal market. Violation of this 'stand-still' provision makes the State aid 'unlawful' or 'illegal'.

According to the jurisprudence of the European Courts this does not mean that the Commission must not assess such unlawful aid, and it does not exclude that such unlawful aid may be declared compatible with the internal market under Article 107(3) TFEU.[43] Furthermore, the Commission cannot order the recovery of unlawful aid without a complete compatibility assessment, unless the requirements of Article 11 of the Procedural Regulation are met.

In many cases, unlawful aid is not the consequence of a deliberate violation by the Member State of its duty to notify the aid measure before implementing it. Rather, it is the result of an assessment of the measure by the Member State which differs from the assessment by the Commission. The Member State may consider a measure to comply with the *market economy investor principle* (see the chapters by Coppi, Kavanagh *et al.* and Lykotrafiti), whereas the Commission may consider that this test is not met and that consequently, the measure is to be considered a State aid. A Member State that considers a measure not to constitute a State aid does not have to notify the measure – but it bears the risk that, once the measure is implemented, the Commission will consider the measure to constitute a State aid, and since it has not been notified, an unlawful aid. Other cases concern the interpretation of existing, approved aid schemes – if the Member State interprets the scope of the approved aid measure to be wider than the Commission, the resulting aid granted to a company will be considered an unlawful aid, since it is not covered by the approved scheme.

According to Article 11 of the Procedural Regulation, the Commission may order the Member State to suspend the unlawful aid until the Commission has taken a final decision and, in exceptional cases, order the provisional recovery of any aid that has been unlawfully granted for the duration of the procedure, and thus order the status *ex ante* to be re-established. The provisional recovery is exceptional, and the Commission does not use it in practice. Rather, it relies on the jurisprudence of the European Courts that have consistently held that it is for the national Courts to ensure that Article 108 TFEU is complied with, and that any unlawful measure be recovered under national law.[44]

One of the consequences of the fact that an aid measure has not been notified, and is being assessed by the Commission as an unlawful aid, is that the deadlines for notified aid do not apply, Article 13(2) of the Procedural Regulation. Consequently, if the Commission does not take a Decision within two months, the aid measure is not deemed compatible with the internal market. There is no possibility for compatibility 'by default' as is the case for notified aid measures.

Another problem relates to the issue of what set of rules applies to an aid that has been granted unlawfully. Normally, the Commission assesses a State aid in accordance with the rules applicable at the time of its final Decision on the compatibility of the aid. In the case of non-notified aid measures, the Commission always assesses the compatibility of unlawful State aid with the common/internal market in accordance with the substantive criteria set out in any instrument *in force at the time when the aid was granted.*[45]

Article 10 of the Procedural Regulation forces the Commission to inquire about unlawful aid, whenever it has in its possession information from whatever source regarding alleged unlawful aid. It shall address a request for information to the Member State concerned. The normal rules applicable to notified aid apply *mutatis mutandis*, except for the deadlines. If the Commission does not obtain satisfactory information from the Member State in cases of unlawful aid, it shall issue an information injunction under Article 10(3) of the Procedural Regulation.

The procedure on non-notified aid is concluded in the same way as a notified aid – no aid decision, positive Decision, or opening of the formal procedure.

III. EXISTING AID AND APPROPRIATE MEASURES

Existing aid is defined in Article 1 (lit. b) of the Procedural Regulation (see part II.i.). Under Article 108(1) TFEU, the Commission must ensure that the application of any aid measure does not become incompatible with the internal market. Consequently, the Commission is reviewing existing aid on an ongoing basis, and it has the right to obtain all pertinent information from the Member State (Article 17 of the Procedural Regulation).

If necessary, the Commission will propose *appropriate measures* that may lead to an adaptation of an existing aid scheme so as to ensure that it remains compatible with the internal market (Article 18 of the Procedural Regulation). If the Member State accepts the appropriate measure, it is bound by it; if the measure is not accepted, the Commission can initiate the formal procedure and impose the adaptation by Decision (Article 19 of the Procedural Regulation).

The possibility of imposing appropriate measures has far reaching consequences. Appropriate measures adopted by the Commission and accepted by the Member States are binding – not only on the Commission and the Member State itself, but also on third parties.[46] In the field of State aid, the Commission is using appropriate measures not only for the adaptation of existing aid schemes, but also to make its State aid policy laid down in frameworks and Guidelines both transparent and binding. Although the frameworks and Guidelines do not constitute secondary legislation under the TFEU, they are nonetheless binding on all parties when Member States have accepted them.

It is important to note that it is not possible to order the recovery of any existing aid by means of appropriate measures, or otherwise. Only unlawful aid, or misused aid, can be recovered.

IV. MISUSE OF AID AND RECOVERY

IV.i. Misuse of Aid

Any State aid that has not been used in accordance with the Decision declaring it compatible with the internal market will have to be recovered. If the Commission considers that there has been a misuse of aid, it will open the formal procedure (Article 16 of the Procedural Regulation). For instance, in a restructuring case in which losses were covered with State aid, the Commission considered that if the total amount of losses had not been achieved, keeping the excess subsidy and using it for other purposes, even in the same restructuring process, would constitute a misuse of aid.[47]

IV.ii. Recovery

Recovery is the logical consequence of an aid that is unlawfully granted and incompatible with the internal market.[48] The recovery aims at reinstating the position '*ex ante*', before the distortion of competition caused by the granting of aid had taken place.

Recovery is only excluded where it would be contrary to a general principle of EU law (Article 14(1) Procedural Regulation) or where it would be entirely impossible.[49] The term 'impossibility' is interpreted very narrowly by the European Courts, it is almost excluded to construe a case where total impossibility would be accepted. Practical administrative difficulties, such as a multitude of beneficiaries and authorities involved, is clearly insufficient to show total impossibility.[50] Recovery is also not impossible if the company has gone bankrupt and ceased its economic activities, since recovery can be achieved by registration as one of the liabilities of the undertaking in bankruptcy procedure.[51]

In this respect, the principle of legitimate expectations and the principle of legal certainty have been invoked, in most cases, without success. In fact, a beneficiary cannot rely on the principle of legitimate expectations or legal certainty where the Member State itself has been at fault:[52] if the measure has not been properly notified,[53] the fact that it was granted by national law does not provide the beneficiary with the protection of legitimate expectations.[54] Similarly, whereas the principle of good administration may be invoked as a fundamental principle of Community law, the long duration of an administrative procedure is not sufficient to prevent the recovery from being enforced.

Furthermore, since recovery is the logical consequence of an unlawful incompatible aid, it cannot be disproportionate, even if it means liquidating the beneficiary.[55] This is so because the recovery only aims at restoring the previous situation.[56] Recovery must be carried out in case of an illegal aid that has been declared compatible with the internal market but where the Decision by the Commission has been annulled; the likelihood of a new positive decision cannot be used as a defence against the recovery.[57]

The amount to be recovered, if it is not included in the Commission Decision, must be determined by the Member State. Recovery of the aid must include interest on the aid, from the time the aid was first granted until the moment the aid is fully recovered (Article 14(2) of the Procedural Regulation). The interest rate to be applied is normally the reference rate applicable to the Member State that granted the aid, irrespective of the currency in which the beneficiary finances itself. The reference rates are communicated by the Commission to the Member States, and are normally fixed in close cooperation with them. Thus, claiming that the interest rate on the basis of the reference rate does not reflect the reality is not considered as a proper defence.[58] The Commission is not under any obligation to fix the interest rate for recovery of the aid in question, given that it is not even required to identify precisely the principle amount of the recoverable aid.[59] If the State aid has benefitted not only a direct beneficiary, but also an indirect beneficiary, it may have to be recovered from the indirect beneficiary.[60]

In case a State aid has been granted unlawfully, but is, or can be declared compatible with the internal market, the amount of interest for the period between the granting of the aid and the positive Decision by the Commission declaring the aid compatible will have to be recovered.[61] This is a clarification of the earlier jurisprudence that seemed to require that the act with which the unlawful aid was granted should be considered null and void. Under the *CELF* and *Wienstrom* judgments, it is now clear that, if the unlawful aid is declared compatible with the internal market, the aid itself need not be recovered; the benefit, however, that consists of the amount of the aid having been at the disposal of the beneficiary during the time between the granting of the aid and the positive decision of the Commission must be recovered from the beneficiary.

It is for the Member State to decide how the unlawful and incompatible aid measure is recovered. Recovery does not necessarily have to be in the form of a cash payment. A Member State is free to choose the means of fulfilling the recovery order, provided that the measures chosen do not adversely affect the scope and effectiveness of EU law.[62]

NOTES

1. Council Regulation (EC) 659/1999, O.J. 1999 L 83/1; the Commission issued an implementing Regulation, Commission Regulation (EC) 774/04, O.J. 2004 L 140/1.
2. Case C-199/06, *CELF* [2008] E.C.R. I-469.
3. Case 6/64, *Costa v. ENEL* [1964] E.C.R. 1141; Case C-39/94, *SFEI* [1996] E.C.R. I-3547, para. 39 et seq.
4. Case 6/64, *Costa v. ENEL* [1964] ECR 1141; Case C-39/94, *SFEI* [1996] E.C.R. I-3547, para. 39 et seq. Cf. also Case T-388/03, *Deutsche Post and DHL v. Commission* [2009] E.C.R. II-199 para. 87 et seq. [On appeal: Case C-148/09 P].
5. Case 301/87, *France v. Commission (Boussac)* [1990] E.C.R. I-307, para. 16.
6. Cf. Article 10 of the Procedural Regulation.
7. Cf. for instance, Case T-20/03, *KAHLA/Thüringen Porzellan GmbH v. Commission* [2008] E.C.R. II- 2305, para. 189 et seq., [On appeal, Case C-537/08 P].
8. Cases T-425/04, T-444/04, T-450/04 and T-456/04, T-425/04, T-444/04, T-450/04 and T-456/04, *France and others v. Commission*, judgment of 21 May 2010, para. 218, n.y.r. [on appeal: Case C-399/10P and C-401/10P].
9. O.J.199L83/1.ThisRegulationwasamendedseveraltimes.Theconsolidatedversioncanbe found at: <http://eur-lex.europa.eu/LexUriServ/LexUriServ.do?uri=CONSLEG:1999R 0659:20070101:EN:PDF>.
10. O.J. 2004 L 140/1.
11. Amended by Commission Regulation (EC) No. 1627/2006, O.J. 2006 L 302/10; Commission Regulation (EC) No. 1935/2006, O.J. 2006 L 407/1; Commission Regulation (EC) No. 271/2008, O.J. 2008 L 82/1; Commission Regulation (EC) No. 1147/2008, O.J. 2008 L 313/1, last amended by Commission Regulation (EC) No. 1125/2009, O.J. 2009 L 308/5. The consolidated version of the text can be found at: <http://eur-lex.europa.eu/LexUriServ/LexUriServ.do?uri=CONSLEG:2004R0794:200 90416:EN:PDF>.
12. Case T-198/01, *Technische Glaswerke Ilmenau* [2004] E.C.R. II-2717, para. 193.
13. Cf. Ortiz Blanco 2006: 22.82.
14. Cf. Bartosch 2007: 474.

15. The statutory State guarantees in favour of public banks in Germany were a prominent example; they were abolished only in 2005. See Commission, State Aid E-10/2000, Decision of 27 March 2002 – *Anstaltslast und Gewährträgerhaftung* (State Guarantees for public credit institutions in Germany), cf. O.J. 2002 C 150/7.
16. See O.J. 2008 L 90/7.
17. Case T-128/98, *Aéroports de Paris* [2000] E.C.R. II-3929, para. 120.
18. OJ 2004 L 140/1.
19. Case T-425/04, *France, France Télécom et al. v. Commission* [2010] judgment of 21 May 2010, n.y.r., para. 218.
20. If a Member State withdraws a notification because it considers the measure not to constitute a State aid, but the Commission disagrees, it is free to continue the investigation. Due to the withdrawal of the notification, the measure would then be a non-notified aid, and the procedure continued as a 'CP' (cas présumé), if no aid has yet been granted, or as a 'NN' (non-notifié) procedure.
21. Case T-375/04, *Scheucher-Fleisch et al. v. Commission* [2009] E.C.R. II-4155, para. 41.
22. Case T-20/03, *KAHLA/Thüringen Porzellan GmbH v. Commission* [2008] E.C.R. II-2305. [On appeal: Case C-537/08 P].
23. In this case the Member State had explained that the law would apply to certain categories of companies, which would not have included the beneficiary; the wording of the law, however, allowed the granting of the aid to the beneficiary.
24. Decisions on individual (*ad hoc*) aid do not pose the same problem, since the company will normally cooperate with the Member State, thus knows the details of the procedure, and is directly and individually concerned by the Decision, can appeal it if it contains unacceptable restrictions. Also, in case of an individual Decision, there is no doubt a company can rely on the principle of legal certainty and the principle of legitimate expectations regarding the contents of the Decision.
25. *Commission Notice on a Simplified Procedure for Certain Types of Aid*, O.J. 2009 C 136/3.
26. *Commission Notice on a Best Practices Code on the Conduct of State Aid Control Proceedings*, [2009] O.J. C 136/13.
27. Case 120/73, *Lorenz* [1973] E.C.R. 1471, para. 3 et. seq.
28. Cf. Article 5 of the Procedural Regulation.
29. Case C-99/98, *Austria v. Commission* [2001] E.C.R. I-1101, para. 61ff.
30. Cf. *Commission Notice on a Best Practices Code*, *loc. cit.*
31. Case T-73/98, *Prayon Rupel* [2001] E.C.R. II-867, para. 44.
32. Case T-73/98, *Prayon Rupel* [2001] E.C.R. II-867, para. 47 ; Case T-46/97, *SIC* [2000] E.C.R. II-2125 para. 71.
33. Cf. Case T-375/04, *Scheucher-Fleisch et al. v. Commission* [2009] E.C.R. II-4155, para. 69 et seq.
34. Cf. Article 6(1) of the Procedural Regulation.
35. Case C-47/91, *Italy v. Commission* [1992] E.C.R. I-4145/4162 para. 27 et seq. Case C-312/90, *Spain v. Commission* [1992] E.C.R. I-4117, para. 19 et seq.
36. CFI, Case T-332/06, *Alcoa Trasformazioni Srl v. Commission* [2009] E.C.R. II-29, para. 36. [On appeal: C -194/09].
37. Case T-198/91, *Technische Glaswerke Ilmenau* [2004] E.C.R. II-2717, para. 192; cf. Ortiz Blanco 2006: 22.82.
38. In exceptional cases, the Commission may refrain from the recovery, cf. Commission O.J. 2004 L 257/11 – France Télécom, where the Commission took the view that its novel approach declaring a mere press announcement by a French Minister to constitute a State aid was unforeseeable and that therefore, no recovery should be ordered. The Commission Decision has been annulled, General Court judgment of 21 May 2010, T-425/04, T-444/04, T-450/04 and T-456/04, *France and France Télécom v. Commission* n.yr. [On appeal: C-399/10 C-401/10].
39. Cf. O.J. 2000 L 165/25 – *Gooding Consumer Electronics Ltd.*
40. O.J. 2003 L 132/1 para. 73 ff. – *Olympic Airways.*

41. O.J. 2008 L 143/31 – *Arcelor Huta Warszawa.*
42. Cf. Commission [2008] O.J. L 239/12 – Automobile Craiova, which took only four and a half months from the opening of the formal procedure to the final decision, due to extreme political pressure, intense cooperation between all parties, and the willingness of the Commission to conclude the procedure quickly so as not to jeopardise the privatisation process.
43. Case C-301/87, *France v. Commission* [1990] E.C.R. I-307. Cf. also Case C-142/87, *Belgium v. Commission* [1990] E.C.R. I-959.
44. Case C-368/04, *Transalpine Ölleitung* [2006] E.C.R. I-9957, paras 38 and 44; Joined Cases C-261/01 and C-262/01, *Van Calster and Cleeren* [2003] E.C.R. I-12249, para. 75; Case C-295/97, *Piaggio* [1999] E.C.R. I-3735, para. 34.
45. *Commission Notice on the Determination of the Applicable Rules for the Assessment of Unlawful State Aid*, O.J. 2002 C 119/22.
46. Cf. Case T-354/05, *Télévision française 1 SA (TF1) v. Commission* [2009] ECR II-471, para. 60 et seq.
47. OJ 2005 L 120/21, annulled by the General Court, Case T-68/05, *Aker Warnow Werft* [2009] E.C.R. II-355.
48. Consistent jurisprudence of the European Courts, cf. for instance, C-214/07, *Commission v. France* [2008] E.C.R. I-8357; Case T-75/03, *Banco Comercial des Açores* [2009] E.C.R. II-143.
49. *Commission v. France*, ibid.
50. Ibid.
51. Case T-81to 83/07, *Jan Rudolf Maas et al v. Commission (KG Holding)* [2009] E.C.R. II-5409. [On appeal: Case C-9/06P *Salazar Brier v. Commission* [2007] E.C.R. I-10357.]
52. Case C-39/06, *Commission v. Germany* [2008] E.C.R. I-93.
53. Cases T-230/01 to T-232/01 and T-267/01 to T-269/01, *Territorio Histórico de Álava* [2009] E.C.R. II-139.
54. Case T-75/03, *Banco Comercial des Açores* [2009] E.C.R. II-143.
55. Case C-419/06, *Commission v. Greece* [2008] E.C.R. I-27.
56. Case T-254/00, *Hotel Cipriani v. Commission* [2008] E.C.R. II 3269 [on appeal: C-71/09 C-73/09 C-76/09].
57. Case C-1/2009, *CELF v. SIDE* judgment of 11 March 2010, n.y.r.
58. Case T-273/06 and 297/06, *ISD Polska and IUD v. Commission* [2009] E.C.R. II-2181 [on appeal: Case C-369/09P].
59. Case T-288/06R, *Regionalny Fundusz Gospodarczy* [2009] E.C.R. II-101.
60. Cf. Case C-520/07 P, *Commission v MTU* [2009] E.C.R. I-8495; Case T-291/06, *Operator ARP v Commission* [2009] E.C.R. II-2275; Case T-445/05, *Assogestioni* [2009] E.C.R. II-289.
61. Case C-199/06, *CELF* [2008] E.C.R. I-469; confirmed by Case C-384/07, *Wienstrom.* [2008] E.C.R. I-10393.
62. Case C-369/07, *Commission v. Hellenic Republic* [2009] E.C.R. I-5703.

REFERENCES

Abbamonte, G. (1997), 'Competitors' rights to challenge illegally granted aid and the problem of conflicting decisions in the field of competition law', *European Competition Law Review* , **17:4**, 87.
Bartosch, A. (2007), 'The Procedural Regulation in State aid matters, a case for profound reform', *European State Aid Law*, **3**, 474–483.
Dashwood, A. (1975), 'Control of State aids in the EEC. Prevention and cure under Article 93', *Common Market Law Review*, **12**, 43.
Flynn, L. (2007), 'Procedures under Articles 88 and 89', *Butterworths Competition Law*, London: Lexis Nexis, Ch.6.

Hancher, L., T. Ottervanger, J.P. Slot (2006), *EC State Aids*, 3 edn, London: Sweet and Maxwell.

Lever, J. (2003), 'The EC State aid regime, the need for reform', in A. Biondi P. Eeckhout and J. Flynn, (eds), *The Law of State Aid in the European Union*, Oxford: OUP.

Matthias-Werner, A. (2006), 'The Procedural Regulation – is the time ripe for a revision?', in M. Sanchez-Rydelski, (ed), *The EC State Aid Regime*, Cambridge: Cameron May/CUP, 631.

Mederer, W. (1996), 'Future of State aid control', *Competition Policy Newsletter*, **3**, 12.

Ortiz Blanco, L.(2006), *European Community Competition Procedure, Part IV*, Oxford: OUP.

Rosenfeld, K. (2000), *Das Verfahrensrecht der gemeinschaftlichen Beihilfenaufsicht*, Berlin: Nomos.

Roth QC, P. and V. Rose (eds) (2008), *Bellamy & Child: European Community Law of Competition*, Oxford: OUP ch. 15.

Sinnaeve, A. and J.P. Slot, (1999), 'The new regulation on State aid procedures', *Common Market Law Review*, **36:6**, 1153.

Sinnaeve, A. (2007), 'State aid procedures, developments since the entry into force of the Procedural Regulation', *Common Market Law Review*, **38:7**, 965–1033.

16 Judicial review of Commission Decisions in State aid

Herwig C.H. Hofmann and Alessandro Morini

This chapter focuses on annulment procedures brought against Commission Decisions under Article 263 TFEU.[1] Reflecting the rapid evolution of key aspects of this litigation, it illustrates and contextualises the background and origins of the problems the case law attempts to address (I) and proposes paths to simplification and rationalisation of the developments of the past years with regard to standing (II) as well as the extent of judicial review (III)[2] before drawing general conclusions for the future role of general principles of law (IV) in this area. The chapter shows the increasing importance of information-related general principles of law in this field.

I. BACKGROUND

Judicial review is an essential aspect of ensuring accountability of the exercise of public power as well as legality of administrative activity, especially, firstly, given that State aid Decisions are often taken in politically highly sensitive areas affecting *inter alia* Member State tax systems, regional policies or incentives for social developments, to name just a few. The importance of effective judicial review arises also, secondly, from the fact that in State aid cases the Commission decides in the context of an investigative and not an adjudicative procedure, requiring comparatively strict oversight over the exercise of far reaching powers conferred on it.

Judicial review in State aid cases, however, takes place in the context of asymmetric information. By nature of the procedural arrangements, the Commission will be made aware by a Member State only of the main issues of an intended aid but an economic and a legal assessment of such planned aid requires near full information about the conditions and the potential effect on the markets. Judicial review of Commission Decisions, in turn is based on Courts obtaining sufficient information about these factors and the Commission Decision in response to it, in order to exercise its review. The more intense the degree of review with regards to the facts and law of the case, the more a Court will require detailed information about the background and motivation of a Commission Decision.

In State aid law, limitations on available information are intensified through a procedure favouring the relation between the Commission and the Member States. Provision of information through Member States may be partial and biased, since a Member State generally has an interest in a specific outcome of the procedure.[3] Private parties such as beneficiaries, their competitors and trade associations are virtually excluded from the preliminary phase of investigation. They enjoy procedural rights, which allow them to learn about the details of an investigation and submit their views only in the context of an in-depth investigation under Article 108(2) TFEU.[4] Member States are thus initially the most valuable source of information for the Commission, which in the first phase is deprived of the contribution of private parties.

In summary, many of the concrete problems in the area of the State aid litigation arise from problems related to the gathering and use of information. The issue of information re-appears throughout this chapter as a central theme in considerations on understanding and improving procedural provisions and judicial review in the State aid arena.

II. LITIGATION AGAINST WHAT BY WHOM? ACTS AND STANDING

In State aid litigation against institutions, standing problems are rife. The reason is the very definition of Article 263, fourth paragraph TFEU requiring that any non-privileged actor display that an individual act or regulatory act which does not require further implementing measures is of direct and individual concern to them.[5] To be able to navigate the complexities of judicial review of Commission Decisions in State aid, two major preliminary aspects have to be understood: first, the question what kind of acts or non-acts can be subject to an action for annulment. This is becoming increasingly difficult to discern given the capacity of measures which are not formally Decisions to affect individuals. Second, the question of standing in which the ever-increasing complexity of the case law must be critically reviewed with regard to legal certainty.[6] We shall address these two related aspects separately.

II.i Acts Subject to Judicial Review

Many of the problems in reviewability of acts and standing stem from the distinction in State aid procedure between preliminary examination and formal investigation. Whilst the first of these phases aims at allowing the Commission to form a *prima facie* opinion on the case, the second actually recognises the rights of third parties, thereby having the effect also of widening the breadth of information to the Commission.[7] Given the formal absence of procedural rights in the phase of preliminary examination and the almost total lack of information obligations in favour of third parties,[8] the major issues in this area appear to stem from Decisions refusing the opening of a formal investigation. Accordingly, the position of complainants,[9] mainly competitors to the beneficiary of the aid, is particularly weak. This remarkably contrasts with the vital role played by these parties within the procedure.[10]

II.i.a.   Opening and closing of procedural steps

The developments of protection of rights of individuals in various steps of the procedure, especially closing a procedure prior to the opening of a formal investigation, have always been problematic. Even before the adoption of Regulation 659/1999,[11] State aid investigation procedures were defined as taking place more or less exclusively between the Commission and Member States. The CJEU was instrumental in defining this position, for example, in *Sytraval* in which it held that 'decisions adopted by the Commission in the field of State aid,' were addressed exclusively to the Member States.[12] A consequence of this is that in the field of State aid the Decision addressed to a Member State could not be considered as an implicit rejection of a complaint by an individual. Although the CJEU thereby confirmed *Plaumann,* requiring proof of direct and individual concern, its approach may be problematic in view of the *IBM* case law.[13] Under the latter test, acts adopted by the EU institutions are reviewable, if they are binding on and capable of affecting the interests of the applicant by bringing about a distinct change in his legal position. In order to determine the capacity of an act to be reviewed, the EU judicature looks at the substance of a contested act, in lieu of the form, as well as the intention of its author.[14]

Under Regulation 659/1999, the situation has become more complex. For example, the Commission is required to examine, without delay, the information made available by a complaint,[15] and conclude the preliminary examination by means of a Decision.[16] This has prompted the EU judicature to apply the *IBM* doctrine in order to ascertain the nature of the act adopted by the Commission to conclude the phase of preliminary examination. Consistently, the General Court in *Deutsche Bahn*[17] has reviewed the acts addressed to the complainant examining whether the Commission adopted *a reasoned and definitive position* on the State measure, in conformity with the requirements of *IBM.*[18] The crucial point in the reasoning of the General Court is that where the Commission had *expressly* held in a letter addressed to the complainant that the State measure did not constitute aid, this would imply that the Commission had actually taken a Decision clearing the measure in the sense of Article 4(2) of Regulation 659/99, and that such Decision is contained in the letter made subject to judicial review. In its case law, the General Court also underlines the exceptional nature of the reviewability of the letters addressed to complainants, explaining that review of these was necessary in case of the absence of a Decision addressed to the Member State.[19] Should the Commission have adopted one, the complainant would be required to challenge the Commission Decision directed at the Member State and not the letter of information.[20] Where therefore an explicit decision towards the Member State exists, a letter to the complainant should be considered as a simple letter communicating that, according to the available information, there are no sufficient grounds for the Commission to take a view on the issue.[21]

While such interpretation of the procedural law in State aids appears to be deeply influenced by the configuration of the State aid procedure as taking place between Commission and Member States, it does not seem to fully comply with the actual rationale designed by the European lawmaker in Regulation 659/1999. The obligation enshrined in Article 10(1) of Regulation 659/99 appears to be focused on a precise and strict duty of diligent investigation,[22] which requires the Commission to thoroughly review and carefully analyse all information provided by the complainant, as well as by all other sources.[23] Similarly, Article 13(1) of Regulation 659/99 urges the institution to conclude its assessment by means of Decision.[24] The two provisions appear to be the poles of a decision-making mechanism based on an adequate stream of information, whereby complainants occupy an important position as sources. In light of this, there does not seem to be much room for a conclusion of the procedure other than by a Decision under Article 4 of Regulation 659/99.

More recently, in this context, the CJEU (in *Athinaïki Techniki*) seems to have considered that preliminary examination must in any case be concluded by a Decision of the Commission. By acknowledging the reviewability of the refusal of the Commission to open a formal investigation, the Court also appears to consider that such a Decision may infringe upon the rationale of the State aid procedure. The rules governing the treatment of complaints, as provided in Articles 10(1) and 13(1) of Regulation 659/1999 actually aim at ensuring that the Commission examines and takes a Decision on the allegedly unlawful State measure, thereby clearing the aid, or, where necessary, opening a formal investigation over it.[25] The logic springing from such provisions reflects the awareness of the risk that the determination not to investigate in-depth the State measure might actually entail that unlawful new aid is granted, as a consequence of the Commission's failure to properly assess the information in its possession. Therefore, given the possibility that the State measure concerned actually is State aid, in view of the Court, the Commission could not close the examination by simply informing the complainant of the lack of all the necessary information to take a Decision. Conversely, the Commission is called to actively cooperate with the complainant, in order to reduce such informational gap. Thus, where the information provided by a complainant is insufficient for the Commission to take a view on an issue, it would be required to invite the complainant to supply additional comments.[26] According to the Court, such obligation results from Article 20(2) of Regulation 659/99. This approach overturns previous case law interpreting Article 20(2) as allowing the Commission to close the procedure by means of a simple communication.

In conclusion, the finding of such a new obligation can be seen as aiming at reinforcing the stream of information initiated by the submission of the complaint, in order to put the institution in the position to adopt a Decision definitively clearing the State measure or, where serious doubts exist as to the compatibility of the Decision, opening formal investigations. Importantly, the Court appears to be fully aware that the weak position of complainants during preliminary examinations could affect their role as sources of precious information for the procedure.[27] Therefore, in *Athinaïki Techniki* the Court consolidated the position of complainants by acknowledging that these, as parties concerned, 'have a right to be *associated with* [the proceedings] in an adequate manner taking into account the circumstances of the case at issue'.[28] Even if such statement does not entail the recognition of any status during preliminary examinations, undoubtedly it represents an important step forward in the consideration of third parties' rights in that phase.

II.i.b.   Old and new aid

The construction of the State aid procedure so far described appears to apply in principle only to cases where information has been adopted on allegedly unlawful new aid. As the General Court clearly stated in *NDSHT*,[29] Article 13(1) of Regulation 659/99 actually prescribes that the Commission adopts a Decision only with respect to new aid, thereby excluding existing aid from the application of these procedural requirements.[30] The role of complainants as information suppliers in the course of State aid proceedings is incompatible with the discretion the Commission generally enjoys when handling existing aid.[31] In turn, such a different attitude towards existing aid is justified in the light of the fact that it is presumed that the aid already has been assessed on the basis of all relevant information.

However understandable this distinction on the legal point may be, the reasoning of the General Court does not seem consistent with the judgments rendered in the field of unlawful new aid. Firstly, the fact that, upon a complaint the Commission qualifies the State measure as existing aid appears to be a reasoned and definitive position of the type envisaged in *Deutsche Bahn*.[32] Nothing seems to oppose application of the latter judgment to the facts of *NDSHT*.

Secondly, the approach of the General Court appears particularly restrictive where compared to the attitude shown by the CJEU in *Athinaïki Techniki*. The reasons underlying the judgment in the latter case actually appear to be fully applicable to the facts in *NDSHT*: a broader involvement of the complainant in the procedure could contribute decisively to improve the stream of information. This, in turn, would help in clarifying whether the measure is existing or illegal new aid. The application of the reasoning in *Athinaïki Techniki* does not appear inconsistent with the qualification of the State measure as existing aid. Consistently, the General Court could have urged the Commission to adopt a proactive stance, thereby requiring further information to the complainant. Conversely, however, the General Court endorsed the traditional interpretation of Article 20(2) of Regulation 659/99, which allows the Commission to close preliminary investigations for not enjoying all the information necessary to take a view on the issue. This conclusion is in contrast with the CJEU approach in *Athinaïki Techniki,* which, before the General Court's decision in *NDSHT,*gave quite a different interpretation of the aforementioned provision.[33] If the distinction between new and existing aid can partially justify the different outcome, it does not appear to allow for such a different interpretation of a provision of the EU legislation. This clearly contrasts with the principle of legal certainty, which the General Court itself appears to carefully respect in this area of law.[34]

Thirdly, the approach of the General Court regarding existing aid, as expressed in *NDSHT*, appears also to be not compatible with that of the CJEU on the same issue. In *CIRFS*, for example, the Court held that the decision to classify an aid as existing aid, thereby taking the view that the aid was not subject to the prior notification procedure provided for by Article 108(3) TFEU, is a final refusal to initiate the procedure provided for by Article 108(2) TFEU.[35] On this basis, it rejected the Commission's argument qualifying the act as a preparatory measure, which, as such, could not have been subject to judicial review.[36]

II.i.c.   Reviewability of informative acts
Informative acts exist in many forms under the title of: Guidelines, circulars, disciplines and others. Information tools have gained great

significance for national authorities.[37] The General Court has confirmed the Commission's competence to adopt such guidelines, as 'such measures reflect the Commission's desire to publish directions on the approach it intends to follow'.[38] Such acts have a particular importance in the area of State aid, in that they codify the rules evolved in day-to-day practice relating to the exercise by the Commission of the powers conferred on it by Article 108 TFEU.[39] This does not make them generally subject to judicial review in themselves. They may indirectly be reviewed through individual cases.[40] The situation will differ, as the example of *CIRFS* shows, where the discipline was not simply a unilateral tool established by the Commission but was more akin to an agreement concluded between the Commission and certain Members States. The Court concluded from this that the 'discipline,' which was contained in a letter sent by the Commission to the Member States, had binding legal effects.[41] Where 'the rules set out in the discipline and accepted by the Member States themselves have the effect, *inter alia*, of withdrawing from certain aid falling within its scope the authorisation previously granted and hence of classifying it as new aid and subjecting it to the obligation of prior notification'.[42] Information plays the key part in understanding this reasoning. While a binding agreement such as that in *CIRFS* can be subject to judicial review, mere unilateral information about future intentions of the Commission cannot.

II.ii.   Standing

While privileged actors like Member States generally do not face any specific difficulties with regard to standing,[43] individual parties (such as beneficiaries and competitors to the beneficiary) or sub-national legal persons (regions, local bodies and authorities), have to prove their direct and individual concern. The very specific relation between the Commission and the Member States, who are officially the parties to a State aid procedure, poses its specific problems to individuals with respect to standing. Individual concern by a private individual is, in the case law of the Courts, generally accepted in two sets of circumstances: either, where a Commission Decision affects them by reason of certain attributes which are particular to the individual, or, where circumstances differentiate and distinguish an individual in the same way as a person would be when being the direct addressee of a Decision.[44] Particular criteria have been developed in the area of State aid review in order to adapt this general approach to the peculiar substantial and procedural features of the policy area. State aid case law on standing often tends to focus on the evaluation of the economic impact of the proposed aid.

II.ii.a.   The position of beneficiaries of aid and of competitors

Sketched in broad strokes, recipients of aid are considered to be substantially affected by the Decision adopted declaring the aid incompatible at the end of an Article 108 (2) TFEU procedure.[45] As already observed, beneficiaries also enjoy standing with respect to decisions to open formal investigations, insofar as the examination concerns unlawful new aid, in which case the extension of the standstill obligation[46] entails substantial effects on the economic sphere of the aid recipients.[47] On the contrary, a Decision opening a formal investigation concerning existing aid does not entail any substantial change in their situation, because here the standstill obligation actually does not apply. Consequently, beneficiaries must show a specific interest to challenge it. Finally, beneficiaries of aid generally do not enjoy standing vis-à-vis Decisions not to open a formal investigation, as such a Decision entails the grant of the aid. However, in the event that the State measure was qualified as aid, though compatible, beneficiaries might be interested in furthering the proceedings, in order to obtain a decision that the Commission completely clears the measure from the qualification of aid. In this case, beneficiaries are required to prove that they have a vested and present interest in the proceedings.[48]

The position of competitors appears weaker than that of beneficiaries. For the purpose of standing, it may be more difficult for competitors both to prove their competitive position and to show that they are individually concerned by a Commission's Decision clearing the State measure. The burden of the *Plaumann* case law would be particularly difficult to bear during the phase of preliminary examination due to the absence of procedural rights of complainants and the extremely limited information available. The lack of information of the complainant appears to be particularly severe. Information accessible to the complaining competitor is necessarily limited to the elements which have been communicated by and exchanged with the Commission in the dialogue which followed the submission of the complaint. In principle, the State aid procedure does not provide for any form of publication of either notified aid or the carrying out of preliminary examinations, subsequent to the submission of a complaint. Decisions not to open formal investigations are published only as a summary notice,[49] while the complainant enjoys a right to be informed of such a Decision.[50] Upon acknowledgment of such weakness, the Court, in the case law *Cook* and *Matra*, has elaborated a more lenient test for the standing of competitors vis-à-vis Decisions not to open formal investigations.[51] Accordingly, competitors (as well as other third parties) may enjoy standing against Decisions not to open a procedure under Article 108(2) TFEU, insofar as these can prove to be concerned parties according to the meaning of Article 108(2) TFEU.[52] Competitors may thus avoid the burdensome test of *Plaumann* and challenge the Decision not to give suite to the proceedings, where they claim the existence of serious difficulties as to the qualification of the measure. The more lenient *Cook* and *Matra* test appears therefore as a remedy found against the peculiar information constraints that a complainant has to bear in the preliminary examination phase.

Crucially, the reasoning laying down the construction of such a lenient standing test is deeply rooted in the acknowledgement that the complainant is not in the position to be fully aware of the particular features of the case. Thus, the complainant could not be able to substantiate why its position is individually concerned *vis-à-vis* the Decision.[53] The test elaborated in *Cook* and *Matra* is thus based on such acknowledgement of the difficulties of obtaining information, which the complainant itself has to bear. Furthermore, this appears to respond to the same logics of the (already described) case law on reviewability of the Commission's Decisions. The lenient test for standing actually allows for the judicial review of the Commission Decision not to look in-depth into the State measure. By means of the application against such Decision, the Courts are able to assess the existence of serious difficulties as to the compatibility of the measure with the common market.[54]

II.ii.b.   The complex role of the parties' pleas for the definition of standing
Notwithstanding the undeniable goodwill of the Court, the application of the *Cook* and *Matra* test for standing has shown itself to be complex. This is true especially vis-à-vis the relationship between the specific requests of the parties, as expressed in the pleas, and the determination of the subject-matter of the application. The subject-matter is actually defined by the specific pleas that the parties submit in their applications for annulment. In general, the parties are obliged to forward pleas supporting their case and to select the arguments to support the pleas. However, the subject-matter of an application for the annulment of a Decision ending the phase of preliminary examination is strictly influenced by the particular nature of the Decision challenged.[55]

Even if the Commission is substantially called to carry out the same evaluations required in the phase of formal investigations, the examination is only preliminary, that is, aimed at letting the institution form a *prima facie* opinion.[56] The Commission is actually urged to open the phase of formal investigation where there are doubts as to the compatibility of the measure with the common/internal market, unless no such doubts are raised as to the fact that the measure is not an aid, or its compatibility with the common/internal market.[57] Thus, the subject-matter of an application for the annulment of a Decision not to open formal investigations is necessarily limited to the review of the potential existence of serious difficulties to determine the compatibility of the aid measure. As a consequence, the main purpose of the parties in challenging such a Decision should be no more than to obtain the opening of a formal investigation, in order to be put in a position to exert the procedural rights conferred upon them by Article 108(2) TFEU.[58]

Therefore, the specific requests presented by the parties in their application against a Decision not to open a formal investigation must aim at proving that serious difficulties exist as to the compatibility of the aid, thereby compelling the Commission to look more thoroughly into the State measure.

A look to the case law shows that the requests of the parties are generally broader than such a definition of the subject-matter, as they include pleas ranging from the claim of infringement of the procedural rights, to issues of substance, such as the application of Article 108(1) and (3) TFEU.[59] Such a wide range of pleas is comprehensible, given that the Commission clears the aid with a Decision similar in content to the Decision adopted at the end of formal investigations. However, as the subject-matter of the dispute is limited, the scope of the judicial review also will be restricted to verifying the existence of serious difficulties and ought not to be extended to a full review of the issues of substance. This should actually take place only once a decision has been adopted following the opening of formal investigations. Otherwise, the Courts would go beyond the determination of the existence of serious difficulties and review the Commission's assessment in light of Article 108(1) and (3) TFEU. Thereby they would effectively replace the potential future Commission decision with their own. This was clearly stated in the Opinion of Advocate General Mengozzi of 17 July 2008 in *British Aggregates Association*:

> [there is] a need to ensure that, where an action is brought by a person who is simply relying on his status as a concerned party within the meaning of [Article 108(2) TFEU], the [Union] judicature's review of the contested decision does not go beyond what is needed to ensure that the procedural rights conferred by that provision are complied with. That would be the case where, rather than merely determining whether the conditions justifying non-initiation of the formal investigation procedure were satisfied – namely the absence of serious difficulties in classifying the measure as aid and/or in assessing its compatibility with the common market – the [Union] judicature were to establish the existence of State aid (or of individual elements of State aid which the Commission had found to be lacking), or to find that the conditions relied upon by the Commission, in declaring the aid compatible with the Treaty, were not satisfied. In such circumstances, the applicant would in fact secure not only initiation of the formal investigation procedure, where appropriate, but the additional result that the Commission would be bound by those

findings on the part of the [Union] judicature and the substance of the decision to be adopted on conclusion of that procedure would, in part at least,
be predetermined; that is to say, the applicant would have brought about the
predetermination of a decision which it would not have been entitled to challenge solely by virtue of its status as a 'concerned party' within the meaning of
[Article 108 (2) TFEU].[60]

In order for the lenient test to apply, the CJEU actually therefore
requires that the parties *expressly* aim at securing the procedural rights
provided for in Article 108 (2) TFEU, thereby obtaining the opening of
formal investigations. This implies that the *locus standi* in State aid cases
under Article 263 TFEU is therefore dependent on the pleadings of the
applicant. Accordingly, these could gain standing only where, in the
application, they expressly plead for the protection of their procedural
rights.[61]

One consequence of this stance is that, where no pleas on this point are
formulated in the application, the Courts could not *construe* the other
ones advanced by the parties as they were conceived to obtain the opening
of formal investigations.[62] The CJEU therefore aims at determining the
subject-matter by channelling the formulation of the pleas with express
references to the protection of procedural rights. This appears to have
clarified the somewhat inconsistent case law of the General Court, which
has sometimes rejected applications lacking any such plea as inadmissible,[63] while on another occasion granting it on the basis of a teleological
reading of the other pleas.[64]

A second consequence results from the specific relationship existing
between the different pleas advanced by the parties. In particular, if applicants advance grounds both on infringement of procedural rights and
on substance, two different tests appear to apply in order to determine
their admissibility. Standing in respect of substantial grounds follows the
Plaumann test, whereas the more lenient *Cook* and *Matra* test applies to
pleas relating to procedural rights.[65] Consideration of the already mentioned lack of information of third parties necessary to meet the test of
Plaumann is evident from the fact that, should demonstration of the individual concern fail, standing could be granted under the *Cook* and *Matra*
test.[66]

Maintaining the parallel tests for standing of *Cook* and *Matra*, and
Plaumann responds to the EU judicature's intention to limit the subject-
matter in preliminary examinations. As the already well-stressed lack of
sufficient information renders it difficult to meet the *Plaumann* test for
standing, the parties are much more likely to challenge the Commission's
Decision arguing infringement of procedural rights. This will entail the
admissibility of the application and, at the same time, the limitation of

proceedings to the assessment of the existence of serious difficulties in the determination of the compatibility of the State measure.

Importantly, the CJEU has clarified that failure to meet the *Plaumann* test does not rule out the application of *Cook* and *Matra*.[67] In accordance with this, should the applicant fail the test in *Plaumann*, it will always be possible to obtain standing under the more lenient test in *Cook* and *Matra*. This, however, still leaves open the question of the relationship between the different pleas presented by the parties. In particular, it is not clear whether failure to meet *Plaumann* should bring the courts to automatically drop the pleas on substance. Recent case law of the General Court, for example in *Kronoply,* seems to indicate that although failure to meet *Plaumann* implies the inadmissibility of pleas on merits, the latter could nonetheless be used by the EU judicature in order to determine the subsistence of serious difficulties in determining the compatibility of the aid with the common market thus warranting the opening of the second phase.[68]

This case law raises the question of a lack of consistency, and even of equity in the treatment of complainants, as based on the different requests they advance in their pleas. If preserving the consistency of the subject-matter of the application, while, at the same time, granting applicants a lenient standing test, constitutes a reasonable ground to frame the *Cook* and *Matra* case law, such choice also implies a heavier burden on applicants. In particular, applicants' lawyers must actually be very careful in shaping the application as, under the current case law, failure to claim infringement of procedural rights practically implies the obligation to satisfy the stricter *Plaumann* test. Furthermore, as Advocate General Sharpston has rightly pointed out, it is difficult to see how an applicant could avoid being drawn into arguments about the merits of a Decision:

> [. . .] when seeking to show that there were still serious difficulties remaining in the Commission's initial assessment of the aid in issue (. . .). It is all too easy for them to slip and find that they are either trapped by the stricter *Plaumann* test, or that they have not done enough to satisfy the Court that there were indeed procedural errors in the decision they wish to contest.[69]

II.ii. c. Legal position of an applicant

As to what more precisely concerns the test enshrined in *Plaumann*, and applied by the CJEU to verify the standing of applicants advancing pleas on substance, the applicant must,[70] in general, demonstrate that its legal position is affected. The beneficiaries of aid schemes have *locus standi* where they are the actual beneficiaries of the aid in question.

It may appear at first sight that in State aid cases brought by competitors, the Court has been comparatively lenient with respect to the standing requirements of the applicant's legal position being affected. Instead the focus seems to have developed towards giving more weight to procedural and economic considerations than to the more dogmatic definition of direct and individual concern applied in other policy areas.[71] In particular, competitors affected only by their competitive relationship to a recipient of aid must not only demonstrate that their market position as competitor is affected in some distant way, but corroborate that the market position was 'substantially' affected by demonstrating the 'magnitude and prejudice' of the aid 'to its market position.'[72] This does not yet answer the question to whether any type of actual or potential competitive relationship between the recipient of an aid and a third party might be sufficient to grant standing against a Decision.

The case law of the CJEU confirms that the competitive relationship is the criterion also to be applied to parties who had been involved in the procedures during a second phase in-depth review of a proposed aid, mentioning explicitly 'the persons, undertakings or associations whose interests might be affected by the grant of the aid, in particular competing undertakings and trade associations'.[73] A competitor will then have standing if he played an active role in the procedure, provided that his market position is significantly affected by the aid which is the subject of the contested Decision.[74]

The case law since *Cofaz* has clarified that the competitive relationship needs to be qualified to fulfil the criteria of individual concern under Article 263(4) TFEU. The mere fact that a contested Decision may have an effect on the competitive relationship is in itself not sufficient even if the party had been participating in a formal investigation.[75] The claimant additionally has to show itself to be individually concerned in a way similar to an addressee of a Decision.[76] Individual concern will be denied if the position of the applicant in the relevant market is not substantially affected by the aid in question.[77] Several factors can be identified in the case law as being relevant in that respect. First, the Court will have to analyse the market situation in question. Only an analysis of the overall market situation will, in its view, allow demonstration of a substantial adverse effect on a competitor's position. It cannot, the CJEU states, be 'simply a matter of the existence of certain factors' indicating a decline in the commercial or financial performance of one competitor due to the aid granted to another.[78]

The overall analysis of the market will consist *inter alia* of factors such as the number of producers which are in competition to another, the smaller the number, the more likely the effect. In *Lenzing,* for example, the Court granted standing finding that the relevant viscose market was characterised by 'a very small number of producers and by serious production overcapacity' increasing the significance of the distortive effect of an aid granted to one of the few producers in the market.[79] In *ARE* on the other hand, an association of small businesses and former land owners, despite having actively participated in a formal investigation, could not show to be individually concerned due to the competitive situation they were in. The Court found that a very large number of competitors, in fact, 'all farmers in the EU' could be regarded as competitors of the beneficiaries of the land acquisition scheme' applied under German law.[80] Similarly, in *Italy and Sardegna* the Court held that a company could not contest 'a Commission decision prohibiting a sectoral aid scheme if it is concerned by that decision solely by virtue of belonging to the sector in question and being a potential beneficiary of the scheme'.[81]

The same reasoning applies to standing by associations, which are 'as a rule, entitled to bring an action for annulment against a final Decision of the Commission in matters of State aid only if the undertakings which it represents or some of those undertakings themselves have *locus standi* or if it can prove an interest of its own'. In *Territorio Histórico de Álava* the Court stated that:

> the adoption of a broad interpretation of the right of associations to intervene is intended to facilitate assessment of the context of such cases whilst avoiding multiple individual interventions which would compromise the effectiveness and proper course of the procedure.[82]

Since standing is to the benefit of the individual claiming it, the burden of proof falls onto third parties to show the individual effect in view of the market situation in the concrete case. All relevant information has therefore to be placed before the Court for evaluation.

II.ii.d.   Overall remarks on standing and reviewability of acts

The construction of the State aid procedure as a procedure between the Commission and Member States appears to internalise some peculiarities of State aid control which date back to the period preceding the adoption of Regulation 659/1999. First, the identification of reviewable acts in principle covers Decisions addressed to Member States concerning State measures.[83] Second, according to Article 108 TFEU, third parties could enjoy procedural rights only once, and if a formal investigation is opened. This in principle imposed the heavy burden of the *Plaumann* test for standing to actions for annulment of decisions clearing the State measure at the end of the preliminary examination.[84] In State aid procedure, third parties are actually considered as mere sources of information[85] and do not enjoy the status of parties in the procedure. Even the exercise of procedural rights, which follows the opening of formal investigations, is conceived as a means principally to ensure the full stream of information.[86]

Such shortcomings in the construction of the procedure appeared to directly impact upon the function of third parties as information providers, reducing the participation of the latter in the procedure and thereby substantively ostracising their potential contributions. As already observed, the outcome of this has been the uncertainty as to the identification of Commission Decisions, which prompted the Courts' searching for remedies against a Decision-making too lacking in crucial information. In light of this, the rebalancing of third parties' rights entailed by the solutions envisaged by the EU judicature is not exclusively to be considered as a purpose itself, but as a means to ensure the effective application of the relevant State aid rules. Importantly, this purpose appears to be common in all the case law on reviewability of acts and standing.[87]

It must be noted that, notwithstanding the praetorian nature of these advancements, the Courts have carefully stuck to the relevant rules and the precedents in case law, so as to ensure consistency with the existing procedural rules and continuity in the jurisprudence.[88] This comprehensible need for consistency is partly the basis of the great complexity which characterises the solutions elaborated by the Courts on these issues.[89] The admissibility criteria actually may differ depending on whether the Decision has been adopted before or after the opening of a formal investigation on the aid. The standing rights further depend on whether the plaintiff only challenges the non-opening of such an in-depth procedure or also the material grounds of a contested decision. This is a situation which is difficult to reconcile with the principle of legal certainty, a key element of the rule of law. Advocate General Jacobs stressed this point by stating that access to the Court is 'an area in which, more than in any other, the law must be clear and consistent'.[90] One of the many practical suggestions was made by Advocate General Bot in *Kronofrance* in which he suggested that the Court:

> make the case law more straightforward and consistent, by defining the conditions of the admissibility of actions brought against State aid decisions only in relation to the purpose of the action, not in relation to the pleas in law invoked in support of it.[91]

This in turn stresses how, notwithstanding its important achievements, judicial review in this particular area of State aid is not capable of fully replacing legislation in the field. It is time the legislation addressed these serious shortcomings of the procedural rules.[92]

III.   EXTENT OF JUDICIAL REVIEW

Judicial review of Commission's Decisions in State aid matters is a central tool of holding the Commission accountable. Judicial review, generally being a key notion to a system of checks and balances and maintaining the rule of law, is especially relevant in State aid matters, given the far reaching investigatory and adjudicatory decision-making powers bundled in the hands of the Commission.[93]

To what extent judicial review takes place vis-à-vis State aid Decisions by the Commission remains unclear when looking at Article 263 TFEU which merely contains a list of grounds of review: lack of competence, infringement of essential procedural requirements, infringement of the Treaty or of any rule of law in relation to its application or misuse of powers.[94] This list stems from the origins of Article 263 TFEU which was initially modelled on the *recours pour excès de pouvoir* before the French Conseil d'Etat. Since its founding days, the EU legal order has strongly evolved. What is left is the original wording which is now little but a shell since the notion of infringement of the Treaty of any rule deriving thereof virtually covers any case one might be able to think of.[95] In today's reality, the key term indicating whether European Courts will engage in only marginal review,[96] or more fully review a Commission Decision, is the notion of discretion.[97] This is not a static concept and in the recent dynamic case law of the Courts has developed quite complex distinctions and particularities, which will be subject of this part of the chapter.

III.i.   Delegation of Decision-making Powers and the Latest Definition of Discretion

Delegation of decision-making powers comes in many forms. Delegation of the most far reaching powers to the administration is often referred to as 'wide discretion.'[98] Discretion can be defined as the conferral of power to take decisions within legally defined limits regarding content and procedure. Key to this notion is that the administration is granted powers to decide about the substance of a certain policy[99] also with a view to future situations.[100] It exists where the broad nature of the provision applied or the analytical process required to subsume the facts of the case under such powers leaves room for either cognitive assessment to appreciate the relevance of factors or volititive assessment such as policy considerations.[101] These responsibilities are in the case law often addressed as matters of specific 'complexity'.[102] The notion of complexity is used as short-hand for the requirement to undertake a balancing decision taking into account a combination of various facts, evaluations of future developments of facts, as well as interests and rights.[103] Despite this, one might legitimately wonder why the fact that a matter contains economically or technically complex considerations should put it beyond the intellectual reach of a Court.[104] After all, one would expect judges to be generally capable of reviewing a Commission file and reconstructing complex situations and their legal assessment.[105] What lies behind the misleading term of 'complexity' is actually a separation of powers consideration that policy decisions or decisions based on specific non-legal expertise should be taken by the institutions which have a competence and the mandate to do so.[106]

Generally, the main consequence of the European Courts' finding that an institution enjoys broad discretion is that the so called 'manifest error of assessment' test is applicable.[107] This test indicates that instead of a full review, the Court will undertake a restricted degree of review under which it will confine itself 'to verifying whether the Commission complied with the relevant rules governing procedure and the statement of reasons, whether the facts on which the contested finding was based have been accurately stated and whether there has been any manifest error of assessment or a misuse of powers'.[108] However, on the other hand, where no discretionary powers have been delegated, that is, no conferral of expedient judgment or evaluation of policies has taken place, administrative decisions are submitted to full review.[109] This means that the Courts should fully review interpretations of the delegating act, the determination of the facts and the ultimate holding that the statutory prerequisites have been met, or not.

Although there is a tendency in the case law to declare either a marginal or a full review,[110] the case law of the European Courts in reality puts less emphasis on a clear definition of theoretical notions. Instead, it aims at adapting the degree of judicial review to the situation.[111] Thus the distinctions between wide discretion, discretion and non-discretion are fluid, and also depend on factors such as the question of whether the situation is one of legislative or administrative context. The true nature of the extent of judicial review is thus found not by the labelling as a power to be discretionary (or not) but as to the effective exercise of judicial review underlying a specific case.

In State aid cases, the identification of cases where discretion exists is especially relevant in the context of the definition of an aid under Article 107 TFEU. The Courts held that the concept of aid is objective, the test being whether a State measure confers an advantage on one or more particular undertakings.[112] Here, the Commission assesses situations in interpretation of the law without enjoying discretion, 'save for particular circumstances owing to the complex nature of the State intervention in question'.[113] These particular circumstances have been found by the case law for example in areas in which the Commission, in order to determine whether investment by the public authorities in the capital of an undertaking, constitutes State aid within the meaning of Article 107 TFEU, considers the so-called 'private investor test'.[114] Further, since in view of the Courts, in the evaluation of State aids under Article 107(3) TFEU and in some cases of Article 107(2) TFEU the Commission must rely on 'complex economic, social, regional and sectoral assessments,' and therefore its Decisions are to be covered by the notion of broad discretion.[115] In recent years, however, a tendency in the case law of the Courts can be observed to increase the level of its judicial review. Two contributing factors may be identified leading to this trend.

The first factor is the approach of reviewing administrative activity including discretionary activity through information-related general principles of law such as the duty of care.[116] Under this principle, an administrative decision-maker, even when granted wide discretion, must make the decision after considering all the relevant factors, including special circumstances affecting the matter.[117] The Courts review whether all of the 'relevant factors and circumstances of the situation the act was intended to regulate' have been taken into consideration, and whether the institution 'was able, without exceeding the bounds of the broad discretion it enjoys in the matter, to reach the conclusion' it had drawn.[118]

The duty of care is thus a principle allowing the Courts to review the *quantity* and to a certain degree the *quality* of the information taken into account by the Commission in a State aid Decision, as can be seen for example in *Sytraval*. The applicant in the case challenged the Commission's Decision rejecting a complaint about the grant of a loan and raise of capital to a competitor wholly controlled by the French State. The General Court had established an expansive reading of the obligations the Commission was under, by stating that under the duty of care, the Commission deciding whether to enter into a second phase of a State aid case, in which the complainant would have had a procedural role to present its arguments, had the 'automatic obligation to examine the objections which the complainant would certainly have raised if it had been given the opportunity of taking cognizance of that information.'[119] Upon appeal of this far reaching view, the CJEU confirmed this by finding that the Commission could be required 'to conduct a diligent and impartial examination of the complaint, which may make it necessary for it to examine matters not expressly raised by the complainant'.[120] Also, where the Commission has entered into a formal investigation, the duty of care obliges the administration maturing a case towards a final decision to conduct its investigation with 'the requisite care, seriousness and diligence so as to be able to assess with full knowledge of the case the factual and legal particulars submitted for its appraisal'.[121]

A second, related, tendency to expansion of judicial review arises by expanding the notion of reviewable 'facts' including applied economic theory, and thus reducing the margin of appreciation which has been submitted to only marginal or limited review.[122] This case law has been developed on the back of the duty to give reasons. In practice this means that where the Court finds in the analysis of the Commission, contradictions, insufficient analysis and substantiation of the relevant facts underlying the Decision,[123] even in an area giving rise to complex economic assessments, the Court will not 'refrain from reviewing the Commission's interpretation of information of an economic nature'.[124] As a consequence, the Courts distinguish the measure of judicial review from the verification of the quantity and quality of the evidence offered to meet the required standard of proof.

Combining these two approaches, the case law of the CJEU has identified several factors to be taken into account. These include first, to analyse whether the evidence relied on by the institution, was 'factually accurate, reliable and consistent'.[125] Secondly, the Court will have to review, whether the evidence presented by the institution in support of its Decision 'contains all the information which must be taken into account in order to assess a complex situation'. Finally, the institution must show that it is 'capable of substantiating the conclusions' drawn from this information.[126]

This standard of review allows the Courts to enter deeply into the reasoning of the Commission in a given administrative Decision, in this case, a State aid Decision. The standard of review is based on a complex obligation of gathering information and the use thereof. These information-related obligations are thus drawn from general principles of law which are upheld also in the presence of a wide margin of discretion of an institution. The CJEU refers to these as 'procedural guarantees of fundamental importance.'[127]

The application of the duty of care combined with far reaching obligations of reasoning have reduced the power of the notion of 'marginal review' to inflict limitations on the degree of judicial review of Commission Decisions in State aid matters. This is an appropriate approach of the Courts in view of the administrative nature of the Commission's exercise of discretionary powers.

Not surprisingly, the test applied by the Courts in review of the factual basis for the exercise of discretion under the duty of care, closely resembles the Courts' three-step test of proportionality. The obligation under the duty of care is linked to the principle of proportionality in so far as it imposes 'an obligation on Community institutions at least to satisfy themselves that the proposed measures are prima facie adequate to attain the legitimate aims pursued.'[128] The CJEU can thus use the information collected by the Commission for the judicial review of all three steps of the proportionality test: *first*, the capability of a measure to contribute to reaching a legitimate policy goal; *secondly*, the review whether the least onerous measure vis-à-vis the Member States' prerogatives and individual rights has been chosen; *thirdly,* the overall balancing for exclusion of extreme cases of imbalance between means and objectives. Given the constitutional basis of the proportionality principle under Article 5(4) TEU, it is a principle very well suited to limit the unwritten concept of the extent of discretionary powers of the Commission in administrative procedures.[129]

III.ii.   Self-limitation of discretion

An important and typical issue arising from the existence of discretionary power is the degree to which the administration can bind itself, in effect restricting its own discretionary range. The most important general principles of law leading to a self-limitation of administrative discretionary powers are the principles of equality, legal certainty and legitimate expectations. In the last few decades, the case law of the CJEU has developed these general principles of law as a question of self-limitation of discretion.[130] 'Self-binding' of the Commission can be discussed in at least five categories: *first*, by the establishment of a decisional practice of an administration, *second,* by creating (internal) administrative guidelines, *third,* by publishing the information that the Commission intends to follow a certain approach and, *fourth*, by entering into administrative agreements and, *fifth,* by publication of information.

With regard to the first three categories, internal administrative guidelines may be used by an institution to lay down 'policy rules' for the exercise of its discretion as a reflection of 'the Commission's desire to publish directions on the approach it intends to follow.'[131] They are 'an instance of the exercise of its discretion and requires only a self-imposed limitation of that power',[132] helping to ensure that an institution 'acts in a manner which is transparent, foreseeable and consistent with legal certainty'.[133] Judicial review of the Commission's exercise of discretion will thus include considering whether it has observed guidelines which the Commission itself has laid down and published either vis-à-vis the Member States or the wider public.[134]

With respect to the fourth possibility of self-limitation of discretionary powers by agreement, the CJEU has developed these notions for example in its case law on Article 108(1) TFEU which provides for agreements 'from which neither the Commission nor a Member State can release itself'.[135] But also self-limitation of discretion by publicised information has been accepted by the case law as a possible method of self-limitation of discretionary powers. For instance, self-binding can also take place through information tools. The difference between pure information and binding administrative guidelines can however be fluid.[136] The approach of the Courts is well established by *CIRFS*,[137] in which the Court assessed a case where the Commission had made a Decision, contrary to its own administrative rule, that a particular undertaking need not submit a notification in respect of State aids received. The CJEU held that the rules relating to a particular economic sector which the Commission had established in a communication on this policy area (a so-called discipline) and which were also accepted by the Member States, have a binding effect. They have to be seen as constituting 'a measure of general application and may not be impliedly amended by an individual decision.'[138] The Commission is bound by the Guidelines and Notices that it issues in the area of supervision of State aid where they do not depart from the rules in the Treaty and are accepted by the Member States and the parties may thus rely on these.[139] The reasons for this are the principles of equal treatment and protection of legitimate expectations. This determination shows very importantly also that the principle of equality also applies to EU institutions.

III.iii.   Review of Discretion in Supervisory Cases: BUPA

The Commission's power to review the legality of aid to be granted by Member States in the context of State aid control under Article 108 TFEU, becomes an interesting constellation for example in the area of Services of General Economic Interest (SGEI) where in turn the Member States have the power to establish and define such services in the context of national law (for further discussion see Chapter 13). These constellations are characterised by a multiple step procedure. In the first step, generally the Member State institutions enjoy discretion to determine a special legal regime for an SGEI.[140] The second step consists of the Commission's supervision of the decisions taken on SGEIs in the context of Article 108(2) and (3) TFEU.

In these contexts, two questions arise with respect to discretionary decision-making. The first question is the extent of the supervision powers. To what degree of control may the Commission subject the original decision by a Member State institution? The second question is to what degree the supervisory decision of the Commission itself is subject to review and how much discretion the supervisory body enjoys in the context of its supervision. At stake is, on one hand, the extent of the Commission's power to take supervisory decisions, and, on the other hand, the freedom of action available to Member States.

In State aids the General Court has held that the review of the

Commission's supervisory assessment of Member State compliance with EU law, in itself must be confined to ascertaining whether the Commission properly found or rejected the existence of a manifest error by the Member State.[141] Supervisory powers by the Commission are 'limited to ascertaining whether there is a manifest error of assessment'.[142] The Commission will review whether the factual premises on which a Member State decision is based is 'manifestly erroneous and whether, second, the system is manifestly inappropriate for achieving the objectives pursued'.[143]

In this framework, the Commission itself enjoys discretion for taking its supervisory decisions if and so far as the supervision activity contains complex economic and ecologic assessments. As a consequence, judicial review of supervisory decisions by the Commission is limited:

> In such a context, review by the Court consists in ascertaining that the Commission complied with the rules of procedure and the rules relating to the duty to give reasons and also that the facts relied on were accurate and that there has been no error of law manifest error of assessment or misuse of powers.[144]

In other words, a Court review of the supervisory decision by the Commission will assess whether the Commission's assessment of the Member State decision is 'sufficiently plausible'.[145]

Inextricably linked to this limitation of Commission review of a Member State decision, where the Member State enjoys discretion, is the burden of proof. Even where a Member State enjoys discretion as to the choice of a policy, it is obliged to justify its choice with respect to its compliance with requirements under Union law. The General Court held in *BUPA* that:

> in absence of such reasons, even a marginal review by the Community institutions (. . .) with respect to a manifest error by the Member State in the context of this discretion would not be possible.[146]

On the other hand, the Commission is obliged to prove the manifest error of the Member State on the basis of erroneous facts and assessments or implausibility of the result established on this factual basis.[147]

When seeing this case law in context, it will not escape the readers' attention that the case law of the European Courts with respect to these multi-level situations is probably not completely established. After all, the same reasons for controlling the Commission's exercise of discretion through an analysis of the information taken into account under the duty of care, when applied by the Commission would also require future justification by the Member States of their exercise of powers to define SGEIs. This would consequently empower the Commission to analyse whether all relevant facts were taken into consideration, whether the Member State could have drawn the conclusions therefrom and whether the possible conclusions supported the final result.

IV. CONCLUDING REMARKS

Most of the problematic issues regarding the structure of judicial review of Commission Decisions in EU State aid control refer to issues of information. EU State aid control is an eminently political policy field, in which the Commission has been granted a very powerful role to establish itself as reviewer of a host of highly sensitive policy areas, key to the exercise of public powers in the Member States. The system which has been established in the EU enhances accountability of Member States' exercise of their powers by requiring them to justify their activity and offer information about objectives, effects and analysis of their activities. It equally requires the Commission in the exercise of its control powers to be open to accountability by justification of its decision-making and reasoning. The notion of information and the rights associated with it through general principles of law increasingly enforced by the European Courts is thus the key to understanding modern judicial review in State aid procedures as well as, we may add, actually more generally EU administrative law. This is the theme under which simplification and rationalisation of the case law of the Courts needs to be understood. It is an area in which the Courts are visibly struggling with adapting the general system of judicial review, especially the annulment procedures, to the specific constellation of participants and individual rights arising in State aid procedures.Problems with regard to the issue of standing arise in no small part due to the specificity that the procedure *de jure* takes place between the EU Commission and one or several Member States, but *de facto* the potential beneficiaries and their competitors have not only a legal but also an economic interest in the outcome of the proceedings between the Commission and the Member States. Complexity of the case law on judicial review in State aid matters further arises from the variation of possible tools the Commission can employ at various stages of the procedure, ranging from pure publication of information, to binding decisions on Member States and finally concluding agreements with one or several Member States. Such factors contribute to a growing complexity in the case law. Such complexity results in dangers to plaintiffs, requiring ever more specialised legal advice to navigate the various dangers of formulating and forwarding one plea rather than another.

Simplification would be key to increasing the transparency of the policy area. Guiding principles for a reform may arise not least from the principle of good administration, as Advocate General Mengozzi most recently reconfirmed.[148] Good administration is thus the theme which should govern decisions about the degree of judicial review reflecting an increasing awareness for general principles of EU law and the role that these play in shaping the legal system.

NOTES

1. Annulment procedures are brought under Article 263 TFEU against Commission Decisions and, exceptionally, also against Decisions of the Council in Article 108(2) 3rd paragraph TFEU. Jurisdiction is split between the CJEU General Court, with the General Court having jurisdiction for all actions for annulment by individual claimants under Article 263 4th paragraph TFEU and the CJEU having jurisdiction for claims by privileged actors, especially Member States, under Article 263 2nd paragraph TFEU and for preliminary reference procedures referred to it by national courts under Article 267 TFEU. Further the CJEU has jurisdiction for actions brought by the Commission against Member State acts or omissions under Article 108(2) 2nd paragraph TFEU.
2. Thereby the contribution does not explicitly address actions for failure to act (Article 265 TFEU), preliminary reference procedures by Member State courts (Article 267 TFEU), actions for damages (Article 340 2nd paragraph TFEU) or actions brought by the Commission against Member States under Article 108 (2) 2nd paragraph TFEU.
3. Bartosch 2007: 481. The author particularly stresses how the introduction of a 'complaints' culture conflicts with the Member States' interest in having fast and smooth procedures, responding to their economic interests (especially attracting investments).
4. Regulation 659/1999 confirms the construction of the State aid procedure, as enshrined in Article 108 TFEU. It contains a few indications allowing for a major involvement of third parties in the procedures, already pending the preliminary examination. As will be explained in the following pages, this can be appreciated with reference to the treatment of complaints. Article 10 of Regulation 659/1999 actually requires the Commission to examine information it has in its possession without delay. Read in light of Article 20(2) of Regulation 659/99, which expressly allows third parties to submit a complaint, the provision acknowledges that complaints submitted by competitors could prove to be important sources of information in order for the Commission to be informed about potentially unlawful aid.
5. It is worth noting that the Treaty of Lisbon 2009 has introduced a significant amendment to the action of annulment, aimed at widening the admissibility of such type of judicial remedy. Thus, under Article 263 TFEU, natural and legal persons also are allowed to bring applications against 'a regulatory act which is of direct concern to them and does not entail implementing measures'. See Balthasar 2010.
6. The issue of standing appears particularly delicate in light of the *TWD* case law, limiting individual access to judicial protection before national courts. Acknowledgment of standing of third parties would actually have the effect of compelling third parties to abide by the two-month period for applying against an act affecting them individually, as provided in Article 263 TFEU. Therefore, recognition of third parties' standing in judicial proceedings against decisions on State aid might turn out to be a double-edged sword. See: Case C-188/92, *TWD Textilwerke Deggendorf v. Germany* [1994] E.C.R. I-833. See Flynn 2004: 293.
7. See Case C-198/91, *Cook v. Commission* [1993] E.C.R. I-2487, para. 22; Case

C-225/91, *Matra v. Commission* [1993] E.C.R. I-3203, para. 16; Case C-367/95 P, *Commission v. Sytraval and Brink's France* [1998] E.C.R. I-1719, para. 38; Case C-78/03 P, *Aktionsgemeinschaft Recht und Eigentum v. Commission* [2005] E.C.R. I-10737, para. 34.

8.   Lack of information appears particularly severe in preliminary examination, whereby neither the case law nor Regulation 659/1999 recognise any obligation to publish notification of an aid measure by the Member States; a short summary only of the Decision clearing the State measure is published in the *Official Journal*; and complainants must be informed that there are insufficient grounds for taking a view over the case (Article 20(2), although such interpretation is questionable in light of the judgment on appeal in Case C-521/06 P, *Athenaïki Techniki v. Commission* [2008] E.C.R. I-5829).

9.   A Decision not to open formal investigation in principle ensures that beneficiaries are able to receive the benefits granted by the State measure. Occasionally this might not be the case where the State measure had been cleared as an aid compatible with the common/internal market. In such a situation, beneficiaries may be interested in a Decision completely clearing the State measure, which actually would avoid this being challenged before national courts. See Case T-141/03, *Sniace v. Commission* [2005] E.C.R. II-1197.

10.   Bartosch 2007: 480.

11.   Council Regulation 659/1999/EC of 22 March 1999 laying down detailed rules for the application of Article 93 of the EC Treaty, O.J. 1999 L 83/1.

12.   Case C-367/95 P, *Commission v. Sytraval and Brink's France* [1998] E.C.R. I-1719, paras. 44–45. By this judgment, the CJEU annulled the General Court's decision which had recognised that a Commission Decision issued upon submission of a complaint by an individual could be considered as a Decision rejecting the complaint, even if formally addressed to a Member State. Case T-95/94, *Sytraval and Brink's France v. Commission* [1995] E.C.R. II-2651, para. 51.

13.   Case 60/81 *IBM v. Commission* [1981] E.C.R. 2639. The Courts have generally applied strictly the *IBM* ruling to acts other than those from Commission Decisions. Judicial review appears to be quite delicate, as the acts adopted by the institutions, even where unable to produce effects to the meaning of *IBM*, touch upon situations whereby the conflicting interests of beneficiaries and competitors are mixed. Therefore, acts have been challenged which, in principle, appear unable to produce legal effects. For example, in *Tramarin* the Commission, by letter, requested Italy to withdraw a regional aid scheme. Such request could not produce any effects, as it took place in the phase of preliminary examination, where Member States are free to comply with such indications, or to leave the original plan unchanged. Nonetheless, the letter was challenged, which ultimately led to the application being dismissed by the General Court. See Order of the General Court in T-426/04, *Tramarin v. Commission* [2005] E.C.R. II-4765, paras. 34–35.

14.   See Case 60/81, *IBM v. Commission* [1981] E.C.R. 2639 paras. 9–10; Case C-147/96, *Netherlands v. Commission* [2000] E.C.R. I-4723, para. 27; Case C-521/06 P, *Athinaïki Techniki v. Commission* [2009] E.C.R. I-5829, para. 42; Case C-362/08 P, *Internationaler Hilfsfonds v. Commission* [2010] E.C.R. I-nyr (Grand Chamber), para. 52. In the light of this, challenge to an act would be admissible where such act represents the final determination of the Commission upon the conclusion of an administrative procedure, and is intended to have legal effects capable of affecting the interests of the complainant.

15.   Article 10(1) of Regulation 659/1999/EC of 22 March 1999 laying down detailed rules for the application of Article 93 of the EC Treaty, O.J. 1999 L 83/1.

16.   Article 13(1) of Regulation 659/1999/EC of 22 March 1999 laying down detailed rules for the application of Article 93 of the EC Treaty, O.J. 1999 L 83/1, referring to Article 4 of the same Regulation to identify the contents of Decisions terminating a preliminary examination. Accordingly, the Commission might clear the State measure, either concluding that it does not constitute State aid (Article 4(2)) or declaring it

aid compatible with the common market (Article 4(3)), or, conversely, finding that there are serious difficulties to determine its compatibility with the common/internal market (Article 4(4)), thereby opening the phase of formal investigation.

17. Case T-351/02, *Deutsche Bahn v. Commission* [2006] E.C.R. II-1047. In *Deutsche Bahn*, the German national railway urged the Commission to look into a tax exemption accorded to some competitors, which allegedly would distort the market. The Commission considered that the State measure at issue complied with Council Directive 92/81 on the harmonisation of the structures of excise duties of mineral oils, it could not be qualified as aid. On this basis, the Commission exposed in a letter to the complainant its intention not to proceed further.

18. Case T-351/02, *Deutsche Bahn v. Commission* [2006] E.C.R. II-1047, paras. 44-45 and 52; also see Order of the General Court in Case T-94/05, *Athinaïki Techniki v. Commission* [2006] E.C.R. II-73, para. 29; Case T-152/06, *NDSHT v. Commission* [2009] E.C.R. II-1517, para. 56.

19. Case T-351/02, *Deutsche Bahn v. Commission* [2006] E.C.R. II-1047, paras. 53-54.

20. Ibid, para. 55.

21. *Deutsche Bahn,* ibid, para. 43; Order of the General Court in Case T-94/05, *Athinaïki Techniki v. Commission* [2006] E.C.R. II-73, para. 29; Case T-152/06, *NDSHT v. Commission* [2009] E.C.R. II-1517, para. 41.

22. Opinion of AG Bot of 3 April 2008 in Case C-521/06 P, *Athinaïki Techniki v. Commission* [2008] E.C.R. I-5829, para. 122.

23. Case T-351/02, *Deutsche Bahn v. Commission* [2006] E.C.R. II-1047, paras. 41, 49 and 52; Opinion of AG Bot of 3 April 2008 in Case C-521/06 P, *Athinaïki Techniki v. Commission* [2008] E.C.R. I-5829, para. 106; Case C-521/06 P, *Athinaïki Techniki v. Commission* [2009] E.C.R. I-5829, para. 37; Case T-152/06, *NDSHT v. Commission* [2009] E.C.R. II-1517, para. 40.

24. Case T-351/02, *Deutsche Bahn v. Commission* [2006] E.C.R. II-1047, para. 42; Opinion of AG Bot of 3 April 2008 in Case C-521/06 P, *Athinaïki Techniki v. Commission* [2008] E.C.R. I-5829, paras. 40 and 60; Case T-152/06, *NDSHT v. Commission* [2009] E.C.R. II-1517, para. 44, whereby the General Court states the difference in the procedure entailed by new and existing aid.

25. See the explanation in *Athinaïki Techniki* ibid, paras. 33-37.

26. Ibid, paras. 38-41. See Jürimäe 2010: 318. Such stance, aiming at obliging the Commission to adopt a positive and proactive attitude towards the applicant has been affirmed in other areas of EU law, for example access to documents. See for instance, in the area of application of access to documents, Case T-42/05, *Williams v. Commission* [2008] E.C.R. II-156.

27. This was already recognised, with specific reference to beneficiaries of aid, in the Opinion of AG Jacobs of 14 April 2005 in Case C-276/03 P, *Scott v. Commission* [2005] E.C.R. I-8437, at para. 74: '[. . .] The very fact that the rights of interested parties – amongst which beneficiaries are not accorded any special treatment – are dealt with in such limited terms in the context of [Article 20 of Regulation 659/1999] is significant when contrasted with the references, omnipresent throughout the rest of the regulation, to the powers and duties of the Commission and the Member States, and to the relations and exchanges between the two.'

28. Case C-521/06 P, *Athinaïki Techniki v. Commission* [2009] E.C.R. I-5829, para. 38.

29. Case T-152/06, *NDSHT v. Commission* [2009] E.C.R. II-1517. See extensively Polverino 2010.

30. Case T-152/06, *NDSHT v. Commission* [2009] E.C.R. II-1517, para. 44: 'The obligation of the Commission to adopt a decision in response to a complaint arises only in the situation envisaged in Article 13 of Regulation 659/1999. Under the second sentence of Article 20(2) of that Regulation, the Commission needs only inform the complainant by letter that there are insufficient grounds for taking a view on the case. The latter situation arises, in particular, where Article 13 does not apply because, in reality, the aid referred to in the complaint is not unlawful aid, but existing aid.'

31. Case T-152/06, *NDSHT v. Commission* [2009] E.C.R. II-1517, para. 57. See the remarks of Polverino 2010: 423.
32. Jürimäe 2010: 321; Polverino 2010: 424.
33. The hearing in *NDSHT* took place before (1 July 2008) the publication of *Athinaïki Techniki* (17 July). Therefore, even if the General Court was not required to reopen the oral procedure following publication of the latter, it anyway had the power to decide to do so. This would probably have helped in achieving a different conclusion, thereby ensuring consistency between the two judgments, and providing useful guidelines on the consequences of the distinction between existing and new aid. See Jürimäe, 2010: 321.
34. See Case T-351/02, *Deutsche Bahn v. Commission* [2006] E.C.R. II-1047, para. 56.
35. Case C-313/90, *CIRFS and Others v Commission* [1993] E.C.R. I-1125, paras. 25–27.
36. On the same issue, see T-190/00, *Regione Siciliana v. Commission* [2003] E.C.R. II-5015, paras. 42–53.
37. See Hofmann 2006b.
38. Case T-187/99, *Agrana Zucker und Stärke v. Commission* [2001] E.C.R. II-1587, para. 56. In Case T-214/95, *Het Vlaamse Gewest v. Commission* [1998] E.C.R. II-717, para. 89, the Court has found that: 'the adoption of such guidelines by the Commission is an instance of the exercise of its discretion and requires only a self-imposed limitation of that power when considering the aids to which the guidelines apply, in accordance with the principle of equal treatment.' See also: Case T-16/96, *Cityflyer Express Ltd.* [1998] E.C.R. II-757, para. 57; Case T-380/94, *AIUFFASS* [1996] E.C.R. II-2169, para. 57. See in general on the admissibility of applications against informative acts: Case C-325/91, *France v. Commission* [1993] E.C.R. I-3283; Case C-303/90, *France v. Commission* [1991] E.C.R. I-5315; Case 310/85, *Deufil v. Commission* [1987] E.C.R. 901; C-351/98, *Spain v. Commission* [2002] E.C.R. I-8031.
39. In Joined Cases C-189/02 P, C-202/02 P, C-205/02 P to C-208/02 P and C-213/02 P, *Dansk Rørindustri and others v. Commission* [2005] E.C.R. I-5425, para. 210, the CJEU held that: 'In adopting such rules of conduct and announcing by publishing them that they will hence forth apply to the cases to which they relate, the institution in question imposes a limit on the exercise of its discretion and cannot depart from those rules under pain of being found, where appropriate, to be in breach of the general principles of law, such as equal treatment or the protection of legitimate expectations. It cannot be excluded that, on certain conditions and depending on their conduct, such rules of conduct, which are of general application, may produce legal effects'. Also see Joined Cases C-182/03 and C-217/03, *Belgium and Forum 187 v. Commission* [2006] E.C.R. I-5479, para. 70. For an exhaustive summary of the limits of Commission's power to adopt and apply informative acts, see Opinion of AG Bot of 6 March 2008 in Joined Cases C-75/05 P and C-80/05P, *Germany v. Kronofrance* [2008] E.C.R. I-6619, paras. 137–148.
40. For greater detail see: Hofmann 2006a; 2006b.
41. Case C-313/90, *CIRFS and Others v. Commission* [1993] E.C.R. I-1125, paras. 35, 36. See also Case C-242/00, *Germany v. Commission* [2002] E.C.R. I-5603, para. 35.
42. Case C-313/90, *CIRFS and Others v. Commission* [1993] E.C.R. I-1125, para. 35.
43. See for example, Case 131/86, *United Kingdom v. Council* [1988] E.C.R. 905, para. 6; Case C-208/99, *Portugal v. Commission* [2004] E.C.R. I-9183, para. 22.
44. See, *inter alia*, Case C-198/91 *Cook v. Commission* [1993] E.C.R. I-2487, para. 20; Case C-525/04 P, *Spain v. Lenzing* [2007] E.C.R. I-9947, para. 30; Case C-78/03P, *Commission v ARE* [2005] E.C.R. I-10737, para. 33; all with reference to Case 25/62, *Plaumann v Commission* [1963] E.C.R. 95, 107.
45. See Quigley 2009: 691. See Case 730/79, *Philip Morris* [1980] E.C.R. 2671 para. 5. In light of the recent case law, this seems to be true both for Decisions concerning individual aid and aid schemes. The CJEU has currently relaxed its initial rigid stance against the standing of third parties proceedings concerning general aid schemes. The restrictive attitude of the Court was based on the general scope of such State

measures: because a Decision entailed legal effects for categories of persons deter-mined in a general and abstract manner, it could not have been regarded as being of individual concern to those persons. See Case 282/85, *DEFI v. Commission* [1986] E.C.R. 2469, para. 16; Order of the CJEU in Joined Cases 67, 68 and 70/85, R *Van der Kooy v. Commission* [1988] E.C.R. 219, para. 15; Case T-398/94, *Kahn Scheppvaart v Commission* [1996] E.C.R. II-477, paras. 37–38 and 41; Joined Cases C-15/98 and C-105/99, *Italy and Sardinia Lines v. Commission* [2000] E.C.R. I-8855, para. 33. The Court appears to have overcome this rigid stance by applying the *Codorniu* case law more relaxed approach on standing in judicial proceedings for annulment of a decision of an institution (Case C-309/89, *Codorniu v. Council* [1994] E.C.R. I-1853, para. 19). For application of the *Codorniu* case law to the standing of beneficiaries of aid schemes, see Joined Cases C-182/03 and C-217/03, *Belgium and Forum 187 v.* Commission [2006] E.C.R. I-5479, para. 58. The Case C-78/03P, *Commission v. Aktiongemeinschaft Recht und Eigentum* [2005] E.C.R. I-10737 is particularly sig-nificant, in that the Court did not follow the indications presented in the Opinion of AG Jacobs of 24 February 2005 in case C-78/03P, *Commission v. Aktiongemeinschaft Recht und Eigentum* [2005] E.C.R. I-10737, paras. 111 and 119. The AG expressly requested application of the *Kahn Scheppvaart* case law and therefore suggested that actual beneficiaries could exist only once the grant of the aid took place. The Court did not take an express position on the point, but did not endorse the solution recom-mended by the Advocate General. This new approach has been confirmed in Case C-487/06P, *British Aggregates Association v. Commission* [2008] E.C.R. I-10505, para. 35.

46. Article 3 of Regulation 659/1999. For a concise and exhaustive review of the standstill obligation in State aid, see Grespan 2008:576.
47. See C-312/90, *Spain v. Commission* [1992] E.C.R. I-4117, paras. 22-25; T-246/99, *Tirrenia v. Commission,* Order of 27 December 2007, para. 43.
48. See Case T-141/03, *Sniace v. Commission* [2005] E.C.R. II-1197, para. 25–26.
49. Article 26(1) of Regulation 659/1999.
50. Article 20(2) of Regulation 659/1999.
51. Case C-225/91, *Matra v. Commission* [1993] E.C.R. I-3203, para. 16; C-198/91, *Cook v. Commission* [1993] E.C.R. I-2487, para. 22; C-367/95P, *Commission v. Sytraval and Brink's France* [1998] E.C.R. I-1719, paras. 38–41; C-78/03P, *Commission v. Aktiongemeinschaft Recht und Eigentum* [2005] E.C.R. I-10737, paras. 34–35; Joined Cases C-75/05P and C-80/05P, *Germany v. Kronofrance* [2008] E.C.R. I-6619, paras. 37–38; Case C-487/06P, *British Aggregates v. Commission* [2008] E.C.R. I-10505, paras. 26–29.
52. See Dony 2007: 432; Flynn 2004: 293.
53. In the Opinion of AG Tesauro in Case C-198/91, *Cook v. Commission* [1993] E.C.R. I-2487, para. 41, AG Tesauro held : '[. . .] on a more general point of view, one must not forget that undertakings challenging a decision not to raise 'objections', in general, as to what concerns the aid, do not enjoy more than the elements communicated by the Commission or described in the summary publication in the Official Journal. These undertakings should therefore not be required – as the Commission appears to require in the present case – to formulate, in their introductory act a precise statement as to the importance and impact of the aid (for instance, the influence of the aid on the costs of production for the beneficiaries, the evolution of market shares or the impact on market exchanges). As it has been mentioned, for the purpose of standing, the plaintiff is required only to demonstrate that it is in a position of being an effective, and not merely marginal, competitor to the undertaking beneficiary of the aid which has been declared compatible. Evidence of this has been fully produced in this case.'
54. The case law of the Courts shows that the Commission has often to face the lack of information during the preliminary examination. This ultimately can imply the adop-tion of Decisions flawed to a certain extent. The fact that the Courts have annulled some of these Decisions highlights that such risk is far from being theoretical. See, for

382   *Research handbook on European State aid law*

example, Case T-49/93, *SIDE v. Commission* [1995] E.C.R. II-2501; Case T-155/98, *SIDE v. Commission* [2002] E.C.R. II-1179.

55. See for example, Case T-193/06, *TF1 v. Commission,* judgment of 13 September 2010, n.y.r., para. 72; Case C-487/06P, *British Aggregates v. Commission* [2008] E.C.R. I-10505, para. 30; C-78/03P, *Commission v. Aktiongemeinschaft Recht und Eigentum* [2005] E.C.R. I-10737, para. 37.

56. See Case C-198/91, *Cook v. Commission* [1993] E.C.R. I-2487, para. 22; Case C-225/9, *Matra v. Commission* [1993] E.C.R. I-3203, para. 16; Case C-390/06, *Nuova Agricast* [2008] E.C.R. I-2577, para. 57.

57. See Case C-198/91, *Cook v. Commission* [1993] E.C.R. I-2487, para. 29; Case C-225/91, *Matra v. Commission* [1993] E.C.R. I-3203, para. 33; Case C-367/95P, *Commission v. Sytraval and Brink's France* [1998] E.C.R. I-1719, para. 39.

58. In Case C-319/07P, *3F v. Commission* [2009] E.C.R. I-5963, para. 35, the CJEU stated this expressly: 'It is true that, as appears from Article 4(3) of Regulation 659/1999, a decision of the Commission not to raise objections is taken where the Commission finds that the notified measure does not raise doubts as to its compatibility with the common market. If an applicant seeks the annulment of such a Decision, he is essentially challenging the fact that the Decision on the aid was adopted without the Commission initiating the formal review procedure, thereby infringing his procedural rights. For his action to be successful, the applicant may attempt to show that the compatibility of the measure in question should have given rise to doubts. The use of such arguments cannot, however, have the consequence of changing the subject-matter of the application or altering the conditions of its admissibility.'

59. See, for example, Case T-158/99, *Thermenhotel Stoiser Franz v. Commission* [2004] E.C.R. II-1; Case T-157/01, *Danske Busvognmaend v. Commission* [2004] E.C.R. II-917; case T-27/02, *Kronofrance v. Commission* [2004] E.C.R. II-4177.

60. Opinion of AG Mengozzi C-487/06P, *British Aggregates Association v. Commission* [2008] E.C.R. I-10505, para. 71.

61. See Case C-78/03P, *Commission v. Aktiongemeinschaft Recht und Eigentum* [2005] E.C.R. I-10737, paras. 65–67; Joined Cases C-75/05 and 80/05, *Germany v. Kronofrance* [2008] E.C.R. I-6619, para. 42-45; Case T-388/02, *Kronoply v. Commission* [2008] E.C.R. II-305, paras. 77–78.

62. See Case C-78/03P, *Commission v. Aktiongemeinschaft Recht und Eigentum [ARE]* [2005] E.C.R. I-10737, paras. 44–45 and 65–67.

63. Case T-266/94, *Skibsvaerftsforeningen and Others v. Commission* [1996] E.C.R. II-1399, para. 45; T-212/00, *Nuove industrie molisane v. Commission* [2002] E.C.R. II-347, para. 45; T-30/03, *SID v. Commission* [2007] E.C.R. II-34, para. 40.

64. In Case T-114/00, *Aktiongemeinschaft Recht und Eigentum v. Commission* [2002] E.C.R. II-5121, para. 49, the General Court held that: 'The pleas for annulment put forward in support for the present action. . . must be construed as seeking to establish that the measures at issue pose serious difficulties as regards their compatibility with the common market, difficulties which place the Commission under an obligation to initiate the formal proceedings.' Also see, in this respect, Case C-198/91, *Cook v. Commission* [1993] E.C.R. I-2487; Case C-225/91, *Matra v. Commission* [1993] E.C.R. I-3203.

65. See Case T-210/02, *British Aggregates v. Commission* [2008] E.C.R. II-2789, para. 54; C-319/07 P, *3F v. Commission* [2009] E.C.R. I-5963, para. 78.

66. Case C-319/07P, *3F v. Commission* [2009] E.C.R. I-5963, paras. 78–81. In the Order of the General Court in Case T-30/03, *SID v. Commission* [2007] E.C.R. II-34 (subsequently appealed by the trade organisation 3F in *3F v. Commission*), the General Court declared the application inadmissible by reason of applicant's failure to satisfy the *Plaumann* test, notwithstanding its being a party concerned according to the meaning of *Cook* and *Matra*. In the Opinion of AG Sharpston of 5 March 2009 in Case C-319/07 P, *3F v. Commission* [2009] E.C.R. I-5963, para. 35, AG Sharpston expressed her worries that the rulings in *Aktiongemeinschaft Recht und Eigentum* and

British Aggregates might imply the application of the *Plaumann* test for standing already in proceedings brought against Decisions adopted at the end of preliminary examination: 'The BAA case was notable in that the applicant there had challenged a decision not to initiate a review on the grounds both that its procedural rights had been infringed and that the Commission had erred on the merits of the Decision. The Court considered together on appeal all the pleas in law raised by the applicant before the Court of First Instance. It seems from that judgment that if a party includes in its challenge a plea as to the merits of the decision itself, the test for standing to be applied is that set out in *Plaumann* and the subsequent line of case-law. Furthermore, this judgment suggests that it would not be possible for the [General Court] to sever the pleas in law brought before it so that, were the applicant in question not to meet the *Plaumann* criteria for admissibility, in relation to the challenge on the merits, the court might consider admissibility within the category of "parties concerned" with respect of the procedural pleas.'

67. Case C-319/07 P, *3F v. Commission* [2009] E.C.R. I-5963, para. 78.

68. In Case T-388/02, *Kronoply v. Commission* [2008] E.C.R. II-305, paras. 82–83, the General Court held that: 'Imposing a limitation to the General Court's power to interpret the pleas of the parties [as determined in *Commission v. Aktiongemeinschaft Recht und Eigentum*] does not affect its capacity to examine the arguments on substance presented by the applicant, with a view to determine whether they could support the argument, equally presented by the applicant, bringing on the existence of serious difficulties which would have justified the opening of a formal investigation [. . .] Consequently, in order to decide on the admissibility of the second plea, the Court must examine the other pleas presented by the applicant against the challenged decision. This will enable the Court to determine whether such pleas [both of which bring on substance, and more precisely concern the existence of a manifest error of fact and violation of Articles 107(1) and 107(3) TFEU] can be linked to the plea of the infringement of the procedural guarantees, in that they would provide information on the existence of a serious difficulty, against which the Commission should have opened the formal procedure of investigation' (unofficial translation from French by the authors). The General Court appears to have confirmed this line of proceeding in Case T-388/03, *Deutsche Post and DHL International v. Commission* [2009] E.C.R. II-199, para. 66 and in Case T-375/04, *Scheuer Fleisch v. Commission* [2009] E.C.R. 4155, para. 62. [On appeal: Case C-47/10P].

69. Opinion of AG Sharpston of 5 March 2009 in Case C-319/07 P, *3F v. Commission* [2009] E.C.R. I-5963, para. 42.

70. Case C-78/03P, *Commission v. ARE* [2005] E.C.R. I-10737, para. 37; Case 169/84, *Cofaz and others v. Commission* [1986] E.C.R. 391, paras. 22–25; Case 25/62, *Plaumann v. Commission* [1963] E.C.R. 95, paras. 9–10.

71. See Case T-380/94, *AIUFFASS and another v. Commission* [1996] E.C.R. II-2169, paras. 44–52; Case T-442/93, *AAC and others v. Commission* [1995] E.C.R. II-1329, paras. 44–53; Case T-149/95, *Ducros v. Commission* [1997] E.C.R. II-2031, paras. 32–42.

72. Case T-193/06, *TF1 v Commission,* judgment of 13 September 2010, n.y.r., paras. 77 and 86.

73. Case 323/82, *Intermills v. Commission* [1984] E.C.R. 3809, para. 16. See also Case C-78/03P, *Commission v. Aktionsgemeinschaft Recht und Eigentum* [2005] E.C.R. I-10737, para. 36; Case T-395/04, *Air One v Commission* [2006] E.C.R. II-1343, para. 36; Case T-167/04, *Asklepios Kliniken v. Commission* [2007] E.C.R. II-2379, para. 49; Case T-30/03, *SID v Commission* [2007] E.C.R. II-34, para. 31, in which the General Court held that the applicant was not affected in its competitive position.

74. Case 169/84, *Cofaz and others v. Commission* [1986] E.C.R. 391, para. 25.

75. Case C-260/05, *Sniace v Commission* [2007] ECR I-10005, paras. 56 and 57; Joined Cases 10 and 18/68, *Eridania and Others v Commission* [1969] E.C.R. 459, para. 7.

76. Case C-106/98P, *Comité d'entreprise de la Societé française de production and Others v. Commission* [2000] E.C.R. I-3659, para. 41.
77. See Case C-260/05, *Sniace v. Commission* [2007] E.C.R. I-10005, paras. 56, 57 and 60.
78. Case C-487/06P, *British Aggregates v. Commission* [2008] E.C.R. I-10505, paras. 47–56; Case C-525/04, *Spain v. Lenzing* [2007] E.C.R. I-9947, paras. 31–38. See also Case C-78/03P *Commission v. Aktionsgemeinschaft Recht und Eigentum* [2005] E.C.R. I-10737, para. 72; Case T-117/04, *Vereniging Werkgroep and Others v. Commission* [2006] E.C.R. II-3861, para. 53.
79. Case C-525/04P, *Spain v. Lenzing* [2007] E.C.R. I-9947, para. 37.
80. C-78/03P, *Commission v. ARE* [2005] E.C.R. I-10737, para. 72.
81. Case C-15/98 and C-105/99, *Italy and Sardegna v. Commission* [2000] E.C.R. I-8855, para. 33 (emphasis added); Joined Cases T-254/00, T-270/00 and T-277/00, *Hotel Cipriani and Italgas v. Commission* [2008] E.C.R. II-3269, at paras. 77 and 78. See, however, Case T-9/98, *Mitteldeutsche Erdoel-Raffinerie GmbH v. Commission* [2001] E.C.R. II-3367, paras. 78–85.
82. Joined Cases T-227/01 to T-229/01, T-265/01, T-266/01 and T-270/01, *Territorio histórico de Álava and Others v. Commission* [2009] n.y.r, para. 84. [On appeal: Cases C-471/09 C-472/09 C-473/09 C-474/09 C-475/09 C-476/09] with reference, *inter alia*, to the Order of the General Court in Case T-201/04, R *Microsoft v. Commission* [2004] E.C.R. II-2977, para. 38.
83. See Case C-367/95P, *Commission v. Sytraval and Brink's France* [1998] E.C.R. I-1719.
84. See Case C-198/91, *Cook v. Commission* [1993] E.C.R. I-2487; Case C-225/91, *Matra v. Commission* [1993] E.C.R. I-3203.
85. See Bartosch 2007: 477; Case T-613/97, *UFEX v. Commission* [2000] E.C.R. II-4055 para. 89.
86. Case T-266/94, *Skibsvaerftsforeningen and Others v. Commission* [1996] E.C.R. II-1399, para. 256; Joined Cases T-371/94 and T-394/94, *British Airways and Others and British Midland Airways v. Commission* [1998] E.C.R. II-2405, para. 59; Case T-366/00, *Scott v. Commission* [2003] E.C.R. II-1763, para. 59.
87. See Opinion of AG Bot of 3 April 2008 in Case C-521/06 P, *Athinaïki Techniki v. Commission* [2008] E.C.R. I-5829, paras. 127–130. There the AG argued that the case law on defence of procedural rights requires that solutions on reviewability of acts offer the same protection to applicants which the Courts grant with respect to standing.
88. See, with respect to reviewability of decisions refusing to open formal investigations, Case T-351/02, *Deutsche Bahn v. Commission* [2006] E.C.R. II-1047, paras. 54–55; Order of the General Court in Case T-94/05, *Athinaïki Techniki v. Commission* [2006] E.C.R. II-73, para. 28; Case C-521/06P, *Athinaïki Techniki v. Commission* [2008] E.C.R. I-5829, para. 52; with respect to standing of complainants in proceedings against the same kind of act, Case C-78/03 P, *Aktionsgemeinschaft Recht und Eigentum v. Commission* [2005] E.C.R. I-10737, para. 35; Joined Cases C-75/05P and 80/05P, *Germany v. Kronofrance* [2008] E.C.R. I-6619, para. 38.
89. For an in-depth, very exhaustive analysis of the most recent case law on issues of reviewability of acts and standing of third parties, see Jürimäe 2010.
90. Opinion of AG Jacobs of 24 February 2005 in Case C-78/03P, *Commission v. Aktionsgemeinschaft Recht und Eigentum* [2005] E.C.R. I-10737, para. 138.
91. Opinion of AG Bot of 6 March 2008 in Joined Cases C-75/05 P and C-80/05 P, *Germany v. Kronofrance and Others* [2008] E.C.R. I-6619, para. 108.
92. Before the adoption of Regulation 659/1999, some cases had actually nudged the legislator in the direction of adopting rules governing the different procedural aspects of State aid procedure: Case T-277/94, *AITEC v. Commission* [1996] E.C.R. II-351, para. 70; Case C-375/95P, *Commission v. Sytraval* [1998] E.C.R. I-1719, para. 44.
93. See in particular an insider's description of the procedure before the Commission in State aid procedure: Grespan 2008: 569–627.

94. See specifically on applications for annulment in State aid Flynn 2004 : 283–285; Dony 2007: 428–472; Grespan 2008: 689–707 ; Quigley 2009: 528.
95. Meij 2009: 10.
96. On the meaning of marginal review, see specifically Gattinara 2006: 454.
97. On discretion, see in general Craig 2006; Ritleng 1999.
98. The basic case on delegation of decision-making powers in this category is Case 9/56, *Meroni & Co, Industrie Metallurgiche SpA v. High Authority* [1958] E.C.R. 133. Therein the CJEU defined limitations to the possibility of delegation of administrative tasks to bodies not established by the founding Treaties, interpreting a '*wide* margin of discretion' as a delegation which 'according to the use which is made of it, make possible the execution of actual economic policy.' This notion of a 'wide margin of discretion' in other cases has been referred to as a 'broad discretion', see for example, Case 69/83, *Luxembourg v. Court of Auditors* [1984] E.C.R. 2447; Case T-54/99, *max.mobil v. Commission* [2002] E.C.R. II-313, para. 58.
99. See, for example, Case C-180/96, *UK v Commission* [1998] E.C.R. I-2265, para. 97; Joined Cases T-481 and 484/93, *Exporteurs in Levende Varkens v. Commission* [1995] E.C.R. II-2941, paras. 91 and 120 both from the policy area of agriculture.
100. See, for example, Case 40/72, *Schroeder v. Germany* [1973] E.C.R. 125, para. 28.
101. Meij 2009: 11.
102. See, for example, Case C-352/98P, *Bergaderm and Goupil v. Commission* [2000] E.C.R. I-5291, para. 46; Case 42/84, *Remia BV and Verenigde Bedrijven Nutricia v. Commission* [1985] E.C.R. 2545, para. 34; Joined Cases 142/84 and 156/84, *BAT and Reynolds v. Commission* [1987] E.C.R. 4487, para. 62; and Case C-194/99P, *Thyssen Stahl v. Commission* [2003] E.C.R. I-10821, para. 78 as well as the Order of the General Court in Case T-271/03, *Deutsche Telekom AG v. Commission* [2008] E.C.R. II-477, which formulated in para. 185: 'it must be borne in mind that, although as a general rule the Community judicature undertakes a comprehensive review of the question whether the conditions for applying the competition provisions of the EC Treaty are met, its review of complex economic appraisals made by the Commission is necessarily limited to verifying whether the relevant rules on procedure and on the statement of reasons have been complied with, whether the facts have been accurately stated and whether there has been any manifest error of appraisal or misuse of powers'.
103. See, for example, Ritleng 1999.
104. See, for example, the case law regarding risk assessment and risk management in which despite the necessity of administrations to undertake 'complex technical and scientific assessments', judicial review was undertaken in a detailed fashion. See, for example, Case 14/78, *Denkavit v. Commission* [1978] E.C.R. 2497, para. 20; Case T-13/99, *Pfizer Animal Health SA v. Council* [2002] E.C.R. II-3305, paras. 154–163.
105. Tiili and Vanhamme 1999:890; Azizi 2009: 316.
106. See, for example, Case T-187/06, *Schräder v. CPVO* [2008] E.C.R. II-3151, paras. 59–63. The case is the first explicitly granting discretionary powers to an agency, potentially in conflict with the *Meroni* doctrine.
107. Joined Cases T-371 and 394/94, *British Airways v. Commission* [1998] E.C.R. II-2405, para. 293.
108. Case C-56/93, *Belgium v. Commission* [1996] E.C.R. I-723, paras. 10 and 11; Joined Cases C-204/00 P, C-205/00 P, C-211/00 P, C-213/00 P, C-217/00 P and C-219/00 P, *Aalborg Portland and Others v. Commission* [2004] E.C.R. I-123, para. 279; Joined Cases C-501/06 P, C-513/06 P, C-515/06 P and C-519/06 P, *GlaxoSmithKline Services v. Commission* [2009] E.C.R. I-9291, para. 85; C-290/07P *Commission v. Scott,* judgment of 2 September 2010, n.y.r., para. 66.
109. See Case C-83/98 P, *France v. Ladbroke Racing and Commission* [2000] E.C.R. I-3271, para. 25; T-296/97, *Alitalia v. Commission* [2000] E.C.R. II-3871, para. 95; Joined Cases T-195/01 R and T-207/01 R, *Government of Gibraltar v. Commission* [2001]

E.C.R. II-3915, para. 75; Case T-366/00, *Scott v. Commission* [2007] E.C.R. II-797, para. 91; Case T-196/04, *Ryanair v. Commission* [2008] E.C.R. II-3643, para. 40.

110. See in general the approach held by the Courts in other areas of EU law: Case C-84/94, *United Kingdom v. Council* [1996] E.C.R. I-5755, para. 58; Case C-233/94, *Germany v. Parliament and Council* [1997] ECR I-2405, paras. 55–56; C-157/96, *National Farmers' Union and Others* [1998] E.C.R. I-2211, para. 61; Joined Cases C-248/95 and C-249/95, *SAM Schiffahrt and Stapf* [1997] E.C.R. I-4475, para. 23; Case C-266/05P, *Sison v. Council* [2007] E.C.R. I-1233, para. 33.

111. The Court has actually shown to be quite attentive to meet the delicate political points in several cases; one of the most important manifestations of such care is the adaptation of the scope of institutional discretion to the particular facts of the case: confront, for instance, Case C-266/05 P, *Sison v. Council* [2007] E.C.R. I-1233, para. 33, whereby the Court appears to invoke the limits of the scope of judicial review against institutional discretion in order to avoid to review a highly political issue (which nonetheless could actually have been dealt by means of a thorough review of fundamental rights protection, in particular as to application of the proportionality test), and Case T-85/09, *Kadi v. Commission*, judgment of 30 September 2010, n.y.r., paras. 142–143. [on appeal Case C-584/10 C-593/10 C-595/10P]. As appears from the last case, the EU judicature's approach to institutional discretion (though elaborated in the framework of the administrative activity) represents a reference for the interpretation of it: see C-525/04P, *Spain v. Lenzing* [2007] E.C.R. I-9947, para. 57.

112. Case C-83/98P, *France v. Ladbroke Racing and Commission* [2000] E.C.R. I-3271, para. 25; Case T-296/97, *Alitalia v. Commission* [2000] E.C.R. II-3871, para. 95; Case T-98/00, *Linde v. Commission* [2002] E.C.R. II-3961, para. 40.

113. Case T-67/94, *Ladbroke Racing v. Commission* [1998] E.C.R. II-1, paras. 52–53; Case T-358/94, *Air France v. Commission* [1996] E.C.R. II-2109, para. 71; Case C-56/93, *Belgium v. Commission* [1996] E.C.R. I-723, paras. 10–11.

114. Case C-56/93, *Belgium v. Commission* [1996] E.C.R. I-723, para. 10; Joined Cases T-126/96 and T-127/96, *Breda Fucine Meridionali and Others v. Commission* [1998] E.C.R. II-3437, para. 5; T-296/97, *Alitalia v. Commission* [2000] E.C.R. II-3871, para. 105; T-301/01, *Alitalia v. Commission* [2008] E.C.R. II-1753, para. 185; T-196/04, *Ryanair v. Commission* [2008] E.C.R. II-3643, para. 41.

115. Case 730/79, *Philip Morris v. Commission* [1980] E.C.R. 2671, para. 17 and 24; Case 310/85, *Deufil v. Commission* [1987] E.C.R. 901, para. 18; Case C-301/87, *France v. Commission* [1990] E.C.R. I-307, para. 49; Joined Cases T-371 and 394/04, *British Airways v. Commission* [1998] E.C.R. II-2405, para. 79; Case C-169/95, *Spain v. Commission* [1997] E.C.R. I-135, para. 18; Case C-355/95P, *TWD v. Commission* [1997] E.C.R. I-2549, para. 26; T-20/03, *Kahla/Thüringen Porzellan v. Commission* [2008] E.C.R. II-2305, para. 115.

116. The general principle of the duty of care is probably best known through the judgment in Case C-269/90, *Technische Universität München v. Hauptzollamt München-Mitte* [1991] E.C.R. I-5469. At para. 14, the CJEU held that 'where the Community institutions have such a power of appraisal, respect for the rights guaranteed by the Community legal order in administrative procedures is of even more fundamental importance. Those guarantees include, in particular, the duty of the competent institution to examine carefully and impartially all the relevant aspects of the individual case, the right of the person concerned to make his views known and to have an adequately reasoned decision.'

117. What factors may or may not be taken into account may be either expressly listed, sometimes exhaustively, in the statute or may be inferred from the statutory goals, or both. They may arise from general principles of law or from specific cross-sectoral Treaty provisions regarding the protection of the environment (Article 6 TFEU) or health protection (Article 168(1) TFEU).

118. Case C-310/04, *Spain v. Council* [2006] E.C.R. I-7285, paras. 98, 117, 121, 122, 124, 128, 131–135.

119. Case T-95/94, *Sytraval and Brink's France v. Commission* [1995] E.C.R. II-2651, para. 66.
120. Case C-367/95P, *Commission v. Sytraval and Brinks France* [1998] E.C.R. I-1719, paras. 60–62, linking this duty to the principle of sound (or good) administration.
121. Case T-206/99, *Métropole Télévision v. Commission* [2001] E.C.R. II-2707, para. 59.
122. This tendency began in the judicial review of merger control cases (Case T-342/99, *Airtours v. Commission* [2002] E.C.R. II-2585; Case T-5/02, *Tetra Laval BV v. Commission* [2002] E.C.R. II-4381, upheld on appeal in Case C-12/03P, *Commission v. Tetra Laval* [2005] E.C.R. I-987; T-351/03, *Schneider Electric v. Commission* [2007] E.C.R. II-2237, expanded to Article 101 and 102 TFEU cases (Case T-54/99, *max.mobil Telekommunikation Service GmbH v. Commission* [2002] E.C.R. II-313; C-141/02, *Commission v. max.mobil Telekommunikation Service* [2005] E.C.R. I-1283) and has also been expanded to State aid cases.
123. Case T-36/99, *Lenzing v. Commission* [2004] E.C.R. II-3597, para. 160.
124. Case C-525/04P, *Spain v. Lenzing* [2007] E.C.R. I-9947, para. 56; Case C-12/03, *Commission v. Tetra Laval* [2005] E.C.R. I-987, para. 39.
125. Case C-525/04P, *Spain v. Lenzing* [2007] E.C.R. I-9947, para. 57.
126. Case C-525/04P, *Spain v. Lenzing* [2007] E.C.R. I-9947, para. 57 referring back to the Cases 98/78, *Racke* [1979] E.C.R. 69, para. 5; Case C-16/90, *Nölle* [1991] E.C.R. I-5163, para. 12; Case C-12/03P, *Commission v. Tetra Laval* [2005] E.C.R. I-987, para. 39; Case C-326/05P, *Industrias Quimicas del Vallés v. Commission* [2007] E.C.R. I-6557, para. 76.
127. Case C-525/04P, *Spain v. Lenzing* [2007] E.C.R. I-9947, para. 58.
128. Opinion of AG Sharpston of 16 March 2006 in Case C-310/04, Spain *v.* Council [2006] E.C.R. I-7285, paras. 80 and 94. The CJEU followed the Advocate General explicitly referring to the duty of care which requires the Commission to collect and to take into account all relevant information prior to taking a discretionary decision (Case C-310/04, *Spain v. Council* [2006] E.C.R. I-7285, para. 133).
129. See also Opinion of AG Kokott of 7 July 2009 in Case C-558/07, *S.P.C.M. and others* [2009] E.C.R. I-5783, paras. 69–77, and the case law referred to in the footnotes.
130. Case 148/73, *Louwage v. Commission* [1974] E.C.R. 81, para. 15; Case 105/75, *Giuffrida v. Council* [1976] E.C.R. 1395, paras. 17–18. This early case law of the CJEU had already begun to invoke the principle of good (or sound) administration.
131. Case T-187/99, *Agrana Zucker und Stärke AG v. Commission* [2001] E.C.R. II-1587, para. 56.
132. Case T-214/95, *Vlaamse Gewest v. Commission* [1998] E.C.R. II-717, paras. 79 and 89; Case C-382/99, *Netherlands v. Commission* [2002] E.C.R. I-5163, para. 24; Case T-87/05, *EDP – Energias de Portugal SA v. Commission* [2005] E.C.R. II-3745, paras. 161–165.
133. The case law is summarised in Joined Cases C-189, 202, 205, 208 and 213/02P, *Dansk Rørindustri and others v. Commission* [2005] E.C.R. I-5425, para. 211 stating that 'In adopting such rules of conduct and announcing by publishing them that they will henceforth apply to the cases to which they relate, the [Commission] imposes a limit on the exercise of its discretion and cannot depart from those rules under pain of being found, where appropriate, to be in breach of the general principles of law, such as equal treatment or the protection of legitimate expectations. It cannot therefore be excluded that, on certain conditions and depending on their conduct, such rules of conduct, which are of general application, may produce legal effects.' See also: Case C-310/99, *Italian Republic v. Commission* [2002] E.C.R. I-2289, para. 52.
134. See, for example, Case C-310/99, *Italian Republic v. Commission* [2002] E.C.R. I-2289, para. 52; Case T-35/99, *Keller v. Commission* [2002] E.C.R. II-261, para. 77. The conditions for the validity of such administrative guidelines is that they 'contain indications as to the direction to be followed' by the Commission and 'do not depart from the Treaty rules" (see also: Case T-187/99, *Agrana Zucker und Stärke AG v. Commission* [2001] E.C.R. II-1587, para. 56) the latter criterion of legality echoing the

principle of *ultra vires*. In addition, the Commission may not through administrative rulemaking amend the provisions of either primary or secondary law.

135. Case C-311/94, *Ijssel-Vliet v. Minister van Economische Zaken* [1996] E.C.R. I-5023, paras. 36 and 37; Case C-313/90, *CIRFS and others v. Commission* [1993] E.C.R. I-1125, paras. 35 and 36. For further detail see Hofmann 2006a: 153–78.

136. The European Courts have interpreted various forms of Commission documents in the same way as they have applied administrative guidelines formally published in the C series of the *Official Journal*. For example, the General Court has treated Commission's statements in the 17th *Report on Competition Policy* as 'guidelines which the Commission follows when implementing the rules of competition in agriculture, which are thus a reference framework known to the Member States, public bodies and the operators concerned' (Case T-190/00, *Regione Siciliana v. Commission* [2003] E.C.R. II-5015, para. 100). Statements in the report on competition policy can thus be regarded as administrative guidelines. The CJEU has taken this approach a step further and regarded Commission statements in the *Bulletin of the European Communities* in a way similar to guidelines (Case C-457/00, *Belgium v. Commission* [2003] E.C.R. I-6931, paras. 6–10, 43, 79 and 97). In that case, Belgium had successfully argued that the Commission had laid out 'its general position with regard to public authorities' holdings in company capital'. The Court found that the Commission was bound to this statement in the same way as to its formal administrative Guidelines.

137. Case C-313/90, *CIRFS and other v. Commission* [1993] E.C.R. I-1125, paras. 32 and 45.

138. Case C-313/90, *CIRFS and other v. Commission* [1993] E.C.R. I-1125, paras. 32 and 45.

139. Case T-176/01, *Ferriere Nord v. Commission* [2004] E.C.R. II-3931, para. 134.

140. Case T-289/03, *BUPA v. Commission* [2008] E.C.R. II-81, paras. 165–169. The same situation exists with respect to the establishment of allocation plans for greenhouse gas allowances on the basis of their local economic and ecologic assessments, see Cases T-374/04, *Germany v. Commission* [2007] E.C.R. II-4431, paras. 77–81; T-183/07, *Poland v. Commission* [2009] E.C.R II-3395, paras. 89–91. [On appeal : Case C-504/09P]; T-263/07, *Estonia v. Commission* [2009] E.C.R. II-3463, paras. 49–69. [On appeal: Case C-505/09P].

141. Case T-289/03, *BUPA v. Commission* [2008] E.C.R. II-81, para. 220.

142. Ibid, para. 169.

143. Ibid, para. 266.

144. Ibid, para. 221.

145. Ibid, para. 266.

146. Ibid, para. 172.

147. Case T-374/04, *Germany v. Commission* [2007] E.C.R. II-4431, para. 79.

148. Opinion of 23 February 2010 in Case C-290/07P, *European Commission v Scott SA* [2010] E.C.R. I-n.y.r, paras. 58–60.

REFERENCES

Azizi, J. (2009), 'The tension between Member States' autonomy and Commission control in State aid matters: Selected aspects', in H. Kanninen, N. Korjus, A. Rosas (eds), *EU Competition Law in Context: Essays in Honour of Virpi Tiili*, Oxford – Portland Oregon: Hart Publishing, 307–320.

Balthasar, S. (2010), 'Locus standi rules for challenges to regulatory Acts by private applicants: The new Art. 263(4) TFEU', *European Law Review*, **35:4**, 342–350.

Bartosch A. (2007), 'The Procedural Regulation in State Aid Matters', *European State Aid Law Quarterly*, **3**, 474–484.

Craig P. (2006), *EU Administrative Law,* Oxford: Oxford University Press.

Dony, M. (in collaboration with F. Renart, and C. Smits) (2007), *Contrôle des aides d'État,* Bruxelles: Institut d'Études européens.

Flynn, L. (2004), 'Remedies in European Courts', in A. Biondi, P. Eeckhout, P and J. Flynn (eds), *The Law of State Aid in the European Union,* Oxford: Oxford University Press, 283–301.

Gattinara G, (2006), 'Judicial protection at European level', in G.L. Tosato and L. Bellodi (eds), *EU Competition Law*, Vol. I, Procedure, Leuven: Clays & Casteels.

Grespan, D. (2008), 'State aid procedure', in W. Mederer, N. Pesaresi, and M. Van Hoof (eds), *EU Competition Law*, Vol IV, Book 1, State Aid, 1st edn, Leuven: Claeys & Casteels, 551–708.

Hofmann, H.C.H. (2006a), 'Negotiated and non-negotiated administrative rule-making – The example of EC competition policy', *Common Market Law Review*, **43,** 153–178.

Hofmann, H.C.H. (2006b), 'Administrative governance in state aid policy', in H.C.H. Hofmann, and A.H. Türk (eds), *EU Administrative Governance*, Cheltenham: Elgar, 185–215.

Jürimäe, K, (2010) 'Standing in State aid cases: What's the state of play?', *European State Aid Law Quarterly,* **9:2,** 303–321.

Meij, A. (2009), 'Judicial review in the EC Courts: *Tetra Leval* and beyond', in: O. Essens, A. Gerbrandy, and S. Lavrijssen, (eds) *National Courts and the Standard of Review in Competition Law and Economic Regulation,* Groningen: Europa Law Publishing.

Polverino, F. (2010), 'Have your day (and say) in Court: the case of existing aid', *European State Aid Law Quarterly*, **9.2,** 419–426.

Quigley, C. (2009), *European State Aid Law and Policy*, 2nd edn, Oxford–Portland Oregon: Hart.

Ritleng D. (1999), 'Le juge communautaire de la légalité et le pouvoir discrétionnaire des institutions communautaires', *Actualité Juridique Droit Administratif*, 645.

Tiili, V. and J. Vanhamme (1999), 'The "Power of Appraisal" (Pouvoir d'Appréciation) of the Commission of the EC vis-à-vis the powers of judicial review of the Communities' Court of Justice and Court of First Instance', *Fordham International Law Journal*, **22**, 885–901.

17 State aid and the role of national courts
Paolisa Nebbia

I. INTRODUCTION

National courts' role in the enforcement of State aid law stems from the direct effect of the prohibition laid down in the last sentence of Article 108(3) TFEU.[1]

While the power to monitor the compatibility of proposed aid with the common/internal market is vested in the Commission, national courts are entrusted with the task of safeguarding the rights of individuals faced with a possible breach by Member States' authorities of the obligation not to grant any aid before it is approved by the Commission (the 'standstill obligation').[2] In principle, such an obligation may be invoked in national courts under two main scenarios: when a competitor of the aid-receiving undertaking resorts to court for the annulment of the aid granted, and when a taxpayer seeks to avoid payment of a tax resulting from the grant of an aid.

National courts may also face State aid issues in cases where the Commission has already ordered recovery: in this instance, claimants would in most cases be applying for the annulment of a national recovery order implementing the Commission Decision or, more rarely, be seeking to recover damages from national authorities for failure to implement a Commission recovery Decision.

The general principle governing such claims is that, in the absence of EU rules, national remedies and national procedural rules must conform to the principles of equivalence (as regards the treatment of comparable but purely national disputes) and effectiveness (that is, national rules must not render, in practice, impossible or excessively difficult the exercise of the rights conferred by EU law). The CJEU has also held that national courts must also take fully into consideration the interests of the EU.[3]

The Commission has been addressing directly the role of national courts since 1995, with its *Notice on cooperation between national courts and the Commission in the State aid field*,[4] introducing mechanisms for cooperation and exchange of information between the Commission and national courts. In 2006, the Commission published a study on the enforcement of State aid law at national level,[5] intended to provide a detailed analysis of private State aid enforcement in different Member States: this revealed that, although between 1999 and 2006 State aid litigation at Member State level had increased significantly,[6] the number of legal challenges aimed at enforcing compliance with the State aid rules is still relatively small. The Commission, however, believes that private enforcement actions can offer considerable benefits for State aid policy and, accordingly, it has issued a second *Notice on the enforcement of State aid law by national courts* (2009 Notice),[7] replacing the 1995 one. The 2009 Notice has a twofold purpose: first, it aims to inform and provide guidance to all relevant parties about the available remedies in case of a breach of the EU State aid rules, including damages claims; second, it purports to clarify the mechanisms for cooperation between the courts and the Commission.

II.   NATIONAL COURTS AND UNLAWFUL STATE AID

II.i.   Determination as to the Existence of a Breach

An infringement of Article 108(3) TFEU occurs either because the aid was not notified at all, or because the Member State implemented it before obtaining the Commission's approval.

The role played by national courts in this context is particularly important from the point of view of competitors and other third parties in the light of the fact that the Commission's powers against unlawful aid are limited: as the ECJ held in its *Boussac*[8] and *Tubemeuse*[9] judgments, the Commission cannot adopt a final Decision ordering recovery merely because the aid was not notified in accordance with Article 108(3) TFEU: while national courts can, and must, limit their scrutiny to determining whether the measure constitutes State aid and whether the standstill obligation applies to it, the Commission must in any case conduct a full compatibility assessment, regardless of whether the standstill obligation has been respected or not. This assessment can be time-consuming and accordingly actions before national courts may be more timely and efficient means of redress for the aggrieved parties than resorting to the Commission.

It must be noted, on the other hand, that the possibility of remedying an infringement of Article 108(3) TFEU at a national level is limited by a series of factors such as lack of transparency in the granting of aid, difference between the various national legal systems and difficulties for national courts in obtaining the necessary information.

A national court called upon to deal with an action based on an infringement of Article 108(3) TFEU would be under a duty to ascertain, in the first place, whether the State measure in dispute constituted 'State aid' within the meaning of Article 107 TFEU. This may involve an obligation to interpret and apply the notion of 'State aid' and to check whether the other criteria of Article 107 TFEU (effect on trade and competition and State origin) are fulfilled. In this case, it is debatable whether the national court should take a position on the law as such or only the individual issue in regard to Article 107 TFEU.[10]

Secondly, if the measure was found to constitute 'aid', the national court would have to determine whether it has been granted in breach of Article 108(3) TFEU, that is, whether it constitutes new or existing aid. Existing aid, which includes aid granted under a scheme which existed before a Member State's accession to the EU or under a scheme previously approved by the Commission, does not need to be notified.

Thirdly, the national court may be called upon to check whether the aid falls within a Block Exemption Regulation: where a measure meets all the prescribed requirements, the Member State is relieved of its obligation to notify the planned aid measure and the standstill obligation does not apply. The adoption of numerous Block Exemptions, triggered by the desire to reduce the Commission's workload, has diluted its ability to ensure monitoring of the compatibility of proposed aid measures with EU law on the basis of the traditional system of *ex ante* monitoring, while on the other hand it has significantly increased the responsibility of national judges.

Nevertheless, when the applicability of a Block Exemption Regulation (or of an existing or approved aid scheme) are being examined, the national court can only determine whether all conditions of the regulation or scheme are met. Where the issues raised at national level concern the validity of a Commission Decision, the national court has no jurisdiction to declare acts of EU institutions invalid,[11] but may or must, in accordance with the second and third paragraphs of Article 267 TFEU refer the matter to the CJEU for a preliminary ruling: under the *TWD*[12] doctrine, however, this is no longer possible where the claimant could undoubtedly have challenged the Commission Decision before the European Courts under Article 263 TFEU, but failed to do so.

In case of doubt concerning the applicability of a Block Exemption Regulation or an existing or approved aid scheme, the national court may ask for the Commission's assistance under section 3 of the 2009 Notice.[13]

Under no circumstances are national courts allowed to decide substantive matters concerning the compatibility of the aid with the common market: this would result in 'the powers exercised by the Commission for the benefit of the Community being rendered ineffective' and in 'setting aside of the division of powers between the Community and the Member

States with respect to the granting of State aid'.[14] As a result, a national administrative authority entrusted with the task of recovering State aid that has been the subject matter of some sort of *ultra vires* assessment by a national court, declaring it compatible with the common market, would not be bound by the principle of *res judicata* in so far as its application would prevent the recovery of State aid granted in breach of EU law.

II.ii. Consequences of Unlawful Aid

Once a national court has come to the conclusion that there has been a breach of the standstill obligation, it is under a duty to 'offer to individuals in a position to rely on such breach the certain prospect that all the necessary inferences will be drawn, in accordance with their national law, as regards the validity of measures giving effect to the aid, the recovery of financial support granted in disregard of that provision and possible interim measures'.[15] While in principle it would be for national law to determine the applicable rules (and the available remedies) for the enforcement of claimant's rights, subject to the principles of equivalence and effectiveness, the CJEU case law, partly drawn upon the principles established with regard to recovery of wrongly paid EU subsidies,[16] has gradually superseded national systems' autonomy. The resulting array of available remedies is now expressly set out in the 2009 Notice.[17]

In the first place, in cases where an unlawful payment is about to be made, national courts must, also by means of an interim order, prevent such payment from taking place.

Where, on the other hand, aid has already been unlawfully granted, courts must in principle order its repayment in accordance with the procedural rules of domestic law. Any other interpretation would encourage the Member States to disregard the prohibition laid down in Article 113(3) TFEU.[18] Member States are free to choose the most suitable means to claim repayment, provided they ensure that the normal market conditions of competition which were distorted by the grant of the aid are restored.[19]

The recovery of aid is not dependent on the substantive issue of its compatibility with Article 87 TFEU: even the Commission's final Decision does not have the effect of regularising *ex post* the implementing measures which were invalid because they had been taken in breach of the prohibition laid down by the last sentence of Article 113(3) TFEU. This principle has been applied in a less stringent manner in the recent case law, which favours an interpretation whereby once the Commission has taken a final Decision, the national court needs to ensure compliance with this rather than with the last sentence of Article 108(3) TFEU. Accordingly, where, by the time that the national court renders its judgment, the Commission has already decided that the aid is compatible with the common market, the national court is no longer under an obligation to order full recovery but may limit the scope of its judgment to the payment of interest for the period of illegality, even in the absence of exceptional circumstances.[20] As a consequence, the Commission Decision may have a certain factual retroactivity.[21]

This solution has been confirmed and reinforced in the *Wienstrom*[22] case, where the CJEU has held that in a situation where the unlawful putting into effect of aid is followed by a positive Commission Decision, the national court is not bound to order the recovery of aid unlawfully granted, but must in any case order the aid recipient to pay interest in respect of the period of unlawfulness and may also be required to uphold claims for compensation for damage caused to third parties by reason of the unlawful nature of the aid.

The CJEU has come to this conclusion by arguing that the purpose of Article 108(3) TFEU is to ensure that compatible aid may alone be implemented; where, however, the Commission adopts a positive Decision, it is then apparent that the purpose referred to has not been frustrated by the premature payment of the aid. The argument indeed assumes that the purpose of Article 108(3) TFEU is that no incompatible aid is paid, but one may argue that the purpose of that provision is (also) to ensure that no aid is paid without the Commission' approval: in this case, allowing the beneficiary to keep the aid would run counter to the spirit of Article 108(3) TFEU. Under the interpretation given by the Court, Member States may be encouraged to grant aid without notifying it: in the event that aid turns out to be incompatible, the only consequence is that the beneficiary will have to pay the relevant interest; meanwhile, it may also have gained a competitive advantage over its rivals by having at its immediate disposal the unnotified benefit, for example, a substantial loan at particularly advantageous conditions, which may be immediately used to renew the production plants.

An ongoing Commission investigation does not release the national court from its obligation to protect individual rights under Article 108(3) TFEU. The national court may not, therefore, simply suspend its own proceedings until the Commission has decided and leave the rights of the claimant unprotected in the meantime:[23] a Decision of this type would, *de facto*, have the same effect as a Decision to refuse the claimant's application and to maintain the benefit of the aid during the period in which implementation is prohibited. The Notice seems to suggest, however, an intermediate route by prescribing that a national court may await the outcome of the Commission's compatibility assessment before adopting a final Decision if it chooses to adopt appropriate interim measures, such as ordering the placement of the funds on a blocked account.[24]

Under the *SFEI*[25] doctrine, in exceptional circumstances recovery of unlawful aid may not be ordered.[26] The legal standard applied in this respect is very strict and is similar to the one applicable under Articles 14 and 15 of Regulation 659/1999.[27] Accordingly, legitimate expectations cannot be pleaded by the beneficiary, since a diligent businessman would have been able to verify whether the aid he received was notified or not. The only case where legitimate expectations could be pleaded seems to be where these have been generated by a specific and concrete fact, for example, if the Commission itself has given precise assurances that the measure in question does not constitute State aid, or that it is not covered by the standstill obligation.[28]

In its decision in *CELF (II)* the CJEU has held that the adoption by the Commission of three successive Decisions declaring aid to be compatible with the common/internal market, which were subsequently annulled by the EU judicature, is not, in itself, capable of constituting an exceptional circumstance such as to justify a limitation of the recipient's obligation to repay that aid, in the case where that aid was implemented contrary to Article 108(3) TFEU. On the contrary, the complexity of the case, far from giving rise to a legitimate expectation, would rather appear likely to increase the recipient's doubts as to the compatibility of the disputed aid. Moreover, so long as the Commission has not taken a decision approving aid, and so long as the period for bringing an action against such a decision has not expired, the recipient cannot be certain as to the lawfulness of the aid, with the result that neither the principle of the protection of legitimate expectations nor that of legal certainty can be relied upon.

When the national court orders the full recovery of the given sum, interest needs to be added so as to neutralise the financial advantage resulting from the premature implementation of the aid, since in the case of notification any payment (if at all) would have taken place later.[29] Even if the entire sum must not be recovered (for example, when the aid has been *ex post* approved by the Commission), the national court is still under an obligation to order recovery of the accrued interest.

The duty of national courts to protect individual rights from violations of the standstill obligation is not limited to passing a final judgment on the lawfulness of the aid: as part of their role under Article 108(3) TFEU, national courts are also required, where appropriate, to take interim measures in accordance with the national procedural framework and subject to the requirements of equivalence and effectiveness. Where, for example, the national judge reaches a reasonable *prima facie* conviction that the measure at stake involves unlawful State aid, the most expedient remedy will be to order the unlawful aid and the illegality interest to be put on a blocked account until final judgment, ie until the time where the national court will conclusively order the funds on the blocked account to be returned to the granting authority or order the funds to be released to the beneficiary.

Interim recovery can also be a very effective instrument in cases where national court proceedings run parallel to a Commission investigation or where the national court seeks clarification from the Commission for the purposes of interpreting the concept of State aid or refers a question to the Court for a preliminary ruling.[30]

Although this is not expressly mentioned among the remedies under the Notice, an action may also be brought by a claimant seeking reimbursement or avoidance of a financial burden which is part of an aid scheme and has not been notified to the Commission. In *Van Caster*,[31] for example, the claimants sought reimbursement of part of the charges levied on them in order to fund an aid scheme which had not been notified to the Commission. The Court held that the prohibition on State aid also includes its method of financing and that the claimants were entitled to reimbursement, even if the scheme was subsequently declared compatible with the common market, as far as charges levied before the decision of compatibility were concerned.[32]

In practice, there are only two cases where taxes or charges imposed selectively may be considered as a State aid:[33] first, where a charge is an 'integral part' of an aid measure, that is, where the charge is designed specifically and exclusively to finance the aid; second, where the imposition of a charge on one group of undertakings, but not on another, is the means by which aid is granted to the non-taxed group. In that case, the aid measure is the tax itself.

In other cases arising from asymmetrical tax imposition, the ECJ has held that those liable to pay a charge cannot simply rely on the argument that the exemption enjoyed by other businesses constitutes State aid in order to avoid payment of that charge or to obtain reimbursement:[34] they have to prove that, under the relevant national rules, the tax revenue is reserved exclusively for funding the unlawful State aid and has a direct impact on the amount of State aid granted in violation of Article 108(3) TFEU.[35]

II.iii.　Damages Claims

Competitors of the beneficiary and any other third parties negatively affected by unlawful State aid[36] may bring damages actions to claim compensation for the loss suffered as a consequence of the unlawful aid either under national or EC law. The 2006 Study, nevertheless, reveals that where actions for damages have been introduced in the Member State, they have had no success.

In an attempt to promote private enforcement of State aid law, the Notice recalls the general conditions governing damages claims elaborated since *Francovich* that would also be applicable to a damages claim based on the infringement of Article 108(3) TFEU. These are:

i) the rule of law infringed must be intended to confer rights on individuals. This condition generates no doubt, as the Court has repeatedly emphasised that national courts play an important role in protecting the rights of individuals affected by unlawful implementation of State aid;[37]

ii) the breach must be sufficiently serious. This requires an assessment of the amount of discretion enjoyed by the infringing authority: where this has no discretion, the mere infringement of Community law may be sufficient to establish the existence of a sufficiently serious breach. The existence of a sufficiently serious breach would therefore be easy to establish in a State aid case, since the authority granting aid has no discretion in deciding whether to notify or not; difficulties may arise only in exceptional circumstances, for example where the Commission itself has given precise assurances that the measure in question does not constitute State aid, or that it is not covered by the standstill obligation.[38]

iii) there must a direct causal link between the breach of the Member State's obligation and the damage suffered by the injured parties. The different methods for assessing the damage suffered are described in some detail in the 2009 Notice,[39] but some useful clues may also be found in the Study, *Quantifying Antitrust Damages*,[40] prepared for the Commission in 2009. In State aid cases, the effect on competitors will typically be to limit their market presence or ability to expand, to force them to exit the market altogether (if they are already in the market), or to prevent them from entering the market in the first place. Harm in these cases will be expressed not only as actual losses (*damnum emergens*) suffered by these competitors, but also as lost profit (*lucrum cessans*). From a legal perspective it is important to determine in each specific case whether this effect falls under actual loss or lost profit, as the evidentiary requirements may be different and the standard of proof may be high, particularly as far as *lucrum cessans* is concerned. On the other hand, the 2009 Notice provides that where the burden of proof as regards a particular claim makes it impossible or excessively difficult for a claimant to substantiate its claim, the Notice requires the national court to use all means available under national procedural law to give the claimant access to the relevant evidence. This can include, where provided for under national law, the obligation for the national court to order the defendant or a third party to make the necessary documents available to the claimant.

While the defendant of a damages claim would naturally be the entity that grants the aid, there may be cases where the claimant may prefer to bring an action against the beneficiary of the aid, for example, on the basis that it failed to verify that the aid had been duly notified to the Commission. The EU machinery for reviewing and examining State aids does not impose any specific obligation on the recipient of aid: the notification requirement and the prior prohibition on implementing planned aid are clearly directed to the Member State and, additionally, the Member State is also the addressee of the decision by which the Commission finds that aid is incompatible with the common market. As a result, EU law does not provide a sufficient basis for the recipient to incur liability where he has failed to verify that the aid received was duly notified to the Commission. That does not, however, prejudice the possible application of national law concerning non-contractual liability. If, according to national law, the acceptance by an economic operator of unlawful assistance of a nature such as to occasion damage to other economic operators may in certain circumstances cause him to incur liability, the principle of non-discrimination may lead the national court to find the recipient of aid paid in breach of Article 113(3) TFEU.

III.   ENFORCEMENT OF COMMISSION RECOVERY DECISIONS

National courts may be confronted with State aid issues in cases where the Commission has already ordered recovery. Although most cases will be actions for the annulment of a national recovery order, third parties can also claim damages from national authorities for failure to implement a Commission recovery Decision, under the same *Francovich* and *Brasserie du Pêcheur* case law. In addition, actions can be brought by the national recovering authority seeking a court order to force an unwilling beneficiary to refund the unduly granted aid, in which case Article 14 of Regulation 659/99 requires the Member State concerned to take all necessary steps which are available in its legal system, including provisional measures.

Recovery Decisions must be issued without delay in accordance with the procedures available under national law, provided they allow for immediate and effective execution of the recovery Decision: where a national procedural rule prevents immediate and/or effective recovery, the national court must leave this provision unapplied. In this respect, the applicable principles of equivalence and effectiveness are the same as the ones described under the previous paragraph.[41]

The Commission set out its policy concerning recovery Decisions in its 2007 Recovery Notice.[42] This restates the major principles laid down by the CJEU in this area, in particular the prohibition on the beneficiary of an aid from challenging the validity of a Commission recovery Decision if he could have challenged it under Article 263 TFEU but failed to do so.[43] Such a rule is based on the consideration that the periods within which legal proceedings must be brought are intended to ensure legal certainty by preventing EU measures which produce legal effects from being called in question indefinitely;[44] to find otherwise would enable the recipient of the aid to overcome the definitive nature which a decision necessarily assumed, by virtue of the principle of legal certainty, once the time limit laid down for bringing proceedings had expired.[45] Claims based on Article 263 TFEU are more likely to be considered admissible where it is not clear whether the claimant can bring a direct action.[46]

IV. COOPERATION BETWEEN THE NATIONAL COURTS AND THE COMMISSION

The Commission may provide assistance to national courts in two different ways, intended to help national courts with an ever-increasing docket on State aid issues.

First, the national court may ask the Commission to transmit relevant information in its possession. This may include both information concerning a pending Commission procedure (for example, whether it has initiated formal investigation; whether it has already taken a Decision; whether a measure has been duly notified) and documents that may be in its possession.

Second, the national court may ask the Commission for an opinion concerning the application of State aid rules. The opinions may, in principle, cover all economic, factual or legal matters which arise in the context of the national proceedings: this includes any doubts as to whether a certain measure qualifies as State aid within the meaning of Article 107 TFEU and, if so, how the exact aid amount is to be calculated; whether an aid measure meets the requirements of a Block Exemption Regulation; whether an aid measure falls under a specific aid scheme which has been notified and approved by the Commission or otherwise qualifies as existing aid. Opinions may be also asked on other matters listed at paragraph 91 of the 2009 Notice, such as clarification as to the existence of 'exceptional circumstances' that may prevent a full recovery order under EU law.

The answers by the Commission are neither binding nor definitive, and do not prevent the national court from making a reference to the CJEU. In practice, this procedure seems to have seldom been used.[47]

As a consequence of the duty of loyal cooperation between the Community Institutions and the Member States under Article 4(3) TEU the Commission must respond as quickly as possible to national courts' requests.[48]

In fulfilling its duty of cooperation, the Commission is committed to safeguarding its own functioning and independence and to remaining neutral and objective and to respecting its duty of professional secrecy. Where the national court requests information covered by professional secrecy to a national court, the Commission will be aware of its obligations to protect secrecy under Article 339 TFEU and will ask it whether it can and will be aware of guarantee the protection of such information. Where the national court cannot offer such a guarantee, the Commission will not transmit the information concerned; where, on the other hand, the national court has offered such a guarantee, the Commission will transmit the information requested.

V. CONCLUSION

Compared to the role played by national courts in the enforcement of other provisions of EC law, in the area of State aid the inroads made into the procedural autonomy of national systems have been significant: not only does the 2009 Notice list expressly what range of remedies judges must put at the parties' disposal, but the need to maintain a highly centralised system has brought the ECJ to interpret rather restrictively the various exceptions that from time to time beneficiaries have put forward before national courts in order to resist repayment: this has been so for the principles of legitimate expectations and *res judicata*, as well as for time limits.

Against this backdrop, one area which is still underdeveloped is that of damages claims: taking into account that, as far as Articles 101 and 102 TFEU are concerned, damages claims constitute an entire policy area, the attention paid to the same matter by the 2009 Notice appears to be scant. This, far from being due to an illogical inconsistency with the EU, can rather be explained by the fact that, in the area of State aid law, the narrative of the EU case law and policy perceives effective judicial protection to the benefit of private individuals not as an end in itself (as the CJEU well expounds in the *Courage*[49] case), but as an ancillary tool for the effective enforcement of the prohibition for Member States to act in a way that distorts the market dynamics.[50]

NOTES

1. Case 120/73, *Lorenz* [1973] E.C.R. 147; C-354/90, *Fédération Nationale de Commerce Extérieur des Produits Alimentaires and Others v France* [1991] E.C.R. I-5505, para. 11. On the contrary, in Case 74/76, *Ianelli e Volpi* [1977] E.C.R. 557 the CJEU held that Article 107(1) TFEU does not have direct effect because there are exceptions and derogations to it and the Commission has a wide discretion, under Article 107(3), to declare aid compatible with the common/internal market.
2. Ibid.
3. Case C-368/04, *Transalpine Ölleitung* [2006] E.C.R. I-9957, para. 48.
4. O.J. C 312/8.
5. Jones Day, Lovells, Allen & Overy, *Study on the enforcement of state aid law at national level*, March 2006, available at: <http://ec.europa.eu/competition/State_aid/studies_reports/studies_reports.html> (last accessed 1 January 2011).
6. This appears to be even more so between 2006 and 2009, especially in France, Italy and Germany: see Lovells *2009 update of the 2006 Study on the enforcement of State aid rules at national level*, October 2009, available at: <http://ec.europa.eu/competition/State_aid/studies_reports/studies_reports.html> (last accessed 1 January 2011).
7. O.J. C 85/1. In October 2010 the Commission published a Handbook, *Enforcement of EU State aid law by national courts.* The Handbook is designed to help national courts in the enforcement of EU State aid law at the national level by bringing the main EU Notices and Regulations relating to State aid of relevance to national judges. In addition to the Commission's Enforcement Notice, which aims at offering national courts practical support in their individual cases and explaining their role as defined by the EU Courts, guidance is also provided with respect to the principles concerning recovery of unlawful aid and the rules for the application of Article 108 TFEU. The Handbook is available at: <http://ec.europa.eu/competition/publications/State_aid/national_courts_booklet_en.pdf> (last accessed 3 January 2011).
8. Case C-301/87, *France v. Commission* [1990] E.C.R. I-307.
9. Case C-148/87, *Belgium v. Commission* [1990] E.C.R. I-959.
10. In Case C-200/97, *Ecotrade* [1998] E.C.R. I-7909 A.G. Fennelly pointed out that a conclusion reached with regard to a specific case should be open to refutation in any other case, provided that the undertaking in question is in a position to demonstrate that the one-off application of the rule in its favour does not constitute aid. The Court's decision, on the other hand, does not introduce that nuance, see Nicolaides *et al.* 2008: 26.05.
11. Case C-119/05, *Lucchini* [2007] E.C.R. I 6199, para. 53.
12. Case C-188/92, *TWD v. Germany* [1994] E.C.R. I-833.
13. Para. 18 of the 2009 Notice.
14. A.G. Geelhoed in *Lucchini*, above n. 11, paras. 69 and 74.
15. *Fédération Nationale de Commerce Extérieur des Produits Alimentaires and Others*, above n. 1, para. 12.
16. Dougan 2004: 343.
17. Remedies that are specifically listed are: preventing the payment of unlawful aid, recovery of unlawful aid (regardless of compatibility), recovery of illegality interest; damages for competitors and other third parties and interim measures against unlawful aid.
18. Thus, if national courts could only order suspension of any new payment, aid already granted would subsist until the Commission's final Decision finding the aid incompatible with the common market and ordering its repayment, see Case C-38/94, *SFEI v. Others* [1996] E.C.R. I-3547, para. 67.
19. Case C-209/00, *Commission v. Germany* [2002] E.C.R. I-11695.
20. See Case C-199/06, *CELF* [2008] E.C.R. I-469, paras. 46–49 and 2009 Notice, para. 34.
21. Heidenhain 2010, p. 775.
22. Case C-384/07, [2008] E.C.R. 10393.
23. Case C-1/09, *CELF II*, judgment of 11 March 2010, paras. 31–32.
24. 2009 Notice, para 62. On the other hand, para. 34 of the 2009 Notice expressly clarifies

that a national court's obligation to order recovery and protect individual rights under Article 108(3) TFEU remains unaffected where the Commission has not yet taken a Decision, regardless of whether a Commission procedure is pending or not.

25.   Case C-38/94, *SFEI v. Others* [1996] E.C.R. I-3547, paras. 70–71.
26.   This would be the case, for example, where the recipient company has been wound up: Case 52/84, *Commission v. Belgium* [1986] E.C.R. 89.
27.   O.J. L 83/1. According to Article 14, the Commission will not require recovery of the aid if this would be contrary to a general principle of EU law. In addition, Article 15 provides for a ten-year limitation period as from the day on which the unlawful aid was awarded to the beneficiary for the recovery of aid.
28.   2009 Notice, para. 33; see also A.G. Jacobs in *SFEI*, above n. 25, para. 68.
29.   The interest rate applied in this context should be determined under the same criteria applied to recovery following a decision of incompatibility defined in Article 14 of the Procedural Regulation and in Article 9 of Regulation 794/2004.
30.   2009 Notice, para. 95 and *SFEI*, above n. 25, paras. 44 and 50 to 53.
31.   Case C-261-262/01 [2003] E.C.R. I-12249.
32.   Cf this with the recent case *Wienstrom*, above n. 22, where no financial charge was imposed on third parties.
33.   Bacon *et al.* 2007: 1225.
34.   See, in particular, Case C-390/98, *Banks* [2001] E.C.R. I-6117, para. 80, and *Distribution Casino France*, paras. 42 and 44, and Joined Cases C-393/04 and C-41/05, *Air Liquide* [2006] E.C.R. I-5293, para. 43.
35.   *Air Liquide Industries Belgium*, ibid, para. 46.
36.   A damages claim may also be brought by third parties other than competitors who have suffered a loss as a result of unlawful aid, for example where the recovery of unlawful aid harms a creditor of the aid beneficiary.
37.   Case C-368/04, *Transalpine Ölleitung in Österreich and Others* [2006] E.C.R. I-9957, paras. 38 and 44.
38.   As per joined Cases C-182/03 and C-217/03, *Belgium and Forum 187 v. Commission* [2006] E.C.R. I-5479, para. 147.
39.   Para. 49.
40.   Available at: <http://ec.europa.eu/competition/antitrust/actionsdamages/index.html> (last accessed 1 January 2011).
41.   An express application of effectiveness to time limits can be found in Case C-24/95, *Alcan* [1997] E.C.R I-1491, where the CJEU held that domestic courts are under a duty to disregard the fact that national authorities have permitted the expiry of domestic limitation periods for the recovery of unlawful aid.
42.   Notice from the Commission towards an effective implementation of Commission decisions ordering Member States to recover unlawful and incompatible aid, O.J. C 272/4.
43.   *TWD v. Germany*, above n. 12 and *Lucchini*, above n. 11.
44.   Case C-239/99, *Nachi Europe GmbH v. Hauptzollamt Krefeld* [2001] E.C.R. I-1197, para. 29.
45.   Note that in Case C-222/04, *Ministero dell'Economia e delle Finanze v. Cassa di Risparmio di Firenze SpA* [2006] E.C.R. I-289, paras. 72–74, the CJEU specified that the *TWD* doctrine is limited to cases where the question seeking determination of the validity of a Decision is being referred at the request of the legal entity which, having had the opportunity to bring proceedings for annulment of that Decision, has not done so within the relevant period. It does not apply, however, where the question is being referred by the national court of its own motion.
46.   C-241/95, *Accrington Beef* [1996] E.C.R. I-6691.
47.   See Jones Day, Lovells, Allen & Overy Study, above n. 5, 43.
48.   The 2009 Notice (para. 84) gives an indicative timeframe of one month from the date of the request.
49.   Case C-453/99, *Courage v. Crehan* [2001] E.C.R. I-6297.
50.   For a more thorough discussion of this point see Nebbia 2008.

REFERENCES

Bacon, K., T. Karalis, and C. Zatschler (2007), 'State Aid', in D. Vaughan and A. Robertson (eds), *Law of the European Union*, Oxford: OUP.

Dougan, M. (2004), *National Remedies Before the Court of Justice*, Oxford: Hart.

Heidenhain, M. (2010), *European State Aid Law Handbook*, Beck, Munich/Oxford: Hart.

Nebbia, P. (2008), 'Do the rules on State aids have a life of their own? National procedural autonomy and effectiveness in the *Lucchini* case', *European Law Review*, **33.3**, 427–438.

Nicolaides, P., M. Kekelis and M. Kleiss (2008), *State Aid policy in the European Community: Principles and Practice*, The Hague: Kluwer.

18 State aid (subsidies) in international trade law

Rike Krämer and Markus Krajewski

> No question in international trade law is as contentious, and as complicated, as the question of subsidies.
>
> Andreas F. Lowenfeld[1]

I. INTRODUCTION

European Union law on State aid cannot be seen in clinical isolation from other transnational regimes applicable to governmental support for domestic economic actors. In particular, as a Member of the World Trade Organization (WTO), the EU must adhere to the rules of the multilateral trading system which apply to subsidies, the term of art for State aid in the WTO context. State aid in the European context is embedded in a multilevel system of disciplines and exceptions determining the legality of governmental support measures and the reactions of States, international institutions and economic actors to these measures. This has three important practical consequences.

First, support measures of EU Member States must not only adhere to EU State aid law, but are also subject to the WTO provisions on subsidies. WTO law is an integral part of EU law and therefore binding on the Member States of the EU (Article 216(2) TFEU). It has the same legal supremacy over domestic law as primary and secondary EU law. Furthermore, all EU Member States are also Members of the WTO and are therefore bound by these rules also in their own right. As a consequence, the legality of a support measure or the possible consequences of that measure may not only depend on EU law but also on WTO rules.

Second, support measures of the EU itself are also covered by WTO rules. As international agreements of the EU the WTO agreements are also binding on the EU organs (Article 216(2) TFEU). EU organs may therefore not adopt any measures which would violate these agreements. In the context of WTO rules on subsidies, this obligation is of particular relevance in the area of agricultural support measures. Furthermore, other countries may react to EU support measures by levying countervailing duties against European products.

Third, conflicts between EU State aid law and WTO rules may be possible. While formal conflicts between EU State aid law and the WTO legal system (for example, an obligation under EU law which would violate WTO law) seem rare, it is conceivable that EU law allows certain measures which the WTO prohibits or which may be subject to countervailing duties. In order to avoid this scenario, WTO Members would have to agree on a reform of the WTO subsidies agreement.

EU and WTO law regarding State aid/subsidies have common or similar elements, but they also differ from each other significantly in some areas. Both regimes aim at a reduction of State aid/subsidies because of their distortive effects on trade and competition. However, they differ in their approach towards subsidies: EU law generally prohibits a large number of State aid measures and only considers those measures as compatible with EU law which do not affect the trade between Member States (Article 107(1) TFEU) or which are specifically justified. WTO law by and large only prohibits export subsidies but allows countervailing measures against a large range of subsidies if they adversely affect the interest of other WTO Members. WTO law may hence seem less strict; it allows countervailing measures which may also have negative effects on international trade. This difference may be explained by the different functions of the two regimes: While the EU system aims at the establishment and maintenance of an internal market with undistorted competition (Article 26(2) TFEU), WTO law is aimed at the liberalisation of trade through the reduction of tariffs and other barriers to trade and the elimination of discriminatory treatment (WTO Agreement, Preamble). The different functions of the two systems and their respective regimes on State aid/subsidies need to be kept in mind when drawing comparisons between the different concepts and rules of WTO and EU law.

This chapter will begin with a short overview of the background and the historical development of the rules on subsidies in the world trading system. After a brief reflection on the political economy of subsidies and trade, Part II will discuss the basic provisions of the GATT regarding subsidies which have been in force since 1948 and still remain the basis of the law of subsidies in the WTO, the development of a first comprehensive set of rules on subsidies in the 1970s and the negotiations on subsidies during the Uruguay Round which led to the adoption of the WTO's Agreement on Subsidies and Countervailing Measures (SCM). Part III will be devoted to the scope of this agreement as defined by the notion of a 'subsidy', an overview of the three categories of subsidies in the SCM (prohibited, actionable and non-actionable subsidies) and the remedies provided for in the SCM. Part III will also discuss some notification and monitoring issues and special provisions for developing countries in the SCM. Parts

IV and V will address rules on subsidies which are excluded from the scope of the SCM, in particular agricultural subsidies which are regulated in the Agreement on Agriculture (AoA) and subsidies regarding trade in services which are subject to the General Agreement on Trade in Services (GATS). The last part of this chapter will briefly discuss the treatment of subsidies in regional trade agreements (RTAs) which are of growing importance for the international trading system. The concluding part will highlight the pertinent features of the law on subsidies in WTO law and compare them to respective elements of EU law on State aids. Comparisons between EU and WTO law will also be incorporated into the analyses throughout this chapter.

II.   BACKGROUND AND HISTORICAL DEVELOPMENT OF THE REGIME ON SUBSIDIES IN THE MULTILATERAL TRADING SYSTEM

II.i.   Political Economy of Subsidies and Trade

Economic theory suggests that subsidies are the least trade-restrictive policy measure affecting imports and exports (Matsushita, Schoenbaum and Mavroidis 2006: 332). They are usually considered less inefficient than quantitative restrictions or tariffs, because their effects on consumer and producer welfare are not as negative as the effects of other trade measures. In a perfect competition model, subsidies to domestic companies will have a positive effect on foreign consumers. Apart from these theoretical considerations, subsidies are also the typical instrument of income redistribution and of offsetting externalities in particular for the production of public goods (Hoekman and Kostecki 2001: 169). Subsidies can also be used for protectionist reasons and may distort the competition between foreign and domestic producers both on the foreign or on the domestic market (Sykes 2003: 2). For example, the potential for market access for foreign steel producers due to a tariff reduction on steel can be nullified by subsidising domestic steel production.

   The rules of the world trading system applicable to subsidies reflect the multitude of the effects and functions of subsidies through an approach which only partly aims at disciplining subsidies as such by prohibiting certain types of disciplines. The other element of the subsidies system is the notion of countervailing duties to subsidies. One of the dominant features of the WTO law on subsidies is that it allows governments to employ duties to offset the effects of subsidies on international trade. The concept of countervailing duties was developed in the first half of the 20th century in US trade policy and was transmitted to the international trading system in the General Agreement on Tariffs and Trade (GATT 1947). Originally, the trading system displayed a lenient approach towards subsidies and contained only few restrictions on their use. It was only in the 1970s and 1980s when the use of subsidies and of countervailing measures, became a problem for the international trading system. This development explains the emergence of the current subsidies regime as displayed in the SCM.

II.ii.   Subsidies and Countervailing Measures in the GATT 1947

At its inception, the multilateral trading regime only contained a require-ment to notify the other contracting parties of the GATT about the introduction or maintenance of subsidies and a requirement to enter into 'discussion' should these subsidies cause serious prejudice to the interests of another country (Article XVI:1 GATT). The rather weak requirement of Article XVI was amended in 1954/1995 with rules on export subsidies in Article XVI:2 to 5 GATT 1947 (Lowenfeld 2008: 219). These provisions discouraged the use of export subsides in primary products and prohibited the use of export subsidies on other products if the subsidy resulted in the sale of the product at a lower price than the comparable price of a like product on the domestic market. It should be noted that this provision did not contain a definition of the term subsidy. A Panel of the GATT parties established in 1961 on the 'Operation of the Provisions of Article XVI' even concluded that 'it was neither necessary nor feasible to seek an agreed interpretation of what constituted a subsidy. It would probably be impossible to arrive at a definition which would at the same time include all measures that fall within the intended meaning of the term in Article XVI without including others not so intended.'[2]

The second provision which refers to subsidies in the GATT is Article VI. This provision contains the requirements for the imposition of coun-tervailing duties. This provision focuses mainly on dumping and anti-dumping measures, but Article VI:3 GATT clearly indicates that a GATT party may impose countervailing duties on products which have been subsidised. Countervailing duty is defined as special duty 'levied with the purpose of offsetting any bounty or subsidy bestowed, directly, or indi-rectly, upon the manufacture, production of export of any merchandise'. Article VI:3 required that any countervailing duty should not go beyond an amount equal to the estimated subsidy. It should be noted that coun-tervailing duties are not restricted to subsidies which are inconsistent with the GATT. The right to levy countervailing duties is not a reaction to the illegality of the subsidies, it is merely a trade measure aimed at offsetting presumably unfair distortions of trade. This two-fold approach of the GATT towards subsidies, prohibiting certain subsidies and allowing countervailing duties under specific situations, was maintained in the Subsidies Code of the Tokyo Round and the WTO's SCM (Lowenfeld 2008: 223).

It should also be noted that Article III:8(b) GATT exempts subsidies to domestic producers from the national treatment provision. In other words, the reservation of subsidies to domestic firms would not be a violation of this principle which generally requires that governments treat foreign products no less favourably than like domestic products.

The GATT provisions on subsidies are formally still in force and they form part of the WTO's law on subsidies. From a practical perspective, they have largely been succeeded by the negotiation results of the Uruguay Round.

II.iii.   The Subsidies Code of the Tokyo Round

As successive rounds of trade negotiations lowered the level of tariffs significantly in the 1960s and 1970s, non-tariff barriers to trade became a major issue of concern. Among those were subsidies and countervailing measures, which is why the trade negotiations of the Tokyo Round (1973–1979) included the development of more elaborated rules on subsidies (Clarke and Horlick 2005: 682). In principle the US were interested in greater disciplines for subsidies in general, while other countries wanted to discipline countervailing duties to a greater extend in particular because such duties became a major trade policy instrument of the United States. The negotiations during the Tokyo Round resulted in the Agreement on Interpretation and Application of Articles VI, XVI and XXIII of the General Agreement on Tariffs and Trade of 1979. As with all Tokyo Round agreements, parties to the GATT could choose whether or not they wanted to adopt this agreement. The majority of developed countries and a number of developing countries accepted the Subsidies Code.

The Subsidies Code maintained the two-track approach already identified in the GATT 1947: First, it contained a number of substantive and procedural requirements for the imposition of countervailing duties. In particular, the Subsidies Code put great emphasis on the proceedings leading to the decision to levy countervailing duties. It required evidence of subsidisation, injury and a causal link between imports and injury. However, the Code did not define those subsidies which were countervailable (Trebilcock and Howse 2005: 264). Second, the Subsidies Code maintained the prohibition of export subsidies, but did not increase its scope to other types of subsidies. The Code elaborated on the requirements of Article XVI GATT. The Code's prohibition did not apply to export subsidies for primary products, in particular agricultural export subsidies and developing countries were also exempted from the prohibition. This two-fold approach reflects the interests of the various actors involved: While the US placed greater emphasis on better disciplines for subsidies in general, the then EC wanted in particular tighter control of countervailing duties.

II.iv Negotiations on Subsidies in the Uruguay Round

The Subsidies Code did not meet the expectations of the EU (Luengo Hernández de Madrid 2007: 83f.). Neither an overall reduction of subsidies nor a decrease in countervailing measures by the US had been achieved. Against this background, the Uruguay Round on multilateral trade negotiations which lasted from 1986 to 1993 included negotiations on the control of subsidies and of countervailing duties. The outcome of the negotiations was the Agreement on Subsidies and Countervailing Measures (SCM). The main innovations of the SCM were the introduction of a definition of subsidies, a so-called traffic light approach and a direct link between this approach and the possibility to impose countervailing duties (Stehn 1996: 6).

The approaches of the EC and the US in these negotiations differed remarkably. Understanding these controversies is essential for an analysis of the differences between European State aid law and subsidy law at the WTO level. As regards the *definition of subsidies*, the US argued for an understanding of subsidies as a cause of market distortion. According to this approach subsidies impede the efficient allocation of resources and should therefore be sanctioned with penalties such as countervailing duties (Antidistortion School) (Hufbauer and Shelton Erb 1984: 21). Furthermore, according to this view, a subsidy exists if it is possible to measure a benefit for firms. Such a benefit is present if the beneficiary received an advantage which he would not have received under normal market conditions (Luengo Hernández de Madrid 2007: 84).

The EC, represented in these negotiations by the Commission, advocated a more differentiated approach. First of all, the EC called for a clear definition of subsidies and an elaboration of how to measure the effect of subsidies in order to reduce the use of countervailing duties by the US. Furthermore, the EU aimed at greater security regarding the conformity of Member States' measures with international subsidy law. Unlike the US the EC was of the opinion that subsidizing can be an option to correct market failures. Accordingly, subsidies should only be prohibited, if the subsidy causes an injury to another Member State industry (Injury-Only School) (Hufbauer and Shelton Erb 1984: 19). In order to identify a subsidy, the EU also proposed the criterion of benefit or financial contribution. In line with its own interpretation of Article 107(1) TFEU the criterion of financial contribution should not be considered fulfilled if a measure did not include any cost or charge on the public account (Luengo Hernández de Madrid 2007: 84ff). The reason for the EC to promote such a seemingly wide interpretation was to reduce the scope of the SCM so that the number of measures adopted by the EC Member States which could be declared subsidies according to the SCM was more limited. If the definition of subsidy in the multilateral trading system would be consistent with the European definition, no subsidy granted legally by the EC Member States would cause countervailing duties from another country, for example, the US.

Eventually, however, the EC had only limited success in exporting its own State aid rules and compromises with the US were necessary.

III. THE AGREEMENT ON SUBSIDIES AND COUNTERVAILING MEASURES (SCM)

The adoption of the SCM agreement was an outcome of the Uruguay Round. Like all other agreements of the Uruguay Round, the SCM had to be accepted by all the Members as part of the WTO's single package. The SCM is a multilateral agreement and hence mandatory for all WTO Members. Generally, the SCM only deals with subsidies granted to producers of non-primary products or industrial products; subsidies to agricultural products typically fall within the scope of the Agreement on Agriculture (AoA).

One main innovation of the SCM was the introduction of a definition of the term subsidy (III.1). Subsidies, as defined by the SCM, have to fulfil the criterion of specificity (III.2). The SCM distinguishes three categories of subsidies (III.3). The agreement also enlarged the scope of the rules applying to countervailing duties and made them more detailed (III.4). Furthermore, the WTO's dispute settlement system applies to subsidies and countervailing measures (III.5), and the monitoring and notification procedure has been extended (III.6). Finally, the SCM includes exceptions for developing countries (III.7).

III.i.   Definition of 'Subsidy'

As one of the main novelties of the SCM, the compromise reached in the Uruguay Round negotiations included a definition of subsidies in Article 1 SCM. According to this provision, a subsidy exists if there is a *financial contribution* by a government (III.1.1.) or *any form of income or price support* (III.1.2.) which confers a *benefit* to certain enterprises (III.1.3.). This wording left the question undecided if a charge on the public account was needed to define a measure as a subsidy or not (Slotboom 2002: 533f). This vagueness is due to the fact that not all divergences in the negotiation process between the EU and the US could be eliminated (Rubini 2005: 159).

III.i.a.   Financial contribution
According to Article 1.1(a)(1) SCM a subsidy shall be deemed to exist if there is a financial contribution by a government or any public body within the territory of a Member State. The provision consists of an exhaustive list[3] mentioning different possibilities of a financial contribution. Article 1.1(a)(1) SCM includes:

(i)   a government practice involves a direct transfer of funds (e.g. grants, loans, and equity infusion), potential direct transfers of funds or liabilities (e.g. loan guarantees);

(ii)   government revenue that is otherwise due is foregone or not collected (e.g. fiscal incentives such as tax credits);

(iii) a government provides goods or services other than general infrastructure, or purchases goods;

(iv)   a government makes payments to a funding mechanism, or entrusts or directs a private body to carry out one or more of the type of functions illustrated in (i) to (iii) above which would normally be vested in the government and the practice, in no real sense, differs from practices normally followed by governments.

Generally, the Appellate Body emphasized in the *Brazil-Aircraft* case that the term 'financial contribution' is different from the term 'benefit': 'We see the issues – and the respective definitions – of a 'financial contribution' and a 'benefit' as two separate legal elements in Article 1.1 of the SCM Agreement, which together determine whether a subsidy exists.' (Appellate Body Report, WT/DS/ 46/AB/R, 1999, paragraph 157). This issue is strongly connected to the question whether the financial contribution is defined by the beneficial effect caused by the governmental measure or by the nature of the action (Rubini 2009: 109). In the case *US-Export Restraints* the Panel opted for the second approach: 'We consider that it cannot be the case that the nature of a Member government's measure under the SCM Agreement is to be determined solely on the basis of the reaction to that measure by those it affects. Rather, the existence of a financial contribution by a government must be proven by reference to the action of the government.' (Panel Report, WT/DS194/R, 1999, paragraph

8.34). In addition, the Panel found that the object and purpose of the SCM Agreement consists in disciplining *certain forms* of government action. Hence, the Panel rejected the opinion, that every government intervention with the potential to distort trade is a subsidy within the meaning of the SCM as suggested in economic theory (paragraph 8.62).

In this context, a parallel with the EU State aid regulation can be drawn. For the definition of a State aid the CJEU does not strictly follow economic theory either and does not declare every government action with the potential to distort trade a State aid.[4]

Another contentious issue was the meaning and role of subparagraph (iv). This paragraph was inserted to avoid circumvention of the SCM by granting subsidies indirectly through a private body. Mainly the interpretation of the terms 'entrust or direct' has been debated. Regarding this topic, the Panel in *US-Export Restraint* stated that both terms contain a *notion of delegation*. Hence, the Panel provided three necessary requirements for the terms: (i) an explicit and affirmative action, be it delegation or command; (ii) addressed to a particular party; and (iii) the object of which action is a particular task or duty.

It can be concluded that the *financial contribution* is defined by the nature of the government action. In the case of Article 1.1(a)(1)(iv) SCM it is furthermore necessary that the government delegates the subsidization to a private body. This is similar as in EU law, where the term 'state' in Article 107 TFEU is interpreted broadly and also includes actions of private bodies entrusted by the state.

III.i.b.   Income or price support
The second alternative of the first element of the definition of a subsidy consists of 'any form of income or price support in the sense of Article XVI of GATT of 1994'. One commentator describes income and price supports as 'forms of government intervention aimed at sustaining the income of a certain category or at maintaining the price of a certain commodity at a given, usually minimum, desired level'. (Rubini 2009: 123). This alternative has played nearly no role in doctrine, the Panels or the Appellate Body reports (Luengo Hernández de Madrid 2007: 119).

III.i.c.   Benefit
Article 1.1(2) SCM states that a subsidy shall be deemed to exist if 'a benefit is thereby conferred'. The term benefit is not defined further. However, some guidelines for the calculation of the 'benefit' are established in Article 14 SCM. In addition, Panels and the Appellate Body interpreted the term in a number of cases. The first case was *Canada-Aircraft*. Here, the Panel stated that 'the ordinary meaning of 'benefit'

clearly encompasses some form of advantage' (WT/DS 70/R, 1999, paras 9.112–9.113). Furthermore, the Panel determined that 'a financial contribution will only confer a "benefit", i.e., an advantage, if it is provided on terms that are more advantageous than those that would have been available to the recipient on the market' (para. 9.112). Moreover the reasoning of the Panel was supported by the wording of Article 14 SCM. For example Article 14(b) provides:

> a loan by a government shall not be considered as conferring a benefit, unless there is a difference between the amount that the firm receiving the loan pays on the government loan and the amount the firm would pay on a comparable commercial loan which the firm could actually obtain on the market. In this case the benefit shall be the difference between these two amounts.

This interpretation of the term 'benefit' has been approved by the Appellate Body in the same case (WT/DS 70/AB/R, 1999, paras 157–158).

In conclusion, the definition of the term 'benefit' requires a comparison, between normal market condition and the situation with the maintenance of the 'financial contribution'. Hence, it must always be considered whether the 'financial contribution' for the recipient is more favourable than market conditions. The term 'State aid' in the EU requires an identical comparison (Luengo Hernández de Madrid 2007: 442f.).

III.i.d.   Charge on the public account

Does the term subsidy necessarily involve a charge on the public account? Due to the divergent opinions during the negotiations on this issue, the question was finally left to the judiciary to decide. The Panels as well as the Appellate Body decided against the 'European way' and interpreted the wording of Article 1 SCM in accordance with the US understanding of subsidies.

The first reports regarding this question were the reports in *Canada-Civilian Aircraft* (WT/DS70/R, 1999 and WT/DS70/AB/R, 1999). In this case, Brazil complained that Canada granted prohibited export subsidies to the Canadian civil aircraft industry. One of the contentious questions was whether a credit should be considered a subsidy even though it did not involve a cost to government. Interestingly, this issue was not debated as a matter of the first element of a subsidy in Article 1 SCM (a 'financial contribution') but with regard to the benefit criterion. The EC participated as a third party in this dispute and declared that 'a cost to government' is a not a question of benefit but of the first element, the 'financial contribution'. In addition the EC was of the opinion that the 'cost to government' is the appropriate measure of a 'financial contribution' (WT/DS70/AB/R, 1999, para. 97). This point was not addressed by either the parties or the DSB organs (Slotboom 2002). The result of the case was the finding that a 'cost to government' is not needed to define the term 'benefit'. The main argument was that the requirement of 'cost to government' for the term 'benefit' 'would exclude from the scope of that term those situations where a "benefit" is conferred by a private body under the direction of government. These situations cannot be excluded from the definition of "benefit" in Article 1.1(b), given that they are specifically included in the definition of "financial contribution" in Article 1.1(a)(iv)' (WT/DS70/AB/R, 1999, para. 160).

To sum up, unlike the European interpretation of the term State aid, starting with *Fediol*,[5] no charge on the public account is required for the definition of the term subsidy in the SCM.

III.ii.   Specificity of the Measure

Another requirement for a subsidy according to Article 1.2 SCM is the specificity of a subsidy. Only 'specific' subsidies shall be subject to the provisions of Part II (prohibited subsidies), Part III (actionable subsidies) and Part V (countervailing duties) of the SCM. The specificity criterion is laid down in Article 2 SCM. The purpose of this criterion is to distinguish between measures of general government market policy and those that are subject to subsidy regulation.

According to Article 2 SCM different subsidies are considered specific. First Article 2.1(a) SCM establishes *de jure* specificity which applies to a subsidy explicitly limited to certain enterprises. Contrary to this, *de facto* specificity, as laid down in Article 2.1(c) SCM, presupposes a subsidy programme that in its appearance is not limited to certain enterprises. The use of such a subsidy programme could be limited to certain enterprises, if for example, the subsidy programme is only or predominantly used by a limited number of certain enterprises or disproportionately large amounts are granted to certain enterprises. In addition Article 2.2 SCM states that general *regional aid* is not specific. Furthermore Article 2.3 SCM establishes that *prohibited subsidies* are always deemed as specific.

Like in EU law, subsidies which are granted on objective criteria governing the eligibility for and the amount of, a subsidy, specificity shall not exist, provided that the eligibility is automatic and that such criteria are strictly adhered to. Translated into European State aid language the term for specificity refers to 'selectivity' (Luengo Hernández de Madrid 2007: 450f.).

III.iii.   Three Categories of Subsidies

The SCM divides subsidies in three categories that might, at first sight, resemble those in Articles 107(2) and (3) of the TFEU. However, the categories of the SCM are not formulated as exceptions as in the EU system, but they follow the so-called 'traffic-light approach' (red, amber, green) referring to the meaning of the three signals in a traffic light at a road intersection. The subsidies are divided into these three categories based on their distorting impact on international trade and competition. Hence, the red category includes prohibited subsidies, that is those considered most harmful for international trade (III.2.1). Such subsidies are completely forbidden, like the illumination of red light prohibits any traffic from proceeding. The second, the amber category includes actionable subsidies (III.2.2). As the amber traffic light admonishes the driver to pass carefully, governments must use actionable subsidies cautiously, since they may distort international competition. The third, green category includes the non-actionable subsidies (III.2.3). Granting those subsidies is regarded as to having no negative effect on competition and is therefore allowed. The last category lapsed in 2000. For the sake of completeness this category will be described briefly, but will not be mentioned in any of the subsequent paragraphs.

Unlike EU law, the SCM does not prohibit all subsidies. Article 107(1) TFEU declares all State aid which distorts or threatens to distort competition by favouring certain undertakings or the production of certain goods as incompatible with the internal market in so far as it affects trade between Member States. In principle all State aid is therefore prohibited and falls within the red category. The Articles 107(2) and (3) establish exceptions. Such a general prohibition is not laid down in the SCM system. However, the green and amber categories parallel in a certain way Article 107(2) and Article 107(3) TFEU (Luengo Hernández de Madrid 2007: 455ff.)

III.iii.a.   Prohibited subsidies (Article 3 SCM)

The first category ('prohibited') according to Article 3 SCM includes two types of subsidies: (1) export subsidies illustratively listed in Annex I and (2) subsidies contingent 'upon the use of domestic over imported goods'. According to Article 2.3 SCM all subsidies falling within the prohibited category are characterized as specific subsidies regardless of their details (Sykes 2003: 15). Examples of export subsidies include internal transport and freight charges on export shipments, provided by governments, on terms more favourable than for domestic shipments. Subsidies which fall into this category have to be withdrawn. The idea of banning such subsidies found strong support among the WTO Members. In a similar way, EU law prohibits this category of subsidies, for example in Article 1 of the Commission Regulation 69/2001 (Rubini 2005: 177). However, in some cases State aid declared compatible with the common/internal market in the EU could represent a prohibited subsidy according to Article 3 SCM. One example could be the case *France* v. *Commission.*[6] In this case, France granted subsidies to book producers for the export of books to non-French-speaking countries, especially to reduce costs for the handling of small orders. The Commission applied the cultural exception clause (Article 107(3)(d) TFEU) and the CJEU confirmed the Commission's Decision. Within the WTO regime such an export subsidy falls in the category of prohibited subsidies, however, unless this question is brought before the WTO dispute settlement organs it will not be adjudicated (*nullum ius sine actione*) (Luengo Hernández de Madrid 2007: 458ff.)

III.iii.b.   Actionable subsidies (Articles 5 and 6 SCM)

The second category ('actionable') according to Article 5 and 6 SCM contains subsidies which adversely affect the interests of another Member. Such an adverse effect could be a material injury to the domestic industry of another Member. A material industry requires an effect on a large group of domestic producers that produce goods similar to the subsidized products (Luengo Hernández de Madrid 2007: 167). Furthermore, evidence of a causal relationship between the subsidized imports and the injury to the domestic industry is necessary (Article 15.5 SCM).

Another adverse effect could be the nullification or impairment of benefits accruing directly or indirectly to other Members under GATT 1994 in particular the benefits of concessions bound under Article II of GATT 1994. Nullification or impairment occur either through non-compliance with the obligation in the Agreement or the violation of duties in the Agreement (Luengo Hernández de Madrid 2007: 168).

Finally, an adverse effect exists whenever the subsidy causes a serious prejudice to the interests of another Member. The criteria for a serious prejudice are laid down in Article 6 SCM. They include, for example, the case where a subsidy is used to cover operating losses sustained by an industry. The *prima facie* presumption of 'serious prejudice' in Article 6.1 SCM became inapplicable in 2000, due to a sunset clause in Article 31 SCM. Nevertheless, its contents can still be used as guidance to define serious prejudice (Luengo Hernández de Madrid 2007: 172). The other parts of Article 6 SCM are still applicable and, unlike Article 6.1, lay down the cases in which a serious prejudice *may exist*.

III.iii.c.   Non-actionable subsidies (Article 8 SCM)

As expected during the negotiations the most difficult category was the green basket of 'non-actionable' subsidies (Article 8). This category was included as a result of European pressure. With the notion of 'non-actionable' subsidies, the EU tried to transpose its State aid exception system to the WTO level in order to create legal security for the EU Member States (Didier 1999: 256). State aid granted legally in the EU should be in compliance with WTO disciplines and not be subject to countervailing duties. The US, in contrast, was reluctant regarding the green basket. In their view such a category would make it easier for Member States to circumvent the SCM by disguising their measures as non-actionable subsidies (Luengo Hernández de Madrid 2007: 87). Due to the reluctance of the US, the review of Article 8 SCM was foreseen after a period of five years (Article 31 SCM). After five years passed, the US was still reluctant to extend the provision. Furthermore, developing countries were concerned that the provision favours developed countries' interests.[7] Until the end of 1999 no consensus about the extension of Article 8 SCM could be found and so the category of non-actionable subsidies lapsed, in 2000 (Rubini 2005: 185). Unlike the SCM, the 'green category' in the EU (Article 107(2) TFEU) is still applicable. As a consequence, the situation which the EU tried to prevent during the negotiations became reality: State aid granted legally in the EU may sometimes not comply with WTO law or trigger countervailing duties.

III.iv. Remedies

The SCM also contains rules on trade remedies. Remedies include measures applicable to prohibited, actionable or non-actionable subsidies respectively (Ehlermann and Goyette 2006: 717). Remedies can be adopted either at the international level through the dispute before the Dispute Settlement Body (DSB) (III.iv.a) or can be pursued at the national level through countervailing duties (III.iv.b). The aim of both possibilities is the same: the correction of the market distortion caused by the subsidy. Countervailing duties only reduce the effect of the subsidy on the national market. In contrast, the withdrawal of the subsidy, reached through a DSB procedure, reduces the effect also on third markets.

III.iv.a. The different procedures before the DSB
The possibilities of claims before the DSB relate to the different categories of subsidies. One difference between the two categories (prohibited and actionable subsidies) is the time frame of such a procedure. The procedure for prohibited subsidies is shorter, e.g. a consultation period of 30 days (Article 4 SCM) instead of 60 days (Article 7 SCM). More importantly, the possible outcome of such a procedure differs.

The procedure for *prohibited subsidies* is established in Article 4 SCM. If the Panel determines that the measure in question is a prohibited subsidy, it has to recommend the withdrawal of the subsidy. The Panel report will be adopted by the DSB unless it is appealed against in which case the WTO's Appellate Body will have to decide on the matter. If a Member does not follow the recommendations of the Panel or Appellate Body's report during the set time period, the DSB can authorize the adoption of appropriate countermeasures (Article 4.10 SCM). One highly contentious issue was the scope of the term 'withdrawn', especially, whether this term includes retroactive repayment (Rubini 2009: 71f.). A WTO panel had the opportunity to clarify this question in the *Australia-Leather* case. In its report of 21 January 2000 (WT/DS126/RW, 2000) the Panel justified the retrospective repayment of a prohibited subsidy with the principle of *effet utile* (WT/DS126/RW, 2000, para 6.24) well known in CJEU jurisprudence (Tietje 2004: 12f). This reasoning nearly caused the rejection of the Report in the DSB.[8] After this strong reaction by the WTO Members, Panels and the Appellate Body eschewed to revert to this case law (Rubini 2009: 71f).

Article 7 SCM defines the procedure for *actionable subsidies*. Once the Panel determines an actionable subsidy the Member has two possibilities to react: The Member (1) can take appropriate steps to remove the adverse effects or (2) can withdraw the subsidy. If the Member does not react appropriately, the DSB can authorize the complaining Member to take countermeasures, unless the DSB decides by consensus to reject the request.

III.iv.b.   Countervailing duties

Another instrument against distortive subsidies provided for in the SCM agreement are countervailing duties on another Members' products. Unlike the withdrawal of a subsidy, countervailing duties only neutralize the effect of the subsidy on the Member's market. The procedure to levy countervailing duties is laid down in the Articles 10 to 23 SCM. They are: (1) evidence of the existence of a specific subsidy, (2) material injury to domestic industry of a Member, (3) a causal link between the subsidized imports and the alleged injury. The procedure to adopt countervailing duties can be initiated by the government itself or by a domestic industry. In addition, the SCM requires that the amount of the countervailing duty must be equal or less than the amount of the subsidy. The calculation methods of the subsidy are also laid down. A countervailing duty cannot be applied longer than five years from its imposition. Finally, the SCM requires that each Member whose national legislation contains provisions on countervailing duty measures shall maintain judicial review of those domestic procedures (Luengo Hernández de Madrid 2007: 193ff.)

In conclusion, unlike in EU law, the withdrawal of the subsidy is not the only possible remedy. Instead, countermeasures, that is, measures authorized by the DSB, or countervailing duties, that is, measures provided for in the SCM, are options within the SCM framework.

III.v. Notification and monitoring

The requirement to notify and monitor already existed in the GATT 1947 (Article XVI:1 GATT), but this procedure was barely used in practice (Luengo Hernández de Madrid 2007: 199). The new provision, which is set out in Article 25 SCM, raised hopes of improvement. It requires that Members shall notify any subsidy until 30 June each year to the SCM Committee (Article 26 SCM). The notifications should be sufficiently specific to enable other Members to evaluate the trade effects and to understand the operation of notified subsidy programmes (Article 25.3 SCM). Unlike in the EU, the SCM does not lay down specific requirements whether a subsidy has to be notified before granted. The only exception is Article 8.3 SCM which requires the notification of non-actionable subsidies before they are granted. Furthermore, interested Members can request information on the nature and extent of any subsidy granted or maintained by another Member (Article 25.8 SCM). Final actions taken with respect to countervailing duties shall also be reported by the Members (Article 25.11 SCM).

III.vi. Exceptions for Developing Countries

Article 27 SCM establishes a few exceptions for developing countries. The prohibition to subsidies exports (Article 3.1(a) SCM) shall not apply for a number of developing countries, mainly least-developed countries referred to in Annex VII (Article 27.2(a) SCM). A country referred to in Annex VII which has reached export competitiveness in one or more products, is required to gradually phase out export subsidies on such products over a period of eight years (Article 27.5 SCM). There are only few exemptions for developing countries concerning the category of actionable subsidies. Only Article 27.13 exempts direct forgiveness of debts, subsidies to cover social costs, in whatever form, including relinquishment of government revenue and other transfer of liabilities when such subsidies are granted within and directly linked to a privatization programme of a developing country. Regarding countervailing duties the SCM only minimally differentiates between developing countries and others. Article 27.10 provides a *de minimis* rule: subsidies granted by a developing country below the threshold cannot be subject of an investigation.

IV.   THE AGREEMENT ON AGRICULTURE (AOA)

Subsidies which affect trade in agriculture are one of the most contentious subjects addressed by the multilateral trading system. In general, two types of measures need to be distinguished: measures which aim at a support of domestic producers and measures which explicitly apply to exports. The former affect competition on the domestic market of the subsidising country; the latter affect the competitive relationship on a foreign market. The WTO's Agreement on Agriculture (AoA) which was also negotiated during the Uruguay Round addresses both types of measures. The AoA does not completely prohibit domestic support measures and export subsidies. Instead, Members schedule reduction commitments which are binding for each Member (Article 3.3 AoA).

As stipulated in Article 3.2 AoA, Members shall not provide support in favour of domestic producers 'in excess of the commitment levels specified' in its schedule. The commitments are expressed in terms of total Aggregate Measurement of Support (AMS) which refers to the annual level of support expressed in monetary terms. Annex 3 of the AoA contains provisions on how to calculate the AMS. Article 6(4) AoA excludes measures which do not go beyond a certain minimum level (*de minimis* threshold) from the scope of the AMS. Furthermore, the AoA's regime on domestic support also relies on a system of 'coloured boxes' picture. Support measures which are part of a production limiting programme ('blue box') are exempt from the inclusion in the calculation of the AMS (Article 6(5) AoA). Similarly, subsidies which are mentioned in Annex 2 are also not part of the obligation to reduce domestic support measures. The measures contained in Annex 2 relate to food security, food aid, direct payments and are hence often referred to as 'green box'. All other measures are subject to the reduction of domestic support.

Export subsidies are covered both by the AoA and the SCM, but the AoA is *lex specialis* and will therefore be applied first (Coppens 2010: 354). Unlike the SCM, the AoA does not completely outlaw export subsidies. Instead Article 3(3) and Article 8 AoA require that Members do not provide export subsidies unless they are in conformity with the commitments as specified in the schedules of the Members. Export subsidies are defined as subsides contingent upon export performance (Article 1(e) AoA). Article 9.1 AoA lists a number of export subsidies which are subject to the reduction commitments under the AoA. These include direct subsidies contingent on export performance, sale or disposal for export by governments at a price lower than the comparable price charged in the domestic garden or payments on the export of an agricultural product (Article 9(1) AoA).

V.   SUBSIDIES REGARDING TRADE IN SERVICES (ART XV GATS)

The SCM and the AoA only apply to subsidies affecting trade in goods. Trade in services is addressed in the General Agreement on Trade Services (GATS). The GATS contains a special provision on subsidies, Article XV GATS. According to paragraph 1 of this provision Members recognize that subsidies may have distortive effects on trade in services. They therefore agreed to 'enter into negotiations with a view to developing the necessary multilateral disciplines to avoid such trade-distortive effects', which shall also address the appropriateness of countervailing procedures (Article XV:1 GATS). Furthermore, Article XV:2 GATS stipulates that a Member which considers that it is adversely affected by a subsidy of another Member may request consultations with that Member. It should be noted that these elements of Article XV GATS resemble the basic rules of Article XVI GATT (see above II.ii.). Furthermore, the GATS does not exempt subsidies from its general obligations such as the most-favoured nation principle and specific commitments such as the national treatment principle. As the GATS does not contain a provision similar to Article III:8(a) GATT which excludes subsidies from national treatment, many WTO Members have excluded the application of national treatment to subsidies in the schedules of specific commitments. Unlike the GATT (and the SCM), the GATS does not include rules on the permissibility of subsidies in services or on possible countervailing measures.

Article XV:1 GATS contains a negotiating mandate which calls for negotiations with a view to developing necessary disciplines to avoid distortive effects and addressing the appropriateness of countervailing procedures. These negotiations have been ongoing in the WTO's Working Party on GATS Rules (WPGR) since 1996. However, the Members of the WPGR are still in the process of exchanging information on subsidies, discussing technical questions and trying to establish a working definition of subsidies in services trade. The duration of the negotiations and its fruitlessness so far indicates that the subject of subsidies with regards to services may be even more contentious than with regards to trade in goods.

VI.   SUBSIDIES DISCIPLINES IN REGIONAL TRADE AGREEMENTS (RTAS)

The growing number of bilateral and regional trade agreements (RTAs) is one of the key challenges to the multilateral trading system. More often than not do the disciplines contained in these agreements go beyond the scope of the respective provisions of WTO law (so-called 'WTO-Plus' approach). Regarding rules on subsidies, the picture is relatively mixed. In general three types of approaches towards subsidies in RTAs can be distinguished.

A first group of agreements does not contain any substantive rules on subsidies at all. For example, the Chapter 19 of the North American Free Trade Agreement (NAFTA) only provides for the review of antidumping and countervailing duty matters based on domestic laws and does not provide for any substantive standards regarding the legality of subsidies.

A second group of RTAs contains rules on subsidies which do not go beyond the approach of the WTO. The agreements signed by the EC/EU seem to be following this approach. For example, the Association Agreement between (the then) EC and Chile of 2002 contains a general reference to the rights and obligations of the partners to WTO rules on subsidies and excludes subsides from the scope of its services chapter. The proposed free trade agreement between the EU and Colombia and Peru seems to follow a similar approach. The EC-CARIFORUM Economic Partnership Agreement of 2008 specifically mentions the phasing out of agricultural export subsidies (Article 28 EC-CARIFORUM EPA), but does not provide for further disciplines and also excludes subsidies from the chapter on services. It is remarkable that the EU does not seem to be able to negotiate subsidies disciplines which are more closely connected with its own internal State aid regime.

Finally, some RTAs contain fully-fledged regimes on subsidies which go beyond the WTO rules as they include disciplines for subsidies on goods and services. For example, the Revised Treaty of Chaguaramas Establishing the Caribbean Community including the CARICOM Single Market and Economy of 2001 contains no less than 21 provisions (Articles 96–115) on subsidies applying to goods and services. These include definition of subsidies, categories and possible reactions to certain types of subsidies. Similarly, the Andean Commission enacted special rules to prevent and correct distortive effects of subsidies in 1999. These rules contain detailed provisions on the definition of a subsidy in general, of actionable and of specific subsidies, and on the calculation of the benefit element of a subsidy. The rules also specify the determination of a damage caused by a subsidy and possible remedies, including preliminary measures.

VII.   CONCLUSION

The preceding brief overview of the main features and elements of the law of subsidies in international trade revealed some important differences between WTO and EU law in this regards: First, the notion of a subsidy seems to be larger than the notion of State aid. In EU law, State aid requires a charge on the public account, a notion which was rejected by the WTO jurisprudence. Furthermore, the legal consequences also differ. Under WTO law, a clear distinction between legal, but still countervailable and illegal subsidies which have to be withdrawn can be seen at work. EU law, however, does not contain a notion of legal State aid which may nevertheless be subject to countervailing duties. This may even lead to conflicting rules, that is, if the measure is justifiable under EU law, but not according to WTO law, the respective country may become an addressee of countervailing duties. So far, this situation has not yet materialized and it remains to be seen if it ever will.

NOTES

1. Lowenfeld (2008: 216).
2. Analytical Index of the GATT, p. 189, available at <http://www.wto.org/english/res_e/booksp_e/gatt_ai_e/art16_e.doc> (last accessed 28 December 2010).
3. Report of the Panel in *US-Export Restraints*, WT/DS194/R, para. 8.69.
4. See the chapters by Bartosch, Coppi, Micheau and Szyszczak in this volume.
5. Case 187/85, [1988] E.C.R. 4155, paras 9 and 11.
6. Case C-332/98, [2000] E.C.R. 1-4833.
7. Minutes of the regular meeting of the Committee on Subsidies and Countervailing Measures held on 1–2 November 1999, G/SCM/M/24.
8. Minutes of the DSB Meeting, held on 11 February 2000, WT/DSB/M75.

REFERENCES

Clarke, Peggy A. and Gary N. Horlick (2005), 'The Agreement on Subsidies and Countervailing Measures', in Patrick F. J. Macrory, Arthur E. Appleton and Michael G. Plummer (eds), *The World Trade Organization: Legal, Economic and Political Analysis, Vol. 1*. New York: Springer, 679–734.

Coppens, Dominic (2010), 'WTO disciplines on export credit support for agricultural products in the wake of the *US – Upland Cotton* case and the Doha Round Negotiations', *Journal of World Trade*, **44**, 349–384.

Didier, Pierre (1999), *WTO Trade Instruments in the EU Law*, London: Cameron May.

Ehlermann, Claus-Dieter and Martin Goyette (2006), 'The interface between EU State aid control and the WTO disciplines on subsidies', *European State Aid Law Quarterly*, **1:2**, 695–718.

Hoekman, Bernard M. and Michel M. Kostecki (2001), *The Political Economy of the World Trading System, The WTO and Beyond*, 2nd edn, Oxford: OUP.

Hufbauer, Gary Clyde and Joanna Shelton Erb (1984), *Subsidies in International Trade*, Cambridge: MIT Press.

Lowenfeld, Andreas F. (2008), *International Economic Law*, 2nd edn, Oxford: OUP.

Luengo Hernández de Madrid and Gustavo E. (2007), *Regulation of Subsidies and State Aids in WTO and EC Law: Conflicts in International Trade Law*, Alphen aan den Rijn: Kluwer Law International.

Matsushita, Mitsuo, Thomas J. Schoenbaum and Petros C. Mavroidis (2006), *The World Trade Organization – Law, Practice, and Policy*, 2nd edn, Oxford: OUP.

Rubini, Luca (2005), 'The international context of EC State aid law and policy: the regulation of subsidies in the WTO', in Andrea Biondi, Piet Eeckhout and James Flynn (eds), *The Law of State Aid in the European Union,* Oxford: OUP, 149–188.

Rubini, Luca (2009), *The Definition of Subsidy and State Aid: WTO and EC Law in Comparative Perspective,* Oxford: OUP.

Slotboom, Marco M. (2002) 'Subsidies in WTO law and in EC law: broad and narrow definitions', *Journal of World Trade* **36**, 517–542.

Stehn, Jürgen (1996) 'Subsidies, countervailing duties, and the WTO: towards an open subsidy club', *Kieler Diskussionsbeiträge: Kiel Discussion Papers*, 1–18.

Sykes, Alan O. (2003), 'The economics of WTO rules on subsidies and countervailing measures' *Chicago John M. Olin Law & Economics Working Paper No 186*, 1–36.

Tietje, Christian (2004), 'Current developments under the WTO Agreement on Subsidies and Countervailing Measures as an example for the functional unity of domestic and international trade', in Christian Tietje, Gerhard Kraft and Rolf Sethe (eds) *Beiträge zum Transnationalen Wirtschaftsrecht*, Halle Wittenberg: Marthin-Luther-Universität Halle Wittenberg, 1–20. <http://www.wirtschaftsrecht.uni-halle.de/Heft26.pdf> (last accessed 28 December 2010).

Trebilcock, Michael J. and Robert Howse (2005), *The Regulation of International Trade*, 3rd edn, London and New York: Routledge.

Index